Managerial Accounting

A Note to Students...

Dear Students of Managerial Accounting,

Managerial Accounting is concerned with using information to effectively plan and control operations and make good business decisions. The overall objective of this book is to provide you with the concepts and tools needed in planning, control, and decision making. I've taught Managerial Accounting for many years, and my former students, many of whom are in senior executive positions, tell me that they've used these concepts and tools throughout their business careers. So, trust me. Work hard in this course, and you will reap major benefits!

In approaching the course, realize that you need to take personal responsibility for your success. Of course your instructor will help you understand the material, but you're the one who must make time to read the material before class and complete all assigned problems and cases. I recommend that you take a three-step approach to the study of each chapter in ***Managerial Accounting***:

- First, skim the chapter for a quick overview.
- Second, read the chapter carefully, and pay particular attention to the illustrations. When you're finished, make sure you understand each of the learning objectives.
- Third, enhance and test your knowledge using the materials within *WileyPLUS*.

If at all possible, you should also form a study group with one or two of your classmates. You'll learn a lot from each other, and going over the homework together may actually be fun!

With my best wishes for success,

Jim Jiambalvo
Dean and Kirby L. Cramer
Chair in Business Administration
Michael G. Foster School of Business
University of Washington

Sixth Edition

Managerial Accounting

James Jiambalvo

University of Washington

WILEY

To my wife, Cheryl

VICE PRESIDENT & DIRECTOR	George Hoffman
EXECUTIVE EDITOR	Michael McDonald
ASSOCIATE DEVELOPMENT EDITOR	Rebecca Costantini
SENIOR CONTENT MANAGER	Dorothy Sinclair
PRODUCTION EDITOR AND MEDIA SPECIALIST	Elena Santa Maria
MARKETING MANAGER	Lauren Harrell
PRODUCT DESIGN MANAGER	Allison Morris
SENIOR PRODUCT DESIGNER	Greg Chaput
DESIGN DIRECTOR	Harry Nolan
COVER AND INTERIOR DESIGNER	Maureen Eide
SENIOR PHOTO EDITOR	Mary Ann Price
COVER PHOTO	Malerapaso/Getty Images, Inc.

This book was set in 10/12 Minion Pro Regular by Aptara, Inc. and printed and bound by Quad Graphics/Versailles. The cover was printed by Quad Graphics/Versailles.

Tape measure icon credit: Image Source/Getty Images

This book is printed on acid free paper.

Founded in 1807, John Wiley & Sons, Inc. has been a valued source of knowledge and understanding for more than 200 years, helping people around the world meet their needs and fulfill their aspirations. Our company is built on a foundation of principles that include responsibility to the communities we serve and where we live and work. In 2008, we launched a Corporate Citizenship Initiative, a global effort to address the environmental, social, economic, and ethical challenges we face in our business. Among the issues we are addressing are carbon impact, paper specifications and procurement, ethical conduct within our business and among our vendors, and community and charitable support. For more information, please visit our website: www.wiley.com/go/citizenship.

BRV: 978-1-119-15801-1
EVAL: 978-1-119-24810-1

The inside back cover will contain printing identification and country of origin if omitted from this page. In addition, if the ISBN on the back cover differs from the ISBN on this page, the one on the back cover is correct.

Printed in the United States of America

10 9 8 7 6 5 4 3 2 1

About the Author

JAMES JIAMBALVO, Dean of the Michael G. Foster School of Business at the University of Washington and Kirby L. Cramer Chair in Business Administration, joined the accounting faculty at Foster after receiving a Ph.D. in accounting from The Ohio State University. A CPA, he has audit experience with the firm of Haskins and Sells (now Deloitte & Touche), and has served on the national academic advisory board of Deloitte & Touche LLP. Dean Jiambalvo has served as chairman of the University of Washington Accounting Department and previously held the PricewaterhouseCoopers and Alumni Endowed Professorship.

Dean Jiambalvo's research has been published in top accounting journals, including *The Accounting Review, Contemporary Accounting Research,* the *Journal of Accounting and Economics*, and the *Journal of Accounting Research*. He is a former associate editor of *The Accounting Review* and has served on the editorial boards of *The Accounting Review, Contemporary Accounting Research,* and the *Journal of Management Accounting Research*.

Dean Jiambalvo has received the Notable Contribution to the Auditing Literature Award, the Burlington Northern Foundation Faculty Achievement Award, the Andrew V. Smith Faculty Development Award, and the Lex N. Gamble Award for Excellence in the Field of E-Commerce. He has also been recognized for his teaching of managerial accounting with the MBA Professor of the Year and Professor of the Quarter awards. He has taught numerous executive education courses, including courses for Alcoa, Boeing, Microsoft, Tyson, and other major firms. He currently serves on the board of Saltchuk Resources.

WHAT'S **NEW?**

WileyPLUS with ORION

WileyPLUS with ORION is an adaptive study and practice tool that helps students build proficiency in course topics. Over 3,500 new questions are available for practice and review.

Updated Design and Content

A redesigned interior and new learning objective structure help students practice their understanding of concepts before they progress to different topics in other learning objectives. This provides a more organized learning experience.

WileyPLUS Solution Walkthrough Videos

Newly created solution walkthrough videos are available within the eText and as homework assistance. Approximately 50 videos are newly available to the Sixth Edition. The videos serve as guides through homework problems and solutions and review chapter-level concepts.

Additional *WileyPLUS* Practice

Students have more opportunities within *WileyPLUS* to practice questions that are similar to the end-of-chapter content before completing homework.

Revised Excel Templates

New Excel templates offer "What if?" scenarios to help students apply their understanding of Excel and chapter concepts from different perspectives.

Links to Practice

New Links to Practice throughout the textbook have an even stronger focus on engaging, real-world issues.

Preface

This book is intended to drive home the fundamental ideas of managerial accounting and motivate students to actually *want* to study the subject. As you will see, the text has a number of unique features that help accomplish these goals. Based on my teaching experience and from what we have heard from professors using the previous editions, we believe students and professors want a textbook that:

- Recognizes that most students will become managers, not accountants
- Focuses attention on decision making
- Stresses the fact that "You Get What You Measure"
- Motivates students to learn managerial accounting by connecting concepts and techniques to the real world
- Recognizes the growing importance of service businesses
- Is clear, concise (can be covered in one semester), and current
- Provides students with ample opportunities to test their knowledge.

Here's how the sixth edition of *Managerial Accounting* reflects these desires.

Recognizes that most students will become managers, not accountants. Most students of introductory managerial accounting will pursue careers as managers, not accountants. Future managers most likely will not need to know the FIFO approach to process costing or how to calculate four overhead variances—so these and other less essential topics are not covered.

Focuses more attention on decision making. Instructors want their students to be able to solve the types of problems that real managers face. This requires that more emphasis be placed on decision making skills. Accordingly, three of the chapters (Chapters 7, 8, and 10) focus specifically on decision making. Additionally, decision making, and the use of incremental analysis, are discussed in the first chapter and integrated throughout the book. By the time students get to Chapter 7 (The Use of Cost Information in Management Decision Making), they will already have a good understanding of costs that are relevant in making a decision. After reading Chapter 7, working homework problems and discussing the material in class, students will have a greater understanding of decision making!

Stresses the fact that "You Get What You Measure" Senior managers know that performance measures greatly affect how subordinates focus their time and attention. Thus, the subject of performance measurement is of great practical importance. In this book, every chapter makes reference to the critical idea that *You get what you measure.* Chapter 12 has an extensive discussion of performance measures.

Motivates students to learn managerial accounting by connecting concepts and techniques to the real world. Business people often say that they wish they had known how important managerial accounting would have been to their success on the job—they would have studied the subject harder in school! Here, every effort is made to convince students that managerial accounting is of critical importance in the real world. *Link to*

Practice boxes relate the text material to real companies. Additionally, each chapter has cases developed with feedback from managers who attested to their realism and relevance. An often-heard comment: "We had that exact situation at my company!"

Recognizes the growing importance of service businesses. In the last 20 years, employment has shifted from manufacturing to the service sector. Now, more than 75% of all jobs are in the service economy. With this in mind, numerous examples of service companies are in the chapter and end-of-chapter materials.

Clear, concise (can be covered in one semester), and current. According to students and faculty who used the previous editions, a major and much appreciated strength of the text is the clear and concise writing style. Discussions are to the point, ideas are illustrated, and examples are presented to make the ideas concrete. The entire text can be comfortably covered in one semester. Coverage is also up-to-date, including: Theory of Constraints, Economic Value Added, The Balanced Scorecard, Strategy Maps, Activity-Based Costing and Activity-Based Management, Why Budget-Based Compensation Can Encourage Padding and Income-Shifting, etc.

Provides students with ample oppourtunities to test their knowledge. In each chapter, students are presented with a feature called *Test Your Knowledge*. At the end of each chapter, there are two comprehensive review problems as well as several multiple choice problems with solutions. These features allow students to assess their understading of the material as they read through the chapter as well as after they have finished reading the entire chapter. The features also set students up for success in completing end-of-chapter assignments.

WILEYPLUS RESOURCES

WileyPLUS is an innovative, research-based online environment for effective teaching and learning. *WileyPLUS* builds students' confidence because it takes the guesswork out of studying by providing students with a clear roadmap: what to do, how to do it, if they did it right. Students will take more initiative, so you'll have greater impact on their achievement in the classroom and beyond.

Instructor Resources

Solutions Manual

The Solutions Manual provides detailed solutions for all end-of-chapter questions, exercises, problems, and cases.

Test Bank

The Test Bank consists of over 2,000 examination questions and exercises accompanied by solutions. Question types include true-false, multiple choice, completion, exercises, and short-answer.

Instructor's Manual

The Instructor's Manual is a comprehensive resource guide designed to assist professors in preparing lectures and assignments. The manual includes chapter reviews, lecture outlines, assignment classification tables, teaching illustrations, and quizzing exercises.

PowerPoint™ Presentations

PowerPoint™ Presentations contain key concepts and images from the textbook.

Student Resources

Study Guide

The Study Guide is comprised of a chapter review with true-false question, multiple-choice exercises, and problems.

Excel Templates

The Excel Templates help students to complete select end-of-chapter exercises and problems identified by an icon in the margin of the textbook.

Acknowledgments

I am indebted to my academic colleagues and former students for enriching my understanding of managerial accounting. The team at Wiley provided expert help, guidance, and support throughout the publication process. In particular, Michael McDonald, executive editor, made a number of valuable suggestions for improving the sixth edition. Other Wiley staff who contributed to the text and media are: Rebecca Costantini, associate development editor; Allie Morris, product design manager; Greg Chaput, senior product designer; Elena Santa Maria, production editor; Maureen Eide, senior designer; Mary Anne Price, senior photo editor.

Other individuals whose input is greatly appreciated are indicated below.

Ancillary Authors, Proofers, and Accuracy Checkers for the Sixth Edition

LuAnn Bean, *Florida Institute of Technology*; Debby Bloom CMA, *CFM*; Bea Chiang, *The College of New Jersey*; Jill Misuraca, *University of Tampa*; Alice Sineath, *University of Maryland University College*; Diane Tanner, *University of North Florida*; Melanie Yon, *WileyPLUS* developer.

Reviewers

The development of this sixth edition of Managerial Accounting benefited greatly from the comments and suggestions of colleagues who teach managerial accounting. I would like to acknowledge the contributions made by the following individuals:

Stephen Asare, *University of Florida*; LuAnn Bean, *Florida Institute of Technology*; Brenda Bradford, *Missouri Baptist University*; Kurt Fanning, *Grand Valley State University*; Amanda Farmer, *University of Georgia, Athens*; Timothy Foley, *University at Albany*; George Gerner, *University at Albany*; John Giles, *North Carolina State University*; Michael Hammond, *Missouri State University*; Catherine Katagiri, *The College of Saint Rose*; Ethan Kinory, *Baruch College*; Curtis Ksenak, *Saint Joseph's College*; Gary Laycock, *Ivy Tech Community College*; Daniel McGeough, *Mt. San Antonio College*; Christopher McKittrick, *North Carolina State University*; James McKittrick, *University of Portland*; Michael Newman, *University of Houston*; Jorge Romero, *Towson University*; Anwar Salimi, *University of Laverne*; Jason Stanfield, *Purdue University, West Lafayette*; Michael Sweeney, *Hillsdale College*; Diane Tanner, *University of North Florida*; Robin Thomas, *North Carolina State University*; Kim Walker, *Johnson C. Smith University*

Prior Edition Reviewers

Ajay Adhikari, *American University;* Gilda Agacer, *Monmouth University;* Natalie Allen, *Texas A&M University;* Sekhar Anantharaman, *Indiana University of Pennsylvania;* Christie Anderson, *Whitworth College*; Walt Austin, *Mercer College*; Noah Barsky, *Villanova University;* Connie Belden, *Butler Community College*; William Blosel, *California University of Pennsylvania;* Cynthia Bolt, *The Citadel—The Military College of South Carolina*; Nat Briscoe, *Northwestern State University*; Wayne Bremser, *Villanova University;* Ann Brooks, *Central New Mexico Community College*; Carol Brown, *Oregon State University;* Leonor Cabrera, *San Mateo County Community College*; Betty Chavis, *California State University, Fullerton*; Richard Claire, *San Mateo County Community College*; Cheryl Crespi, *Central Connecticut State University;* Terry Dancer, *Arkansas State University*; Carleton Donchess, *Bridgewater State College*; Bob Everett, *Lewis and Clark Community College*; Anthony Fortner, *Carl Albert College*; Cynthia Greeson, *Ivy Tech Community College*; Rosalie Hallbauer, *Florida Memorial University;* Deborah Hanks, *Cardinal Stritch University;* Candice Heino, *Anoka-Ramsey Community College*; Dave Henderson, *College of Charleston*; Carol Hutchinson, *Asheville-Buncombe Technical Community College*; Ron Krug, *Allegony College of Maryland*; D. Jordan Lowe, *Arizona State University;* Steven Markoff, *Montclair State University;* Laurie McWhorter, *Mississippi State University;* Cathy Montesarchio, *Broward Community College*; Carmen Morgan, *Oregon Institute of Technology*; Al Oddo, *Niagara University;* Nick Powers, *Devry University—Chicago;* Denise C. Probert, *Viterbo College*; Dr. Anwar Y. Salimi, *California State University, Pomona*; Betty Saunders, *University of North Florida;* Charles Stanley, *Baylor University;* Sakaran Venkateswar, *Trinity University;* Jeffery Yost, *College of Charleston*; Christian E. Wurst Jr., *Temple University*

Contents

1
MANAGERIAL ACCOUNTING IN THE INFORMATION AGE 2

2

JOB-ORDER COSTING FOR MANUFACTURING AND SERVICE COMPANIES 36

3

PROCESS COSTING 86

4

COST-VOLUME-PROFIT ANALYSIS 122

5 VARIABLE COSTING 174

6 COST ALLOCATION AND ACTIVITY-BASED COSTING 204

7

THE USE OF COST INFORMATION IN MANAGEMENT DECISION MAKING 254

8

PRICING DECISIONS, CUSTOMER PROFITABILITY ANALYSIS, AND ACTIVITY-BASED PRICING 294

9

CAPITAL BUDGETING AND OTHER LONG-RUN DECISIONS 326

10

BUDGETARY PLANNING AND CONTROL 368

11

STANDARD COSTS AND VARIANCE ANALYSIS 414

12 DECENTRALIZATION AND PERFORMANCE EVALUATION 450

Chapters 13 & 14 Available in *WileyPLUS*

13

STATEMENT OF CASH FLOWS 496

14

ANALYZING FINANCIAL STATEMENTS: A MANAGERIAL PERSPECTIVE 530

List of Cases

Each chapter of *Managerial Accounting* includes one or more cases that:

- Promote critical thinking and decision making skills.
- Provide an opportunity for group work and/or written communication work.
- Integrate information from other business disciplines.

CHAPTER 1

1–1: LOCAL 635

A union is disputing "cost of meal" charges to hotel employees.

1–2: BOSWELL PLUMBING PRODUCTS

A senior manager wants to know a product's cost. But the "cost" information needed depends on the decision the senior manager is facing.

CHAPTER 2

2–1: ETHICS CASE: BRIXTON SURGICAL DEVICES

To meet an aggressive earnings target, two senior executives are planning to increase production to "bury" fixed overhead costs in inventory.

2–2: YSL MARKETING RESEARCH

A marketing research firm is considering various costs when bidding on a job.

2–3: DUPAGE POWDER COATING

A company's product costs are being distorted by its approach to overhead allocation.

CHAPTER 3

3–1: TECH-TONIC SPORTS DRINK

A producer of a sports drink is considering alternative treatments for the cost of lost units.

3–2: JENSEN PVC

A company is considering lowering prices to increase sales and reduce unit costs by making better use of excess capacity.

CHAPTER 4

4–1: ROTHMUELLER MUSEUM

A curator at a museum is trying to estimate the financial impact of a planned exhibit.

4–2: MAYFIELD SOFTWARE, CUSTOMER TRAINING

The customer training facility of a software company is showing a loss. The manager needs to determine the number of classes that must be offered to break even.

4–3: KROG'S METALFAB, INC.

A company is estimating the lost profit related to fire damage so it can submit an insurance claim.

CHAPTER 5

5–1: MICROIMAGE TECHNOLOGY, INC.

A start-up company has a negative gross margin and it appears that "the more it sells, the more it loses." Use of variable costing reveals that this is not the case.

5–2: RAINRULER STAINS

A variable-costing income statement is used to show the financial impact of sales related to a new customer category.

CHAPTER 6

6–1: EASTSIDE MEDICAL TESTING

This case presents a service company example of ABC.

6–2: QuantumTM

This case shows how ABC affects product costs and considers the use of ABC information in decision making.

CHAPTER 7

7–1: PRIMUS CONSULTING GROUP

A consulting firm is considering a client offer of a fee that is less than standard rates.

7–2: FIVE STAR TOOLS

A tool manufacturer is faced with a production constraint, and needs to consider the financial impact of a plan to deal with the situation.

CHAPTER 8

8–1: PRESTON CONCRETE

The company is considering moving away from its cost-plus pricing approach when an increase in interest rates reduces housing starts and the demand for concrete.

8–2: GALLOWAY UNIVERSITY MEDICAL CENTER PHARMACY

A university hospital pharmacy is considering the profit implications of alternative approaches to encouraging prescription renewals from "out-of-area" patients.

CHAPTER 9

9–1: ETHICS CASE: JUNIPER PACKAGING SOLUTIONS

A plant manager is considering a plan to circumvent a freeze on capital expenditures.

9–2: SERGO GAMES

A game company is considering outsourcing manufacturing of CDs.

CHAPTER 10

10–1: ETHICS CASE: COLUMBUS PARK—WASTE TREATMENT FACILITY

The manager of a waste treatment facility is planning to pad costs in her budget because the city controller is likely to cut whatever budget is submitted.

CHAPTER 11

CHAPTER 12

For Cases in Chapters 13 and 14 go to www.wiley.com/college/jiambalvo

CHAPTER 13

CHAPTER 14

1

MANAGERIAL ACCOUNTING IN THE INFORMATION AGE

What type of job will you hold in the future?

You may be a marketing manager for a consumer electronics firm, you may be the director of human resources for a biotech firm, or you may be the president of your own company. In these and other managerial positions you will have to plan operations, evaluate subordinates, and make a variety of decisions using accounting information. In some cases, you will find information from your firm's balance sheet, income statement, statement of retained earnings, and statement of cash flows to be useful. However, much of the information in these statements is more relevant to *external* users of accounting information, such as stockholders and creditors. In addition, you will need information prepared specifically for firm managers, the *internal* users of accounting information. This type of information is referred to as managerial accounting information.

If you are like most users of this book, you have already studied financial accounting. Financial accounting stresses accounting concepts and procedures that relate to preparing reports for external users of accounting information. In comparison, **managerial accounting** stresses accounting concepts and procedures that are relevant to preparing reports for internal users of accounting information. This book is devoted to the subject of managerial accounting, and this first chapter provides an overview of the role of managerial accounting in planning, control, and decision making. The chapter also defines important cost concepts and introduces key ideas that will be emphasized throughout the text. The chapter ends with a discussion of the information age and the impact of information technology on business, a framework for ethical decision making, and the role of the controller as the top management accountant. Note that you can enhance and test your knowledge of the chapter using Wiley's online resources and the self-assessment quiz at the end of the chapter. The end-of-chapter material also includes two solved review problems.

Monkey Business Images/Shutterstock

LEARNING OBJECTIVES

1. Explain the primary goal of managerial accounting and distinguish between financial and managerial accounting.
2. Define cost terms used in planning, control, and decision making.
3. Explain the two key ideas in managerial accounting.
4. Discuss the impact of information technology on business processes and the interactions companies have with suppliers and customers.
5. Describe a framework for ethical decision making and discuss the duties of the controller.

LEARNING OBJECTIVE 1

Explain the primary goal of managerial accounting and distinguish between financial and managerial accounting.

GOAL OF MANAGERIAL ACCOUNTING

Virtually all managers need to plan and control their operations and make a variety of decisions. The goal of managerial accounting is to provide the information they need for **planning, control**, and **decision making**. If *your* goal is to be an effective manager, a thorough understanding of managerial accounting is essential.

Planning

Planning is a key activity for all companies. A plan communicates a company's goals to employees aiding coordination of various functions, such as sales and production. A plan also specifies the resources needed to achieve company goals.

Budgets for Planning. The financial plans prepared by managerial accountants are referred to as **budgets**. A wide variety of budgets may be prepared. For example, a *profit budget* indicates planned income, a *cash-flow budget* indicates planned cash inflows and outflows, and a *production budget* indicates the planned quantity of production and the expected costs.

Consider the production cost budget for the Surge Performance Beverage Company. In the coming year, the company plans to produce 5,000,000 12-ounce bottles of beverage. This amount is based on forecasted sales. To produce this volume, the company estimates it will spend $1,500,000 on bottles, $400,000 on ingredients, $150,000 on water, and pay workers at its bottling plant $300,000. It also expects to pay $60,000 for rent, incur $80,000 of depreciation of equipment, and pay $100,000 for other miscellaneous costs. The production cost budget presented in Illustration 1-1 summarizes this information. This budget informs the managers of Surge about how many bottles the company intends to produce and what the necessary resources will cost.

Control

Control of organizations is achieved by evaluating the performance of *managers* and the *operations* for which they are responsible. The distinction between evaluating managers and evaluating the operations they control is important. Managers are evaluated to determine how their performance should be rewarded or punished, which in turn motivates them to perform at a high level. Based on an evaluation indicating good performance, a manager might receive a substantial bonus. An evaluation indicating a manager performed poorly might lead to the manager being fired. In part because evaluations of managers are typically tied to compensation and promotion opportunities, managers work hard to ensure that they will receive favorable evaluations. (Of course, managers

ILLUSTRATION 1-1

Production cost budget

Surge Performance Beverage Company
Budgeted Production Costs
For the Year Ended December 31, 2017

Budgeted Production	**5,000,000 Bottles**
Cost of bottles	$1,500,000
Ingredient cost	400,000
Water	150,000
Labor cost	300,000
Rent	60,000
Depreciation	80,000
Other	100,000
Total budgeted production cost	$2,590,000

may also work hard because they love their jobs, receive respect from coworkers, or value the sense of accomplishment from a job well done!)

Operations are evaluated to provide information as to whether they should be changed or not (i.e., expanded, contracted, or modified in some way). An evaluation of an operation can be negative even when the evaluation of the manager responsible for the operation is basically positive. For example, the manager of one of the two bottling plants at Surge Performance Beverage Company may do a good job of controlling costs and meeting deadlines, given that the plant is old and out-of-date. Still, senior management may decide to close the plant because, given the outdated equipment in the plant, it is not an efficient operation. In this scenario, the manager receives a positive evaluation whereas the operation receives a negative evaluation.

Company plans often play an important role in the control process. Managers can compare actual results with planned results and decide whether corrective action is necessary. If actual results differ from the plan, the plan may not have been followed properly; the plan may have not have been well thought out; or changing circumstances may have made the plan out-of-date.

Illustration 1-2 presents the major steps in the planning and control process. Once a plan has been made, actions are taken to implement it. These actions lead to results that are compared with the original plan. Based on this evaluation, managers are rewarded (e.g., given substantial bonuses or promoted if performance is judged to be good) or punished (e.g., given only a small bonus, given no bonus, or even fired if performance is judged to be poor). Also, based on the evaluation process, operations may be changed. Changes may consist of expanding (e.g., adding a second shift), contracting (e.g., closing a production plant), or improving operations (e.g., training employees to do a better job answering customer product inquiries). Changes may also consist of revising an unrealistic plan.

Performance Reports for Control. The reports used to evaluate the performance of managers and the operations they control are referred to as **performance reports**. Although there is no generally accepted method of preparing a performance report, such reports frequently involve a comparison of current-period performance with performance in a prior period or with planned (budgeted) performance.

ILLUSTRATION 1-2

Planning and control process

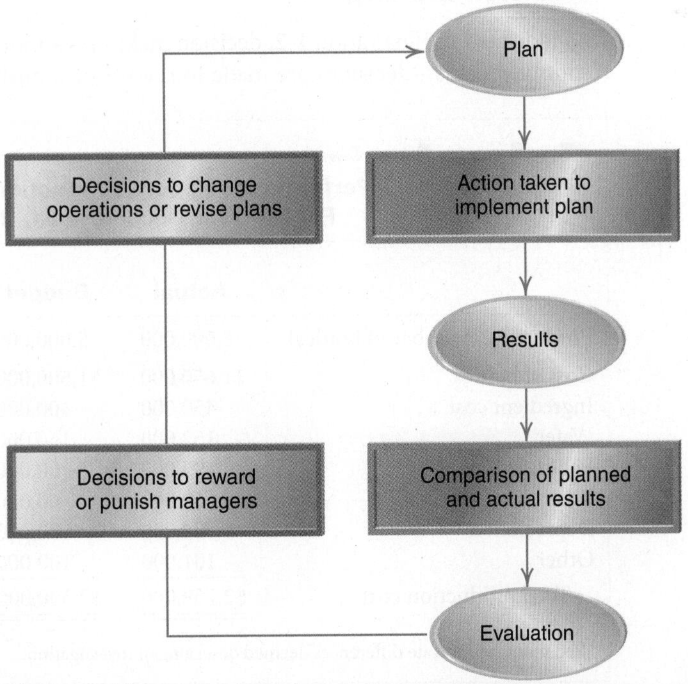

Suppose, for example, that during 2017, Surge Performance Beverage Company actually produced 5,000,000 bottles and incurred these costs:

Cost of bottles	$1,650,000
Ingredient cost	450,000
Water	152,000
Labor cost	295,000
Rent	60,000
Depreciation	80,000
Other	101,000
Total actual production cost	$2,788,000

A performance report comparing these actual costs to the budgeted costs is presented in Illustration 1-3.

Typically, performance reports only suggest areas that should be investigated; they do not provide definitive information on performance. For example, the performance report presented in Illustration 1-3 indicates that something may be amiss in the control of bottle and ingredient cost. Actual costs are $150,000 more than planned for bottles and $50,000 more than planned for ingredients. There are many possible reasons why these costs are greater than the amounts budgeted. Perhaps the price of bottles or key ingredients increased, or perhaps bottles were damaged in the production process. Management must investigate these possibilities before taking appropriate corrective action.

Although performance reports may not provide definitive answers, they are still extremely useful. Managers can use them to flag areas that need closer attention and to avoid areas that are under control. It would not seem necessary, for example, to investigate labor, rent, depreciation, or other costs, because these costs are either equal to or relatively close to the planned level of cost. Typically, managers follow the principle of **management by exception** when using performance reports. This means that managers investigate departures from the plan that appear to be exceptional; they do not investigate minor departures from the plan.

Decision Making

As indicated in Illustration 1-2, decision making is an integral part of the planning and control process—decisions are made to reward or punish managers, and decisions are

ILLUSTRATION 1-3

Performance report

SURGE PERFORMANCE BEVERAGE COMPANY

Performance Report, Production Costs
For the Year December 31, 2017

	Actual	Budget	Difference (Actual Minus Budget)
Production (number of bottles)	5,000,000	5,000,000	-0-
Cost of bottles	$1,650,000	$1,500,000	$150,000*
Ingredient cost	450,000	400,000	50,000*
Water	152,000	150,000	2,000
Labor cost	295,000	300,000	(5,000)
Rent	60,000	60,000	-0-
Depreciation	80,000	80,000	-0-
Other	101,000	100,000	1,000
Total production cost	$2,788,000	$2,590,000	$ 198,000

*Red numbers indicate differences deemed deserving of investigation.

made to change operations or revise plans. Should a firm add a new product? Should it drop an existing product? Should it manufacture a component used in assembling its major product or contract with another company to produce the component? What price should a firm charge for a new product? These questions indicate just a few of the key decisions that confront companies. How well they make these decisions will determine future profitability and, possibly, the survival of the company. Recognizing the importance of making good decisions, we devote all of Chapters 7, 8, and 9 to the topic. Below you'll see that one of the two key ideas of managerial accounting relates to decision making and its focus on so-called incremental analysis. Finally, at the end of each chapter, there is a feature called Making Business Decisions. This feature will remind you of how the chapter material is linked to decision making, and it will summarize the knowledge and skills presented in the chapter that will help you make good decisions as a manager.

TEST YOUR **KNOWLEDGE**

With respect to managerial accounting, which of the following statements are valid?

a. Budgets are used for planning.

b. Performance reports are used for control.

c. A goal of managerial accounting is to provide information useful in decision making.

d. All of the above are valid statements.

Correct answer is d.

A Comparison of Managerial and Financial Accounting

As suggested in the opening of this chapter, there are important differences between managerial and financial accounting:

1. Managerial accounting is directed at internal rather than external users of accounting information.
2. Managerial accounting may deviate from generally accepted accounting principles (GAAP).
3. Managerial accounting may present more detailed information.
4. Managerial accounting may present more nonmonetary information.
5. Managerial accounting places more emphasis on the future.

Internal versus External Users. Financial accounting is aimed primarily at external users of accounting information, whereas managerial accounting is aimed primarily at internal users (i.e., company managers). External users include investors, creditors, and government agencies, which need information to make investment, lending, and regulatory decisions. Their information needs differ from those of internal users, who need information for planning, control, and decision making.

Need to Use GAAP. Much of financial accounting information is required. The Securities and Exchange Commission (SEC) requires large, publicly traded companies to prepare reports in accordance with generally accepted accounting principles (GAAP). Even companies that are not under the jurisdiction of the SEC prepare financial accounting information in accordance with GAAP to satisfy creditors. Managerial accounting, however, is completely optional. It stresses information that is *useful* to internal managers for planning, control, and decision making. If a company believes that deviating from GAAP will provide more useful information to managers, GAAP need not be followed.

Detail of Information. Financial accounting presents information in a highly summarized form. Net income, for example, is presented for the company as a whole. To run a company, however, managers need more detailed information; for example, information about the cost of operating individual departments versus the cost of operating the company as a whole or sales broken out by product versus total company sales.

Emphasis on Nonmonetary Information. Both managerial and financial accounting reports generally contain monetary information (information expressed in dollars, such as revenue and expense). But managerial accounting reports often contain a substantial amount of additional nonmonetary information. The quantity of material consumed in production, the average time taken to process a customer service call, and the number of product defects are examples of important nonmonetary data that appear in managerial accounting reports.

Emphasis on the Future. Financial accounting is primarily concerned with presenting the results of past transactions. Managerial accounting, however, places considerable emphasis on the future. As indicated previously, one of the primary purposes of managerial accounting is planning. Thus, managerial accounting information often involves estimates of the costs and benefits of future transactions.

Similarities between Financial and Managerial Accounting

We should not overstate the differences between financial accounting and managerial accounting in terms of their respective user groups. Financial accounting reports are aimed *primarily* at external users, and managerial accounting reports are aimed *primarily* at internal users. However, managers also make significant use of financial accounting reports, and external users occasionally request financial information that is generally considered appropriate for internal users. For example, creditors may ask management to provide them with detailed cash-flow projections.

TEST YOUR **KNOWLEDGE**

Which of the following is **false?**

a. Compared to financial accounting, managerial accounting places more emphasis on generally accepted accounting principles (GAAP).

b. Compared to financial accounting, managerial accounting may present more nonmonetary information.

c. Compared to financial accounting, managerial accounting places more emphasis on the future.

d. Compared to financial accounting, managerial accounting may present more detailed information.

Correct answer is a.

LEARNING OBJECTIVE 2

Define cost terms used in planning, control, and decision making.

COST TERMS USED IN DISCUSSING PLANNING, CONTROL, AND DECISION MAKING

When managers discuss planning, control, and decision making, they frequently use the word *cost*. Unfortunately, what they mean by this word is often ambiguous. This section defines key cost terms so that you will have the accounting vocabulary necessary to begin discussing issues related to planning, control, and decision making. The treatment will be brief because we will return to these cost terms and examine them in detail in later chapters.

Variable and Fixed Costs

The classification of a cost as variable or fixed depends on how the cost changes in relation to changes in the level of business activity.

Variable Costs. Costs that increase or decrease in proportion to increases or decreases in the level of business activity are **variable costs**. Material and direct labor are generally considered to be variable costs because in many situations they fluctuate in proportion to changes in production (business activity). Suppose that for Surge Performance Beverage Company, the cost of bottles, ingredients, water, and labor are variable costs and in the prior month, when production was 400,000 bottles, costs were $120,000 for bottles, $32,000 for ingredients, $12,000 for water, and $24,000 for labor. How much variable cost should the company plan on for the current month if production is expected to increase by 20 percent, to 480,000 bottles? Since the variable costs change in proportion to changes in activity, if production increases by 20 percent, these costs should also increase by 20 percent. Thus, the cost of bottles should increase to $144,000, the cost of ingredients should increase to $38,400, the cost of water to $14,400, and the cost of labor to $28,800.

	PRIOR MONTH		CURRENT MONTH	
Production	400,000 Bottles	Per Unit	480,000 Bottles	Per Unit
Variable costs:				
Cost of bottles	$120,000	$0.30	$144,000	$0.30
Ingredient cost	32,000	0.08	38,400	0.08
Water	12,000	0.03	14,400	0.03
Labor cost	24,000	0.06	28,800	0.06
Total variable cost	$188,000	$0.47	$225,600	$0.47

Note that although the *total variable cost* increases from $188,000 to $225,600 when production changes from 400,000 to 480,000 units, the *variable cost per unit* does not change. It remains $0.47 per bottle. With variable cost of $0.47 per bottle, variable cost increases by $37,600 (i.e., $0.47 × 80,000) when production increases by 80,000 bottles.

Fixed Costs. Costs that remain constant when there are changes in the level of business activity are **fixed costs**. Depreciation and rent are costs that typically do not change with changes in business activity. Suppose that in the prior month, Surge Performance Beverage Company incurred $20,000 of fixed costs including $5,000 of rent, $6,667 of depreciation, and $8,333 of other miscellaneous fixed costs. If the company increases production to 480,000 bottles in the current month, the levels of rent, depreciation, and other fixed costs incurred should remain the same as when production was only 400,000 bottles. However, with fixed costs, the cost per unit does change when there are changes in production. When production increases, the constant amount of fixed cost is spread over a larger number of units. This drives down the fixed cost per unit. With an increase in production from 400,000 to 480,000 units, *total fixed costs* remains at $20,000. Note, however, that *fixed cost per unit* decreases from $0.0500 per unit to $0.0417 per unit.

	PRIOR MONTH		CURRENT MONTH	
Production	400,000 Bottles	Per Unit	480,000 Bottles	Per Unit
Fixed costs:				
Rent	$ 5,000	$0.0125	$ 5,000	$0.0104
Depreciation	6,667	0.0167	6,667	0.0139
Other	8,333	0.0208	8,333	0.0174
Total fixed cost	$20,000	$0.0500	$20,000	$0.0417

Sunk Costs

Costs incurred in the past are referred to as **sunk costs**. These costs are not relevant for decision making because they do not change when decisions are made. For example, suppose you buy a ticket to a play for $30. Before the play, you run into a friend who invites you to a party. If you go to the party, you won't be able to attend the play. The cost of the ticket is irrelevant to the decision as to whether you should go to the party. What matters is how much you will enjoy the party versus the play and how much you can *sell* the ticket for (not how much you *paid* for it). Whether you go to the play or go to the party, you are out $30 (the price of the ticket to the play, which is sunk).

Opportunity Costs

The value of benefits forgone when one decision alternative is selected over another is an **opportunity cost**. For example, suppose Surge Performance Beverage Company refuses an order to produce 50,000 bottles for a grocery chain because taking on the order will require the company to miss delivery deadlines on orders already taken. Suppose the order would have generated $50,000 of additional revenue (the product sells for $1 per bottle) and $23,500 of additional costs. Then the opportunity cost (the net benefit forgone) associated with meeting current delivery deadlines is $26,500 ($50,000 – $23,500).

LINK TO **PRACTICE**

Long Supply Chains Create Opportunity Costs

Today, much of the textiles sold in the United States come from China and other Asian countries. Labor is relatively cheap in Asia, and the direct cost of shipping isn't that significant. Given this, why are some U.S. companies considering manufacturing closer to home—such as in Mexico? The reason is opportunity costs. With a long-distance supplier in, say, China, there may be a lack of reliability due to misunderstandings and the inability of the purchaser to directly monitor the production process. Further, the distance shipped creates delays in getting products to market. Both of these situations create opportunity costs. Wrong colors and errors in stitching patterns may mean lost sales, as may delays in getting textiles into the hands of consumers. These lost sales are opportunity costs associated with the decision to use a supplier located thousands of miles away.

Source: Peter T. Leach, "What Goes Around Comes Around: Long Supply Chains Can Create Opportunity Costs," *Gulf Shipper* (December 2007), 6–9.

Direct and Indirect Costs

Costs that are directly traceable to a product, activity, or department are **direct costs. Indirect costs** are those that either cannot be directly traced to a product, activity, or department or are not worth tracing. The distinction between a direct and an indirect cost depends on the object of the cost tracing. For example, Surge Performance Beverage

ILLUSTRATION 1-4
Insurance as both a direct and indirect cost

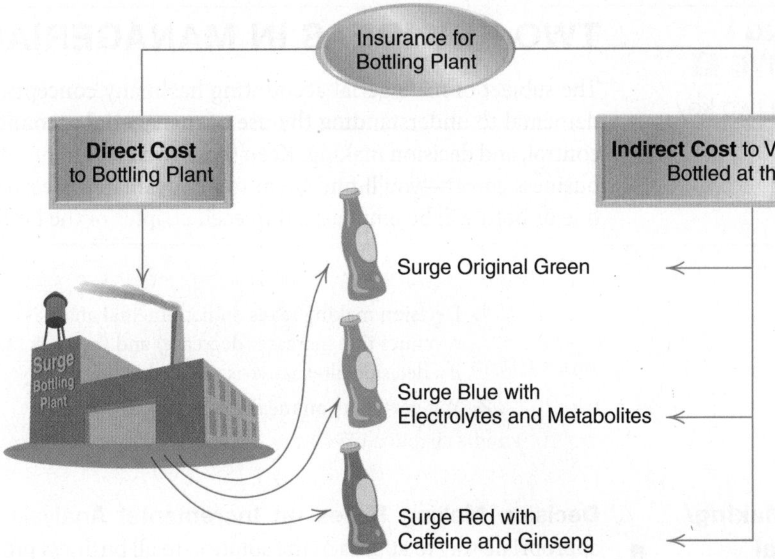

Company has a production facility in Memphis for which it incurs insurance costs. The insurance cost related to the Memphis plant is obviously a direct cost of the Memphis plant. However, the insurance cost is an indirect cost with respect to the individual types of sports drinks produced in the Memphis plant because *direct* tracing of the insurance cost to each type of drink is not possible. This situation is presented in Illustration 1-4.

Controllable and Noncontrollable Costs

A manager can influence a **controllable cost** but cannot influence a **noncontrollable cost**. The distinction between controllable and noncontrollable costs is especially important when evaluating a manager's performance. A manager should not be evaluated unfavorably if a noncontrollable cost sharply increases.

As an example of controllable and noncontrollable costs, consider a plant supervisor. This individual influences labor and material costs by scheduling workers and ensuring an efficient production process. Thus, labor and material costs are the supervisor's controllable costs. However, the supervisor cannot determine insurance for a plant. A plant manager or an insurance specialist makes decisions regarding insurance. Therefore, insurance cost is a supervisor's noncontrollable cost but a plant manager's or an insurance specialist's controllable cost.

TEST YOUR **KNOWLEDGE**

Susan Evans paid a $5,000 nonrefundable fee to attend a 5-day management seminar on leadership, hosted by the Bradford College of Business. After registering for the course, her boss asked Susan to be the lead consultant on a project with a major client and, unfortunately, the start of the engagement conflicted with the seminar. Her boss, however, said that she'd be happy to ask another coworker to be the lead if Susan still wanted to attend the seminar.

With respect to the decision Susan faces (go to the seminar or take the lead position on a consulting engagement), the $5,000 cost of the seminar is:

a. A variable cost. b. A fixed cost.
c. A sunk cost. d. An opportunity cost.

Correct answer is c.

LEARNING OBJECTIVE 3

Explain the two key ideas in managerial accounting.

TWO KEY IDEAS IN MANAGERIAL ACCOUNTING

The subject of managerial accounting has many concepts. However, two ideas are fundamental to understanding the use of managerial accounting information in planning, control, and decision making. Keep these two ideas in mind as you progress through your business career—you'll find them to be invaluable! Because the ideas are so important, one or both will be emphasized in each chapter of the book and identified with an icon.

1. Decision making relies on incremental analysis—an analysis of the revenues that increase (decrease) and the costs that increase (decrease) if a decision alternative is selected.
2. You get what you measure!

Decision Making/ Incremental Analysis

Decision Making Relies on Incremental Analysis. Incremental analysis is the appropriate way to approach the solution to all business problems. Essentially, **incremental analysis** involves the calculation of the difference in revenue and the difference in cost between decision alternatives. The difference in revenue is the **incremental revenue** of one alternative over another, whereas the difference in cost is the **incremental cost** of one alternative over another. If an alternative yields an incremental profit (the difference between incremental revenue and incremental cost), it is the preferred alternative. In the simplified example that follows, decision alternative 1 should be selected because, compared with alternative 2, it yields an incremental profit of $3,000.

COMPARISON OF DECISION ALTERNATIVES

	ALTERNATIVE 1		ALTERNATIVE 2			
Revenue	$15,000	–	$10,000	=	$5,000	Incremental Revenue
Cost	8,000	–	6,000	=	2,000	Incremental Cost
Profit	$ 7,000	–	$ 4,000	=	$3,000	Incremental Profit

Although the idea is simple, implementing it in practice can be difficult—that's why we devote all of Chapters 7, 8, and 9 to decision making. For now, let's look at a decision facing Surge Performance Beverage Company to gain a better understanding of incremental analysis.

Recall that at Surge Performance Beverage Company, the budgeted annual production costs for 5,000,000 bottles was $2,590,000:

Production	5,000,000 bottles
Cost of bottles	$1,500,000
Ingredient cost	400,000
Water	150,000
Labor cost	300,000
Rent	60,000
Depreciation	80,000
Other	100,000
Total production cost	$2,590,000
Cost per unit	$ 0.518

Currently, Surge sells its product only to grocery and health food stores, at $1 per bottle. Now assume that Surge is approached by Costless, a company that sells products in no-frills, self-service warehouse facilities. Costless offers to buy 200,000 bottles in the coming year, but only if the price is reduced to $0.75 per bottle. In this case there are two decision alternatives: (1) stick with the status quo and decline the offer, or (2) accept the offer.

If the offer is accepted, incremental revenue (the increase in revenue due to accepting the offer versus declining the offer) will be $150,000 and incremental cost (the increase in cost due to accepting the offer versus declining the offer) will be $94,000. Thus, the incremental profit of accepting the offer is $56,000. Assuming that the company has the capacity to produce the additional 200,000 bottles and that other orders will not have to be turned down if this large order is accepted (i.e., assuming that there are no opportunity costs), Surge Performance Beverage Company should accept this order.

Incremental revenue ($.75 × 200,000 bottles)		$150,000
Less incremental costs:		
Increase in cost of bottles ($.30 × 200,000)	$60,000	
Increase in cost of ingredients ($.08 × 200,000)	16,000	
Increase in cost of water ($.03 × 200,000)	6,000	
Increase in cost of labor ($.06 × 200,000)	12,000	94,000
Incremental profit		$ 56,000

Note that in the analysis, we use only four of the production cost items (cost of bottles, cost of ingredients, cost of water, and cost of labor). These are the only costs that increase with the new order, because all other costs (rent, depreciation, and other) are fixed and will not increase with an increase in production. Therefore, they are not incremental costs and are not relevant to the decision at hand. Think about rent expense. If the special order is rejected, rent expense will be $60,000. If the special order is accepted, rent expense will still be $60,000. Since rent expense does not change, it is not incremental, and it is not relevant in analyzing the decision.

YOU GET WHAT YOU MEASURE

You Get What You Measure! The second key idea in managerial accounting is "You get what you measure!" In other words, performance measures greatly influence the behavior of managers.

You Get What You Measure!
Performance Measures Drive Behavior

PERFORMANCE MEASURES	POTENTIAL ACTIONS OF MANAGERS
Customer satisfaction at auto repair shop	Give customers a loaner car while auto is being repaired
Injuries on the job at home construction site	Develop training program for new employees at construction site
Sales to new customers of office supply company	More sales calls on potential versus current customers

Companies can select from a vast number of performance measures when deciding how they want to assess performance. Profit, market share, sales to new customers, product development time, number of defective units produced, and number of late deliveries are examples of measures in common use. Because rewards often depend on how well an employee performs on a particular measure, employees direct their attention to what is measured and may neglect what isn't measured.

For example, suppose that at Surge Performance Beverage Company, sales to new customers is introduced as a primary measure of the performance of the sales manager. How would this influence the behavior of the sales manager? Most likely, this measure will lead the manager to spend more time developing business with new customers. Although that may be just what senior management desires from the performance measure, it could lead to problems. Suppose a sales manager greatly reduces the time spent attending to the needs of existing customers, and the company loses the business of several key accounts. To avoid this and other unintended consequences, companies need to develop a balanced set of performance measures and avoid placing too much emphasis on any single measure.

TEST YOUR KNOWLEDGE

Jason Deen is the owner of Deen's Custom Motorcycles. Recently, his cousin, Jake, crashed his bike and brought it in for repairs. Jason offered to fix the bike and charge his cousin for just the incremental costs.

Which of the following is an incremental cost associated with the repair job?

a. Depreciation on tools.
b. Salary paid to the accountant at Deen's.
c. Required parts.
d. Utilities (e.g., heat and electricity).

Correct answer is c.

LINK TO PRACTICE

Problems Related to the Wrong Performance Measures

As documented by Dean Spitzer, a performance measurement thought leader, in his book *Transforming Performance Measurement,* bad things can happen when the wrong performance measure is used to evaluate employees. For example, he notes that at an insurance company known for its customer focus, digital scoreboards were mounted at a call center and reported on the average wait time for teams to respond to customer calls. The idea was to motivate employees to respond quickly to incoming calls. But to do this, employees quickly and incompletely answered customer calls so they could get off the line and pick up the next incoming call. The result was that customers frequently had to call back to get additional information, and that certainly didn't lead to customer satisfaction.

When the CEO of the company realized the problem, the "wait time" measure was replaced with "percentage of callers who complete their business on the first call with no need for additional follow-up."

LEARNING OBJECTIVE 4

Discuss the impact of information technology on business processes and the interactions companies have with suppliers and customers.

THE INFORMATION AGE AND MANAGERIAL ACCOUNTING

In recent years, advances in information technology have radically changed access to information and, as a consequence, the business landscape—so much so that the current business era is frequently referred to as the *information age.* Since managerial accounting is about *providing information* in order to plan and control operations and to make decisions, part and parcel of an understanding of managerial accounting is an understanding of the impact of information technology on business processes and the interactions companies have with suppliers and customers. These topics are discussed in this section.

ILLUSTRATION 1-5
The value chain

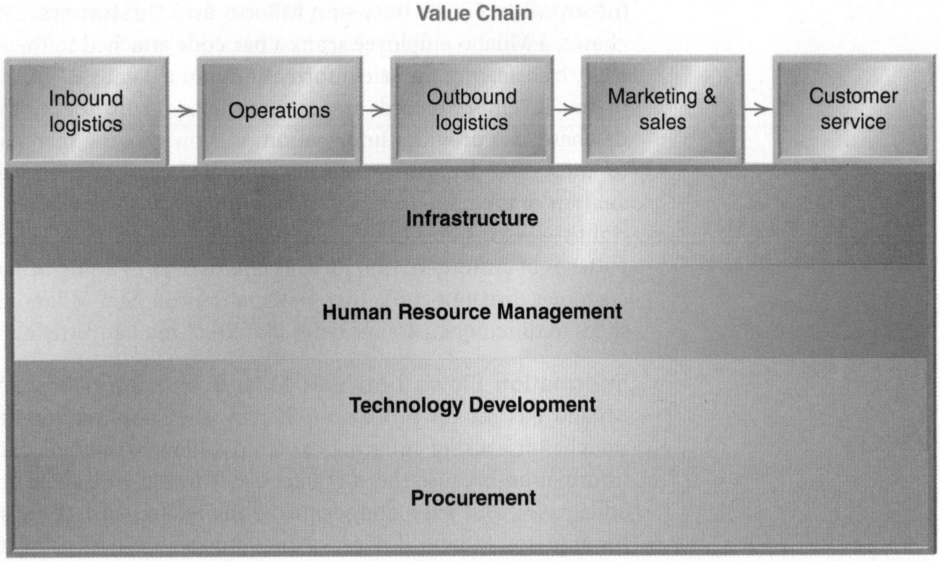

Impact of Information Technology on Management of the Value Chain

The **value chain** comprises the fundamental activities a firm engages in to create value. The idea was developed by Michael Porter in his groundbreaking book, *Competitive Advantage*. According to Porter, firms engage in a series of primary and secondary activities. The primary activities are inbound logistics (receiving and storing goods and materials), operations to transform materials into finished products, outbound logistics (storing and shipping products to customers), marketing and sales, and after-sale customer service. (See Illustration 1-5.) The secondary activities include firm infrastructure (e.g., accounting, finance, and legal affairs), human resource management (e.g., hiring, training, benefits administration), technology development, and procurement of goods and services. When the value to the customer of receiving products and services exceeds the cost of these activities, firm value is created.

Information flows up and down a company's value chain and also between the company and its suppliers and between the company and its customers. Illustration 1-6 shows this for Milano Clothiers. Milano has 35 stores throughout the United States and annual sales of over $800 million. For Milano to be successful, its suppliers must provide high-quality items, on time, to the right location, at a reasonable price. Also, Milano's own operations must be efficient. It must be able to market effectively and offer products that customers want. How can Milano ensure that this happens? The key is to take advantage of information flows up and down the value chain and between Milano and its suppliers and between Milano and its customers. This is where advances in information technology are having an impact. Note that in Illustration 1-6, the lines between suppliers and Milano and between customers and Milano are dashed lines. These represent the fact that the organizational boundaries are somewhat permeable because a lot of information is being transmitted both ways. Let's see some examples of how this works.

ILLUSTRATION 1-6
Information flows within Milano and between Milano and its suppliers and Milano and its customers

Information Flows between Milano and Customers. When customers make purchases, a Milano employee scans a bar code attached to the sale item, thereby automatically transferring the sale information into a database. This information can be used to update inventory records and ensure the company does not run out of "hot" items. The database also provides information on slow-moving merchandise that Milano can sell to a discount department store so that it doesn't take up valuable floor space. Further analysis of the sales data can reveal regional tastes in clothes, helping Milano to buy the right styles for stores in different parts of the country. Milano may also track the buying patterns of customers who identify themselves by using Milano's credit card or a special customer discount card. This information can help Milano direct targeted selling messages to different customer types via direct-mail advertising.

Information Flows between Milano and Suppliers. With several key suppliers, Milano has set up processes whereby the suppliers monitor Milano's sales of their merchandise using information from Milano's internal database. Milano shares this information because the suppliers use it to improve their production scheduling, gain efficiencies, and pass along some of the related cost savings to Milano in the form of lower prices. Milano also tracks the status of its orders using its suppliers' websites. Thus, Milano knows the exact time merchandise will be arriving at each of its locations, and this information is available any time of the day. Milano uses this information, in part, to time its advertising campaigns.

Using Information Technology to Gain Internal Efficiencies. Internally, Milano uses information technology to automate purchasing and accounts payable, sales and customer billing, as well as other accounting and finance functions. While in the past the company could not close its books until 1 month after year-end, it can now close in a week. This provides senior managers with timely information on the company's profitability and allows the company to provide timely financial reports to shareholders and creditors. The company has over 2,000 employees. Each employee has access to a company human resources (HR) Web site that provides comprehensive information on company policies and allows employees to select from a menu of alternative health and retirement plans. The launch of the Web site has eliminated the need for five full-time HR staff who previously responded to employee questions and processed paperwork.

Software Systems That Impact Value Chain Management

Companies use a variety of software systems to process information and improve the operation of the value chain. Here, we briefly discuss three systems: **enterprise resource planning (ERP) systems, supply chain management (SCM) systems**, and **customer relationship management (CRM) systems.**

Enterprise Resource Planning Systems. ERP systems grew out of material requirements planning (MRP) systems that have been used since the 1960s. MRP systems computerized inventory control and production planning. Key features included an ability to prepare a master production schedule and a bill of materials and generate purchase orders. ERP systems update MRP systems with better integration, relational databases, and graphical user interfaces. ERP components now include accounting and finance, human resources, and other applications including SCM and CRM, which are discussed next.

Supply Chain Management Systems. Supply chain management (SCM) is the organization of activities between a company and its suppliers in an effort to provide for the profitable development, production, and delivery of goods to customers. By sharing information, production lead times and inventory holding costs have been reduced, while on-time deliveries to customers have been improved. SCM software systems support the planning of the best way to fill orders and help tracking of products and components among companies in the supply chain. Walmart and Procter & Gamble (P&G) are two companies that have become well known for their cooperation in the use of SCM. When P&G products are scanned at a Walmart store, P&G receives information on the sale via satellite and, thus, knows when to make more product and the specific Walmart stores to which the product should be shipped. Related cost savings are passed on, at least in part, to Walmart customers.

Customer Relationship Management Systems. CRM systems are used to manage information related to a variety of customer interactions. At their heart is a database of many, if not all, customer interactions. Company employees (and, in some cases, customers) can access this database for many purposes, including these:

- Salespeople can examine the history of all sales calls made to customers and customers' responses. This allows the sales force to personalize their messages so that they match a specific customer's needs.
- Analysis of data in the CRM system can support targeted direct-mail advertising, taking into account customers' past purchases.
- A CRM system can be used to suggest future purchases to customers based on their past purchases. This is a well-known feature of the CRM system at Amazon.com.
- A CRM system can allow customers to track the status of their orders. For example, the CRM system used by FedEx allows customers to track their shipments.
- A CRM system can allow customers to access information on product updates. For example, Canon has a CRM system that allows customers to update printer drivers.

LINK TO **PRACTICE**

Casinos Manage with Data from CRM Systems

Casinos have been leaders in using data collected from their CRM systems in marketing decisions. Some give customers a card that they can use as they bet, buy meals, buy spa services, and pay for golf outings. Information from applying for and using the card includes patron age and home location, e-mail address, number and length of visits, retail purchase data, food and beverage data, table game preference, and slot machine denomination preference.

Casinos can use this information to determine which customers are most profitable and then target them with promotions that encourage repeat visits. These promotions can be sent via e-mail since the customer's e-mail address is available. As another example, if a casino learns that a customer plays golf, then the casino can offer a discount on this activity. This would be especially profitable if a golf outing caused a customer to stay 2 or 3 days longer at the casino and gamble.

Customers who are especially profitable, such as those who play higher-denomination slot machines, would also be offered incentives and advertising stressing the excitement and glamour of playing slots. Individuals who avoided playing slot machines but loved playing blackjack might be sent ads stressing the excitement and glamour of playing this game. And individuals like me won't be sent any incentives since I don't find gambling to be either exciting or glamorous!

TEST YOUR **KNOWLEDGE**

Which of the following is **false?**

a. Companies use CRM systems to manage information related to customers.
b. Supply chain management systems may be used to share information with suppliers.
c. Enterprise resource planning systems may include CRM and SCM applications.
d. CRM systems are primarily used to manage information generated by suppliers.

Correct answer is d.

LEARNING OBJECTIVE 5

Describe a framework for ethical decision making and discuss the duties of the controller.

ETHICAL CONSIDERATIONS IN MANAGERIAL DECISION MAKING

Remember that when we discuss decision making throughout this book, we will focus on incremental analysis as the approach to making good decisions. However, in addition to performing incremental analysis, it is equally important that managers consider the ethical aspects of their decisions. Why focus on ethics? First and foremost, ethical decision making is simply the right thing to do. But additionally, when managers behave ethically, they gain the confidence of their customers, suppliers, subordinates, and company stockholders, and that confidence is likely to translate into gains to the bottom line and to their company's stock price.

Ethical and Unethical Behavior

Ethical behavior requires that managers recognize the difference between what's right and what's wrong and then make decisions consistent with what's right. In recent years, we've witnessed a plethora of disclosures, indictments, and convictions, indicating that key managers in major companies either can't tell right from wrong or don't care to make decisions consistent with what's right. Some examples:

> Enron managers misled investors by hiding debt in so-called special-purpose entities. Kenneth Lay, Enron's CEO, touted Enron's stock to employees just weeks before the energy company imploded, leaving many with worthless 401(k) retirement accounts. Lay was found guilty of securities fraud and related charges. He faced a sentence of more than 20 years but died of a heart attack in 2006, prior to sentencing.
>
> WorldCom, America's number two long-distance company, disclosed the biggest case of fraudulent accounting in U.S. history, with profits overstated by billions. The result—the company declared bankruptcy and laid off 17,000 employees. Bernard Ebbers, CEO of WorldCom, received a 25-year prison sentence in 2005.
>
> Dennis Kozlowski, who made more than $300 million as head of Tyco, was charged with conspiring with art dealers to avoid sales tax on art he bought for $13.2 million. Tyco's share price took a nosedive following the disclosure. In 2005, Kozlowski was convicted for misappropriations of corporate funds including granting himself unauthorized bonuses and having millions of dollars of personal expenses paid by Tyco, including a $15,000 umbrella stand and a $6,000 shower curtain. He was sentenced to a jail term of 8 to 20 years.

Sarbanes-Oxley Act. The abuses just cited, along with others, led Congress to enact the Sarbanes-Oxley Act in July 2002. This law, named after Senator Paul Sarbanes and Representative Michael Oxley, has changed the financial reporting landscape for public companies and their auditors. Some of the act's most important provisions are:

- A requirement that chief executive officers and chief financial officers of a company certify that, based on their knowledge, their financial statements do not contain any untrue statements or omissions of material facts that would make the statements misleading.
- A ban on certain types of work by the company's auditors to ensure their independence. For example, the act bans auditors from performing bookkeeping services and designing or implementing financial information systems for clients.
- Longer jail sentences and larger fines for corporate executives who knowingly and willfully misstate financial statements. Fines now run up to $5 million and jail terms up to 20 years.
- A requirement that companies report on the existence and reliability of their internal controls as they relate to financial reports.

The cost of complying with Sarbanes-Oxley has been substantial. According to a survey conducted by Charles River Associates of 90 companies with average annual gross revenue of $8.1 billion, the average cost to comply with the act in the first year was $7.8 million. This amount should be contrasted with the $63 billion lost by shareholders in Enron. Will the net benefits of Sarbanes-Oxley outweigh the costs? Time will tell. There is no doubt, however, that the act has reminded corporate leaders that they have a clear obligation to ensure that financial statements do not mislead investors. And the act has put needed distance between senior managers and auditors of publicly traded companies.

In addition to conspicuous and rather clear-cut examples of unethical behavior, some companies and individuals have been accused of paying unconscionably low wages to workers in undeveloped countries, using child labor, endangering the environment with toxic chemicals, and bribing officials to promote sales abroad. But are these accusations clearly indicative of ethical lapses? Low wages are better than no wages, and, while child labor is reprehensible, the additional income earned by a child may save a family from starvation. The point is that ethical dilemmas are often complex and the situations managers face are often gray rather than black and white. When this is the case, a framework for ethical decision making may help understanding of "what's right."

LINK TO **PRACTICE**

Feds Investigating Walmart Over Bribery in Mexico

Wouldn't it have been wonderful if corporate wrongdoing had ceased after the events at Enron, WorldCom, and Tyco? Unfortunately, that hasn't been the case. Here's an example of more recent alleged wrongdoing:

In 2012, the Justice Department began a criminal investigation of Walmart related to allegations the company paid more than $24 million in bribes to Mexican officials for construction permits. Such bribes would be a violation of the U.S. Foreign Corrupt Practices Act (FCPA). The probe expanded to China, India, and Brazil and is ongoing as of 2015. Walmart spent $439 million in FCPA investigation and compliance costs in 2013 and 2014. And the company estimates such costs will exceed $200 million in fiscal 2015!

Sources: Asri Horwithz and Jia Lynn Yang, "Wal-Mart Faces Criminal Probe into Bribery Allegations," *The Washington Post*, April 24, 2012; David Voreaqcos and Renee Dudley, "Wal-Mart Says Bribe Probe Cost $439 Million in Two Years," *Bloomberg News*, March 26, 2014.

A Framework for Ethical Decision Making

The following framework for ethical decision making consists of seven questions.[1] Hopefully, answering these questions will serve as an aid in identifying "what's right." But certainly, answering them doesn't guarantee ethical decision making.

A Seven-Question Framework for Ethical Decision Making

When evaluating a decision, ask:

1. What decision alternatives are available?
2. What individuals or organizations have a stake in the outcome of my decision?
3. Will an individual or an organization be harmed by any of the alternatives?
4. Which alternative will do the most good with the least harm?
5. Would someone I respect find any of the alternatives objectionable?

After deciding on a course of action, but before taking action, ask:

6. At a gut level, am I comfortable with the decision I am about to make?
7. Will I be comfortable telling my friends and family about this decision?

ANY QUESTIONS?

Q: Why focus on the seven-question framework for ethical decision making? Many, if not most, companies have written codes of ethics, so when managers make decisions, they just need to consult their company's code to determine whether their decision stacks up to what's right in their company's environment.

A: Managers should definitely be familiar with their company's code of ethics. However, codes of ethics aren't always good guides to ethical behavior. Part of the problem is that codes often specify what can't be done rather than what should be done. And some codes focus more on ensuring that decisions are legal rather than right!

A number of exercises, problems, and cases in the end-of-chapter material present ethical dilemmas, and you should refer to this framework when preparing your answers to them. Alternatively, you may wish to consider other ethical perspectives. A large amount of material is available on the Web to help your understanding of ethical decision making.

IMA Statement of Ethical Professional Practice

The Institute of Management Accounting (IMA) is a professional organization that focuses, as its name indicates, on management accounting. One of the contributions of the IMA is the development of a Statement of Ethical Professional Practice, which is presented in the appendix to this chapter. The IMA has also developed an ethics helpline that members can call to discuss ethical dilemmas they face at their companies. Callers are assigned a code number to preserve anonymity and are then referred to a counselor

[1]Developing these questions was aided by three resources located on the Web. The first is *A Guide to Moral Decision Making* by Chris MacDonald in the Department of Bioethics at Dalhousie University. The second is material developed by the W. Maurice Young Centre for Applied Ethics at the University of British Columbia, and the third is *Complete Guide to Ethics Management: An Ethics Toolkit for Managers*, by Carter MacNamera.

LINK TO **PRACTICE**

Are the Procurement Practices of the Hershey Company Ethical?

The Hershey Company is the largest producer of chocolates in North America. Like most other producers of chocolate, Hershey relies on cocoa sourced from West Africa, which accounts for approximately 80 percent of the world's cocoa. This is controversial, however, because West Africa's cocoa production involves widespread use of child labor. And, in many cases, the children are exposed to dangerous pesticides used because of the extent of crop infestations.

What should Hershey do about this? Some critics are calling on Hershey to purchase fair-trade cocoa. In a fair-trade system, Hershey would pay a higher price, enabling small producers to afford adult workers, make important improvements in their farming practices, and support development of schools and hospitals.

In 2010, Hershey issued a corporate social responsibility report in which it said, "As the largest chocolate producer in the United States and one of the largest in the world, the well-being of the global cocoa supply chain is of vital importance to us. Even as we seek to assure a continuing supply of high-quality cocoa, we embrace our responsibility to ensure that the cocoa we buy is grown and harvested in a sustainable manner." In 2013, amid growing protests (including removal of Hershey's high-end Scharffen Berger brand from Whole Foods), Hershey vowed to use only fair-trade cocoa by 2020.

who explains how the dilemma relates to the provisions of the standards of ethical professional practice.

The IMA also publishes *Strategic Finance Magazine* and *Management Accounting Quarterly*, and since 1973 it has conducted a comprehensive examination to test what knowledge a management accountant must have in order to be successful in a complex and fast-changing business world. More than 3,000 individuals take the exam each year. Those who pass the exam are issued a Certificate in Management Accounting and are proud to indicate the designation Certified Management Accountant (CMA) on resumes and business cards. For details on student and professional memberships in the IMA and information on the CMA examination, visit the IMA Web site (www.imanet.org).

TEST YOUR **KNOWLEDGE**

Which of the following is **false?**

a. Ethical behavior requires an assessment of what's right and what's wrong.
b. The seven-question framework for ethical decision making requires asking if you are comfortable with your decision at a "gut level."
c. Ethical dilemmas are often complex without answers that are clearly right.
d. The Sarbanes-Oxley Act insured that business leaders would behave ethically.

Correct answer is d.

THE CONTROLLER AS THE TOP MANAGEMENT ACCOUNTANT

Who is responsible for preparing the information needed for planning, control, and decision making? In most organizations, the top managerial accounting position is held by the controller. The **controller** prepares reports for planning and evaluating company activities (e.g., budgets and performance reports) and provides the information needed to make management decisions (e.g., decisions related to purchasing office equipment or decisions related to adding or dropping a product). The controller also has responsibility

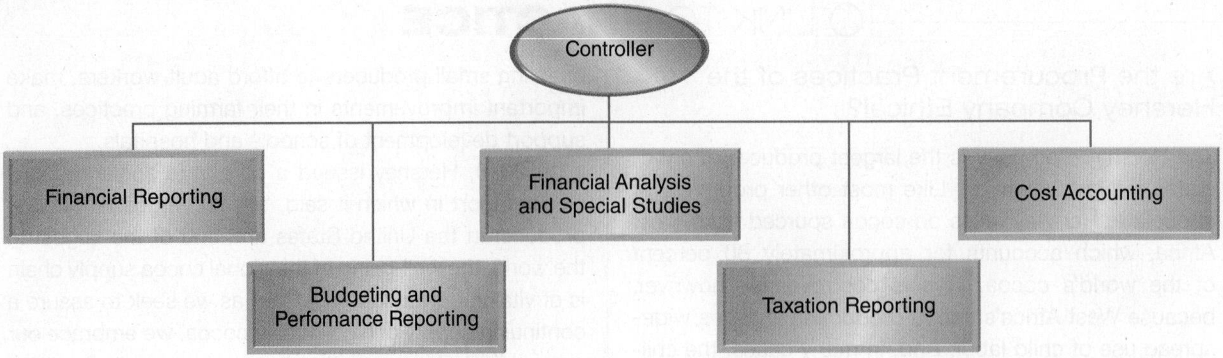

ILLUSTRATION 1-7
Organization chart for the controller's office

for all financial accounting reports and tax filings with the Internal Revenue Service and other taxing agencies, as well as coordinating the activities of the firm's external auditors.

A simplified example of the organization chart for the controller's office is shown in Illustration 1-7. Note that one of the areas reporting to the controller is cost accounting. Most medium-size and large manufacturing companies have such a department. Cost accountants estimate costs to facilitate management decisions and develop cost information for purposes of valuing inventory.

Many companies seeking to fill the position of controller send a clear message to applicants: "Bean counters need not apply!" This means that they want a managerial accountant who does more than concentrate on tracking costs ("counting beans"). They want an individual who will be an integral part of the top management team.

It is obvious that if you want a high-level career in managerial accounting, you will need strong accounting skills. But this is not enough. To be an important player on the management team, you will need the skills required of all high-level executives: excellent written and oral communication skills, solid interpersonal skills, and a deep knowledge of the industry in which your firm competes.

In addition to the position of controller, many companies have positions called treasurer and chief information officer (CIO). The **treasurer** has custody of cash and funds invested in various marketable securities. In addition to money management duties, the treasurer generally is responsible for maintaining relationships with investors, banks, and other creditors. Thus, the treasurer plays a major role in managing cash and marketable securities, preparing cash forecasts, and obtaining financing from banks and other lenders. The **chief information officer (CIO)** is the person responsible for a company's information technology and computer systems. Both the controller and the treasurer report to the **chief financial officer (CFO)**, who is the senior executive responsible for both accounting and financial operations. At some companies, the CIO also reports to the CFO. However, as we saw earlier, information technology is playing a critical role in managing the value chain. Therefore, it's not surprising that the CIO is frequently part of the senior management team reporting directly to the chief executive officer (CEO).

TEST YOUR **KNOWLEDGE**

The top managerial accountant is typically the:

a. Controller. b. Chief financial officer.
c. Chief information officer. d. Treasurer.

Correct answer is a.

Decision Making INSIGHT

As discussed in this chapter, decisions are made to reward or punish managers and to change operations or revise plans. Should a company add a new product? Should it drop an existing product? Should a company outsource a business process or perform it internally? What price should a company charge for a new product? Appropriate answers to these types of questions are critical to firm profitability, and much of this book will focus on how to address them. While gut feeling will always play a role in decision making, so too will careful analysis. The type of analysis we focus on is called incremental analysis, which is an analysis of the costs and revenues that change when one decision alternative is selected over another.

SUMMARY OF LEARNING OBJECTIVES

LEARNING OBJECTIVE 1 State the primary goal of managerial accounting and distinguish between financial and managerial accounting.

The primary goal of managerial accounting is to provide information that helps managers plan and control company activities and make business decisions.

The financial plans prepared by managerial accountants are referred to as budgets. These plans help employees understand company goals and what resources are needed to achieve them.

Control of organizations is achieved by evaluating the performance of managers and the operations for which they are responsible. The reports used to evaluate the performance of managers and the operations they control are referred to as performance reports. Often the reports compare current period performance with performance in a prior period or to planned (budgeted) performance. Since evaluations affect the rewards and punishments managers receive, the evaluation process causes them to work hard to receive good evaluations. Evaluations may also lead to modifications in operations, as needed.

Managerial accounting differs from financial accounting in many ways. A key difference is that managerial accounting stresses information that is useful to firm managers, whereas financial accounting stresses information that is useful to external parties. In addition, financial accounting information must be prepared in accordance with GAAP, but managerial accounting information need not be.

LEARNING OBJECTIVE 2 Define cost terms used in planning, control, and decision making.

A number of cost terms are used in discussing planning, control, and decision making. The terms include *variable cost* (a cost that changes in proportion to a change in business activity), *fixed cost* (a cost that does not change in response to a change in business activity), *sunk cost* (a cost incurred in the past), *opportunity cost* (a benefit forgone by selecting one decision alternative over another), *direct cost* (a cost that is directly traceable to a product, activity, or department), *indirect cost* (a cost that is not directly traceable to a product, activity, or department or is not worth tracing), *controllable cost* (a cost that a manager can influence), and *noncontrollable cost* (a cost that a manager cannot influence).

LEARNING OBJECTIVE 3 Explain the two key ideas in managerial accounting.

The first key idea is "Decision making relies on incremental analysis." This means that the solution to business problems involves the calculation of the difference in revenue (incremental revenue) and the difference in costs (incremental costs) between decision alternatives. The second key idea is "You get what you measure!" In other words, how companies measure performance affects how managers behave. This can create problems if managers spend too much time focused on any single performance measure.

LEARNING OBJECTIVE 4 Discuss the impact of information technology on, business processes and the interactions companies have with suppliers and customers.

Information technology is having a profound effect on the value chain and on company interactions with suppliers and customers. Companies use IT to coordinate activities with suppliers and to gain information on customers. IT is also being used to improve the internal processes of companies.

LEARNING OBJECTIVE 5 Describe a framework for ethical decision making and discuss the duties of the controller.

The framework for ethical decision making consists of seven questions. See page 20.

The controller is the top management accountant in most organizations. The controller is responsible for preparing reports for planning and evaluating company activities and for preparing information and reports needed to make management decisions. In contrast to the controller, the treasurer is responsible for maintaining relationships with investors, banks, and other creditors. The treasurer also has custody of cash and funds invested in various marketable securities. The chief information officer (CIO) is responsible for information technology. The controller and the treasurer report to the chief financial officer (CFO), who is the senior executive responsible for accounting and financial operations. The CIO has historically reported to the CFO, but the trend today is for the CIO to report to the chief executive officer (CEO).

APPENDIX

IMA STATEMENT OF ETHICAL PROFESSIONAL PRACTICE[2]

Members of IMA shall behave ethically. A commitment to ethical professional practice includes: overarching principles that express our values, and standards that guide our conduct.

Principles

IMA's overarching ethical principles include: Honesty, Fairness, Objectivity, and Responsibility. Members shall act in accordance with these principles and shall encourage others within their organizations to adhere to them.

Standards

A member's failure to comply with the following standards may result in disciplinary action.

I. Competence. Each member has a responsibility to:

1. Maintain an appropriate level of professional expertise by continually developing knowledge and skills.
2. Perform professional duties in accordance with relevant laws, regulations, and technical standards.
3. Provide decision support information and recommendations that are accurate, clear, concise, and timely.
4. Recognize and communicate professional limitations or other constraints that would preclude responsible judgment or successful performance of an activity.

II. Confidentiality. Each member has a responsibility to:

1. Keep information confidential except when disclosure is authorized or legally required.
2. Inform all relevant parties regarding appropriate use of confidential information. Monitor subordinates' activities to ensure compliance.
3. Refrain from using confidential information for unethical or illegal advantage.

III. Integrity. Each member has a responsibility to:

1. Mitigate actual conflicts of interest. Regularly communicate with business associates to avoid apparent conflicts of interest. Advise all parties of any potential conflicts.
2. Refrain from engaging in any conduct that would prejudice carrying out duties ethically.
3. Abstain from engaging in or supporting any activity that might discredit the profession.

IV. Credibility. Each member has a responsibility to:

1. Communicate information fairly and objectively.
2. Disclose all relevant information that could reasonably be expected to influence an intended user's understanding of the reports, analyses, or recommendations.
3. Disclose delays or deficiencies in information, timeliness, processing, or internal controls in conformance with organization policy and/or applicable law.

Resolution of Ethical Conflict

In applying the Standards of Ethical Professional Practice, you may encounter problems identifying unethical behavior or resolving an ethical conflict. When faced with ethical issues,

[2]Institute of Management Accountants Statement of Ethical Professional Practice. Adapted with permission.

you should follow your organization's established policies on the resolution of such conflict. If these policies do not resolve the ethical conflict, you should consider the following courses of action:

1. Discuss the issue with your immediate supervisor except when it appears that the supervisor is involved. In that case, present the issue to the next level. If you cannot achieve a satisfactory resolution, submit the issue to the next management level. If your immediate superior is the chief executive officer or equivalent, the acceptable reviewing authority may be a group such as the audit committee, executive committee, board of directors, board of trustees, or owners. Contact with levels above the immediate superior should be initiated only with your superior's knowledge, assuming he or she is not involved. Communication of such problems to authorities or individuals not employed or engaged by the organization is not considered appropriate, unless you believe there is a clear violation of the law.
2. Clarify relevant ethical issues by initiating a confidential discussion with an IMA Ethics Counselor or other impartial advisor to obtain a better understanding of possible courses of action.
3. Consult your own attorney as to legal obligations and rights concerning the ethical conflict.

REVIEW PROBLEM 1

Sterling Auto Detail is currently open Monday through Friday. In the past year, income before taxes was as follows:

Numbers of cars detailed		**2,080**
Revenue		$ 468,000
Less operating expenses:		
Supplies (polish, wax, etc.)	$ 5,824	
Salaries of detailers	104,000	
Water and other variable costs	12,480	
Supervisor's salary	65,000	
Rent	36,000	
Depreciation	5,000	
Other fixed costs	1,050	229,354
Income before taxes		$ 238,646

Quincy Davis, the owner of Sterling, is considering extending the workweek through Saturday. If he takes this action, he'll hire a part-time employee for $300 per day to act as the Saturday manager so the supervisor still can have Saturday off. Quincy estimates that his company will detail an additional 10 cars per Saturday, 52 weeks per year.

REQUIRED

a. Calculate the annual incremental revenue associated with being open on Saturday.

b. Calculate the incremental cost associated with being open on Saturday.

c. Ignoring taxes, what is the incremental profit? Should Quincy open the business on Saturdays?

ANSWER

a. The price of a detail is $225 ($468,000 ÷ 2,080). In total, 520 (10 × 52) additional cars will be detailed. Thus, annual incremental revenue is $117,000 ($225 × 520).

b. The incremental cost per detail job is as follows:

Supplies (polish, wax, etc.) ($5,824 ÷ 2,080)	$ 2.80
Salaries of detailers	50.00
Water and other variable costs	6.00
	$ 58.80
Thus, the incremental cost per year is:	
520 details × $58.80	$30,576
Incremental cost of Saturday manager ($300 × 52 days)	15,600
Total incremental cost per year	$46,176

c. The incremental profit is $70,824 ($117,000 – $46,176), suggesting that Quincy should stay open on Saturdays.

REVIEW PROBLEM 2

Brennan Wealth Planning offers financial advice to high-net-worth individuals. Services include tax advice, estate planning, and advice regarding the allocation of investments so that they are consistent with customers' risk profiles. Financial advisors at the firm also sell investments and insurance products to customers. All advisors are paid a base salary plus a bonus based on the total revenue they generate.

Hampton Financial Services is very similar to Brennan. However, at this firm, financial advisors are paid a base salary plus a bonus based solely on customer satisfaction.

REQUIRED

Discuss the concept of "You get what you measure!" and comment on how this may affect customers at the two companies.

ANSWER

The idea behind "You get what you measure!" is that performance measures drive the behavior of managers. At Brennan, financial advisors have a clear incentive to sell as many services and products as possible—even if customers don't need the services. At Hampton, financial advisors have a strong incentive to make customers happy with the advice and the services they receive. Thus, it is quite possible that their customers will receive less biased recommendations and have high levels of satisfaction.

KEY TERMS

Budgets (4)
Chief financial officer (CFO) (22)
Chief information officer (CIO) (22)
Controllable cost (11)
Controller (21)
Customer relationship management (CRM) systems (16)
Direct costs (10)
Enterprise resource planning (ERP) systems (16)
Fixed costs (9)
Incremental analysis (12)
Incremental cost (12)
Incremental revenue (12)
Indirect costs (10)
Management by exception (6)
Managerial accounting (12)
Noncontrollable cost (11)
Opportunity cost (10)
Performance reports (5)
Supply chain management (SCM) systems (16)
Sunk costs (10)
Treasurer (22)
Value chain (15)
Variable costs (9)

SELF-ASSESSMENT (Answers Below)

1. The primary goal of managerial accounting is to:

a. Provide information to current and potential investors in the company.

b. Provide information to creditors as well as current and prospective investors.

c. Provide information to creditors, taxing authorities, and current and prospective investors.

d. Provide information for planning, control, and decision making.

2. Match the following terms with the management activities described below:
   a. Planning
   b. Control
   c. Decision making
      (1) This management activity involves changing operations, revising plans, or rewarding/punishing managers.
      (2) This management activity compares actual results with planned outcomes as a basis for corrective action.
      (3) This management activity formulates goals, communicates them to employees, and specifies the resources needed to achieve them.
3. Which of the following statements about budgets is **false**?
   a. Budgets may be expressed in dollars, quantities, or both.
   b. Budgets may reflect projected revenues, projected expenses, projected cash flows, or projected quantities of inputs or outputs.
   c. Budgets must be prepared in accordance with GAAP.
   d. Budgets are useful both for planning and control.
4. Which of the following statements is **false**?
   a. Managerial accounting statements do not necessarily comply with GAAP.
   b. Financial accounting statements normally reflect more detail than would be found in managerial accounting reports.
   c. Managerial accounting reports emphasize future activities and future costs.
   d. Financial accounting data are directed primarily at external users rather than internal users.
5. Which of the following is most likely to be a variable cost?
   a. Depreciation.
   b. The cost of material used in production.
   c. Rent.
   d. Advertising.
6. Which of the following is most likely to be a fixed cost?
   a. The cost of material used in production.
   b. Rent.
   c. Assembly labor cost.
   d. Commissions.
7. Costs incurred in the past are:
   a. Opportunity costs.
   b. Direct costs.
   c. Sunk costs.
   d. Variable costs.
8. ____________ costs are directly traceable to a product, activity, or department, whereas ____________ costs are not.
9. The salary a student forgoes while in college is an example of:
   a. Opportunity cost.
   b. Direct cost.
   c. Sunk cost.
   d. Variable cost.
10. Which of the following is **not** one of the seven questions in the framework for ethical decision making?
   a. Will an individual or an organization be harmed by any of the decision alternatives?
   b. Would someone I respect find any of the alternatives objectionable?
   c. At a gut level, am I comfortable with the decision I am about to make?
   d. Are any of the alternatives illegal?

ANSWERS TO SELF-ASSESSMENT

1. d **2.** (1)-c, (2)-b, (3)-a **3.** c **4.** b **5.** b **6.** b **7.** c **8.** direct, indirect **9.** a **10.** d

QUESTIONS

1. What is the goal of managerial accounting?
2. In a performance report, current-period performance is compared with some benchmark. What might be a useful benchmark?
3. List three differences between financial and managerial accounting.
4. List three examples of nonmonetary information that might appear in a managerial accounting report.
5. Explain the difference between fixed and variable costs.
6. Consider the manager of the home appliance department at a Sears store. For this manager, list a cost that is controllable and a cost that is noncontrollable.

7. What is incremental analysis? How is the concept used in decision making?

8. What is meant by the statement "You get what you measure!"?

9. How have changes in information technology impacted management of the value chain?

10. If an action is legal, is it necessarily ethical? Explain.

EXERCISES

GROUP WORK

EXERCISE 1-1. You Get What You Measure [LO 3] A key idea in this book is that "You get what you measure!" Essentially, this means that performance measures have a great influence on the behavior of managers.

REQUIRED

Select a company with which you are familiar. Identify three performance measures that the company might use. For each measure, identify a favorable outcome and an unfavorable outcome that might occur because the measure is used to evaluate manager performance.

WRITING

EXERCISE 1-2. Sunk Cost [LO 2] Rachel Cook owns Campus Copies, a copy business with several high-speed copy machines. One is a color copier that was purchased just last year at a cost of $25,000. Recently a salesperson got Rachel to witness a demo of a new $23,000 color copier that promises higher speed and more accurate color representation. Rachel is interested but she can't get herself to trade in a perfectly good copier for which she paid $25,000 and replace it with one that will cost $23,000.

REQUIRED

Write a paragraph explaining why the cost of the old copier is irrelevant to Rachel's decision.

ETHICS

EXERCISE 1-3. [LO 4] Guthrie Wilson is an accountant at Bellwether Systems, a company that sells and installs customer relationship management (CRM) systems. The company sells third-party software at cost plus 25 percent and charges a fee of $300 per hour of installation/integration time spent on each engagement. Recently Guthrie's boss asked him to charge 60 hours of time to the Bradley account when the time was actually worked servicing the IMG account. The rationale: "Look, IMG is a struggling start-up and they can barely afford our service. We ran over our time estimate due to some unforeseen problems, and they'll balk if we charge them for all of our time. Bradley, on the other hand, is a highly profitable company, and we're providing services that are going to make them even more profitable. They'll have no problem with their bill."

REQUIRED

Review the IMA's ethical standards in the appendix. What do the standards suggest that Guthrie should do to resolve the issue he's facing?

EXERCISE 1-4. Information Age [LO 4] The Wellington Hotel is a posh hotel in Manhattan that uses a customer relationship management (CRM) system to track customer preferences and purchases. Provide two examples of specific information the CRM system might capture and how the hotel could use the information to enhance revenue and/or the customer experience.

EXERCISE 1-5. Budgets [LO 1] Megan Kelly is the chief financial officer of a chain of 25 drugstores. Explain how she can use budgets in both planning profit and controlling operations.

EXERCISE 1-6. Performance Reports [LO 1] Which of the following statements related to performance reports is **false**?

a. Performance reports may provide a comparison of actual performance with planned performance.

b. Performance reports may provide a comparison of actual performance with performance in a prior period.

c. If actual costs exceed planned costs in a performance report, this clearly indicates managerial incompetence.

d. Performance reports are used to evaluate managers and the operations they control.

EXERCISE 1-7. Performance Reports [LO 1] At Designs by Deirdre, the budgeted income statement for December 2017 indicated sales of $600,000 and cost of sales of $400,000. Actual sales and cost of sales were $700,000 and $425,000, respectively. Should Deirdre Nelson, owner of the company, be concerned that cost of sales is $25,000 greater than planned? Explain the basis for your answer.

EXERCISE 1-8. Financial versus Managerial Accounting [LO 1] Bob Stevens is taking Managerial Accounting at State University next term and asked his friend, Summer Adams, who has already taken the course, to explain its focus. "Are we going to learn more about balance sheets and income statements? Is it just an extension of the financial accounting course I had last year?"

REQUIRED

Assume the role of Summer and explain the focus of managerial accounting and some of the ways it differs from financial accounting.

EXERCISE 1-9. Financial versus Managerial Accounting [LO 1] Consider a large manufacturing company like Boeing that rewards its sales force with bonuses based on sales. For this purpose, should the company record sales when orders are placed or, to be consistent with GAAP, wait until orders are delivered?

EXERCISE 1-10. Cost Terms [LO 2] Identify each of the following statements with fixed costs or variable costs by writing "fixed" or "variable" in the space provided.

______ **a.** A cost that varies in total with changes in the activity level.

______ **b.** A cost that varies on a per-unit basis with changes in the activity level.

______ **c.** A cost that remains fixed per unit with changes in the activity level.

______ **d.** A cost that remains fixed in total with changes in the activity level.

EXERCISE 1-11. Cost Terms [LO 2] Indicate whether each of the following costs is most likely a fixed cost or a variable cost by writing "fixed" or "variable" in the space provided.

______ **a.** Assembly labor.

______ **b.** The cost of material used in production.

______ **c.** Rent.

______ **d.** Depreciation.

______ **e.** Fuel cost at an airline.

EXERCISE 1-12. Cost Terms [LO 2] Explain how a cost can be controllable at one administrative level and noncontrollable at another administrative level.

EXERCISE 1-13. Sunk Cost [LO 2, 3] Peter Takesha, the manager of testing services at a medical diagnostics firm, purchased a new lab testing machine last year for $30,000. This year a new machine, which is faster and more reliable than Peter's current model, is on the market. In deciding whether to purchase the new machine, should Peter consider how much he paid for the old machine? Should he consider the value of the old machine in the used equipment market?

EXERCISE 1-14. Opportunity Costs [LO 2] Parrish Plumbing provides plumbing services to residential customers from Monday through Friday. Ken Parrish, the owner, believes that it is important for his employees to have Saturday and Sunday off to spend with their families. However, he also recognizes that this policy has implications for profitability, and he is considering staying open on Saturday.

Ken estimates that if his company stays open on Saturday, it can generate $2,500 of daily revenue each day for 52 days per year. The incremental daily costs will be $700 for labor, $500 for parts, $100 for transportation, and $200 for office staff. These costs do not include a share of monthly rent or a share of depreciation related to office equipment.

Ken is determined not to have employees work on Sunday, but he would like to know the opportunity cost of not working on Saturday. Provide Ken with an estimate of the opportunity cost, and explain why you do not have to consider rent or depreciation of office equipment in your estimate.

EXERCISE 1-15. Opportunity Cost [LO 2] Zachary made plans to visit a friend in New York during the Memorial Day weekend. However, before the trip, his employer asked him if he would work overtime for 16 hours at $35 per hour during the weekend. What will be the opportunity cost if Zachary decides to visit his friend in New York?

EXERCISE 1-16. Incremental Analysis [LO 2, 3] Wilmington Chemicals produces a chemical, PX44, which is used to retard fading in exterior house paint. In the past year, the company produced 200,000 gallons at a total cost of $1,200,000 ($6 per gallon). The company is currently considering an order for 15,000 gallons from a paint company in Canada. (To date, Wilmington has not sold the product in markets outside the United States.) Explain why the incremental cost associated with this order is likely to be less than $90,000.

EXERCISE 1-17. Incremental Analysis [LO 3] In the past year, Williams Mold & Machine had sales of $7,000,000 and total production costs of $5,000,000. In the coming year, the company believes that sales and production can be increased by 25 percent, but this will require adding a second production shift to work from 4:00 P.M. to 1:00 A.M.

REQUIRED

a. Indicate three production costs that are likely to increase because of the addition of a second production shift.

b. Suggest a production cost that most likely will not increase when the second shift is added.

EXERCISE 1-18. You Get What You Measure! [LO 3] At LA Porsche, customers receive an online survey asking them to rate their satisfaction after every car service. How is this measure likely to affect the financial welfare of Hulmut Schmidt, manager of the service department? List three actions that Hulmut can take to ensure the ratings indicate that customers are very satisfied.

ETHICS **EXERCISE 1-19. [LO 5]** Shauna Miller is an accountant at Western Building Supplies. Recently, in the course of her normal processing of transactions and related documents, she noticed that two of her company's top sales executives were taking the purchasing agents of important customers on lavish golf vacations to Hawaii. The average cost was over $6,000 per person per trip.

Review the Institute of Management Accountant's Statement of Ethical Professional Practice in the appendix to this chapter. As a member of the IMA, does Shauna have any specific obligations related to her discovery? What steps should she consider?

EXERCISE 1-20. Duties and Skills of Controller [LO 5] Search the Web for a company seeking to hire a controller. What duties does it specify, and what skills does it want the controller to have?

EXERCISE 1-21. Career Connection Select one or two concepts from this chapter and describe how you might use those concepts in your future career. Briefly describe the career or job you will be performing. Then specifically describe the type of situation for which the concept could be applied. Also include a discussion of how use of the concept would allow you to make informed decisions or improve your job performance. Envision specific instances where these concepts would be useful to you.

PROBLEMS

EXCEL

PROBLEM 1-1. Budgets in Managerial Accounting [LO 1, 2] Santiago's Salsa is in the process of preparing a production cost budget for May. Actual costs in April were:

Santiago's Salsa
Production Costs
April 2017

Production	25,000 Jars of Salsa
Ingredient cost (variable)	$20,000
Labor cost (variable)	12,000
Rent (fixed)	5,000
Depreciation (fixed)	6,000
Other (fixed)	1,000
Total	$44,000

REQUIRED

a. Using this information, prepare a budget for May. Assume that production will increase to 30,000 jars of salsa, reflecting an anticipated sales increase related to a new marketing campaign.

b. Does the budget suggest that additional workers are needed? Suppose the wage rate is $20 per hour. How many additional labor hours are needed in May? What would happen if management did not anticipate the need for additional labor in May?

c. Calculate the actual cost per unit in April and the budgeted cost per unit in May. Explain why the cost per unit is expected to decrease.

EXCEL

PROBLEM 1-2. Incremental Analysis [LO 2, 3] Consider the production cost information for Santiago's Salsa in Problem 1-1. The company is currently producing and selling 325,000 jars of salsa annually. The jars sell for $5.00 each. The company is considering lowering the price to $4.60. Suppose this action will increase sales to 375,000 jars.

REQUIRED

a. What is the incremental cost associated with producing an extra 50,000 jars of salsa?

b. What is the incremental revenue associated with the price reduction of $0.40 per jar?

c. Should Santiago's lower the price of its salsa?

PROBLEM 1-3. Budgets in Managerial Accounting [LO 1, 2] Matthew Gabon, the sales manager of Office Furniture Solutions, prepared the following budget for 2017:

Sales Department
Budgeted Costs, 2017
(Assuming Sales of $10,000,000)

Salaries (fixed)	$400,000
Commissions (variable)	150,000
Advertising (fixed)	75,000
Charge for office space (fixed)	3,000
Office supplies & forms (variable)	2,000
Total	$630,000

After he submitted his budget, the president of Office Furniture Solutions reviewed it and recommended that advertising be increased to $100,000. Further, she wanted Matthew to assume a sales level of $11,000,000. This level of sales is to be achieved without adding to the sales force.

Matthew's sales group occupies approximately 250 square feet of office space out of total administrative office space of 20,000 square feet. The $3,000 space charge in Matthew's budget is his share (allocated based on relative square feet) of the company's total cost of rent, utilities, and janitorial costs for the administrative office building.

REQUIRED

Prepare a revised budget consistent with the president's recommendation.

PROBLEM 1-4. Performance Reports [LO 1] A performance report that compares budgeted and actual profit in the sporting goods department of Maxwell's Department Store for the month of December follows:

Maxwell's Department Store
Sporting Goods
Performance Report December 2017

	Budget	Actual	Difference
Sales	$700,000	$775,000	$75,000
Less:			
Cost of merchandise	350,000	430,000	80,000
Salaries of sales staff	70,000	78,000	8,000
Controllable profit	$280,000	$267,000	($13,000)

REQUIRED

a. Evaluate the department in terms of its increases in sales and expenses. Do you believe it would be useful to investigate either or both of the increases in expenses?

b. Consider storewide electricity cost. Would this cost be a controllable or a noncontrollable cost for the manager of sporting goods? Would it be useful to include a share of storewide electricity cost on the performance report for sporting goods?

PROBLEM 1-5. Performance Reports [LO 1, 2] At the end of 2017, Cyril Fedako, CFO for Central Products, received a report comparing budgeted and actual production costs for the company's plant in Forest Lake, Minnesota:

Manufacturing Costs
Forest Lake Plant
Budget versus Actual 2017

	Budget	Actual	Difference (Actual Minus Budget)
Materials	$3,200,000	$3,500,000	$300,000
Direct labor	2,300,000	2,500,000	200,000
Supervisory salaries	475,000	500,000	25,000
Utilities	125,000	135,000	10,000
Machine maintenance	350,000	380,000	30,000
Depreciation of building	90,000	90,000	-0-
Depreciation of equipment	250,000	255,000	5,000
Janitorial	220,000	235,000	15,000
Total	$7,010,000	$7,595,000	$585,000

His first thought was that costs must be out of control since actual costs exceed the budget by $585,000. However, he quickly recalled that the budget was set assuming a production level of 60,000 units. The Forest Lake plant actually produced 65,000 units in 2017.

REQUIRED

a. Given that production was greater than planned, should Cyril expect that all actual costs will be greater than budgeted? Which costs would you expect to increase, and which costs would you expect to remain relatively constant?

PROBLEM 1-6. Financial versus Managerial Accounting [LO 1, 2, 3] Linda Vendetto is the manager of contact lenses and related products sold online by a large retail chain (think Walmart.com). In this capacity, she is responsible for approximately 250 different products.

REQUIRED

a. Explain why the level of detail in the company's income statement, balance sheet, and statement of cash flows is not sufficient for Linda to manage her operation.

b. List three nonfinancial measures that Linda may find useful to manage her operation.

c. Linda's own performance is evaluated, in part, based on customer satisfaction ratings. What can Linda do to improve performance on this measure?

d. List three likely costs in Linda's operation and indicate whether they are fixed or variable.

PROBLEM 1-7. You Get What You Measure! [LO 3] Each year the president of Smart-Toys Manufacturing selects a single performance measure and offers significant financial bonuses to all key employees if the company achieves a 10 percent improvement on the measure in comparison to the prior year. She recently said, "This focuses my managers on a single, specific target and gets them all working together to achieve a major objective that will increase shareholder value."

Sarabeth Robbins is a new member of the company's board of directors, and she has begun to question the president's approach to rewarding performance. In particular, she is concerned that placing too much emphasis on a single performance measure may lead managers to take actions that increase performance in terms of the measure but decrease the value of the firm.

REQUIRED

a. What negative consequence might occur if the performance measure is sales to new customers ÷ total sales in the current year versus the prior year? (*Note:* To receive a bonus, managers would need to increase this ratio compared with the prior year.)

b. What negative consequence might occur if the performance measure is cost of goods sold ÷ sales in the current year versus the prior year? (*Note:* To receive a bonus, managers would need to decrease this ratio compared with the prior year.)

c. What negative consequence might occur if the performance measure is selling and administrative expenses ÷ sales in the current year versus the prior year? (*Note:* To receive a bonus, managers would need to decrease this ratio compared with the prior year.)

PROBLEM 1-8. Incremental Analysis [LO 2, 3] The Riverview Hotel is a deluxe four-star establishment. Late on Friday, it had 20 of its 300 rooms available when the desk clerk received a call from the Pines Hotel. The Pines Hotel made a booking error and did not have room for four guests (each of whom had a "confirmed" room). The Pines wants to send its customers to the Riverview but pay the rate the guests would have been charged at the Pines ($160 per room) rather than paying the normal rate of $260 per room at the Riverview.

REQUIRED

a. If the Riverview accepts the guests, what will be the incremental revenue?

b. Provide examples of incremental costs that the Riverview will incur if it accepts the guests.

c. In your opinion, will the incremental revenue be greater than the incremental cost?

ETHICS **PROBLEM 1-9. Ethics and Code of Conduct [LO 5]** Search the Web for the Code of Conduct for Sears Holdings Corporation (the parent company for Sears and Kmart). For each of the following cases, indicate whether it is allowable under the Code of Conduct. In your answer, cite specific language in the code.

a. A purchasing agent is negotiating with two suppliers A and B. The agent tells supplier B the bid price offered by supplier A in an effort to get B to lower its bid.

b. An employee is running for city council and distributes materials supporting his campaign via company email.

c. A purchasing agent accepts samples of various clothing items.

d. An employee writes an anonymous blog on her experience at Sears that provides insights into the company's strategy for success.

CASE

1-1 LOCAL 635 [LO 2, 5]

Local 635 represents kitchen workers at hotels in several southern cities. Part of their labor agreement states that workers "shall receive one free meal per shift up to a cost of $12, with any cost over $12 being deducted from wages paid to said employee."

A labor dispute arose at the Riverside Hotel shortly after it was opened in June. Kitchen workers who ate dinner on the late shift found that their wages were reduced by $10 for each meal they consumed at the hotel during their dinner break. Josh Parker, a line cook, stated the widely held belief of the workers. "There's no way these dinners cost the Riverside Hotel $12 to make, let alone $22. This is just another case of management trying to rip us off. Take last night. I had the prime rib dinner. The piece of meat cost about $7 and the salad less than $1. That's only $8 in total. Really, there aren't any other costs to speak of. The cook, well, he's going to be working in the kitchen and getting paid for 8 hours whether he makes my meal or not. This claim that my meal cost $22 is baloney!"

Management of the Riverside Hotel sees the situation differently. Take the case of Josh's dinner. In presenting the hotel's case to a labor arbitration board, Sandy Ross, manager of the hotel, explained, "Look, that dinner goes for $32 on the menu so assigning a cost of $22 represents a very good value to the kitchen workers. The contention that the meal only costs $8 is nonsense. True, the meat costs $7 and the salad ingredients cost $1, but there's also the labor costs related to preparing the meal and the numerous overhead costs, like the cost of the oven that the prime rib is cooked in. That oven cost more than $20,000. And there's heat, light, power, etc. Each meal we prepare should be assigned part of these overhead costs. And don't forget that when the worker finishes his or her meal, someone has to clean up. That costs money too. When you add up all of these items, a prime rib dinner easily adds up to $22!"

REQUIRED

a. List examples of costs at the Riverside Hotel that are variable, fixed, and sunk. Provide an example of an opportunity cost.

b. What is the source of conflict between labor and management? What changes would you recommend in the wording of the labor agreement?

CASE

1-2 BOSWELL PLUMBING PRODUCTS [LO 3]

Boswell Plumbing Products produces a variety of valves, connectors, and fixtures used in commercial and residential plumbing applications. Recently a senior manager walked into the cost accounting department and asked Nick Somner to tell her the cost of the D45 valve. Nick quickly replied, "Why do you want to know?" Noticing that the manager appeared somewhat startled by this question, he explained, "The cost information you need depends on the decision you're going to make. You might be thinking of increasing a scheduled production run of 3,000 D45s by 100 units or scheduling an additional production run, or you might even be thinking of dropping the product. For each of these decisions, the cost information that you need is different."

REQUIRED

Using the concept of incremental analysis, expand on Nick's response of, "Why do you want to know?" What cost information would be relevant to a decision to drop the product that would not be relevant to a decision to increase a production run by 100 units?

2

JOB-ORDER COSTING FOR MANUFACTURING AND SERVICE COMPANIES

While working in the software industry, Bob Williams spent his limited free time restoring an old wooden motorboat.

After 15 years at Mayfield Software, Bob was able to retire and pursue his love affair with old boats on a full-time basis. He's now the new owner of Eastlake Motorboat Company, a small (and, heretofore, barely profitable) manufacturer of custom-built wooden motorboats patterned after the classic lake cruisers built in the 1930s through the 1950s.

During his first week on the job, he had a lunch meeting with his accountant, Nancy Young, and expressed his interest in two key drivers of company success—cost estimation and pricing.

"Nancy, I know that before we take an order and set a price for a custom boat, we estimate material, labor, and overhead costs. What I want to do is look at what the boats are actually costing us and compare the actual costs to estimates. I think one of our problems may be that we are underestimating cost and pricing too low. How hard will it be to put together some cost data for a number of recent orders so I can get a handle on this?"

"Not hard at all," Nancy replied. "We have what's called a job-order costing system that tracks the cost of each custom boat. I can get you the material later this afternoon."

"That's great, Nancy. And while you're at it, maybe you can bring me up to speed on how the costing system works. As you know, my background is in computer programming, and I'm afraid I don't know a lot about accounting. Do you think you can help me out with the basics?"

"You bet," Nancy assured him. "In fact, when we get back to the office, let's grab a cup of coffee and I'll begin your accounting education. Before long, you'll know the difference between product and period costs, fixed and variable costs, and how the job cost sheets relate to inventory on our balance sheet. Frankly, I'm really glad you're interested in the accounting side of things. The previous owner was great with boats but never paid much attention to financial information. That's probably one of the main reasons the company never really prospered."

To determine the cost of manufactured products like the boats made by Eastlake Motorboat, companies use a **product costing system**, an integrated set of documents, ledgers, accounts, and accounting procedures used to measure and record the cost of manufactured products. In this chapter, we consider cost classifications for manufacturing firms and how the costs of manufactured products are reflected in a company's financial statements. In particular, we consider a type of product costing system referred to as a job-order costing system. While the primary example in the chapter focuses on a manufacturing firm, Eastlake Motorboat Company, job-order costing also applies to service companies that need to calculate the cost of services they provide to customers. Thus, as we will discuss, job-order costing is used by law firms, consulting firms, hospitals, auto repair shops, and other service companies. Finally, we address modern manufacturing practices and how they are helping companies succeed in a competitive global economy. These practices are important to the study of managerial accounting because they affect the type and amount of costs and, to some extent, the design of the product costing system.

Rhoberazzi/iStock/Getty Images Plus

LEARNING OBJECTIVES

1 Distinguish between manufacturing and nonmanufacturing costs and between product and period costs.

2 Discuss the three inventory accounts of a manufacturing firm and describe the flow of product costs in a manufacturing firm's accounts.

3 Discuss the types of product costing systems and explain the relation between the cost of jobs and the Work in Process Inventory, Finished Goods Inventory, and Cost of Goods Sold accounts.

4 Describe how direct material, direct labor, and manufacturing overhead are assigned to jobs.

5 Explain the role of a predetermined overhead rate in applying overhead to jobs, and explain the treatment of the difference between actual overhead and overhead allocated to jobs using a predetermined rate.

6 Explain how service companies can use job-order costing to calculate the cost of services provided to customers.

7 Discuss modern manufacturing practices and how they affect product costing.

LEARNING OBJECTIVE 1

Distinguish between manufacturing and nonmanufacturing costs and between product and period costs.

COST CLASSIFICATIONS FOR MANUFACTURING FIRMS

Companies need to know the cost of their products so that they can set prices, calculate profit when products are sold, and assess the reasonableness of the costs incurred in manufacturing products. Determining the cost of items a merchandising firm purchases from a supplier is relatively easy. The cost of the items is the purchase price plus shipping charges. Determining the cost of items a manufacturing firm produces is more complex. Using both labor and machinery, a manufacturing firm converts raw materials into finished goods. Complexity arises because the costs of the resources used in production must be assigned to the units produced.

Merchandising and manufacturing firms are compared in Illustration 2-1. This section discusses the broad classifications of manufacturing and nonmanufacturing costs. It also discusses product and period costs, which are other ways in which costs can be classified.

Manufacturing Costs

Manufacturing costs (also known as product costs) are all the costs associated with the production of goods. They include three cost categories: direct material, direct labor, and manufacturing overhead.

Direct Material. **Direct material cost** is the cost of all materials and parts that are directly traced to items produced. For the Eastlake Motorboat Company, a manufacturer of motorboats, direct material includes the wood, the steering assembly, the motor, and a variety of other items.

ILLUSTRATION 2-1

Comparison of merchandising and manufacturing firms

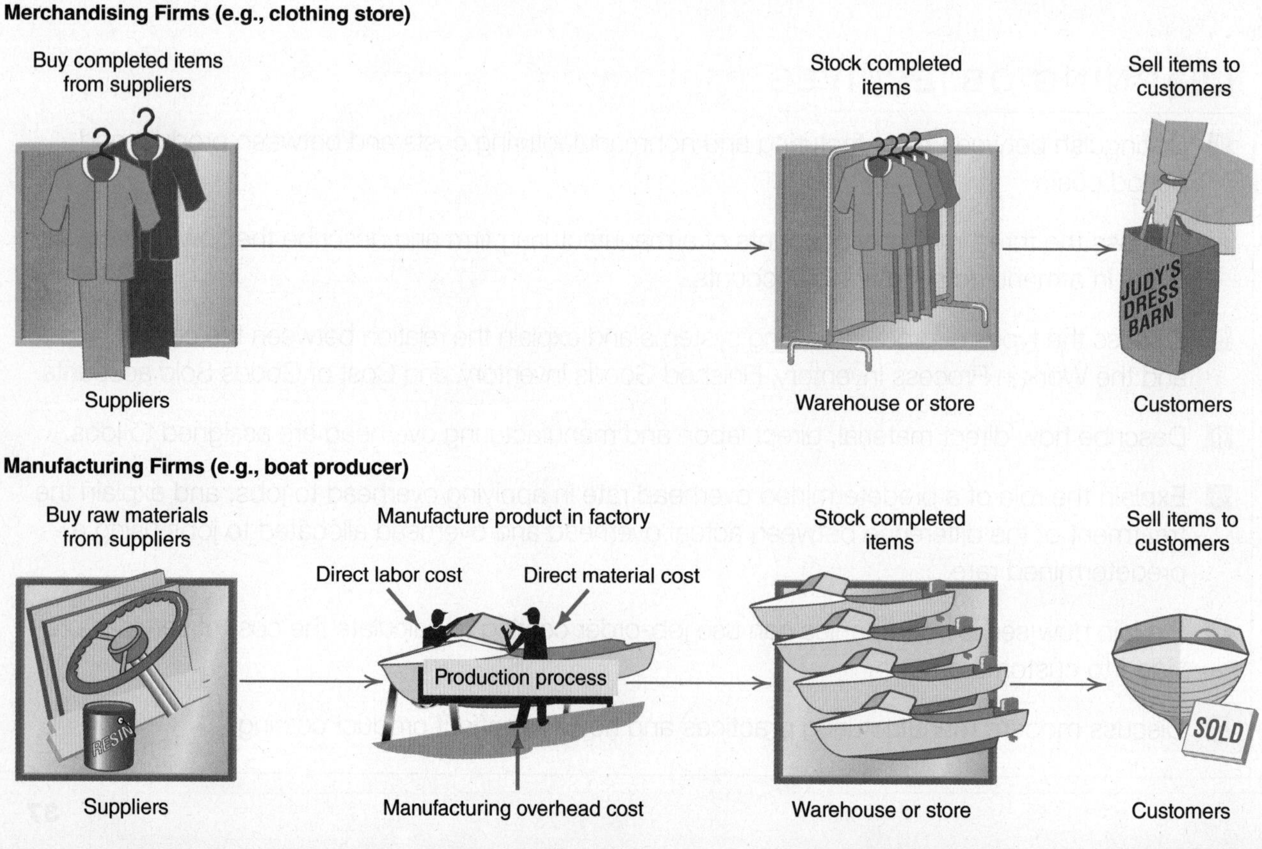

Direct material cost often does not include the cost of minor materials, such as screws and glue. Although such minor material costs could be traced to a particular boat, tracing the costs may not be worth the time it would take to do so. Materials that are not directly traced to a product are referred to as **indirect materials**.

Direct Labor. **Direct labor cost** is the cost of labor that is directly traced to items produced. The Eastlake Motorboat Company's direct labor includes the labor cost of the workers directly involved in constructing each motorboat. It probably does not include the cost of production supervisors, such as the salary of Carl Jensen, the master builder. This manager supervises the production of 10 or more different boats at once. He spends 5 minutes to an hour on a job before directing his attention to another job or to other aspects of production, such as scheduling workers and ordering equipment. It would be very difficult, if not impossible, to directly trace the time Carl spends scheduling workers to individual jobs. And although it might be possible to directly trace the time he spends supervising production of a particular job, it may not be worthwhile to do so. Labor costs that are not traced directly to products produced are referred to as **indirect labor costs**.

Manufacturing Overhead. **Manufacturing overhead** is the cost of all manufacturing activities other than direct material and direct labor. It includes indirect material and indirect labor, which were explained earlier, as well as a wide variety of other cost items. For the Eastlake Motorboat Company, manufacturing overhead includes the costs of screws, glue, varnish, supervisor salary, depreciation of tools, depreciation of the building where manufacturing takes place, utilities, and a number of other items. Illustration 2-2 lists some common manufacturing overhead costs.

Nonmanufacturing Costs

Nonmanufacturing costs (also known as period costs) can be defined simply as all costs that are not associated with the production of goods. These costs typically include selling and general and administrative costs.

Selling Costs. **Selling costs** include all the costs associated with securing and filling customer orders. Thus, selling costs include advertising costs, sales personnel salaries, depreciation of automobiles and office equipment used by the sales force, and costs of storing and shipping finished goods.

General and Administrative Costs. **General and Administrative Costs** are all the costs associated with the firm's general management. These costs include the salaries of the company president and accounting personnel, depreciation of the general office building, depreciation of office equipment used by general managers, and the cost of supplies used by clerical employees.

In many cases, a cost is classified by its use rather than by its specific nature. Consider janitorial costs. Janitorial costs associated with maintaining a production area

ILLUSTRATION 2-2

Common manufacturing overhead costs

Indirect factory labor	Power, heat, and light in the factory
Indirect material	Depreciation of factory equipment
Overtime premium	Depreciation of plant
Nightshift premium	Insurance on plant and factory equipment
Vacation and holiday pay for factory workers	Repair of factory equipment
Social Security and Medicare taxes for factory workers	Maintenance of factory building and grounds
Health insurance for factory workers	Property taxes related to the factory

are classified as a manufacturing costs (specifically, manufacturing overhead). In contrast, janitorial costs associated with maintaining the general office building are classified as nonmanufacturing costs (specifically, General and Administrative Costs).

ANY QUESTIONS?

Q: I see that in Illustration 2-2, overtime premium is listed as manufacturing overhead. Why is that? Can't we directly trace overtime to specific jobs worked on after 5 P.M., or on weekends or holidays when overtime is paid?

A: The fact that a specific job is worked on after 5 P.M. or on a weekend or holiday doesn't necessarily mean that it's a job that *caused* overtime premium to be incurred. Plant supervisors try to schedule jobs in a way that's efficient. It could be that a particular job is worked on after 5 P.M. simply because it's efficient to make it the last job worked on during the day. Because of the difficulty of assigning overtime to specific jobs that *caused* it, most companies simply spread overtime premium among all jobs by including it in manufacturing overhead.

Product and Period Costs

As mentioned previously, costs that are classified as manufacturing and nonmanufacturing costs can also be classified as product and period costs. This latter distinction is made to emphasize differences in the timing of when costs are recognized as expenses. Product costs are identified with goods produced and expensed when goods are sold. Period costs are identified with accounting periods and expensed in the period incurred.

Product Costs. Product costs are those costs assigned to goods produced. Thus, the terms *product costs* and *manufacturing costs* are used interchangeably. Both include direct material, direct labor, and manufacturing overhead. Product costs are considered an asset (inventory) until the finished goods are sold. When the goods are sold, the product costs are expensed. Thus, direct labor costs incurred in 2016 to produce goods sold in 2017 do not reduce income until 2017, the year of the sale. This ensures a proper matching of revenue with the costs necessary to produce it.

Period Costs. Period costs are identified with accounting periods rather than with goods produced. Selling and general and administrative costs (nonmanufacturing costs) are period costs. We recognize period costs as expenses in the period incurred. For example, rent paid on an *office building* is a period cost and becomes an expense in the period incurred. In contrast, the rent paid on a *factory building* is a product cost and becomes an expense when goods are sold. Differences between product and period costs are summarized in Illustration 2-3.

ILLUSTRATION 2-3
Relationships among cost categories

	Type of Cost	When Expensed
	Product costs	
Manufacturing costs	Direct material Direct labor Manufacturing overhead	Expensed when goods are sold
	Period costs	
Nonmanufacturing costs	Selling cost General and Administrative cost	Expensed in period in which they are incurred

TEST YOUR KNOWLEDGE

Which of the following is not a product cost?

a. Depreciation of manufacturing equipment.

b. Indirect materials.

c. Insurance on manufacturing equipment.

d. Bonuses and compensation to the company president.

Correct answer is d.

PRODUCT COST INFORMATION IN FINANCIAL REPORTING AND DECISION MAKING

Decision Making/ Incremental Analysis

Manufacturing companies need product cost information in order to prepare financial statements in accordance with generally accepted accounting principles (GAAP). GAAP requires that inventory on the balance sheet and cost of goods sold on the income statement be presented using full cost information. **Full cost** means that product cost includes both variable and fixed manufacturing overhead as well as direct material and direct labor, which are generally variable costs.

Product cost information is also needed for a variety of managerial decisions. Often the product cost information needed for management decision making is different from the product cost information produced for external financial reports. Recall from Chapter 1 that decision making relies on incremental analysis—an analysis of the revenues that increase (decrease) and the costs that increase (decrease) if a decision alternative is selected. In most cases, in order to perform incremental analysis, you need to separate fixed and variable cost components. For example, suppose Bob Williams, the owner of Eastlake Motorboat Company, is considering taking out an advertisement in *Wooden Boat Magazine*. The ad will cost $25,000, and Bob believes it will result in at least one additional order for a custom boat. On average, Eastlake boats sell for $90,000. Thus, he expects that there will be $90,000 of incremental revenue and $25,000 of incremental costs related to the ad. But what about incremental production costs?

LINK TO PRACTICE

Product and Period Costs at SpaceX

SpaceX designs, manufactures, and launches rockets and spacecraft, and it was the first *private* company to return a spacecraft from low-Earth orbit. Subsequently, the company has delivered cargo to the International Space Station multiple times.

Classify each of the following costs as a product or period cost for SpaceX:

1. Cost of producing components such as nozzles through which gases are discharged to generate thrust.
2. Cost of rocket engine design.
3. Salary of plant manager.
4. Salary of marketing vice president.
5. Cost of testing rocket engine prior to shipment.
6. Salary of the division president.
7. Cost of legal staff who draft contracts.

Answer: (1) Product, (2) Product, (3) Product, (4) Period, (5) Product, (6) Period, (7) Period.

Bob knows that, on average, the production cost of a boat includes $25,000 of direct material cost, $20,000 of direct labor cost, and $30,000 of manufacturing overhead. Thus, the full production cost of a boat is $75,000.

Direct material	$25,000
Direct labor	20,000
Manufacturing overhead	30,000
	$75,000

It may appear that Bob should not place the ad because the revenue of $90,000 is less than the cost of advertising and the cost of producing the boat, which is $100,000 ($25,000 of advertising and $75,000 of production costs). However, suppose Bob analyzes production costs and concludes that while direct material and direct labor are incremental costs, only 10 percent of manufacturing overhead, or $3,000, is incremental. The reason for this is that much of manufacturing overhead includes fixed costs, such as depreciation on equipment, depreciation on production facility, the salary of the master builder, and other fixed cost items.

Let's perform incremental analysis and see whether Bob should place the ad:

Incremental revenue		$ 90,000
Incremental cost:		
Cost of advertisement		(25,000)
Incremental production costs		
Direct material	$25,000	
Direct labor	20,000	
Manufacturing overhead	3,000	(48,000)
Incremental profit		$ 17,000

As indicated, incremental revenue exceeds incremental cost, and there will be an incremental profit of $17,000. Thus, Bob should place the ad. The important point here is that product cost information produced for external reporting purposes may not be appropriate for management decisions unless it is modified or adjusted.

LEARNING OBJECTIVE 2
Discuss the three inventory accounts of a manufacturing firm and describe the flow of product costs in a manufacturing firm's accounts.

BALANCE SHEET PRESENTATION OF PRODUCT COSTS

As noted earlier, product costs are treated as an asset until the finished goods are sold. In this section, we learn how product costs appear on the balance sheet in three asset accounts related to inventory: Raw Materials, Work in Process, and Finished Goods. In the next section, we discuss how costs flow from one account to another. Then we turn our attention to how the costs are reflected on a company's income statement.

The **Raw Materials Inventory** account includes the cost of materials on hand that are used to produce a company's products. For the Eastlake Motorboat Company, steering assemblies, motors, wood, screws, varnish, and glue are included in Raw Materials Inventory.

Work in Process Inventory is the inventory account for the cost of goods that are only partially completed. For example, suppose that at the end of the year, the Eastlake

ILLUSTRATION 2-4

Balance sheet presentation of inventory accounts

Eastlake Motorboat Company

Balance Sheet
As of December 31, 2017

Assets			**Liabilities and Stockholders' Equity**	
Cash		$ 20,000	Accounts payable	$ 10,000
Accounts receivable		40,000	Notes payable	60,000
Inventory			Long-term debt	100,000
Raw Materials	$ 30,000		Common stock	400,000
Work in Process	50,000		Retained earnings	70,000
Finished Goods	100,000	180,000		
Equipment (net)		400,000	Total liabilities and	
Total Assets		$640,000	stockholders' equity	$640,000

Motorboat Company has 10 partially completed boats. The cost of direct material, direct labor, and manufacturing overhead incurred to bring the boats to their current state of partial completion is included in Work in Process.

Finished Goods Inventory is the account for the cost of all items that are complete and ready to sell. Suppose that at the end of the year, the Eastlake Motorboat Company has four boats that are completed and ready to sell. Finished Goods includes the cost of direct material, direct labor, and manufacturing overhead incurred to bring those boats to their finished state. A simplified balance sheet showing the three inventory accounts is presented in Illustration 2-4.

FLOW OF PRODUCT COSTS IN ACCOUNTS

In an accounting system, product costs flow from one inventory account to another. Illustration 2-5 shows the flow of product costs in the accounts.

The cost of *direct* material used reduces the Raw Material Inventory account and increases Work in Process Inventory. *Indirect* material used, however, is not added directly to Work in Process; instead, it is accumulated in Manufacturing Overhead. The amount of direct labor used increases Work in Process, but indirect labor is not added directly to Work in Process. Like indirect material, indirect labor is accumulated in Manufacturing Overhead. The cost accumulated in Manufacturing Overhead, which includes indirect material, indirect labor, and a variety of other overhead costs, is also added to Work in Process.

Once items are finished, the cost of the completed items is transferred from Work in Process into Finished Goods. The cost of items completed is referred to as **cost of goods manufactured**. When the completed items are sold, the cost of the items sold is transferred from Finished Goods into Cost of Goods Sold.

INCOME STATEMENT PRESENTATION OF PRODUCT COSTS

When finished goods are sold, the cost of the inventory sold is considered an expense and must be removed from Finished Goods Inventory and charged to Cost of Goods Sold. This provides a matching of revenue (sales dollars) with the cost of producing the revenue (the cost of goods sold).

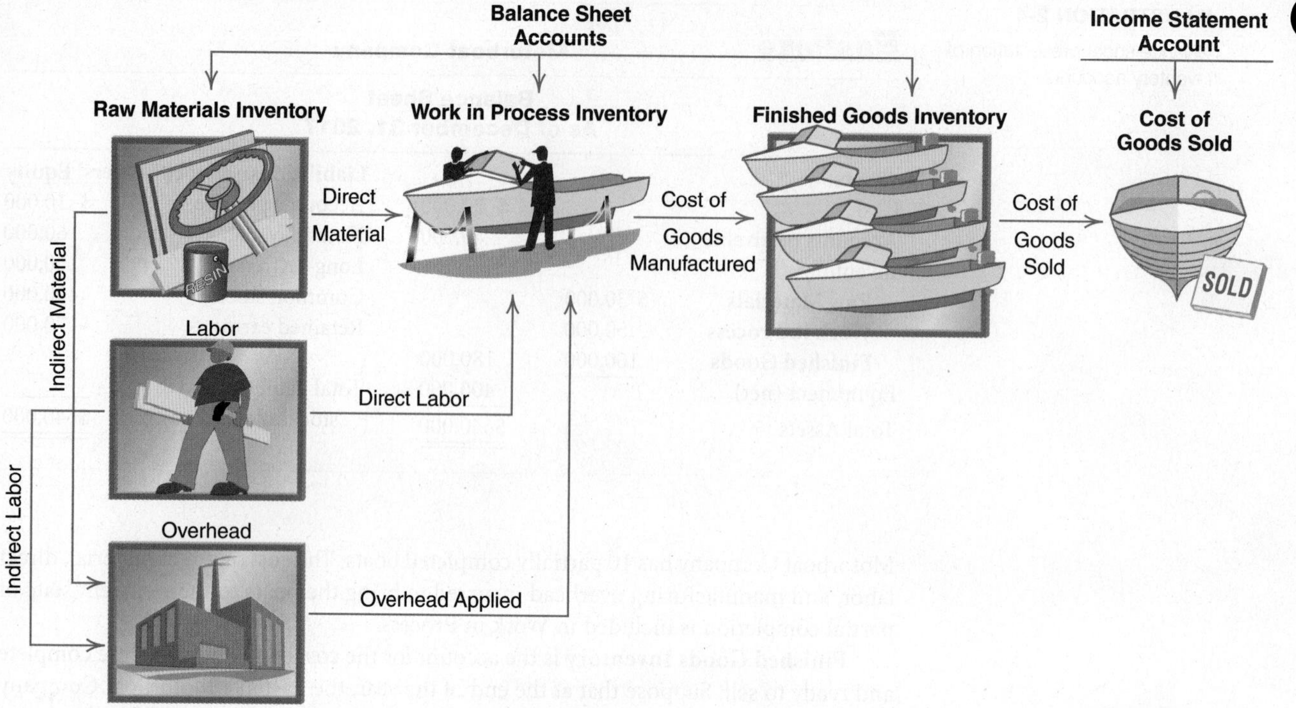

ILLUSTRATION 2-5
Flow of product costs in accounts

Cost of Goods Manufactured. Before cost of goods sold can be calculated, however, we must calculate cost of goods manufactured. Recall that cost of goods manufactured is the cost associated with items completed during a period. Cost of goods manufactured can be calculated using a simple formula. It is equal to the beginning balance in Work in Process plus current manufacturing costs (direct material, direct labor, and manufacturing overhead incurred in the current period) minus the ending balance in Work in Process.

Beginning Balance in Work in Process + **Current Manufacturing Costs** − **Ending Balance in Work in Process** = **Cost of Goods Manufactured**

Direct Material
Direct Labor
Manufacturing Overhead

Cost of Goods Sold. Once cost of goods manufactured is known, cost of goods sold can also be calculated using a simple formula. It is equal to the beginning balance in finished goods plus the cost of goods manufactured minus the ending balance in finished goods.

Beginning Balance in Finished Goods + **Cost of Goods Manufactured** − **Ending Balance in Finished Goods** = **Cost of Goods Sold**

Illustration 2-6 presents a schedule of cost of goods manufactured and a simplified income statement showing cost of goods sold for the Eastlake Motorboat

ILLUSTRATION 2-6

Schedule of cost of goods manufactured and an income statement showing cost of goods sold

Eastlake Motorboat Company

Schedule of Cost of Goods Manufactured
For the Year Ended December 31, 2017

Beginning balance in Work in Process Inventory			$ 40,000
Plus current manufacturing costs:			
Direct material		$ 600,000	
Direct labor		480,000	
Manufacturing overhead			
Heat, light, and power	$ 15,000		
Rent for production facility	45,000		
Depreciation of equipment	50,000		
Supervisor Salary	150,000		
Other	460,000	720,000	1,800,000
Total			1,840,000
Less ending balance in Work in Process Inventory			50,000
Cost of goods manufactured			**$1,790,000**

Income Statement
For the Year Ended December 31, 2017

Sales		$ 2,160,000
Less cost of goods sold:		
Beginning finished goods inventory	$ 80,000	
Add cost of goods manufactured	**1,790,000**	
Cost of goods available for sale	1,870,000	
Less ending finished goods inventory	76,000	**1,794,000**
Gross profit		366,000
Less nonmanufacturing expenses:		
Selling and administrative expenses		220,000
Net Income		$ 146,000

Company. Note that in the income statement, the sum of the beginning balance in Finished Goods plus the cost of goods manufactured is referred to as the **cost of goods available for sale.**

TEST YOUR **KNOWLEDGE**

The formula to determine cost of goods sold is:

a. Beginning Work in Process Inventory + Cost of goods manufactured – Ending Finished Goods Inventory.

b. Beginning Work in Process Inventory + Cost of goods manufactured – Ending Work in Process Inventory.

c. Beginning finished goods inventory + Cost of goods manufactured – Ending Finished Goods Inventory.

d. Beginning Work in Process Inventory + Current manufacturing costs – Ending Work in Process Inventory.

Correct answer is c.

LEARNING OBJECTIVE 3

Discuss the types of product costing systems and explain the relation between the cost of jobs and the Work in Process, Inventory, Finished Goods Inventory, and Cost of Goods Sold accounts.

TYPES OF COSTING SYSTEMS

As noted in the introduction to this chapter, companies use product costing systems (an integrated set of documents, ledgers, accounts, and accounting procedures) to measure and record the cost of manufactured products. There are two major product costing systems: job-order costing systems and process costing systems. The best system to use depends on the type of manufacturing.

Companies that produce individual products or batches of products that are unique use a **job-order costing system**. This is the case when a company manufactures goods to a customer's unique specifications. Companies using job-order systems include construction companies, producers of equipment and tools, shipbuilding companies, and printing companies. In the context of job-order costing, a **job** is an individual product or batch for which a company needs cost information. When the items that make up the job are completed and sold, the company can match the cost of the job with the revenue it produced and obtain an appropriate measure of gross profit.

Companies that use a **process costing system** generally produce large quantities of identical items. Such companies include metal producers, chemical producers, and producers of paints and plastics. Products such as chemicals, paints, and plastics pass through uniform and continuous production operations. Costs are accumulated by each operation, and the unit cost of items is determined by dividing the costs of the production operations by the large number of identical items produced:

$$\text{Unit cost of items produced} = \frac{\text{Total cost of production}}{\text{Total number of units produced}}$$

In a process costing system, there is no need to trace costs to specific items produced, since all items are identical. It is sufficient to assign each item its average unit cost of production. You will learn more about process costing systems in Chapter 3. The sections that follow focus on job-order costing.

OVERVIEW OF JOB COSTS AND FINANCIAL STATEMENT ACCOUNTS

As previously discussed, product costs include three cost items: direct material, direct labor, and manufacturing overhead. In a job-order costing system, the cost of a job is the sum of these three cost items. Thus, a job-order system must be able to relate these costs to specific jobs (see Illustration 2-7).

LINK TO **PRACTICE**

Examples of Companies Using Job-Order and Process Costing Systems

Which of the following companies use job-order systems and which ones use process costing systems to determine product cost?

Companies

Grand Banks Yachts
Jones Soda Company
Dow Chemical Company
Pfizer, Inc.
Goodyear Tire and Rubber Company
Cray, The Supercomputer Company
Learjet, a subsidiary of Bombardier Aerospace,
Precision Castparts, a manufacturer of custom metal components

Answer: Job-order companies are Grand Banks, Cray, Learjet, and Precision Castparts. Process costing companies are Jones Soda, Dow Chemical, Pfizer, and Goodyear.

ILLUSTRATION 2-7
Relating product costs to jobs

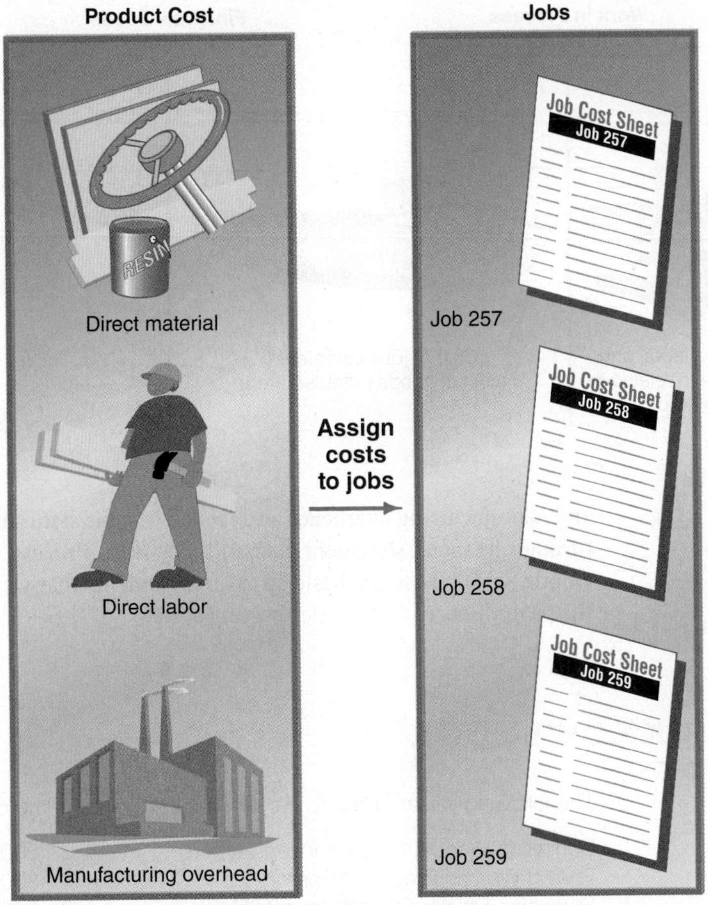

You should also recall that product costs are reflected in Work in Process Inventory and Finished Goods Inventory on the balance sheet and in Cost of Goods Sold on the income statement. In a job-order costing system, Work in Process will include the cost of all jobs that are currently being worked on (i.e., are in process). Finished Goods will include the cost of all jobs that are completed but not yet sold. Cost of Goods Sold will include the cost of all jobs that are sold during the accounting period (see Illustration 2-8).

Cost flow through a job-order costing system is based on the status of jobs. First, direct material, direct labor, and manufacturing overhead costs related to jobs being worked on are added to the Work in Process Inventory account. When specific jobs are completed, the costs of those jobs (referred to as the costs of goods manufactured) are deducted from Work in Process Inventory and added to the Finished Goods Inventory account. When specific jobs are sold, the costs of those jobs are removed from Finished Goods Inventory and added to Cost of Goods Sold. These cost flows are indicated in Illustration 2-9.

As you read the following material, keep in mind the components of a job-order costing system: (a) the items making up the costs of a job (direct material, direct labor,

ILLUSTRATION 2-8
Job costs and financial statement accounts

Work in Process Inventory	Finished Goods Inventory	Cost of Goods Sold
Cost of jobs being worked on	Cost of jobs completed but not yet sold	Cost of jobs sold

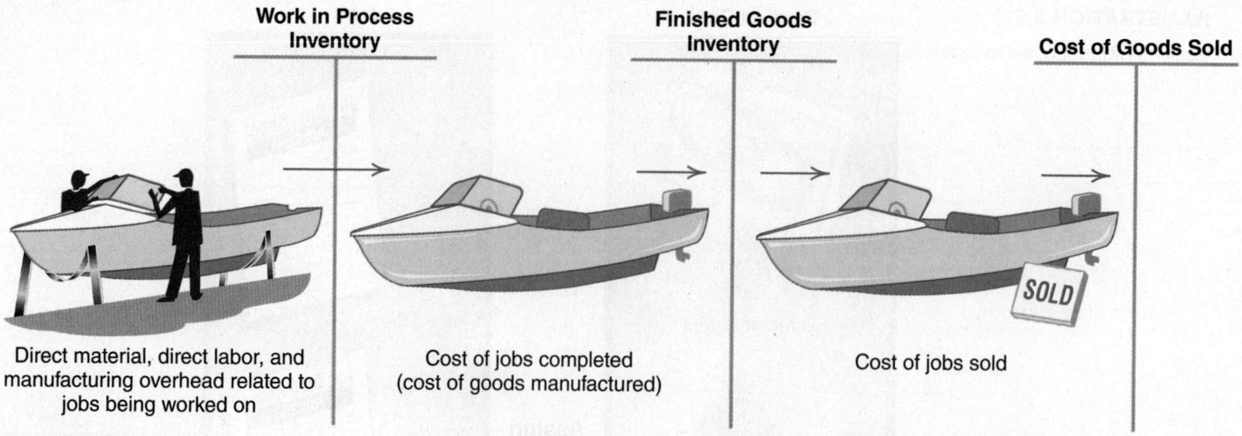

ILLUSTRATION 2-9

Flow of costs in job-order system

and manufacturing overhead) and (b) the way the status of jobs triggers the flow of costs through financial statement accounts (Work in Process, Finished Goods, and Cost of Goods Sold). These are basic structural elements that we build on in our discussion of the procedures of a job-order costing system.

TEST YOUR **KNOWLEDGE**

The following values relate to Royal Custom Molds for the current year:

Beginning Work in Process Inventory	$ 200,000
Ending Work in Process Inventory	$ 300,000
Beginning Finished Goods Inventory	$ 600,000
Ending Finished Goods Inventory	$ 900,000
Cost of Goods Manufactured	$4,000,000

Based on this information, what is cost of goods sold?

a. $3,900,000
b. $3,700,000
c. $1,200,000
d. $ 100,000

Correct answer is b.

LEARNING OBJECTIVE 4

Describe how direct material, direct labor, and manufacturing overhead are assigned to jobs.

JOB-ORDER COSTING SYSTEM

Job-order costing operations begin when a company decides to produce a specific product for stock (i.e., with no specific buyer in mind for the item) or in response to an order for a custom product. For example, an electric motor manufacturer decides to build five model XL25 motors for stock, a print shop receives an order for 20,000 spring catalogs from a clothing manufacturer, or a residential construction company receives an order to build a summer home.

If the company decides to accept the order, a job cost sheet is prepared. A **job cost sheet** is a form, typically computer generated, used to accumulate the cost of producing the item or items ordered (i.e., the cost of the job). Illustration 2-10 shows a job cost

ILLUSTRATION 2-10

Top of first page and bottom of last page of job cost sheets

Eastlake Motorboat Company

65 Shore Place
Kirkland, Washington 98006

Job number: 20126 Requested Delivery Date: 5/30 Date Started: 4/15 Date Completed: 5/25

Customer: Mary and John Hughes, 647 Circle Drive, Redmond, Washington 98042

Description: 18-foot runabout, mahogany hull, 75 h.p. inboard, deluxe interior (cream/maroon)

	Direct Materials		Direct Labor			Manufacturing Overhead
Date	Requisition number	Cost	Labor report number	Hours	Cost	$57.60 per direct labor hour
4/15	255	1,542.68	105	24	880.00	$1,362.40
4/16	261	5,450.00	106	12	432.00	691.20
4/17	266	4,225.42	107	15	576.00	864.00
4/18	272	1,820.65	108	7	262.50	403.20
4/19	282	436.80	109	9	297.50	518.40
4/22	289	854.64	110	4	140.00	230.40
4/23	295	1,620.22	111	5	175.00	288.00
			(last page of job cost report)			
5/25	382	655.50	133	4	160.00	230.40
		Total 24,500.50		Total 568	21,025.30	Total 32,716.80

Cost summary

Direct materials	$24,500.50
Direct labor	21,025.30
Manufacturing overhead	32,716.80
	$78,242.60

sheet for a custom product to be built by Eastlake Motorboat Company. The job is identified by a job number: 20126. How specific amounts end up on the job cost sheet will be explained later. For now, simply note that the job cost sheet contains detailed information on the three categories of product costs: direct material, direct labor, and manufacturing overhead.

Direct Material Cost

A **material requisition form** is used to request the release of materials from a company's storage area. Illustration 2-11 shows a material requisition form for Eastlake Motorboat Company job 20126. The form lists the type, quantity, and cost of material as well as the number of the job requiring the materials. Because the form includes the job number, it can be used to trace material cost to specific jobs. Requiring a supervisor's signature helps to prevent the unauthorized issuance of material.

Each material requisition form is listed in summary form on the job cost sheet. For example, on material requisition form number 255, presented in Illustration 2-11, the total cost of items requested amounts to $1,542.68. When these items are released

ILLUSTRATION 2-11
Material requisition form

Eastlake

Material requisition number 255
Job number 20126
Date 4/15

Item	Description	Cost
T5627	Floor tarp	$ 246.36
L2005	120 feet mahogany planking	1,296.32
		$1,542.68

Approved by: *Carl Jensen*

from storage, the total cost is posted to the job cost sheet (see Illustration 2-10) and cross-referenced by the material requisition number.

Removal of materials from storage for use on a specific job decreases Raw Materials and increases Work in Process Inventory. Periodically (daily, weekly, or monthly), the total cost of materials issued to jobs is calculated and recorded in the company accounts. Suppose $60,000 of materials are issued to specific jobs. The entry to record this is:

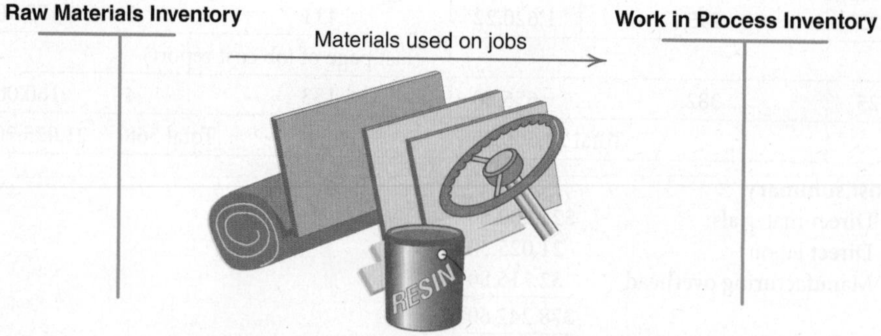

(date)	Work in Process Inventory	60,000.00	
	Raw Materials Inventory		60,000.00
	To record raw materials used		

Direct Labor Cost

Workers in a company that uses a job-order costing system fill out **time tickets** (also called job tickets or work tickets) to keep track of the amount of time spent on each job. Illustration 2-12 shows a time ticket for Eastlake Motorboat Company job 20126. If there are many workers on a particular job, individual time tickets may not be posted directly to job cost sheets since that would produce too much detail. Illustration 2-13 presents a daily labor cost summary by job. As you can see, time ticket number 1587 is just one of three time tickets indicating work performed on job number 20126 on April 15. In total, on April 15, 24 hours were spent on job 20126 at a cost of $880.00. The total labor cost traced to job 20126 ($880.00) is the amount posted to the job cost sheet (see Illustration 2-10).

ILLUSTRATION 2-12
Labor time ticket

Eastlake

Time ticket number 1587
Employee number 21 — Grade 3
Job number 20126 — Date 4/15
Time start 8:00 — Time stop 5:00
Total hours 8

Journal Entry to Record Direct Labor. Periodically, the amount of direct labor cost attributed to jobs being worked on must be debited to Work in Process. Suppose $40,000 of direct labor cost is incurred. The appropriate journal entry is:

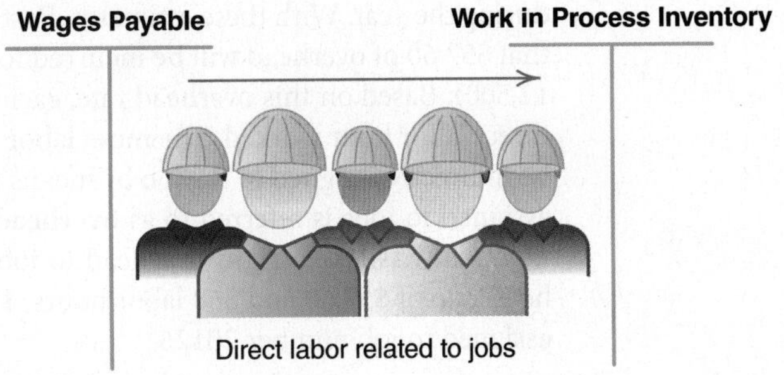

(date)	Work in Process Inventory	40,000.00	
	Wages Payable		40,000.00
	To record direct labor cost		

ILLUSTRATION 2-13
Daily labor cost summary

Eastlake **Motorboat Company**

Daily labor report number: 105 **Date: 4/15/2017**

Job	Time ticket	Hours	Grade	Rate	Cost
20124	1583	8	4	42.00	$ 336.00
20124	1582	5	3	37.00	185.00
20124	1583	3	2	31.00	93.00
		16			**614.00**
20125	1584	3	3	37.00	111.00
20125	1585	5	2	31.00	155.00
		8			**266.00**
20126	1586	8	4	42.00	336.00
20126	1587	8	3	37.00	296.00
20126	1588	8	2	31.00	248.00
		24			**880.00**
				Total daily labor	$1,760.00

Manufacturing Overhead

So far, we have traced raw material and direct labor costs to jobs. The final and more complex cost component to assign is manufacturing overhead, which we discuss in a general way here before going into more detail later in this chapter and in Chapter 6.

Recall that manufacturing overhead costs are not directly traced to goods produced. For that reason, an indirect method of assigning overhead costs to jobs is needed. The basic approach involves assigning overhead to jobs based on some characteristic that jobs share in common, such as direct labor hours or direct labor cost. The common characteristic is referred to as an **allocation base**. Essentially, the allocation base spreads the overhead among the various jobs.

An **overhead allocation rate** is calculated by dividing estimated overhead costs by the estimated quantity of the allocation base. For example, suppose Eastlake Motorboat Company anticipates $720,000 of manufacturing overhead and 12,500 direct labor hours during the year. With these estimates, Eastlake's accountant, Nancy Young, can calculate that $57.60 of overhead will be incurred for every direct labor hour worked ($720,000 ÷ 12,500). Based on this overhead rate, each job will receive $57.60 of overhead for every direct labor hour worked. The more labor hours spent on a job, the more overhead will be indirectly assigned to the job by means of the overhead rate. The amount of overhead assigned to jobs is referred to as **overhead applied**. Look back at Illustration 2-10 and note that Eastlake assigns overhead to jobs on the basis of labor hours. With an overhead rate of $57.60 and 568 labor hours, $32,716.80 of manufacturing overhead will be assigned to job number 20126.

Journal Entries to Record Manufacturing Overhead. Recording manufacturing overhead is a two-step process. First, when actual overhead costs are incurred, they are debited to the Manufacturing Overhead account. Second, when overhead is applied to jobs, the Manufacturing Overhead account is credited, and Work in Process Inventory is debited.

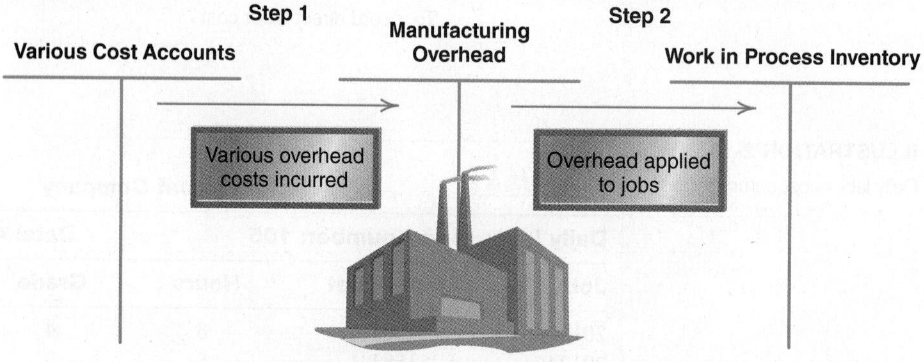

Step 1. Overhead costs include depreciation of manufacturing equipment, utilities related to manufacturing, indirect materials, and a variety of other costs. Therefore, the credit side of the entry to record manufacturing overhead can include a large number of accounts. Suppose $4,000 of depreciation, $1,000 of utility costs, $1,000 of indirect materials, and $60,000 of various other overhead costs are incurred. The journal entry to record these costs is:

(date)	Manufacturing Overhead	66,000.00	
	Accumulated Depreciation		4,000.00
	Utilities Payable		1,000.00
	Raw Materials Inventory		1,000.00
	Accounts Payable		60,000.00
	To record overhead costs incurred		

Step 2. The total amount of estimated overhead costs applied to jobs is calculated periodically, and an entry is made to take the cost out of Manufacturing Overhead and debit it to Work in Process. Suppose $60,000 of overhead is applied to jobs. The journal entry is:

(date)	Work in Process Inventory	60,000.00	
	Manufacturing Overhead		60,000.00
	To record overhead costs applied to jobs		

Assigning Costs to Jobs: A Summary

Direct material costs are traced to jobs using material requisition forms. Direct labor costs are traced to jobs using labor time tickets. Manufacturing overhead costs cannot be directly traced to jobs. Instead, they are assigned to jobs using an overhead rate that is multiplied by each job's measure of the allocation base. Illustration 2-14 summarizes the methods used to relate manufacturing costs to jobs.

EASTLAKE REVISITED: USING JOB COST INFORMATION

At this point we have reviewed a good deal of financial accounting information related to job-order costing systems. Of what use is all this information to management? Let's consider Eastlake Motorboat Company to illustrate.

ILLUSTRATION 2-14
How manufacturing costs are related to jobs

Recall from the chapter-opening vignette that Bob Williams, the new owner of Eastlake Motorboat, is concerned that his company is underestimating costs and setting prices too low for its custom boats. Using information from job-cost sheets, his accountant, Nancy Young, prepared an analysis of estimated and actual cost for three recent jobs (see Illustration 2-15). Using this information, Bob can see that his hunch is right: Actual costs are higher than estimated. The information indicates that, in particular, there has been a problem in estimating material costs; on average, these costs have been running 14 percent higher than estimated.

The problem is reflected in the difference between the estimated and actual profit margin percentages [(Price – Cost) ÷ Price]. For example, consider job 20124. Based on estimated costs, the company would have earned a profit margin of 22 percent. However, due primarily to the difference between estimated and actual material cost, the actual profit margin is only 16 percent.

	Estimate	Actual
Sales price	$115,000	$115,000
Less:		
Material	27,000	31,600
Labor	24,100	25,200
Overhead	38,078	39,816
Total	89,178	96,616
Profit margin	$25,822	$18,384
Profit margin as % of sales	22%	16%

Armed with the knowledge that costs have been underestimated, Bob can work to improve the estimation process, especially with respect to cost of materials. However,

ILLUSTRATION 2-15

Analysis of estimated and actual costs for Eastlake Motorboat

Eastlake Motorboat Company

	Material	Labor	Overhead		
Job 20126				**Price**	$102,000
Estimated	22,000.00	21,200.00	33,600.00	**Est. margin**	25%
Actual	24,500.00	21,025.00	33,219.00	**Act. margin**	23%
Difference	(2,500.00)	175.00	381.00	**Difference**	–2%
Percent of estimate	–11%	1%	1%		
Job 20125				**Price**	105,000
Estimated	25,000.00	22,500.00	35,550.00	**Est. margin**	21%
Actual	28,600.00	23,500.00	37,130.00	**Act. margin**	15%
Difference	(3,600.00)	(1,000.00)	(1,580.00)	**Difference**	–6%
Percent of estimate	–14%	–4%	–4%		
Job 20124				**Price**	115,000
Estimated	27,000.00	24,100.00	38,078.00	**Est. margin**	22%
Actual	31,600.00	25,200.00	39,816.00	**Act. margin**	16%
Difference	(4,600.00)	(1,100.00)	(1,738)	**Difference**	–6%
Percent of estimate	–17%	–5%	–5%		
Total estimated	74,000.00	67,800.00	107,228.00		
Total actual	84,700.00	69,725.00	110,165.00		
Total Difference	(10,700.00)	(1,925.00)	(2,937.00)		
Percent of estimate	–14%	–3%	–3%		

Note: Actual overhead is applied using a predetermined rate times actual labor hours.

should he raise prices consistent with higher estimated cost? That's a complex question. The fact that his costs have been higher than planned doesn't necessarily mean prices have been too low.

Decision Making/ Incremental Analysis

As explained more fully in Chapter 8, in addition to considering production cost, when setting prices, managers need to consider what customers are willing to pay. Let's look at job 20124. Suppose the customer for this boat was only willing to pay $115,000. Should Bob have turned down the sale? Probably not.

Remember that when making a decision, we need to perform incremental analysis. Let's assume that only 10 percent of overhead is variable and the remainder is composed of fixed costs, such as depreciation and the salary of the master builder. In this case, the incremental costs of the job are $31,600 for materials, $25,200 for direct labor, and $3,982 for manufacturing overhead. This totals to $60,782. The incremental profit of the job is $54,218, and turning the job down would have hurt financial performance.

Incremental revenue		$115,000
Incremental cost:		
Direct material	31,600	
Direct labor	25,200	
Manufacturing overhead	3,982	60,782
Incremental profit		$ 54,218

In adjusting prices, Bob will have to be careful that he doesn't turn down business that will actually improve profitability.

RELATION BETWEEN THE COSTS OF JOBS AND THE FLOW OF COSTS IN WORK IN PROCESS, FINISHED GOODS, AND COST OF GOODS SOLD

Earlier in the chapter, we discussed in general terms how product costs flow in the accounts of a manufacturing firm (see Illustration 2-5). Now that we have a good understanding of the cost of a job, we can make a link between the cost of jobs and cost flows. When a company begins work on a job, production costs are applied to Work in Process using journal entries such as those illustrated earlier. When jobs are completed, Work in Process is reduced and Finished Goods is increased. When completed jobs are sold, Finished Goods is reduced by the cost of the completed jobs sold and the Cost of Goods

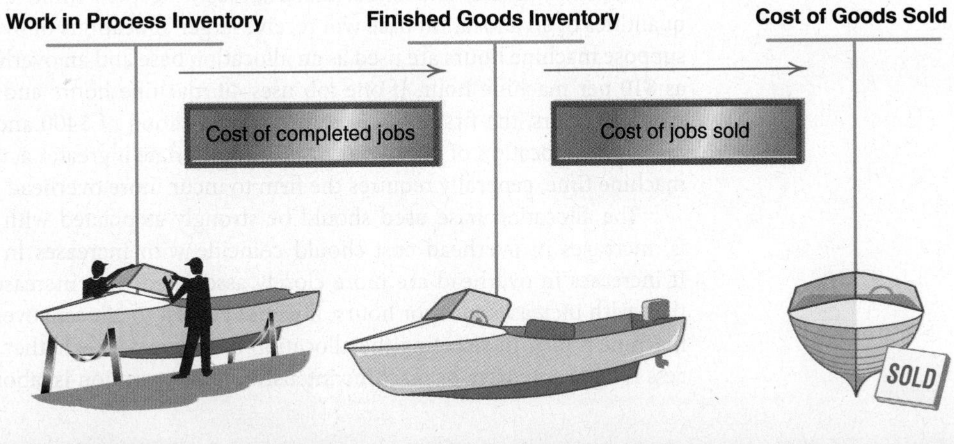

Sold account is increased. Suppose the cost of jobs completed is $160,000 and the cost of jobs sold is $85,000. The journal entries are:

(date)	Finished Goods Inventory	160,000	
	Work in Process Inventory		160,000
	To record cost of jobs completed		
(date)	Cost of Goods Sold	85,000	
	Finished Goods Inventory		85,000
	To record cost of goods sold expense		

ALLOCATING OVERHEAD TO JOBS: A CLOSER LOOK

We have seen how direct material, direct labor, and manufacturing overhead are accumulated in a job-order costing system. However, in discussing the process of assigning manufacturing overhead to specific jobs and recording overhead in various accounts, referred to as **overhead allocation**, we did not go into much detail. It's time for a more thorough discussion.

Overhead Allocation Rates

Because cost items that make up overhead are related only indirectly to jobs being produced, some means of allocating or assigning overhead costs to jobs must be developed. As mentioned, overhead costs are allocated to jobs by means of an overhead allocation rate. The rate is calculated as the ratio of overhead costs to activity. Common measures of activity include direct labor hours, direct labor cost, machine hours, and direct material cost. Recall that the measure of these activities is referred to as the allocation base.

$$\text{Overhead allocation rate} = \frac{\text{Overhead cost}}{\text{Allocation base}}$$

Suppose a company had $50,000 of overhead cost and used 10,000 labor hours during the year. In this example, an average *actual* overhead cost per labor hour of $5 ($50,000 ÷ 10,000) can be calculated, and overhead can be assigned to jobs based on the amount of labor hours worked on each job. For example, if a particular job required 100 labor hours, it would receive an overhead allocation of $500 (100 × $5).

The Overhead Allocation Base

In choosing among alternative allocation bases (such as direct labor hours, direct labor cost, machine hours, and direct material cost), keep in mind that jobs with greater quantities of an allocation base will receive larger allocations of overhead. For example, suppose machine hours are used as an allocation base and an overhead rate is calculated as $10 per machine hour. If one job uses 40 machine hours and another job uses 20 machine hours, the first job will receive an allocation of $400 and the second job will receive an allocation of only $200. This is appropriate if greater activity, as measured by machine time, generally requires the firm to incur more overhead cost.

The allocation base used should be strongly associated with overhead cost. That is, increases in overhead cost should coincide with increases in the allocation base. If increases in overhead are more closely associated with increases in machine hours than with increases in labor hours, it would be best to allocate overhead on the basis of machine hours. In selecting the allocation base, consider whether the production process is labor intensive or machine intensive. If an operation is labor intensive (i.e., large quantities of labor are used to produce most jobs), then direct labor hours or direct labor cost is likely to be a reasonable allocation base. If an operation is highly mechanized, then machine hours are likely to be a reasonable allocation base.

YOU GET WHAT YOU MEASURE

In selecting an allocation base, you also need to remember that "You get what you measure!" Manufacturing managers try to reduce costs because it reflects well on their managerial skill. If labor hours are used as the overhead allocation base, managers may try to cut labor to reduce overhead charges to the jobs for which they are responsible. Similarly, if machine hours are used, managers may try to reduce machine run time. But if labor or machine time is reduced, will overhead costs be reduced? That's not clear, because, at least in the short run, much of the overhead cost may be fixed. Thus, apparent cost savings may not be realized. In other words, the costing system will make it appear that costs are decreasing when in fact they are not.

For example, suppose the performance of Carl Jensen, the master builder at Eastlake Motorboat Company, is evaluated in terms of building boats below the cost estimated in pricing custom orders. Carl is a supervisor, and his salary is included in manufacturing overhead. He knows that overhead costs of $57.60 per direct labor hour are assigned to each boat. On job 20130, estimated cost was $75,000 and, although the boat is only 80 percent complete, costs assigned to the job are already around $70,000.

To cut costs, Carl personally works on completing the boat and assigns craftsmen to other jobs, saving 40 direct labor hours. This results in the following apparent cost savings:

Direct labor (80 hours × $38 per hour)	$3,040
Overhead (40 × $57.60)	2,304
Total apparent savings	$5,344

Now let's ask ourselves: "How much cost did reducing direct labor hours really save the company?" The answer, as in many cases, is "It depends!" Suppose the company isn't at capacity and craftsmen typically work and get paid for a 40-hour workweek. There is no overtime. In this case, no direct labor is being saved by Carl taking over for craftsmen on job 20130.

And how much overhead is saved by reducing direct labor? Let's assume that 90 percent of overhead is fixed. Then clearly the most overhead saved is 10 percent of the $2,304 of overhead, or $230. Thus, in this case, Carl has pulled himself away from his important job of supervising workers in order to look better with respect to his performance measure. And the accounting system is making it look like he has indeed saved $5,344 when he may have saved only $230 or less! Why did this happen? The performance measure used to evaluate Carl led him to cut direct labor even when it apparently wasn't a good idea. This clearly makes the point that "You get what you measure!" It's critical to carefully consider the effects of performance measures on the behavior of managers.

Activity-Based Costing (ABC) and Multiple Overhead Rates

Many companies allocate overhead to jobs using a single overhead rate with an allocation base of direct labor. However, overhead costs are created by a variety of factors, and allocating costs just on the basis of labor, or any single allocation base, may seriously distort product costs.

Activity-based costing (ABC) is a method of assigning overhead costs to products using a number of different allocation bases. In the ABC approach, the major activities that create overhead costs are identified. The costs of the major activities are grouped into so-called **cost pools**. Multiple overhead rates are calculated by dividing the amount of each cost pool by a measure of its corresponding activity (referred to as a **cost driver**).

Overhead is then assigned to a product based on how much of each activity (cost driver) it caused. The topic of ABC costing is examined in detail in Chapter 6.

TEST YOUR **KNOWLEDGE**

Which of the following is false with respect to manufacturing overhead?

a. Manufacturing overhead is allocated to jobs using a predetermined overhead rate.

b. A predetermined overhead rate is calculated by dividing estimated overhead by an estimate of the allocation base.

c. The difference between overhead applied and actual overhead may be closed to either Cost of Goods sold or apportioned among Cost of Goods Sold, Work in Process, and Finished Goods.

d. Actual overhead is a cost indicated on a Job Cost Sheet.

Correct answer is d.

LEARNING OBJECTIVE 5

Explain the role of a predetermined overhead rate in applying overhead to jobs, and explain the treatment of the difference between actual overhead and overhead allocated to jobs using a predetermined rate.

PREDETERMINED OVERHEAD RATES

Companies can develop overhead rates by dividing *actual* overhead by the *actual* level of the allocation base. Most companies do not follow this practice, however, because total actual overhead cost and the total actual level of the allocation base are not known until the end of the accounting period, making it impossible to determine the actual overhead rate until that time. In many cases, however, an immediate cost figure is also needed to determine the profitability of jobs.

Typically, then, overhead rates are based on *estimates* of overhead cost and *estimates* of the level of the allocation base rather than on *actual* costs and quantities. Overhead rates calculated in this way are referred to as **predetermined overhead rates** (also called budgeted overhead rates). Once the estimated overhead cost and estimated allocation base are established, the predetermined overhead rate is obtained by dividing the estimated overhead by the estimated level of the allocation base:

$$\text{Predetermined overhead rate} = \frac{\text{Estimated total overhead cost}}{\text{Estimated level of alloction base}}$$

Let's return to our example of Eastlake Motorboat Company. Suppose management estimates that $720,000 of total manufacturing overhead will be incurred in the coming year and that 12,500 labor hours will be required. In that case, the predetermined overhead rate is $57.60 per labor hour ($720,000 ÷ 12,500), and a job requiring 600 direct labor hours to complete would be allocated $34,560.00 of overhead ($57.60 × 600 labor hours).

The estimated or budgeted overhead cost and the estimated level of the allocation base are generally estimated for a year so that the overhead allocation rate stays the same from month to month. If a shorter period, such as one month, were used, the overhead rate would fluctuate from month to month, causing identical jobs produced in different months to have different costs. This happens because some overhead charges only occur in certain months. For example, in summer months, extra power costs may be incurred because the plant is air-conditioned. Another reason for fluctuation in a shorter period of time is that overhead includes both variable and fixed cost items. When *expected* levels of the allocation base decrease, the *expected* amount of variable overhead also decreases. However, the expected amount of fixed overhead does not decrease. Thus, the overhead rate is likely to be higher in slow months.

Eliminating Overapplied or Underapplied Overhead

As indicated earlier, recording manufacturing overhead is a two-step process. First, the *actual* costs of various overhead items are accumulated in the Manufacturing Overhead account. Second, overhead is applied to individual jobs using the predetermined overhead rate. This increases Work in Process and decreases Manufacturing Overhead. Thus, two types of entries are made to the Manufacturing Overhead account: The debit entries record actual overhead costs incurred, and the credit entries record the amount of overhead applied to jobs in process.

Manufacturing Overhead	
Actual overhead costs incurred	Overhead costs applied to jobs

Unless *estimated* overhead equals *actual* overhead and the estimated level of the allocation base equals the actual level of the allocation base, the amount of overhead applied to jobs using a predetermined overhead rate will not equal actual overhead cost incurred. Because estimates are seldom perfectly accurate, there is likely to be a difference between the debits to manufacturing overhead (recording actual overhead costs) and the credits to manufacturing overhead (recording the amount of overhead applied to jobs using the predetermined overhead rate). The difference is referred to as **underapplied overhead** if actual overhead is greater than the amount of overhead applied and as **overapplied overhead** if actual overhead is less than the amount applied.

At the end of the accounting period, the amount of under- or overapplied overhead is equal to the balance in Manufacturing Overhead. This account must be closed, and accounts must be adjusted to reflect actual overhead costs. If a reasonable job of estimation has been done in developing the predetermined overhead rate, the amount of over- or underapplied overhead will not be large. In this case, most companies simply close the account and adjust Cost of Goods Sold.

For example, suppose a company had $50,000 of actual overhead and applied $48,000 to jobs using a predetermined overhead rate. In this case, overhead is underapplied by $2,000, the debit balance in the manufacturing overhead account. To close the account, the following journal entry is made:

(date)	Cost of Goods Sold	2,000.00	
	Manufacturing Overhead		2,000.00
	To close manufacturing overhead and eliminate underapplied overhead		

Theoretically, the amount of under- or overapplied overhead should be apportioned among Work in Process, Finished Goods, and Cost of Goods Sold. This follows from the fact that use of a predetermined rate results in job costs that differ from the actual cost of jobs by the amount of over- or underapplied overhead. Because the cost of jobs is reflected in Work in Process, Finished Goods, and Cost of Goods Sold, all of these accounts should be adjusted to reflect actual overhead costs.

Apportioning costs among Work in Process, Finished Goods, and Cost of Goods Sold can be accomplished based on the relative cost recorded in these accounts. For example, suppose a company has Work in Process of $10,000, Finished Goods of $10,000, Cost of Goods Sold of $20,000, and underapplied overhead of $2,000. The apportionment rate would be $.05 for each dollar in the accounts (i.e., $2,000 ÷ $40,000). Thus, Work in Process would receive $500, Finished Goods would receive $500, and Cost of Goods sold $1,000. The following journal entry would be made:

(date)	Work in Process Inventory	500.00	
	Finished Goods Inventory	500.00	
	Cost of Goods Sold	1,000.00	
	Manufacturing Overhead		2,000.00
	To apportion underapplied overhead		

Whether the amount of over- or underapplied overhead is applied to Cost of Goods Sold or apportioned among Work in Process, Finished Goods, and Cost of Goods Sold depends on the dollar value of over- or underapplied overhead. If the amount is immaterial (i.e., relatively small), it is sufficient for practical purposes simply to debit (for underapplied overhead) or credit (for overapplied overhead) the amount to Cost of Goods Sold. If the amount is material (i.e., relatively large), it should be apportioned among Work in Process, Finished Goods, and Cost of Goods Sold.

TEST YOUR **KNOWLEDGE**

Overapplied overhead is.

a. Overhead applied to production greater than actual overhead.
b. Overhead in excess of standard overhead.
c. Equal to the predetermined overhead rate.
d. Overhead in excess of the amount in the previous period.

Correct answer is a.

LEARNING OBJECTIVE 6

Explain how service companies can use job-order costing to calculate the cost of services provided to customers.

JOB-ORDER COSTING FOR SERVICE COMPANIES

All the examples used so far have involved manufacturing companies, but many service companies also use job-order costing (e.g., hospitals, law firms, accounting firms, consulting companies, and repair shops). For example, a hospital might want to know the cost of treating a patient. In this case, the patient becomes a "job," and costs incurred in treating the patient (cost of physician and nursing care, cost of medicine, cost of X-rays, etc.) are accumulated on a report much like a job cost sheet used in a manufacturing setting. Repair shops also use job costing systems. When you bring your car in for service, the repair shop traces labor and parts to a job cost sheet that becomes your bill. Typically, these shops do not assign overhead to jobs. Rather, they mark up the charges for labor and parts to cover overhead and generate profit.

Consider the company Kendall/Allan, a consulting firm that specializes in installing computer information systems. Each consultant keeps track of his or her time and at the end of the month fills out a time sheet that indicates how much time was spent on each consulting engagement. For purposes of the company's accounting system, each consulting engagement is considered to be a "job." The data from the time sheets are then posted on job cost sheets (see Illustration 2-16). Consultants also keep track of so-called billable items that include the cost of software and training manuals provided to customers. These costs are also entered on job cost sheets. Note that this is much like the accumulation of direct labor and direct materials on the job cost sheets of manufacturing firms.

To allocate overhead to jobs, Kendall/Allan must develop a predetermined overhead rate using estimated overhead and an allocation base. Overhead for the company would include depreciation of the company's office building; depreciation of computers, fax machines, and other office equipment; utilities; salaries of office staff; and other indirect costs. The company has decided that these overhead costs are most highly associated with the salaries paid to consultants. At the start of the year, the company estimates that overhead will be $4,000,000 and consultants' salaries will be $20,000,000. Thus, the predetermined overhead rate is 20 percent of consultants' salaries. As indicated in Illustration 2-16, consultants' salaries charged to the job performed for Design Works, Inc. are $2,782.25. Therefore, $556.45 of overhead is assigned to this job (.20 × $2,782.25). In total, the cost of the job for Design Works is $9,332.55, and this is made up of $2,782.25 of consultant cost, $5,993.85 of billable items, and $556.45 of overhead.

Comprehensive Example

To expand your understanding of how job-order costing applies to service companies, let's work through a more comprehensive example. India Call Management Services (ICMS) is a company located in Bangalore, India. It provides call service management to 26 large companies located primarily in the United States and the United Kingdom. Each customer is considered a "job," and the cost of the job is determined monthly. The amount charged to each customer is negotiated annually, and ICMS tries to earn a return of 30 percent above full cost. It is important for ICMS to determine the cost of servicing each customer so that customer profitability can be assessed. If it turns out that actual costs are higher or lower than anticipated when the annual contract was negotiated, the company will take this into account when contracts come up for renegotiation.

ILLUSTRATION 2-16

Job cost sheet for a service firm

Kendall/Allan, Consulting

Client Design Works, Inc.

Engagement Installation of billing system linked to existing G/L program.

Consultant time

Reference	Date	Name	Hours	Rate	Total
S325	15-Feb	S. Wilson	8.0	45.50	$ 364.00
S325	15-Feb	H. Starr	8.0	65.50	524.00
S326	16-Feb	S. Wilson	8.0	45.50	364.00
S326	16-Jan	H. Starr	8.0	65.50	524.00
S326	16-Feb	J. Kendall	3.5	125.00	437.50
S327	19-Feb	S. Wilson	8.0	45.50	364.00
S328	20-Feb	S. Wilson	4.5	45.50	204.75
				Total	2,782.25

Billable items

Reference	Description		Total
E8102	SQA software		5,868.25
E8156	SQA training manual		125.60
		Total	5,993.85
Overhead	(20% of consultant salary)		556.45
		Total cost	$9,332.55

One of ICMS's customers is RCP Communications. The contract with this company is $4.2 million per year, or $350,000 per month. In early July, ICMS determined the cost of providing services to RCP Communications. Illustration 2-17 shows the analysis.

The call center employs 60 operators over three shifts dedicated to the RCP account. The operators are paid, on average, $15.75 per hour. Thus, the job is charged $151,200 of operator cost.

The operators process calls at 20 workstations that are dedicated to the RCP account. In total, the 20 workstations cost $500,000, and each workstation has a 4-year life. Thus, depreciation for a month is $10,416.67.

ICMS operates out of a 60,000-square-foot facility with annual depreciation of $1,000,000. This depreciation is allocated to the RCP account based on the square feet occupied by the 20 workstations, which is 2,000. For one month, the allocation is $2,777.78.

Each of the three shifts has a supervisor who is paid $4,500 per month. Thus, $13,500 of supervisory salary is assigned to the RCP account.

Finally, all remaining costs of operating the call center are assigned using an overhead allocation rate of $1.053 per dollar of operator salary. The rate was determined as follows. At the start of the year, ICMS estimated that the annual amount of all costs other than operator salary, depreciation of workstations, depreciation of facility, and shift supervisor salary would amount to $38,782,800. Additionally, the company estimated that annual operator salaries would be $36,843,660. With this information, the rate was calculated to be $1.053 per dollar of operator salary (i.e., $38,782,800 ÷ $36,843,600).

Is RCP a profitable customer? Note that the total cost of the job for June was $337,108.50. The monthly revenue for the job is $350,000, which is one-twelfth of the annual revenue of $4.2 million. With profit on the job equal to $12,891.95 ($350,000 – $337,108.50), the mark up over cost is only 3.8 percent, which is much lower than the company's goal of 30 percent. This information will be very useful the next time the contract is up for negotiation—especially if RCP Communications presses for price concessions!

($350,000.00 – $337,108.50) ÷ $337,108.50 = .038

ILLUSTRATION 2-17

Job-order cost for call center

India Call Management Services

ICMS—Simply the Best

Customer: RCP Communications	
Call center operators	
60 operators × 160 hours × $15.75 per hour	$151,200.00
Depreciation associated with	
20 workstations costing $500,000 in total	
($500,000 ÷ 4-year life) ÷ 12 months	10,416.67
Annual depreciation of $1,000,000 for 60,000-square-foot building	
2,000-square feet occupied by 20 workstations	
(($1,000,000 ÷ 60,000 square feet) ÷ 12 months) × 2,000 square feet	2,777.78
3 shift supervisors × $4,500 monthly salary	13,500.00
Other overhead allocated at $1.053 × operator salary	
$1.053 × $151,200	159,213.60
Total	$337,108.05

TEST YOUR KNOWLEDGE

Which of the following is false?

a. Service companies may use job-order costing.
b. Service companies may use a predetermined overhead rate.
c. Job-order costing is used by manufacturing firms, not service firms.
d. A consulting firm may use a job-order costing system.

Correct answer is c.

LEARNING OBJECTIVE 7

Discuss modern manufacturing practices and how they affect product costing.

MODERN MANUFACTURING PRACTICES AND PRODUCT COSTING SYSTEMS

To compete effectively in a global economy, many U.S. manufacturers made fundamental changes in their operations and business philosophies starting in the late 1980s. These changes in the manufacturing environment affect the types of costs that are incurred and, to some extent, the way the costs are recorded in the product costing system.

Here we briefly discuss three of the major changes: just-in-time production, computer-controlled manufacturing, and total quality management. The purpose of the discussion is to make sure you have a basic understanding of the setting in which companies are calculating product costs. In addition, you need to speak the language of top management and operating personnel if you want to have a significant impact on important decisions. Increasingly, the language includes references to just-in-time production, computer-controlled manufacturing, and total quality management.

Just-in-Time (JIT) Production

Japanese companies, following the lead of Toyota Motor Company, were the first to use an innovative manufacturing system referred to as a **just-in-time (JIT)** system. One important goal of such manufacturing systems is to minimize inventories of raw materials and work in process. Companies with JIT systems make arrangements with suppliers to deliver materials just before they are needed in the production process. In addition, when products need to be manufactured on multiple production lines (e.g., first a production line that involves welding and then a production line that involves machining), production on one line is scheduled so that operations are completed just in time to meet the requirements of the next production line. With such a system, there is no buildup of raw material and work in process inventories to clog the factory floor. It is partly for this reason that JIT systems are also referred to as lean production systems. With JIT, there is no "fat" associated with wasted space and excess investment in inventory.

JIT is, however, much more than an effort to reduce companies' investments in inventory. The goals of a JIT system are to develop a balanced production system that is flexible and allows for smooth, rapid flow of materials. To achieve these goals, companies using JIT concentrate on improving quality (since quality problems disrupt the production system), eliminating production breakdowns, and preventing missed delivery deadlines by suppliers. To improve coordination with suppliers, many companies are using the Internet to link their production facilities to suppliers (see the discussion in Chapter 1 on supply chain management). Dramatic improvements in manufacturing performance have been attributed to use of JIT

LINK TO **PRACTICE**

Lean Principles Are Not Just for Manufacturing Firms

While Lean principles were developed by manufacturing firms such as Toyota, they have been widely adopted by service firms such as banks and hospitals. According to blogger Ann All, the president of Seattle Children's Hospital says that Lean improvement efforts cut costs per patient by 3.7 percent, for a savings of $23 million. And the hospital saved $180 million in capital expenditures by using its facilities more efficiently. According to Ms. All, Akron Children's Hospital performed an overhaul of its process for sterilizing instruments, which helped it avoid a $3.5 million expansion of its surgery department.

Source: Ann All, *Hospitals Use Lean Principles to Achieve Efficiency Gains,* July 14, 2010.

production. Some companies report 90 percent reductions in production lead time, 89 percent reductions in work in process, and 80 percent reductions in space required for production.[1]

JIT can also have an effect on product costing. What happens to over- or underapplied overhead when a company uses a JIT system? With a JIT system, Work in Process and Finished Goods Inventory balances are generally quite small compared to the balance in Cost of Goods Sold. Thus, the difference between assigning all of over- or underapplied overhead to Cost of Goods Sold or allocating it among Work in Process, Finished Goods, and Cost of Goods Sold is likely to be quite small. Thus, simply charging the amount to Cost of Goods Sold is expedient and appropriate.

Lean Manufacturing. Closely related to JIT is the concept of lean manufacturing. Indeed, some authors use the terms interchangeably. However, most people associate JIT with an intense focus on inventory management, while they associate lean with eliminating waste across the value chain.

Computer-Controlled Manufacturing

Many manufacturing companies are also using highly automated **computer-controlled manufacturing systems**. Using computers to control equipment, including robots, generally increases the flexibility and accuracy of the production process. But while state-of-the-art equipment and computer-controlled systems may help firms meet the challenge of global competition, they also have a significant effect on the composition of product costs.

Survey data indicate that, on average, product costs in recent years have consisted of 53 percent material, 15 percent direct labor, and 32 percent overhead. Some highly automated companies, such as Hewlett-Packard, however, report that direct labor accounts for as little as 3 percent of total production costs. Decreasing labor costs are causing many companies to reconsider their overhead allocation bases. Currently, the most commonly used allocation bases for assigning overhead to jobs are direct labor hours and direct labor cost. However, in highly mechanized companies where direct labor is a small part of total manufacturing costs, using labor as an allocation base is generally not appropriate.

[1]See for example, "The Just-In-Time Breakthrough: Implementing the New Manufacturing Basics," Edward J. Hay, 1988, John Wiley & Sons.

LINK TO PRACTICE

Just-in-Time or Just-in-Case

Companies that have adopted just-in-time systems have generally found that they create shareholder value by reducing their investment in inventory and by eliminating costs associated with non–value-added activities. However, in some cases it makes sense to hold substantial buffer inventory (i.e., inventory that buffers the company from shocks to the smooth flow of inventory).

Here are some examples when holding more buffer inventory is appropriate:

- Expected price increases may make investing in an inventory buildup a good financial move.
- If a company's supplier is in an undeveloped country with poor infrastructure, it makes sense to hold more inventory. Think about what would happen if a bridge collapsed and needed materials could not reach the port on a timely basis.
- If a company's supplier is in an area where weather can disrupt transportation, it also makes sense to hold more inventory. As in the last point, what would happen if a snowstorm shut down highways and disrupted the flow of components needed for production?
- A terrorist attack or pandemic flu outbreak could severely disrupt the supply chain of a company. But should a company hold more inventory in light of these potential catastrophes? Obviously, companies have to weigh the cost of holding more inventory against the low probability but high cost of such disastrous events.

The need for buffer inventory was very apparent after the 2011 earthquake and tsunami in Japan. As a result of the disaster, many factories, ports, and roads were closed, impacting shipments of parts to the U.S. and other countries.

Source: The Associated Press, "Japan Crisis Disrupts Firms' Supply Routes," *The Seattle Times*, (March 17, 2011), A14.

Investing in state-of-the-art equipment also changes the mix of fixed and variable costs. When equipment is substituted for labor, fixed costs generally increase and variable costs decrease.

Total Quality Management

To survive in an increasingly competitive environment, firms realize that they must produce high-quality products. An increasing number of companies have instituted **total quality management (TQM)** programs to ensure that their products are of the highest quality and that production processes are efficient. Currently, there is no generally agreed-on "right" way to institute a TQM program. However, most companies with TQM develop a company philosophy that stresses listening to the needs of customers, making products right the first time, reducing defective products that must be reworked, and encouraging workers to continuously improve their production processes.

Indeed, some TQM programs are referred to as continuous quality improvement programs. At Marlow Industries, a manufacturer of thermoelectric cooling devices, workers sign a Quality Pledge that reads: "I pledge to make a constant, conscious effort to do my job right today, better tomorrow, recognizing that my individual contribution is critical to the success of Marlow Industries."

The results of an effective TQM program can be impressive. In a relatively early effort, Sundstrand Data Control, a manufacturer of electronic instruments in Washington state, found that its TQM program reduced rework on some instrument production lines by 66 percent and scrap costs by 60 percent. The company also

LINK TO PRACTICE

Can There Be Too Much Emphasis on Quality?

YOU GET WHAT YOU MEASURE

In Chapter 1 we identified a key idea in managerial accounting: You get what you measure! Many companies have quality measures, but can there be too much emphasis on quality?

Consider the case of Wallace Company, a Texas-based industrial distributor of pipes, valves, and fittings that launched a "quality at all cost" campaign. Apparently, the campaign was successful, since the company won the prestigious Malcolm Baldrige National Quality Award. However, in the year the company won the award, it had a $691,000 loss on sales of $88 million. While racking up financial losses, the company was processing 100 requests a day for information about its quality programs! John Wallace, CEO, noted: "We spent too much time telling the story [*about quality*] and should have been out drumming up more business."

The point of this example is not to suggest that emphasis on high quality is a bad idea—far from it. For example, General Electric has a quality program aimed at reducing product defects, which is called the Six Sigma Program. This program is cited as a major factor in GE's continuing earnings growth. However, companies must balance the emphasis on quality measures with an emphasis on measures of financial performance, measures of innovation, and measures of customer satisfaction. Otherwise, they may end up producing a high-quality product that customers don't want or for which customers are unwilling to pay a premium price.

Courtesy Baldridgoz National Quality Program/ National Institute of Standards and Technology.

Baldrige Award.

Perhaps not surprisingly, given the financial difficulties of the Wallace Company and others that have won the Baldrige Award, the criteria for winning the award have shifted. There is now less emphasis on quality and more emphasis on financial results. In 1988, when the Baldrige Award was launched, the word *quality* appeared 13 times in the point scoring summary. In 2001, the word *quality* does not appear even once in the scoring summary. And in 2001, 450 out of the 1,000 maximum points for winning the award relate to financial performance!

Source: "Is the Baldrige Award Still About Quality?" Richard Schonberger, qualitydigest.com, www.qualitydigest.com/dec01.html/baldrige.html.

reduced cycle time (the time it takes to produce a product from beginning to end) by 90 percent.[2]

How does TQM affect product costing systems? Strong advocates would argue that without TQM, there is no need for product costing, since companies without TQM will not survive! Undoubtedly there is some truth to this position. In addition, TQM affects product costing by reducing the need to track the cost of scrap and rework related to each job. If TQM is able to reduce these costs to an insignificant level, the benefit of tracking the costs is unlikely to exceed the cost to the accounting system.[3]

Decision Making INSIGHT

When using job cost information to make a decision, care must be taken because some costs going into a job are fixed (e.g., depreciation on equipment that is included in manufacturing overhead) and some costs are variable (e.g., direct material costs). Thus, the *full cost* of a job is not the same as the *incremental* cost of a job.

[2] Steve Wilhelm, "Quality Program Keeps Spreading at Sundstrand, "*Puget Sound Business Journal* 11, No. 52 (May 13, 1991), Sec. 1, p. 17.

[3] Many service firms, such as banks, insurance companies, and hospitals, have adopted the TQM programs initially developed by manufacturers. TQM is especially popular in the healthcare field.

TEST YOUR **KNOWLEDGE**

Which of the following is false?

a. Use of computer-controlled manufacturing systems is likely to increase fixed costs.
b. Companies that utilize JIT are likely to have more raw materials inventory.
c. Companies that utilize JIT are likely to close the difference between actual overhead and overhead applied using a predetermined overhead rate to cost of goods sold.
d. A singular focus on quality could be counterproductive.

Correct answer is b.

SUMMARY OF **LEARNING OBJECTIVES**

LEARNING OBJECTIVE 1 Distinguish between manufacturing and nonmanufacturing costs and between product and period costs.

Manufacturing costs include all the costs associated with the production of goods. They include direct material, direct labor, and manufacturing overhead. Nonmanufacturing costs are all the costs not associated with the production of goods. Selling and general and administrative costs are nonmanufacturing costs. Costs can also be classified as either product costs or period costs. Product costs are identical to manufacturing costs and include direct labor, direct material, and manufacturing overhead. Product costs are considered an asset (inventory) until finished goods are sold. When the goods are sold, the product costs are expensed. Period costs, however, are expensed in the period in which they are incurred. Period costs include both selling and general and administrative costs, which are also referred to as nonmanufacturing costs.

LEARNING OBJECTIVE 2 Discuss the three inventory accounts of a manufacturing firm and describe the flow of product costs in a manufacturing firm's accounts.

The three inventory accounts are Raw Materials Inventory, Work in Process Inventory, and Finished Goods Inventory. Raw Materials Inventory includes the cost of the materials on hand that are used to produce a company's products. Work in Process Inventory is the inventory account for the cost of goods that are only partially completed. Finished Goods Inventory is the account for the cost of all items that are complete and ready to sell.

As they are incurred, product costs are assigned to Work in Process Inventory. When the items in work in process are completed, the cost of the completed items is removed from Work in Process and added to Finished Goods. When the finished goods are sold, the cost of the items sold is removed from Finished Goods and added to Cost of Goods Sold Expense. Thus, product costs become an expense when completed items are sold.

LEARNING OBJECTIVE 3 Discuss the types of product costing systems and explain the relation between the cost of jobs and the Work in Process Inventory, Finished Goods Inventory, and Cost of Goods Sold accounts.

There are two types of product costing systems: job-order systems and process costing systems. Companies using job-order systems generally produce individual products or batches of products that are unique. Companies using process costing systems generally produce large quantities of identical items in a continuous production operation.

Work in Process Inventory includes the cost of all jobs that are currently being worked on; Finished Goods Inventory includes the cost of all jobs that are completed but not yet sold; and Cost of Goods Sold includes the cost of all jobs that are sold during the accounting period.

LEARNING OBJECTIVE 4 Describe how direct material, direct labor, and manufacturing overhead are assigned to jobs.

Job cost sheets track the direct material, direct labor, and manufacturing overhead cost of each job. Direct material cost is traced to jobs by means of material requisition forms. Direct labor is traced to jobs by means of labor time tickets. Manufacturing overhead is applied to jobs using an overhead rate.

LEARNING OBJECTIVE 5 Explain the role of a predetermined overhead rate in applying overhead to jobs and explain how the difference between actual overhead and overhead allocated to jobs using a predetermined rate is treated.

Most companies apply overhead to jobs using a predetermined overhead rate rather than an actual overhead rate. Actual overhead cannot be determined until the end of the accounting period, and companies cannot wait until the end of the period before applying overhead to jobs.

If the amount of overhead applied to inventory does not equal actual overhead, the difference must be apportioned among Work in Process, Finished Goods, and Cost of Goods Sold. This adjusts the accounts to reflect actual overhead costs. If the amount of under- or overapplied overhead is small, the balance can be closed to Cost of Goods Sold.

LEARNING OBJECTIVE 6 Explain how service companies can use job-order costing to calculate the cost of services provided to customers.

Much like manufacturing firms, service companies such as hospitals, law firms, accounting firms, consulting companies, and repair shops use job-order costing. Using job-order costing, they assign wages, various material costs, and overhead to "jobs." Consider a consulting firm that provides services to various clients. A specific engagement (e.g., installation of a computer information system) for a specific client is a "job." Using job-order costing, the salaries of consultants are charged to the job as well as any materials provided to the client. Materials might include training manuals or software. Overhead, such as depreciation of office equipment, utilities, and the salaries of office staff, is assigned to a job using a predetermined overhead rate.

LEARNING OBJECTIVE 7 Discuss modern manufacturing practices and how they affect product costing.

U.S. companies face stiff competition from companies abroad. In response, many have adopted manufacturing systems that minimize inventories of raw materials and work in process. In addition, many companies have become highly automated and have instituted total quality management programs. JIT production systems have reduced inventory levels, automation has increased levels of overhead and fixed costs, and total quality management programs have reduced product defects and waste.

REVIEW PROBLEM 1

Ellie Richard's Commercial Flooring installs stone, tile, and carpet flooring in office buildings, condominiums, and restaurants. The company traces labor and materials to each job, but overhead is assigned based on labor hours. At the start of the year, the company estimated overhead as follows:

Rent	$ 35,000
Depreciation of trucks	25,000
Depreciation of equipment	5,000
Supervisor salaries	150,000
Other overhead	20,000
	$235,000

Total labor hours were estimated to be 11,520.

During the first week in December, the company started and completed a job installing black granite tiles in the remodeled lounge of Joey D's Restaurant. In total, the job took 36 hours. The average wage rate of installers is $35 per hour. Materials for the job including tiles and grouting cost $7,500.

REQUIRED

a. What is the cost of the job?

b. Assuming that the company charges $80 per installer hour plus the cost of materials, with a markup of 30 percent, what was the profit on the job?

ANSWER

a. The overhead rate is $20.40 per labor hour ($235,000 ÷ 11,520 labor hours). Thus, the cost of the job is:

Labor	
36 hours × $35 per hour	$1,260.00
Materials	7,500.00
Overhead	
$20.40 × 36 hours	734.40
Total	$9,494.40

b. Charges are $12,630. Thus, the profit on the job is $3,136.60.

Labor $80 × 36 hours	$ 2,880.00
Materials $7,500 × 1.3	9,750.00
Total charges	12,630.00
Less cost of job	(9,494.40)
Profit	$ 3,135.60

REVIEW PROBLEM 2

Herbert Plumbing Products produces a variety of valves, connectors, and fixtures used in commercial and residential plumbing applications. The company has a just-in-time inventory and production system, and it has relatively small amounts of material, work in process, and finished goods inventory.

At the end of October, the company had $20,000 of raw material inventory. In addition, jobs 281 and 282 were in process and job 279 was complete and awaiting shipment. The job cost sheets for these jobs were as follows:

End of October

	Direct Material	Direct Labor	Overhead	Total	Job Status
Job 279	$50,000	$15,000	$30,000	$ 95,000	Finished but not shipped
Job 281	20,000	5,000	10,000	35,000	In process
Job 282	60,000	20,000	40,000	120,000	In process

During November, the company began work on Jobs 283, 284, and 285. The status of the jobs at the end of November is as follows:

End of November

	Direct Material	Direct Labor	Overhead	Total	Job Status
Job 279	$50,000	$15,000	$30,000	$ 95,000	Shipped
Job 281	25,000	8,000	16,000	49,000	Shipped
Job 282	62,000	21,000	42,000	125,000	Shipped
Job 283	30,000	20,000	40,000	90,000	Shipped
Job 284	80,000	30,000	60,000	170,000	Shipped
Job 285	15,000	10,000	20,000	45,000	In process

Also during November, Herbert Plumbing Products purchased $120,000 of materials and incurred $130,000 of actual overhead costs. The company charges over- or underapplied overhead to Cost of Goods Sold.

REQUIRED

Assume that all material used in November is direct.

a. What is the balance in Raw Materials Inventory at the end of November?

b. What is the balance in Work in Process Inventory at the end of November?

c. What is the balance in Finished Goods Inventory at the end of November?

d. What is the cost of goods manufactured for the month of November?

e. What is the cost of goods sold for the month of November?

ANSWER

a. The beginning balance in raw materials inventory is $20,000.

Purchases are $120,000.

Inventory used in November:

Job 281	$ 5,000
Job 282	2,000
Job 283	30,000
Job 284	80,000
Job 285	15,000
Total	$132,000

Beginning balance + Purchases – Amount used = Ending balance

$20,000 + $120,000 – $132,000 = **$8,000**

b. The ending balance in Work in Process Inventory is the cost of jobs in process at the end of November. This is the cost of job 285, which is **$45,000.**

c. The ending balance in Finished Goods Inventory is the cost of jobs that are completed but not shipped. Since all completed jobs have been shipped, the balance is zero.

d. The beginning balance in Work in Process Inventory is:

Job 281	$ 35,000
Job 282	120,000
Total	**$155,000**

Additional costs added during November are:

Material cost		$ 132,000 per part **a**
Direct labor cost		
Job 281	$ 3,000	
Job 282	1,000	
Job 283	20,000	
Job 284	30,000	
Job 285	10,000	64,000
Overhead		
Job 281	6,000	
Job 282	2,000	
Job 283	40,000	
Job 284	60,000	
Job 285	20,000	$ 128,000
	Total	**$324,000**

The ending balance in Work is Process Inventory is **$45,000** per part **b.**

Beginning balance in WIP Inventory + Current manufacturing costs – Ending balance in WIP Inventory = Cost of goods manufactured

$155,000 + $324,000 – $45,000 = **$434,000**

e. Beginning balance in Finished Goods Inventory is the cost of job 279, which is $95,000. Cost of Goods Manufactured is $434,000, per part **d.**

Ending balance in Finished Goods Inventory is zero, per part **c.**

Beginning balance in Finished Goods Inventory + Cost of goods manufactured – Ending balance in Finished Goods Inventory = Cost of goods sold

$95,000 + $434,000 – 0 = **$529,000**

Alternatively, we could simply add up the cost of jobs shipped this period:

Job 279	$ 95,000
Job 281	49,000
Job 282	125,000
Job 283	90,000
Job 284	170,000
Total	**$529,000**

Note, however, that actual overhead is $130,000, while overhead applied to production at the standard rate of $2 per dollar of direct labor is $128,000 per part d. Thus, cost of goods sold must be increased by $2,000.

Cost of goods sold = $529,000 + $2,000 = **$531,000**

KEY TERMS

Activity-based costing (ABC) (57)
Allocation base (52)
Computer-controlled manufacturing systems (64)
Cost driver (57)
Cost of goods available for sale (45)
Cost of goods manufactured (43)
Cost pools (57)
Direct labor cost (39)
Direct material cost (38)
Finished Goods Inventory (43)
Full cost (41)
General and Administrative Costs (39)
Indirect labor costs (39)
Indirect materials (39)
Job (46)
Job cost sheet (48)
Job-order costing system (46)
Just-in-time (JIT) (63)
Manufacturing costs (38)
Manufacturing overhead (39)
Material requisition form (49)
Nonmanufacturing costs (39)
Overapplied overhead (59)
Overhead allocation (56)
Overhead allocation rate (52)
Overhead applied (52)
Period costs (40)
Predetermined overhead rates (58)
Process costing system (46)
Product costing system (36)
Product costs (40)
Raw Materials Inventory (42)
Selling costs (39)
Time tickets (50)
Total quality management (TQM) (65)
Underapplied overhead (59)
Work in Process Inventory (42)

SELF-ASSESSMENT (Answers Below)

1. Which of the following is a period cost?
a. Raw materials costs.
b. Manufacturing plant maintenance.
c. Wages for production-line workers.
d. Salary for the vice president of finance.

2. Full costing includes which of the following in determining product cost?
a. Only variable costs of production.
b. Only fixed costs of production.
c. Administrative overhead.
d. All fixed and variable costs of production.

3. Cost of Goods Sold is $200,000, the beginning balance in Finished Goods Inventory is $50,000, the ending balance in Finished Goods Inventory is $100,000, and the ending balance in Work in Process Inventory is $10,000. What is Cost of Goods Manufactured?
a. $100,000
b. $250,000
c. $50,000
d. None of these answer choices is correct.

4. The beginning balance in Finished Goods Inventory is $50,000, the ending balance in Finished Goods Inventory is $100,000, and Cost of Goods Manufactured is $200,000. What is Cost of Goods Sold?
a. $100,000
b. $250,000
c. $150,000
d. None of the above.

5. Which entity would most likely use a job-order costing system?
a. Textile manufacturer.
b. Concrete block producer.
c. Petroleum refiner.
d. Antique automobile restorer.

6. The predetermined overhead rate is determined as:
a. Estimated overhead costs divided by estimated allocation base.
b. Actual overhead costs divided by estimated allocation base.
c. Estimated overhead costs divided by actual allocation base.
d. Actual overhead costs divided by actual allocation base.

7. Overhead is overapplied if:
   a. The actual overhead rate is greater than the budgeted overhead rate.
   b. The Manufacturing Overhead account has a credit balance at the end of the period.
   c. The actual overhead rate is greater than the rate used in prior periods.
   d. The overhead rate is material.
8. Compared to traditional methods of allocating overhead, activity-based costing (ABC) uses:
   a. More allocation bases.
   b. Only allocation bases related to direct labor.
   c. Machine hours as an allocation base.
   d. None of these answer choices is correct.
9. Service companies:
   a. Do not use job-order costing.
   b. Often use job-order costing.
   c. Do not cost their services.
   d. Produce durable products.
10. All of the following are true about just-in-time (JIT) production **except**:
    a. JIT seeks to minimize inventories of raw materials and work in process.
    b. JIT is often referred to as "fat" production.
    c. JIT companies concentrate on improving quality.
    d. JIT companies need dependable suppliers.

ANSWERS TO SELF-ASSESSMENT

1. d **2.** d **3.** b **4.** c **5.** d **6.** a
7. b **8.** a **9.** b **10.** b

QUESTIONS

1. What is the difference between manufacturing and nonmanufacturing costs?
2. What is the difference between product and period costs?
3. Identify the two most common types of product costing systems and discuss the manufacturing environments associated with each system.
4. What is a job cost sheet? What information does it contain?
5. Why do companies apply overhead to jobs using a predetermined (budgeted) overhead rate instead of applying actual overhead to jobs?
6. Discuss an important characteristic of a good overhead allocation base.
7. Some modern, capital-intensive production facilities have significantly reduced the proportion of direct labor cost to total production cost. Discuss the effect this might have on the selection of an allocation base for the application of overhead.
8. When might it be necessary to assign over- or underapplied overhead to Finished Goods, Work in Process, and Cost of Goods Sold?
9. Would an unexpected increase in sales and production result in underapplied or overapplied overhead? Explain.
10. As companies move to computer-controlled manufacturing systems, what happens to the mix of product costs (direct material, direct labor, and manufacturing overhead)?

EXERCISES

GROUP WORK

EXERCISE 2-1. You Get What You Measure! [LO 4] Consider three very similar companies. Company A allocates manufacturing overhead to jobs using labor hours as the allocation base; Company B allocates manufacturing overhead to jobs using machine hours as the allocation base; and Company C allocates manufacturing overhead to jobs using material cost as the allocation base.

REQUIRED

Explain why, in spite of the fact that the companies are very similar, supervisors at Company A are very focused on controlling labor, whereas supervisors at Company B are very focused on controlling machine run time, and supervisors at Company C are very focused on controlling material costs. Use the concept of "You get what you measure!" in your answer.

WRITING **EXERCISE 2-2. Just-in-Time Manufacturing and Assigning Over- or Underapplied Overhead [LO 5, 7]** At Star Plastics, the balance in manufacturing overhead (which represents over- or underapplied overhead) is always closed to Cost of Goods Sold. This is done even when the balance is relatively large. Suzette Barger, the controller, explains that this makes sense because Star uses a just-in-time (JIT) manufacturing system and jobs are shipped to customers within hours of being completed.

REQUIRED

Write a paragraph elaborating on the justification provided by Suzette Barger. Why is there no need to apportion the balance in manufacturing overhead among Work in Process, Finished Goods, and Cost of Goods Sold?

EXERCISE 2-3. Applying Overhead to Jobs [LO 4, 5] At Precision Custom Molds, manufacturing overhead was estimated to be $20,000,000 at the start of the year and direct labor hours were estimated to be 200,000. Overhead is applied to jobs using a predetermined overhead rate with direct labor hours as the allocation base. During the current year, Job 525 was assigned 25 labor hours. How much overhead was applied to this job?

EXERCISE 2-4. Product Costing Systems [LO 3] For the list of product manufacturers below, indicate whether a job-cost system (J) or a process-cost system (P) would be most appropriate.

_____ **a.** Chemicals processor

_____ **b.** Paint manufacturer

_____ **c.** Law firm

_____ **d.** Producer of molds used by other manufacturing firms to shape their products

_____ **e.** Dog food producer

_____ **f.** Custom home builder

EXERCISE 2-5. Inventory-Related Accounts [LO 1, 2] Place Y (yes) beside the general ledger accounts related to inventory in a job-order cost system and N (no) by those that are not.

_____ **a.** Raw Materials Inventory

_____ **b.** Administrative Expense

_____ **c.** Work in Process Inventory

_____ **d.** Finished Goods Inventory

_____ **e.** President's salary

_____ **f.** Cost of Goods Sold

_____ **g.** Manufacturing overhead

_____ **h.** Advertising expense

EXERCISE 2-6. Recording Material Cost in Job-Order Costing [LO 2, 4] During the month of August, Star Plastics had material requisitions for $200,000 of materials related to specific jobs and $10,000 of miscellaneous materials classified as overhead.

REQUIRED

Prepare journal entries to record the issuance of materials during August.

EXCEL **EXERCISE 2-7. Recording Material Cost in Job-Order Costing [LO 2, 4]** Five material requisitions (MR) forms were received by the materials storeroom of the Saint Louis Foundry during the first week of 2014. MR101 was for $250 of direct materials for job number 1501. MR102 was for $350 of direct materials for job number 1502. MR103 was for $100 of indirect materials issued to the factory floor. MR 104 was for $400 of direct materials issued to job number 1501. MR105 was for $500 of direct materials issued to job number 1503.

REQUIRED

Prepare summary journal entries to record the issuance of these materials. (*Hint*: There should be a separate journal entry for direct and indirect materials.)

EXERCISE 2-8. Recording Labor Cost in Job-Order Costing [LO 2, 4] During the month of August, Star Plastics had $70,000 of labor costs that were traced to specific jobs. The company also had $50,000 of indirect labor related to supervisory pay.

REQUIRED

Prepare journal entries to record labor cost during August. (*Hint*: There should be separate journal entries for direct and indirect labor.)

EXCEL **EXERCISE 2-9. Recording Labor Cost in Job-Order Costing [LO 2, 4]** Johnson Products had the following labor time tickets for the month of February:

Ticket #	Employee #	Pay Rate	Hours Worked	Job #
2101	011	$10.00	110	201
2102	008	21.00	90	201
2103	011	12.00	40	201
2104	008	20.00	50	202
2105	008	18.00	70	203

REQUIRED

a. Calculate the amount of direct labor cost assigned to each job.

b. Summarize the labor time tickets and prepare a journal entry to record direct labor for the month.

EXERCISE 2-10. Overhead Allocation Bases [LO 5] Lawler Manufacturing Company expects annual manufacturing overhead to be $900,000. The company also expects 60,000 direct labor hours costing $1,800,000 and machine run time of 30,000 hours.

REQUIRED

Calculate predetermined overhead allocation rates based on direct labor hours, direct labor cost, and machine time.

EXERCISE 2-11. Service Company Allocation of Overhead [LO 4, 5, 6] Franklin Computer Repair treats each repair order as a job. Overhead is allocated based on the cost of technician time. At the start of the year, annual technician wages were estimated to be $800,000, and company overhead was estimated to be $500,000.

REQUIRED

a. Discuss why use of a predetermined overhead rate would be preferred to assigning actual overhead to repair jobs.

b. Suppose a job required parts costing $200 and technician time costing $100. What would be the total cost of the job?

EXCEL **EXERCISE 2-12. Allocating Manufacturing Overhead to Jobs [LO 4, 5]** Webber Fabricating estimated the following annual hours and costs:

Expected annual direct labor hours	40,000
Expected annual direct labor cost	$ 625,000
Expected machine hours	20,000
Expected material cost for the year	$ 800,000
Expected manufacturing overhead	$1,000,000

REQUIRED

a. Calculate predetermined overhead allocation rates using each of the four possible allocation bases provided.

b. Determine the cost of the following job (number 253) using each of the four overhead allocation rates:

Job 253	
Direct materials	$3,000
Direct labor (150 hrs @ $12/hr)	$1,800
Machine hours used	150

EXERCISE 2-13. Recording Actual Overhead and Overhead Applied to Jobs [LO 2, 4, 5] During the month of August, Star Plastics applied overhead to jobs using an overhead rate of $3 per dollar of direct labor. Direct labor in August was $100,000. Actual overhead in August was $260,000. Assume that actual overhead was composed of the following items.

Indirect materials	$ 40,000
Indirect labor	80,000
Utilities	25,000
Depreciation	60,000
Repair expense	55,000
Total	$260,000

REQUIRED

a. Prepare a journal entry to record overhead applied to jobs.

b. Prepare a journal entry to record actual overhead.

EXERCISE 2-14. Closing the Manufacturing Overhead Account [LO 5] Refer to the information in Exercise 2-13.

REQUIRED

a. Determine the balance in manufacturing overhead, and prepare a journal entry to close the balance to cost of goods sold.

b. Why is it important to close the balance in manufacturing overhead?

c. Assume that Star Plastics uses a JIT inventory system. What is the justification for assigning the balance in manufacturing overhead to Cost of Goods Sold rather than apportioning it to Work in Process, Finished Goods, and Cost of Goods Sold?

EXERCISE 2-15. Cost of Jobs [LO 4, 5] Milton Company is a steel fabricator, and job 325 consists of producing 500 steel supports for Wendell Construction Company. Overhead is applied on the basis of direct labor hours, using a predetermined overhead rate of $25 per hour. Direct costs associated with Job 325 are: direct materials, $10,000; direct labor, 250 hours at $16 per hour.

REQUIRED

Calculate the cost of Job 325.

EXERCISE 2-16. Service Company Use of Predetermined Overhead Rate [LO 4, 5, 6] Smith and Baker Legal Services employs five full-time attorneys and nine paraprofessionals. Budgeted salaries are $100,000 for each attorney and $50,000 for each paraprofessional. Budgeted indirect costs (e.g., rent, secretarial support, copying, etc.) are $210,000. The company traces the cost of attorney and paraprofessional time to each client and uses the total to assign indirect costs.

REQUIRED

What amount of indirect cost would be assigned if services to a client required $25,000 of attorney cost and $20,000 of paraprofessional cost? (Round overhead rate to 2 decimal places.)

EXERCISE 2-17. Underapplied and Overapplied Manufacturing Overhead [LO 8] Injection Molding Services uses a job-order costing system. The account balances at the end of the period for the product cost-related accounts are as follows:

Raw Materials Inventory	$300,000
Work in Process Inventory	500,000
Finished Goods Inventory	600,000
Cost of Goods Sold	900,000
Manufacturing Overhead (credit)	90,000

REQUIRED

Prepare a journal entry to close the manufacturing overhead account assuming that the amount ($90,000) is material.

EXERCISE 2-18. Modern Manufacturing Practices [LO 7] Just-in-time production systems seek to reduce the amount of material, work in process, and finished goods inventory. However, companies must hold some amount of inventory to buffer themselves from various negative events. List three such events and briefly indicate why they require holding a buffer inventory.

EXERCISE 2-19. Incremental Analysis and Overhead Allocation [LO 4] At the start of the year, Vencor Company estimated manufacturing overhead to be $2,000,000. Eighty percent of the overhead is fixed and relates to depreciation of equipment. The remaining 20 percent is variable. The company estimated machine hours to be 100,000 and thus used a predetermined overhead rate of $20 per machine hour.

During the year, the company devised a new way to sequence movements of material among the machines, which resulted in a savings of 30,000 machine hours.

REQUIRED

Estimate the amount of manufacturing overhead that the company would save related to the reduction in machine hours. Why is the savings less than $20 per machine hour?

EXERCISE 2-20. Career Connection Select one or two concepts from this chapter and describe how you might use those concepts in your future career. Briefly describe the career or job you will be performing. Then specifically describe the type of situation for which the concept could be applied. Also include a discussion of how use of the concept would allow you to make informed decisions or improve your job performance.

PROBLEMS

EXCEL

PROBLEM 2-1. Cost of Goods Manufactured, Cost of Goods Sold, and Income [LO 2] The following information is available for Satterfield's Custom Glass for the fiscal year ending December 31, 2017:

Beginning balance in Work in Process Inventory	$ 210,000
Ending balance in Work in Process Inventory	300,000
Beginning balance in Finished Goods Inventory	500,000
Ending balance in Finished Goods Inventory	400,000
Direct material cost	2,500,000
Direct labor cost	3,000,000
Manufacturing overhead	1,700,000
Selling and administrative expenses	1,350,000
Sales	8,500,000

REQUIRED

a. Prepare a schedule of cost of goods manufactured.

b. Prepare an income statement for fiscal 2017. Ignore income taxes.

PROBLEM 2-2. Cost of Goods Manufactured and Cost of Goods Sold [LO 2] Terra Cotta Designs manufactures custom tiles. The following information relates to the fiscal year ending December 31, 2017:

Beginning balance in Raw Material Inventory	$ 450,000
Purchases of raw material	1,500,000
Ending balance in Raw Material Inventory	200,000
Beginning balance in Work in Process Inventory	650,000
Ending balance in Work in Process Inventory	350,000
Direct labor cost	2,500,000
Manufacturing overhead applied	650,000
Beginning balance in Finished Goods Inventory	750,000
Ending balance in Finished Goods Inventory	350,000
Sales	7,000,000
Selling expenses	500,000
General and administrative expenses	850,000

REQUIRED

a. Prepare a schedule of cost of goods manufactured. Assume that there are no indirect material costs.

b. Prepare an income statement for fiscal 2017. Ignore income taxes.

EXCEL **PROBLEM 2-3. Job-Order Costing: Inventory Accounts and Cost of Goods Sold [LO 4]** Smith Die Company manufactures cutting dies for the shoe industry. Each set of dies is custom designed to a customer's templates. During the first week of May, six orders were received from customers. They were assigned job numbers 1005 to 1010. The following transactions occurred during the first week of May:

Smith Die purchased steel on account from Eastern City Steel costing $5,500. The company received and paid for supplies (indirect materials) from Mallard Supply costing $2,400.

Material requisitions indicated that materials were issued to the factory floor as follows:

Job No.	Direct Materials	Indirect Materials
1005	$ 650	
1006	850	
1007	1,550	
1008	650	
1009	450	
1010	350	
Totals	$4,500	$1,000

The labor time ticket summary reflected the following costs for the week:

Job No.	Direct Labor	Indirect Labor
1005	$1,600	
1006	2,000	
1007	3,300	
1008	1,400	
1009	900	
1010	700	
Totals	$9,900	$6,500

Overhead was applied to all jobs in process at 180 percent of direct labor cost. Jobs 1005, 1006, 1007, and 1008 were completed and transferred to finished goods. Jobs 1009 and 1010 were still in process at the end of the week. Jobs 1005, 1006, 1007, and 1008 were shipped to customers and billed at 150 percent of total job cost.

REQUIRED

a. Calculate the total cost of each job.

b. Prepare journal entries to record the above information.

PROBLEM 2-4. Job Cost Sheets and Inventory Accounts [LO 2, 4] Renton Custom Windows produces custom windows for business and residential customers who supply Renton with architectural specifications.

At the start of 2017, three jobs were in process:

Cost incurred as of 1/1/2017	
Job 258	$5,000
Job 259	6,000
Job 260	3,500

Also at the start of 2017, one job was completed and awaiting shipment:

Cost incurred as of 1/1/2017	
Job 257	$9,000

During 2017, the company incurred the following costs:

Direct material	$ 750,000
Direct labor	1,650,000
Manufacturing overhead	2,150,000

At the end of 2017, two jobs were in process:

Cost incurred as of 12/31/2017	
Job 345	$2,500
Job 346	5,900

In addition, four jobs were completed and awaiting shipment:

Cost incurred as of 12/31/2017	
Job 341	$1,500
Job 342	3,300
Job 343	2,400
Job 344	4,500

REQUIRED

a. What are the beginning and ending balances in Work in Process Intenvory?

b. What are the beginning and ending balances in Finished Goods Intenvory?

c. What is Cost of Goods Sold? What job numbers likely relate to the balance in Cost of Goods Sold?

PROBLEM 2-5. Various Predetermined Overhead Rates for Job-Order Costing [LO 4, 5] Retter Shoe Company has expected overhead costs of $12,000,000. The majority of the overhead costs are incurred providing production support to the direct labor force. Direct labor rates vary from $10 to $20 per hour, and more complex tasks are assigned to more skilled workers who have higher pay rates. Retter projects direct labor costs of $4,800,000 and 300,000 direct labor hours. More complex tasks require proportionally more support than do the less complex tasks.

Each model/size of shoe is produced in a single production run and constitutes a job. During the year, the company produced 9,000 pairs of the model K25, size 8 dress shoe. A total of 11,000 direct labor hours, costing $165,000, were assigned to the job.

REQUIRED

a. Determine the amount of overhead assigned to the model K25, size 8 dress shoe, using both direct labor hours and direct labor cost as the allocation base.

b. Justify selection of either direct labor hours or direct labor cost as the allocation base.

PROBLEM 2-6. Job Costs Using Different Overhead Rates [LO 4, 5] Custom Auto Parts manufactures parts to order for antique cars. Custom Auto Parts makes everything from fenders to engine blocks. Each customer order is treated as a job. The company currently has two jobs, Job 9823 and Job 9824, that are complete, although overhead has not yet been applied. The company wants to know what each job's cost would be under alternative overhead allocation rates based on: (1) direct labor cost, (2) direct labor hours, and (3) machine hours. Estimates for this year are as follows:

Direct labor cost	$300,000
Direct labor hours	25,000
Machine hours	8,000
Overhead costs	$200,000

Depreciation on machinery accounts for 75 percent of the overhead costs. The job-cost sheets show:

	Job 9823	Job 9824
Direct material	$1,000	$2,000
Direct labor cost	$1,400	$1,400
Direct labor hours	150	130
Machine hours	130	270

REQUIRED

a. Determine the overhead allocation rate under the three suggested allocation bases. Round to two decimal places.

b. Calculate the cost of Job 9823 and Job 9824 using each of the three bases. Round to nearest dollar.

c. Discuss which allocation base appears preferable.

PROBLEM 2-7. Underapplied or Overapplied Overhead [LO 5] In the past year, Oak Crafters Cabinets had total revenue of $2,500,000, cost of goods sold of $1,000,000 (before adjustment for over- or underapplied overhead), administrative expenses of $600,000, and selling expenses of $400,000. During the year, overhead was applied using a predetermined rate of 75 percent of direct labor cost. Actual direct labor was $700,000. Actual overhead was $450,000. The ending balances in the inventory accounts (prior to adjustment for overapplied overhead) are:

Raw Materials Inventory	$32,000
Work in Process Inventory	80,000
Finished Goods Inventory	48,000

REQUIRED

a. Calculate net income treating the amount of overrapplied overhead as immaterial and assigning it to Cost of Goods Sold.

b. Calculate net income treating the amount of overapplied overhead as material and apportioning it to the appropriate inventory accounts and Cost of Goods Sold. Round proportions to 3 decimal places. Round adjustments to the nearest whole dollar.

c. Discuss the impact of the alternative treatments.

PROBLEM 2-8. Underapplied or Overapplied Overhead [LO 5] World Window Company produces custom windows to specifications provided by architects. At the end of its accounting period, its account balances indicated the following:

Raw Materials Inventory	$ 80,000
Work in Process Inventory	66,000
Finished Goods Inventory	44,000
Cost of Goods Sold	440,000
Manufacturing Overhead (credit balance)	50,000

REQUIRED

a. Determine the adjusted balances of the accounts if the balance in Manufacturing Overhead is considered immaterial in amount and assigned to Cost of Goods Sold.

b. Determine the adjusted balances of the accounts if the balance in Manufacturing Overhead is considered material in amount. Round to the nearest whole dollar.

PROBLEM 2-9. Job Costing (Service Example) [LO 4, 5, 6] LaPlatt & Associates is an accounting firm that provides audit, tax, and accounting services to medium-size retail companies. It employs 50 professionals (10 partners and 40 associates) who work directly with clients. The average expected total compensation per professional for the year is $120,000. The services of LaPlatt are in high demand, and each professional works for clients to their maximum of 1,600 billable hours. All professional salaries are traced to individual client service summaries. All costs other than professional salaries are included in a single indirect cost pool (professional support). The indirect costs are assigned to service summaries using professional hours as the allocation base. The expected amount of indirect costs for the year is $5,200,000.

REQUIRED

a. Compute the budgeted indirect cost rate per hour of professional service.

b. LaPlatt & Associates is bidding on tax and audit services for a potential client that are expected to require 100 hours of professional service time. Calculate the estimated cost of the work using average professional wage rates and basing indirect costs on estimated service time.

PROBLEM 2-10. Recording Inventory-Related Costs [LO 2, 4] Fill in the missing information:

Raw Materials Inventory

Beginning Balance	30,000	
Purchases	40,000	(a)
Ending Balance	15,000	

Work in Process Inventory

Beginning Balance	80,000	
DM	(a)	(b)
DL	45,000	
OH	63,000	
Ending Balance	82,000	

Manufacturing Overhead

70,000	60,000
	(d)

Finished Goods Inventory

Beginning Balance	95,000	
	(b)	(c)
Ending Balance	110,000	

Cost of Goods Sold

(c)	
(d)	

PROBLEM 2-11. Recording Inventory Costs [LO 4, 5] Vulcan Molding produces molded rubber components. At the start of the year, the company estimated that it would incur $3,500,000 of direct labor cost and $9,000,000 of manufacturing overhead. Overhead is allocated to production on the basis of direct labor cost. Actual materials used during the year were $5,750,000, actual direct labor cost was $4,000,000, and actual overhead was $11,000,000.

REQUIRED

a. Calculate the overhead rate for the current year. Round to 2 decimal places.

b. Prepare the journal entry to record use of direct material.

c. Prepare the journal entry to record direct labor.

d. Prepare the journal entry to record manufacturing overhead applied to production.

e. Prepare the journal entry to close the balance in manufacturing overhead to cost of goods sold.

PROBLEM 2-12. Multiple Overhead Rates [LO 4, 5] Vulcan Molding has three production departments: A, B, and C. At the start of the year, the company estimated that it would incur $3,080,000 of direct labor cost and $10,000,000 of manufacturing overhead as follows:

	Dept. A	Dept. B	Dept. C	Total
Estimated Overhead	$4,000,000	$3,000,000	$3,000,000	$10,000,000
Estimated Direct Labor	$1,200,000	$ 630,000	$1,250,000	$3,080,000
Overhead Rate	$3.33	$4.76	$2.40	$3.25

Along with many others, Vulcan Molding worked on the following three jobs during the year:

Direct Labor Cost

	Dept. A	Dept. B	Dept. C	Total
Job 201	$9,500	$3,000	$4,500	$17,000
Job 202	$5,000	$6,500	$9,000	$20,500
Job 203	$2,000	$5,000	$2,000	$ 9,000

REQUIRED

a. Calculate the overhead that would be assigned to each job assuming the company uses one plant-wide overhead allocation rate based on expected labor cost.

b. Calculate the overhead that would be assigned to each job assuming the company uses a separate overhead allocation rate for each production department based on direct labor cost.

c. Which is preferable: a single overhead rate or separate rates by production department? Explain.

PROBLEM 2-13. Comprehensive Job-Order Costing Problem [LO 2, 4, 5] Lane Confectioners produces special orders of sugar candies and chocolates for airlines and hotels. During March, Lane purchased, on credit, 2,100 pounds of confectioner's sugar at $.80 per pound, 2,300 pounds of granulated sugar at $.90 per pound, 900 pounds of chocolate at $4.00 per pound, and 300 pounds of caramel at $1.50 per pound from Seattle Confectionery Supply. In addition, it purchased for cash 60 dozen eggs at $.85 per dozen and 90 pounds of paraffin at $.50 per pound from PMG Foods.

The beginning balances in the inventory accounts were:

Raw Materials Inventory	$2,500
Work in Process Inventory	6,500
Finished Goods Inventory	9,000

The ending balances in the inventory accounts were:

Raw Materials Inventory	$3,500
Work in Process Inventory	5,000
Finished Goods Inventory	6,000

Direct labor costs were $5,400 for 450 hours, indirect labor costs were $2,500, utilities were $400, rent was $750, and other overhead costs totaled $5,000. Manufacturing overhead is applied at $17 per direct labor hour. Sales during the month were $35,000, and selling and administration expenses were $9,000. (Assume that all of the above were noncash transactions.)

REQUIRED

a. Prepare journal entries to record the transactions for the month of March. Assume that over- or underapplied overhead is closed to Cost of Goods Sold.

b. Prepare an income statement for the month of March.

PROBLEM 2-14. Selection of an Overhead Allocation Base [LO 4, 5] Wolf Manufacturing expects the following overhead costs in the current year:

Indirect material	$ 45,000
Indirect labor	55,000
Depreciation of machinery	160,000
Repair and maintenance on machinery	135,000
Utilities and taxes	55,000
Total	$450,000

It expects to use 25,000 direct labor hours at a cost of $525,000 and 15,000 machine hours during the year.

REQUIRED

Justify the selection of an appropriate allocation base and calculate the predetermined overhead allocation rate.

PROBLEM 2-15. Applying Overhead in a Service Company [LO 5, 6] The following cost data relate to the office overhead costs of the Charles Wright Tax Preparation Company during the just-completed year:

Overhead costs incurred:	
Office rent	$ 25,000
Office supplies	6,000
Utilities, office	15,000
Salary, office manager	55,000
Salary, receptionist	35,000
Depreciation—office equipment	10,000
Software licensing fees	24,000
Other miscellaneous expenses	30,000
Total overhead costs	$200,000

The company uses a predetermined overhead rate to apply overhead cost to each tax job. The rate for the year was $6 per tax-preparer hour. A total of 35,000 tax preparer hours was recorded for the year.

REQUIRED

Compute the amount of under- or overapplied overhead cost for the year.

PROBLEM 2-16. Predetermined Overhead Rates in a Service Company; Over- or Underapplied Overhead [LO 5, 6] Rosemont Music is a musical instrument repair facility located in Akron, Ohio. The repair shop uses a job-order costing system and applies overhead costs to repair jobs on the basis of repair technician hours. The following estimates were used in preparing the predetermined overhead rate at the beginning of the year:

Repair technician hours	10,000
Estimated overhead costs	$170,000

During the year, the opening of another musical instrument repair shop in the same area resulted in fewer repair jobs being worked at Rosemont Music. The company's cost records revealed the following actual cost and operating data for the year:

Technician hours	7,000
Overhead costs	$140,000

REQUIRED

a. Compute the company's predetermined overhead rate.

b. Compute the under- or overapplied overhead.

c. Assume that the company closes any under- or overapplied overhead directly to Cost of Goods Sold. Prepare the appropriate journal entry.

PROBLEM 2-17. Service Company Use of Predetermined Overhead Rate [LO 4, 5, 6] Southwest Community Hospital uses a job-order costing system to track charges for each patient. The following charges relate to Candice O'Dea, who had laparoscopic knee surgery:

Pharmacy	$ 450
Sterile supply	1,500
Supplies, other	4,500
Operating room service (nursing staff)	4,500
Anesthesia	1,500
Anesthesiologist	3,500

Southwest charges patients for the use of the operating room based on a predetermined overhead rate. The estimated overhead costs of the operating room are $5,500,000, and the activity base is available hours of 2,000. Note that the hospital does not charge for the services of the surgeon. These charges are billed directly by the surgeon.

REQUIRED

a. Calculate the predetermined overhead rate for the operating room, and determine the charge to Candice. Assume that her surgery took 3 hours in the operating room.

b. Calculate the total cost for the knee surgery.

CASE

2-1 ETHICS CASE: BRIXTON SURGICAL DEVICES [LO 4, 5]

Brixton Surgical Devices, a public company with sales of over $900,000,000, is one of the world's largest producers of surgical clamps, saws, screws, and stents. Its business involves production of both stock items and custom pieces for doctors at research hospitals.

At the end of the third quarter of 2017, it became clear to Ed Walters, chief operating officer, and Robin Smith, chief financial officer, that the company would not make the aggressive annual earnings target specified by the board of directors. In consequence, Ed and Robin would not receive bonuses, which historically had averaged about 35 percent of their base compensation. The two devised the following strategy.

"Here's what we'll do," suggested Ed. "We've never offered our customers a discount. Let's change that right now. We'll offer a 25 percent discount on all orders placed in October and November for delivery in December of 2017."

"That will certainly boost fourth-quarter sales," said Robin. "But you know, it won't really increase total sales. It'll just transfer some sales from the first quarter of 2018 to the fourth quarter of 2017. Of course, 2017 is where we need earnings to hit our bonus target. Hey, I've got another idea. We can also jack up production of our stock items in the fourth quarter. With our high-priced production equipment, we've got a ton of overhead. But the more we produce, the more overhead we can bury in inventory. With lower unit costs and higher sales, profit will go way up. Let's get going on execution. I've got to get the marketing people working on the promotion, and you've got to update the production schedule. This could end up being our best year ever in terms of bonuses!"

REQUIRED

Are the proposed actions of Ed and Robin ethical? What is the likely effect of their actions on shareholder value?

CASE

2-2 YSL MARKETING RESEARCH [LO 6]

YSL Marketing Research is a small firm located in Seattle, Washington. On behalf of its clients, the firm conducts focus group meetings, telephone and mail opinion surveys, and evaluations of marketing strategies. The firm has three partners and six nonpartner professionals. At the start of the year, the company estimated total professional compensation (for the three partners and six nonpartner professionals) to be $1,600,000.

To evaluate the profitability of its engagements, the firm traces actual professional compensation to each engagement along with so-called direct charges. Direct charges consist of travel costs and costs of conducting surveys (e.g., paper and postage). In addition, each engagement receives an allocation of overhead based on professional compensation charges. Overhead consists of all support costs including rent, utilities, and depreciation of office equipment. At the start of the year, these costs were estimated to be $496,000.

Recently, Connie Bachmann, a YSL partner, was asked to conduct a survey for Surenex, a new high-tech company. Connie is excited about this opportunity since she expects that this hot small company will, in 3 to 5 years, become a hot big company with premium billing opportunities. At this point, however, Connie wants to quote a low fee since Surenex has cash-flow problems and is clearly unwilling to pay YSL's normal rates. On most jobs, YSL's fee is 1.5 times professional compensation. In addition, the company is reimbursed for all out-of-pocket costs related to travel and paper and postage costs for surveys. YSL is in high demand, and if it undertakes the Surenex job, it will have to turn down another potential client.

Connie estimates that the Surenex engagement will require the following costs in addition to overhead support costs:

Connie Bachmann (partner), 40 hours at a salary averaging $120 per hour = $4,800.

Ambrose Bundy (professional staff), 100 hours at a salary of $40 per hour = $4,000.

Direct charges for actual travel, mailing, and postage = $3,000.

Total of above = $11,800.

REQUIRED

a. Calculate the expected full cost of the Surenex engagement, including an allocation of overhead. Round answer to nearest dollar and predetermined overhead rate to two decimal places.

b. What is the lowest amount that Connie can bill on this engagement without hurting company profit?

c. In deciding on a price for the engagement, what should Connie consider in addition to the amount calculated in (b)?

CASE

2-3 DUPAGE POWDER COATING [LO 4, 5]

DuPage Powder Coating applies powder coating finishes to a variety of materials and parts used by small and medium-size manufacturing firms. Essentially, powder coating involves the application of powder (finely divided particles of organic polymer containing pigments, fillers, and additives) to a surface, after which the powder is fused into a continuous film by the application of heat or radiant energy. The process results in a durable finish that resists rust.

In prior years, finishes were applied by hand, and manufacturing overhead was allocated to jobs based on direct labor hours. (The rate was $12 per hour based on overhead of $1,080,000 and 90,000 direct labor hours.) At the start of the current year, the company purchased and installed a computer-controlled electrostatic powder coating system at a cost of $1,800,000. With a five-year life, the equipment adds $360,000 a year to manufacturing overhead. (Thus, expected total overhead is now $1,440,000.) However, labor has been reduced by 25,000 hours per year (because the equipment reduces the need for labor). At an average wage rate of $20 per hour, $500,000 of wages are expected to be saved in the current year.

While the company purchased a computer-controlled system including a new spray chamber, it kept its old spray booth and manual equipment for use on small jobs.

DuPage Powder Coating has just received an order from Cedargreen Enterprises (a small manufacturer of outdoor furniture) to powder coat 4 tables and 16 chairs. On small orders such as this, DuPage uses its old spray booth and manual equipment rather than the new computer-controlled system. Material cost for the job will be $500, and 7 labor hours are required.

Small jobs like the one for Cedargreen are worked on while the computer-controlled electrostatic system is being changed over (cleaning, different colors, etc.) between large jobs.

REQUIRED

a. Based on the limited information, estimate the full cost of the job in the current year. Assume the company uses one company-wide overhead rate.

b. What would have been the cost of the job in part (a) in the prior year?

c. Bill McCally, plant manager, observed: "Last year, jobs like the one we did for Cedargreen Enterprises cost less. But I know we're not less efficient at handling small jobs. We use the same equipment, the same labor, and the same products on small jobs this year as last year, and yet the accounting system is making small jobs look more expensive!"

Explain why the accounting system is making small jobs appear to be more costly in the current year.

d. Does the fact that small jobs have a higher cost in the current year suggest that prices for small jobs should be increased?

3

PROCESS COSTING

Stacy Brannen was just completing a tour at Kent Chemical Company's Midwest plant.

Only 2 weeks ago, Stacy had graduated from State University with a degree in mechanical engineering, and now she was nearing the end of her first day on the job at Kent. The assistant plant manager, Bill Merton, conducted the tour and pointed out the steps involved in processing paints, stains, and wood preservatives.

Although the tour concentrated on the equipment used in the production processes, Stacy found herself wondering how the cost of products was determined. "Bill, can you give me a rough idea of how you calculate product costs?" she asked. "I noticed, for example, that to end up with a gallon of wood preservative ready to ship, we perform both mixing and packaging operations. With labor, material, and overhead added in these separate operations, is assigning costs to wood preservative a difficult job?"

"Well," Bill replied, "let's see if we can catch Walter Hunt before he goes home for the day. He's the plant controller, and no one can do a better job than Walt of explaining how we do product costing at Kent Chemical."

The type of product costing system used at Kent Chemical Company is a process costing system. Such systems are in common use by companies that produce large numbers of homogeneous items in a continuous production process. Companies using process costing include producers of paints, plastics, paper products, cereals, cosmetics, and metals. Thus, well-known companies like DuPont, the Quaker Oats Company, and the Ralston Purina Company use process costing. This chapter introduces you to the essential elements of a process costing system.

Science Photo Library/Shutterstock

LEARNING OBJECTIVES

1 Describe how products flow through departments and how costs flow through accounts.

2 Discuss the concept of an equivalent unit and calculate the cost of goods completed and the ending Work in Process balance in a processing department.

3 Prepare a production cost report.

DIFFERENCE BETWEEN JOB-ORDER AND PROCESS COSTING SYSTEMS

As explained in Chapter 2, there are two primary systems for calculating the cost of inventory: a job-order system and a process costing system. In a job-order system, each unique product or batch is a "job" for which the company needs cost information. Therefore, it is necessary to trace manufacturing costs to specific jobs. When jobs are completed, the costs of the jobs are removed from Work in Process and included in Finished Goods. When completed jobs are sold, the costs of the jobs are removed from Finished Goods and included in Cost of Goods Sold.

Process costing, in contrast, is essentially a system of averaging. Dividing production costs by the total number of homogeneous items produced results in an average unit cost. When items are completed, multiplying the number of units completed by the average unit cost determines the costs to be removed from Work in Process Inventory and included in Finished Goods Inventory. When items are sold, multiplying the number of units sold by the average unit cost determines the costs to remove from Finished Goods Inventory and include in Cost of Goods Sold. Illustration 3-1 presents a comparison of job-order and process costing systems. The remainder of the chapter describes process costing systems in more detail.

ANY QUESTIONS?

Q: I noticed that some companies produce a large number of *somewhat* identical items. For example a company may produce thousands of very similar laptop computers. Different models may have the same case, keyboard, and screen, but one may have a faster processor and more memory than the other. Or consider a producer of Cabernet wine. Two of the company's wines could be similar in all respects except one is aged in French oak barrels while the other is aged in American oak barrels. What do these companies use, process costing or job-order costing?

A: Good observation! In practice, firms frequently use a hybrid system that combines features of job-order costing and process costing. The hybrid system is called operations costing. In operations costing, conversion costs are assigned to products, as in process costing. Different materials, however, are assigned to products, as in job-order costing. Those of you who become managers most likely won't need to know much more than this. Those of you who plan on becoming accountants will receive more information in your cost accounting course.

LINK TO PRACTICE

What Type of Costing System Is Used by ExxonMobil Corporation for the Product Mobil 1?

ExxonMobil is one of the world's largest companies engaged in the exploration, production, and sale of crude oil and natural gas. The company also manufactures numerous petroleum products.

Courtesy AmSoil

One product you may have heard of is Mobil 1, the world's leading synthetic motor oil. What type of costing system do you think the company uses for this product? Large quantities of identical units are produced in continuous production processes. So, to account for the cost of Mobil 1, ExxonMobil uses process costing.

ILLUSTRATION 3-1

Comparison of job-order and process costing systems

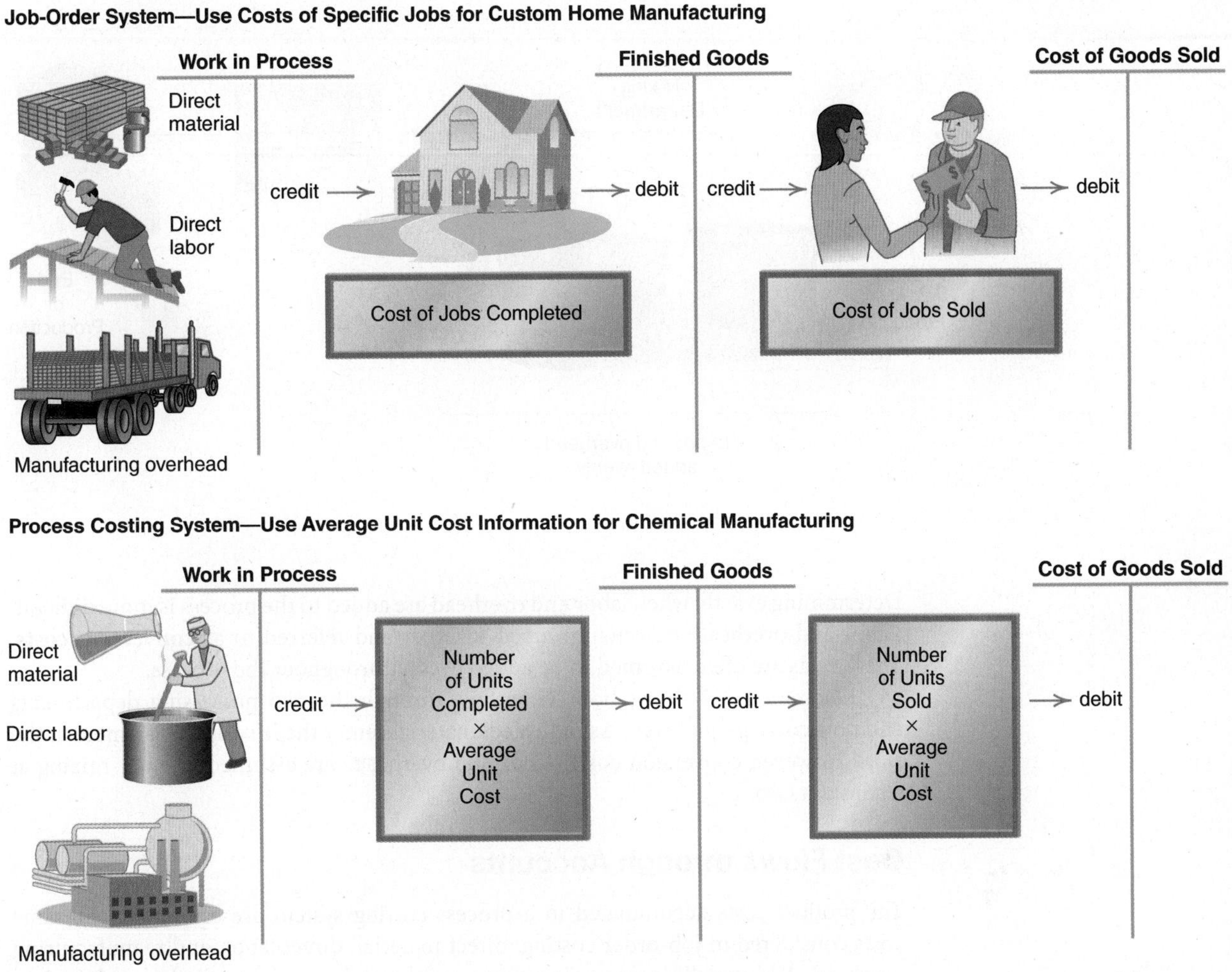

LEARNING OBJECTIVE 1

Describe how products flow through departments and how costs flow through accounts.

PRODUCT AND COST FLOWS

Just as a product passes through several departments before it is completed, costs flow through several accounts before the product costs of the product is recorded in finished goods. Here we discuss the flow of products through departments and the flow of costs through accounts of companies that use process costing.

Product Flows through Departments

In the manufacturing operations of a company using process costing, a product typically must pass through two or more departments, and costs are accumulated in each department. The Kent Chemical Company manufactures wood preservative in two departments: mixing and packaging. After chemical materials are blended in the Mixing Department, the liquid preservative is transferred to the Packaging Department, where it is placed in plastic containers. Materials, labor, and overhead are added at different stages in each processing department.

Generally, identifying the stage when materials enter the production process is easy. In the Mixing Department, the chemical materials are added at the start of the process.

ILLUSTRATION 3-2
Flow of items through processing departments

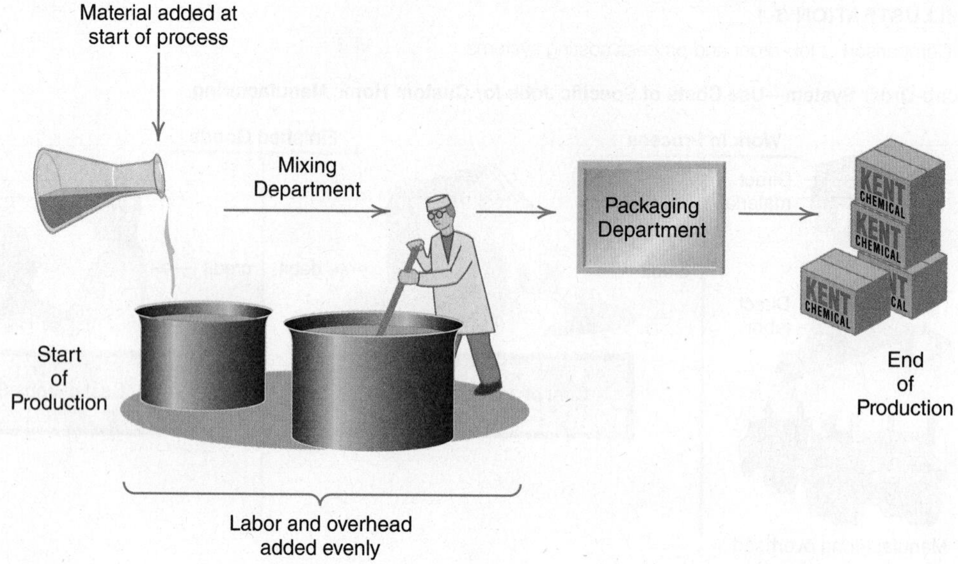

Determining exactly when labor and overhead are added to the process is more difficult. Labor and overhead are often grouped together and referred to as **conversion costs**. These costs are often assumed to be added evenly throughout the process.

Illustration 3-2 shows how items flow through the two processing departments and how costs are incurred. As indicated, materials enter the Mixing Department at the start. However, conversion costs (labor and overhead) are assumed to enter mixing at a constant rate.

Cost Flows through Accounts

The product costs accumulated in a process costing system are essentially the same costs considered in job-order costing: direct material, direct labor, and manufacturing overhead. Additionally, a processing department may have a cost called **transferred-in cost**. This is the cost incurred in one processing department that is transferred to the next processing department. For example, at Kent Chemical, the cost incurred in the Mixing Department is transferred to the Packaging Department. In essence, the cost transferred in from Mixing becomes a material cost added to Packaging. However, it is called a "transferred-in" cost.

LINK TO PRACTICE

Virtual Plant Tour for Company Using Process Costing

Process costing is used by companies that produce large numbers of homogeneous items in a continuous production process. Have you ever been in a plant that has such a production process? If not, take a virtual tour of one.

Endot Industries is a producer of pipes used to move liquids and gas and as conduit for pulling wires in construction projects. A tour of the company is available at Endot Industries' company website.

Each processing department accumulates product cost in a separate departmental Work in Process account. The sum of the departmental Work in Process accounts is the amount in Work in Process for the entire company. The following entries illustrate the flow of costs between processing departments.

Direct Material. Suppose that $142,000 of direct materials are used during April in the Mixing Department of Kent Chemical Company. The following entry would be appropriate for this transaction:

(date)	Work in Process, Mixing	142,000	
	Raw Materials		142,000
	To record use of raw material		

Direct Labor. Suppose that $62,200 of direct labor costs are incurred during April in the Mixing Department. The following entry would be appropriate for this transaction:

(date)	Work in Process, Mixing	62,200	
	Wages Payable		62,200
	To record direct labor cost		

Manufacturing Overhead. To assign overhead to products in a process costing system, a company may use either actual overhead costs or a predetermined overhead rate. Unless the amount of overhead cost and the level of production are fairly constant from month to month, using actual overhead costs results in substantial fluctuations in the unit cost of goods produced. For this reason, most companies use a predetermined overhead rate.

Suppose that at the start of the year, the Mixing Department estimates it will incur $2,160,000 of overhead cost and $720,000 of direct labor cost. Using direct labor as an allocation base, the department calculates a predetermined overhead rate of $3 for each dollar of direct labor cost (i.e., $2,160,000 ÷ $720,000). Assuming $62,200 of direct labor cost was incurred in the month of April, $186,600 of overhead ($62,200 × $3 = $186,600) would be assigned to Work in Process that month.

(date)	Work in Process, Mixing	186,600	
	Manfacturing Overhead		186,600
	To record manufacturing overhead applied to Work in Process		

Transferred-in Cost. When one processing department completes its work, the items are transferred to the next department along with their related cost. As mentioned earlier, this cost is referred to as *transferred-in* cost. Suppose that during April, the Mixing Department completes units with a cost of $360,000. The completed units are transferred to the Packaging Department, and the related cost becomes a transferred-in cost to packaging. The entry to record the transfer is:

(date)	Work in Process, Packaging	360,000	
	Work in Process, Mixing		360,000
	To record transfer of units from Mixing to Packaging		

The flow of costs between departmental Work in Process accounts is presented in Illustration 3-3.

ILLUSTRATION 3-3
Flow of costs between processing departments

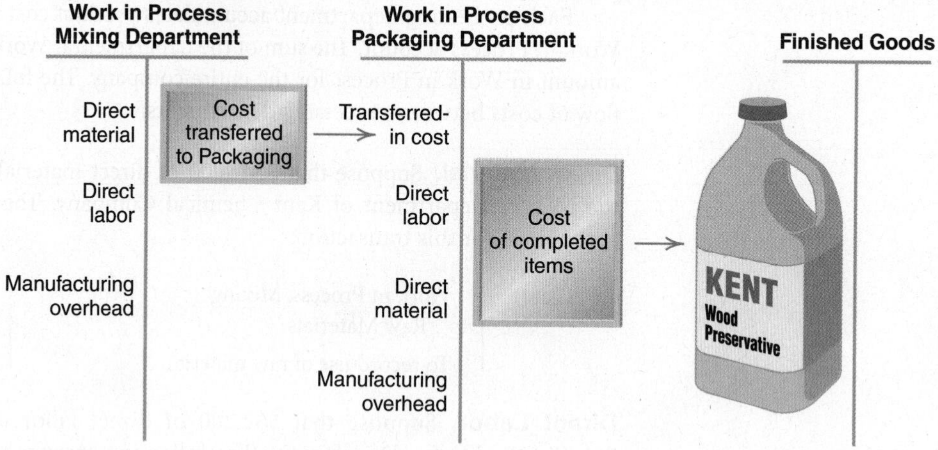

LEARNING OBJECTIVE 2

Discuss the concept of an equivalent unit and calculate the cost of goods completed and the ending Work in Process balance in a processing department.

CALCULATING UNIT COST

Process costing, as we have seen, is essentially a system of averaging. This section shows how to calculate an average unit cost in a process costing system.[1] First, however, we must explain an essential concept in process costing—the concept of an equivalent unit.

Equivalent Units

In calculating the average unit cost, it is necessary to convert the number of partially completed units in Work in Process to an equivalent number of whole units. Otherwise, the denominator in the average unit cost calculation will be misstated. When partially completed units are converted to a comparable number of completed units, they are referred to as **equivalent units**. For example, if 100 units in Work in Process are 50 percent completed, then they are equivalent to 50 completed units (100 × 50%), as shown in Illustration 3-4.

The number of equivalent units in Work in Process may be different for material and conversion costs. This is because material and conversion costs enter the production process at different times. For example, suppose that at the end of July, the Mixing Department at Kent Chemical has 100 gallons (units of production) of wood preservative in Work in Process that are 50 percent through the mixing process. Further, assume that materials enter into the process at the start, while conversion costs enter evenly throughout the process. Even though the units are only halfway through the process, they have received 100 percent of material since material was added immediately at the start of the process (see Illustration 3-2). Therefore, with respect to material cost, there are 100 equivalent units in Work in Process. However, because the units are only halfway through the process, they have received only 50 percent of the labor and overhead needed for completion. Since the 100 gallons are only 50 percent complete

ILLUSTRATION 3-4
How equivalent units are calculated

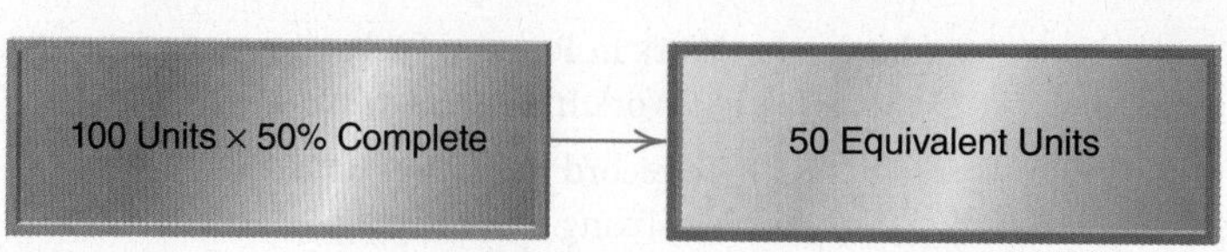

[1]The approach we take is referred to as the weighted average method. Other approaches, such as the first-in, first-out method, are also used. These methods are discussed in cost accounting textbooks.

ILLUSTRATION 3-5

Differences in equivalent units for material and conversion costs, assuming material added at start of process

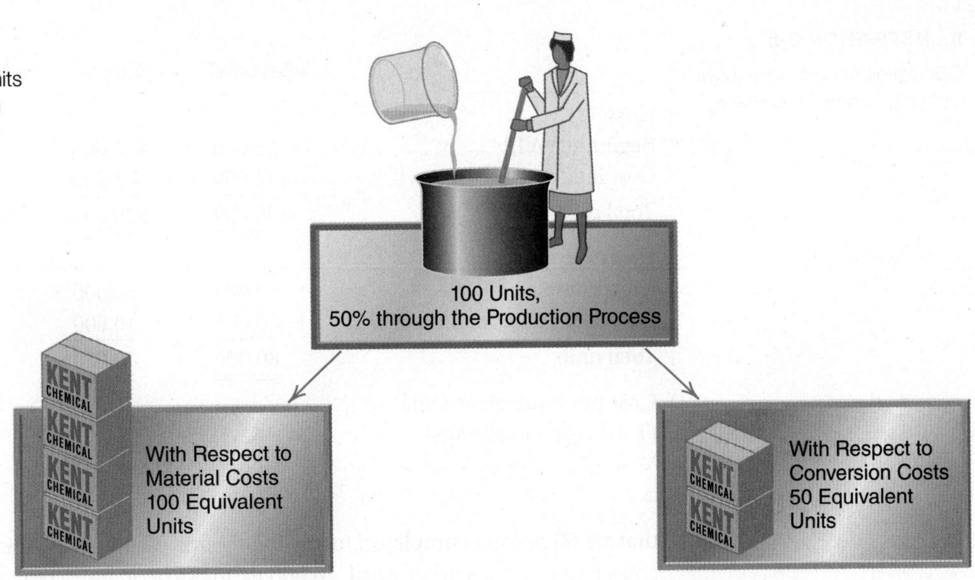

with respect to conversion costs, there are 50 equivalent units for labor and overhead (see Illustration 3-5).

Cost per Equivalent Unit

The average unit cost in a process costing system is referred to as a **cost per equivalent unit**. The formula for determining the cost per equivalent unit is:

$$\text{Cost per equivalent unit} = \frac{\text{Cost in beginning WIP} + \text{Cost incurred in current period}}{\text{Units completed} + \text{Equivalent units in ending WIP}}$$

The numerator contains the cost in beginning Work in Process (WIP) plus the cost incurred in the current period. This amount represents the total cost for which a processing department must account in each period. The total cost is divided by the units completed plus the equivalent units in ending work in process. The result is a cost per equivalent unit amount that can be used to spread the cost at the start of the period and the cost incurred during the period over the units completed and the units in process at the end of the period.

TEST YOUR KNOWLEDGE

At Rainier Chemical, conversion costs (labor and overhead) enter evenly throughout the production process. At the end of the year, 200 units in work in process are 80 percent complete. With respect to conversion costs, how many equivalent units are in Work in Process?

a. 200. b. 160. c. 360. d. 280.

Correct answer is b.

CALCULATING AND APPLYING COST PER EQUIVALENT UNIT: MIXING DEPARTMENT EXAMPLE

Next, we consider cost per equivalent unit calculations for the Mixing Department of Kent Chemical Company. At the start of April, the Mixing Department has on hand beginning Work in Process inventory consisting of 10,000 gallons of wood preservative

ILLUSTRATION 3-6

Calculation of cost per equivalent unit, Mixing Department

	Material	Labor	Overhead	Total
Cost				
Beginning WIP	$ 18,000	$ 7,800	$ 23,400	$ 49,200
Cost incurred during April	142,000	62,200	186,600	390,800
Total cost	$160,000	$70,000	$210,000	$440,000
Units				
Units completed	60,000	60,000	60,000	
Equivalent units, ending WIP	20,000	10,000	10,000	
Total units	80,000	70,000	70,000	
Cost per Equivalent Unit				
(Total cost ÷ total units)	$2 +	$1 +	$3 =	$6

that are 80 percent complete. During the month, 70,000 gallons are started and 60,000 are completed. At the end of April, 20,000 gallons are on hand that are 50 percent complete. The cost in beginning Work in Process consists of $18,000 of material cost, $7,800 of labor cost, and $23,400 of overhead cost. During April, the Mixing Department incurs $142,000 of material cost and $62,200 of labor cost. Because the Mixing Department's predetermined overhead rate is $3 for each dollar of labor cost, $186,600 ($3 × $62,200) of overhead is applied to production during the month.

The cost per equivalent unit calculations for the Mixing Department is presented in Illustration 3-6. The cost of material includes the $18,000 in beginning Work in Process and the $142,000 of material cost incurred during April. The total of $160,000 is divided by 80,000 units, the sum of the number of units completed (60,000 gallons) and the equivalent units in ending Work in Process (20,000 gallons). Dividing total cost by the total number of units yields a cost per equivalent unit for materials of $2. A similar procedure is used to find the cost per equivalent unit for labor and overhead cost.

Let's look more closely at the equivalent units used in these calculations. Note that at the end of April, there are 20,000 units on hand that are only 50 percent through the mixing process. However, since material cost enters at the start of the mixing process, the 20,000 units are 100 percent complete with respect to material cost. Thus, there are 20,000 equivalent units in ending Work in Process for materials. In contrast, for both labor and overhead, the 20,000 units on hand are only 50 percent complete, so they correspond to only 10,000 equivalent units.

As shown in the last line of Illustration 3-6, the total cost per equivalent unit is $6, consisting of $2 of material cost, $1 of labor cost, and $3 of overhead cost. These unit cost figures can be used to calculate the cost of goods completed and transferred out of the Mixing Department and the cost of ending Work in Process.

TEST YOUR **KNOWLEDGE**

At Rainier Chemical, labor cost in beginning Work in Process at the start of April was $50,000, and $450,000 of labor was incurred during the month. At the end of April, 200 units are in WIP, and they are 80 percent complete with respect to labor. During this month, 840 units were completed. What is the cost per equivalent unit for labor?

a. $225. b. $481. c. $536. d. $500.

Correct answer is d. ($50,000 + $450,000) ÷ [840 + (200 × .8)]

Cost Transferred Out

Recall that 60,000 gallons were completed by the Mixing Department during April and transferred to the Packaging Department. We know that the unit cost is \$6. Therefore, \$360,000 of cost (60,000 gallons × \$6) is related to the units completed and transferred out. The entry at the end of April to record the transfer was presented earlier and is repeated here:

(date)	Work in Process, Packaging	360,000	
	Work in Process, Mixing		360,000
	To record transfer of units from Mixing to Packaging		

Ending Work in Process

The ending balance in Work in Process in the Mixing Department is \$80,000. This balance is made up of 20,000 equivalent units for material at \$2 per equivalent unit, 10,000 equivalent units for labor at \$1, and 10,000 equivalent units for overhead at \$3.

Ending Balance in Work in Process, Mixing	
Material (20,000 equiv. units at \$2)	\$40,000
Labor (10,000 equiv. units at \$1)	10,000
Overhead (10,000 equiv. units at \$3)	30,000
Total	\$80,000

Here is a summary of the cost activity for the Mixing Department resulting in the \$80,000 ending balance in Work in Process:

Work in Process, Mixing

	Beginning balance	49,200	
Cost added	Material	142,000	360,000 Cost transferred out
	Labor	62,200	
	Overhead	186,600	
	Ending balance	80,000	

LEARNING OBJECTIVE 3
Prepare a production cost report.

PRODUCTION COST REPORT

A **production cost report** is an end-of-the-month report for a process costing system that provides a reconciliation of units and a reconciliation of costs as well as the details of the cost per equivalent unit calculations. The reconciliations help ensure that mistakes are not made in calculations. A production cost report for the Mixing Department of

ILLUSTRATION 3-7

Production cost report, Mixing Department

Production Cost Report
Mixing Department
April

Unit Reconciliation				
Units in beginning WIP (100% material, 80% conversion costs)				10,000
Units started during April				70,000
Units to account for				80,000
Units completed and transferred to packaging				60,000
Units in ending WIP (100% material, 50% conversion costs)				20,000
Units accounted for				80,000
Cost per Equivalent Unit Calculation				
	Material	**Labor**	**Overhead**	**Total**
Cost				
Beginning WIP	$ 18,000	$ 7,800	$ 23,400	$ 49,200
Cost incurred during April	142,000	62,200	186,600	390,800
Total	$160,000	$70,000	$210,000	$440,000
Units				
Units completed	60,000	60,000	60,000	
Equivalents units, ending WIP	20,000	10,000	10,000	
Total	80,000	70,000	70,000	
Cost per equivalent unit	$2	$1	$3	$6
Cost Reconciliation				
Total cost to account for				$440,000
Cost of completed units transferred to Packaging (60,000 × $6)				$360,000
Cost of ending WIP				
Material (20,000 equivalent units × $2)			$40,000	
Labor (10,000 equivalent units × $1)			10,000	
Overhead (10,000 equivalent units × $3)			30,000	80,000
Total cost accounted for				$440,000

Kent Chemical Company is provided in Illustration 3-7. The unit cost calculations in the production report are identical to the ones just presented. We will concentrate now on the reconciliation of units and the reconciliation of costs.

Reconciliation of Units

Assuming no units are lost (e.g., due to evaporation, damage, or theft), the number of units in beginning Work in Process inventory plus the number of units started during the period should be equal to the number of units completed plus the number of units in Work in Process at the end of the period. For the Mixing Department, 10,000 units were in beginning inventory and 70,000 units were started during the period, which means that 80,000 units must be accounted for. Since 60,000 units were completed and 20,000 units are in Work in Process at the end of the period, all of the units are accounted for.

Units in beginning Work in Process	10,000		Units completed	60,000
+ Units started	70,000	=	+ Units in ending Work in Process	20,000
	80,000			80,000

Reconciliation of Costs

For each period, the total cost that must be accounted for is the sum of the costs in beginning Work in Process and the costs incurred during the period. In the Mixing Department, this amounts to $440,000. The cost must be either transferred out with the completed units or remain in ending Work in Process inventory. The amount transferred out is $360,000, and the amount in ending Work in Process inventory is $80,000. Because their sum is $440,000, the total amount of cost is accounted for.

Cost in beginning Work in Process	$ 49,200		Cost transferred out	$360,000
+ Cost incurred during the period	390,800	=	+ Cost in ending Work in Process	80,000
	$440,000			$440,000

BASIC STEPS IN PROCESS COSTING: A SUMMARY

Unless process costing is approached in a systematic way, it is easy to get lost in the calculations. Here is a summary of the basic steps presented earlier. As you can see, each of the steps is performed when the production cost report is prepared.

Step 1. Account for the number of physical units. The number of units at the start of the period plus the number of units started during the period should equal the number of units completed plus the number of units in ending Work in Process.

Step 2. Calculate the cost per equivalent unit for material, labor, and overhead. Remember that cost (numerator in the calculation) includes both beginning cost and cost incurred during the period. The number of equivalent units (denominator in the calculation) includes both the number of units completed and the number of equivalent units in ending Work in Process.

Step 3. Assign cost to items completed and items in ending Work in Process. The cost of items completed is simply the product of the total cost per equivalent unit and the number of units completed. The cost of items in Work in Process is the sum of the products of equivalent units in process and cost per equivalent unit for material, labor, and overhead.

Step 4. Account for the amount of product cost. The cost of beginning inventory plus the cost incurred during the period should equal the amount of cost assigned to completed items plus the amount of cost assigned to items in ending Work in Process.

KENT CHEMICAL REVISITED: ANSWERING STACY'S QUESTION

Recall that in the scenario at the beginning of the chapter, Stacy Brannen asked how the cost of products like wood preservative are calculated at the Kent Chemical Company. At this point you should be able to answer that question. Essentially, material, labor, and overhead costs are accumulated in each processing department. In each department, the cost per equivalent unit is calculated for material, labor, and overhead (Step 2 in the previous section). Then the costs per equivalent unit are used to determine the cost of items completed and the cost of ending Work in Process (Step 3).

DEALING WITH TRANSFERRED-IN COST: PACKAGING DEPARTMENT EXAMPLE

As previously noted, companies using process costing systems generally use several processes to make their products. When items are completed in one processing department, the cost of the completed units is transferred to the next processing department. This procedure is repeated until the units are completed in the last process. At that point, the cost of the items is transferred to finished goods.

Here we consider an example to illustrate the method for dealing with cost transfers. The example involves the Packaging Department of Kent Chemical. To calculate product costs in the Packaging Department, we will use the same procedures already used to calculate product costs in the Mixing Department, thereby providing you with another opportunity to enhance your understanding of process costing.

Step 1. In working through the Packaging Department example, it will be helpful to examine the information provided in the Production Cost Report for the Packaging Department (see Illustration 3-8). At the start of April, the Packaging Department has 15,000 gallons that are 50 percent through the packaging operation. During the month of April, the department receives 60,000 gallons from the Mixing Department. There are now 75,000 gallons to account for. At the end of April, 5,000 gallons are 40 percent complete, and 70,000 gallons are completed and transferred to finished goods, which accounts for the total of 75,000 gallons. Reconciling the physical number of units is the first of the four steps in solving a process costing problem and is shown in the quantity reconciliation section of the Production Cost Report (see Illustration 3-8).

Step 2. The second step is to calculate the cost per equivalent unit. The beginning balance in Work in Process includes $10,500 of material cost, $4,500 of labor, $9,000 of overhead, and $92,250 of cost transferred in from the Mixing Department. In addition, $49,500 of material cost, $27,900 of labor cost, $55,800 of overhead, and $360,000 of cost transferred in from the Mixing Department were incurred during the month of April. The sum of these costs is divided by the number of completed units plus the equivalent units in ending Work in Process for each cost category. As the Production Cost Report shows, this yields cost per equivalent unit values of $.80 for material, $.45 for labor, $.90 for overhead, and $6.03 for transferred-in cost. Note that the calculation for material assumes that material is added at the start of the packaging process—thus the 5,000 units in ending Work in Process are 100 percent complete with respect to materials.

Because it was not covered in the previous example, note especially the calculation of cost per equivalent unit for transferred-in cost. The sum of

ILLUSTRATION 3-8

Production cost report, Packaging Department

Production Cost Report
Packaging Department
April

Unit Reconciliation

Units in beginning WIP (100% material, 50% conversion costs)	15,000
Units received from Mixing during April	60,000
Units to account for	75,000
Units completed and transferred to finished goods	70,000
Units in ending WIP (100% material, 40% conversion costs)	5,000
Units accounted for	75,000

Cost per Equivalent Unit Calculation

	Material	Labor	Overhead	Trans. In	Total
Cost					
Beginning WIP	$10,500	$ 4,500	$ 9,000	$ 92,250	$116,250
Cost incurred during April	49,500	27,900	55,800	360,000	493,200
Total	$60,000	$32,400	$64,800	$452,250	$609,450
Units					
Units completed	70,000	70,000	70,000	70,000	
Equivalent units, ending WIP	5,000	2,000	2,000	5,000	
Total	75,000	72,000	72,000	75,000	
Cost per equivalent unit	$0.80	$0.45	$0.90	$6.03	$8.18

Cost Reconciliation

Total cost to account for		$609,450
Cost of completed units transferred to Finished Goods (70,000 × $8.18)		$572,600
Cost of ending WIP		
Material (5,000 equivalent units × $0.80)	$ 4,000	
Labor (2,000 equivalent units × $0.45)	900	
Overhead (2,000 equivalent units × $0.90)	1,800	
Transferred-in (5,000 equivalent units at $6.03)	30,150	36,850
Total cost accounted for		$609,450

transferred-in cost in beginning Work in Process ($92,250) plus the cost transferred-in during April ($360,000) is the numerator of the calculation ($452,250). The denominator (75,000 units) is the sum of the units completed (70,000) plus the equivalent units in ending Work in Process (5,000). The result is a cost per equivalent unit for transferred-in cost of $6.03.

One aspect of the calculation may be confusing: the equivalent units in ending Work in Process. At the end of April, there are 5,000 units in process that are only 40 percent through the packaging process. However, these units are 100 percent complete with respect to transferred-in cost, because they were transferred in with all of the Mixing Department cost that they will receive. Therefore, there are 5,000 equivalent units in ending Work in Process for transferred-in cost.

Step 3. The third step in solving the process costing problem is to assign cost to items completed and items in ending Work in Process. The cost of the completed items is $572,600. As indicated in the Production Cost Report (see Illustration 3-8), this is computed as the cost per equivalent unit ($8.18) times the number of units completed (70,000). Once the units are completed in the Packaging Department, they include the cost of both the mixing operation and the packaging operation and they are ready to be transferred to Finished Goods. The entry to record the transfer is:

(date)	Finished Goods	572,600	
	Work in Process, Packaging		572,600
	To record cost of units completed and transferred to Finished Goods		

The cost of ending Work in Process is composed of material, labor, overhead, and transferred-in cost. For each cost category, the equivalent units in ending Work in Process are multiplied by the cost per equivalent unit. As indicated in the production cost report, the sum of the cost categories is the ending balance of $36,850.

Step 4. The fourth and final step is to account for the amount of product cost. The cost of beginning inventory ($116,250) plus the amount of cost incurred during the period ($493,200) is the total cost that must be accounted for ($609,450). As indicated in the production cost report, this is accounted for by the cost of the completed items ($572,600) plus the cost of ending Work in Process ($36,850).

TEST YOUR **KNOWLEDGE**

The packaging department at Rainier Chemical had no beginning Work in Process inventory at the start of April. During April, the department received $300,000 of transferred-in cost from the Mixing Department. During April, the department completes 600 units, and 200 are in Work in Process. Packaging has not yet started on the in-process units since they were received right before the plant closed on April 30. With respect to transferred-in cost, the 200 units in work in process are:

a. Equivalent to 200 completed units.
b. Equivalent to 0 completed units.
c. Equivalent to 100 completed units.
d. Identical to the equivalent units for conversion costs.

Correct answer is a.

PROCESS COSTING AND INCREMENTAL ANALYSIS

Decision Making/ Incremental Analysis

Recall from Chapter 1 that whenever we make a decision, we need to perform incremental analysis. That is, we need to determine the *change* in revenue and the *change* in cost, assuming a particular decision alternative is selected. If the net change is positive, the decision alternative is "good" since it will have a positive impact on firm profit. If the net change is negative, the decision alternative is "bad" in that it will have a negative impact on firm profit.

When using process costing information (or, for that matter, job-order costing information) to make a decision, we have to be careful to recognize that the cost per unit is typically the average of fixed and variable costs. Thus, it does not measure the change in cost associated from producing an additional unit. Let's consider a simplified example to clarify this point. Later in Chapter 7, we'll go into more detail on decision making with product cost information.

Suppose that a company has no beginning Work in Process inventory and no ending Work in Process inventory for 2017. During 2017, the company incurs $100,000 of direct material cost, $200,000 of direct labor cost, and $300,000 of manufacturing overhead in producing 200,000 units that sell for $3.25 per unit. Further, let's assume that material and labor are variable costs and, for simplicity, that manufacturing overhead is completely fixed. In this case, the annual profit for 2017 is $50,000, as follows:

	200,000 UNITS	PER EQUIVALENT UNIT
Direct material cost	$100,000	$0.50
Direct labor cost	200,000	1.00
Manufacturing overhead cost	300,000	1.50
Total	$600,000	$3.00

Current selling price $3.25
Profit = Sales − Cost
= ($3.25 × 200,000) − $600,000
= $50,000

Now suppose that the company is considering *decreasing* its price to $2.90 for 2018 and expects that demand for its product will increase 75,000 units to 275,000. Note that the price of $2.90 is less than the cost per equivalent unit in 2017 so it might appear that decreasing the price is a poor decision. However, to evaluate the decision properly, we must perform incremental analysis.

New revenue ($2.90 × 275,000)		$797,500
Old revenue ($3.25 × 200,000)		650,000
Incremental revenue		$147,500
New cost		
Material: variable ($0.50 × 275,000)	$137,500	
Labor: variable ($1.00 × 275,000)	275,000	
Overhead: fixed	300,000	$712,500
Old Cost		600,000
Incremental cost		$112,500
Net change		$ 35,000

Note that at the new price, revenue will increase by $147,500. However, costs will increase by only $112,500. Thus, there will be a net *benefit* of $35,000 associated with decreasing the price to $2.90 even though it is below the old cost per unit of $3.00! We can see this only by performing incremental analysis. And in performing incremental analysis, we must take into account that some of the costs are variable (material and labor) and some costs are fixed (manufacturing overhead). We would have made a serious error if we had assumed that the new cost would be $825,000 (i.e., $3.00 × 275,000). Costs won't increase by $3.00 per unit because $1.50 of the old unit cost is actually fixed.

"YOU GET WHAT YOU MEASURE!" AND MANUFACTURING PROCESSES

YOU GET WHAT YOU MEASURE

Cost information for a manufacturing firm can be quite useful, as we just saw with the pricing decision in the previous section. Additionally, nonmonetary performance measures can help a manufacturing company create value. For example, a key nonmonetary measure for Kent Chemical is the safety measure *reportable instance*. A reportable instance is an occurrence that could have or did lead to harm and that could have been prevented by a change in how an operation or task was performed. For example, if an employee handling a chemical in the mixing process burned her hand because she was not wearing protective gloves, this would be a reportable instance.

If this performance measure is viewed as important (which would certainly be the case if the number of reportable instances is tied to bonuses!), then employees will pay more attention to safety, reduce the number of reportable instances, and create value related to fewer insurance claims and days off recovering from injuries.

The important point to remember is that manufacturing companies can create value by measuring performance related to important company goals. If safety is important, then they should develop and report safety measures, such as *number of reportable instances*. If the time it takes to package 4,000 1-gallon containers of wood preservative is important, the company should measure that time and make sure employees know how they are performing with respect to the measure.

Decision Making INSIGHT

Just as with job-order costing, process costing systems provide information on the *full* cost of units produced rather than their *incremental* cost. Since decision making relies on incremental analysis, care must be taken not to treat full cost as if it were incremental cost.

SUMMARY OF **LEARNING OBJECTIVES**

LEARNING OBJECTIVE 1 Describe how products flow through departments and how costs flow through accounts.

Process costing systems are used to accumulate the cost of inventory in companies that produce large numbers of identical items. Typically, several distinct processes are used to produce the items. When units are completed in one process, the cost of the units is transferred to the next process. This procedure is repeated until the units are completed in the last process. Along with transferred-in costs, each process may add its own material, labor, and overhead costs.

LEARNING OBJECTIVE 2 Discuss the concept of an equivalent unit and calculate the cost of goods completed and the ending Work in Process balance in a processing department.

Units in work in process are not equal to fully completed units. Therefore, in calculating the average cost per unit, it is necessary to express these partially completed units in terms of equivalent whole units.

Process costing is essentially a system of averaging. The average unit cost is referred to as the cost per equivalent unit. It equals the sum of beginning Work in Process costs and current-period costs divided by the sum of units completed and equivalent units in ending Work in Process.

To calculate the cost of completed items, the total cost per equivalent unit is multiplied by the number of units completed. To calculate the cost of units in Work in Process, it is necessary to multiply the number of equivalent units in process by the cost per equivalent unit separately for each cost category (i.e., material, labor, overhead, and transferred-in cost). This is necessary because the units in Work in Process at the end of the period may be completed to different degrees with respect to each of these costs.

LEARNING OBJECTIVE 3 Prepare a production cost report.

A production cost report provides a reconciliation of units in beginning inventory and units started to units in ending inventory and units completed. This report also provides a reconciliation of costs in beginning inventory and costs added during the period to costs in ending inventory and costs transferred out.

REVIEW PROBLEM 1

K/9 Plus Dog Treats has two departments, Mixing and Packaging. The Packaging Department started in December with work in process inventory of 20,000 pounds (a 1-pound bag is a unit of production). The units had $12,000 of transferred-in costs but no costs from Packaging.

During December, Packaging received 100,000 more pounds from Mixing and additional transferred-in cost of $54,000. Packaging also incurred $17,250 of material cost, $13,800 of labor, and $8,050 of overhead during the month of December.

At the end of December, Packaging had work in process inventory of 5,000 pounds. These units were zero percent complete with respect to material, labor, and overhead in Packaging (they had just been received from Mixing and had not been worked on by that department).

REQUIRED

Prepare a production cost report for Packaging for the month of December.

K/9 Plus Dog Treats
Production Cost Report
Packaging Department December

Unit Reconciliation

Units in beginning WIP	20,000
Units started	100,000
Units to account for	120,000
Units completed*	115,000
Units in ending WIP	5,000
Units accounted for	120,000

*Units completed = 120,000 units to account for −5,000 in ending WIP = 115,000.

Cost per Equivalent Unit Calculation

	Material	Labor	Overhead	Trans. In	Total
Cost					
Beginning WIP	$ -0-	$ -0-	$ -0-	$12,000	$ 12,000
Cost incurred in December	17,250	13,800	8,050	54,000	93,100
Total	$17,250	$13,800	$8,050	$66,000	$105,100
Units					
Units completed	115,000	115,000	115,000	115,000	
Equivalent units in ending WIP	-0-	-0-	-0-	5,000	
Total	115,000	115,000	115,000	120,000	
Cost per equivalent unit	$0.15	$0.12	$0.07	$0.55	$0.89

Cost Reconciliation

Total cost to account for	$105,100
Cost of completed units transferred to Finished Goods (115,000 × $0.89)	$102,350
Cost of ending WIP ($0.55 transferred-in cost × 5,000)	2,750
Total cost accounted for	$105,100

REVIEW PROBLEM 2

Little Gardener Company produces an environmentally safe general-purpose plant food that can be used on flower beds and in vegetable gardens. The company operates two departments, Mixing and Packaging. Liquid plant food is prepared in the Mixing Department and packaged in 1-gallon containers in the Packaging Department. Material is added at the start of each process, and labor and overhead are added evenly throughout the processes. All units are completed each month in Packaging. Therefore, there is no ending Work in Process in this department.

The following information is related to production in February:

Unit Information (gallons)	Mixing	Packaging
Beginning Work in Process		
(Mixing)	2,000	
(Packaging)		-0-
Started during March	60,000	61,000
Ending Work in Process		
(Mixing: 100% material, 60% conversion costs)	1,000	
(Packaging)		-0-

Cost Information, Beginning Work in Process		
Direct material	$4,000	$-0-
Direct labor	800	-0-
Manufacturing overhead	1,120	-0-
Transferred-in cost	-0-	-0-
Cost added during February		
Direct material	$120,000	$18,300
Direct labor	30,000	3,050
Manufacturing overhead	42,000	6,100
Transferred-in cost	-0-	?

REQUIRED

Prepare production cost reports for Mixing and Packaging for the month of February.

Little Gardener Company
Production Cost Report
Mixing Department
February

Unit Reconciliation	
Units in beginning WIP	2,000
Units started during February	60,000
Units to account for	62,000
Units completed	61,000
Units in ending WIP (100% material, 60% conversion costs)	1,000
Units accounted for	62,000

Cost per Equivalent Unit Calculation

	Material	Labor	Overhead	Total
Cost				
Beginning WIP	$ 4,000	$ 800	$ 1,120	$ 5,920
Cost incurred during February	120,000	30,000	42,000	192,000
Total	$124,000	$30,800	$43,120	$197,920

	Material	Labor	Overhead	Total
Units				
Units completed	61,000	61,000	61,000	
Equivalent units, ending WIP	1,000	600	600	
Total	62,000	61,600	61,600	
Cost per equivalent unit	$2.00	$0.50	$0.70	$3.20
Cost Reconciliation				
Total cost to account for				$197,920
Cost of completed units transferred to Finished Goods (61,000 × $3.20)				$195,200
Cost of ending WIP				
Material (1,000 equivalent units × $2)			$2,000	
Labor (600 equivalent units × $0.50)			300	
Overhead (600 equivalent units × $0.70)			420	2,720
Total cost accounted for				$197,920

Little Gardener Company
Production Cost Report
Packaging Department
February

Unit Reconciliation	
Units in beginning WIP	–0–
Units started	61,000
Units to account for	61,000
Units completed	61,000
Units in ending WIP	–0–
Units accounted for	61,000

Cost per Equivalent Unit Calculation

	Material	Labor	Overhead	Trans. In	Total
Cost					
Beginning WIP	$ –0–	$ –0–	$ –0–	$ –0–	$ –0–
Cost incurred during February	18,300	3,050	6,100	195,200	222,650
Total	$18,300	$3,050	$6,100	$195,200	$222,650
Units					
Units completed	61,000	61,000	61,000	61,000	
Equivalent units, ending WIP	–0–	–0–	–0–	–0–	
Total	61,000	61,000	61,000	61,000	
Cost per equivalent unit	$0.30	$0.05	$0.10	$3.20	$3.65
Cost Reconciliation					
Total cost to account for					$222,650
Cost of completed units transferred to Finished Goods (61,000 × $3.65)					$222,650
Cost of ending WIP					–0–
Total cost accounted for					$222,650

KEY TERMS

Conversion costs (90)
Cost per equivalent unit (93)
Equivalent units (92)
Production cost report (95)
Transferred-in cost (90)

SELF-ASSESSMENT (Answers Below)

1. Which of the following characteristics are associated with a process costing system? (Choose all that apply).
   - **a.** Heterogeneous products.
   - **b.** Homogeneous products.
   - **c.** Continuous production.
   - **d.** Discontinuous production.
   - **e.** Costs are traced to jobs.
   - **f.** Costs are traced to processing departments.
2. The best example of a business requiring a process costing system would be a:
   - **a.** Custom cabinet shop.
   - **b.** Antique furniture restorer.
   - **c.** Soap manufacturer.
   - **d.** Automobile repair shop.
3. The costs in a process cost system are traced to:
   - **a.** Specific jobs.
   - **b.** Specific customers.
   - **c.** Specific company administrators.
   - **d.** Specific production departments.
4. Match the following terms with the definitions in the numbered list below.
   - **a.** Conversion costs
   - **b.** Equivalent units
   - **c.** Transferred-in costs
   - **d.** Cost per equivalent unit
   - **(1)** The costs associated with units received from a preceding department for further processing.
   - **(2)** The unit cost in a process costing system.
   - **(3)** The costs associated with changing units of direct materials into finished products; they include both direct labor and manufacturing overhead.
   - **(4)** The quantity of partially completed units expressed in terms of whole units.
5. Determine the amount of conversion cost in the following list of costs.

a. Direct material	$25,000
b. Direct labor	$35,000
c. Manufacturing overhead	$45,000
d. Selling expenses	$10,000
e. Administrative expenses	$50,000

6. If raw materials are introduced into a production department at the beginning of the process, which statement is correct about the equivalent units in ending Work in Process for materials?
   - **a.** All of the units in Work in Process are 100 percent complete with respect to materials.
   - **b.** All of the units in Work in Process are 50 percent complete with respect to materials.
   - **c.** Equivalent units of materials are not a function of when the materials are entered into the process.
   - **d.** All of these choices are correct.
7. A transfer of units from Production Department 1 to Production Department 2 would be recorded as a:
   - **a.** Debit to Work in Process, Department 1; credit to Work in Process, Department 2.
   - **b.** Debit to Work in Process, Department 2; credit to Work in Process, Department 1.
   - **c.** Debit to Cost of Goods Sold; credit to Work in Process, Department 1.
   - **d.** Debit to Cost of Goods Sold; credit to Work in Process, Department 2.
8. The unit reconciliation section of a production cost report includes all of the following **except**:
   - **a.** Beginning units in process.
   - **b.** Ending units in process.
   - **c.** Units in finished goods.
   - **d.** Units completed and transferred out.
   - **e.** Units started during the period.
9. The units as shown in the unit reconciliation section of a production cost report are:
   - **a.** Equivalent units of production.
   - **b.** Units without regard to stage of completion.
   - **c.** Units complete as to materials.
   - **d.** Units complete as to prime costs.
10. Transferred-in costs occur in:
    - **a.** All production departments.
    - **b.** The first and last production departments.
    - **c.** All production departments after the first.
    - **d.** None of these answer choices is correct.

ANSWERS TO SELF-ASSESSMENT

1. b, c, f **2.** c **3.** d **4.** (1)-c, (2)-d, (3)-a, (4)-b **5.** $80,000 **6.** a **7.** b **8.** c **9.** b **10.** c

QUESTIONS

1. Explain the major differences between job-order and process costing systems.
2. Identify three types of manufacturing companies for which process costing would be an appropriate product costing system. What characteristic(s) do the products of these companies have that would make process costing a good choice?
3. Explain the concept of an "equivalent unit," including how it is calculated.
4. What is meant by the term *conversion costs*?
5. What is meant by the term *transferred-in cost*?
6. Why are units often in a different stage of completion with respect to raw materials and conversion costs?
7. What items of production cost make up the "costs to account for" in a production cost report?
8. What is accomplished by preparing a reconciliation of the physical units as a part of the production cost report?
9. Do transferred-in costs occur in all departments of a manufacturer using a process costing system? Explain.
10. What are the four steps involved in the preparation of a production cost report?

EXERCISES

GROUP WORK
ETHICS

EXERCISE 3-1. Equivalent Units [LO 2] Techno Enterprises is a manufacturer of microchips (referred to as chips). Its production process is complex and involves more than 100 steps, starting with production of small, round silicon wafers and ending with chips being put into individual packages that protect them and provide connections to the products for which the chips are developed. The company uses a process costing system and has always made the simplifying assumption that wafers in production, but not yet finished, are 50 percent complete with respect to conversion costs.

In the current year, the company has struggled due to a decline in computer sales and reduced demand for chips. To boost profit, the company has decided to start a very large number of wafers into production in the last few days of the year. Due to the use of ceramic carriers and other high-performance features, the Techno Enterprises production process typically takes 30 days.

REQUIRED

Explain why starting a large number of wafers into production will boost profit even though the chips that ultimately result from the wafers are ones that have not been sold or even completed. Is the company's approach to boosting profit ethical?

WRITING

EXERCISE 3-2. Cost per Equivalent Units [LO 2] Write a paragraph explaining the calculation of the cost per equivalent unit (i.e., explain what goes in the numerator and what goes in the denominator of the calculation). Be sure to explain why the denominator may be different for the cost per equivalent unit of material and the cost per equivalent unit of labor and overhead.

EXERCISE 3-3. Cost Flows through Accounts [LO 1] What are the four cost items that may enter a processing department?

EXERCISE 3-4. Physical Flow of Units [LO 3] In each case below, fill in the missing amount.

Case #1	Work in Process, October 1	5,000 gallons
	Units started during October	?
	Units completed during October	15,000 gallons
	Work in Process, October 31	2,500 gallons
Case #2	Work in Process, March 1	16,000 tons
	Units started during March	4,000 tons
	Units completed during March	14,400 tons
	Work in Process, March 31	?
Case #3	Work in Process, December 1	300,000 pounds
	Units started during December	950,000 pounds
	Units completed during December	?
	Work in Process, December 31	350,000 pounds

EXCEL **EXERCISE 3-5. Unit Reconciliation [LO 3]** During August the Panama Paint Company completed 90,000 cans of paint. At the beginning of August, the company had 850 units that were 75 percent complete with respect to material and 50 percent complete with respect to conversion costs. During the month, the company started production of 95,000 units.

REQUIRED

How many units were in Work in Process at the end of August?

EXERCISE 3-6. Unit Reconciliation [LO 3] During August, Wilson Lubricant completed 31,000 gallons of product. At the start of August there were 4,500 gallons in Work in Process, and at the end of August, there were 7,000 gallons in Work in Process.

REQUIRED

How many gallons of product were started during the month of August?

EXERCISE 3-7. Cost per Equivalent Unit [LO 2] The balance in beginning Work in Process at Bing Rubber Company for direct labor was $140,000. During the month of March, an additional $800,000 of direct labor was incurred, and 35,000 pounds of rubber were produced. At the end of March, 10,000 pounds of rubber were in process and the units were 50 percent complete. At the start of March, the company had 6,000 pounds of rubber that were 40 percent complete.

REQUIRED

Calculate the cost per equivalent unit for labor, assuming that labor is added uniformly throughout the production process.

EXCEL **EXERCISE 3-8. Cost Reconciliation [LO 3]** During December, Western Solvent completed 40,000 units. At the end of December, there were 10,000 units in ending Work in Process that were 30 percent complete with respect to labor and overhead and 100 percent complete with respect to material. During the month of December, the company incurred $260,000 of material cost, $120,000 of labor cost, and $161,000 of manufacturing overhead. Costs per equivalent unit for material, labor, and manufacturing overhead equal $6, $3, and $4, respectively.

REQUIRED

Calculate the amount of material cost, labor cost, and overhead cost in beginning Work in Process inventory.

EXERCISE 3-9. Calculation of Equivalent Units [LO 2] The McMillian Tire Company produces tires used on small trailers. The month of June ended with 600 tires in process, 90 percent complete as to direct materials, and 50 percent complete as to conversion costs; 2,000 tires were transferred to finished goods during the month, and 2,400 were started during the month. The beginning Work in Process inventory was 60 percent complete as to direct materials and 40 percent complete as to conversion costs.

REQUIRED

Determine the denominators to be used in the calculations of cost per equivalent unit for materials and conversion costs.

EXERCISE 3-10. Reconciliation of Units and Costs [LO 2] At the start of July, the Classic Car Wax Company had beginning Work in Process of 2,500 units that were 90 percent complete with respect to material and 45 percent complete with respect to conversion costs. The cost of the units was $7,000 ($5,000 of material and $2,000 of conversion costs). During the month, the company started production of 40,000 units and incurred $224,500 of material cost and $91,750 of labor and overhead. Costs per equivalent unit were $6.00 for material and $2.50 for labor and overhead (conversion costs). The cost of items completed was $314,500 ($222,000 for materials and $92,500 for labor and overhead). Units in ending Work in Process are 25 percent complete with respect to material and 10 percent complete with respect to conversion costs.

REQUIRED

a. Prepare a reconciliation of units.

b. What is the cost of ending Work in Process?

EXERCISE 3-11. Costing Units Completed and Ending Work in Process [LO 2] For the month of September, the Wilber Pickle Company had cost per equivalent unit of $0.80 for materials (pickles, vinegar, spices, etc.) and $.90 for conversion costs (labor and overhead). At Wilber Pickle, units are measured in quarts. The company began the month with 600 quarts of pickles. By the end of the month, the company had completed 4,500 quarts, and 950 quarts were in process. The in-process units were 100 percent complete with respect to material and 75 percent complete with respect to labor and overhead.

REQUIRED

Determine the cost of the ending Work in Process inventory and the cost of items completed and transferred to Finished Goods inventory. Round answers to the nearest dollar.

EXERCISE 3-12. Costing Units Completed and Ending Work in Process [LO 2] Magi-Clean Vacuum produces a single product, a vacuum cleaner, in a continuous production process. At the beginning of production, 85 percent of materials are added; the other 15 percent are added immediately before transfer to the finished goods warehouse. Conversion costs are assumed to be added evenly throughout the process. At the end of February, there were 20 vacuums in process, 80 percent complete as to labor and overhead. Ninety-five vacuums were completed during the month. Assume that direct materials cost per equivalent unit during February was $2,050, labor cost per equivalent unit was $800, and overhead per equivalent unit was $1,500.

REQUIRED

Determine the cost of the ending Work in Process inventory and the cost of items completed and transferred to Finished Goods inventory.

EXERCISE 3-13. Costing Units Completed and Ending Work in Process [LO 2] At the start of November, Penco Refinery had Work in Process inventory consisting of 4,000 units that were 90 percent complete with respect to materials and 50 percent complete with respect to conversion costs. The cost of the units was $43,000 ($30,000 of material cost and $13,000 of labor and overhead). During November, the company started 44,000 units and incurred $421,990 of material cost and $394,880 of labor and overhead. The company completed 45,000 units during the month, and 3,000 units were in process at the end of November. The units in ending Work in Process were 85 percent complete with respect to materials and 45 percent complete with respect to conversion costs.

REQUIRED

a. Calculate the cost per equivalent unit for materials and conversion costs.

b. Calculate the cost of items completed during November.

c. Calculate the cost of ending Work in Process.

d. Round cost per equivalent unit calculations to the nearest cent and cost of work in process to the nearest dollar.

EXERCISE 3-14. Quantity Schedule and Equivalent Units [LO 3] The Simon Fishing Company processes salmon for various distributors. The two departments involved are Cleaning and

Packing. The next table summarizes the data related to pounds of salmon processed in the Cleaning Department during June:

	Pounds of Salmon	Percent Complete*
Work in Process, June 1	40,000	50%
Started into processing during June	500,000	—
Work in Process, June 30	30,000	75%

*Labor and overhead only

All materials are added at the beginning of the process in the Cleaning Department.

REQUIRED

Prepare a reconciliation of units and a computation of equivalent units for June for the Cleaning Department.

EXERCISE 3-15. Calculation of Equivalent Units [LO 2, 3] Tempe Chemicals refines a variety of chemicals for cleaning products. The following data are from the company's Greenville plant:

Work in Process, May 1	2,300,000 gallons
Direct material	100% complete
Conversion costs	40% complete
Units started in process during May	770,000 gallons
Work in Process, May 31	235,000 gallons
Direct material	100% complete
Conversion costs	60% complete

REQUIRED

Compute the equivalent units for direct material and conversion costs for the month of May.

EXERCISE 3-16. Physical Flow and Equivalent Units [LO 1, 2] The Sacramento plant of Montero Food Corporation produces a gourmet cheese. The following data pertain to the year ended December 31, 2017:

		Percentage of Completion	
	Units	Direct Material	Conversion Costs
Work in process, January 1	45,000 lb	65%	85%
Work in process, December 31	60,000 lb	80%	45%

During the year, the company started 200,000 pounds of material into production.

REQUIRED

Prepare a schedule analyzing the physical flow of units and computing the equivalent units for both direct material and conversion costs for the year.

EXERCISE 3-17. Cost per Equivalent Unit [LO 2] The Amigo Glass Company manufactures glass for sliding glass doors. At the start of August 2,000 units were in process. During August, 15,000 units were complete and 3,000 units were in process at the end of August. These in-process units were 100 percent complete with respect to material and 40 percent complete with respect to conversion costs. Other information is as follows:

Work in process, August 1:	
Direct material	$50,000
Conversion costs	$45,000
Costs incurred during August:	
Direct material	$200,000
Conversion costs	$280,000

REQUIRED

Calculate the cost per equivalent unit, for both direct material and conversion costs, during August.

EXERCISE 3-18. Incremental Analysis Woodinville Cement uses a process costing system. In 2017, the company produced and sold 100,000 bags of cement and incurred the following costs:

	Total	Per Equivalent Unit
Direct material	$ 25,000	$0.25
Direct labor	100,000	1.00
Manufacturing overhead	200,000	2.00
Total	$325,000	$3.25

The current selling price is $4 per unit, and the profit for 2017 was ($4 × 100,000) – $325,000 = $75,000. Sales projections for 2017 at the current price look flat, but the sales manager believes that if the sales price is reduced to $3.75, sales volume would increase by 12,000 units. Assume that direct material and direct labor are variable costs and that manufacturing costs are primarily fixed. Should Woodinville Cement lower the price?

PROBLEMS

EXCEL

PROBLEM 3-1. Comprehensive Problem, One Department [LO 2] Regal Polish manufactures a single product in one department and uses a process costing system. At the start of May, there were 11,000 units in process that were 100 percent complete with respect to direct material and 60 percent complete with respect to conversion costs (labor and overhead). During the month, the company began production of 105,000 units. Ending Work in Process inventory consisted of 5,100 units that were 100 percent complete with respect to material and 70 percent complete with respect to conversion costs.

Cost Information	Beginning Work in Process	Costs Added in May
Direct material	$4,000	$76,040.00
Direct labor	200	8,957.60
Manufacturing overhead	300	10,002.30
Total	$4,500	$94,999.90

REQUIRED

a. Calculate the cost per equivalent unit for each of the three cost items and in total. Round to 2 decimal places.

b. Calculate the cost of items completed in May and the cost of ending Work in Process. Round to 2 decimal places.

c. Reconcile the sum of the two costs in part b to the sum of beginning Work in Process and costs added in May.

PROBLEM 3-2. Comprehensive Problem, One Department [LO 2] Marquita Filters produces an air filter for use in jet aircraft. Parts are added at several points in the production process. In August, production began with 600 filters in Work in Process, 80 percent complete as to materials and 70 percent complete as to labor and overhead. During the month, an additional 2,700 units were started into production. Seven hundred filters were in Work in Process at the end of the month, and they were 70 percent complete as to materials and 60 percent complete as to labor and overhead.

Cost Information for August	Beginning Work in Process Inventory	Cost Added in August
Direct material	$ 45,000	$267,090
Direct labor	11,000	76,580
Manufacturing overhead	80,000	496,820
Total	$136,000	$840,490

REQUIRED

a. Calculate the cost per equivalent unit for each of the three cost items and in total. Round to 2 decimal places.

b. Calculate the cost of items completed in August and the cost of ending Work in Process inventory. Round to 2 decimal places.

c. Reconcile the sum of the two costs in part b to the sum of beginning Work in Process and costs added in August.

PROBLEM 3-3. Production Cost Report [LO 2, 3] Kao Tiles is a specialized producer of ceramic tiles. Its production process involves highly skilled workers and top-quality ceramic crafters. Work in Process is relatively large because each tile is in process for up to 3 weeks because of art, mold work, and drying time. October began with 5,000 units (a unit is one ceramic tile) in process, on average 65 percent complete as to direct materials and 35 percent complete as to conversion costs; 6,000 units were started during the month, and ending Work in Process inventory consisted of 7,000 units that were on average 75 percent complete as to direct materials and 50 percent complete as to conversion costs.

Cost Information	Beginning Work in Process	Costs Added in October
Direct material	$170,000	$ 422,000
Direct labor	160,000	1,055,000
Manufacturing overhead	50,000	107,500

REQUIRED

a. Prepare a production cost report for the month of October.

b. Prepare the journal entry to recognize the transfer of the units completed and transferred to finished goods during October.

PROBLEM 3-4. Production Cost Report [LO 2, 3] Aussie Yarn is a U.S. producer of woolen yarn made from wool imported from Australia. Raw wool is processed, spun, and finished before being shipped out to knitting and weaving companies. Material is added in the beginning of processing, and conversion costs are added evenly throughout processing.

Aussie began the month of August with 7,000 units in process that were 100 percent complete as to materials and 70 percent complete as to labor and overhead. It started 34,000 units into production during the month of August of which 8,000 remained in ending Work in Process inventory and were 50 percent complete as to conversion costs. The cost data are as follows:

Beginning work in process:	
Direct materials	$ 6,000
Direct labor	2,000
Manufacturing overhead	2,500
	$10,500
Costs added during August:	
Direct materials	$26,390
Direct labor	12,430
Manufacturing overhead	14,520
	$53,340

REQUIRED

Prepare a production cost report for the month of August.

PROBLEM 3-5. Journal Entries in Process Costing [LO 1] Lakeland Solvent produces a single product in two departments. The following costs relate to April:

	Department 1	Department 2
WIP, March 31	$ 24,000	$ 44,000
Costs added during April		
Direct material	80,000	15,000
Direct labor	40,000	70,000
Manufacturing overhead	220,000	100,000
Transferred-in costs	N/A	?
WIP, April 30	–0–	30,000

REQUIRED

Prepare journal entries to record:

a. The issuance of direct material.

b. The cost of direct labor (credit wages payable).

c. The application of manufacturing overhead.

d. The transfer of cost associated with units completed in both departments.

PROBLEM 3-6. Journal Entries in Process Costing [LO 1] The Wilmont Box Company produces a single box used by AirSpeed, an express shipping company. Wilmont uses a just-in-time system and has almost no inventories of material, work in process, or finished goods. Indeed, the balances are so small that the company treats them as zero for purposes of its accounting reports.

During July, the company produced and shipped 125,000 boxes at a cost of $0.90 per box. The cost consisted of 40 percent material cost, 15 percent labor cost, and 45 percent manufacturing overhead.

REQUIRED

Prepare journal entries to record:

a. The issuance of direct material.

b. The cost of direct labor (credit wages payable).

c. The application of manufacturing overhead.

d. The completion of units in process and their transfer to finished goods.

e. Cost of goods sold.

EXCEL **PROBLEM 3-7. Production Cost Report, Missing Data [LO 2, 3]** Classic 50s Flooring produces linoleum flooring. Below is a partial production cost report for the Mixing Department. In the report, a unit is a gallon of linoleum cement (a mixture of linseed oil, pine resin, and wood flour).

Production Cost Report
Mixing Department
June

Quantity Reconciliation	
Units in beginning WIP	700
Units started	2,700
Units to account for	3,400
Units completed	2,300
Units in ending WIP (100% material, 70% conversion costs)	(a)
Units accounted for	(b)

Cost per Equivalent Unit Calculation

	Material	Labor	Overhead	Total
Cost				
Beginning WIP	$ 475	$ 1,200	$ 2,400	$ 4,075
Cost incurred during June	4,125	11,610	23,830	39,565
Total	$4,600	$12,810	$26,230	$43,640
Units				
Units completed	2,300	2,300	2,300	
Equivalent units, ending WIP	(c)	(d)	(e)	
Total	(f)	(g)	(h)	
Cost per equivalent unit	(i)	(j)	(k)	(l)

REQUIRED

Fill in the missing data (items a through l). Round to 2 decimal places.

PROBLEM 3-8. Production Cost Report, Missing Information [LO 2, 3] Marion Chemicals produces a chemical used as a base in paints. In the manufacturing process, all materials are added at the start of the process, whereas labor and overhead are added evenly throughout production.

REQUIRED

Fill in the missing information in Marion's Production Cost Report for the month of December.

Marion Chemicals
Production Cost Report
December 2017

Unit Reconciliation	
Units in beginning WIP (100% material, 10% conversion costs)	8,000
Units started during December	?
Units to account for	?
Units completed	?
Units in ending WIP (100% material, 20% conversion costs)	5,000
Units accounted for	?

Cost per Equivalent Unit Calculation

	Material	Labor	Overhead	Total
Cost				
Beginning WIP	$45,200	$10,500	$26,300	$ 82,000
Cost incurred in December	?	?	?	?
Total	?	?	?	?
Units				
Units completed	?	?	?	
Equivalent units, ending WIP	?	?	?	
Total	?	?	?	
Cost per equivalent unit	$1.80	$1.40	$2.64	?

Cost Reconciliation		
Total cost to account for		$3,020,640
Cost of completed items		$3,007,600
Cost of ending WIP		
Material	$?	
Labor	?	
Overhead	?	?
Total cost accounted for		$3,020,640

PROBLEM 3-9. Comprehensive Problem, Two Departments [LO 2, 3] Simply Shine Shampoo is manufactured in two departments: Mixing and Packing. Once the shampoo mixture is completed in the Mixing Department, it is sent to Packaging, where a machine fills and seals individual bottles, which are then passed to a machine that places the bottles in individual boxes.

The following information is related to production in March:

	Mixing	Packing
Unit Information		
Beginning WIP		
(Mixing: 100% material, 90% conversion costs)	15,000	
(Packing: 60% material, 50% conversion costs)		14,500
Started during March:	660,000	63,000
Ending WIP		
(Mixing: 100% material, 70% conversion costs)	40,000	
(Packing: 80% material, 60% conversion costs)		38,000
Cost Information, Beginning Work in Process		
Direct material	$ 8,500	$ 925
Direct labor	1,200	60
Manufacturing overhead	2,500	115
Transferred-in cost	—	3,805
Cost Added during March		
Direct material	$254,750	$ 88,941
Direct labor	78,360	12,626
Manufacturing overhead	130,700	18,914
Transferred-in cost	—	450,850

REQUIRED

Prepare production costs reports for Mixing and Packing for the month of March. (Round costs per unit to two decimal places and cost reconciliation amounts to nearest dollar.)

PROBLEM 3-10. Comprehensive Problem, Two Departments [LO 2, 3] The Carnival Caramel Company makes a high-quality caramel candy. The manufacturing process involves mixing ingredients (Mixing Department) and shaping the processed mixture into 1-pound balls (Shaping Department), which are sold to retail outlets. No additional material is added in the shaping process. The following information is related to production in March:

	Mixing	Shaping
Unit Information		
Beginning WIP		
(Mixing: 100% material, 70% conversion costs)	5,000	
(Shaping: 80% conversion costs)		5,000
Started during March	45,000	?
Ending WIP		
(Mixing: 100% material, 50% conversion costs)	3,000	
(Shaping: 60% conversion costs)		1,500

	Mixing	Shaping
Cost Information, Beginning Work in Process		
Direct material	$ 4,000	—
Direct labor	1,600	$ 800
Manufacturing overhead	1,900	600
Transferred-in cost	—	4,420
Cost Added during March		
Direct material	$45,500	—
Direct labor	23,135	$13,592
Manufacturing overhead	25,745	9,166
Transferred-in cost	—	?

REQUIRED

Prepare production cost reports for Mixing and Shaping for the month of March. In your calculations, round to two decimal places.

PROBLEM 3-11. Production Report [LO 2, 3] Tropical Sun makes suntan lotion in two stages. The lotion is first blended in the Blending Department and then bottled and packed in the Bottling Department. The following information relates to the operations of the Blending Department for May.

		Percent Completed	
	Units	Materials	Conversion
Beginning WIP	7,500	80%	55%
Started into production	97,000		
Completed and transferred out	92,500		
Ending WIP	12,000	65%	20%
		Costs ($)	
Beginning WIP		$ 7,000	$ 8,000
Costs added during May		$106,339	$143,840

REQUIRED

Prepare a production report for the Blending Department for May. (Round cost percent to two decimal places and cost reconciliation amounts to nearest dollar.)

PROBLEM 3-12. Determination of Production Costs [LO 2, 3] The Kioda Corporation assembles various components used in the electronics industry. The company's major product, a computer chip, is the result of assembling three parts: X1, Y2, and Z3. The following information relates to production in January:

- Beginning Work in Process inventory: 6,000 units, 85 percent complete as to conversion; costing $330,000 (direct materials, $260,000; conversion costs, $70,055).
- Production started: 33,000 units.
- Production completed: 29,500 units.
- Ending Work in Process inventory: 9,500 units, 55 percent complete as to conversion.
- Direct materials used: X1,$295,000; Y2, $750,000; Z3, $490,170.
- Hourly wages of direct laborers, $25; total direct-labor payroll, $162,500.
- Overhead application rate: $70 per direct-labor hour.

REQUIRED

All parts are introduced at the beginning of Kioda's manufacturing process; conversion costs are incurred uniformly throughout production.

a. Calculate the total cost of direct material and conversion during January.

b. Determine the cost of goods completed during the month.

c. Determine the cost of the work in process inventory on January 31.

PROBLEM 3-13. Conversion Costs [LO 2, 3] Hartwell Drug Company produces a supplement to improve bone density. Conversion costs are added evenly throughout the production process. The following information is available for March:

	Units
Units (gallons) in process, March 1 (40% complete)	600
Units started in March	1,000
Units in process, March 31 (80% complete)	300

	Costs
Conversion costs in WIP, March 1	
Labor	$ 36,000
Overhead	6,000
Labor costs in March (5,100 hours)	102,600
Overhead in March	47,900

REQUIRED

a. Compute the number of units completed in March.

b. Compute the cost per equivalent unit for conversion costs.

c. Compute the conversion costs included in units completed in March.

d. Compute the conversion costs included in units in process at the end of March.

PROBLEM 3-14. Production Cost Report [LO 2, 3] Sassy Cotton produces fine cotton fabrics. The cotton is processed and finished before being shipped out to clothing companies. Material is added in the beginning of processing, and conversion costs are added evenly throughout processing.

At the beginning of July, Sassy had 8,000 units in process that were 100 percent complete as to material and 40 percent complete as to labor and overhead. The company started 31,000 units into production during the month of July. At the end of July, 8,500 units were in ending Work in Process inventory and were 60 percent complete as to conversion costs. Cost data are as follows:

Beginning Work in Process:	
Direct materials	$7,500
Direct labor	3,400
Manufacturing overhead	2,200
Costs added during July:	
Direct materials	$33,060
Direct labor	10,484
Manufacturing overhead	17,024

REQUIRED

Prepare a production cost report for the month of July.

PROBLEM 3-15. Comprehensive Problem, One Department [LO 2, 3] Lindy Manufacturing uses a process costing system to track the production of the single product it makes in one department. At the start of November, there were 8,000 units in process that were 100 percent complete for direct material and 70 percent complete for conversion costs (labor and overhead). Lindy began the production of 83,000 units during the month. In ending Work in Process inventory, there were 1,800 units that were 100 percent complete for material and 80 percent complete for conversion costs.

Cost Information	Beginning Work in Process	Costs Added in November
Direct material	$3,000	$71,620
Direct labor	300	8,764
Manufacturing overhead	200	13,396
	$3,500	$93,780

REQUIRED

a. Calculate the cost per equivalent unit for each of the three cost item and in total.

b. Calculate the cost of the units completed in November and the cost of ending Work in Process inventory.

c. Reconcile the sum of the two costs in part b to the sum of beginning Work in Process and costs added in November.

PROBLEM 3-16. Comprehensive Problem [LO 2, 3] The Newberry Company accumulates costs for its product using a process costing system. Direct materials are added at the beginning of the production process, and conversion occurs evenly throughout the production process. Below is information related to May.

Unit Information	
Work in Process, May 1 (75% complete)	40,000
Units started during May	90,000
Total to account for	130,000
Units completed	110,000
Units in ending WIP (45% complete)	20,000
Units accounted for	130,000

Cost Information

	Direct Material	Conversion	Total
Work in Process, May 1	$43,000	$340,300	$383,300
Cost incurred during May	87,000	733,080	820,080

REQUIRED

a. Compute the cost per equivalent unit for material and for conversion costs for May.

b. Compute the costs of units completed during May.

c. Compute the cost of work in process at the end of May.

d. Prepare a journal entry to record the cost of goods completed.

PROBLEM 3-17. Journal Entries in Process Costing [LO 1] Douglas Basket produces a specialty basket used by a gift basket company, Yours Truly Gifts. Douglas uses a just-in-time system and has very little inventories of material, work in process, or finished goods. Since the balances are so small, the company carries them at zero for purposes of accounting.

During August, the company produced and shipped 150,000 baskets at a cost of $1.75 per basket. The cost was made up of 55 percent material cost, 25 percent labor cost, and 20 percent manufacturing overhead.

REQUIRED

Prepare journal entries to record:

a. The issuance of direct material.

b. The cost of direct labor (use wages payable).

c. The application of manufacturing overhead.

d. The completion of units in process and their transfer to finished goods.

e. Cost of goods sold.

PROBLEM 3-18. You Get What You Measure! The Plastic Glow Company makes glow sticks. It uses a process costing system and has had a just-in-time inventory policy. The plant has a capacity to produce 500,000,000 units a year but currently operates at 300,000,000 units per year. Direct material and direct labor costs are variable, and manufacturing overhead is primarily fixed. Production costs for 2017 are as follows:

Number of units produced and sold	300,000,000
Direct materials	$ 15,000,000
Direct labor	30,000,000
Manufacturing overhead	105,000,000
Total costs	$150,000,000
Equivalent cost per unit	$0.50

Jim Taylor, the president, receives a bonus each year based on net operating profit and would like to reduce costs in 2018 so that profit will increase. He decides to take advantage of the excess plant capacity and increase production to 350,000,000 even though he expects the company will be unable to increase unit sales in 2018.

REQUIRED

a. If Jim increases production to 350,000 units per year, what will be the new equivalent cost per unit?

b. Would increasing the production level be a good idea? Why or why not?

CASE

3-1 TECH-TONIC SPORTS DRINK [LO 2, 3]

The Western Beverage Company is marketing a new product, Tech-Tonic Sports Drink Syrup. The product sells for $16 per gallon, and in recent months the company has had sales of more than 525,000 gallons per month. Consumers mix 1 part syrup with 5 parts water to make a drink that "replenishes vital bodily fluids following exertion."

At the start of April, there were 200,000 gallons in beginning Work in Process. The product was 100 percent complete with respect to material and 50 percent complete with respect to conversion costs. During April, 500,000 gallons were started. Of the 700,000 units to account for, 100,000 gallons remained in process at the end of April. These units were 100 percent complete with respect to material and 20 percent complete with respect to conversion costs; 300,000 gallons were completed during April and, unfortunately, 300,000 gallons were lost owing to worker error. The production process calls for sodium to be added at the start of the process. On two separate occasions, a new worker added too much sodium, and batches were ruined. The errors were not identified until the end of the production process when batches were tested for quality assurance. Needless to say, the worker was fired.

The controller of Western Beverage, Gunther Bergman, is considering two ways to treat the cost of the "lost" units. One approach is to "bury" the cost in the units completed and the units in process. This would result in cost of units completed of $1,669,000 and cost of ending Work in Process of $222,600 calculated as follows.

Approach No. 1

Tech-Tonic Sports Drink Syrup
Production Cost Report
April

Quantity Reconciliation	
Units in beginning WIP (100% material, 50% conversion costs)	200,000
Units started	500,000
Units to account for	700,000
Units completed	300,000
Units in ending WIP (100% material, 20% conversion costs)	100,000
Lost units	300,000
Units accounted for	700,000

Cost per Equivalent Unit Calculation

	Material	Labor	Overhead	Total
Cost				
Beginning WIP	$110,000	$ 50,000	$100,000	$ 260,000
Cost incurred during April	450,000	373,000	800,000	1,623,000
Total	$560,000	$423,000	$900,000	$1,883,000
Units				
Units completed	300,000	300,000	300,000	
Equivalent units, ending WIP	100,000	20,000	20,000	
Total	400,000	320,000	320,000	
Cost per equivalent unit	$1.40	$1.32	$2.81	$5.53

Cost Reconciliation

Total cost to account for		$1,883,000
Cost of completed units transferred to Finished Goods (300,000 × $5.53)		$1,659,000
Cost of ending WIP		
Material (100,000 equivalent units × $1.40)	$140,000	
Labor (20,000 equivalent units × $1.32)	26,400	
Overhead (20,000 equivalent units × $2.81)	56,200	222,600
		$1,881,600
Difference due to rounding		1,400
Total cost accounted for		$1,883,000

A second approach involves identifying the lost units for April. The result is a cost of units completed equal to $879,000, cost of Work in Process equal to $122,600, and cost of lost units equal to $879,000, which will be charged to Cost of Goods Sold.

Approach No. 2

Tech-Tonic Sports Drink Syrup
Production Cost Report
April

Quantity Reconciliation

Units in beginning WIP (100% material, 50% conversion costs)	200,000
Units started	500,000
Units to account for	700,000
Units completed	300,000
Units in ending WIP (100% material, 20% conversion costs)	100,000
Lost units	300,000
Units accounted for	700,000

Cost per Equivalent Unit Calculation

	Material	Labor	Overhead	Total
Cost				
Beginning WIP	$110,000	$ 50,000	$100,000	$ 260,000
Cost incurred during April	450,000	373,000	800,000	1,623,000
Total	$560,000	$423,000	$900,000	$1,883,000
Units				
Units completed	300,000	300,000	300,000	
Equivalent units, ending WIP	100,000	20,000	20,000	
Lost units	300,000	300,000	300,000	
Total	700,000	620,000	620,000	
Cost per equivalent unit	$0.80	$0.68	$1.45	$2.93

	Material	Labor	Overhead	Total
Cost Reconciliation				
Total cost to account for				$1,883,000
Cost of completed units transferred to Finished Goods (300,000 × $2.93)				879,000
Cost of lost units (300,000 × $2.93)				879,000
Cost of ending WIP				
Material (100,000 equivalent units × $0.80)			$80,000	
Labor (20,000 equivalent units × $0.68)			13,600	
Overhead (20,000 equivalent units × $1.45)			29,000	122,600
				$1,880,600
Difference due to rounding				2,400
Total cost accounted for				$1,883,000

REQUIRED

a. Assume that 80 percent of the units completed in April are sold in that month. What will be the difference in reported profit between the two approaches?

b. Which approach is most appropriate from a conceptual standpoint?

c. Senior managers at Western Beverage receive monthly bonuses determined as a percent of profit in excess of a targeted level of profit. Which method will they favor?

CASE

3-2 JENSEN PVC [LO 2]

Jensen PVC, Inc., produces polyvinyl chloride (PVC) irrigation pipes. In 2017, the cost of producing a foot of pipe was $0.30, and the selling price was $0.39 per foot. In 2018, production costs increased to $0.40 per foot, although the selling price remained at $0.39.

	2017	2018
Selling price	$0.39	$0.39
Production cost	0.30	0.40

The increase in cost was obvious. Material and labor had remained fairly constant per foot of pipe, but overhead costs, which were $0.15 per foot in 2017, had increased to $0.25 in 2018. The problem was that most overhead costs were fixed, but output had decreased due to weak crop prices and a corresponding decrease in spending on irrigation projects. Bob Elger, CFO of Jensen, reviewed the data generated by the company's process costing system.

In 2017, overhead costs in all of the company's departments (mixing, extrusion, cutting, and packing) were $1,500,000, and pipe production was 10,000,000 feet. In 2018, overhead costs were still approximately $1,500,000, but pipe production decreased to 6,000,000 feet. At a recent meeting of the senior management team, Bob noted: "The problem is that we're not making use of capacity. We could easily produce 15,000,000 feet of pipe given our state-of-the-art equipment, but we're operating at less than 50% of capacity."

REQUIRED

Bob estimates that to sell 15,000,000 feet of pipe in the current market, the company would have to lower its price to $0.35 per foot, which is even lower than its current cost per foot of $0.40. Would decreasing the price be a good decision?

4

COST-VOLUME-PROFIT ANALYSIS

Mary Stuart is the vice president of operations for CodeConnect, a company that manufactures and sells bar code readers.

As a senior manager, she must answer a variety of questions dealing with planning, control, and decision making. Consider the following questions that Mary has faced:

PLANNING. Last year, CodeConnect sold 20,000 bar code readers at $200 per unit. The cost of manufacturing these items was $2,940,000, and selling and administrative costs were $766,800. Total profit was $293,200. In the coming year, the company expects to sell 25,000 units. What level of profit should be in the budget for the coming year?

CONTROL. In April, production costs were $250,000. In May, costs increased to $260,000, but production also increased from 1,750 units in April to 2,000 units in May. Did the manager responsible for production costs do a good job of controlling costs in May?

DECISION MAKING. The current price for a bar code reader is $200 per unit. If the price is increased to $225 per unit, sales will drop from 20,000 to 17,000. Should the price be increased?

The answer to each of these questions depends on how costs and, therefore, profit change when volume changes. The analysis of how costs and profit change when volume changes is referred to as **cost-volume-profit (CVP) analysis.** In this chapter, we develop the tools to analyze cost-volume-profit relations. These tools will enable you to answer questions like the ones listed above—questions managers face on a daily basis.

Paul Bradbury/Getty Images

LEARNING OBJECTIVES

1 Identify common cost behavior patterns, and estimate the relation between cost and activity using account analysis and the high-low method.

2 Perform cost-volume-profit analysis for single and multiple products.

3 Discuss the effect of operating leverage, and use the contribution margin per unit of the constraint to analyze situations involving a resource constraint.

LEARNING OBJECTIVE 1

Identify common cost behavior patterns, and estimate the relation between cost and activity using account analysis and the high-low method.

COMMON COST BEHAVIOR PATTERNS

To perform cost-volume-profit (CVP) analysis, you need to know how costs behave when business activity (e.g., production volume and sales volume) changes. This section describes some common patterns of cost behavior. These patterns may not provide exact descriptions of how costs behave in response to changes in volume or activity, but they are generally reasonable approximations involving variable costs, fixed costs, mixed costs, and step costs.

Variable Costs

As mentioned in Chapter 1, **variable costs** are costs that change in proportion to changes in volume or activity. Thus, if activity increases by 10 percent, variable costs are assumed to increase by 10 percent. Some common variable costs are direct and indirect materials, direct labor, energy, and sales commissions.

Exactly how activity should be measured in analyzing a variable cost depends on the situation. At McDonald's restaurants, food costs vary with the number of customers served. At United Airlines, fuel costs vary with the number of miles flown. In these situations, number of customers and number of miles are good measures of activity.

Let's consider an example using CodeConnect, the company introduced in the beginning of the chapter. Suppose that CodeConnect has variable production costs equal to $91 per bar code reader. In this case, total variable cost at a production level of 1,000 units (the measure of activity) is equal to $91,000 ($91 × 1,000), while total variable cost at 2,000 units is equal to $182,000 ($91 × 2,000). A graph of the relation between total variable cost and production is provided in Illustration 4-1. The slope of the straight line in the figure measures the change in cost per unit change in activity. Note that while total variable cost increases with production, variable cost per unit remains at $91.

ILLUSTRATION 4-1

Variable cost behavior at CodeConnect

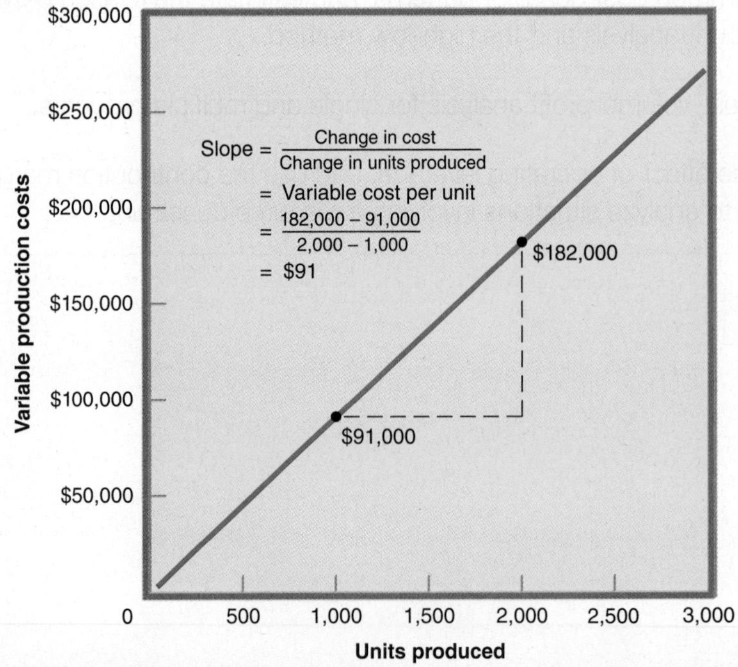

ILLUSTRATION 4-2
Fixed cost behavior at CodeConnect

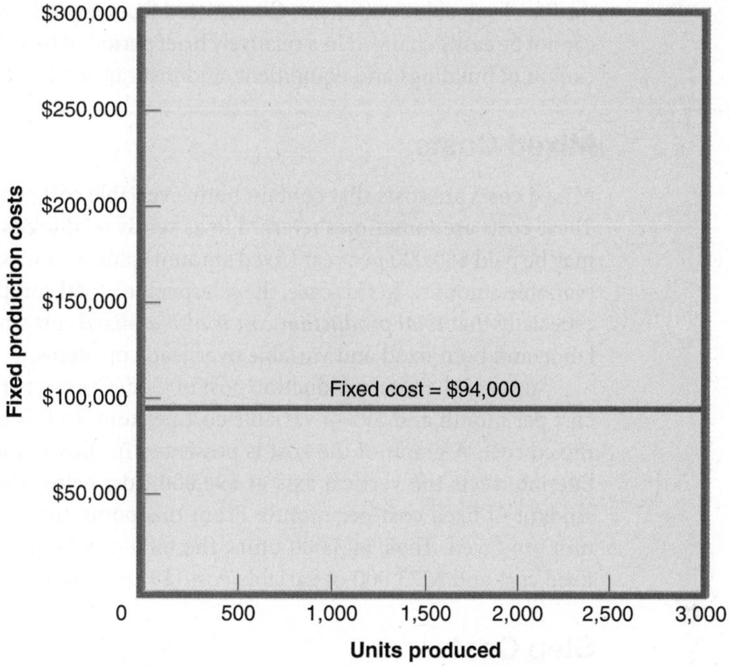

Fixed Costs

Recall from Chapter 1 that **fixed costs** are costs that do not change in response to changes in activity levels. Some typical fixed costs are depreciation, supervisory salaries, and building maintenance. Suppose that CodeConnect has $94,000 of fixed costs per month. A graph of the relation between the company's fixed cost and production is provided in Illustration 4-2. As you can see, whatever the number of units produced, the amount of total fixed cost remains at $94,000. However, the amount of fixed cost per unit does change with changes in the level of activity. When activity increases, the amount of fixed cost per unit decreases because the fixed cost is spread over more units. For example, at 1,000 units, the fixed cost per unit is $94 ($94,000 ÷ 1,000), whereas at 2,000 units, the fixed cost per unit is only $47 ($94,000 ÷ 2,000).

Discretionary versus Committed Fixed Costs. In the short run, some fixed costs can be changed while others cannot. **Discretionary fixed costs** are those fixed costs that management can easily change in the short run. Examples include advertising, research and development, and repair and maintenance costs. Some companies cut back on these expenditures when sales drop so that profit trends stay roughly constant. That, however, may be shortsighted since a cut in research and development can have a negative effect on long-run profitability, and a cut in repair and maintenance can have a negative effect on

LINK TO PRACTICE

Using Less Water but Paying Higher Rates!

As reported by the Associated Press, residents of Austin, Texas, are becoming victims of their own success at conserving water. Due to conservation efforts, the city's water utility had a $27 million loss in annual water sales. But less water use doesn't reduce the utility's fixed costs. Thus, the somewhat counterintuitive result is that the utility is now considering raising rates to cover its costs. To the rate-payers this must seem like another example of "no good deed goes unpunished!"

Source: Associated Press, February 25, 2014, kxan.com.

the life of valuable equipment. **Committed fixed costs**, however, are those fixed costs that cannot be easily changed in a relatively brief period of time. Such costs include rent, depreciation of buildings and equipment, and insurance related to buildings and equipment.

Mixed Costs

Mixed costs are costs that contain both a variable cost element and a fixed cost element. These costs are sometimes referred to as **semivariable costs**. For example, a salesperson may be paid $80,000 per year (fixed amount) plus commissions equal to 1 percent of sales (variable amount). In this case, the salesperson's total compensation is a mixed cost. Note especially that *total production cost is also a mixed cost* since it is composed of material, labor, and both fixed and variable overhead cost items.

Suppose the total production cost of CodeConnect is composed of $94,000 of fixed cost per month and $91 of variable cost per unit. In this case, total production cost is a mixed cost. A graph of the cost is presented in Illustration 4-3. Note that the total cost line intersects the vertical axis at $94,000 (just below the $100,000 point). This is the amount of fixed cost per month. From this point, total cost increases by $91 for every unit produced. Thus, at 3,000 units, the total cost is $367,000, composed of $94,000 of fixed cost and $273,000 of variable cost ($91 × 3,000).

Step Costs

Step costs are those costs that are fixed for a range of volume but increase to a higher level when the upper bound of the range is exceeded. At that point, the costs again remain fixed until another upper bound is exceeded. Step costs are often classified as either

ILLUSTRATION 4-3
Mixed cost behavior

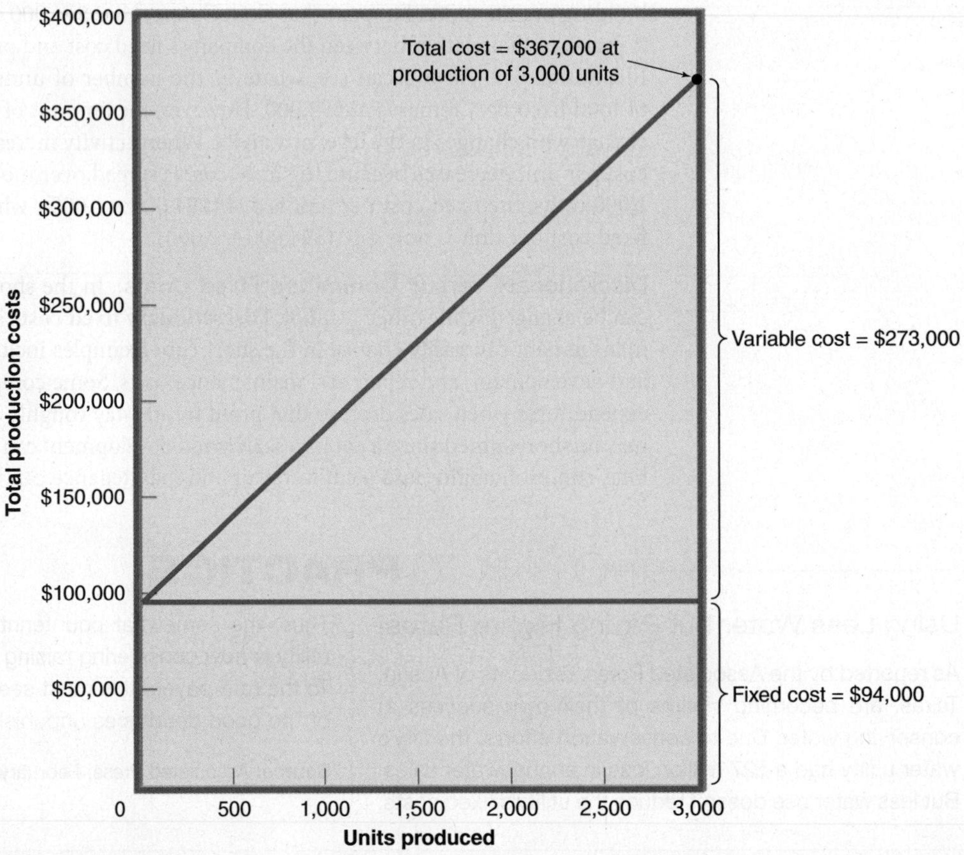

step variable costs or **step fixed costs**, depending on the range of activity for which the cost remains fixed. If the range is relatively small, the cost is considered to be a step variable cost. If the range is relatively large, the cost is considered to be a step fixed cost.

An example of a step variable cost at CodeConnect is the salary of individuals who test the bar code readers before they leave the factory. Testers are paid $4,000 per month, and each can test 300 units per month. A graph of this cost is presented in Illustration 4-4.

Given that the range of activity is relatively small before costs jump up to a higher level (i.e., the steps are small), step variable costs can often be well approximated as simply variable costs (i.e., costs that change in proportion to activity).

An example of a step fixed cost is the cost of plant supervisors. CodeConnect can produce up to 3,000 bar code readers using one supervisor whose monthly salary is $7,000. However, to produce 3,001 to 6,000 bar code readers, the company must add a second shift. Now, another supervisor is needed, bringing the total cost for plant supervisors to $14,000. To produce more than 6,000 bar code readers, the company must add a third shift and a third supervisor. Now supervisor salaries will increase to $21,000. A graph of this cost is presented in Illustration 4-5.

Note that the steps in Illustration 4-5 are much wider than those in Illustration 4-4. Given this, the cost is not close to being a variable cost.

Relevant Range

The **relevant range** is the range of activity for which cost behavior assumptions are reasonably valid. We might assume, for example, that plant supervisory salaries are fixed even though we know they are step costs. If production is only going to be between 3,001 and 6,000 units (the relevant range), then the assumption that supervisor salaries are fixed at $14,000 per month is valid. Making the assumption that the cost is fixed at $14,000 would, however, not be valid if we went above or below this range. See Illustration 4-6.

ILLUSTRATION 4-4

Testing as a step variable cost

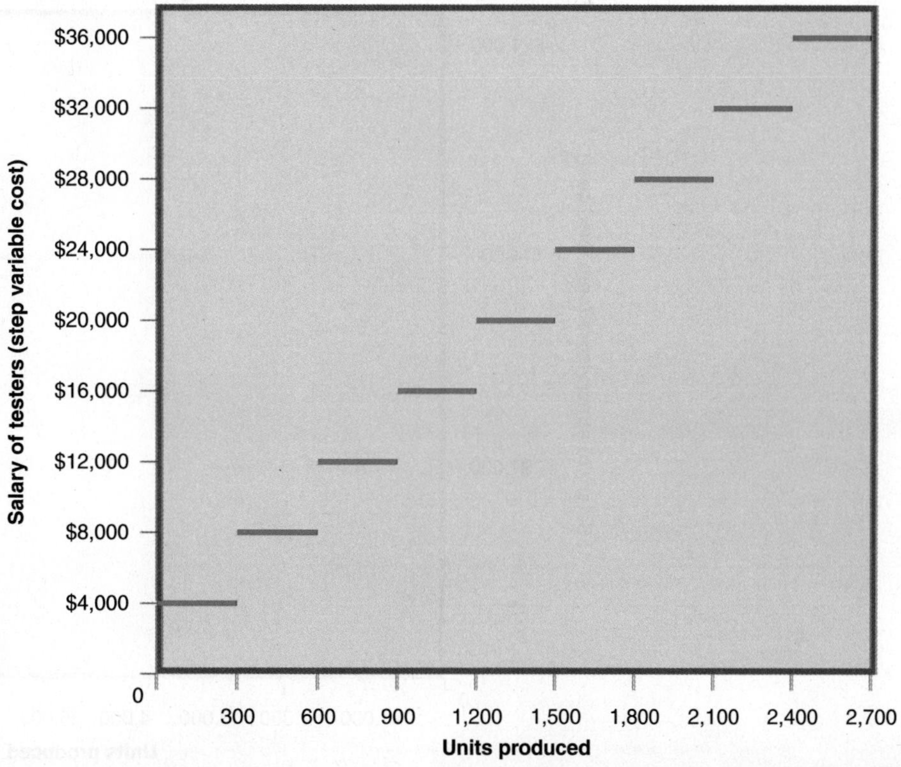

ILLUSTRATION 4-5
Salaries of plant supervisors (step fixed cost)

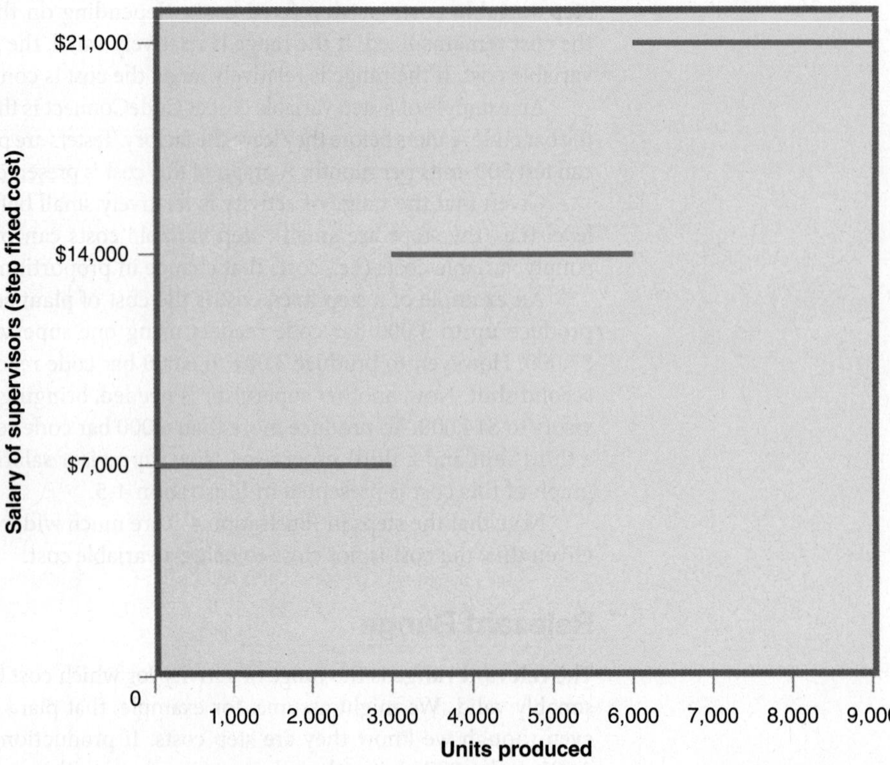

ILLUSTRATION 4-6
Relevant range

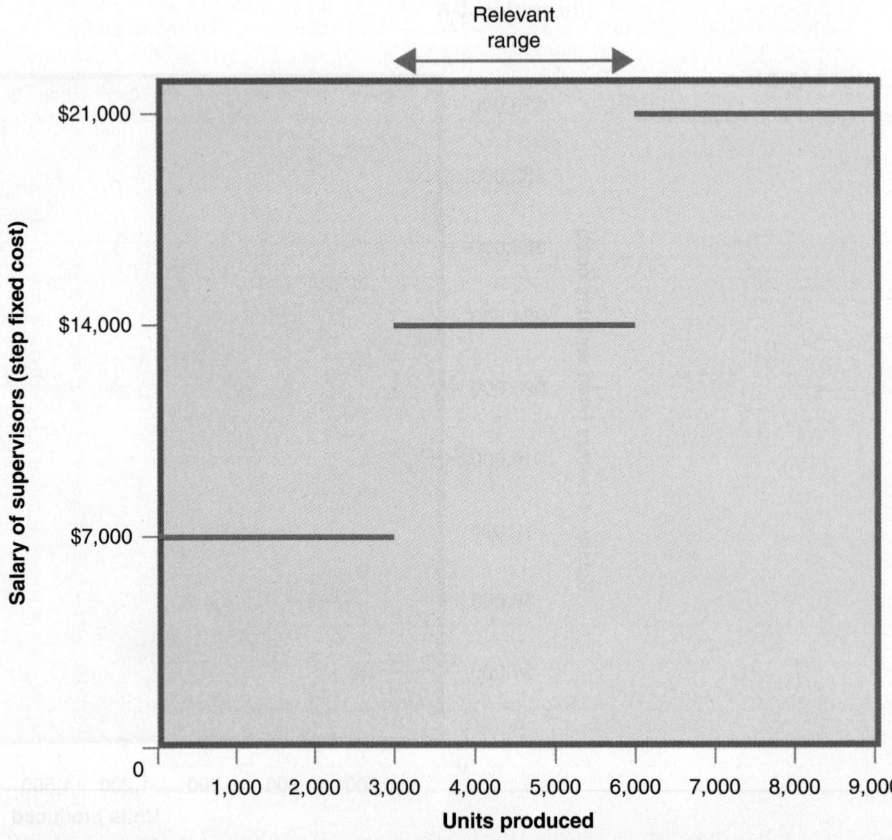

ANY QUESTIONS?

Q: Is direct labor always a variable cost?

A: While we typically think of labor as a variable cost, it could also be a fixed cost. In some countries, such as Japan and Korea, companies are very reluctant to lay off workers when business decreases, and they are hesitant to increase labor when demand increases. Thus, for many companies in Japan and Korea, labor is a fixed cost. In the United States, companies are more willing to hire and fire with fluctuations in demand, making labor more reasonably approximated as a variable cost. But some U.S. companies are so highly automated that they can accommodate wide fluctuations in volume with the same workforce, and for them, labor is more reasonably approximated as a fixed cost. To determine whether labor is variable or fixed for a particular company, you must analyze the unique situation facing the company. Also, keep in mind the notion of a relevant range. Within a particular range of activity, labor may be fixed, but it may jump to a higher level if the company exceeds the upper limit of the range.

COST ESTIMATION METHODS

In order to predict how much cost will be incurred at various activity levels (a critical part of CVP analysis), you must know how much of the total cost is fixed and how much is variable. In many cases, cost information is not broken out in terms of fixed and variable cost components; therefore, you must know how to estimate fixed and variable costs from available information. In this section, we cover three techniques for estimating the amount of fixed and variable cost: account analysis, the high-low method, and regression analysis.

Account Analysis

Account analysis is the most common approach to estimating fixed and variable costs. This method requires that a manager use professional judgment to classify costs as either fixed or variable. The total of the costs classified as variable can then be divided by a measure of activity to calculate the variable cost per unit of activity. The total of the costs classified as fixed provides the estimate of fixed cost.

To illustrate, let's return to the CodeConnect example. For the month of May, the cost of producing 2,000 units of the DX375 bar code reader was $265,000. Account analysis would require a detailed analysis of the accounts that comprise the $265,000 of production costs. Suppose the costs were as follows:

	MAY
Production in units	2,000
Production cost	
Component cost	$130,600
Assembly labor	32,400
Utilities	7,100
Rent	22,000
Depreciation of assembly equipment	72,900
Total production cost	$265,000

Using professional judgment, you may decide that component cost and assembly labor are variable costs and all other items are fixed costs. In this case, variable and fixed costs are estimated as in Illustration 4-7. Total production costs would be estimated as $102,000 of fixed cost per month plus $81.50 of variable cost for each unit produced.

ILLUSTRATION 4-7
Estimate of variable and fixed costs

Variable Cost Estimate

Component cost	$130,600	
Assembly labor	32,400	
Total	$163,000	(a)
Production	2,000	(b)
Variable cost per unit	$ 81.50	(a) ÷ (b)

Fixed Cost Estimate

Utilities	$ 7,100
Rent	22,000
Depreciation	72,900
Total per month	$102,000

Although Illustration 4-7 classifies each individual cost item as either 100 percent fixed or 100 percent variable, the account analysis method does not require that this be so. For example, there may be reason to believe that at least part of utilities is also variable. In this case, the manager can use his or her judgment to refine estimates using account analysis. Suppose the manager believes that approximately 50 percent of utilities are variable. As indicated in Illustration 4-8, the revised estimate of total variable cost would then amount to $166,550, or $83.28 per unit, whereas the revised estimate of fixed costs per month would amount to $98,450.

ILLUSTRATION 4-8
Revised estimate of variable and fixed costs

Variable Cost Estimate

Component cost	$130,600	
Assembly labor	32,400	
Utilities (50% of $7,100)	3,550	
Total	$166,550	(a)
Production	2,000	(b)
Variable cost per unit	$ 83.28	(a) ÷ (b)

Fixed Cost Estimate

Utilities (50% of $7,100)	$ 3,550
Rent	22,000
Depreciation	72,900
Total per month	$ 98,450

With these estimates we can project what costs will be at various levels of production. For example, how much cost can CodeConnect expect to incur if 2,500 units are produced? With 2,500 units, variable costs are estimated as $208,200 and fixed costs per month are estimated as $98,450. Therefore, total cost of $306,650 would be expected, as shown:

Expected Monthly Cost of 2,500 Units; DX375 Bar Code Reader	
Variable cost (2,500 × $83.28)	$208,200
Fixed cost per month	98,450
Total	$306,650

The account analysis method is subjective in that different managers viewing the same set of facts may reach different conclusions regarding which costs are fixed and which costs are variable. Despite this limitation, most managers consider it an important tool for estimating fixed and variable costs.

Scattergraphs

In some cases, you may have cost information from several reporting periods available in order to estimate how costs change in response to changes in activity. Weekly, monthly, or quarterly reports are particularly useful sources of cost information. In contrast, annual reports are not as useful because the relation between costs and activity is generally not consistent or stable over several years.

Suppose the monthly production and cost information provided in Illustration 4-9 is available for CodeConnect. We can gain insight into the relation between production cost and activity by plotting these costs and activity levels. The plot of the data is referred to as a **scattergraph**. The scattergraph for the data in Illustration 4-9 is presented in Illustration 4-10.

Typically, as in Illustration 4-10, scattergraphs are prepared with costs measured on the vertical axis and activity level measured on the horizontal axis. Each point on the scattergraph represents one pair of cost and activity values. The graphical features in spreadsheet programs such as Excel® make the preparation of a scattergraph very easy. Essentially, all you need to do is input the data, and then you can rely on the spreadsheet to plot it accurately.

The methods we use to estimate cost behavior assume that costs are linear. In other words, they assume that costs are well represented by straight lines. A scattergraph is useful in assessing whether this assumption is reasonable. The plot in Illustration 4-10 suggests that a linear approximation is quite reasonable since the data points line up in an approximately linear fashion. The scattergraph is also useful in assessing whether there are any outliers. Outliers are data points that are markedly at odds with the trend of other data points. Here there are no obvious outliers.

High-Low Method

With the same type of data as that described previously, we can estimate the fixed and variable components of cost at various activity levels using the **high-low method**. This

ILLUSTRATION 4-9
Monthly production cost information

Month	Production	Cost
January	750	$ 170,000
February	1,000	175,000
March	1,250	205,000
April	1,750	250,000
May	2,000	265,000
June	2,250	275,000
July	3,000	400,000
August	2,750	350,000
September	2,500	300,000
October	1,250	210,000
November	1,000	190,000
December	500	150,000
Total	20,000	$2,940,000

ILLUSTRATION 4-10
Scattergraph of cost and production information

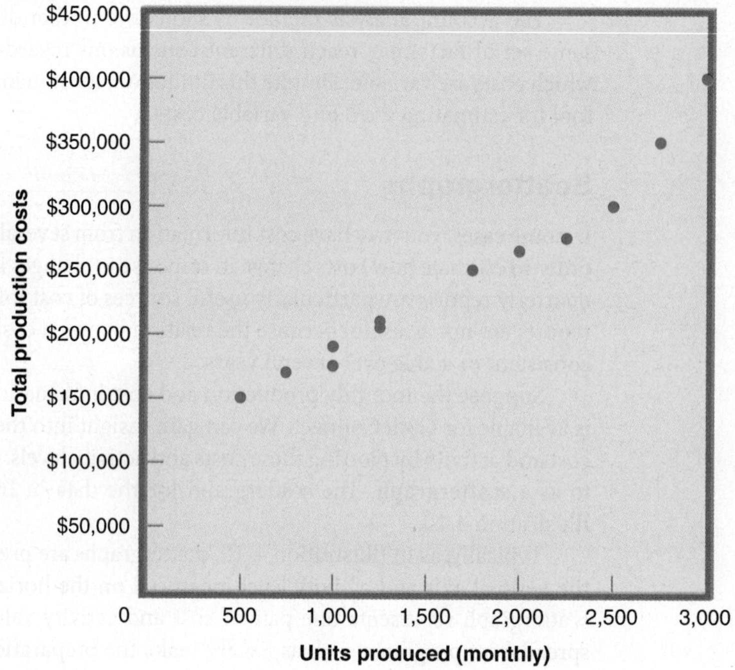

method fits a straight line to the data points representing the highest and lowest levels of activity. The slope of the line is the estimate of variable cost (because the slope measures the change in cost per unit change in activity), and the intercept (where the line meets the cost axis) is the estimate of fixed cost.

We'll use the data in Illustration 4-9 to describe the high-low method. Note in Illustration 4-9 that the highest level of activity is a production level of 3,000 units in July with a corresponding cost of $400,000. The lowest level of activity is a production level of 500 units in December with a corresponding cost of $150,000. Thus, a line connecting these points looks like the one in Illustration 4-11.

We can calculate the slope of the line in Illustration 4-11 fairly easily. The slope is equal to the change in cost divided by the change in activity. In moving from the lowest level of activity to the highest level of activity, the cost changes by $250,000 and activity changes by 2,500 units. Thus, the estimate of variable cost (the slope) is $100 per unit.

$$\text{Estimate of variable cost} = \frac{\text{Change in cost}}{\text{Change in activity}}$$

$$\text{Estimate of variable cost} = \frac{\text{Cost at highest level of activity} - \text{Cost at lowest level of activity}}{\text{Highest level of activity} - \text{Lowest level of activity}}$$

$$\text{Estimate of variable cost} = \frac{\$400{,}000 - \$150{,}000}{3{,}000 - 500}$$

$$\text{Estimate of variable cost} = \frac{\$250{,}000}{2{,}500} = \$100 \text{ per unit}$$

Once we obtain an estimate of variable cost, we can use it to calculate an estimate of fixed cost (the intercept of the line). The fixed cost equals the difference between total cost and estimated variable cost. For example, at the lowest level of activity (500 units), total cost

ILLUSTRATION 4-11

High-low estimate of production costs

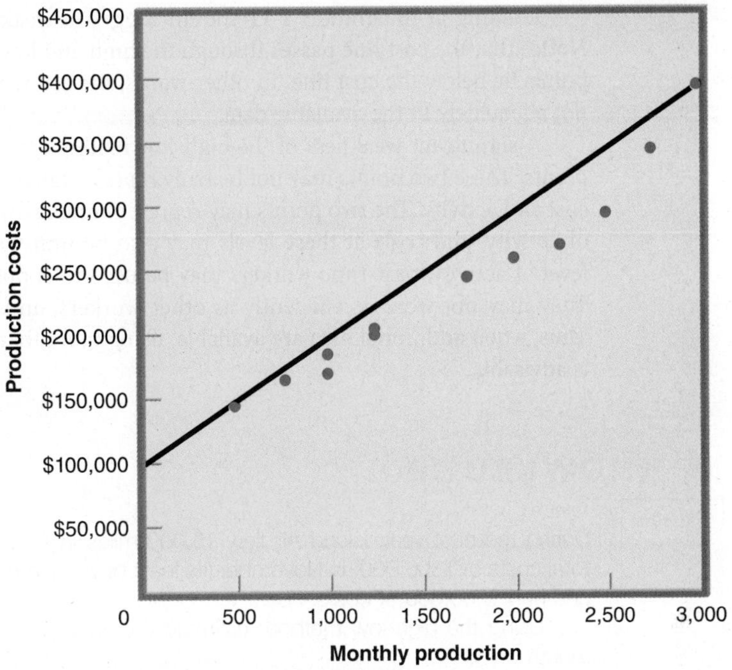

is $150,000. Since variable cost is $100 per unit, variable cost is $50,000 of the total cost. Thus, the remaining cost of $100,000 must be the amount of fixed cost. As indicated in the following calculation, we arrive at the same fixed cost amount ($100,000) whether we work with the lowest or the highest level of activity.

ESTIMATE USING LOWEST ACTIVITY		ESTIMATE USING HIGHEST ACTIVITY	
Total cost	$150,000	Total cost	$400,000
Less: Estimated variable cost (500 × $100)	50,000	Less: Estimated variable cost (3,000 × $100)	300,000
Estimated fixed cost per month	$100,000	Estimated fixed cost per month	$100,000

Be sure to note that because monthly data—the data from Illustration 4-9—are used in this example, the fixed costs calculated are the fixed costs *per month*. If annual data were used, the fixed costs calculated would be the fixed costs *per year*.

Refer to Illustration 4-11, which shows the high-low line for the cost and activity data from Illustration 4-9. We can describe the total cost at any point along this line by using the following equation:

$$\text{Total cost} = \text{Fixed cost} + (\text{Variable cost per unit} \times \text{Activity level in units})$$

Thus, we can use the equation to derive an estimate of total cost for a given activity level. For example, at an activity level of 1,500 units, we would estimate that $250,000 of cost would be incurred:

$$\begin{aligned}\text{Total cost} &= \$100{,}000 + (\$100 \times 1{,}500)\\ &= \$100{,}000 + \$150{,}000\\ &= \$250{,}000\end{aligned}$$

Looking at Illustration 4-11 should suggest a weakness of the high-low method. Notice that the cost line passes through the high and low data points but the other data points lie below the cost line. In other words, the estimate represented by the line does not adequately fit the available data.

A significant weakness of the high-low method, then, is that it uses only two data points. These two points may not be truly representative of the general relation between cost and activity. The two points may represent unusually high and unusually low levels of activity, and costs at these levels may also be unusual. For example, at the highest level of activity, part-time workers may be used to supplement the normal workforce. They may not work as efficiently as other workers, and costs may be unusually high. Thus, when additional data are available, using more than two data points for estimates is advisable.

TEST YOUR **KNOWLEDGE**

During the past year, Island Air flew 15,000 miles in August (its busiest month) and had total costs of $300,000. In November (its least busy month), the company flew 5,000 miles and had $200,000 of costs.

Using the high-low method, estimate the variable cost per mile and fixed cost per month.

a. $20 of variable cost per mile and $100,000 of fixed costs per month.
b. $15 of variable cost per mile and $250,000 of fixed costs per month.
c. $10 of variable cost per mile and $150,000 of fixed costs per month.
d. $5 of variable cost per mile and $250,000 of fixed costs per month.

Correct answer is c ($300,000 − $200,000) ÷ (15,000 − 5,000) = $10; FC = $200,000 − (5,000 × $10) = $150,000.

Regression Analysis

Regression analysis is a statistical technique that uses all the available data points to estimate the intercept and slope of a cost equation. The line fitted to the data by regression is the best straight-line fit to the data. Software programs to perform regression analysis are widely available and are included in spreadsheet programs like Excel. How to use Excel to conduct regression analysis is explained in the appendix to this chapter. The topic of regression analysis is covered in introductory statistics classes. For our purposes, we simply note that application of regression analysis to the data in Illustration 4-9 yields the following equation:

$$\text{Total cost} = \text{Fixed cost} + (\text{Variable cost per unit} \times \text{Activity level in units})$$
$$\text{Total cost} = \$93{,}619 + (\$90.83 \times \text{Activity level in units})$$

Thus, at a production level of 1,500 units, the amount of total cost estimated is $229,864:

$$\text{Total cost} = \$93{,}619 \text{ of fixed cost} + (\$90.83 \times 1{,}500)$$
$$= \$229{,}864$$

This is less than the $250,000 estimated using the high-low cost equation.

A graph of the regression analysis estimate of cost is presented in Illustration 4-12. Notice that the regression line fits the available data better than the line estimated

ILLUSTRATION 4-12
Regression analysis estimate of production cost

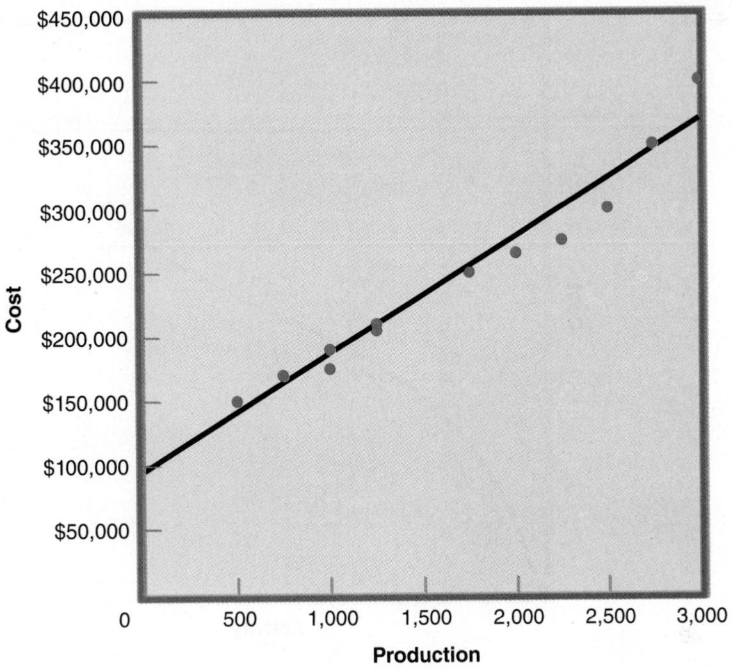

with the high-low method. Because the regression line is more consistent with the past data of the company, it probably will provide more accurate predictions of future costs.

The Relevant Range and Cost Estimation

When working with estimates of fixed and variable costs, remember that they are valid for only a limited range of activity which, you recall, we refer to as the relevant range. Outside the relevant range, the estimates of fixed and variable costs may not be very useful. Often managers are not confident using estimates of fixed and variable costs when called upon to make predictions for activity levels that have not been encountered in the past. Since the activity levels have not been encountered in the past, past relations between cost and activity may not be a useful basis for estimating costs in this situation. For example, a manager at CodeConnect may not feel confident using the regression estimates of $93,619 fixed cost and $90.83 variable cost per unit to estimate total cost for a production level of 4,000 units. As indicated in Illustration 4-9, the highest prior level of production was 3,000 units; thus, 4,000 units is outside the relevant range.

In some cases, actual costs behave in a manner that is different from the common cost behavior patterns that we have discussed. All of those patterns imply linear (straight-line) relations between cost and activity. In the real world, some costs are nonlinear. When companies produce unusually large quantities, for example, production may not be efficient, resulting in costs increasing more rapidly than the rate implied by a straight line. This may not be a serious limitation for a straight-line approach as long as the predictions and estimates are restricted to the relevant range. Consider Illustration 4-13. Note that although the relation between cost and activity is nonlinear, within the relevant range, a straight line would closely approximate the relation between cost and activity.

ILLUSTRATION 4-13
Relevant range

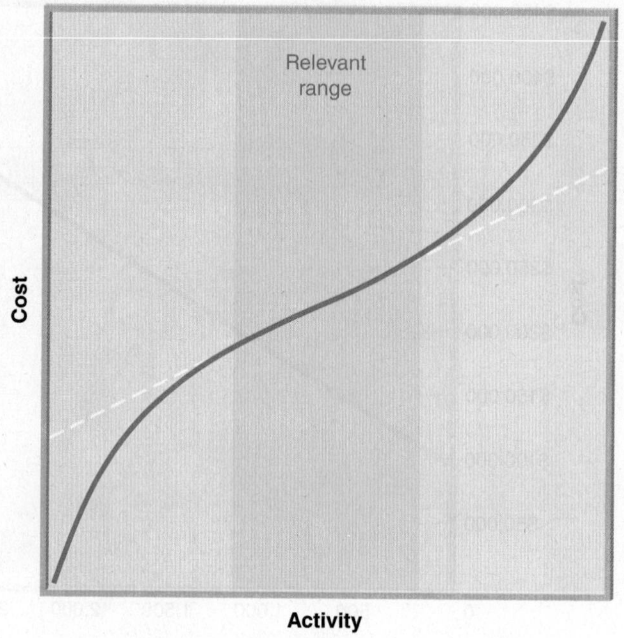

TEST YOUR **KNOWLEDGE**

Last month, Venture Trucking logged 80,000 miles delivering goods for various customers. Costs for the month were:

Fuel	$30,000
Maintenance	10,000
Tires	4,000
Driver salaries	60,000
Insurance	5,000
Depreciation	10,000
Office expenses	6,000
Permits	3,000

Fuel, maintenance, tires, and driver salaries are considered to be variable costs while all other costs are fixed. Using account analysis, what is variable cost per mile and fixed costs per month?

Based on this information, what is cost of goods sold?

a. Variable = $1.30 per mile; fixed = $24,000 per month.
b. Variable = $1.20 per mile; fixed = $24,000 per month.
c. Variable = $1.50 per mile; fixed = $22,000 per month.
d. Variable = $1.40 per mile; fixed = $20,000 per month.

Correct answer is a.

LEARNING OBJECTIVE 2

Perform cost-volume-profit analysis for single and multiple products.

COST-VOLUME-PROFIT ANALYSIS

Once fixed and variable costs have been estimated, **cost-volume-profit analysis (CVP)** can be conducted. Basically, CVP analysis is any analysis that explores the relation among costs, volume or activity levels, and profit.

The Profit Equation

Fundamental to CVP analysis is the profit equation. The **profit equation** states that profit is equal to revenue (selling price times quantity), minus variable cost (variable cost per unit times quantity), minus total fixed cost:

$$\textbf{Profit} = \textbf{SP}(x) - \textbf{VC}(x) - \textbf{TFC}$$

where

$$x = \text{Quantity of units produced and sold}$$
$$SP = \text{Selling price per unit}$$
$$VC = \text{Variable cost per unit}$$
$$TFC = \text{Total fixed cost}$$

Break-Even Point

One of the primary uses of CVP analysis is to calculate the break-even point. The **break-even point** is the number of units that must be sold for a company to break even—to neither earn a profit nor incur a loss. The break-even point is shown in the profit graph presented in Illustration 4-14. At the point where sales revenue equals total cost (composed of fixed and variable costs), the company breaks even.

To calculate the break-even point, we simply set the profit equation equal to zero, because by definition the break-even point is the point at which profit is zero. Then we insert the appropriate selling price, variable cost, and fixed cost information and solve for the quantity (x).

Let's consider an example. Mary Stuart, the VP of operations at CodeConnect, wants to know the break-even point for the company's model DX375 bar code reader. This will help her assess the possibility of incurring a loss for this product. Suppose CodeConnect sells this model for $200 per unit. Mary uses account analysis and estimates that variable production costs will be $81.50 per unit and fixed production costs

ILLUSTRATION 4-14

Profit graph and break-even point

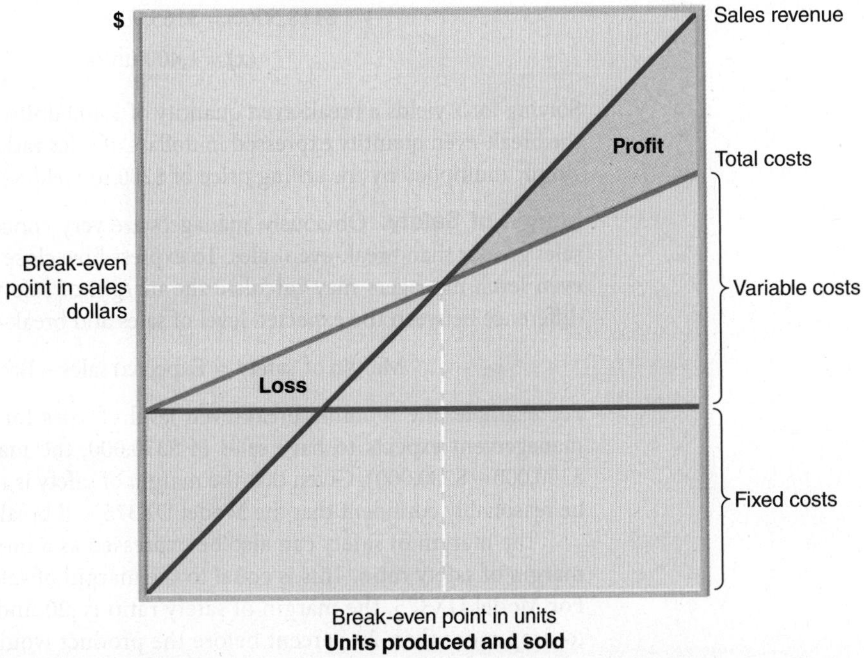

LINK TO PRACTICE

Breaking Even on a Golf Course Is Harder than Making Par

While most golfers dream of shooting a round of golf below par, many golf course administrators dream of a year when profit is above break-even. Making a profit on a golf course is a difficult business, and recent years have seen more course closures than openings. What can a manager do to increase the profitability of a golf course and ensure the break-even point is reached? The key, not surprisingly, is to increase the number of rounds played. Some ideas to increase rounds:

- Lower rates after 3 P.M.
- Offer frequent player discount cards.
- Offer a senior discount.
- Use course marshals to improve the pace of play and eliminate waiting between holes. (No one likes to wait!)
- Market to corporations that have golf outings.
- Develop a golf program for juniors.

will be $102,000 per month. There are also $63,900 of fixed selling and administrative costs each month. Thus, total fixed costs are $165,900.

Selling price per unit	$ 200.00
Variable cost per unit	81.50
Fixed production cost per month	$102,000.00
Fixed selling and administrative costs per month	63,900.00
Total fixed costs	$165,900.00

How many units must be sold to break even in a given month? To answer this question, we solve the profit equation for a particular value of x:

$$\text{Profit} = \text{SP}(x) - \text{VC}(x) - \text{TFC}$$
$$0 = \$200(x) - \$81.50(x) - \$165{,}900$$
$$\$118.50(x) = \$165{,}900$$
$$(x) = 1{,}400 \text{ units}$$

Solving for x yields a break-even quantity of 1,400 units. If management prefers to have the break-even quantity expressed in dollars of sales rather than in units, the quantity is simply multiplied by the selling price of $200 to yield $280,000.

Margin of Safety. Obviously, managers are very concerned that they have a level of sales greater than break-even sales. To express how close they expect to be to the break-even level, managers may calculate the margin of safety. The **margin of safety** is the difference between the expected level of sales and break-even sales:

$$\text{Margin of safety} = \text{Expected sales} - \text{Break-even sales}$$

For example, the monthly break-even level of sales for Model DX375 is $280,000. If management expects to have sales of $350,000, the margin of safety is $70,000 (i.e., $350,000 – $280,000). Given that the margin of safety is relatively high, Mary Stuart can be reasonably confident that the Model DX375 will break even.

The margin of safety can also be expressed as a ratio called, not surprisingly, the margin of safety ratio. This is equal to the margin of safety divided by expected sales. For Model DX375, the margin of safety ratio is .20, indicating that sales would have to drop more than 20 percent before the product would show a loss. Obviously, the higher the margin of safety ratio, the more likely that profit will exceed the break-even level.

$$\text{Margin of safety ratio} = \frac{\text{Margin of safety}}{\text{Expected sales}}$$

$$\text{Margin of safety ratio} = \frac{\$70{,}000}{\$350{,}000} = .20$$

Contribution Margin

The profit equation can be rewritten by combining the terms containing x in them to yield the **contribution margin** per unit—the difference between the selling price (SP) and variable cost per unit (VC).

$$\text{Profit} = \text{SP}(x) - \text{VC}(x) - \text{TFC}$$

$$\text{Profit} = (\text{SP} - \text{VC})(x) - \text{TFC}$$

$$\text{Profit} = \text{Contribution margin per unit}(x) - \text{TFC}$$

For CodeConnect's model DX375 bar code reader, the selling price is $200.00 and the variable cost is $81.50. Thus, the contribution margin is:

Selling price per unit	$200.00
Variable cost per unit	(81.50)
Contribution margin per unit	$118.50

The contribution margin per unit measures the amount of incremental profit generated by selling an additional unit. This may not be obvious at first glance, but consider what happens when sales and production increase by one unit. The firm benefits from revenue equal to the selling price, ($200.00) but it also incurs increased costs equal to the variable cost per unit ($81.50). Fixed costs are unaffected by changes in volume, so they do not affect the *incremental* profit associated with selling an additional unit. Thus, the net benefit of producing and selling an incremental unit is $118.50 (i.e., $200.00 – $81.50). Note that if we multiply the contribution margin per unit by the number of units sold, we obtain the incremental profit related to the units sold.

For example, suppose Mary Stuart wanted to know how much incremental profit would be generated by selling 100 more units. Multiplying the 100 units by the contribution margin per unit ($118.50) indicates that the total incremental profit would be $11,850:

Number of units sold	100.00
Contribution margin per unit	× $118.50
Incremental profit related to selling 100 units	$11,850

Units Needed to Achieve Profit Target. If we solve the profit equation for the sales quantity in units (x), we get a handy formula for calculating the break-even level of sales in units or for calculating the number of units needed to achieve a specified or target level of profit.

$$\text{Unit sales } (x) \text{ needed to attain specified profit} = \frac{\text{TFC} + \text{Profit}}{\text{SP} - \text{VC}}$$

$$\text{Unit sales } (x) \text{ needed to attain specified profit} = \frac{\text{TFC} + \text{Profit}}{\text{Contribution margin per unit}}$$

For CodeConnect, the amount of fixed cost is $165,900 per month. With a selling price of $200 and variable costs of $81.50, the contribution margin per unit is $118.50. Using the formula implies that 1,400 units must be sold to break even each month.

$$1{,}400 = \frac{\$165{,}900 + 0}{\$118.50} = \frac{\text{TFC} + \text{Profit}}{\text{Contribution margin per unit}}$$

Now suppose that the management of CodeConnect wants to know how many units must be sold to achieve a profit of $35,550 in a given month. Using the formula implies that 1,700 units must be sold to achieve a profit of $35,550:

$$1{,}700 = \frac{\$165{,}900 + \$35{,}550}{\$118.50}$$

Contribution Margin Ratio

The **contribution margin ratio** measures the amount of incremental profit generated by an additional dollar of sales. It is equal to the contribution margin per unit divided by the selling price:

$$\text{Contribution margin ratio} = \frac{\text{SP} - \text{VC}}{\text{SP}}$$

For the model DX375 bar code reader, the contribution margin ratio is:

$$\frac{\$200.00 - \$81.50}{\$200.00} = .5925$$

This indicates that the company earns an incremental $0.5925 for every dollar of sales. Thus, if Mary Stuart wanted to know how much incremental profit would be generated by have sales increase by $10,000, the answer to her question is easily obtained by multiplying the contribution margin ratio by sales, yielding $5,925:

$$.5925 \times \$10{,}000 = \$5{,}925$$

Dollar Sales Needed to Achieve Profit Target. We can also solve the profit equation to determine the dollar level of sales needed to break even or achieve a specified or target level of profit. The formula ends up being equal to profit plus fixed cost divided by the contribution margin ratio:

$$\text{Dollar sales needed to attain specified profit} = \frac{\text{TFC} + \text{Profit}}{\text{Contribution margin ratio}}$$

Recall that the contribution margin ratio tells us how much incremental profit we earn per dollar of sales. So if we divide this into the sum of profit plus fixed cost, we'll get the dollar level of sales needed to cover fixed costs and generate the specified profit.

Let's apply the formula to calculate the amount of sales dollars needed to earn a profit of $35,550 in a given month for CodeConnect. Its contribution margin ratio is .5925 (Contribution margin of $118.50 ÷ Selling price of $200). Thus, sales of $340,000 are needed:

$$\$340{,}000 = \frac{\$165{,}900 + \$35{,}550}{.5925}$$

"What If" Analysis

The profit equation also can show how profit will be affected by various options under consideration by management. Such analysis is sometimes referred to as **"what if" analysis** because it examines *what* will happen *if* a particular action is taken.

Change in Fixed and Variable Costs. Suppose CodeConnect is currently selling 3,000 units per month at a price of $200. Variable costs per unit are $81.50, and total fixed costs are $165,900 per month. Management is considering a change in the production process that will increase fixed costs per month by $50,000 to $215,900 but decrease variable costs to only $80 per unit. How would this change affect monthly profit? Using the profit equation, and assuming that there will be no change in the selling price or the quantity sold, profit under the alternative will be equal to $144,100:

$$\text{Profit} = \$200(3{,}000) - \$80(3{,}000) - \$215{,}900 = \$144{,}100$$

Without the change, profit will equal $189,600:

$$\text{Profit} = \$200(3{,}000) - \$81.50(3{,}000) - \$165{,}900 = \$189{,}600$$

The change in the production process would actually lower profit, so it appears not to be advisable.

Change in Selling Price. Any one of the variables in the profit equation can be considered in light of changes in the other variables. For example, suppose CodeConnect's management wants to know what the selling price would have to be to earn a profit of $200,000 if 3,000 units are sold in a given month. To answer this question, all of the relevant information is organized in terms of the profit equation, and then the equation is solved for the selling price:

$$\$200{,}000 = \text{SP}(3{,}000) - \$81.50(3{,}000) - \$165{,}900$$
$$\text{SP}(3{,}000) = \$610{,}400$$
$$\text{SP} = \$203.47$$

TEST YOUR KNOWLEDGE

Matthews Consulting charges $300 per hour. It has fixed costs of $600,000 per month and no variable costs. How many hours must the company work to earn a monthly profit of $900,000?

a. 5,000. b. 2,000. c. 3,000. d. 6,000.

Correct answer is a ($600,000 + $900,000)/$300.

MULTIPRODUCT ANALYSIS

The previous examples illustrate CVP analysis for a single product. But CVP analysis can be extended easily to cover multiple products. In the following sections, we examine the use of the contribution margin and the contribution margin ratio in performing CVP analysis for a company with multiple products.

Contribution Margin Approach

If the products a company sells are similar (e.g., various flavors of ice cream, various types of calculators, various models of similar boats), the weighted average contribution margin per unit can be used in CVP analysis. Let's consider a simple example. Suppose that Rohr Watch Company produces two model watches: Model A has an automatic movement and displays the date as well as time. Model B displays the date, time, and moon phase. Model A sells for $2,000 and requires $800 of variable cost per watch. Model B sells for $3,000 and requires $1,200 of variable cost per watch. Further, Rohr typically

ILLUSTRATION 4-15
Calculation of weighted average contribution margin per unit

Rohr Watch Company

	Contribution Margin Model A	Contribution Margin Model B
Selling price	$2,000	$3,000
Variable cost	800	1,200
Contribution margin	$1,200	$1,800

$$\text{Weighted average contribution margin per unit} = \frac{2(\$1{,}200) + 1(\$1{,}800)}{3}$$
$$= \$1{,}400 \text{ per unit}$$

sells two Model A watches for every Model B watch sold. To calculate the weighted average contribution margin per unit, the fact that twice as many A watches as B watches are sold must be taken into account. Since two Model A watches are sold for each Model B, the contribution margin of A is multiplied by 2 and the contribution margin of B is multiplied by 1. The sum is then divided by 3 to yield the weighted average contribution margin per unit of $1,400. (See Illustration 4-15.)

Now suppose the Rohr Watch Company has fixed costs equal to $3,500,000. How many watches must be sold for the company to break even? Working with the weighted average contribution margin, the break-even point is 2,500 watches.

$$\text{Break-even sales in units} = \frac{\text{Total fixed costs} + \text{Profit}}{\text{Weighted average contribution margin per unit}}$$

$$2{,}500 = \frac{\$3{,}500{,}000 + 0}{\$1{,}400}$$

These 2,500 units would be made up of the typical two-to-one mix. Thus, Rohr must sell 1,667 Model A's (two-thirds of 2,500) and 833 Model B's (one-third of 2,500) to break even.

Contribution Margin Ratio Approach

If the products that a company sells are substantially different, CVP analysis should be performed using the contribution margin ratio. Consider a large store like Walmart, which sells literally thousands of different products. In this setting, it does not make sense to ask how many *units* must be sold to break even or how many *units* must be sold to generate a profit of $100,000. Because the costs and selling prices of the various items sold are considerably different, analyzing these types of questions in terms of number of units is not useful. Instead, these questions are addressed in terms of sales dollars. It is perfectly reasonable to ask how much *sales* must be to break even or how much *sales* must be to generate a profit of $100,000. To answer these questions, the contribution margin ratio rather than the contribution margin per unit is used.

Suppose Gilbert and Gibbs, a store that sells outdoor living products, is interested in using CVP analysis to analyze its four product lines, which include garden tools, outdoor furniture, barbecues, and patio entertainment items such as glasses, plates, and outdoor lighting. The company is only 2 years old, and last year was the first time it performed an analysis of fixed and variable costs and product-line profitability. The resulting report is shown in Illustration 4-16.

ILLUSTRATION 4-16

Profitability analysis of product lines

Gilbert and Gibbs

	Garden Tools	Outdoor Furniture	Barbecues	Entertainment Items	Total
Sales	$950,000	$2,500,000	$1,400,000	$1,600,000	$6,450,000
Less variable costs:					
Cost of goods sold	665,000	1,800,000	910,000	640,000	4,015,000
Incentive compensation tied to sales	95,000	250,000	140,000	160,000	645,000
Miscellaneous variable costs	12,000	13,000	11,000	10,000	46,000
Total variable costs	772,000	2,063,000	1,061,000	810,000	4,706,000
Contribution margin	178,000	437,000	339,000	790,000	1,744,000
Contribution margin ratio	0.1874	0.1748	0.2421	0.4938	0.2704
Less direct fixed costs:					
Sales staff salaries	75,000	120,000	96,000	103,000	394,000
Product-line specific advertising	20,000	35,000	25,000	10,000	90,000
Total direct fixed costs	95,000	155,000	121,000	113,000	484,000
Product-line profit	$ 83,000	$ 282,000	$ 218,000	$ 677,000	$1,260,000
Less common fixed costs:					
Advertising					220,000
Utilities					35,000
Rent					185,000
Management salaries					625,000
Other common fixed costs					55,000
Total common fixed costs					1,120,000
Profit					$ 140,000

Let's review it. From sales of each product line, the company subtracts variable costs to identify the contribution margin. The contribution margin is then divided by sales to identify the contribution margin ratio. The same procedure can be followed to identify the contribution margin ratio for the entire company. Given the information in the report, what is the break-even level of sales for Gilbert and Gibbs?

To answer this question, the total amount of fixed costs is divided by the contribution margin ratio for the company. Total fixed costs are composed of the direct fixed costs associated with the four product lines plus the common fixed costs. Common fixed costs are related to resources that are shared but not directly traced to the product lines. Examples are advertising, utilities, and salaries of managers. Because the contribution margin of the company is .2704 and total fixed costs are $1,604,000 ($484,000 of direct fixed costs and $1,120,000 of common fixed costs), the break-even level of sales is $5,931,953:

$$\text{Break-even sales} = \frac{\text{Total fixed costs}}{\text{Contribution margin ratio}}$$

$$\text{Break-even sales} = \frac{\$1{,}604{,}000}{.2704} = \$5{,}931{,}953$$

We can also easily calculate the break-even point for the various product lines. For example, the break-even level of sales for garden tools is \$506,937:

$$\text{Break-even sales} = \frac{\$95{,}000}{.1874} = \$506{,}937$$

Note that when we calculate the break-even level of sales for garden tools, we only consider the direct fixed costs related to this product line (\$95,000) since the common fixed costs cannot be directly traced to it or any other product line.

The contribution margin ratio can also be used to analyze the effect on income of a change in total company sales. Suppose in the coming year, management believes that total company sales will increase by 20 percent and is interested in assessing the effect of this increase in overall company profitability. A 20 percent increase in sales is \$1,290,000. The weighted average contribution margin ratio of .2704 indicates that the company generates \$0.2704 of incremental profit on each dollar of sales. Thus, income will increase by \$348,816:

$$.2704 \times \$1{,}290{,}000 = \$348{,}816$$

Note that this approach makes one very important assumption: When overall sales increase, sales of garden tools, outdoor furniture, barbecues, and entertainment items will increase in the same proportion as the current mix. If this assumption is not warranted, then the contribution margin ratios of the four product lines must be weighted by their share of the increase. For example, suppose the company believes sales will increase by \$1,290,000 but expects the increase will be made up of a \$258,000 increase in garden tools, a \$387,000 increase in outdoor furniture, a \$516,000 increase in barbecues, and a \$129,000 increase in entertainment items. To calculate the effect on profit, the contribution margin ratios of the specific product lines must be used. The expected increase in profit is \$304,621.

Product Line	**Increase in Sales**	**Contribution Margin Ratio**	**Increase in Profit**
Garden Tools	\$ 258,000	0.1874	\$ 48,349
Outdoor Furniture	387,000	0.1748	67,648
Barbecues	516,000	0.2421	124,924
Entertainment Items	129,000	0.4938	63,700
	\$1,290,000		\$304,621

Why did this analysis yield a smaller increase in profit compared to the preceding analysis? The preceding analysis assumed the increase in sales would be proportionate to the current mix of product-line sales (\$6,450,000 × .20). With the current mix, entertainment items make up approximately 25 percent of sales. Now we are assuming that entertainment items are only 10 percent of sales (\$129,000 ÷ \$1,290,000), so relatively less is being sold of the product line with the highest contribution margin ratio. If relatively less of this high-margin line is sold, profit will be less.

Decision Making/ Incremental Analysis

Before leaving the Gilbert and Gibbs example, let's see how the contribution margin ratio can help a manager make decisions that increase company profit. Suppose Sarah Williams, the store manager, is considering ways to increase profit in the coming year. Which product line do you think she should emphasize? As indicated in Illustration 4-16, entertainment items have the highest contribution margin ratio. For this product line, the company earns $0.49 on every dollar of sales. The next highest line is barbecues, which earns only $0.24 on a dollar of sales. The contribution margin ratio tells us that if we can get a dollar of incremental sales by emphasizing a product, we definitely want to emphasize entertainment items. But what does it mean to "emphasize" a product? A critical aspect in retail is the positioning of products within the store, and the prime area is usually near the entrance. Because many shoppers don't make it halfway through the store, Sarah needs to place the entertainment items where they will be seen. Also, she may want to spend relatively more money making the display of entertainment items particularly attractive. Remember, she makes almost 50 cents on each dollar of sales for this product line.

YOU GET WHAT YOU MEASURE

If you refer to Illustration 4-16, you will see that under each product line, there is an expense for incentive compensation equal to 10 percent of sales. This is the incentive compensation paid to the sales people in the product-line departments. Obviously, this incentive encourages them to provide good service to customers and generate sales in their respective departments. Sarah Williams, the store manager, currently does not receive incentive compensation, but the owner of the company is considering such an arrangement. Do you think Sarah's incentive compensation should be tied to sales or to the contribution margin?

Any answer to this question is bound to be subjective, but a good case can be made for measuring and compensating Sarah's performance based on the total contribution margin generated by the store. We don't want Sarah to get overly focused on sales, since all sales dollars are not equal. Sales of entertainment items generate more profit per dollar of sales than all other product lines, and sales of outdoor furniture generate less profit per dollar of sales than all other product lines. If Sarah is evaluated with respect to the contribution margin, she will pay close attention to how much contribution margin is generated and come up with ideas to increase this measure. That's exactly what the owner of Gilbert and Gibbs would want Sarah to do.

TEST YOUR KNOWLEDGE

Refer to the information in Illustration 4-16. What level of sales is needed to generate a profit of $288,800 across the four product lines?

a. $6,000,000. b. $6,500,000. c. $7,000,000. d. $7,500,000.

Correct answer is c ($484,000 + $1,120,000 + $288,800) ÷ .2704.

ASSUMPTIONS IN CVP ANALYSIS

Whenever CVP analysis is performed, a number of assumptions are made that affect the validity of the analysis. Perhaps the primary assumption is that costs can be accurately separated into their fixed and variable components. In some companies, this is a very difficult and costly task. A further assumption is that the fixed costs remain fixed and the variable costs per unit do not change over the activity levels of interest. With large changes in activity, this assumption may not be valid. When performing multiproduct CVP analysis, an important assumption is that the mix remains constant. In spite of these assumptions, most managers find CVP analysis to be a useful tool for exploring various profit targets and for performing "what if" analysis.

LINK TO PRACTICE

Deciding to Use the Contribution Margin per Unit or the Contribution Margin Ratio

Baskin-Robbins

At an ice cream company like Baskin-Robbins, it is very reasonable for managers to use either the weighted average contribution margin per unit or the weighted average contribution margin ratio in CVP analysis. For example, a manager might want to know the effect on profit of a 1,000,000-gallon increase in sales. Assuming the weighted average contribution margin is $5 per gallon, profit is expected to increase by $5,000,000. A manager might also want to know the effect on profit of a $1,000,000 increase in sales. Assuming a weighted average contribution margin ratio of $0.30, profit is expected to increase by $300,000.

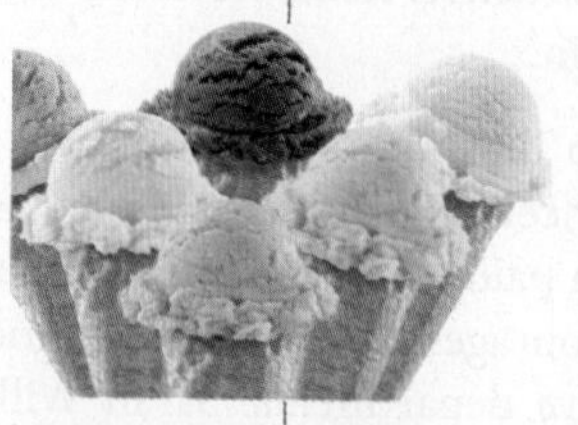

istockphoto/Getty Images, Inc.

Sears

A manager of a Sears store would focus on the weighted average contribution margin ratio, not the weighted average contribution margin per unit. Unlike the units at an ice cream store, the various units at a Sears store are quite different. It doesn't make sense to use a weighted average contribution margin *per unit* when the units are as diverse as refrigerators and shirts. Instead, a manager of a Sears store will focus on the weighted average contribution margin ratio. It would be reasonable for a manager at Sears to ask, "What is the weighted average contribution margin ratio for our store?" and use that number to estimate the increase in profit if the store can increase sales by $20,000,000. Assuming the contribution margin ratio is .20, the expected increase would be $4,000,000.

CODECONNECT EXAMPLE REVISITED: ANSWERING MARY'S QUESTIONS

Recall that at the beginning of the chapter, Mary Stuart of CodeConnect was faced with several questions related to planning, control, and decision making. Let's go back to these questions and make sure we can answer them.

Planning. Last year, CodeConnect sold 20,000 bar code readers at $200 per unit. The cost of manufacturing these items was $2,940,000, and selling and administrative costs were $766,800. Total profit was $293,200. In the coming year, the company expects to sell 25,000 units. What level of profit should be in the budget for the coming year?

Assume that the $2,940,000 of production costs consist of variable production costs of $81.50 per unit and fixed production costs of $1,224,000 per year. Further, assume that all selling and administrative costs are fixed and equal to $766,800 per year. In this case, expected profit is $805,822.

$$\text{Selling price}(x) - \text{Variable cost}(x) - \text{Fixed production costs}$$
$$- \text{Fixed selling and administration costs} = \text{Profit}$$
$$\$200(25{,}000) - \$81.50(25{,}000) - \$1{,}224{,}000 - \$766{,}800 = \$971{,}700$$

Control. In April, production costs were $250,000. In May, costs increased to $260,000, but production also increased from 1,750 units in April to 2,000 units in May. Did the manager responsible for product costs do a good job of controlling costs in May?

LINK TO PRACTICE

Which Firm Has the Higher Contribution Margin Ratio?

The following list identifies six pairs of firms with different contribution margin ratios (contribution margin per dollar of sales). For each pair, identify the firm with the higher contribution margin ratio.

Companies

McDonald's versus United Airlines
Ford Motor Company versus Kroger (a large grocery chain)
Oracle (a large software company) versus Sears
Nordstorm (a chain of clothing stores) versus E*Trade (an online brokerage firm)
Coca-Cola versus Walmart

Answer: United Airlines; Ford Motor Company; Oracle; E*Trade; Coca-Cola

Assume that production costs are estimated to be $81.50 per unit of variable cost and $102,000 of fixed costs per month. Then, the expected cost for producing 2,000 bar code readers is $265,000:

$$\text{Variable cost}(x) + \text{Fixed cost} = \text{Total cost}$$
$$\$81.50(2{,}000) + \$102{,}000 = \$265{,}000$$

Because actual costs are slightly less than expected costs, it appears (based on this limited analysis) that the manager responsible for product costs has done a reasonable job of controlling them.

Decision Making/ Incremental Analysis

Decision Making. The current price for a bar code reader is $200 per unit. If the price is increased to $225 per unit, sales will drop from 20,000 to 17,000. Should the price be increased?

Before answering this question, recall an idea we discussed in Chapter 1: All decisions rely on incremental analysis. For the pricing decision, we can perform an incremental analysis using the contribution margin. Currently, the contribution margin per unit is $118.50 (i.e., $200 – $81.50). Thus, the *total* contribution margin is 20,000 units times $118.50, which equals $2,370,000. If the selling price increases to $225, the contribution margin per unit will increase to $143.50 (i.e., $225 – $81.50). Thus, the *total* contribution margin will increase to $143.50 times 17,000 units, which is $2,439,500. The increase suggests that increasing the selling price is warranted although the effect on profit will be relatively minor. Why aren't fixed costs considered in this analysis? The fixed costs in this decision don't enter into the analysis because they are not incremental costs. Irrespective of the price, the company will have the same level of fixed costs.

Incremental Analysis

Total contribution margin	=	(Selling price – Variable cost)	× Number of units
$2,370,000	=	($200 – $81.50)	× 20,000 Original price of $200
$2,439,500	=	($225 – $81.50)	× 17,000 New price of $225
$ 69,500	= Incremental profit with new price		

LEARNING OBJECTIVE 3

Discuss the effect of operating leverage, and use the contribution margin per unit of the constraint to analyze situations involving a resource constraint.

OPERATING LEVERAGE

We will cover two additional topics before concluding our discussion of CVP analysis. First, we'll discuss the concept of operating leverage, and then we'll address constraints on output. **Operating leverage** relates to the level of fixed versus variable costs in a firm's cost structure. Firms that have relatively high levels of fixed costs are said to have high operating leverage. To some extent, firms can control their level of operating leverage. For example, a firm can invest in an automated production system using robotics, thus increasing its fixed costs while reducing labor, which is a variable cost. The level of operating leverage is important because it affects the change in profit when sales change. Consider two firms with the same level of profit but different mixes of fixed and variable cost:

	FIRM 1	FIRM 2
Sales	$10,000,000	$10,000,000
Variable cost	5,000,000	7,000,000
Contribution margin	5,000,000	3,000,000
Fixed costs	3,000,000	1,000,000
Profit	$ 2,000,000	$ 2,000,000

Suppose there is a 20 percent increase in sales. Which firm will have the greatest increase in profit? If Firm 1 has a 20 percent increase in sales, its profit will increase by $1,000,000 (i.e., 20% × the contribution margin), which represents a 50 percent increase in profit. Firm 2, however, will have a profit increase of only $600,000, or 30 percent. Now suppose there is a 20 percent decrease in sales. Which firm will have the greatest decrease in profit? Again, the answer is Firm 1. This is because it has relatively more fixed costs (higher operating leverage).

Firms that have high operating leverage are generally thought to be more risky because they tend to have large fluctuations in profit when sales fluctuate. However, suppose you are very confident that your firm's sales are going to increase. In that case you would want high operating leverage because the large positive fluctuation in sales will lead to a large positive fluctuation in profit. Unfortunately, many, if not most, managers are not highly confident that their firm's sales will only increase!

A final point on operating leverage: Because of fixed costs in the cost structure, when sales increase by 10 percent, profit will increase by more than 10 percent. The only

LINK TO PRACTICE

Impact of Operating Leverage at Vulcan Materials

Vulcan Materials is the largest producer of construction aggregates (crushed stone, sand, and gravel) in the U.S. Because of its reliance on heavy equipment, the company has significant operating leverage. Thus, when sales increase, profit is likely to increase at a higher rate.

Sales increased from $2.41 billion in 2012 to $2.63 billion in 2013—an increase of 9 percent. Gross profit, however, went from $334.0 million in 2012 to $426.9 million in 2013—an increase of 28 percent! It's important to remember that for firms that have high operating leverage, while profit may increase dramatically when sales increase, it is also the case that profit may decrease dramatically if sales decline.

LINK TO PRACTICE

Fixed Costs Too High—Make Them Variable!

A company with high fixed costs is risky. If its sales decline, profit will take a big hit. Firms, however, can take steps to reduce their fixed costs. In fact, they may be able to turn fixed costs into variable costs. Two strategies for doing this are incentive compensation and outsourcing:

1. Offer employees incentive compensation in lieu of a higher base. Suppose a senior sales executive makes $200,000 in annual base salary. That's a fixed cost. But suppose you could get the executive to accept a base salary of $100,000 and, in addition, receive incentive compensation equal to 1 percent of her sales. If sales go up, you pay her more. If sales go down, you pay her less. Now compensation that was fixed is at least partially variable.
2. Many companies outsource activities such as payroll processing and customer call center services, to turn fixed costs into variable costs. For example, much of the cost of processing payroll transactions is fixed (e.g., fixed wages, depreciation of office equipment and furniture, etc.). But if payroll is outsourced, a company may pay a fee based on the number of payroll transactions. So with outsourcing, the fixed costs become variable.

time that you expect profit to increase by the same percent as sales is when all costs are variable. If all costs vary in proportion to sales (i.e., all costs are variable), then profit will vary in proportion to sales.

CONSTRAINTS

In many cases (e.g., owing to shortages of space, equipment, or labor), there are constraints on how many items can be produced or how much service can be provided. Under such constraints, the focus shifts from the *contribution margin per unit* to the *contribution margin per unit of the constraint*. For example, suppose a company can produce either Product A or Product B using the same equipment. The contribution margin of A is $200, whereas the contribution margin of B is only $100. However, there are only 1,000 machine hours available, and Product A requires 10 hours of machine time to produce one unit while Product B requires only 2 hours per unit. In this simplified case, the company would only produce Product B. Although its contribution margin is smaller ($100 versus $200), it contributes $50 per machine hour, whereas Product A contributes only $20 per machine hour. In total, with 1,000 available machine hours, Product A can generate $20,000 of contribution margin while B can generate $50,000 of contribution margin.

	PRODUCT A	PRODUCT B
Selling price	$500	$300
Variable cost	300	200
Contribution margin	$200	$100
Time to produce 1 unit	10 hours	2 hours
Contribution margin per hour	$20	$50
Contribution margin given 1,000 available hours	$20,000	$50,000

Decision Making INSIGHT

In the chapter, we learned how to estimate fixed and variable costs using account analysis, the high-low method, and regression analysis. (This latter method is covered in the appendix.) All of these methods make the assumption that prior costs are good predictors of future costs. However, decisions that involve significant increases in sales or production may cause prior "fixed" costs to jump to a higher level. This might be due, for example, to the need to hire an additional supervisor.

SUMMARY OF LEARNING OBJECTIVES

LEARNING OBJECTIVE 1 Identify common cost behavior patterns and estimate the relation between cost and activity using account analysis and the high-low method.

Common cost behavior patterns include those involving variable, fixed, mixed, and step costs. Variable costs are costs that change in proportion to changes in volume or activity. Fixed costs are constant across activity levels. Mixed costs contain both a variable cost component and a fixed cost component. Step costs are fixed for a range of volume but increase to a higher level when the upper bound of the range is exceeded.

Managers use account analysis, the high-low method, and regression analysis to estimate the relation between cost and activity. Account analysis requires that the manager use his or her judgment to classify costs as either fixed or variable. The high-low method fits a straight line to the costs at the highest and the lowest activity levels. Regression analysis provides the best straight-line fit to prior cost/activity data.

LEARNING OBJECTIVE 2 Perform cost-volume-profit analysis for single and multiple products.

Once fixed and variable costs have been estimated, cost-volume-profit analysis can be performed. CVP analysis makes use of the profit equation:

$$\text{Profit} = \text{SP}(x) - \text{VC}(x) - \text{TFC}$$

to perform "what if" analysis. The effect of changing various components of the equation can be explored by solving the equation for the variable affected by the change. Specific examples include solving for the break-even point or solving the equation to determine the level of volume required to achieve a certain level of profit. The number of units that must be sold or the sales dollars needed to achieve a specified profit level can be determined using the following formulas:

$$\text{Number of units} = \frac{\text{Fixed cost} + \text{Profit}}{\text{Contribution margin}}$$

$$\text{Sales dollars} = \frac{\text{Fixed cost} + \text{Profit}}{\text{Contribution margin ratio}}$$

The case of multiple products is easily addressed by using the weighted average contribution margin per unit or the weighted average contribution margin ratio.

LEARNING OBJECTIVE 3 Discuss the effect of operating leverage and use the contribution margin per unit of the constraint to analyze situations involving a resource constraint.

Operating leverage relates to the level of fixed versus variable costs in a company's cost structure. The higher the level of fixed costs, the greater the operating leverage. Also, the higher the operating leverage, the greater the percentage change in profit for a given percentage change in sales. Firms with high operating leverage are generally considered to be more risky than firms with low operating leverage.

When there is a constraint, the focus shifts from the contribution margin per unit to the contribution margin per unit of the constraint. The product that has the highest contribution margin per unit of the constraint should be produced because it will generate the greatest contribution to covering fixed costs and generating a profit.

APPENDIX

USING REGRESSION IN EXCEL TO ESTIMATE FIXED AND VARIABLE COSTS

In this appendix, we will see how to use the Regression function in Excel to estimate fixed and variable costs using the data for CodeConnect presented in Illustration 4-9. As you will see, the spreadsheet program makes *performing* regression analysis very easy. However, it doesn't make *understanding* regression analysis easy! While we will discuss the interpretation of the output of the regression program, it would be wise to consult the treatment of regression analysis in an introductory statistics book before doing any real-world analysis.

Setting Up the Spreadsheet

Open a spreadsheet and enter the cost and production data from Illustration 4-7 in columns A and B. (See Illustration A4-1.) Now click on the data tab and then click on Data Analysis. From Data Analysis, select Regression. (*Note:* If you do not see Data Analysis in the data tab, click on Add-Ins and install the Analysis ToolPak.)

ILLUSTRATION A4-1

Selecting the regression function

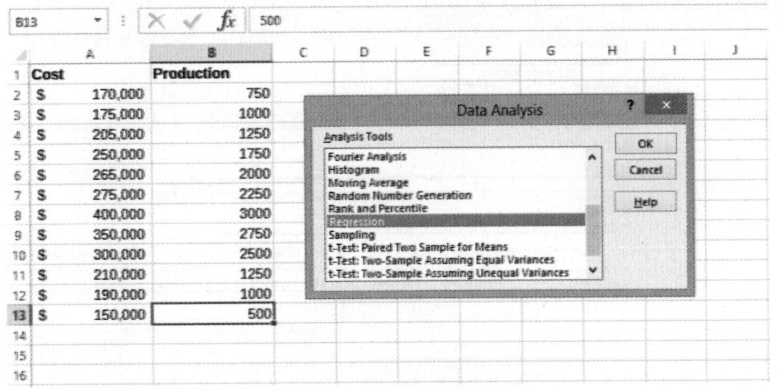

Once the Regression program opens, under *Input Y*, scroll down from A1 to A13. Note that this includes the heading "Cost." Under *Input X*, scroll down from B1 to B13. Note that this includes the heading "Production." Click Labels, which indicates that you have labels for Production and Cost data columns.

Under *Output Options*, click New Worksheet and give the worksheet a name. Under *Residuals*, click Line Fit Plot. This indicates that you want a plot of the data and the regression line. At this point your spreadsheet should look like the one in Illustration A4-2. Now click OK, and the Regression program will yield the output presented in Illustration A4-3.

Interpreting the Output of the Regression Program

Let's interpret the most critical elements of the regression output.

The Plot. The plot of the data and the plot of the regression line indicate that the data line up quite close to the regression line. This suggests that a straight-line fit to the data will be quite successful.

R Square. R Square is a statistical measure of how well the regression line fits the data. Specifically, it measures the percent of variance in the dependent variable (cost in the current case) explained by the independent variable (production). R Square ranges from a low of 0, indicating that there is no linear relation between cost and production, to a high of 1, indicating that there is a perfect linear relation between cost and production. In the current case, R Square is .96, which is quite high. This reinforces our conclusion from looking at the plot of the data and the plot of the regression line that there is a strong linear relation between cost and production.

Intercept and Slope of the Regression Line. The intercept of the regression line is interpreted as the estimate of fixed cost while the slope of the regression line is interpreted as the variable cost per unit. The output from the regression indicates that the intercept is $93,618.78

ILLUSTRATION A4-2

Input cost and production values in the regression program

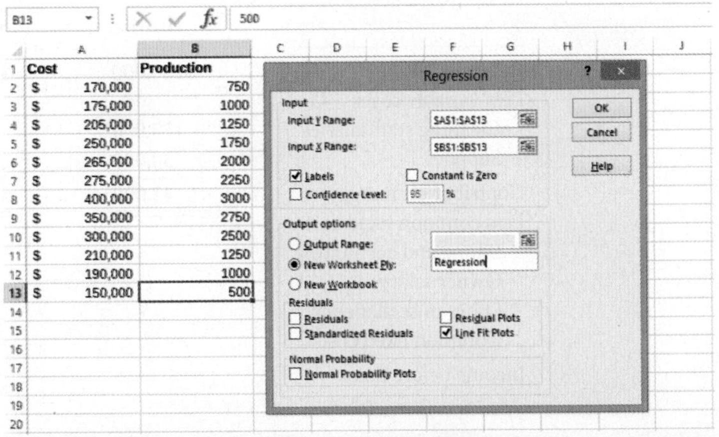

ILLUSTRATION A4-3
Viewing the output

SUMMARY OUTPUT

Regression Statistics	
Multiple R	0.979872122
R Square	0.960149376
Adjusted R Square	0.956164313
Standard Error	16069.6
Observations	12

ANOVA

	df	SS	MS	F	Significance F
Regression	1	62217679558	62217679558	240.9370988	2.51545E-08
Residual	10	2582320442	258232044.2		
Total	11	64800000000			

	Coefficients	Standard Error	t Stat	P-value	Lower 95%	Upper 95%	Lower 95.0%	Upper 95.0%
Intercept	93618.78453	10799.64948	8.668687325	5.79022E-06	69555.66595	117681.9031	69555.66595	117681.9031
Production	90.82872928	5.851556463	15.52214865	2.51545E-08	77.79064898	103.8668096	77.79064898	103.8668096

RESIDUAL OUTPUT

Observation	Predicted Cost	Residuals
1	161740.3315	8259.668508
2	184447.5138	-9447.513812
3	207154.6961	-2154.696133
4	252569.0608	-2569.060773
5	275276.2431	-10276.24309
6	297983.4254	-22983.42541
7	366104.9724	33895.02762
8	343397.7901	6602.209945
9	320690.6077	-20690.60773
10	207154.6961	2845.303867
11	184447.5138	5552.486188
12	139033.1492	10966.85083

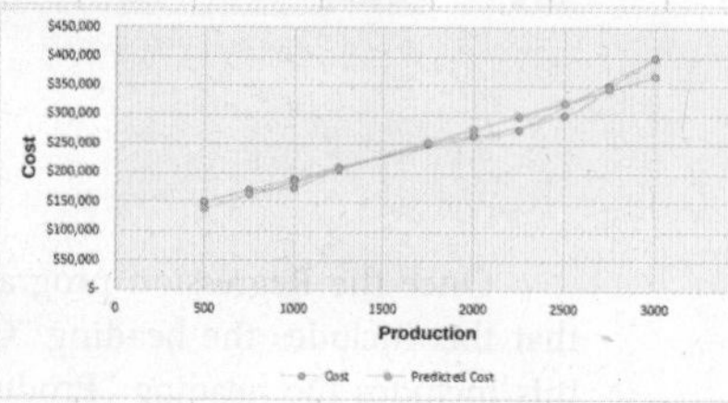

while the coefficient on production (the slope of the regression line) is $90.83. Thus, the regression line indicates that:

$$\text{Cost} = \$93{,}618.78 + \$90.83\,(\text{Production})$$

P-Value. The p-values corresponding to the intercept and the slope measure the probability of observing values as large as the estimated coefficients when the true values are zero. In other words, there is some probability that even when the true fixed cost is zero, we will observe an estimate as large as $93,618.78. We would, of course, like this probability to be quite low (at least less than .05). In the current case, the probability is very low (.00000579). Likewise, the probability that we will observe an estimate as large as $90.83 when the true variable cost per unit is zero is also very low (.0000000252). Thus, it seems highly unlikely that either the true fixed cost is zero or that the true variable cost per unit is zero.

REVIEW PROBLEM 1

Potter Janitorial Services provides cleaning services to both homes and offices. In the past year, income before taxes was $4,250, as follows:

	Home	Office	Total
Revenue	$250,000	$425,000	$675,000
Less variable costs:			
Cleaning staff salaries	175,000	276,250	451,250
Supplies	30,000	42,500	72,500
Contribution margin	$ 45,000	$106,250	151,250
Less common fixed costs:			
Billing and accounting			25,000
Owner salary			90,000
Other miscellaneous			
Common fixed costs			32,000
Income before taxes			$ 4,250

For the coming year, Janice Potter, the company owner, would like to perform CVP analysis. She has asked you to help her address the following independent questions.

REQUIRED

a. What are the contribution margin ratios of the Home and Office segments, and what is the overall contribution margin ratio?

b. Assuming that the mix of home and office services does not change, what amount of revenue will be needed for Janice to earn a salary of $125,000 and have income before taxes of $4,000?

c. Suppose staff salaries increase by 20 percent. In this case, how will break-even sales in the coming year compare to the prior year?

ANSWER

a. Contribution margin ratio for Home = $45,000 ÷ $250,000 = .18
Contribution margin ratio for Office = $106,250 ÷ $425,000 = .25
Overall contribution margin ratio = $151,250 ÷ $675,000 = .22407

b. ($25,000 + $125,000 + $32,000 + $4,000) ÷ .22407 = $830,097.73

c. Break-even in the prior year = ($25,000 + $90,000 + $32,000) ÷ .22407 = $656,045.
If staff salaries increase by 20 percent, then the contribution margin ratios will be as follows:

	Home	Office	Total
Revenue	$250,000	$425,000	$675,000
Less variable costs:			
Cleaning staff salaries	210,000	331,500	541,500
Supplies	30,000	42,500	72,500
Contribution margin	10,000	51,000	61,000
Contribution margin ratios	0.0400	0.1200	0.09037

In this case, the break-even level of sales will be = ($25,000 + $90,000 + $32,000) ÷ .09037 = $1,626,646.01. Obviously, a 20 percent increase in staff salaries will have a very significant impact on the break-even level of sales.

REVIEW PROBLEM 2

The Antibody Research Institute (ARI) is a biotechnology company that develops humanized antibodies to treat various diseases. Antibodies are proteins that bind with a foreign substance, such as a virus, and render it inactive. The company operates a research lab in Boston and currently employs 23 scientists. Most of the company's work involves development of humanized antibodies for specific pharmaceutical companies. Revenue comes from this contract work and from royalties on products that ultimately make use of ARI-developed antibodies.

In the coming year, the company expects to incur the following costs:

Expense Summary

Salaries of 23 research scientists	$2,760,000
Administrative salaries	785,000
Depreciation of building and equipment	3,200,000
Laboratory supplies	765,000
Utilities and other miscellaneous (fixed) expenses	285,000
Total	$7,795,000

Annual contract revenue is projected to be $4,000,000. The company also anticipates royalties related to the sale of Oxacine, which is a product that will come to market next year. Oxacine is marketed by Reach Pharmaceuticals and makes use of an antibody developed under contract with ARI. The product is scheduled to sell for $120 per unit, and ARI will receive a royalty of 20 percent of sales. ARI, in turn, has a contractual commitment to pay 10 percent of royalties it receives (i.e., 10 percent of the 20 percent) to the scientists who were on the team that developed the antibody.

REQUIRED

a. How many units of Oxacine must be sold for ARI to achieve its break-even point?

b. Reach Pharmaceuticals has projected annual sales of 180,000 units of Oxacine. Assuming this level of sales, what will be the before-tax profit of ARI?

c. What if Reach Pharmaceuticals sells only 160,000 units of Oxacine? Assuming that the average salary of scientists is $120,000, how many scientists must be "downsized" to achieve the break-even point?

d. Do you consider ARI to be high or low with respect to operating leverage? Explain.

ANSWER

a. $4,000,000 + .20($120)(Q) − .10(.20)($120)(Q) − $7,795,000 = $-0-
$21.6(Q) = $3,795,000
Q = 175,694.44

b. $4,000,000 + .20($120)(180,000) − .10(.20)($120)(180,000) − $7,795,000 = $93,000

c. $4,000,000 + .20($120)(160,000) − .10(.20)($120)(160,000) − $7,795,000 = ($339,000)
Average salary = $2,760,000 ÷ 23 = $120,000
($339,000) ÷ $120,000 = (2.825)
This implies that approximately three scientists must be "downsized."

d. ARI is extremely high with respect to operating leverage since costs other than royalty payments to scientists are generally fixed. The fact that the costs are fixed does not mean, however, that they cannot be cut. Some costs such as the salaries of the scientists are discretionary fixed costs. Other costs such as depreciation are committed fixed costs.

KEY TERMS

Account analysis (129)
Break-even point (137)
Committed fixed costs (126)
Contribution margin (139)
Contribution margin ratio (140)
Cost-volume-profit (CVP) analysis (136)
Discretionary fixed costs (125)
Fixed costs (125)
High-low method (131)
Margin of safety (138)
Mixed costs (126)
Operating leverage (148)
Profit equation (137)
Regression analysis (134)
Relevant range (127)
Scattergraph (131)
Semivariable costs (126)
Step costs (126)
Step fixed costs (127)
Step variable costs (127)
Variable costs (124)
"What if" analysis (140)

SELF-ASSESSMENT (Answers Below)

1. At Branson Corporation, the selling price per unit is $800 and variable cost per unit is $500. Fixed costs are $1,000,000 per year. In this case, the contribution margin per unit is:

a. $300.
b. $0.375.
c. 2,500 units.
d. None of the answer choices is correct.

2. At Branson Corporation, the selling price per unit is $800 and variable cost per unit is $500. Fixed costs are $1,000,000 per year. Assuming sales of $3,000,000, profit will be:

a. $125,000.
b. $680,000.
c. $750,000.
d. None of the answer choices is correct.

3. The contribution margin ratio measures:
   a. Profit per unit.
   b. Contribution margin per dollar of sales.
   c. Profit per dollar of sales.
   d. The ratio of variable to fixed costs.

4. In March, Octavius Company had the following costs related to producing 5,000 units:

Direct materials	$60,000
Direct labor	20,000
Rent	5,000
Depreciation	4,000

Estimate variable cost per unit using account analysis.
   a. $17.80.
   b. $4.00.
   c. $5.80.
   d. $16.00.

5. Using the following production/cost data, estimate variable cost per unit using the high-low method:

Month	Production	Cost
January	2,000	$20,000
February	2,500	$21,000
March	3,000	$23,000
April	1,900	$18,500

   a. $4.00.
   b. $3.70.
   c. $4.20.
   d. $4.09.

6. At Branson Corporation, the selling price per unit is $800 and variable cost per unit is $500. Fixed costs are $1,000,000 per year. In this case, the break-even point is approximately:
   a. 3,333 units.
   b. 6,667 units.
   c. 5,500 units.
   d. None of the answer choices is correct.

7. Consider the sales and variable cost information for the three departments at Fortesque Drug in May:

	Drugs	Cosmetics	Housewares
Sales	$80,000	$40,000	$30,000
Variable cost	40,000	15,000	25,000
Contribution margin	$40,000	$25,000	$ 5,000

Based on this information, estimate the increase in profit for a $10,000 increase in sales (assuming that the sales mix stays the same).
   a. $4,667.
   b. $5,667.
   c. $3,334.
   d. None of the answer choices is correct.

8. Consider the sales and variable cost information in Question 7. Assuming that total fixed costs at Fortesque Drug are $30,000 per month, what is the break-even level of sales in dollars?
   a. $86,326.
   b. $45,876.
   c. $72,284.
   d. $64,286.

9. If a firm has relatively high operating leverage, it has:
   a. Relatively high variable costs.
   b. Relatively high fixed costs.
   c. Relatively low operating expenses.
   d. Relatively high operating expenses.

10. Product A has a contribution margin per unit of $500 and requires 2 hours of machine time. Product B has a contribution margin per unit of $1,000 and requires 5 hours of machine time. How much of each product should be produced, given there are 100 hours of available machine time?
   a. 50 units of A.
   b. 25 units of B.
   c. 50 units of A and 25 units of B.
   d. None of the answer choices is correct.

ANSWERS TO SELF-ASSESSMENT

1. a **2.** a **3.** b **4.** d **5.** d **6.** a
7. a **8.** d **9.** b **10.** a

QUESTIONS

1. Define the term *mixed cost* and provide an example of such a cost.
2. Distinguish between discretionary and committed fixed costs.
3. Provide two examples of costs that are likely to be variable costs.
4. Provide two examples of costs that are likely to be fixed costs.
5. Explain why total compensation paid to the sales force is likely to be a mixed cost.
6. Explain how to use account analysis to estimate fixed and variable costs.
7. Explain the concept of a relevant range.

8. What is the difference between the contribution margin and the contribution margin ratio?

9. In a multiproduct setting, when would it not be appropriate to focus on a weighted average contribution margin per unit?

10. Which company would have higher operating leverage: a software company that makes large investments in research and development or a trucking company that relies on owner-operators (i.e. individuals who own and drive their own truck). Why?

EXERCISES

GROUP WORK

EXERCISE 4-1. Operating Leverage [LO 3] John Diaz is the president of Pacific Refrigeration. The company has 2,000 employees and manufactures and sells a variety of refrigeration units for commercial use. Recently, the company experienced large losses due to a downturn in the economy and a subsequent decline in sales. John thinks the losses were particularly large because his company has too many fixed costs.

REQUIRED

a. Expand on John's thought. How are the large losses related to fixed costs?

b. Identify a way that John can turn potential fixed costs into variable costs.

WRITING

EXERCISE 4-2. Contribution per Unit and Contribution Margin Ratio [LO 2] Consider two companies, Oakland Hill Golf Course and Brooks Men's Clothing.

REQUIRED

Which company is more likely to focus on the contribution margin per unit, and which is more likely to focus on the contribution margin ratio in cost-volume-profit analysis? Explain. (*Note:* A unit at the Oakland Hills Golf Course is a round of golf. A unit at Brooks Men's Clothing is an article of apparel.)

EXERCISE 4-3. Cost-Volume-Profit Analysis [LO 2] Watson's Fish Company buys whole salmon from various fishermen at $4 per pound and sells the fish to restaurants for $6 per pound. Its fixed costs are $20,000 per month.

REQUIRED

How many pounds must be sold to break even, and how many pounds must be sold to earn a profit of $10,000 per month?

EXERCISE 4-4. Cost Behavior [LO 1] Information for three costs incurred at Boole Manufacturing in the first quarter follows:

	Month	Cost	Units Produced
Depreciation	January	$575,000	6,500
	February	$575,000	9,500
	March	$575,000	12,500
Direct labor	January	$234,000	6,500
	February	$342,000	9,500
	March	$450,000	12,500
Telecommunications	January	$249,000	6,500
	February	$327,000	9,500
	March	$405,000	12,500

REQUIRED

Plot each cost, making the vertical axis cost and the horizontal axis units produced. Classify each cost (depreciation, direct labor, and telecommunications) as either fixed, variable, or mixed.

EXERCISE 4-5. High-Low Method [LO 1] Campus Copy & Printing wants to predict copy machine repair expense at different levels of copying activity (number of copies made). The following data have been gathered:

Month	Copy Machine Repair Expense	Copies Made
May	$ 9,000	300,000
June	13,000	550,000
July	22,000	950,000
August	17,000	750,000
September	10,500	400,000

REQUIRED

Determine the fixed and variable components of repair expense using the high-low method. Use copies made as the measure of activity. Round cost per copy to two decimal places.

EXERCISE 4-6. High-Low Method [LO 1 and Appendix] Madrigal Theater Company is interested in estimating fixed and variable costs. The following data are available:

	Cost	No. of Tickets Sold
January	$160,000	19,000
February	190,000	22,000
March	215,000	28,000
April	217,000	29,000
May	209,500	29,500
June	194,500	24,500
July	240,000	35,000
August	172,000	20,000
September	185,000	22,000
October	202,000	26,000
November	191,500	23,500
December	207,000	30,000

REQUIRED

a. Use the high-low method to estimate fixed cost per month and variable costs per ticket sold [i.e., estimate a and b in the equation Cost = a + (b × # of tickets) using the high-low method].

b. Madrigal Theater Company is considering an advertising campaign that is expected to increase annual sales by 15,000 tickets. Assume that the ticket selling price is $25. Ignoring the cost of the advertising campaign, what is the expected increase in profit associated with the advertising campaign?

c. (Optional) Repeat part a using regression analysis. In light of the result, how would you answer part b? Round unit variable cost to five decimal places.

EXCEL **EXERCISE 4-7. Scattergraph [LO 1]** Reef Office Supplies is interested in estimating the relationship between customer service costs and sales. The following data are available:

Month	Customer Service Cost	Sales
May	$9,740	$170,000
June	$10,100	$210,000
July	$10,690	$230,000
August	$12,750	$255,000
September	$13,830	$275,000

REQUIRED

a. Prepare a scattergraph of customer service cost (vertical axis) and sales (horizontal axis).

b. Comment on whether there appears to be a linear relation between cost and sales and whether any of the observations appear to be outliers.

EXERCISE 4-8. Account Analysis [LO 1] Reef Office Supplies is interested in estimating the cost involved in hiring new employees. The following information is available regarding the costs of operating the Human Resource department at Reef Office Supplies in May, when there were 60 new hires:

Human Resources Department

May	
Staff wages	$30,000
Manager salary	7,500
Office supplies	300
Depreciation of office equipment	500
Share of building cost (based on square feet occupied by Human Resources)	2,000
Total	$40,300

REQUIRED

a. Use account analysis to determine fixed cost per month and variable cost per new hire. Assume that only staff wages and office supplies are variable costs.

b. The company is planning to hire 75 employees in June. Estimate the total cost of Human Resources for June.

c. What is the expected incremental cost associated with hiring 15 more employees than were hired in May?

EXERCISE 4-9. Account Analysis [LO 1, 2] Madrigal Theater Company is interested in estimating fixed and variable costs. The following data are available for the month of December:

	Number of Tickets Sold	Cost
December	4,200	$365,400
Detail of Cost:		
Author royalties/fees*		$ 80,000
Wages (actors, ticket office, ushers, etc.)		165,000
Rent		60,000
Utilities		7,000
Food and beverages		29,400
Depreciation—theater equipment		14,000
Owner's salary		10,000
Total		$365,400

*Author royalties/fees are fixed because the theater pays for the right to put on the play; royalties and fees are not paid based on the number of tickets sold.

REQUIRED

a. Use account analysis to estimate fixed cost per month and variable cost per tickets sold [i.e., estimate a and b in the equation Cost = a + (b × Sales)]. Assume the only variable cost are in food and beverages.

b. Assume that the selling price per ticket is $25. Additionally, on average each ticket holder spends $10 on food and beverages. Based on your answer to part a, what is your estimate of the contribution margin ratio at Madrigal Theater?

EXERCISE 4-10. Account Analysis [LO 1] Lopez Mfg. is interested in estimating fixed and variable manufacturing costs using data from October. Based on judgment, the plant manager classified each manufacturing cost as fixed, variable, or part fixed and part variable:

	Units Produced	Cost	
October	1,500	$136,100	
Detail of Cost:			**Cost Behavior**
Material		$ 63,000	Variable
Direct labor		24,000	Variable
Depreciation		8,000	Fixed
Phone		300	Fixed
Other utilities		4,500	20% Fixed
Supervisory salaries		25,200	75% Fixed
Equipment repair		6,500	20% Fixed
Indirect materials		600	Variable
Factory maintenance		4,000	80% Fixed
Total		$136,100	

REQUIRED

a. Use account analysis to estimate fixed cost per month and variable cost per unit produced.

b. Based on your answer to part a, what is your estimate of the incremental cost of producing 500 units?

EXERCISE 4-11. CVP Analysis [LO 2] Gabby's Wedding Cakes creates elaborate wedding cakes. Each cake sells for $600. The variable cost of making the cakes is $250, and the fixed cost per month is $8,750.

REQUIRED

a. Calculate the break-even point for a month in units.

b. How many cakes must be sold to earn a monthly profit of $7,000?

EXCEL

EXERCISE 4-12. CVP Analysis, Profit Equation [LO 2] Lake Stevens Marina has estimated that fixed costs per month are $350,000 and variable cost per dollar of sales is $0.30.

REQUIRED

a. What is the break-even point per month in sales dollars?

b. What level of sales dollars is needed for a monthly profit of $70,000?

c. For the month of July, the marina anticipates sales of $1,000,000. What is the expected level of profit?

EXERCISE 4-13. Contribution Margin [LO 2] Rhetorix, Inc., produces stereo speakers. The selling price per pair of speakers is $1,000. The variable cost of production is $300 and the fixed cost per month is $49,000.

REQUIRED

a. Calculate the contribution margin associated with a pair of speakers.

b. In August, the company sold eight more pairs of speakers than planned. What is the expected effect on profit of selling the additional speakers?

c. Calculate the contribution margin ratio for Rhetorix associated with a pair of speakers.

d. In October, the company had sales that were $10,000 higher than planned. What is the expected effect on profit related to the additional sales?

EXERCISE 4-14. Margin of Safety [LO 2] Rhetorix, Inc. produces stereo speakers. The selling price per pair of speakers is $1,000. The variable cost of production is $300 and the fixed cost per month is $49,000. For November, the company expects to sell 125 pairs of speakers.

REQUIRED

a. Calculate expected profit.

b. Calculate the margin of safety in dollars. (Round any percentage to two decimal places and round dollar answers to the nearest dollar.)

EXERCISE 4-15. "What If" Analysis [LO 2] Rhetorix, Inc., produces stereo speakers. The selling price per pair of speakers is $1,000. The variable cost of production is $300 and the fixed cost per month is $49,000.

REQUIRED

Calculate the expected profit for November, assuming that the company sells 125 pairs of speakers as planned (see Exercise 4-14), but the selling price changes to $1,200.

EXERCISE 4-16. Multiproduct, Contribution Margin Ratio [LO 2] Wilde Home & Garden is organized into three departments. The following sales and cost data are available for the prior year:

	Dept. A	Dept. B	Dept. C	Total
Sales	$450,000	$600,000	$750,000	$1,800,000
Less variable costs	270,000	450,000	450,000	1,170,000
Contribution margin	180,000	150,000	300,000	630,000
Less fixed costs	70,000	90,000	100,000	260,000
Profit	$110,000	$ 60,000	$200,000	$ 370,000

REQUIRED

a. What is the weighted average contribution margin ratio?

b. What level of sales is needed to earn a profit of $440,000 assuming the current mix?

c. Wilde Home & Garden places an advertisement in the local paper each week. All else equal, which two departments would you emphasize in the advertisement? Explain.

EXERCISE 4-17. Operating Leverage [LO 2, 3] Refer to the data in Exercise 4-16. (Round all decimal answers to four places and all dollar answers to the nearest dollar.)

REQUIRED

a. Calculate profit as a percent of sales in the prior year.

b. Suppose sales in the current year increase by 15 percent. Calculate profit as a percent of sales for the new level of sales and explain why the percent is greater than the one calculated in part a.

EXERCISE 4-18. Constraints [LO 3] Dvorak Music produces two durable music stands:

	Stand A	Stand B
Selling price	$110	$100
Less variable costs	50	64
Contribution margin	$ 60	$ 36

Stand A requires 2 labor hours and stand B requires 1 labor hour. The company has only 350 available labor hours per week. Further, the company can sell all it can produce of either product.

REQUIRED

a. Which stand(s) should the company produce?

b. What would be the incremental benefit of obtaining 15 additional labor hours?

PROBLEMS

PROBLEM 4-1. Cost Behavior [LO 1] The Hotel Majestic is interested in estimating fixed and variable costs so that the company can make more accurate projections of costs and profit. The hotel is in a resort area that is particularly busy from November through February. In July and August, however, the hotel has only a 50 percent occupancy rate.

REQUIRED

Classify each of the following costs as fixed (F), variable (V), or mixed (M) with respect to the number of hotel guests per month:

_____ **a.** Depreciation of the building

_____ **b.** Salaries of restaurant staff

_____ **c.** Salaries of administrative staff (hotel manager, desk clerks, accountants, etc.)

_____ **d.** Soap, shampoo, and other toiletries in rooms

_____ **e.** Laundry costs (cost of linens, cleaning products, depreciation of laundry equipment, etc.)

_____ **f.** Food and beverage costs

_____ **g.** Grounds maintenance

PROBLEM 4-2. Account Analysis [LO 1, 2] Lancer Audio produces a high-end DVD player that sells for $1,300. Total operating expenses for July were as follows:

Units produced and sold	150
Component costs	$ 71,000
Supplies	2,500
Assembly labor	25,000
Rent	2,300
Supervisor salary	5,600
Electricity	350
Telephone	280
Gas	300
Shipping	2,000
Advertising	2,600
Administrative costs	15,000
Total	$126,930

REQUIRED

a. Use account analysis to determine fixed cost per month and variable cost per DVD player. Assume assembly labor in a variable cost.

b. Project total cost for August, assuming production and sales of 175 units.

c. What is the contribution margin per DVD player?

d. Estimate total profit, assuming production and sales of 175 units.

e. Lancer Audio is considering an order for 120 DVD players, to be produced in the next 10 months, from a customer in Canada. The selling price will be $1,050 per unit (well under the normal selling price). However, the Lancer Audio brand name will not be attached to the product. What will be the impact on company profit associated with this order?

PROBLEM 4-3. High-Low, Break-Even [LO 1, 2] Lancer Audio produces a high-end DVD player that sells for $1,300. Total operating expenses for the past 12 months are as follows:

	Units Produced and Sold	Cost
August	165	$140,345
September	130	116,990
October	150	130,650
November	145	127,670
December	155	133,790
January	170	143,910
February	140	123,520
March	150	130,950
April	145	127,385
May	150	129,865
June	140	122,720
July	135	120,255

REQUIRED

a. Use the high-low method to estimate fixed and variable costs.

b. Based on these estimates, calculate the break-even level of sales in units. (Round to the nearest whole unit.)

c. Calculate the margin of safety for the coming August assuming estimated sales of 175 units.

d. Estimate total profit assuming production and sales of 175 units.

e. Comment on the limitations of the high-low method in estimating costs for Lancer Audio.

PROBLEM 4-4. Regression Analysis (see Appendix) [LO 1 and Appendix] Lancer Audio produces a high-end DVD player that sells for $1,300. Total operating expenses for the past 12 months are as follows:

	Units Produced and Sold	Cost
August	165	$140,345
September	130	116,990
October	150	130,650
November	145	127,670
December	155	133,790
January	170	143,910
February	140	123,520
March	150	130,950
April	145	127,385
May	150	129,865
June	140	122,720
July	135	120,255

REQUIRED

a. Use regression analysis to estimate fixed and variable costs. Round to two decimal places.

b. Compare your estimates to those obtained using account analysis (Problem 4-2) and the high-low method (Problem 4-3). Which method provides the best estimates of fixed and variable costs? (Round all answers to the nearest dollar.)

PROBLEM 4-5. Break-Even, "What If" [LO 2] Michael Bordellet is the owner/pilot of Bordellet Air Service. The company flies a daily round trip from Seattle's Lake Union to a resort in Canada.

In 2016, the company reported an annual income before taxes of $120,403, although that included a deduction of $70,000, reflecting Michael's salary:

Revenue ($360 × 1,560 passengers)		$561,600
Less costs:		
Pilot (owner's salary)	$ 70,000	
Fuel (35,657 gallons × $4.15)	147,977	
Maintenance (variable)	127,920	
Depreciation of plane	25,000	
Depreciation of office equipment	2,800	
Rent expense	40,000	
Insurance	20,000	
Miscellaneous (fixed)	7,500	441,197
Income before taxes		$120,403

Revenue of $561,600 reflects six round trips per week for 52 weeks with an average of five passengers paying $360 each per round trip (6 × 52 × 5 × $360 = $561,600). The flight to the resort is 400 miles one way. With 312 round trips (6 per week × 52 weeks), that amounts to 249,600 miles. The plane averages 7 miles per gallon.

REQUIRED (Round all monetary calculations to the nearest cent and all trips to the nearest whole trip.)

a. How many round trips is Michael currently flying, and how many round trips are needed to break even?

b. How many round trips are needed so that Michael can draw a salary of $110,000 and still not show a loss?

c. What is the average before-tax profit of a round trip flight in 2016?

d. What is the incremental profit associated with adding a round-trip flight?

EXCEL **PROBLEM 4-6. Account Analysis, High-Low, Contribution Margin [LO 1, 2]** Information on occupancy and costs at the Light House Hotel for April, May, and June are indicated below:

	April	May	June
Occupancy	1,700	1,850	1,950
Day manager salary	$ 4,500	$ 4,500	$ 4,500
Night manager salary	3,900	3,900	3,900
Cleaning staff	15,960	16,275	16,590
Depreciation	12,500	12,500	12,500
Complimentary continental breakfast: food and beverages	5,050	5,205	5,225
Total	$41,910	$42,380	$42,715

REQUIRED

a. Calculate the fixed costs per month and the variable cost per occupied room using account analysis for April. Round to two decimal places.

b. Calculate the fixed costs per month and the variable cost per occupied room using the high-low method.

c. Average room rates are $120 per night. What is the contribution margin per occupied room? In answering this question, use your variable cost estimate from part b.

PROBLEM 4-7. Fixed and Variable Costs, the Profit Equation [LO 1, 2] Last year, Emily Sanford had a booth at the three-day Indianapolis Craft Expo, where she sold a variety of silver jewelry handcrafted in India. Her before-tax profit was as follows:

Sales	$21,000
Less:	
Cost of jewelry sold	11,550
Gross margin	9,450
Less other expenses:	
Registration fee	1,800
Booth rental (6% sales)	1,260
Salary of Mindy Orwell	450
Before tax profit	$ 5,940

Mindy Orwell is a friend who takes care of the booth for approximately 5 hours, from 9 A.M. until 2 P.M. Emily takes over from 2 P.M. until closing at 9 P.M. Emily has added several new designs to her collection and anticipates that in the coming year, her sales will increase by 20 percent, to $25,200. In light of this, she has forecasted before-tax profit as follows:

Before-tax profit in prior year	$ 5,940	a
Sales in prior year	21,000	b
Before-tax profit per dollar of sales	0.2829	a ÷ b
Forecasted sales	$25,200	
Profit per dollar of sales	0.2829	
Forecasted before-tax profit	$ 7,129	

REQUIRED

a. What is the fundamental assumption that Emily is making, and why is it obviously wrong?

b. Prepare a more appropriate forecast of before-tax profit related to the Indianapolis Craft Expo.

PROBLEM 4-8. The Profit Equation [LO 1, 2] Gaming Solutions is a small company that assembles PCs to gamer customer specifications. The company buys all of its component parts from Northern Oregon Computer Warehouse. In the past year, the company had the following before-tax profit:

Sales		$1,800,000
Less:		
Cost of components	$1,080,000	
Staff salaries	280,000	
Rent	40,000	
Utilities	8,000	
Advertising	7,000	1,415,000
Operating profit before bonuses		385,000
Less:		
Staff bonuses		115,500
Profit before taxes and owner draw		$ 269,500

The company, owned by Steven Rich, has seven full-time employees. These employees are each paid a base salary of $40,000 per year. In addition, they receive a bonus equal to 30 percent of operating profits before bonuses. Owner draw is the amount Steven pays himself out of company profits.

The company is in the process of planning profit for the coming year. Northern Oregon Computer Warehouse has agreed that their prices to Gaming Solutions will be reduced by 20 percent on all purchases over $1,000,000.

REQUIRED

Estimate profit before taxes and owner draw for five levels of sales: $1,600,000; $1,700,000; $1,800,000; $1,900,000; and $2,000,000. (Round all calculations to the nearest dollar.)

EXCEL **PROBLEM 4-9. High-Low, Profit Equation [LO 1]** Crux, Inc., produces amplifiers. Each unit sells for $900. Below is information on production/sales and costs for 2016:

	Production and Sales in Units	Production Costs	Selling and Admin. Costs
January	105	$ 88,860	$ 23,570
February	117	97,600	25,200
March	97	83,007	22,495
April	106	89,600	23,720
May	115	96,200	24,950
June	125	103,500	26,250
July	128	105,670	26,690
August	132	108,550	27,200
September	138	112,978	28,030
October	126	104,200	26,400
November	124	102,750	26,150
December	108	91,050	23,990
Total	1,421	$ 1,183,965	$ 304,645
Average cost per unit		$833.19141	$214.38776

REQUIRED

a. Use the high-low method to identify the fixed and variable cost components for both production costs and selling and administrative costs.

b. The company estimates that production and sales in 2017 will be 1,650 units. Based on this estimate, forecast income before taxes for 2017.

PROBLEM 4-10. High-Low Method, Scattergraph, Break-Even Analysis [LO 1, 2] FirstTown Mortgage specializes in providing mortgage refinance loans. Each loan customer is charged a $500 loan processing fee by FirstTown when the loan is processed. FirstTown's costs over the past year associated with processing the loans follow:

	Loans Processed	Cost
January	190	$50,030
February	170	48,550
March	200	50,810
April	211	51,012
May	235	52,012
June	285	54,530
July	310	55,725
August	240	54,420
September	219	51,180
October	185	49,700
November	175	49,000
December	180	49,290

REQUIRED

a. Use the high-low method to estimate fixed and variable costs.

b. Based on these estimates, calculate the number of loans that must be made to break even. (Round to the nearest whole unit.)

c. Estimate total profit in a month when 275 loans are processed. (Round to the nearest dollar.)

d. Prepare a scattergraph of loan processing cost (vertical axis) and number of loans processed (horizontal axis).

e. Comment on whether the high-low method produces a reasonable estimate of costs. Look at whether the relationship between the number of loans processed and the cost is linear. Are there any outliers? Does an outlier affect the high-low estimate?

PROBLEM 4-11. Break-Even Analysis, Margin of Safety, Increase in Profit [LO 2] Edison Entrepreneur Services, Inc., is a legal services firm that files the paperwork to incorporate a business. Edison charges $1,200 for the incorporation application package and plans to file 1,600 applications next year. The company's projected income statement for the coming year is:

Sales	$1,920,000
Less variable expenses	1,184,000
Contribution margin	736,000
Less fixed expenses	300,000
Operating income	$ 436,000

REQUIRED

a. Compute the contribution margin per application and calculate the break-even point in number of applications. (Round to the nearest whole unit, since it is not possible to file a partial application.) Calculate the contribution margin ratio (round to four decimal places) and the break-even sales revenue (round to the nearest dollar).

b. What is the current margin of safety in terms of the number of units? What is the current margin of safety in terms of sales dollars?

c. If Edison wants to have operating income of $500,000 next year, how many applications must it process? (Round to the nearest whole unit.) What dollar level of sales is required to achieve operating income of $500,000? (Round to the nearest dollar.)

d. The office manager for Edison has proposed that Edison increase advertising (a fixed cost) for the upcoming year by $75,000; she feels that this increase in advertising will lead to an increase in sales of $300,000. Prepare a new projected income statement for this proposal. Should Edison increase its advertising to this new level?

PROBLEM 4-12. Multiproduct CVP [LO 2] Fidelity Multimedia sells audio and video equipment and car stereo products. After performing a study of fixed and variable costs in the prior year, the company prepared a product-line profit statement as follows:

Fidelity Multimedia
Profitability Analysis
For the Year Ended December 31, 2017

	Audio	Video	Car	Total
Sales	$3,250,000	$1,950,000	$1,300,000	$6,500,000
Less variable costs:				
Cost of merchandise	1,920,000	1,374,000	617,000	3,911,000
Salary, part-time staff	192,500	108,000	59,000	359,500
Total variable costs	2,112,500	1,482,000	676,000	4,270,500
Contribution margin	1,137,500	468,000	624,000	2,229,500
Less direct fixed costs:				
Salary, full-time staff	325,000	240,000	220,000	785,000
Total	$ 812,500	$ 228,000	$ 404,000	$1,444,500
Less common fixed costs:				
Advertising				115,000
Utilities				25,000
Other administrative costs				570,000
Total common fixed costs				710,000
Profit				$ 734,500

REQUIRED

a. Calculate the contribution margin ratios for the audio, video, and car product lines.

b. What would be the effect on profit of a $125,000 increase in sales of audio equipment compared with a $125,000 increase in sales of video equipment or a $125,000 increase in sales of car equipment? Based on this limited information, which product line would you recommend expanding?

c. Calculate the break-even level of sales dollars for the company as a whole. (Round to the nearest dollar.)

d. Calculate sales needed to achieve a profit of $1,800,000, assuming the current mix. (Round to the nearest dollar.)

e. Determine the sales of audio, video, and car products in the total sales amount calculated for part d. (Round to the nearest dollar.)

EXCEL **PROBLEM 4-13. Multiproduct, Contribution Margin Ratio [LO 2, 3]** ComputerGuard offers computer consulting, training, and repair services. For the most recent fiscal year, profit was $328,100, as follows:

	Consulting	Training	Repair	Total
Sales	$600,000	$525,000	$375,000	$1,500,000
Less variable costs:				
Salaries	300,000	210,000	225,000	735,000
Supplies/parts	24,000	39,000	75,000	138,000
Other	1,200	2,700	5,000	8,900
Contribution margin	$274,800	$273,300	$ 70,000	618,100
Less common fixed costs:				
Rent				55,000
Owner's salary				212,000
Utilities				13,000
Other				10,000
Profit				$ 328,100

REQUIRED

a. Linda O'Flaherty, the owner of ComputerGuard, believes that in the coming year, she can increase sales by 15 percent. Assuming the current mix of services, what will be the percentage increase in profit associated with a 15 percent increase in sales? Why will profit increase at a greater percent than sales? Round contribution margin ratio to six decimal places, and increased profit to nearest dollar.

b. If Linda were to focus on the contribution margin per unit (rather than the contribution margin ratio), what would be a likely unit of service?

PROBLEM 4-14. Multiproduct, Contribution Margin [LO 2] National Tennis Racquet Co. produces and sells three models:

	Smasher	Basher	Dinker	Total
Units sold	2,000	3,000	3,000	8,000
Sales	$150,000	$180,000	$120,000	$450,000
Less variable costs	80,000	75,000	35,000	190,000
Contribution margin	$ 70,000	$105,000	$ 85,000	260,000
Less common fixed costs				140,000
Profit				$120,000

REQUIRED (Round all percentages to two decimal places and monetary calculations to the nearest dollar.)

a. What is the weighted average contribution margin per unit?

b. Calculate the break-even point in units assuming the current mix.

c. What would be the number of Smashers, Bashers, and Dinkers in the break-even level of sales?

d. What is the weighted average contribution margin ratio?

e. What level of sales (in dollars) would be needed to earn a profit of $125,000, assuming the current mix? Round to nearest dollar.

f. What would be the sales (in dollars) of Smashers, Bashers, and Dinkers for total sales calculated in part e?

PROBLEM 4-15. Operating Leverage [LO 3] Equillion, Inc., and Storis, Inc., are two companies in the pharmaceutical industry. Equillion has relatively high fixed costs related to research and development. Storis, however, does little research and development. Instead, the company pays for the right to produce and market drugs that have been developed by other companies. The amount paid is a percent of sales. Thus, Storis has relatively high variable costs and relatively low fixed costs:

	Equillion, Inc.	Storis, Inc.
Sales	$150,000,000	$150,000,000
Less variable costs	37,500,000	90,000,000
Less fixed costs	90,000,000	37,500,000
Profit	$ 22,500,000	$ 22,500,000

REQUIRED

a. Which company has the higher operating leverage?

b. Calculate the expected percentage change in profit for a 20 percent increase (and for a 20 percent decrease) in sales for each company. (Round to the nearest percentage.)

c. Which company is more risky?

PROBLEM 4-16. Value of Loosening a Constraint [LO 3] For the past 3 years, Rhetorix, Inc., has produced the model X100 stereo speaker. The model is in high demand, and the company can sell as many pairs as it can produce. The selling price per pair is $900. Variable costs of production are $300, and fixed costs per year are $720,000. Each pair of speakers requires 5 hours of assembly time. Currently the company has five assembly workers who are highly skilled and can work a total of 12,500 hours per year. With a tight labor market, the company finds it difficult to hire additional assembly workers (at the current rate of $40 per hour) with the skill needed to assemble the X100. Jurgis Rand, the owner of Rhetorix, is considering offering assembly workers an overtime premium of $20 per hour (wages in excess of regular hourly wages) to get them to work more than 12,500 hours per year. In thinking about how much to offer, Jurgis performed the following calculation:

Sales (2,500 units × $900)	$2,250,000
Less variable costs (2,500 × $300)	750,000
Less fixed costs	720,000
Profit	$ 780,000
Profit/assembly hours ($780,000 ÷ 12,500)	$62.40 per assembly hour

After seeing this calculation, Jurgis decided to offer an overtime premium of $20 per hour to his assembly workers. Jurgis reasoned: "This is a great deal. The workers make an extra $20 per hour, and I'll still make an extra $42.40 per hour." The $42.40 is equal to the profit per assembly hour minus the extra labor cost ($62.40–$20.00).

REQUIRED

a. How much would profit increase if 5 more assembly hours were available at the regular hourly wage for assembly workers?

b. Compare your answer in part a to the answer that Jurgis would provide to the question in part a (i.e., $62.40 × 5 = $312). What is the flaw in Jurgis's calculation of the value of additional assembly time?

c. Suppose Jurgis pays assembly workers $20.00 per hour of overtime premium. On average, what will be the incremental benefit to Jurgis of an hour of extra assembly time?

PROBLEM 4-17. Constraints [LO 3] Fleet Valley Shoes produces two models: the Nx100 (a shoe aimed at competitive runners) and the Mx100 (a shoe aimed at fitness buffs). Sales and costs for the most recent year are indicated:

	Nx100	Mx100
Sales (pairs)	20,000	80,000
Sales	$3,000,000	$8,800,000
Variable costs	(700,000)	(1,200,000)
Contribution margin	2,300,000	7,600,000
Fixed costs	(20,000)	(1,500,000)
Profit	$2,280,000	$6,100,000
Assembly time per pair	3 hours	2 hours
Profit per assembly hour	$38.00	$37.50
CM per assembly hour	$38.33	$47.50

REQUIRED

a. Suppose the company has 200,000 assembly hours available. Further, management believes that at least 4,000 pairs of each model must be produced so that the company has a presence in both market segments. How many pairs of each model should be produced in the coming year?

b. Suppose management decides that at least 6,000 pairs of each model must be produced. What is the opportunity cost of this decision versus requiring only 4,000 pairs?

PROBLEM 4-18. Regression Analysis (see Appendix), Profit Equation [LO 1 and Appendix] Cindy Havana is a vice president of finance for Captain Wesley's Restaurant, a chain of 12 restaurants on the East Coast, including five restaurants in Florida. The company is considering a plan whereby customers will be mailed coupons in the month of their birthday, entitling them to 20 percent off their total bill. The cost of the mailing (printing, paper, postage, etc.) is estimated to be $500,000. Cindy estimates that the campaign will result in an annual increase in sales of $3,000,000 at normal prices ($2,400,000 after the 20 percent discount).

As part of her analysis of the financial impact of the plan, Cindy ran a regression of total monthly operating costs on sales using data from the past year. The results of this analysis are indicated in the Summary Output table (see next page):

	Operating Costs	Sales
January	$ 3,809,720	$ 4,141,000
February	3,850,000	4,065,000
March	3,969,000	4,410,000
April	4,007,225	4,502,500
May	3,895,000	4,750,000
June	4,221,240	4,852,000
July	4,343,200	4,880,000
August	4,177,360	4,747,000
September	4,070,000	4,625,000
October	4,035,600	4,484,000
November	3,795,850	4,265,000
December	4,105,200	4,665,000
	$48,279,395	$54,386,500

Summary Output

Regression Statistics	
Multiple R	0.839596802
R Square	0.70492279
Adjusted R Square	0.675415069
Standard Error	97375.78793
Observations	12

	Coefficients	*Standard Error*	*t Stat*	*P-value*
Intercept	1617476.445	493020.2996	3.28075	0.00827844
Sales	0.530824334	0.108604516	4.887682	0.000634652

REQUIRED

Based on the limited information provided, give Cindy an estimate of the net effect of the coupon campaign on annual profit. (Ignore taxes.)

CASE

4-1 ROTHMUELLER MUSEUM [LO 1, 2]

In 1928, Francis P. Rothmueller, a Northwest railroad magnate, established an endowment to fund the Rothmueller Museum in Minneapolis. The museum currently has a $30 million endowment, but it also has substantial operating costs and continues to add to its eclectic collection that encompasses paintings, photographs, drawings, and design objects post-1900. Annual earnings from the endowment (approximately $2,500,000 in 2016) are not sufficient to cover operations and acquisitions, and the museum's trustees and president are conscious of the need to generate income from admissions, special exhibits, and museum store sales.

Alice Morgan, photographic curator, is in the process of planning an exhibition of Ansel Adams photographs that will run from September through November 2017. Below is a preliminary budget, prepared by Alice, of revenue and costs associated with the exhibition:

Revenue (10,000 × $15)		$150,000	1
Less:			
Lease of photographs from other museums and collectors	$100,000		2
Packing and transportation of photographs from other museums and collectors	5,000		3
Event insurance	4,000		4
Alice Morgan salary (25%)	15,000		5
William Jacob salary (25%)	13,000		6
Guard service	12,000		7
Installation costs	2,000		8
Advertising	7,000		9
Exhibition printed programs	4,000	162,000	10
Profit (loss)		($ 12,000)	

1. Estimated attendance is 10,000, and admission to the exhibit is $15.
2. Some photographs will come from the Rothmueller collection while others will be leased from other museums and collectors.
3. Cost of packing and transportation to and from Rothmueller.
4. Insurance to cover photographs during the run of the exhibition.
5. Twenty-five percent of annual salary for Alice Morgan, head photography curator.
6. Twenty-five percent of annual salary for William Jacob, assistant photography curator.
7. Cost of guard service for exhibition.
8. Painting of exhibition room to off-white background.
9. Advertising in newspapers and public radio.
10. Cost of programs describing the work of Ansel Adams and pictures at exhibition.

ADDITIONAL INFORMATION

In preparing the budget, Alice assigned 25 percent of her and her assistant's annual salaries to the exhibition since they will each spend approximately 3 months on the project. An admission fee of $6 is charged to enter the museum, and attendance at the exhibition is an additional $15 per person. Approximately one-fifth of the individuals who are estimated to attend the exhibition would have come to the museum whether the exhibition was being held or not. (Alternatively, four-fifths of the individuals are coming specifically to attend the exhibition.)

Analysis of prior data indicates that 20 percent of individuals make a purchase at the museum store, and the average purchase price is $8. The store has a 30 percent gross margin (sales minus cost of sales) and profit (sales minus cost of sales minus staff salaries and other operating costs) per dollar of sales of 5 percent.

REQUIRED

a. Prepare an analysis of the financial impact of the exhibition on the Rothmueller Museum, assuming attendance is 10,000. Does offering the exhibition appear to be a good decision from a financial standpoint?

b. How many people must attend the exhibition for its financial impact to be profit neutral (i.e., the museum will not be better or worse off financially)?

CASE

4-2 MAYFIELD SOFTWARE, CUSTOMER TRAINING [LO 2]

Marie Stefano is the group director of customer training for Mayfield Software. In this capacity, she runs a center in Kirkland, Washington, that provides training to employees of companies that use Mayfield's inventory control, customer management, and accounting software products. Her group employs a receptionist and an office manager/bookkeeper, and she has arrangements with several part-time trainers who are hired on an as-needed basis. (They are all retired employees of Mayfield Software.) Trainers are paid $4,000 per daylong class. Mayfield is a decentralized company, and Marie is given considerable authority to advertise and conduct classes as she sees fit.

Report of Operating Results, 2016

Revenue		$6,120,000
Less operating costs:		
Trainer costs	$3,400,000	
Director salary	180,000	
Receptionist	60,000	
Office manager	80,000	
Utilities, phone, etc.	38,000	
Lease expense related to computers, servers, etc.	400,000	
Rent	100,000	
Operating manuals for participants	510,000	
Postage, envelopes, paper, etc.	12,750	
Advertising	160,000	
Total operating costs		4,940,750
Profit before central charges		1,179,250
Central charges		1,224,000
Group profit		($ 44,750)

During 2016, the group conducted 850 day-long classes with an average enrollment of 20 students paying $360. The group's Report of Operating Results for 2016 is detailed above.

ADDITIONAL FACTS

1. All equipment is leased on a yearly basis. Costs include 100 workstations for students (one workstation for every seat in each of the four 25-student classrooms), plus servers and other miscellaneous equipment. While average class enrollment is 20 students, some classes are full (25 students), and classes are cancelled if enrollment is fewer than 15 students. Classes typically are held Monday through Friday, although some classes are held on Saturdays and Sundays.
2. Rent relates to the training center in Kirkland, which is not part of Mayfield's main campus located in Bellevue, Washington.
3. Advertising costs relate to the cost of monthly advertisements in trade journals such as *Tech Worker* and *Inventory Management*. These ads provide information on upcoming training sessions.
4. Operating manuals are provided to each participant.
5. Postage, envelopes, and paper costs relate primarily to billing companies for employees who participate in classes. This cost varies with the number of participants.
6. Central charges are assigned to each group at Mayfield Software based on actual sales. The allocation relates to costs incurred for the benefit of the company as a whole, including salaries of the CEO and company president, legal costs, costs related to the company's central office building, brand advertising, and so on. The charge is 20 percent of revenue.

REQUIRED

a. As indicated, the training group suffered a loss in 2016. Thus, unbeknownst to Marie, Mayfield management is considering shutting down the training center. Given the results of 2016, what would be the effect on Mayfield Software's total company profit in 2017 if the training center is closed at the start of the year?

b. Given the current room configuration and approach to allocation of central charges (20 percent of revenue), calculate the number of classes that must be offered (with an average enrollment of 20 students) for Marie's group to break even on the Report of Operating Results.

c. Recalculate your answer to part b assuming Marie can lower the amount paid to instructors to $3,500 per class. Should Marie seriously pursue this option?

d. Mayfield Software is releasing version 4.0 of CustomerTrack in 2017. Marie believes that this will create a demand for 30 additional daylong classes with an average enrollment of 20 students per class. What effect will this have on "group profit" on Marie's Report of Operating Results? Assume that instructors will be paid $4,000 per class.

CASE

4-3 KROG'S METALFAB, INC. [LO 1, 2]

John Krog is president, chairman of the board, production supervisor, and majority shareholder of Krog's Metalfab, Inc. He formed the company in 1991 to manufacture custom-built aluminum storm windows for sale to contractors in the greater Chicago area. Since that time the company has experienced tremendous growth and currently operates two plants: one in Chicago, the main production facility, and a smaller plant in Moline, Illinois. The company now produces a wide variety of metal windows, framing materials, ladders, and other products related to the construction industry. Recently the company developed a new line of bronze-finished storm windows, and initial buyer reaction has been quite favorable. The company's future seemed bright, but on January 3, 2016, a light fixture overheated causing a fire that virtually destroyed the entire Chicago plant. Three days later, Krog had moved 50 percent of his Chicago workforce to the Moline plant. Workers were housed in hotels, paid overtime wages, and provided with bus transportation home on weekends. Still, the company could not meet delivery schedules because of reduced operating capacity, and total business began to decline. At the end of 2016, Krog felt that the worst was over. A new plant had been leased in Chicago, and the company was almost back to normal.

Finally, Krog could turn his attention to a matter of considerable importance: settlement with the insurance company. The company's policy stipulated that the building and equipment loss be calculated at replacement cost. This settlement had been fairly straightforward, and the proceeds had aided the rapid rebuilding of the company. A valued feature of the insurance policy was "lost profit" coverage. This coverage was to "compensate the company for profits lost due to reduced operating capacity related to fire or flood damage." The period of "lost profit" was limited to 12 months. Interpreting the exact nature of this coverage proved to be difficult. The insurance company agreed to reimburse Krog for the overtime premium, transportation, and housing costs related to operating out of the Moline plant. These expenses obviously minimized the damages related to the 12 months of lost or reduced profits. But was the company entitled to any additional compensation?

Krog got out the latest edition of *Construction Today*. According to this respected trade journal, sales of products similar to products produced by Krog's Metalfab had increased by 7 percent during 2016. Krog felt that were it not for the fire, his company could also have increased sales by this percentage.

Income statement information is available for 2015 (the year prior to the fire) and 2016 (the year during which the company sustained "lost profit"). The expenses in 2016 include excess operating costs of $250,000. Krog has documentation supporting these items, which include overtime costs, hotel costs, meals, and such related to operating out of Moline. The insurance company is quite willing to pay for these costs since they reduced potential lost profit.

The chief accountant at Krog, Peter Newell, has estimated lost profit to be only $34,184. Thus, he does not feel that it's worthwhile spending a lot of company resources trying to collect more than the $250,000. Peter arrived at his calculation as follows:

Sales in 2015	$5,091,094
Predicted sales in 2016, assuming a 7% increase	$5,447,471
Actual sales in 2016	3,857,499
(A) Lost sales	1,589,972
(B) Profit in 2015 as a percentage of 2015 sales ($109,495 ÷ 5,091,094)	.0215
Lost profit (A × B)	$ 34,184

REQUIRED

a. Mr. Krog is not convinced by Peter's analysis and has turned to you, an outside consultant, to provide a preliminary estimate of lost profit. Using the limited information contained in the financial statements for 2015 and 2016, estimate lost profits. (*Hint:* You can proceed as follows.)

STEP 1. Determine the level of fixed and variable costs in 2015 as a function of sales. You can use account analysis, the high-low method, or regression if you are familiar with that technique. If you use account analysis, assume that cost of goods sold and selling expense are variable costs and administrative expense is a fixed cost.

STEP 2. Predict what sales would have been in 2016 if there was no fire. Using this level of sales and the fixed and variable cost information from Step 1, estimate what profit would have been in 2016.

STEP 3. The difference between actual profit in 2016 and the amount estimated in Step 2 is lost profit.

b. Based on your preliminary analysis, do you recommend that Mr. Krog aggressively pursue a substantial claim for lost profit?

c. What is the fundamental flaw in Peter Newell's analysis?

Krog's Metalfab
Income from Operations, 2015 and 2016

2015	January	February	March	April	May	June	July	August	September	October	November	December	Total
Sales	$501,260	$349,260	$361,250	$303,685	$435,650	$511,650	$561,625	$603,210	$421,210	$331,025	$330,009	$381,260	$5,091,094
Less:													
Cost of goods sold	392,036	441,570	334,030	321,131	371,140	406,065	422,007	440,620	370,434	332,255	333,134	354,053	4,518,475
Selling expense	21,200	15,720	15,535	13,300	18,425	21,472	23,590	25,020	17,795	14,383	14,301	16,383	217,124
Administrative expense	20,500	20,500	20,500	20,500	20,500	20,500	20,500	20,500	20,500	20,500	20,500	20,500	246,000
Total expense	433,736	477,790	370,065	354,931	410,065	448,037	466,097	486,140	408,729	367,138	367,935	390,936	4,981,599
Income from operations	$ 67,524	($128,530)	($ 8,815)	($ 51,246)	$ 25,585	$ 63,613	$ 95,528	$117,070	$ 12,481	($ 36,113)	($ 37,926)	($ 9,676)	$ 109,495

2016	January	February	March	April	May	June	July	August	September	October	November	December	Total
Sales	$447,252	$236,362	$291,370	$216,265	$278,165	$316,441	$357,662	$453,245	$363,772	$315,427	$264,273	$317,265	$3,857,499
Less:													
Cost of goods sold	395,445	311,800	330,720	301,232	327,776	343,590	357,880	395,442	362,254	340,732	320,800	343,583	4,131,254
Selling expense	19,340	10,900	13,110	10,105	12,582	14,112	15,760	19,583	16,005	14,072	12,026	14,149	171,744
Administrative expense	22,300	23,515	23,910	24,650	23,745	24,790	23,745	23,522	23,670	22,791	22,709	22,990	282,337
Total expense	437,085	$346,215	$367,740	$335,987	$364,103	$382,492	397,385	438,547	401,929	377,595	355,535	380,722	4,585,335
Income from operations	$ 10,167	($109,853)	($ 76,370)	($119,722)	($ 85,938)	($ 66,051)	($ 39,723)	$ 14,698	($ 38,157)	($ 62,168)	($ 91,262)	($ 63,457)	($ 727,836)

5

VARIABLE COSTING

In 2015, the all-tube amplifier produced by ClausenTube received rave reviews and the company was able to sell all 5,000 units it produced, generating company profit of $3,500,000.

Based on these results, ClausenTube increased production to 6,000 units in the subsequent year but was able to sell only 4,800 units. This performance, however, was considered quite good given that the economy had slipped in the third and fourth quarters.

In early January of 2017, Robert Clausen, company president and founder, reviewed financial performance for 2016. Surprisingly, profit had actually increased slightly to $3,528,000. Robert was confused and wasted no time calling Leslie Anders, the company controller. "What's going on?" Robert asked in a voice that hinted at his irritation. "Sales are down, the production process and prices haven't changed, and yet profit is up! How confident are you in the income numbers? There must be a significant error somewhere."

"I know this result looks bizarre," Leslie replied. "But it's not due to an error in the accounting department. It's due to the fact that our financial statements are prepared using what's called full, or absorption, costing. That's the method most companies use for external reporting to shareholders and creditors. If your schedule permits, let's meet this afternoon and I'll show you an analysis that explains what happened. There's a method called variable costing that we could use for internal reporting purposes which wouldn't produce such puzzling results. Maybe we should consider adopting it. I really think it can help us do a better job managing the business."

In this chapter, we will discuss the differences between full costing and variable costing and gain an understanding of why profit is up at ClausenTube even though sales are down. We will also see how a variable costing income statement can support accurate planning and good decision making, two activities that are jeopardized if managers rely on full cost information.

jakkapan21/iStock/Getty Images Plus

LEARNING OBJECTIVES

1. Explain the difference between full (absorption) and variable costing and prepare an income statement using variable costing.

2. Discuss the effect of production on full and variable costing income; explain the impact of JIT (just-in-time) on the difference between full and variable costing income; and discuss the benefits of variable costing for internal reporting purposes.

LEARNING OBJECTIVE 1

Explain the difference between full (absorption) and variable costing and prepare an income statement using variable costing.

FULL (ABSORPTION) AND VARIABLE COSTING

Income statements of manufacturing firms prepared for *external* purposes use full costing (also called **absorption costing**). In **full costing**, inventory costs include direct material, direct labor, and all manufacturing overhead. Direct material and direct labor are generally variable costs, but manufacturing overhead includes both variable and fixed cost elements. Thus, fixed and variable costs are commingled, or combined, and it is very difficult to untangle the costs to perform "what if" analysis that requires separating fixed and variable costs. An alternative to full costing for internal reporting purposes is variable costing. In **variable costing**, only variable production costs are included in inventory costs. All fixed production costs are treated as period costs and expensed in the period incurred.

As shown in Illustration 5-1, the only difference between the two methods is their treatment of fixed manufacturing overhead. Under the full costing method, these costs are included in inventory. They enter into the determination of expense only when the inventory is sold. Under the variable costing method, fixed manufacturing costs enter into the determination of expense in the same way as other, nonmanufacturing period

ILLUSTRATION 5-1

Comparison of full and variable costing

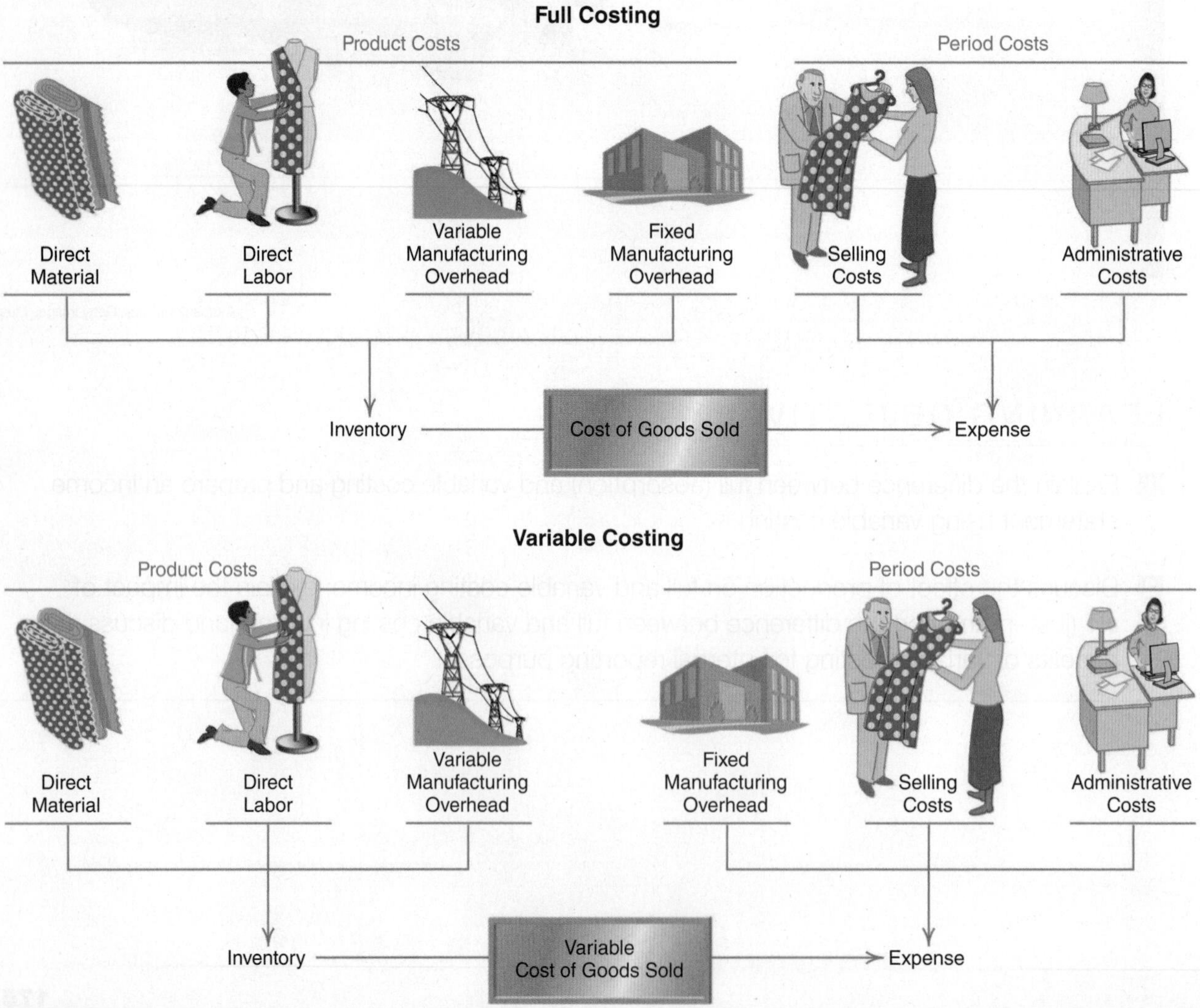

costs. Consider depreciation, which usually is a fixed cost component of manufacturing overhead. Under full costing, some portion of depreciation for the period remains in ending inventory when some of the items produced are not sold. Under the variable costing method, however, the total amount of depreciation is treated as an expense of the period.

Variable Costing Income Statement

If variable costing is used, an income statement can be prepared that classifies all expenses in terms of their cost behavior, either fixed or variable. With the variable expenses separated from the fixed expenses, a contribution margin can be presented. The contribution margin information will allow readers of the income statement to make reasonable estimates of how much profit will change with a change in sales.

A comparison of a variable costing income statement and an income statement typical for a manufacturing firm using full costing is presented in Illustration 5-2. Suppose sales of the Lee Dress Manufacturing Company are expected to increase by $10,000,000. What is the expected increase in profit? This can't be determined from the full costing income statement because we don't know which costs are fixed and which costs are variable. However, using the variable costing income statement, we can easily calculate the contribution margin ratio as the contribution margin divided by sales, which equals 65 percent. If sales increase by $10,000,000, profit is estimated to increase by $6,500,000:

$$\text{Contribution margin ratio} = \frac{\text{Contribution margin}}{\text{Sales}}$$

$$\text{Contribution margin ratio} = \frac{\$65{,}000}{\$100{,}000} = 0.65$$

Increase in sales	$10,000,000
Contribution margin ratio	× 0.65
Increase in contribution margin	$ 6,500,000

Note that the full costing income statement at the top of Illustration 5-2 cannot be used to estimate the increase in profit due to a $10,000,000 increase in sales. The reason is that cost of goods sold includes both fixed and variable costs. Obviously, the fixed costs won't increase if sales increase, but the problem is that we don't know how much of cost of goods sold is fixed—or variable, for that matter—under full costing.

Also note that in the variable costing income statement, we assume that some of the Lee Dress Manufacturing Company's selling and administrative costs are fixed and some are variable. Given this, it is important that we break out the fixed and variable components of selling and administrative costs so that we can calculate the contribution margin ratio. This ratio, as we just saw, allows us to do profit planning and answer questions like, "By how much will profit increase if sales increase by $10,000,000?"

LINK TO **PRACTICE**

German Companies More Likely to Use Variable Costing

In a survey yielding responses from 148 German companies and 130 U.S. firms, two accounting researchers found that German firms are much more likely than American companies to use variable costing (52 percent versus 21 percent). One German respondent stated that variable costing makes fixed overhead more visible. A U.S. respondent who uses variable costing stated that he prefers variable costing because, at his company, volumes vary a lot from period to period. If fixed costs were allocated to products, unit costs would be distorted.

Source: Kip Krumwiede and Augustin Suessmair, "Getting Down to Specifics on RCA," *Strategic Finance*, June 2007, pp. 50–55.

ILLUSTRATION 5-2
Comparison of income statements prepared using full and variable costing

Income Statement Prepared Using Full Costing
Lee Dress Manufacturing Company
Income Statement
For the Year Ended December 31, 2017

In Thousands		
Sales		$100,000
Less cost of goods sold		30,000
Gross margin		70,000
Less selling and administrative expense:		
Selling expense	$18,000	
Administrative expense	12,000	30,000
Net income		$ 40,000

Income Statement Prepared Using Variable Costing
Lee Dress Manufacturing Company
Income Statement
For the Year Ending December 31, 2017

In Thousands		
Sales		$100,000
Less variable costs:		
Variable cost of goods sold	$20,000	
Variable selling expense	10,000	
Variable administrative expense	5,000	35,000
Contribution margin		65,000
Less fixed costs:		
Fixed manufacturing expense	10,000	
Fixed selling expense	8,000	
Fixed administrative expense	7,000	25,000
Net income		$ 40,000

LEARNING OBJECTIVE 2
Discuss the effect of production on full and variable costing income; explain the impact of JIT (just-in-time) on the difference between full and variable costing income; and discuss the benefits of variable costing for internal reporting purposes.

EFFECTS OF PRODUCTION ON INCOME FOR FULL VERSUS VARIABLE COSTING: THE CLAUSENTUBE EXAMPLE

To examine in detail the differences between full and variable costing, let's consider the case of ClausenTube presented at the start of the chapter. The amplifiers produced by the company sell for $2,000 per unit. The variable production costs of each unit include the following: direct material (various tubes and other components), $600; direct labor, $225; and variable manufacturing overhead, $75. In addition, $1,200,000 of fixed manufacturing overhead is incurred each year. Selling expense is composed of $40 per unit sold of variable expense and $100,000 of fixed expense. Administrative expenses are all fixed and equal to $500,000:

Selling price per unit		$2,000
Variable production costs per unit:		
Direct material	$600	
Direct labor	225	
Variable overhead	75	900
Variable selling expense per unit		40
Contribution margin per unit		$1,060
Fixed manufacturing overhead		$1,200,000
Fixed selling expense		$100,000
Fixed administrative expense		$500,000

LINK TO PRACTICE

Overproduction to Avoid Showing a Loss

In a 2006 study, Sugata Roychowdhury found evidence indicating firms that would have shown a loss were able to increase earnings and avoid a loss by producing more goods than necessary. Overproduction lowers the cost per unit and cost of goods sold, since fixed costs are spread over more units.

Source: Sugata Roychowdhury, "Earnings Management Through Real Activities Manipulation," *Journal of Accounting and Economics*, 2006, pp. 335–370.

Quantity Produced Equals Quantity Sold

In 2017, there is no beginning inventory of finished goods; 5,000 units are produced, and 5,000 units are sold. Illustration 5-3 provides a comparison of full costing and variable costing income statements for this situation. The full cost of production is $5,700,000. This includes $4,500,000 of variable production cost ($900 × 5,000 units) and $1,200,000 of fixed manufacturing overhead. With 5,000 units produced, this results in a unit cost of $1,140:

$$\frac{\text{Variable production cost} + \text{Fixed production cost}}{\text{Units Produced}} = \text{Unit cost under full costing}$$

$$\frac{\$4{,}500{,}000 + \$1{,}200{,}000}{5{,}000} = \$1{,}140 \text{ per unit}$$

Because 5,000 units are sold, cost of goods sold is $5,700,000 ($1,140 × 5,000 units).

ILLUSTRATION 5-3
Full versus variable costing when units produced equal units sold

ClausenTube
Income Statements
For the Year Ended December 31, 2015

Full Costing		
Sales ($2,000 × 5,000 units)		$10,000,000
Cost of goods sold ($1,140 × 5,000 units)		5,700,000
Gross margin		4,300,000
Less selling and administrative expense:		
Selling expense	$ 300,000	
Administrative expense	500,000	800,000
Net income		$ 3,500,000

Notes: Units produced and sold both equal 5,000.
Selling expense = $100,000 + ($40 × 5,000 units).

Variable Costing		
Sales ($2,000 × 5,000 units)		$10,000,000
Less variable costs:		
Variable cost of goods sold ($900 × 5,000 units)	$4,500,000	
Variable selling costs ($40 × 5,000)	200,000	4,700,000
Contribution margin		5,300,000
Less fixed costs:		
Fixed production costs	1,200,000	
Fixed selling costs	100,000	
Fixed administrative costs	500,000	1,800,000
Net income		$ 3,500,000

Note: Units produced and sold both equal 5,000.

Selling expense is equal to $100,000 of fixed selling expense plus $40 per unit of variable selling expense for a total of $300,000:

Variable selling expense ($40 × 5,000 units)	$200,000
Fixed selling expense	100,000
Total selling expense	$300,000

Taking into account fixed administrative expense of $500,000, net income is $3,500,000.

Now let's consider the variable costing income statement in Illustration 5-3. The variable cost of production is only $900 per unit and variable selling expense is $40 per unit. With 5,000 units sold, variable expenses are $4,700,000. Thus, as indicated in the illustration, the contribution margin is $5,300,000. With fixed production cost of $1,200,000, fixed selling expense of $100,000, and fixed administrative expense of $500,000, net income is equal to $3,500,000, which is the same as net income calculated using full costing.

Decision Making/ Incremental Analysis

As we've just seen, when the quantity produced equals the quantity sold, there is no difference between net income calculated using full versus variable costing. Since all units produced are sold, no fixed cost ends up in ending inventory. Thus, the only difference between the two methods in this situation is that variable costing breaks out total costs into both fixed and variable costs and provides a contribution margin. That, however, is not a trivial difference since the contribution margin can be very helpful in planning and decision making. Suppose, for example, that ClausenTube is considering an advertising campaign that will cost $100,000 and is expected to increase sales by $200,000. What will be the impact on income (a planning question), and should the company undertake the marketing plan (a decision question)?

Using the variable costing income statement, we can easily calculate the contribution margin ratio to be 0.53:

$$\frac{\text{Contribution margin}}{\text{Sales}} = \frac{\$5{,}300{,}000}{\$10{,}000{,}000} = 0.53$$

With this information, we can estimate that if sales increase by $200,000, incremental profit will be $6,000:

Increase in sales	$200,000
Contribution margin ratio	× 0.53
Increase in contribution margin	106,000
Less increased marketing costs	100,000
Increase in profit	$ 6,000

Given that the impact on profit is positive, deciding to undertake the marketing plan is appropriate, and ClausenTube can update its financial plans accordingly.

Now suppose that the variable costing income statement is not available and ClausenTube managers rely on the information in the full costing income statement. How will they calculate the impact of the marketing plan? There are two assumptions they might make—both of which are wrong! First, they might assume that the cost of goods sold is entirely variable and, further, is the only variable cost. In this case, they will estimate that profit will increase by $0.43 for every dollar of sales, which, as we know, is too low:

$$\frac{\text{Gross margin}}{\text{Sales}} = \frac{\$4{,}300{,}000}{\$10{,}000{,}000} = 0.43$$

Second, they might assume that *all* costs are variable, in which case net income is equivalent to the contribution margin. In this case, they will estimate that profit will increase by only $0.35 for every dollar of sales, which is also too low:

$$\frac{\text{Net income}}{\text{Sales}} = \frac{\$3{,}500{,}000}{\$10{,}000{,}000} = 0.35$$

The point is that having a variable costing income statement can be very useful for planning and decision making. Not having one may lead managers to make assumptions that are incorrect, leading to poor plans and poor decisions.

Quantity Produced Is Greater Than Quantity Sold

In the previous section, we saw that when the quantity produced is equal to the quantity sold, there is no difference between income computed using full costing or using variable costing. Such is not the case if the quantity produced is *greater* than the quantity sold. In this case, income will be greater using full costing as opposed to variable costing. Let's see why this is the case.

Recall that in 2016, ClausenTube increased production to 6,000 units but sold only 4,800 due to a weakening economy. Illustration 5-4 provides a comparison of full costing and variable costing income statements for this situation. The full cost of production is $6,600,000. This includes $5,400,000 of variable production cost ($900 × 6,000 units) and $1,200,000 of fixed manufacturing overhead. With 6,000 units produced, this results in a unit cost of $1,100:

$$\frac{\text{Variable production cost} + \text{Fixed production cost}}{\text{Units produced}} = \text{Unit cost under full costing}$$

$$\frac{\$5{,}400{,}000 + \$1{,}200{,}000}{6{,}000} = \$1{,}100 \text{ per unit}$$

ANY **QUESTIONS?**

Q: If variable costing is so great for internal reporting purposes, why isn't it used for external reporting purposes? Don't external users want useful information?

A: Generally accepted accounting principles (GAAP) imply that variable costing is not acceptable for external reporting purposes. Since it's not allowed, it isn't used! But that leads one to wonder why this is the case. Shouldn't GAAP be formulated to provide useful information? Perhaps a better answer is that company managers may be concerned that variable cost information will prove helpful to competitors who, with the variable cost information, will have better insight into a rival company's cost structure. Another reason is that separating costs into fixed and variable components may be quite subjective. As we saw in Chapter 4, the most common way of classifying costs as fixed and variable is account analysis. In that method, costs are simply classified using management's subjective judgment.

ILLUSTRATION 5-4
Full versus variable costing when units produced are greater than units sold

ClausenTube
Income Statements
For the Year Ended December 31, 2016

Full costing		
Sales ($2,000 × 4,800 units)		$9,600,000
Cost of goods sold ($1,100 × 4,800 units)		5,280,000
Gross margin		4,320,000
Less selling and administrative expense:		
Selling expense	$ 292,000	
Administrative expense	500,000	792,000
Net income		$3,528,000
Notes: 6,000 units produced and 4,800 units sold. Selling expense = $100,000 + ($40 × 4,800 units).		
Variable Costing		
Sales ($2,000 × 4,800 units)		$9,600,000
Less variable costs:		
Variable cost of goods sold ($900 × 4,800 units)	$4,320,000	
Variable selling costs ($40 × 4,800)	192,000	4,512,000
Contribution margin		5,088,000
Less fixed costs:		
Fixed production costs	1,200,000	
Fixed selling costs	100,000	
Fixed administrative costs	500,000	1,800,000
Net income		$3,288,000
Note: 6,000 units produced and 4,800 units sold.		
Full costing income is greater than variable costing income		**$ 240,000**

In the previous year, the unit cost was $1,140. Unit costs have decreased because production has increased, spreading fixed costs out over more units. Because 4,800 units are sold, cost of goods sold is $5,280,000. Net income amounts to $3,528,000.

Now let's consider the variable costing income statement in Illustration 5-4. The variable cost of production is only $900 per unit and variable selling costs are $40 per unit. With 4,800 units sold, variable expenses are $4,512,000. Thus, as indicated in the illustration, the contribution margin is $5,088,000. With fixed production costs of $1,200,000, fixed selling costs of $100,000, and fixed administrative costs of $500,000, net income is equal to $3,288,000, which is $240,000 less than the income computed using full costing.

Let's see why income is higher using full costing. Recall that the difference between full and variable costing is that under full costing, inventory cost includes fixed manufacturing overhead whereas under variable costing, fixed manufacturing overhead is expensed as a period cost. Illustration 5-5 presents a comparison. Note that the $240,000 difference in ending inventory values completely accounts for the difference in income under the two methods.

Quantity Produced Is Less Than Quantity Sold

We have just seen that if the quantity produced equals the quantity sold, then full and variable costing yield the same reported income (see Illustration 5-3). If the quantity produced is greater than the quantity sold, full costing yields a higher income, because some fixed

ILLUSTRATION 5-5

Inventory cost under full and variable costing

Full Costing Inventory Value		
Cost per Unit		
Direct material per unit	$ 600	
Direct labor per unit	225	
Variable manufacturing overhead	75	
Fixed manufacturing overhead ($1,200,000 ÷ 6,000 units)	200	
Total	$1,100	
Ending Inventory Value ($1,100 × 1,200 units)	$1,320,000	
Variable Costing Inventory Value		
Cost per Unit		
Direct material per unit	$ 600	Difference of $240,000 due to $200 per unit of fixed manufacturing overhead in ending inventory under full costing ($200 × 1,200 units = $240,000)
Direct labor per unit	225	
Variable manufacturing overhead	75	
Total	$ 900	
Ending Inventory Value ($900 × 1,200 units)	$1,080,000	

manufacturing overhead is in ending inventory under full costing while the entire amount is treated as a period expense under variable costing (see Illustrations 5-4 and 5-5). Now, what is the case if the quantity produced is less than the quantity sold? To sell more than produced, a company must have some beginning inventory. The recorded value of that beginning inventory will be greater with full costing since full costing includes fixed manufacturing overhead and variable costing does not. Thus, when the beginning inventory is charged to cost of goods sold, the charge will be higher under full costing. The result: Income is lower under full costing when the quantity produced is less than the quantity sold.

Suppose that in 2017, ClausenTube produces 6,000 units but sells 7,200 units. Recall that 1,200 units are left over from the prior year. Now cost of goods sold under full costing includes 1,200 units at $1,100 per unit from beginning inventory and 6,000 units at $1,100 from current-period production. As indicated in Illustration 5-6, total cost of goods sold is equal to $7,920,000 under full costing.

The difference in incomes between full and variable costing is $240,000 ($5,832,000 under variable costing – $5,592,000 under full costing). This, as we've already said, is due to the fact that beginning inventory includes fixed manufacturing overhead under full costing while beginning inventory under variable costing does not.

Note that the difference between the beginning inventory values accounts for the $240,000 difference in incomes:

Beginning inventory under full costing	$1,320,000
Beginning inventory under variable costing	1,080,000
Difference	$ 240,000

To summarize, here are the comparative effects of production on income for the two methods:

Condition	**Result**
Units produced equal units sold	No difference in income
Units produced exceed units sold	Full costing yields higher income
Units produced are less than units sold	Variable costing yields higher income

ILLUSTRATION 5-6
Full versus variable costing when units produced are less than units sold

ClausenTube
Income Statements
For the Year Ended December 31, 2017

Full Costing		
Sales ($2,000 × 7,200 units)		$14,400,000
Cost of goods sold		
1,200 units × $1,100	$1,320,000	
6,000 units × $1,100	6,600,000	7,920,000
Gross margin		6,480,000
Less selling and administrative expense:		
Selling expense	$ 388,000	
Administrative expense	500,000	888,000
Net income		$ 5,592,000
Notes: 6,000 units produced and 7,200 sold.		
Selling expense = $100,000 + ($40 × 7,200 units).		
Variable Costing		
Sales ($2,000 × 7,200 units)		$14,400,000
Less variable costs:		
Variable cost of goods sold		
1,200 units × $900	$1,080,000	
6,000 units × $900	5,400,000	6,480,000
Variable selling costs ($40 × 7,200)		288,000
Contribution margin		7,632,000
Less fixed costs:		
Fixed production costs	1,200,000	
Fixed selling costs	100,000	
Fixed administrative costs	500,000	1,800,000
Net income		$ 5,832,000
Note: 6,000 units produced and 7,200 sold.		
Variable costing income is greater than full costing income		$ 240,000

Explaining What Happened at ClausenTube

Recall the scenario at the start of the chapter. Robert Clausen had just called his controller and asked her to explain why profit increased even though the company sold fewer units in 2016 compared to 2015 and had not changed its price or its production processes. It is hoped that the answer is now apparent. In 2016, the company produced a lot more units than it sold. The high level of production reduced cost per unit because fixed manufacturing overhead was spread out over more units. The low unit cost led to a low cost of goods sold value, but the company ended up with a substantial ending inventory balance.

LINK TO **PRACTICE**

Cut in Production at John Deere Likely to Hurt Profit Margin

At the start of 2015, John Deere forecasted a 20 percent decline in agriculture and turf equipment sales. That's likely to increase cost per unit as fixed costs are spread over fewer units. The end result is a likely decline in Deere's profit margin (the ratio of gross profit to sales).

Source: Trefis Team, "Why 2015 Might Not Be a Good Year For Deere," *Forbes Online* (January, 2, 2015).

If the company had been using variable costing, Robert Clausen would have seen profit decline, just as he expected. Note that per Illustration 5-3, income under variable costing in 2015 when sales were 5,000 units was $3,500,000. Per Illustration 5-4, income under variable costing in 2016 when sales were only 4,800 units was only $3,288,000. That's because variable costing does not allow fixed manufacturing overhead to be "buried" in ending inventory. Rather, with variable costing, the entire amount is treated as a period expense.

Impact of JIT on the Income Effects of Full versus Variable Costing

As discussed in Chapter 2, many companies have adopted just-in-time (JIT) inventory management systems. Companies that use JIT may have very low inventory levels since they don't produce until they are ready to sell their products. The result is that the units they produce are approximately equal to the units they sell. Thus, the difference between variable costing income and full costing income is likely to be very small for companies that use JIT.

TEST YOUR **KNOWLEDGE**

Kincade Faucets produces a variety of faucets for residential and commercial use. At the start of the year, the company had Finished Goods Inventory of $1,000,000. At the end of the year, the company had Finished Goods Inventory of $1,400,000. During the year, the company incurred $400,000 of depreciation expense on its manufacturing equipment.

How much depreciation expense will be in Finished Goods Inventory under variable costing?

a. $285,714.
b. $0.00.
c. Neither of the answer choices is correct.

Correct answer is b.

BENEFITS OF VARIABLE COSTING FOR INTERNAL REPORTING

There are two primary benefits associated with using variable costing for internal reporting purposes. Both are discussed in this section.

Variable Costing Facilitates CVP Analysis

Variable costing separates fixed and variable costs, a necessary step in performing cost-volume-profit (CVP) analysis and, relatedly, planning and decision making. We discussed this point earlier, but it's worth repeating. Managers simply can't estimate accurately the impact of changes in volume on cost and profit unless they know which costs are fixed and which costs are variable. Consider the full costing income statement in Illustration 5-4 and ask yourself, "What would be the impact on profit of a $100,000 increase in sales?" Unfortunately, the question cannot be answered with any assurance using the full cost information. We don't know which costs are fixed and which are variable so we don't know which ones will increase with the increase in sales.

Now consider the variable costing income statement. We can easily see that the contribution margin ratio is .53 (i.e., $5,088,000 ÷ $9,600,000). Thus, we can easily estimate a $53,000 increase in profit with a $100,000 increase in sales.

VARIABLE COSTING LIMITS MANAGEMENT OF EARNINGS VIA PRODUCTION VOLUME

YOU GET WHAT YOU MEASURE

Because the performance of managers is often evaluated in relation to earnings, managers may have an incentive to artificially inflate profit by producing more units than they can sell. Using variable costing to calculate earnings, however, limits this option. Suppose a manager expects sales to be 1,000 units. The selling price is $100 per unit, variable production costs are $50 per unit, and fixed production costs are $45,000. If the manager produced 1,000 units, profit would be equal to $5,000 (i.e., 1,000 × ($100 – $50) – $45,000) under both the full costing method and the variable costing method. The manager may realize, however, that if the full costing method is used, part of the fixed costs can be assigned to ending inventory, thereby transferring the expense to a future period. Thus, if the manager produces 2,000 units, profit will be $22,500 higher because half of the fixed costs will be included in the 1,000 units remaining in ending inventory. Of course, this is a short-run strategy, because eventually the inventory buildup will be noticed. However, the manager may hope to be working for a different company by that time with a great track record as a manager at the former company! Note that the strategy of producing more than you can sell will not increase income under the variable costing method, because under that method, none of the fixed costs can be included in ending inventory.

Decision Making INSIGHT

A variable costing income statement facilitates decision making by breaking out the total contribution margin. If we divide the contribution margin by sales, we have the contribution margin ratio, and we can use it to analyze the impact of changes in sales on profit. Since many decisions affect sales, being able to estimate the impact of changes in sales on profit greatly facilitates decision making.

SUMMARY OF LEARNING OBJECTIVES

LEARNING OBJECTIVE 1 Explain the difference between full (absorption) and variable costing and prepare an income statement using variable costing.

In full costing, product costs include direct material, direct labor, and variable and fixed manufacturing overhead. In variable costing, fixed manufacturing overhead is not included in product cost. Rather, it is treated as a period expense.

In a variable costing income statement, variable and fixed costs are segregated. All variable expenses are deducted from sales to yield a contribution margin. Then fixed expenses are deducted from the contribution margin to yield net income.

LEARNING OBJECTIVE 2 Discuss the effect of production on full and variable costing income; explain the impact of JIT (just-in-time) on the difference between full and variable costing income; and discuss the benefits of variable costing for internal reporting purposes.

If the quantity produced equals the quantity sold, there is no difference in income. If the quantity produced exceeds the quantity sold, full costing income is higher than variable costing income. If the quantity produced is less than the quantity sold, full costing income is less than variable costing income.

With a JIT system, there is often little difference between the quantity produced and the quantity sold. Thus, there is likely to be only a small difference between full and variable costing income when companies use JIT.

Finally, remember that variable costing results in a contribution margin, which is useful in planning and decision making. Also, variable costing income cannot be managed up (inflated) by producing more units than needed.

REVIEW PROBLEM 1

Albert Pernelli, a well-known consultant, was hired to "turn around" Inlet Steel Plate. In the year prior to his arrival, the company produced and sold 60,000 tons of steel plate for $800 per ton. The company has $20,000,000 of fixed manufacturing costs and $400 per ton of variable manufacturing costs. Selling and administrative costs are essentially fixed and amount to $9,000,000. At the end of the year, the company had a loss of $5,000,000, as follows:

Sales (60,000 tons × $800)	$48,000,000
Less cost of goods sold ($20,000,000 fixed + ($400 × 60,000 tons))	44,000,000
Gross margin	4,000,000
Less selling and administrative costs	9,000,000
Net loss	($ 5,000,000)

Upon arriving at Inlet Steel Plate, Albert noted that the company was operating substantially below capacity due to a weak market for steel plate. He decided that the company had to take advantage of its capacity and ordered the company to increase production of steel plate to 90,000 tons. He also cut advertising and laid off white-collar workers, saving the company $2,000,000. Although sales remained at 60,000 tons, profit went from a loss of $5 million to a gain of $3,666,667! Albert received a large fee and added to his reputation as a "turnaround genius."

REQUIRED

a. Assuming no changes in price or the company's cost structure, show the calculation of income under Albert's "leadership."

b. How much fixed cost is buried in ending inventory?

c. Did Albert really create value for the company?

ANSWER

a. Calculation of unit cost of production

Fixed cost	$20,000,000	
Variable costs		
($400 × 90,000 tons)	36,000,000	
Total	$56,000,000	
Number of tons	÷ 90,000	
Cost per ton	$ 622.2222	per ton

Calculation of net income:

Sales (60,000 tons × $800)	$48,000,000
Less cost of goods sold	
($622.2222 × 60,000 tons)	$37,333,332
Gross margin	10,666,668
Less selling and administrative costs	7,000,000
Net income	$ 3,666,668

b. Fixed cost buried in ending inventory

Amount of fixed cost	$20,000,000
Production (tons)	÷ 90,000
Fixed cost per ton	$ 222.2222
Tons in ending inventory	
(90,000 – 60,000)	× 30,000
Fixed cost in ending inventory	
(30,000 × $222.2222)	$ 6,666,666

c. It's hard to see that Albert really created shareholder value. Most of the increase in profit is due to burying $6.7 million of fixed costs in ending inventory. Albert did increase profit by

$2,000,000 due to cutting advertising and laying off white-collar workers, but this may be a short-run savings. Indeed, cutting advertising may actually hurt long-run profitability.

REVIEW PROBLEM 2

Butler Manufacturing produces fireproof data storage containers that sell for $6,000 each. The company has the following cost structure:

Manufacturing costs:	
Direct material per unit	$ 1,000
Direct labor per unit	2,000
Variable manufacturing overhead per unit	500
Total variable manufacturing costs per unit	$ 3,500
Fixed manufacturing overhead per year	$2,000,000
Selling costs:	
Variable selling costs per dollar of sales	$ 0.10
Fixed selling costs per year	$ 600,000
Administrative costs:	
Fixed administrative costs per year	$ 800,000

At the start of 2017, there was no beginning inventory. During 2017, the company produced and sold 2,000 units. During 2018, the company produced 2,500 units but still sold only 2,000 units.

REQUIRED

a. Calculate the full manufacturing cost per unit for 2017 and 2018.

b. Prepare full costing income statements for 2017 and 2018.

c. Calculate the variable manufacturing cost per unit for 2017 and 2018.

d. Prepare variable costing income statements for 2017 and 2018.

e. Reconcile the difference in net income for 2018 between the full costing and the variable costing approaches.

ANSWER

a. Full Manufacturing Cost per Unit in 2017

Direct material per unit	$1,000
Direct labor per unit	2,000
Variable manufacturing overhead per unit	500
Fixed manufacturing overhead per unit ($2,000,000 ÷ 2,000 units)	1,000
Total	$4,500

Full Manufacturing Cost per Unit in 2018

Direct material per unit	$1,000
Direct labor per unit	2,000
Variable manufacturing overhead per unit	500
Fixed manufacturing overhead per unit ($2,000,000 ÷ 2,500 units)	800
Total	$4,300

b. Income for 2017 Using Full Costing

Sales ($6,000 × 2,000 units)		$12,000,000
Cost of goods sold ($4,500 × 2,000 units)		9,000,000
Gross margin		3,000,000
Less selling and administrative expense:		
Selling expense ($600,000 + (.10 × $12,000,000))	$1,800,000	
Administrative expense	800,000	2,600,000
Net income		$ 400,000

Note: Units produced and sold both equal 2,000.

Income for 2018 Using Full Costing

Sales ($6,000 × 2,000 units)		$12,000,000
Cost of goods sold ($4,300 × 2,000 units)		8,600,000
Gross margin		3,400,000
Less selling and administrative expense:		
Selling expense ($600,000 + (.10 × $12,000,000))	$1,800,000	
Administrative expense	800,000	2,600,000
Net income		$ 800,000

Note: 2,500 units produced and 2,000 units sold.

c. Variable Manufacturing Cost per Unit in 2017 and 2018

Direct material per unit	$1,000
Direct labor per unit	2,000
Variable manufacturing overhead per unit	500
Total	$3,500

d. Income for 2017 and 2018 Using Variable Costing

Sales ($6,000 × 2,000 units)		$12,000,000
Less variable costs:		
Variable cost of goods sold ($3,500 × 2,000 units)	$7,000,000	
Variable selling costs (.10 × $12,000,000)	1,200,000	8,200,000
Contribution margin		3,800,000
Less fixed costs:		
Fixed production costs	2,000,000	
Fixed selling costs	600,000	
Fixed administrative costs	800,000	3,400,000
Net income		$ 400,000

e. $800 of fixed manufacturing overhead per unit × 500 units in ending inventory = $400,000.

KEY TERMS

Absorption costing (176)

Full costing (176)

Variable costing (176)

SELF-ASSESSMENT (Answers Below)

1. Full costing differs from variable costing in that:
   a. Full costing excludes selling costs from consideration.
   b. Full costing excludes administrative costs from consideration.
   c. Full costing includes variable manufacturing overhead in inventory.
   d. Full costing includes fixed manufacturing overhead in inventory.

2. If units produced exceed units sold:
   a. Full costing yields a higher income than variable costing.
   b. Full costing yields a lower income than variable costing.
   c. Full costing and variable costing yield the same income.

3. Use of a just-in-time inventory management system is likely to:
   a. Increase the difference between variable and full costing income.
   b. Decrease the difference between variable and full costing income.
   c. Have no effect on the difference between variable and full costing income.

4. A benefit of variable costing for internal reporting purposes is that it:
   a. Facilitates CVP analysis.
   b. Limits the ability to inflate income by producing more units than needed for current sales.
   c. Allows management to manage net income.
   d. Allows two of the answer choices.

5. If units produced are less than units sold:
   a. Full costing yields a higher income than variable costing.
   b. Full costing yields a lower income than variable costing.
   c. Full costing and variable costing yield the same income.

The following information applies to Questions 6–10.

Ajax Manufacturing has the following cost structure:

Direct material	$10
Direct labor	20
Variable manufacturing overhead	5
Total variable manufacturing costs per unit	$35
Fixed manufacturing overhead per year	$100,000
Fixed selling and administrative expense per year	$200,000

6. Assume that Ajax produces 10,000 items and sells 8,000 items. In this case, the full costing value of ending inventory is:
   a. $70,000.
   b. $90,000.
   c. $130,000.
   d. $140,000.
7. Assume that Ajax produces 10,000 items and sells 8,000 items. In this case, the variable costing value of ending inventory is:
   a. $70,000.
   b. $90,000.
   c. $130,000.
   d. $140,000.
8. Assume that Ajax produces 10,000 items and sells 8,000 items. In this case, the full costing value of cost of goods sold is:
   a. $360,000. b. $350,000. c. $300,000. d. $280,000.
9. Assume that Ajax produces 10,000 items and sells 8,000 items. In this case, the variable cost of goods sold is:
   a. $360,000. b. $350,000. c. $300,000. d. $280,000.
10. Assume that Ajax produces 10,000 items and sells 8,000 items. The selling price of Ajax's product is $90 per unit. In this case, the contribution margin on the income statement prepared using variable costing is:
   a. $350,000. b. $440,000. c. $550,000. d. $700,000.

ANSWERS TO SELF-ASSESSMENT

1. d 2. a 3. b 4. d 5. b 6. b
7. a 8. a 9. d 10. b

QUESTIONS

1. Explain the difference between variable costing and full costing.
2. Explain why income computed under full costing will exceed income computed under variable costing if production exceeds sales.
3. What are the benefits of variable costing for internal reporting purposes?
4. Why would the difference between income computed under full costing and income computed under variable costing be relatively small if a company used a JIT inventory management system?
5. Explain why the ending inventory balance (assuming it is not zero) computed under full costing will always be greater than the ending inventory balance computed under variable costing.
6. If a company produces 50,000 units and sells 46,000 units during a period, which method of computing net income will result in the higher net income? Why?
7. If a company produces less than it sells (the extra units sold are from beginning inventory), which method of computing net income will result in the higher net income? Why?
8. Explain how fixed manufacturing costs are treated under variable costing. How are fixed manufacturing costs treated under full costing?
9. If fixed manufacturing overhead per unit under full costing is multiplied by the change units in inventory between the beginning of the period and the end of the period, what does the resulting number represent?
10. Explain how a manufacturing company can "bury" fixed production costs in ending inventory under full costing.

EXERCISES

GROUP WORK

EXERCISE 5-1. [LO 2] A key idea in this book is that decision making relies on incremental analysis.

REQUIRED

Explain how the use of variable costing can support appropriate decisions using incremental analysis.

WRITING

EXERCISE 5-2. [LO 2] In a normal year, Wilson Industries has $24,000,000 of fixed manufacturing costs and produces 60,000 units. In the current year, demand for its product has decreased, and it appears that the company will be able to sell only 50,000 units. Senior managers are concerned, in part because their bonuses are tied to reported profit. In light of this, they are considering keeping production at 60,000 units.

REQUIRED

Write a paragraph explaining why increasing production beyond the quantity needed for current sales will increase profit, and calculate the impact of producing 10,000 "extra" units. Is the managers' proposed action in the best interest of shareholders?

EXERCISE 5-3. [LO 1] Mendel Manufacturing produces composite window frames for airline manufacturing companies. At the start of the year, the company had no beginning inventory. During the year, the company manufactured 5,000 units and sold 4,000. Direct material costs were $500,000, direct labor was $400,000, variable manufacturing overhead was $800,000, and fixed manufacturing overhead was $1,000,000.

REQUIRED

Calculate cost per unit under full costing and under variable costing.

EXCEL

The following information relates to Exercises 5-4 through 5-10:

Xenoc produces stereo speakers. The selling price per pair of speakers is $1,800. There is no beginning inventory.

Costs involved in production are:	
Direct material	$ 150
Direct labor	200
Variable manufacturing overhead	100
Total variable manufacturing costs per unit	$ 450
Fixed manufacturing overhead per year	$600,000
In addition, the company has fixed selling and administrative costs:	
Fixed selling costs per year	$210,000
Fixed administrative costs per year	$110,000

EXERCISE 5-4. [LO 1] During the year, Xenoc produces 1,500 pairs of speakers and sells 1,200 pairs.

REQUIRED

What is the value of ending inventory using full costing?

EXERCISE 5-5. [LO 1] During the year, Xenoc produces 1,500 pairs of speakers and sells 1,200 pairs.

REQUIRED

What is the value of ending inventory using variable costing?

EXERCISE 5-6. [LO 1] During the year, Xenoc produces 1,500 pairs of speakers and sells 1,200 pairs.

REQUIRED

What is cost of goods sold using full costing?

EXERCISE 5-7. [LO 1] During the year, Xenoc produces 1,500 pairs of speakers and sells 1,200 pairs.

REQUIRED

What is cost of goods sold using variable costing?

EXERCISE 5-8. [LO 1] During the year, Xenoc produces 1,500 pairs of speakers and sells 1,200 pairs.

REQUIRED

What is net income using full costing?

EXERCISE 5-9. [LO 1] During the year, Xenoc produces 1,500 pairs of speakers and sells 1,200 pairs.

REQUIRED

What is net income using variable costing?

EXERCISE 5-10. [LO 1, 2] During the year, Xenoc produces 1,500 pairs of speakers and sells 1,200 pairs.

REQUIRED

How much fixed manufacturing overhead is in ending inventory under full costing? Compare this amount to the difference in the net incomes calculated in Exercises 5-8 and 5-9.

EXCEL **The following information relates to Exercises 5-11 through 5-18:**

Summit Manufacturing produces snow shovels. The selling price per snow shovel is $30. There is no beginning inventory.

Costs involved in production are:	
Direct material	$ 5
Direct labor	4
Variable manufacturing overhead	3
Total variable manufacturing costs per unit	$ 12
Fixed manufacturing overhead per year	$180,000

In addition, the company has fixed selling and administrative costs of $160,000 per year.

EXERCISE 5-11. [LO 1] During the year, Summit produces 50,000 snow shovels and sells 45,000 snow shovels.

REQUIRED

What is the value of ending inventory using full costing?

EXERCISE 5-12. [LO 1] During the year, Summit produces 50,000 snow shovels and sells 45,000 snow shovels.

REQUIRED

What is the value of ending inventory using variable costing?

EXERCISE 5-13. [LO 1, 2] During the year, Summit produces 50,000 snow shovels and sells 45,000 snow shovels.

REQUIRED

Calculate the difference in full costing net income and variable costing net income without preparing either income statement.

EXERCISE 5-14. [LO 1] During the year, Summit produces 50,000 snow shovels and sells 45,000 snow shovels.

REQUIRED

What is cost of goods sold using full costing?

EXERCISE 5-15. [LO 1] During the year, Summit produces 50,000 snow shovels and sells 45,000 snow shovels.

REQUIRED

What is cost of goods sold using variable costing?

EXERCISE 5-16. [LO 1] During the year, Summit produces 50,000 snow shovels and sells 45,000 snow shovels.

REQUIRED

What is net income using full costing?

EXERCISE 5-17. [LO 1] During the year, Summit produces 50,000 snow shovels and sells 45,000 snow shovels.

REQUIRED

What is net income using variable costing?

EXERCISE 5-18. [LO 1, 2] During the year, Summit produces 50,000 snow shovels and sells 45,000 snow shovels.

REQUIRED

How much fixed manufacturing overhead is in ending inventory under full costing? Compare this amount to the difference in the net incomes calculated in Exercise 5-13.

PROBLEMS

EXCEL

PROBLEM 5-1. Variable and Full Costing: Sales Constant but Production Fluctuates [LO 1, 2] Spencer Electronics produces a wireless home lighting device that allows consumers to turn on home lights from their cars and light a safe path into and through their homes. Information on the first 3 years of business is as follows:

	2017	2018	2019	Total
Units sold	20,000	20,000	20,000	60,000
Units produced	20,000	25,000	15,000	60,000
Fixed production costs	$750,000	$750,000	$750,000	
Variable production costs per unit	$ 150	$ 150	$ 150	
Selling price per unit	$ 250	$ 250	$ 250	
Fixed selling and administrative expense	$220,000	$220,000	$220,000	

REQUIRED

a. Calculate profit and the value of ending inventory for each year using full costing.

b. Explain why profit fluctuates from year to year even though the number of units sold, the selling price, and the cost structure remain constant.

c. Calculate profit and the value of ending inventory for each year using variable costing.

d. Explain why, using variable costing, profit does not fluctuate from year to year.

EXCEL **PROBLEM 5-2. Variable and Full Costing: Sales and Production Fluctuate [LO 1, 2]** Hamilton Stage Supplies is a manufacturer of a specialized type of light used in theaters. Information on the first 3 years of business is as follows:

	2017	2018	2019	Total
Units sold	5,000	5,000	5,000	15,000
Units produced	5,000	6,000	4,000	15,000
Fixed production costs	$50,000	$50,000	$50,000	
Variable production costs per unit	$ 75	$ 75	$ 75	
Selling price per unit	$ 225	$ 225	$ 225	
Fixed selling and administrative expenses	$ 5,000	$ 5,000	$ 5,000	

REQUIRED

a. Calculate profit and the value of ending inventory for each year using full costing. Round cost percent to two decimal places.

b. Explain why profit fluctuates from year to year even though the number of units sold, the selling price, and the cost structure remain constant.

c. Calculate profit and the value of ending inventory for each year using variable costing.

d. Explain why, using variable costing, profit does not fluctuate from year to year.

PROBLEM 5-3. Variable and Full Costing: Earnings Management with Full Costing; Changes in Production and Sales [LO 1, 2] Firemaster BBQ produces stainless steel propane gas grills. The company has been in operation for 3 years, and sales have declined each year due to increased competition. The following information is available:

	2017	2018	2019	Total
Units sold	30,000	27,000	25,000	82,000
Units produced	30,000	30,000	22,000	82,000
Fixed production costs	$30,000,000	$30,000,000	$30,000,000	
Variable production costs per unit	$ 1,000	$ 1,000	$ 1,000	
Selling price per unit	$ 2,500	$ 2,500	$ 2,500	
Fixed selling and administrative expense	$ 350,000	$ 350,000	$ 350,000	

REQUIRED

a. Calculate profit and the value of ending inventory for each year under full costing.

b. Calculate profit and the value of ending inventory for each year under variable costing.

c. Explain how management of Firemaster could manipulate earnings in 2018 by producing more units than are actually needed to meet demand. Could this approach to earnings management be repeated year after year?

PROBLEM 5-4. Variable and Full Costing: Earnings Management with Full Costing; Changes in Production and Sales [LO 1, 2] Sampson Steel produces high-quality worktables. The company has been in operation for 3 years, and sales have declined each year due to increased competition. The following information is available:

	2017	2018	2019	Total
Units sold	10,000	9,000	8,000	27,000
Units produced	10,000	10,000	7,000	27,000
Fixed production costs	$350,000	$350,000	$350,000	
Variable production costs per unit	$ 100	$ 100	$ 100	
Selling price per unit	$ 350	$ 350	$ 350	
Fixed selling and administrative expenses	$300,000	$300,000	$300,000	

REQUIRED

a. Calculate profit and the value of ending inventory for each year under full costing.

b. Calculate profit and the value of ending inventory for each year under variable costing.

c. Explain how management of Sampson could manipulate earnings in 2018 by producing more units than are actually needed to meet demand. Could this approach to earnings management be repeated year after year?

PROBLEM 5-5. Variable and Full Costing: Income Effect of Clearing Excess Inventory [LO 1, 2] The following information is available for Skipper Pools, a manufacturer of above-ground swimming pool kits:

	2017	2018	Total
Units produced	12,000	8,000	20,000
Units sold	10,000	10,000	20,000
Selling price per unit	$ 4,000	$ 4,000	
Direct material per unit	$ 800	$ 800	
Direct labor per unit	$ 1,500	$ 1,500	
Variable manufacturing overhead per unit	$ 300	$ 300	
Fixed manufacturing overhead per year	$2,400,000	$2,400,000	
Fixed selling and administrative expense per year	$1,500,000	$1,500,000	

In its first year of operation, the company produced 12,000 units but was able to sell only 10,000 units. In its second year, the company needed to get rid of excess inventory (the extra 2,000 units produced but not sold in 2017), so it cut back production to 8,000 units.

REQUIRED

a. Calculate profit for both years using full costing.

b. Note that profit has declined in 2018. Is company performance actually worse in 2018 compared to 2017?

c. Calculate profit for both years using variable costing.

d. Does variable costing profit present a more realistic view of firm performance in the 2 years? Explain.

PROBLEM 5-6. Variable and Full Costing: Income Effect of Clearing Excess Inventory [LO 1, 2] The following information is available for Dunworth Canoes, a company that builds inexpensive aluminum canoes:

	2017	2018	Total
Units produced	21,000	15,000	36,000
Units sold	18,000	18,000	36,000
Selling price per unit	$ 500	$ 500	
Variable production costs per unit	$ 200	$ 200	
Direct material per unit	$ 80	$ 80	
Direct labor per unit	$ 50	$ 50	
Variable manufacturing overhead per unit	$ 70	$ 70	
Fixed manufacturing overhead per year	$630,000	$630,000	
Fixed selling and administrative expense per year	$200,000	$200,000	

In its first year of operation, the company produced 21,000 units but was able to sell only 18,000 units. In its second year, the company needed to get rid of excess inventory (the extra 3,000 units produced but not sold in 2017) so it cut back production to 15,000 units.

REQUIRED

a. Calculate profit for both years using full costing.

b. Note that profit has declined in 2018. Is company performance actually worse in 2018 compared to 2017?

c. Calculate profit for both years using variable costing.

d. Does variable costing profit present a more realistic view of firm performance in the 2 years? Explain.

PROBLEM 5-7. Reconciling Variable and Full Costing Income [LO 1] Miller Heating is a small manufacturer of auxiliary heaters. The units sell for $300 each. In 2017, the company produced 1,000 units and sold 800 units. There was no beginning inventory. Below are variable and full costing income statements for 2017.

Income Statement Prepared Using Variable Costing
Miller Heating Company
Income Statement
For the Year Ending December 31, 2017

Sales		$240,000
Less variable costs:		
Variable cost of goods sold	$32,000	
Variable selling expense	16,000	48,000
Contribution margin		192,000
Less fixed costs:		
Fixed manufacturing expense	50,000	
Fixed selling expense	20,000	
Fixed administrative expense	30,000	100,000
Net income		$ 92,000

Income Statement Prepared Using Full Costing
Miller Heating Company
Income Statement
For the Year Ending December 31, 2017

Sales		$240,000
Less cost of goods sold		72,000
Gross margin		168,000
Less selling and administrative expenses:		
Selling expense	$36,000	
Administrative expense	30,000	66,000
Net income		$102,000

REQUIRED

Reconcile the difference in profit between the two income statements.

PROBLEM 5-8. Reconciling Variable and Full Costing Income [LO 1] The Octavius Company produces a 10-inch chef knife used by commercial chefs. The knives sell for $50 each. In 2017, the company produced 50,000 units and sold 45,000 units. There was no beginning inventory. Following are variable and full costing income statements for 2017.

Income Statement Prepared Using Variable Costing
Octavius Company
Income Statement
For the Year Ending December 31, 2017

Sales		$2,250,000
Less variable costs:		
Variable cost of goods sold	$650,000	
Variable selling expense	150,000	800,000
Contribution margin		1,450,000
Less fixed costs:		
Fixed manufacturing expense	600,000	
Fixed selling expense	150,000	
Fixed administrative expense	100,000	850,000
Net income		$ 600,000

Income Statement Prepared Using Full Costing
Octavius Company
Income Statement
For the Year Ending December 31, 2017

Sales		$2,250,000
Less cost of goods sold		1,190,000
Gross margin		1,060,000
Less selling and administrative expenses:		
Selling expense	$300,000	
Administrative expense	100,000	400,000
Net income		$ 660,000

REQUIRED

Reconcile the difference in profit between the two income statements.

PROBLEM 5-9. Using Information from a Variable Costing Income Statement to Make a Decision [LO 1, 2] Below is a variable costing income statement for the Wilner Glass Company, a maker of bottles for the beverage industry. For the coming year, the company is considering hiring two additional sales representatives at $80,000 each for base salary. The company anticipates that each sales representative will generate $900,000 of incremental sales.

Wilner Glass Company
Income Statement
For the Year Ending December 31, 2017

Sales		$20,000,000
Less:		
Variable cost of goods sold	$8,000,000	
Variable selling expense	4,000,000	12,000,000
Contribution margin		8,000,000
Less:		
Fixed production expense	2,600,000	
Fixed selling expense	1,800,000	
Fixed administrative expense	3,000,000	7,400,000
Net income		$ 600,000

REQUIRED

a. Calculate the impact on profit of the proposed hiring decision. Should the company hire the two additional sales representatives?

b. Consider the analysis of the decision performed by the company's chief accountant and compare it to your analysis in part a. What is the fundamental flaw in the chief accountant's work?

Analysis by Chief Accountant

Incremental sales	$1,800,000
Income per dollar of sales in 2017 ($600,000 ÷ $20,000,000)	0.03
	54,000
Less increase in base salary	160,000
Effect on profit	($ 106,000)

PROBLEM 5-10. Using Information from a Variable Costing Income Statement to Make a Decision [LO 1, 2] Below is a variable costing income statement for Trio Office Supplies, a company well known for its quality high-volume automatic staplers. For the coming year, the company is considering hiring three additional sales representatives at $150,000 each in base salary. The company anticipates that each sales representative will generate $400,000 of incremental sales.

Trio Office Supplies
Income Statement
For the Year Ending December 31, 2017

Sales		$30,000,000
Less:		
Variable cost of goods sold	$15,000,000	
Variable selling expense	3,000,000	18,000,000
Contribution margin		12,000,000
Less:		
Fixed production expense	2,000,000	
Fixed selling expense	1,500,000	
Fixed administrative expense	3,000,000	6,500,000
Net income		$ 5,500,000

REQUIRED

a. Calculate the impact on profit of the proposed hiring decision. Should the company hire the three additional sales representatives?

b. Consider the analysis of the decision performed by the company's chief accountant and compare it to your analysis in part a. What is the fundamental flaw in the chief accountant's work?

Analysis by Chief Accountant

Incremental sales	$1,200,000
Income per dollar of sales in 2017: ($5,500,000 ÷ $30,000,000)	.183
Net increase in income from sales	219,600
Less increase in base salary	450,000
Effect on profit	($ 230,400)

PROBLEM 5-11. Variable versus Full Costing Income and Earnings Management [LO 1, 2] The Renton Tractor Company was formed at the start of 2015 and produces a small garden tractor. The selling price is $4,800, variable production costs are $2,000 per unit, fixed production costs are

$6,400,000 per year, and fixed selling and administrative costs are $3,600,000 per year. Data below indicate net income for 2015–2017 under full costing.

In 2015 and 2016, Edward Vendon was the president of Renton Tractor. The board of directors was generally pleased with the company's performance under his leadership—the company hit the break-even point in its first year of operation and had a modest profit in 2016. Edward quit at the end of 2016 and went on to start an e-commerce company selling used cars on the Internet. His replacement, Zac Dalton, was apparently not as successful as Ed. Zac argued that he was improving the company by getting rid of excess inventory, but the board noted that the company showed a $2,360,000 loss in the first year of his leadership.

	2015	2016	2017
Production (units)	4,000	4,000	2,000
Sales (units)	3,000	3,300	3,700
Production cost per unit	$ 3,600	$ 3,600	$ 5,200
Sales	$14,400,000	$15,840,000	$17,760,000
Less cost of goods sold	10,800,000	11,880,000	16,520,000
Gross margin	3,600,000	3,960,000	1,240,000
Less selling and administrative expense	3,600,000	3,600,000	3,600,000
Net income (loss)	$ -0-	$ 360,000	($ 2,360,000)

REQUIRED

a. Recalculate net income for all 3 years using variable costing.

b. Based on the limited information available, comment on the relative job performance of Ed and Zac.

c. Note that under full costing, the company is showing a substantial loss in 2017. Based on the limited information available, does it appear that the company should get out of the tractor business?

PROBLEM 5-12. Variable versus Full Costing Income and Earnings Management [LO 1, 2] Hawthorne Golf, the maker of a sought-after set of golf clubs, was formed in 2012. The selling price for each golf club set is $1,700, variable production costs are $900 per unit, fixed production costs are $2,100,000 per year, and fixed selling and administrative costs are $2,250,000 per year. Data below indicate net income for 2015–2017 under full costing.

In 2015 and 2016, Milo Hawthorne, Jr., was the president of Hawthorne Golf. The board of directors was generally pleased with the company's performance under his leadership—the company hit the break-even point in its first year of operation and had a modest profit in 2016. Milo quit at the end of 2016 and went on to buy a golf course and open a pro shop. His replacement, Daryl Selmer, was apparently not as successful as Milo. Daryl argued that he was improving the company by getting rid of excess inventory, but the board noted that the company showed a $350,000 loss in the first year of his leadership.

	2015	2016	2017
Production (units)	7,000	7,000	2,500
Sales (units)	4,500	5,500	6,500
Production cost per unit (full cost)	$ 1,200	$ 1,200	$ 1,740
Sales	$7,650,000	$9,350,000	$11,050,000
Less cost of goods sold	5,400,000	6,600,000	9,150,000
Gross margin	2,250,000	2,750,000	1,900,000
Less selling and administrative expenses	2,250,000	2,250,000	2,250,000
Net income (loss)	$ -0-	$ 500,000	($ 350,000)

REQUIRED

a. Recalculate net income for all 3 years using variable costing.

b. Based on the limited information available, comment on the relative job performance of Milo and Daryl.

c. Note that under full costing, the company is showing a substantial loss in 2017. Based on the limited information available, does it appear that the company should get out of the golf club business?

PROBLEM 5-13. Reconciling Variable and Full Costing Income [LO 1, 2] The following information relates to Jarden Industries for fiscal 2017, the company's first year of operation:

Units produced	150,000
Units sold	120,000
Units in ending inventory	30,000
Fixed manufacturing overhead	$900,000

REQUIRED

a. Calculate the amount of fixed manufacturing overhead that would be expensed in 2017 using full costing.

b. Calculate the amount of fixed manufacturing overhead that would be expensed in 2017 using variable costing.

c. Calculate the amount of fixed manufacturing overhead that would be included in ending inventory under full costing and reconcile it to the difference between parts a and b.

PROBLEM 5-14. Reconciling Variable and Full Costing Income [LO 1, 2] The following information relates to Sinclair Industries for fiscal 2017, the company's first year of operation:

Units produced	500,000
Units sold	450,000
Units in ending inventory	50,000
Fixed manufacturing overhead	$1,500,000

REQUIRED

a. Calculate the amount of fixed manufacturing overhead that would be expensed in 2017 using full costing.

b. Calculate the amount of fixed manufacturing overhead that would be expensed in 2017 using variable costing.

c. Calculate the amount of fixed manufacturing overhead that would be included in ending inventory under full costing and reconcile it to the difference between parts a and b.

PROBLEM 5-15. Variable and Full Costing Income: Comprehensive Problem [LO 1, 2] The following information relates to Porter Manufacturing for fiscal 2017, the company's first year of operation:

Selling price per unit	$ 150
Direct material per unit	$ 75
Direct labor per unit	$ 30
Variable manufacturing overhead per unit	$ 5
Variable selling cost per dollar of sales	$ 0.05
Annual fixed manufacturing overhead	$2,750,000
Annual fixed selling expense	$1,500,000
Annual fixed administrative expense	$ 900,000
Units produced	250,000
Units sold	230,000

REQUIRED

a. Prepare an income statement using full costing.

b. Prepare an income statement using variable costing.

c. Calculate the amount of fixed manufacturing overhead that will be included in ending inventory under full costing and reconcile it to the difference between income computed under variable and full costing.

PROBLEM 5-16. Variable and Full Costing Income: Comprehensive Problem [LO 1, 2] The following information relates to Dorian Industrial for fiscal 2017, the company's first year of operation:

Units produced	420,000
Units sold	400,000
Selling price per unit	$ 50
Direct material per unit	$ 15
Direct labor per unit	$ 5
Variable manufacturing overhead per unit	$ 2
Variable selling cost per unit	$ 0.20
Annual fixed manufacturing overhead	$1,260,000
Annual fixed selling expense	$ 300,000
Annual fixed administrative expense	$ 100,000

REQUIRED

a. Prepare an income statement using full costing.

b. Prepare an income statement using variable costing.

c. Calculate the amount of fixed manufacturing overhead that will be included in ending inventory under full costing and reconcile it to the difference between income computed under variable and full costing.

PROBLEM 5-17. Variable and Full Costing Income: Comprehensive Problem [LO 1, 2] The following information relates to Jorgensen Manufacturing for calendar year 2017, the company's first year of operation:

Units produced	8,000
Units sold	7,000
Selling price per unit	$ 4,500
Direct material per unit	$ 2,000
Direct labor per unit	$ 1,200
Variable manufacturing overhead per unit	$ 900
Variable selling cost per unit	$ 225
Annual fixed manufacturing overhead	$800,000
Annual fixed selling and administrative expense	$400,000

REQUIRED

a. Prepare an income statement using full costing.

b. Prepare an income statement using variable costing.

c. Calculate the amount of fixed manufacturing overhead that will be included in ending inventory under full costing and reconcile it to the difference between income computed under variable and full costing.

d. Suppose that the company sold 8,000 units during the year. What would the variable costing net income have been? What would the full costing net income have been?

PROBLEM 5-18. Variable and Full Costing Income: Comprehensive Problem; Break-even Calculation [LO 1, 2] The following information relates to Axar Products for calendar year 2017, the company's first year of operation:

Units produced	20,000
Units sold	18,000
Selling price per unit	$ 30
Direct material per unit	$ 6
Direct labor per unit	$ 4
Variable manufacturing overhead per unit	$ 2
Variable selling cost per unit	$ 3
Annual fixed manufacturing overhead	$160,000
Annual fixed selling and administrative expense	$ 80,000

REQUIRED

a. Prepare an income statement using full costing.

b. Prepare an income statement using variable costing.

c. Using the variable costing income statement, calculate the company's break-even point in sales dollars and in units. Can the break-even point be calculated easily using the full costing income statement? Why or why not?

CASE

5-1 MICROIMAGE TECHNOLOGY, INC. [LO 1, 2]

MicroImage Technology, Inc. produces miniature digital color cameras that can be attached to endoscopes and other medical devices. The cameras sell for $215 per unit and are disposed of after each use. For 2017, the company's first full year of operation, the company had sales of 80,000 units and a net loss of $9,810,000, as follows:

MicroImage Technology, Inc.
Income Statement
For the Year Ended December 31, 2017

Sales		$17,200,000
Less cost of goods sold		18,360,000
Gross profit (loss)		(1,160,000)
Less selling and administrative expenses:		
Selling expense	$3,750,000	
Administrative expense	4,900,000	8,650,000
Net loss		($ 9,810,000)

The company is closely held, with six major inventors. Early in the first quarter of 2018, Warren Logan, company CFO, was preparing to meet with them to present profitability estimates for the coming 2 years. He expected the meeting to be somewhat hostile. Two days before, he had received an email from one of the investors, Sanjay Patel:

> Warren:
> I expected a net loss but not this big. And I certainly didn't expect a negative gross profit! It looks like the more we sell, the more we'll lose. I hope you come to the investor meeting next week with some explanations and some better numbers.
> SP

In preparing for the meeting, Warren assembled the following information based on results for 2017:

Units sold	80,000
Units produced	80,000
Selling price	$ 215
Manufacturing costs:	
Direct material costs	$ 1,280,000
Direct labor costs	1,200,000
Variable manufacturing overhead:	
Equipment maintenance	160,000
Inspection costs	400,000
Miscellaneous variable manufacturing overhead	320,000
Fixed manufacturing overhead:	
Rent	1,800,000
Depreciation	5,000,000
Supervisory salaries	4,500,000
Miscellaneous fixed manufacturing overhead	3,700,000
	$18,360,000

Selling expenses	
Variable selling expense:	
Shipping	$ 280,000
Commissions	800,000
Travel	120,000
Fixed selling expense:	
Salaries	1,900,000
Miscellaneous fixed selling expense	650,000
	$ 3,750,000

Administrative expenses (all fixed)	
Research and development	$ 2,700,000
Administrative salaries not related to R&D	1,300,000
Miscellaneous administrative expense	900,000
	$ 4,900,000

REQUIRED

a. Recast the full costing income statement for 2017 into a variable costing format. Does it appear, as Sanjay Patel contends, that the more the company sells, the more it loses?

b. Based on the previous information, calculate sales in dollars and units needed to break even in 2018.

c. Warren Logan, CFO, has developed assumptions that he believes are reasonable for 2018 and 2019. Using these assumptions, prepare budgeted income statements for 2018 and 2019 using the variable costing method. Are the major investors likely to find forecasted profits encouraging?

Assumptions for 2018

1. The company will hire two additional sales managers at a base salary of $90,000 each.
2. R&D will be cut by $1,100,000.
3. Unit sales will increase by 30 percent.

Assumptions for 2019

1. The company will hire one additional sales manager at a base salary of $90,000.
2. R&D will be increased by $600,000 over 2018.
3. Unit sales will increase by 60 percent over 2018.

CASE

5-2 RAINRULER STAINS [LO 1, 2]

RainRuler Stains produces a variety of exterior wood stains that have excellent coverage and longevity. In 2017, the company produced and sold 310,000 gallons of stain. There was no beginning inventory. Income for the year was as follows:

RainRuler Stains
Income Statement
For the Year Ended December 31, 2017

Sales		$4,650,000
Less cost of goods sold		3,300,000
Gross profit		1,350,000
Less selling and administrative expenses:		
Selling expense	$870,000	
Administrative expense	360,000	1,230,000
Net income		$ 120,000

In the past, the company has marketed its product only to independent hardware stores in Oregon, Washington, and Idaho. Recently, however, Reggie Sherman, VP of marketing, has negotiated deals with several large construction companies. He estimates that these deals will increase annual sales by 70,000 gallons but at a reduced price of $12 per gallon. (The price in 2017 to hardware stores was $15 per gallon, and this will not be affected by the new deals.)

At a recent meeting of the company's senior management team, Reggie presented a rough estimate of the financial impact of selling through the new channel:

Additional sales (gallons)	70,000
Selling price per gallon	$ 12.00
Incremental revenue	$840,000
Gross profit per dollar of sales ($1,350,000 ÷ $4,650,000)	0.2903
Incremental profit	$243,852

Since the incremental profit was more than two times as large as current net income, most of the managers present at the meeting expressed their hearty congratulations. Jennifer Jones, a summer intern and assistant to the company controller, Ed Flemming, thought Reggie's estimate was more than a little rough. After the meeting, she approached her boss and expressed her misgivings. "Ed, according to our previous discussions, fixed production costs related to rent, depreciation, and other items are about $1,362,500 per year. Reggie's analysis assumes that there aren't any fixed manufacturing overhead items. And I know our shipping costs, which are included in selling expense, are around $0.70 per gallon. Reggie's analysis assumes all selling expense is fixed. It's probably the case that almost all of our administrative expense is fixed, but that's clearly not accurate for selling expense. How about if I recast our income statement in a contribution margin format—you know, using variable costing—and use that as a basis to estimate the impact of the new channel sales?" Ed quickly agreed to Jennifer's proposal.

REQUIRED

Assume the role of Jennifer and prepare an income statement for 2017 using variable costing. Then use information on that statement as a basis for estimating the annual impact on profit of sales to construction companies.

6

COST ALLOCATION AND ACTIVITY-BASED COSTING

McMaster Screen Technologies produces a variety of touch-screen displays used in phones, kiosks, automobile navigation devices, and numerous other applications.

Approximately 80 percent of McMaster's revenue comes from producing screens in large numbers for touch-screen phones and automobile navigation devices. The other 20 percent is related to low-volume orders for kiosks, custom electronic equipment, and military applications.

In recent months, Michael Soma, the CFO at McMaster, has become concerned about the apparent profitability of several products. In particular, some high-volume products, such as the Model ND32 touch screen used in automobile navigation systems, are barely breaking even, while low-volume products, such as the Model MK420 touch screen used in a military targeting device, are selling for much more than the cost of production. This surprised Michael because the company has worked hard to reduce production inefficiencies, and he thought that would translate into high-volume products that were quite profitable. On the other hand, the company had just begun manufacturing for military applications that required new production techniques to meet stringent quality standards. Hence he suspected that production inefficiencies would keep gross profit low for more than a year for military-related products.

Michael knows that manufacturing overhead is allocated to products based on labor cost. The approach is simple, but he suspects it may be causing allocations of costs that are too high for the Model ND32 and too low for the Model MK420.

Firms that produce more than one product or that provide more than one type of service invariably have indirect costs because resources are shared by the products or services (e.g., two different products may be manufactured using the same piece of equipment). Various departments may also have common or shared resources (e.g., the marketing and human resources departments may share a high-speed copy machine). Because indirect costs associated with shared resources cannot be directly traced to products or services, some means of assigning them must be developed. The process of assigning indirect costs is referred to as **cost allocation**, which we first discussed in Chapter 2. Unfortunately, cost allocation frequently results in problems like the one faced by Michael Soma. To prepare yourself to deal with them, you need a good understanding of why and how costs are allocated. Providing you with that understanding is the purpose of this chapter. One of the key points of the chapter is that costs are allocated for a variety of purposes; allocations that are adequate for one purpose may not be adequate for another purpose.

Many managers have expressed concern that the way overhead is typically allocated may seriously distort product cost for manufacturing firms. The problem arises because most product costing systems allocate overhead using measures related to production volume. This is the case at McMaster Screen Technologies, where manufacturing overhead is allocated based on labor cost. However, many overhead costs are not proportional to volume. Activity-based costing (ABC) is an approach to allocating overhead costs that addresses this problem. We briefly discussed ABC in Chapter 2. Here you will gain a better understanding of the general process of cost allocation, which allows for a more detailed treatment of ABC.

In our discussion of ABC, we will build on the McMaster Screen Technologies example. However, it is important to note that ABC is not restricted to manufacturing firms. Banks, hospitals, insurance companies, and other service firms find that ABC provides insight into the costs of providing services to customers. Several of the problems and cases at the end of this chapter are in a service firm context and will provide you with an opportunity to generalize the ideas of ABC to this important business setting.

Shironosov/iStock/Getty Images Plus

LEARNING OBJECTIVES

1. Explain why indirect costs are allocated, describe the cost allocation process, and discuss allocation of service department costs.
2. Identify potential problems with cost allocation, discuss activity-based costing (ABC) and cost drivers, and distinguish activity-based costing (ABC) from activity-based management (ABM).

LEARNING OBJECTIVE 1

Explain why indirect costs are allocated, describe the cost allocation process, and discuss allocation of service department costs.

PURPOSES OF COST ALLOCATION

Companies allocate costs to products, services, and departments for four major reasons: (1) to provide information needed to make appropriate decisions, (2) to reduce the frivolous use of common resources, (3) to encourage managers to evaluate the efficiency of internally provided services, and (4) to calculate the "full cost" of products for financial reporting purposes and for determining cost-based prices (see Illustration 6-1). We will now discuss each of these purposes.

To Provide Information for Decision Making

When managers use a company resource and receive an allocation of its cost, they are, in essence, receiving a charge for use. For example, when Malinda Smith, a product manager at Mayfield Software, asks the art department to design a prototype box for a product under development, she will likely receive an allocation, on her product-line profit and loss statement, of costs incurred in the art department. The more artwork she orders, the more cost she will receive, reducing the profit for which she is responsible. But what is the appropriate allocation?

From a decision-making standpoint, the allocated cost should measure the opportunity cost of using a company resource. Let's see why this is the case. Suppose the art department has excess capacity and the design work does not create additional costs other than very minor material cost. In this case, the opportunity cost is approximately zero, and the appropriate allocation is also zero. Malinda's company, after all, does not want to discourage her from using the art department's services since this use does not lead to additional costs.

Suppose, however, the art department is extremely busy. If it takes on Malinda's job, other work will be delayed. In fact, a different product-line manager will be forced to go outside the company to get artwork done on time, incurring a cost of $5,000. In this case, Malinda's use of a company resource has led to a $5,000 opportunity cost. Thus, $5,000 would be an appropriate allocation, or charge, to Malinda's operation. If she does not believe that the art department's services represent a $5,000 benefit to her operation, then she will not demand these services, and the other product manager can make use of them and avoid incurring $5,000 of costs outside the company.

Although allocated costs should measure the opportunity cost of using a company resource, in practice this is difficult to operationalize. One reason is that the opportunity cost may quickly change. For example, on Wednesday, the art department may be dealing with a rush job and working overtime. But by Friday, the rush job may be completed,

ILLUSTRATION 6-1

Reasons firms allocate costs

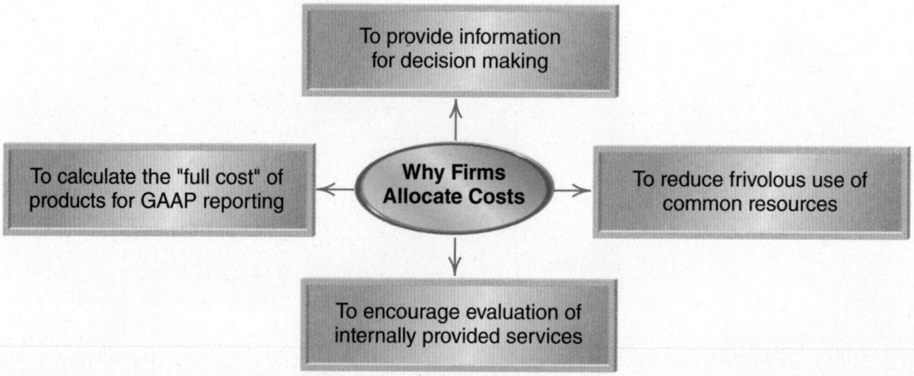

and there may be excess capacity. Thus, the opportunity cost would be much higher on Wednesday than on Friday.

Still, the opportunity cost idea is a useful benchmark. Whenever you are discussing allocations of cost, you should ask yourself, "How close is this allocation to the opportunity cost of use?" The closer it is, the better the allocation.

To Reduce Frivolous Use of Common Resources

As already noted, allocated costs serve as charges, or fees, for use of internal resources or services. Consider a company that runs a computer network used by all three of its divisions. Almost all of the costs associated with running the network are fixed, and they amount to $100,000 per year. Some accountants would argue that because these costs are fixed, the divisions should not be charged for using the network since use creates no incremental cost. However, if the three divisions do not incur any charge for using the network, they may tend to use it for frivolous or nonessential purposes (e.g., playing computer games, sending unnecessary e-mail, or accessing streaming video or otherwise creating unnecessary loads on network traffic).

This situation may not seem to be that detrimental to the company's welfare. After all, the costs associated with the network are primarily fixed. If frivolous use does not create additional costs, why discourage it? The reason is that frivolous use may have hidden costs. The primary hidden cost in the example is slower service to departments that need to use the network when it is being used unnecessarily by another department. In other words, an opportunity cost is associated with the use of the network.

One way to eliminate frivolous use is to charge for the use of centrally provided services. And one of the most common ways to charge for use is to allocate the cost of the service. For example, suppose Division 1 plans to use the network for 1,000 hours per year, Division 2 plans to use it for 1,000 hours, and Division 3 for 2,000 hours. A charge of $25 per hour ($100,000 ÷ 4,000 hours) could be assessed. Note that this rate would allocate the entire cost of the network ($100,000) among the three users, assuming that their plans worked out as expected. Divisions 1 and 2 would each be charged $25,000, and Division 3 would be charged $50,000. If division managers knew that this method of cost allocation would be used, they would have an incentive to reduce their division's frivolous use of the network, because use of the network reduces the reported profit of their division.

To Encourage Evaluation of Services

Cost allocation is also useful because it encourages managers to evaluate the services for which they are being charged. If no costs are allocated to users of centrally administered services, such as computer services or janitorial services, then the users of the services do not have an incentive to evaluate these services carefully. After all, the services are free. However, if the users are charged for the services (i.e., if they receive an allocation of the cost of the services), then the users have a strong incentive to look critically at the services and consider the possibility of lower-cost alternatives. If lower-cost alternatives exist, the users will certainly bring them to the company's attention. The company can then evaluate whether the services are being provided in an efficient manner.

Let's reconsider the example of Malinda Smith, a product manager at Mayfield Software, who is being charged for using the company's art department to design packaging for a product she manages. Suppose she receives a charge of $5,000 and believes that if she purchased the service outside the company, the cost would be only $2,000. In this case, she is likely to bring this matter to the attention of higher-level company officials who will encourage the manager of the art department to lower that operation's costs, perhaps by reducing head count or replacing staff who are inefficient. If the costs of the art department cannot be lowered, the company may consider shutting down the service and using an independent design firm.

To Provide "Full Cost" Information

As we have mentioned, GAAP requires full costing for external reporting purposes. Indirect production costs must be allocated to goods produced to meet this requirement. In addition, full cost information is required when a company has an agreement whereby the amount of revenue received depends on the amount of cost incurred. For example, defense contractors with the federal government often have contracts that specify they will be paid the cost of production as well as some fixed amount or percentage of cost. Such contracts are commonly called "cost-plus" contracts. An interesting feature of these contracts is that the cost of production specified often includes not only manufacturing costs but also a share of general and administrative costs. Thus, a substantial amount of cost allocation is required to assign indirect manufacturing costs and indirect general and administrative costs to the contract work.

A major problem with cost-plus contracts is that they create an incentive to allocate as much cost as possible to the goods produced on a cost-plus basis and little cost to goods that are not produced on a cost-plus basis. The more cost allocated to cost-plus contracts, the higher the amount paid to the company.

In spite of this limitation, cost-plus contracts serve a useful purpose. Without the assurance that they will be reimbursed for their costs and that they will earn some profit, many manufacturers would not be willing to bear the financial risks associated with producing state-of-the-art products for the government, using untried technologies. For example, not many companies would be willing to develop a new fighter aircraft without assurance that they would be reimbursed for all costs incurred in its development.

LINK TO **PRACTICE**

Cost-plus Contracts Create Incentive to Misallocate Costs

Government contracts issued by the Department of Defense are often so-called *cost-plus contracts*. Under such contracts, companies that supply the Department of Defense are reimbursed for their direct costs as well as reasonable overhead (their costs), and they also receive an amount for profit (the "plus" part of the cost-plus contract).

These contracts create an incentive for suppliers to allocate costs to government contracts that more properly should be charged to their non-government contracts. The reason—the more costs they allocate to government contracts, the higher their reimbursement. To thwart this fraudulent practice, the government passed the False Claims Act, which allows whistleblowers (informants) to receive 15 to 30 percent of any recovery. Since informants may collect millions of dollars, the Act is generally considered to be quite effective in bringing fraud to light!

TEST YOUR **KNOWLEDGE**

Indirect costs are allocated to products, services, and departments in order to:

a. Improve decision making.
b. Reduce frivolous use of resources.
c. Encourage evaluation of services.
d. Provide "full cost" information.
e. All of these answer choices are correct.

Correct answer is e.

ILLUSTRATION 6-2
The cost allocation process

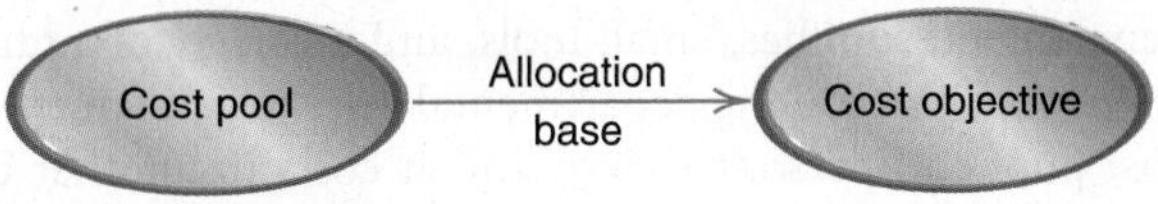

PROCESS OF COST ALLOCATION

We have seen that cost allocation is often necessary. But how is it achieved? The cost allocation process has three steps: (1) identify the cost objectives, (2) form cost pools, and (3) select an allocation base to relate the cost pools to the cost objectives. The three steps are shown in Illustration 6-2.

Determining the Cost Objective

The first step in the cost allocation process is to determine the product, service, or department that is to receive the allocation. The object of the allocation is referred to as the **cost objective**. For example, if a company allocates depreciation of a drilling press to products such as flanges and brackets, the products are the cost objectives. If computer-processing costs are allocated to the contracts worked on by a computer-aided design group, the contracts are the cost objectives. If a bank allocates general and administrative costs to product lines (e.g., loan services and estate-planning services), the product lines are the cost objectives (see Illustration 6-3).

Forming Cost Pools

The second step in the cost allocation process is to form **cost pools**. A cost pool is a grouping of individual costs whose total is allocated using one allocation base. For example, all of the costs in the maintenance department could be treated as a cost pool. In this case, the cost pool would include the wages of workers in the maintenance

ILLUSTRATION 6-3
Cost objectives

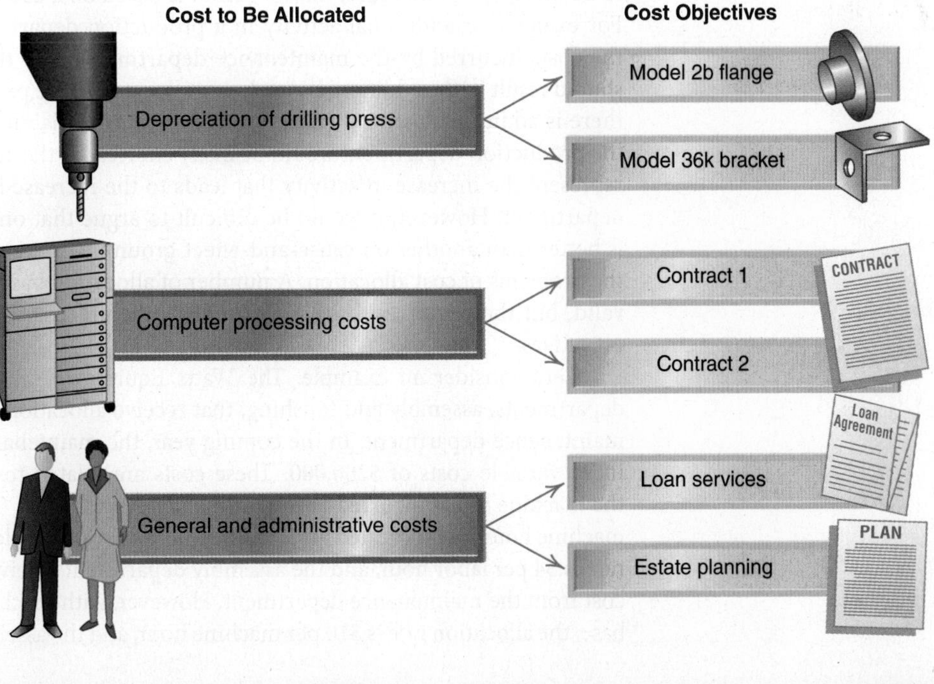

department, supplies, small tools, and a variety of additional cost items. Cost pools are often formed along departmental lines (e.g., maintenance department costs in one cost pool and personnel department costs in another cost pool). They may also be formed according to major activities. For example, costs related to equipment setups, a major activity in most manufacturing firms, are in one cost pool, and costs related to inspecting products for defects, another major activity, are in another cost pool.

The overriding concern in forming a cost pool is to ensure that the costs in the pool are homogeneous, or similar. One way to determine whether these costs are homogeneous is to compare the allocations with the allocations that result from breaking the pool up into smaller pools and using a variety of allocation bases. If there is not a substantial difference in the allocations, then, for practical purposes, the costs in the pool are considered to be homogeneous.

Some manufacturing companies include all manufacturing overhead (power costs, computing costs, material handling costs, etc.) in a single cost pool. However, allocations from a large pool containing costs related to very different activities are not likely to provide useful information. (We discuss this problem later in the chapter.) Although use of a single cost pool for overhead seems too broad, exactly how many cost pools are appropriate is not clear. Managers must make a cost-benefit decision. More pools involve more analysis and record keeping, which is costly. However, more pools also result in the benefit of more accurate information.

Selecting an Allocation Base

The third step in the allocation process is to select an allocation base that relates the cost pool to the cost objectives. The allocation base must be some characteristic that is common to all of the cost objectives. If the cost objectives are manufactured products, then direct labor hours, direct labor cost, and machine hours are examples of characteristics that could be used as allocation bases. If the cost objectives are the divisions of a multidivisional firm, then sales dollars, total assets, and divisional profit are examples of characteristics that could be used as allocation bases.

Deciding which of the possible allocation bases to use is not an easy matter. Ideally, the allocation base selected should relate costs to cost objectives that *caused* the costs to be incurred. In this case, the allocation is based on a **cause-and-effect relationship**. For example, if additional activity in a production department causes an increase in the costs incurred by the maintenance department, then the allocation base selected should result in the additional costs being allocated to the production department when there is additional activity. Direct labor hours, direct labor cost, or machine hours in the production department would be likely choices for the allocation base because they represent the increase in activity that leads to the increase in cost in the maintenance department. However, it would be difficult to argue that one of these allocation bases is better than another on cause-and-effect grounds. As we will see next, this is one of the problems of cost allocation. A number of allocation bases may appear to be equally valid, but they may result in substantially different costs being assigned to the cost objectives.

Let's consider an example. The Watts Equipment Company has two producing departments, assembly and finishing, that receive allocations of indirect costs from the maintenance department. In the coming year, the maintenance department expects to incur variable costs of $200,000. These costs are related to both the labor hours and the machine hours incurred in the producing departments. The quantities of labor and machine hours are indicated here. With labor hours as the allocation base, the allocation rate is $4 per labor hour, and the assembly department receives an $80,000 allocation of cost from the maintenance department. However, with machine hours as the allocation base, the allocation rate is $10 per machine hour, and the assembly department receives a

$110,000 allocation of cost from the maintenance department. The $30,000 difference in the allocations occurs even though both labor hours and machine hours are reasonable allocation bases to use.

	Labor Hours	Allocations	Machine Hours	Allocations
Assembly	20,000	$ 80,000	11,000	$110,000
Finishing	30,000	120,000	9,000	90,000
Total	50,000	$200,000	20,000	$200,000
Allocation rate	$4 per labor hour		$10 per machine hour	

When indirect costs are fixed, establishing cause-and-effect relationships between costs and cost objectives is not feasible. In these cases, accountants turn to other criteria, such as relative benefits, ability to bear costs, and equity. Unfortunately, these terms are rather vague and difficult to implement in an unambiguous manner.

The **relative benefits approach to allocation** suggests that the base should result in more costs being allocated to the cost objectives that benefit most from incurring the cost. This might suggest, for example, that computer costs should be allocated to departments based on time spent using the computer, since greater use implies greater benefit. However, this could result in fixed computer cost being allocated to departments that did not exist when the computer was acquired (and so could not have caused the cost of the computer to be incurred).

The **ability to bear costs** notion suggests that the allocation base should result in more costs being allocated to products, services, or departments that are more profitable. Because they are more profitable, they can *bear* the increased costs from the higher allocations.

The **equity approach to allocation** suggests that the base should result in allocations that are perceived to be fair or equitable. Obviously, this is a difficult criterion to apply, because different individuals have different perceptions of what is equitable.

LINK TO PRACTICE

llocating Costs to Federal Contracts

archers at the University of Washington hare lab space, supplies, support staff, and ources while working on various federal grants tracts. Because of this, they must allocate costs e specific grants and contracts.

For example, syringes may be used in a variety of experiments related to various grants but, due to cost, the lab does not directly trace individual syringes to specific grants. Instead, the cost of syringes is allocated based on the relative number of experiments conducted under each grant. Here are some additional examples of allocation bases used to allocate costs to grants:

- The cost of computer equipment is allocated based on the number of hours used for each project.
- The cost of personality tests is allocated based on the number of clients served.
- The cost of renting space is allocated based on the number of full-time equivalent researchers working on each project.
- The cost of lab supplies is allocated based on the relative time the principal investigator spends on each project.

Source: Grant and Contract Accounting, *Cost Allocation Policy,* University of Washington, Office of Financial Management, October 12, 2006.

ALLOCATING SERVICE DEPARTMENT COSTS

The organizational units in most manufacturing firms can be classified as either production departments or service departments. Production departments engage in direct manufacturing activity, whereas service departments provide indirect support. For example, in a furniture manufacturing company, the assembly and finishing departments are production departments, whereas maintenance, janitorial, personnel, cafeteria, cost accounting, and power are service departments. Cost pools are often formed by service departments, and these costs are allocated to production departments—the cost objectives. Ultimately, production departments allocate their costs to specific products.

Direct Method of Allocating Service Department Costs

The method of allocating service department costs that we cover is called the direct method. In the **direct method of allocating cost**, service department costs are allocated to production departments but not to other service departments.[1] Thus, even though the janitorial department provides a service to the personnel department, under the direct method no janitorial costs are allocated to the personnel department. The process is diagrammed in Illustration 6-4. The illustration includes no arrow between janitorial costs and personnel costs because there is no allocation of costs between the janitorial service department and the personnel department.

We'll consider an example involving the Mason Furniture Company. Suppose the company's janitorial costs are $100,000. The company decides to allocate these costs to assembly and finishing based on the number of square feet in each production department. Since assembly has 20,000 square feet and finishing has 30,000 square feet, the allocation rate is $2 per square foot ($100,000 ÷ 50,000 square feet). Assembly receives an allocation of $40,000 (20,000 square feet × $2), and finishing receives an allocation of $60,000 (30,000 square feet × $2).

Now suppose the personnel costs at Mason are $200,000. These costs are allocated based on the number of employees in each production department. The assembly department h
60 employees, and the finishing department has 40 employees. Thus, the allocation
personnel costs is $2,000 per employee ($200,000 ÷ 100 employees). The assembl
ment receives an allocation of $120,000 (60 × $2,000), and the finishing departme
an allocation of $80,000 (40 × $2,000). The allocations are presented in Illustrati

ILLUSTRATION 6-4

Allocating service department costs with the direct method

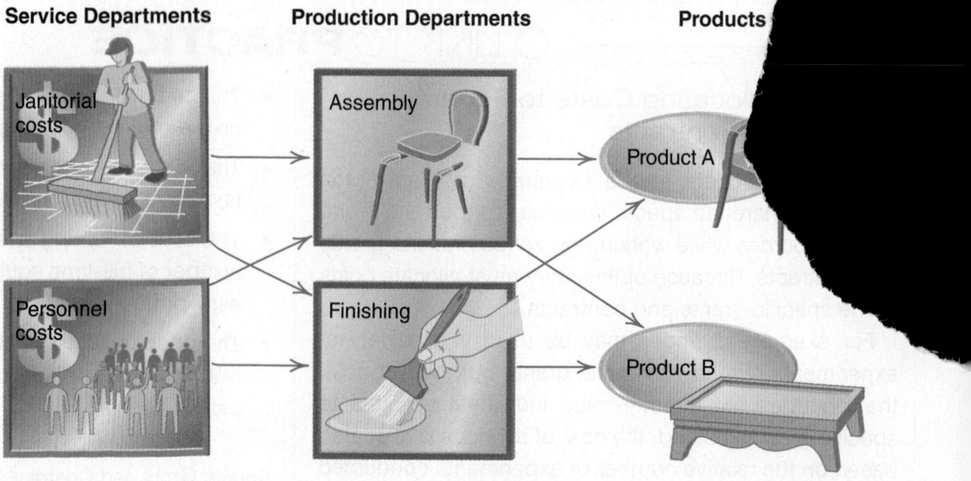

[1] Alternatives to the direct method that recognize that service departments make use of each other's resources (such as the sequential and the reciprocal methods) are covered in cost accounting texts.

ILLUSTRATION 6-5
Direct allocations of service department costs for Mason Furniture

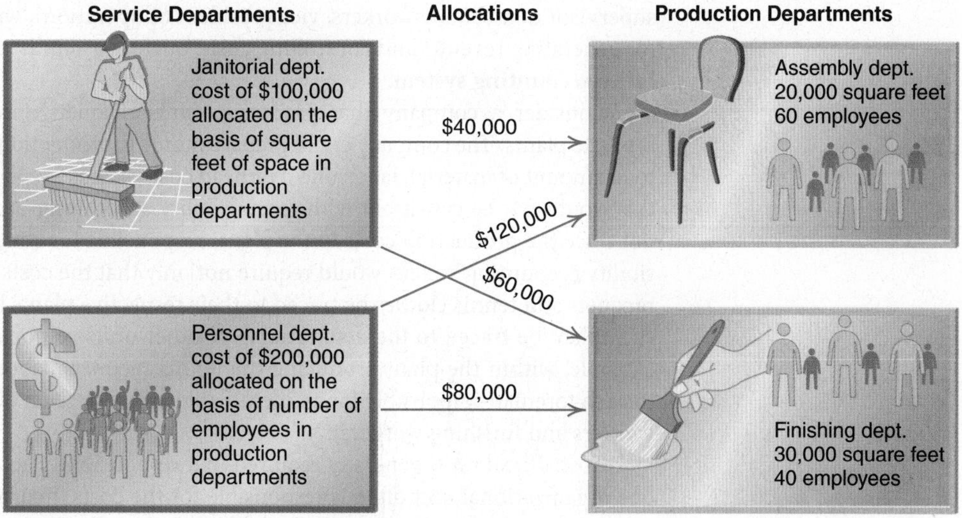

Allocating Budgeted and Actual Service Department Costs

It is generally a good idea to allocate budgeted rather than actual service department costs. If budgeted costs are allocated, service departments cannot pass on the cost of inefficiencies and waste. For example, suppose at the start of the year, budgeted costs in the janitorial department are $100,000, and the accounting department informs assembly and finishing that they will receive allocations of $2 per square foot ($100,000 ÷ 50,000 square feet).

But suppose that the janitorial department actually incurs $130,000 of cost ($30,000 more than planned) due to a lack of good cost control. If actual costs are allocated, the janitorial department can pass the extra costs on to the production departments by allocating $2.60 per square foot ($130,000 ÷ 50,000 square feet). The managers of assembly and finishing would strongly resist the higher charge. Obviously, they would not want their costs to be increased simply because some other department was not performing its job efficiently. This problem is avoided if only budgeted costs are allocated; in that case, the janitorial department must stick to the allocation of $2 per square foot.

LEARNING OBJECTIVE 2
Identify potential problems with cost allocation, discuss activity-based costing (ABC) and cost drivers, and distinguish activity-based costing (ABC) from activity-based management (ABM).

PROBLEMS WITH COST ALLOCATION

Our discussion so far has focused on ideas about how costs should be allocated. In practice, when costs are allocated, a number of problems may arise. Here we discuss problems brought about by: (1) allocations of costs that are not controllable, (2) arbitrary allocations, (3) allocations of fixed costs that make the fixed costs appear to be variable costs, (4) allocations of manufacturing overhead to products using too few overhead cost pools, and (5) use of only volume-related allocation bases.

Responsibility Accounting and Controllable Costs

In Chapter 1 we learned that one of the primary uses of managerial accounting is to evaluate the performance of managers and the operations under their control. Performance evaluation is facilitated by a system of accounting that traces revenues and costs to organizational units (e.g., departments and divisions) and individuals (e.g., plant manager, supervisor of assembly workers, vice president of operation), with related responsibility for generating revenue and controlling costs. Such a system is referred to as a **responsibility accounting system.**

Consider a company that produces tennis racquets and tennis clothes in two separate plants. The company could prepare monthly production cost reports that list the total amount of material, labor, and overhead cost for the two plants combined. However, this would *not* be consistent with responsibility accounting because the reports would not trace the production costs to the plants responsible for controlling them. A responsibility accounting system would require not only that the costs of producing the tennis racquets and tennis clothes be traced to their respective plants but also that the costs in each plant be traced to the departments or other units responsible for those costs. For example, within the plant producing the tennis racquets, labor costs should be traced to each foreman responsible for an identifiable group or team of workers (e.g., assembly workers and finishing workers).

Cost allocation is generally required in a responsibility accounting system because one organizational unit often is responsible for the costs incurred by another organizational unit. For example, activity in a production department increases the costs incurred in the machine repair department. Because the production department is responsible for the incurrence of costs in the machine repair department, the production department's performance reports should reflect some share of the machine repair department cost. This can be achieved by allocating machine repair department costs to the production department.

Some allocations of costs, however, are not consistent with a responsibility accounting system. Most accountants believe that managers should be held responsible only for costs they can control. These costs, called **controllable costs**, are affected by the manager's decisions. Allocating the cost of a building to the performance report of a supervisor responsible for controlling labor costs is not appropriate because the supervisor cannot control building costs.

If allocated costs beyond the manager's control appear on his or her performance reports, they may cause considerable frustration. Managers want their performance evaluations to reflect their own strengths and weaknesses. In some cases, managers are allocated costs beyond their control simply to make them aware that the costs exist and must be covered by the firm's revenue. In such situations, the costs should be clearly labeled noncontrollable, indicating to the manager that company officials are aware that the items are not affected by his or her decisions. This should minimize possible resentment.

Arbitrary Allocations

In practice, cost allocations are the topic of numerous and often heated discussions. Managers may feel that their departments receive unnecessarily large allocations of indirect costs, causing the departments to appear less profitable. Governmental agencies that have cost-plus contracts may feel that products produced by contractors on a cost-plus basis receive allocations of indirect costs that are unfairly high. Unfortunately, such discussions are likely to continue in the future. The reason is that allocations of costs are to a great extent inherently arbitrary.

In almost all cost allocation situations, determining the one "true," "correct," or "valid" allocation is not possible. As noted earlier in the chapter, various allocation bases (e.g., labor hours, labor cost, and machine hours) may be equally justifiable but may result in substantially different allocations. These situations naturally lead managers to support the allocation that makes their performance look best and reject allocations that cast an unfavorable light on their performance.

LINK TO PRACTICE

Disputes over Allocations not Limited to the Private Sector

Disputes over allocations of cost are not limited to the private sector. In Brooksville County, Florida, a civic activist, Janey Baldwin, questioned allocations of costs to county enterprise funds. These funds are set up much like a private business and provide services that are financed through user fees.

Baldwin questioned why 100 percent of the assistant county attorney's salary was allocated to the utilities department (an enterprise fund operation) when the attorney also worked for the county planning and zoning department. Baldwin observed, "This cost allocation system has run amok." Seemingly an easy solution would be to allocate the attorney's salary based on the time spent working on issues related to individual departments. But what if the utilities department has money to cover its allocation but the allocation and planning and zoning does not? Then, a "political" solution might be sought in which the cost is simply charged to the department with the largest budget. That solution, while simple, is likely to lead to a cost allocation dispute.

Source: Michael Bates, "County to Examine Cost Allocations," *Hernado Today*, June 4, 2008.

Unitized Fixed Costs and Lump-Sum Allocations

One of the most significant problems associated with cost allocation is due to the fact that the allocation process may make fixed costs appear to be variable costs. This happens when fixed costs are **unitized**—that is, stated on a per unit basis. To illustrate the problem, consider the Smith Tool Company, which has two divisions. At the start of each year, the company estimates the amount of general and administrative costs that are incurred centrally on behalf of the operations of both divisions. Such costs include administrative salaries, clerical costs, central accounting costs, and a variety of others, all of which are essentially fixed in the short run. In the current year, these costs are expected to amount to $2,000,000. Smith has decided that it would be useful for the divisions to know that these costs are being incurred on their behalf. Therefore, it allocates the costs among the divisions based on their relative sales. In the current year, divisional sales are expected to be $50,000,000. Thus, Smith has decided to allocate general and administrative costs to the divisions at a rate of $0.04 per dollar of sales (i.e., $2,000,000 ÷ $50,000,000).

We have said that the general and administrative costs are essentially fixed, but how will they appear to the division managers? Let's look, for instance, at Bob Gallegos, the manager of the Carpenter Division, which produces a variety of carpenter tools (e.g., hammers, saws, and drills). Bob observes that as divisional revenue increases, the allocated costs increase. Thus, to him, the costs appear to be variable. This may lead Bob to make decisions that are not in the best interest of the company as a whole but that appear to maximize divisional profitability. For example, suppose the Carpenter Division is considering producing a new hammer that will sell for $20. At this price, the division expects to sell 100,000 units. Production of the hammer will require $12 of direct material cost, $6 of direct labor cost, and an increase in manufacturing overhead costs of $130,000. An analysis of the effect on the profit of the Carpenter Division is presented in Illustration 6-6.

ILLUSTRATION 6-6
Problem of unitized fixed costs

Sales of hammers (100,000 × $20)		$2,000,000
Less: additional costs		
Direct material (100,000 × $12)	$1,200,000	
Direct labor (100,000 × $6)	600,000	
Additional manufacturing overhead cost	130,000	1,930,000
Real increase in profit		$ 70,000
Less: allocated fixed costs		
($2,000,000 increase in sales × $.04)		80,000
Perceived loss on sale of hammers		($ 10,000)

As indicated in the illustration, sales of the hammer are expected to result in an increase of $2,000,000 in sales. There will also be a $1,800,000 increase in variable costs (direct material and direct labor) and a $130,000 increase in manufacturing overhead cost. Thus, production and sale of the hammer will result in a $70,000 increase in profit. From this information, the hammer appears to be a profitable addition to the product line of the division. However, will the manager of the division be motivated to produce the hammer? Probably not.

The reason is that, with the increase in sales, the division will receive a larger allocation of central general and administrative costs. With an allocation rate of $.04 per dollar of sales and an expected increase in sales of $2,000,000, the division would expect its allocated costs to increase by $80,000. To the manager of the division, the additional allocated costs appear to be variable even though, in fact, they are fixed (i.e., central administration salaries, clerical costs, and accounting costs will not increase if the hammer is produced). The result is that the manager of the division would expect production of the hammer to result in a loss of $10,000 ($70,000 – $80,000) for the division.

To remedy this problem, allocations of *fixed costs* must be made in such a way that they *appear fixed* to the managers whose departments receive the allocations. This is achieved by **lump-sum allocations** of fixed costs. A lump-sum allocation is an allocation of a predetermined amount that is not affected by changes in the activity level of the organizational unit receiving the allocation. Resources are acquired taking into account the long-run needs of users. Thus, allocations of fixed costs should be based on the projected long-run needs that lead managers to incur the costs. For example, suppose the Smith Tool Company purchases a computer to serve each of its two divisions. Purchase of the computer results in annual fixed costs of $40,000. In deciding what type of computer to purchase, management estimated that the Carpenter Division would use the computer for 2,000 hours per year and the Specialty Tools Division would use the computer for 3,000 hours per year. Thus, allocating $16,000 to the Carpenter Division ($40,000 × 2/5) and $24,000 to the Specialty Tools Division ($40,000 × 3/5) is appropriate.

Lump-sum allocations generally should remain the same year after year, even though, over time, the activity of the organizational units involved may deviate from expectations. Suppose, for example, that the Carpenter Division expanded and required 3,000 hours of computer time per year, whereas the Specialty Tools Division lost business and required only 2,000 hours. Should the lump-sum allocations of the two divisions be reversed? Probably not. Reversing the allocations would make it appear to the managers of the two divisions that their allocations do indeed depend on their activity levels. In other words, the fixed costs would again appear to be variable. If lump-sum allocations of *fixed* costs are to *appear fixed*, the amount of the allocation must not depend on changes in activity.

It follows that, with lump-sum allocations, the allocations of a division do not depend on the activity level of other divisions. Suppose the activity of the Carpenter Division stayed at 2,000 hours, but the activity level of the Specialty Tools Division decreased from 3,000 hours to 2,000 hours. If the cost of the computer were allocated based on current activity levels, the amount allocated to the Carpenter Division would increase from $16,000 to $20,000, in spite of the fact that its use of the computer had not changed. Obviously, this could cause considerable dissatisfaction on the part of the manager of the Carpenter Division. It could also make planning more difficult, because the costs of the division would depend on the activity of other divisions. This is not the case with a lump-sum allocation. Once the amount of the lump sum is determined, it does not vary in response to changes in activity.

How can lump sum allocations improve a manager's decisions? Refer back to the decision Bob Gallegos at the Carpenter Division of the Smith Tool Company faced regarding sale of a new hammer. If the general and administrative costs at Smith Tool Company are allocated on a lump-sum basis and the amount allocated to the Carpenter Division is $700,000 regardless of its activity, then Bob will perceive that general and administrative costs are indeed fixed. Thus, he will correctly determine that, in the interest of maximizing divisional profit, the hammer should be produced because it contributes $70,000 toward covering the allocated costs that will be incurred whether or not the hammer is produced.

The Problem of Too Few Cost Pools

Some companies assign overhead to products using only one or two overhead cost pools. Although the approach has the benefit of being simple and easy to use, product costs may be seriously distorted when only a small number of cost pools are used.

Consider the problem in the context of the Reed Manufacturing company, which manufactures products in two departments: assembly and finishing. Reed has total manufacturing overhead of $1,000,000 and each year the company incurs 50,000 labor hours. If the company includes all overhead in one cost pool and allocates overhead using labor hours, the overhead rate will be $20 per labor hour ($1,000,000 ÷ 50,000 labor hours). Now suppose that of the $1,000,000 of overhead, $600,000 is incurred in assembly and $400,000 is incurred in finishing. Furthermore, assembly requires 40,000 labor hours and finishing requires only 10,000 labor hours. You can see that overhead per labor hour is much less expensive in the assembly department: $15 per labor hour in assembly versus $40 per labor hour in finishing (see Illustration 6-7).

Now assume that Reed produces two products (A and B). Each product requires 25,000 labor hours. However, Product A requires 16,000 hours of assembly time and 9,000 hours of finishing time whereas Product B requires 24,000 hours of assembly time and 1,000 hours of finishing time. How much overhead will be allocated to each product if all overhead is included in a single cost pool and allocated on the basis of labor hours? The answer is that both products will receive the same allocation. They both require a total of 25,000 of total labor hours, and use of a single cost pool allocates the average cost per labor hour. Both will be allocated $500,000 of overhead ($20 per hour × 25,000 hours).

Which product is being undercosted and which product is being overcosted when using a single cost pool? Product A is undercosted because it requires relatively more production time in finishing, which is a high-cost department in terms of overhead cost (but it receives the average overhead allocation of $20 per hour). Product B is overcosted because it requires relatively more production time in assembly, which is a relatively

ILLUSTRATION 6-7

Overhead rates and product costs using one versus two cost pools

One cost pool

$$\frac{\text{Total overhead}}{\text{Total labor hours}} = \frac{\$1{,}000{,}000}{50{,}000} = \$20 \text{ per labor hour}$$

Overhead allocated to Product A = $20 × 25,000 labor hours = $500,000
Overhead allocated to Product B = $20 × 25,000 labor hours = $500,000

Two cost pools

$$\frac{\text{Assembly overhead}}{\text{Assembly labor hours}} = \frac{\$600{,}000}{40{,}000} = \$15 \text{ per assembly labor hour}$$

$$\frac{\text{Finishing overhead}}{\text{Finishing labor hours}} = \frac{\$400{,}000}{10{,}000} = \$40 \text{ per finishing labor hour}$$

Overhead allocated to Product A
$15 per assembly labor hour × 16,000 assembly hours = $240,000
$40 per finishing labor hour × 9,000 assembly hours = $360,000 → $600,000

Overhead allocated to Product B
$15 per assembly labor hour × 24,000 assembly hours = $360,000
$40 per finishing labor hour × 1,000 assembly hours = $40,000 → $400,000

cheap department in terms of overhead (but it receives the average overhead allocation of $20 per hour).

Reed's problem is easily solved by setting up separate cost pools for overhead in each department. Note that when two cost pools are used, Product A receives an allocation of $600,00 versus only $500,000 when a single cost pool is used (see Illustration 6-7.) And when two cost pools are used, Product B's allocation is reduced from $500,000 to $400,000. Generally speaking, using more cost pools will result in more accurate allocations of costs.

Using Only Volume-Related Allocation Bases

We now turn to a final problem involved in cost allocations. Some manufacturing companies allocate manufacturing overhead to products using only measures of production volume (e.g., direct labor or machine hours) as allocation bases. However, not all overhead costs vary with volume. We discuss this issue in the next section along with activity-based costing (ABC), because ABC solves the problem.

ACTIVITY-BASED COSTING

Activity-based costing (ABC) is a relatively recent development in managerial accounting, and it has received a tremendous amount of attention from both academics and practitioners interested in improving managerial accounting information.[2] We introduced ABC in Chapter 2, dealing with job-order costing. Now we discuss it in more detail.

The Problem of Using Only Measures of Production Volume to Allocate Overhead

Manufacturing companies commonly use direct labor hours, direct labor cost, and machine hours as allocation bases when assigning overhead to products. Each of these items is a measure of production volume. Because most companies continue to allocate overhead using only measures of production volume as allocation bases, we refer to this approach as the traditional approach. The problem with the traditional approach is that it assumes that all overhead costs are proportional to production volume. By proportional, we mean that, for example, when volume increases by 20 percent, overhead increases by 20 percent; when volume increases by 50 percent, overhead increases by 50 percent; and so forth. However, many overhead costs (such as the cost of setting up equipment for a production run, the cost of inspecting raw materials, and the cost of handling materials) are not proportional to volume. In fact, many overhead costs are affected by product complexity rather than volume. The result is that simple high-volume products are often overcosted whereas complex low-volume products are undercosted.

Consider the overhead costs created by starting up a production line. Both a high-volume product (which is associated with a large amount of labor and machine time) and a low-volume product (which is associated with a small amount of labor and machine time) may require the same amount of setup time and setup cost. However, since setup costs (along with all other overhead) are allocated only on the basis of production volume, the high-volume product will receive a larger *allocation* of setup cost. Thus, the high-volume product is overcosted. Let's see how the ABC approach avoids this problem.

---

[2]Credit for developing activity-based costing is usually given to Robin Cooper and Robert Kaplan. See R. Cooper, "The Rise of Activity-Based Costing—Part One: What Is an Activity-Based Cost System?" *Journal of Cost Management,* Summer 1988, pp. 45–54, and R. Cooper and R. Kaplan, "How Cost Accounting Distorts Product Costs," *Management Accounting,* April 1988, pp. 20–27.

TEST YOUR KNOWLEDGE

Which of the following is *not* a volume-related cost driver?

a. Direct labor hours.
b. Direct labor cost.
c. Machine time.
d. Time to set up a production run.

Correct answer is d.

The ABC Approach

In the ABC approach, companies identify the major activities that cause overhead costs to be incurred. Some of these activities are related to production volume, but others are not. The costs of the resources consumed performing these activities are grouped into cost pools. Finally, the costs are assigned to products using a measure of activity referred to as a **cost driver** (an allocation base in an ABC system). The steps involved in the ABC approach, then, are:

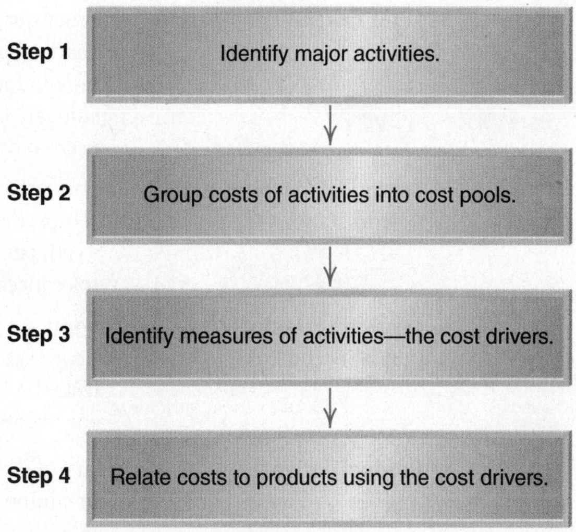

Some common activities and associated cost drivers are listed in Illustration 6-8. Note that some of the cost drivers are volume related; machine hours and assembly labor hours are examples. Other cost drivers are not related to production volume; one example is the number of inspections. Some low-volume products that involve complex or fragile parts may need a large number of inspections, whereas some high-volume products that involve simple or rugged parts may need relatively few inspections. Number of setups, as suggested earlier, is another cost driver that may not be related to volume. Both low-volume and high-volume products may require the same number of setups.

Each firm must decide how many separate activities (and related cost pools and cost drivers) to identify. If too many activities are identified, the system will be unnecessarily costly and confusing. For example, consider a company that produces 200 products and identifies 100 key activities. This company must account for 20,000 (200 × 100) product-activity relations. On the other hand, if too few activities are used, the ABC system is not likely to produce accurate data. Most companies that design ABC systems use 25 to 100 distinct activities.[3]

[3] See R. Cooper, R. Kaplan, L. Maisel, E. Morrissey, and R. Oehm, "Implementing Activity-Based Cost Management: Moving from Analysis to Action," *Institute of Management Accountants,* October 1993, p. 13.

ILLUSTRATION 6-8

Common activities and associated cost drivers

Hierarchy of Activities	Major Activities	Associated Costs	Cost Driver
Unit Level	Handling materials and parts	Labor cost for workers handling material and parts; depreciation of equipment used to move material and parts (e.g., depreciation of forklifts); fuel to run material handling equipment; etc.	Number of material requisitions
	Producing goods using manufacturing equipment	Labor costs for individuals operating machinery; depreciation of machines; energy used to run machines; machine maintenance; insurance for machinery; etc.	Number of machine hours
	Packing customer orders	Labor cost for packing workers; cost of packing materials; etc.	Number of boxes shipped
Batch Level	Processing purchase orders for materials and parts	Labor cost for workers determining order quantities, contracting with vendors, and preparing purchase orders; forms; amortization of software and computer equipment used in order processing; etc.	Number of purchase orders
	Setting up machines and workstations	Labor cost for workers involved in setups; depreciation of tools used to adjust machines and measure tolerances; etc.	Number of setups
	Inspecting products for quality control	Labor costs for inspectors; depreciation of equipment used to test whether items meet customer specifications; etc.	Number of inspections
Product Level	Product design	Salary of designers; depreciation of equipment used by designers; miscellaneous supplies used by designers	Number of hours worked by designers
Facility Level	Factory administration	Salary of plant manager; salary of assistant to the plant manager depreciation of office equipment	This is likely to be arbiitrary

Hierarchy of Activities. Sometimes managers classify activities into a hierarchy of unit-level activities, batch-level activities, product-level activities, and facility-level activities.

Unit-level activities are activities that are required to produce an incremental unit of product. In Illustration 6-8, handling materials and parts would likely be a unit-level activity since, to produce more units, more materials and parts must be handled. Producing goods using manufacturing equipment and packing customer orders would also be unit level activities (assuming that each unit is packed in an individual box).

Batch-level activities are activities that are required to produce another batch of a product, regardless of how many units are in the batch. In Illustration 6-8, processing purchase orders and setting up machines are examples of batch-level activities. Inspecting products would also be a batch-level activity, assuming that inspections are performed on a small sample of a batch. If every unit were inspected, then inspection would be a unit-level activity.

Product-level activities are activities that are required to initiate production of product, regardless of the number of units or batches. In Illustration 6-8, product design would be an example of a product-level activity.

Facility-level activities are activities that support all other activities. Factory administration is an example in Illustration 6-8. In most, if not all, cases, charging the cost of facility-level activities to products is arbitrary, with no real cause-and-effect relationship. Thus, some companies do not assign the cost of facility-level activities to products.

Relating Cost Pools to Products Using Cost Drivers

Let's take a moment to look at the last step in the ABC approach: relating cost pools to products using cost drivers as the allocation bases. Understanding how this step is accomplished will allow us to move on to a comprehensive example.

Kim Electronics produces a variety of electronic products ranging from simple handheld calculators to hard disk drives. Inspection to ensure that products are of high quality is a major activity at Kim. In the coming year, the company expects to incur inspection costs of $2,500,000. Forty workers are employed in the inspection process, and they are expected to perform 1,000,000 product inspections in the coming year. Using inspection cost as a cost pool and the number of inspections as a cost driver, the company arrives at a rate of $2.50 per inspection for purposes of allocating inspection costs to products.

Kim produces 20,000 Model ZX disk drives. Each drive is inspected three times during the production process, and various functions are tested for conformance with rigorous standards set by the company. How much of the total $2,500,000 inspection cost will be allocated to the Model ZX? With 20,000 disk drives and three inspections per drive, a total of 60,000 inspections will be performed. A rate of $2.50 per inspection implies that $7.50 of inspection cost will be allocated to each disk drive ($2.50 rate × 3 inspections) for a total of $150,000 ($7.50 × 20,000). A similar approach will be taken to determine the amount of inspection cost to be allocated to the other products produced by Kim.

Budgeted inspection cost	$2,500,000
Divided by budgeted number of inspections	1,000,000
Cost per inspection	$2.50
Times number of inspections per unit for the Model ZX disk drive	3
Inspection cost per unit for Model ZX	$7.50

The ABC Approach at McMaster Screen Technologies: A Comprehensive Example

Our comprehensive example of the ABC approach uses the situation faced by McMaster Screen Technologies presented at the start of the chapter. As you read through the example, make sure you can explain why using the ABC approach reduces the cost of the high-volume product (the Model ND32 touch screen used in automobile navigation devices) and increases the cost of the low-volume product (the MK420 touch screen used in a military targeting device).

McMaster's Costs under the Traditional Approach. For product costing purposes, McMaster traces labor and material costs directly to products produced. Manufacturing overhead is allocated to products based on labor cost. At the start of 2016, estimated manufacturing overhead was $100,000,000 and estimated labor cost was $25,000,000. Thus, the overhead allocation rate was $4 per dollar of labor.

For 2016, the following costs and revenues are expected from sale of the Model ND32 and the Model MX420:

	Model ND32 Touch Screen for Auto Navigation System	Model MX420 Touch Screen for Military Targeting Device
Number of Units	**45,000**	**50**
Sales revenue	$21,375,000	$112,500
Less:		
Direct labor	2,025,000	2,600
Direct material	9,450,000	16,500
Overhead ($4 × direct labor)	8,100,000	10,400
Total cost	19,575,000	29,500
Gross profit	$ 1,800,000	$ 83,000
Selling price per unit	$ 475	$2,250
Cost per unit	(435)	(590)
Gross profit per unit	$ 40	$ 1,660
Gross profit as a % of sales	8.42%	73.78%

Note that the overhead allocated to the Model ND32 Display, $8,100,000, is equal to the overhead rate of $4 per dollar of labor times the $2,025,000 of direct labor incurred in production of the display used in an automobile navigation system. Also recall that Michael Soma, the CFO at McMaster Screen Technologies, suspects that the relatively low gross profit (less than 10 percent of sales) may be due to problems with the costing system in use. Furthermore, he is somewhat surprised that the company is able to earn such a high gross profit on the display used in a military targeting device (more than 70 percent of sales). While this product has a relatively high selling price, the low-volume product required new production techniques to meet stringent quality standards and he suspected that production inefficiencies would keep gross profit low for more than a year.

McMaster's Costs under the ABC Approach. The CFO is right to be concerned about the product costing system at McMaster. The company's approach to allocating overhead assumes that all overhead is proportional to a single measure of production volume—labor cost. However, overhead is likely caused by several key activities.

Suppose the CFO authorizes a study of how the costs of the Model ND32 touch screen and the Model MX420 touch screen will change if an ABC approach is taken. The study determines that the $100,000,000 of overhead cost is related to the seven cost drivers identified in Illustration 6-9. As indicated in the illustration, setup costs are related to the number of setups, material ordering costs are related to the number of purchase orders, material handling costs are related to the number of material requisitions, machinery costs are related to the number of machine hours, inspection costs are related to the number of inspections, and design costs are related to the number of design hours. All other overhead is categorized in a cost pool simply referred to as "Other." McMaster has decided that "manufacturing complexity" is a major factor contributing to the incurrence of other overhead costs. The cost driver for complexity is the number of workstations required to produce a product. Products that require more workstations to produce are more complex and cause more overhead.

ILLUSTRATION 6-9

Overhead cost items and cost drivers

Major Activities	Annual Cost	Cost Driver	Estimated Annual Activity	Cost per Driver Unit
Setting up production line	$10,000,000	Number of setups	1,000	$10,000 per setup
Ordering materials	$ 4,000,000	Number of purchase orders	24,242	$165 per purchase order
Handling materials	$ 5,000,000	Number of material requisitions	14,286	$350 per requisition
Running machines	$45,000,000	Number of machine hours	30,000	$1,500 per machine hour
Inspection	$18,000,000	Number of inspections	40,000	$450 per inspection
Design	$15,000,000	Number of design hours	176,471	$85 per design hour
Other	$ 3,000,000	Number of workstations used across all products	1,000	$3,000 per workstation

Note that in constructing the table in Illustration 6-9, we are following the steps in the ABC process that we previously discussed. We start by identifying major activities (Step 1). We then group associated costs into cost pools (Step 2), and we identify measures of the activities—the cost drivers (Step 3). Now we'll turn to relating the costs to specific products using the cost drivers (Step 4). This last step is shown in Illustration 6-11.

Manufacturing the Model ND32 touch screen used in an automotive navigation system requires 20 setups, 250 purchase orders, 180 material requisitions, 500 machine hours, 450 inspections, 60 design hours, and 20 workstations. Manufacturing the Model MX420 touch screen used in a military targeting device requires 2 setups, 30 purchase orders, 5 material requisitions, 8 machine hours, 50 inspections, 325 design hours, and 30 workstations. This information is summarized in Illustration 6-10.

Using this information, we can calculate the cost per unit of the Model ND32 and the Model MX420 touch screens assuming the company changes to an ABC system. The calculations are presented in Illustration 6-11. With the ABC approach, the cost of the Model ND32 used in an automobile navigation system drops from $435.00 to $284.37 per unit, whereas the cost of the Model MX420 used in a military targeting device increases from $590.00 to $3,958.50 per unit:

	Model ND32 Touch Screen for Auto Navigation	Model MX420 Touch Screen for Military Targeting Device
Cost per unit using traditional approach to allocating overhead	$435.00	$ 590.00
Cost per unit using ABC approach	$284.37	$3,958.50

ILLUSTRATION 6-10

Production information for 45,000 Model ND32 displays and 50 Model MX420 displays

	Model ND32 Touch Screen for Auto Navigation	Model MX420 Touch Screen for Military Targeting Device
Number of setups	20	2
Number of purchase orders	250	30
Number of material requisitions	180	5
Number of machine hours	500	8
Number of inspections	450	50
Number of design hours	60	325
Number of workstations used in production	20	30

ILLUSTRATION 6-11

Costs of Model ND32 and Model MX420 using an ABC approach

	Model ND32 Touch Screen for Auto Navigation System		Model MX420 Touch Screen for Military Targeting Device
Number of Units	**45,000**	**Number of Units**	**50**
Direct labor	$ 2,025,000	Direct labor	$ 2,600
Direct material	9,450,000	Direct material	16,500
Overhead:		Overhead:	
Setup cost (20 × $10,000)	200,000	Setup cost (2 × $10,000)	20,000
Material ordering cost (250 × $165)	41,250	Material ordering cost (30 × $165)	4,950
Material handling cost (180 × $350)	63,000	Material handling cost (5 × $350)	1,750
Machine costs (500 × $1,500)	750,000	Machine costs (8 × $1,500)	12,000
Inspection costs (450 × $450)	202,500	Inspection costs (50 × $450)	22,500
Design costs (60 × $85)	5,100	Design costs (325 × $85)	27,625
Other (20 × $3,000)	60,000	Other (30 × $3,000)	90,000
Total overhead	1,321,850	Total overhead	178,825
Total cost	$12,796,850	Total costs	$ 197,925
Selling price per unit	$ 475.00	Selling price per unit	$ 2,250.00
Cost per unit	284.37	Cost per unit	3,958.50
Gross profit per unit	$ 190.63	Gross profit (loss) per unit	($1,708.50)
Gross profit as a % of sales	40%	Gross profit (loss) as a % of sales	(76%)

Recall that the Model ND32 sells for $475 per unit. The ABC approach reveals that this high-volume product is very profitable. However, even though the Model MX420 sells for $2,250 per unit, the ABC approach revels that the selling price does not come close to covering the full cost of this low-volume product.[4] The CFO's intuition that the traditional product costing system at McMaster might be providing misleading information was correct. Because the traditional system only allocated costs using a volume-related allocation base (direct labor cost), the high-volume product (touch screen used in automobile navigation systems) was overcosted and did not appear to be particularly profitable. The low-volume product (touch screen used in military targeting device) was undercosted and appeared to be highly profitable when, in fact, it was not covering its full cost.

TEST YOUR **KNOWLEDGE**

Compared to a traditional cost allocation system that allocates costs to products based on labor hours, an ABC system is likely to:

a. Allocate more costs to high-versus low-volume products.
b. Allocate less costs to high-versus low-volume products.
c. Allocate the same amount of costs to high-and low-volume products.
d. Allocate less costs to highly specialized products.

Correct answer is b.

[4] The fact that costs exceed revenue for the Model MX420 does not necessarily imply that the product should be dropped immediately. Some of the costs included in the cost of this product (e.g., depreciation) will exist whether the model is produced or not. See the discussion in Chapter 7 dealing with cost information and management decisions.

Pros and Cons of ABC

Although, as you can see, ABC offers some real advantages, it is not without problems. This section describes two major benefits of ABC and two major limitations.

LINK TO PRACTICE

Avoiding a Disastrous Decision by Using ABC

Mike Paris is a principal at Paris Consultants, a Hinsdale, Illinois, firm that performs ABC consulting. Here's one of his war stories on how ABC saved a client from a potentially disastrous decision:

A gear maker produces standard industrial gearboxes and very large specially engineered ring gears for ships and mining machinery. The special-gear business employed 86 engineers and a technically trained sales force, which ran up lots of sales-related travel costs. The standard gearboxes, however, required just four engineers, and sales expenses were minimal since most sales were to distributors and by catalog.

The indirect costs averaged a worrisome 40 percent and were badly skewed. Burden rates were allocated on the basis of direct labor hours worked. Despite the 86:4 engineering ratio, the big special gears required less labor than the standard gearboxes. The accounting system shifted a large chunk of the big special gears' overhead costs for engineering, sales, and tooling onto the standard products because they used more total direct labor.

PhotoDisc, Inc./Getty Images

This led management to believe the standard gears lost money when the truth was they were very profitable. The big gears lost money. The company almost sold the profitable part of its business to focus on specials that were killing them. Until we pointed out the unintended cross-subsidy, no one perceived the competitive advantages and disadvantages.

Source: Michael Paris and Dan Brassard, "Reading Between the Numbers," *Strategic Finance,* December 2004, pp. 41–45. Copyright © 2004 by the Institute of Management Accountants. Used with permission from *Strategic Finance*, published by the IMA, Montvale, NJ, USA, www.imanet.org, www.strategicfinancemag.com.

Benefits. ABC is less likely than traditional costing systems to undercost complex, low-volume products and overcost simple, high-volume products. This follows because ABC uses more cost drivers to assign costs and the drivers are not necessarily volume related.

A second benefit is that ABC may lead to improvements in cost control. With ABC, managers see costs broken out by a number of activities rather than buried in one or two overhead cost pools. Unless managers know the costs of setups, inspections, order taking, stocking, moving inventory, and other key activities, they are not likely to see a need to improve efficiency and reduce these costs.

Recall that under its traditional overhead allocation system, managers at McMaster Screen Technologies knew that overhead was $100,000,000 in total. What they didn't know was the cost of the key activities that determine total overhead. With the ABC system, however, they now know that: (1) setup costs are $10,000,000 in total or $10,000 per setup; (2) material ordering costs are $4,000,000 or $165 per purchase order; (3) material handling costs are $5,000,000 in total or $350 per requisition; (4) machine-related costs are $45,000,000 or $1,500 per machine hour; (5) inspection costs are $18,000,000 in total or $450 per inspection; (6) design costs are $15,000,000 in total or $85 per design hour; and (7) other overhead is $3,000,000 in total or $3,000 per workstation. One can easily imagine a manager saying, "Wow, I had no idea we were spending $5 million on material handling. We've got to be able to get this cost down below $275 per requisition. Let's take a look at the steps involved in material handling and cost them out. Now that I think of it, we have 15 people working the receiving dock, and they don't seem that busy. Maybe that's a place to start."

Limitations. A major disadvantage of ABC is its expense; an ABC system is more costly to develop and maintain than a traditional costing system. Consider an ABC system with 20 cost pools applied to 100 different products. Assigning costs to each of the 20 pools will be costly, and then 2,000 allocations will have to be made (20 pools × 100 products) to assign costs to products.

Decision Making/ Incremental Analysis

Perhaps the major limitation of ABC is that, in practice, it is used to develop the *full cost* of products. Because full costs include allocations of costs that are fixed (e.g., depreciation of plant and equipment and supervisory salaries), the cost per unit generated by the ABC system does not measure the incremental costs needed to produce an item. And incremental information is what is needed to make decisions. (Remember that Chapter 1 made this point: Decision making relies on incremental analysis.)

Consider the example of the Model MX420 touch screen produced by McMaster Screen Technologies analyzed in the previous section. The ABC system indicated that the cost per unit was $3,658.50 and that the selling price was only $2,250.00. However, will McMaster's costs really increase by $3,068.50 if another screen is produced? The answer is no. Much of the cost of producing the screen relates to depreciation on equipment that has already been incurred. This cost is not just fixed, it's also sunk, and sunk costs are not relevant for decisions since they're not incremental. Thus, in many cases, ABC does not provide clear-cut information applicable to decision making. Do the disadvantages of ABC outweigh the advantages? After assessing the pros and cons, we can reasonably conclude that, for companies that don't use the information in an overly simplistic way (i.e., treat the full cost information as if it were incremental cost information), an ABC system is likely to be quite beneficial.

ANY QUESTIONS?

Q: According to this book, a major limitation of ABC is that it doesn't distinguish between fixed and variable costs. Isn't there a simple fix to this problem? Just separate fixed costs and variable costs in each cost pool and allocate the variable costs per unit of each cost driver to products, but don't allocate the fixed costs on a per unit basis.

A: Your idea is a good one. Most likely, managers would find the variable cost per setup, the variable cost per material requisition, the variable cost per inspection, and so forth, to be very useful information. Unfortunately, the simple fix you suggest isn't common in practice. Perhaps this is due to the fact that, in practice, the fix isn't all that simple—a great deal of analysis would be needed to separate fixed and variable costs in each overhead cost pool.

ACTIVITY-BASED MANAGEMENT

Activity-based management (ABM) is a management tool that involves analyzing and costing activities with the goal of improving efficiency and effectiveness. As you would expect, ABM is closely related to ABC, but the two schemes differ in their primary goals. Whereas ABC focuses on activities with the goal of measuring the costs of products and services produced by them, ABM focuses on activities with the goal of managing the activities themselves. This difference is shown graphically in Illustration 6-12.

To clarify the difference, consider activities involved in setting up equipment for a production run. ABC seeks to measure the cost of setups and then assign a cost to products based on how many setups each product requires. The goal of ABM, however, is to improve the efficiency and effectiveness of the activities. Thus, for example, ABM would focus on ways to improve the setup process and ways to eliminate the demand for setup activity (thus reducing setup cost).

Managers using ABM want to know the costs of activities because this information may provide insight into how well the activities are being performed. For example, by knowing the cost of setups, managers can benchmark performance by comparing setup costs at one plant to setup costs at another plant. If the costs per setup are much higher at Plant A than at Plant B (and the plants are producing similar items), there is a good chance that costs are out of control in Plant A. In essence, ABM supports the management dictum that you can't manage what you can't measure. In other words, you need to know the costs of activities before you can do a good job managing them. ABM is discussed in more detail in the appendix to this chapter.

LINK TO PRACTICE

Banks and Other Service Companies Use ABM

Although ABC and ABM were initially implemented at manufacturing firms, service companies have jumped on the bandwagon. Recall that a previous Link to Practice noted a healthcare organization's use of ABC. Banks and other service firms also are using ABM. Consider Allied Irish Banks. In 2006, the company used ABM in its money transmission and lending operation to gain insights into the cost structure of its processes. The bank, which has 47 outlets, is analyzing the processing of checks and the handling of loan applications.

To help, accomplish this task, the company uses activity analysis software. According to the bank's senior accountant, the ABM analysis has identified a number of processes that can be reengineered to improve efficiency, and related savings have already justified the investment in the software.

Source: Christian Annesley, "Bank Tracks Costs by Activity Tool," *Computer Weekly*, January 24, 2006, p. 5.

ILLUSTRATION 6-12
Comparison of ABC and ABM

ABC focus is better costing of products and services.
Resources are traced to activities to facilitate costing of products and services.

ABM focus is improvement of efficiency and effectiveness of activities.
Resources are traced to activities to facilitate evaluation of activities.

LINK TO PRACTICE

ABC Points to Process Improvement and Cost Control

When AIRCO, a manufacturer of industrial air conditioning units, conducted an ABC study, it identified eight cost pools and associated cost drivers. With overhead broken out by key activities, the company gained an important insight—material handling activities accounted for 55 percent of total overhead expenditures. This encouraged the company to streamline material handling by reducing the distance from storage to the manufacturing floor. The feasibility of an automatic material handling system was also considered.

Source: Heather Nactmann and Mohammad Hani Al-Rifai, "An Application of Activity-Based Costing in the Air Conditioner Manufacturing Industry," *Engineering Economist* 49, 2004, pp. 221–236.

REMEMBER—YOU GET WHAT YOU MEASURE!

YOU GET WHAT YOU MEASURE

Before concluding our discussion of cost allocation, let's return to one of the key points raised in Chapter 1: You get what you measure! How does this point relate to cost allocation? Allocations affect the profit that managers have reported on their performance reports. Thus, managers pay attention to controlling the allocation base, since more use of the allocation base results in higher costs and lower profit.

Consider two companies that are initially identical. Company A allocates production overhead based on labor hours, whereas Company B allocates production overhead based on machine hours. Managers at both companies must make decisions about how much labor and equipment to use in their production processes. All else being equal, the managers at Company A will view labor as more expensive because when they use more labor to make products, the products receive higher allocations of overhead. Managers at Company B will view equipment as more expensive because when they use more machine time to produce products, the products receive higher allocations of overhead. Thus, over time, we might expect the managers of Company A to increase use of equipment and the managers of Company B to increase use of labor to produce their products.

Similarly, if you calculate overhead using the number of setups as the allocation base, managers are likely to want to reduce the number of setups. If you calculate overhead using the number of inspections as the allocation base, managers are likely to want to reduce the number of inspections. And if you calculate overhead using labor costs as the allocation base, managers are likely to want to reduce labor costs. These actions, which are driven by the way companies measure profit, are not necessarily good or bad. For example, it may be useful to *reduce* the number of inspections in order to reduce cost, but it might also be useful to *increase* the number of inspections in order to increase product quality. The point is not that the number of setups, the number of inspections, or labor costs are or are not good allocation bases. The point is that the choice of an allocation base affects other management decisions in ways that may not be obvious.

Decision Making INSIGHT

Decision making relies on incremental analysis. A potential problem with cost allocation is that it may make a fixed cost appear to be a variable cost and, therefore, incremental. Suppose, for example, that fixed costs are allocated based on sales dollars. This makes it appear that if sales increase, the costs will increase. When making decisions using cost information that involves allocation, beware!

SUMMARY OF LEARNING OBJECTIVES

LEARNING OBJECTIVE 1 Explain why indirect costs are allocated, describe the cost allocation process, and discuss allocation of service department costs.

Indirect costs are allocated to provide information for decision making, to calculate the full cost of products, to reduce the frivolous use of common resources, and to encourage managers to evaluate the efficiency of internally provided services. From a decision-making standpoint, the allocation should measure the opportunity cost of using a company resource. However, this is difficult to operationalize in practice, since opportunity costs often change quickly.

The cost allocation process has three steps: (1) identify the cost objectives, (2) form cost pools, and (3) select an allocation base to relate the costs to the cost objectives.

Service department costs are allocated to production departments, which in turn allocate these costs to products. The direct method allocates service department costs to production departments but not to other service departments.

LEARNING OBJECTIVE 2 Identify potential problems with cost allocation, discuss activity-based costing (ABC) and cost drivers, and distinguish activity-based costing (ABC) from activity-based management (ABM).

A number of problems are associated with cost allocation in practice: (1) the allocated costs may not be controllable by the manager receiving the allocation; (2) allocations may be arbitrary; (3) allocations may make fixed costs appear to be variable; (4) allocations may be made using too few cost pools; and (5) allocation may be made using only volume-related allocation bases.

Activity-based costing (ABC) is a costing method that recognizes that costs are caused by activities. Measures of the key activities that cause costs to be incurred are referred to as cost drivers. The cost drivers are used as the allocation bases to relate indirect costs to products. Unlike traditional systems, ABC does not focus solely on volume-related cost drivers.

Whereas ABC focuses on the costs of activities in order to develop the cost of goods and services produced by the activities, ABM focuses on the costs of activities in order to help manage the activities themselves (you can't manage what you can't measure).

APPENDIX

ACTIVITY-BASED MANAGEMENT

LEARNING OBJECTIVE A1

Understand the four steps involved in an ABM study.

Activity-based management is a method of activity analysis aimed at improving the efficiency and effectiveness of business processes. Let's look at two process improvement examples that will help make the goal of ABM more concrete. Then we'll discuss a four-step approach to conducting an ABM study.

Consider the activity *shipping goods to stores* conducted by a large retailer with multiple stores. This activity involves having suppliers unload deliveries at the company's warehouse. Subsequently, goods are moved from the warehouse to the company's trucks and sent to stores. How could this process be improved? Walmart uses *cross-docking,* whereby deliveries from suppliers are loaded directly from suppliers' trucks onto Walmart trucks and then sent to stores. With this approach, there is no need to move products into and around a warehouse.

As another example, consider the activity *checking into a hotel.* A number of hotels have improved this process using computer technology. Based on information obtained from initial visits, a computerized database knows customer preferences for room location and for a smoking versus nonsmoking room. Credit card information, addresses, and phone numbers are also in the database. With this information readily available, hotel workers at the registration desk can check customers in more rapidly and in a way that recognizes their individual preferences, leading to gains in customer loyalty.

Hopefully, these two examples have provided some insight into the goal of an ABM study: process improvement. Now let's discuss a four-step process for conducting one. In our discussion, we'll consider the case of Mattress Warehouse, a discount store that sells beds and mattresses. The company has a single warehouse and 15 stores in the Dallas/Fort Worth area. Stores do not hold inventory except for display. Thus, all shipments originate from the warehouse. The company offers free delivery within 100 miles of any store and, for the first time in its 25-year history, has decided to study the delivery process to determine its cost and identify potential improvements. Solutions Analysis, a consulting firm, has been hired to undertake the study.

Step 1: Determine Major Activities

The first step in the ABM study is to determine major activities. This is usually accomplished through interviews and observation. Solutions Analysis has determined that the key activities are:

a. Determine customer locations, determine availability of stock, and prepare delivery schedules.

b. Pick orders from warehouse.

c. Load trucks.

d. Deliver merchandise.

e. Return merchandise to stock if not acceptable to customer or customer not home to receive delivery.

f. Wash delivery trucks (performed each night).

g. Schedule trucks for routine service (e.g., oil change) and nonroutine repairs.

Step 2: Identify Resources Used by Each Activity

The second step is to identify the resources used by each activity. Let's consider the resources used by activities (e) and (f).

Return Merchandise to Stock If Not Acceptable to Customer or Customer Not Home to Receive Delivery. Solutions Analysis has determined that in a typical month, 25 orders are returned because customers receive a slightly different mattress or box spring than expected. For example, a customer may have picked out a mattress in the store with blue stitching, but the one delivered has red stitching. Or the model name on the mattress delivered is different (due to a change by the manufacturer) from the model name on the mattress in the store, although items are identical in all other respects. Additionally, 40 orders are returned each month due to customers not being home to receive delivery. The monthly cost of this activity is $2,050.

Wash Delivery Trucks. Solutions Analysis has determined that each of the 15 delivery trucks is washed each night. Costs include the salaries of three employees, supplies, depreciation, water, and other miscellaneous costs. The total cost is $8,450 each month.

Monthly Cost of Returning Merchandise to Stock When Not Acceptable to Customer or Customer Is Not Home to Receive Delivery

Salaries related to returning merchandise to stock (15 hours × $20)	$ 300
Costs to process paperwork for corrected shipment	250
Salaries to re-pick shipment (10 hours × $20)	200
Transportation cost to re-ship order (includes fuel, repair cost, and driver salary)	1,300
Total	$2,050

Monthly Cost to Wash 15 Delivery Trucks

Monthly salaries (three full-time employees)	$7,500
Supplies	450
Depreciation of equipment	300
Water and other miscellaneous costs	200
Total	$8,450

Step 3: Evaluate the Performance of the Activities

Once Solutions Analysis has determined the cost of key activities, it can turn its attention to an evaluation of them. This is the third step in an ABM study. One way the company can do this is by benchmarking the activities against similar activities performed by other clients it has dealt with. For example, Solutions Analysis now knows that it costs the company $101,400 a year ($8,450 × 12 months) to wash its 15 trucks. That's $6,760 per truck. From its work with other retail companies that perform delivery services, it has calculated an average cost of under $3,000 per truck. Thus, the cost of this activity to Mattress Warehouse appears to be too high.

ILLUSTRATION A6-1

Possible process improvements for Mattress Warehouse

- Ask the sales force to discuss the possibility of minor variations in stitching color with customers. If customers have a strong preference, confirm current colors with warehouse before shipping. This should reduce returns.
- Have a clerk call customers the day before a delivery to confirm that the customers will be home. This should reduce the problem of customers not being home to accept deliveries.
- Reduce staffing in the wash operation from three full-time employees to two full-time employees. This will save approximately $2,500 per month. Alternatively, consider outsourcing the wash operation.

Step 4: Identify Ways to Improve the Efficiency and/or Effectiveness of the Activities

The most satisfying part of the ABM process is identifying ways to improve the efficiency and/or effectiveness of activities, the fourth and last step of the ABM process. Pause for a minute and consider the two activities analyzed. Can you suggest any process improvements?

To identify process improvements, the consultants at Solutions Analysis would think about best practices they've identified at other clients, they would brainstorm with each other, and they would solicit input from managers at Mattress Warehouse. Possible improvements are listed in Illustration A6-1.

CONCLUSION

It is hoped that this brief treatment of ABM has provided you with insight into the nature of an ABM study.[5] Unlike ABC, which is focused on better costing of goods and services, ABM is focused on process improvements. Still, ABM, like ABC, requires costing activities. Once activities are costed, a manager conducting an ABM study can identify the so-called low-hanging fruit. That is, the manager can identify activities whose costs are large and apparently out of line. These are the activities that deserve immediate management attention.

One reason ABM studies have become so popular is that they often generate very substantial financial returns. Consider the case of Mattress Warehouse. If it turns out that eliminating one employee from the wash operation is appropriate, the company will save $2,500 per month, or $30,000 per year. Over 5 years, that's $150,000. To analyze the wash operation, a consultant from Solutions Analysis likely spent less than eight hours and billed Mattress Warehouse less than $4,000.

[5]These books will provide you with additional information on activity-based management: Judith J. Baker, *Activity-Based Costing and Activity-Based Management for Health Care,* Gaithersburg, MD: Aspen Publishers (1998); James A. Brimson and John Antos, *Activity-Based Management*, New York: John Wiley and Sons (1994); and Robin Cooper, Robert Kaplan, Lawrence Maisel, Eileen Morrissey, and Ronald Oehm, *Implementing Activity-Based Cost Management: Moving from Analysis to Action,* Montvale, NJ: Institute of Management Accountants (1992).

REVIEW PROBLEM 1

Wilton International is a large conglomerate with divisions that produce chemicals, tires, specialty metals, and pharmaceuticals. Two years ago, the chief financial officer noted that the company paid consultants more than $6,000,000 per year to help solve problems related to manufacturing efficiency, employee motivation, investment decisions, and a variety of other matters. The $6,000,000 in charges reflect average fees of approximately $240 per hour. The CFO decided that substantial funds could be saved by setting up an internal consulting group. Accordingly, five senior consultants from a respected firm were hired to run an internal consulting group at an average salary of $300,000 per year. These new managers hired 15 staff consultants at an average salary of $100,000 per year. Thus, the company had 20 full-time internal consultants at a yearly cost of only $3,000,000. The 20 individuals can work approximately 37,974 hours per year in total.

In the first year of the consulting group, the CFO sent out a notice to all divisions that they would no longer be allowed to hire outside consultants for work that could be performed by the internal group. Further, each division was to be charged a flat annual fee for use of the consultants based on their relative size (measured in sales dollars) over the past four years. With this approach, the allocation was as follows:

	Allocation
Chemicals	$ 300,000
Tires	600,000
Specialty metals	900,000
Pharmaceuticals	1,200,000
Total	$3,000,000

With this allocation, the division managers made frequent demands for the services of the consultants. Indeed, because of the demand for the services of the internal consultants, there were frequent delays, often exceeding one month.

The following year, the CFO changed the method of allocation to a charge for hours worked. Since costs were $3,000,000 and 38,000 hours were available, the charge was $79 per hour. With this charge, demand for consulting services declined drastically. In fact, the average consultant was only charging 70 percent of available hours. Further, all requests for service were easily answered within a day or two.

REQUIRED

a. Explain the difference in demand under the two allocation schemes.

b. Is the current charge of $79 per hour more or less than the opportunity cost of providing consulting services?

c. Because, at a charge equal to the actual hourly wage paid to consultants, demand is less than internal consulting capacity, the CFO is considering closing the internal consulting department. Based on the limited information provided, what would you advise?

ANSWER

a. The initial allocation is a lump-sum allocation to each division based on average sales over the past 4 years. This appears to be an ability to bear allocation. The result: excess demand and delays resulting in an opportunity cost that exceeds the zero incremental charge for use. Excess demand isn't surprising when the incremental charge for service is zero. "Does your office chair squeak? If so, call a consultant to fix it!" "Would you like to have someone do market research for a product that you think has a low probability of market acceptance? Call in the consultants—it won't cost anything so you might as well get more information!"

b. The new allocation is $79 per hour, which was calculated as the $3,000,000 annual cost divided by 37,974 hours. With this allocation, there is a drastic decline in requests and only 70 percent of available consulting time is used. This suggests that the opportunity cost of use is less than $79. (If there was a need for consulting time with a benefit exceeding $79, then, presumably, the manager with the need would call on the consultants.)

c. In the past, the company used only 25,000 hours of outside consultant time ($6,000,000 ÷ $240 per hour). Perhaps the company just hired too many internal consultants. In this case, the company should downsize consulting to, say, 25,000 hours.

Alternatively, one could argue that the situation is just right. At many firms, consultants don't work more than 70 percent of their available time on billable projects because they need time for training, and they need some slack or they won't be able to respond on a timely basis when a new project comes along.

Perhaps the company shouldn't worry too much about the fact that only 70 percent of consultant time is being used. After all, the company is saving $3,000,000 per year. The key question should be:

Is their service of high quality? The CFO should have a meeting with representatives from the divisions and get their feedback on the quality of the services provided by the internal consultants.

REVIEW PROBLEM 2

Bender Electric Motors produces electric motors used by home appliance and other manufacturing companies. Each motor is built to customer specifications although the number of units requested may vary from 1 to as many as 2,000.

Bender has recently adopted an activity-based costing system with the following overhead costs and drivers.

Cost Pool	Annual Amount	Annual Activity	Cost Driver
Direct labor related	$ 400,000	$1,000,000	Direct labor cost
Material ordering	100,000	5,000	Purchase orders
Material inspection	600,000	4,000	Receiving reports
Equipment setup	200,000	1,000	Setups
Quality control	400,000	2,000	Inspections of motors
Machine related	800,000	40,000	Machine hours
Miscellaneous	400,000	$4,000,000	Product costs other than miscellaneous overhead
Total overhead	$2,900,000		

Recently the company received an order from Kromer's Department Stores for 10 identical motors for use in a holiday display. Bender estimates the following costs and activities related to the order:

Material cost	$500
Labor cost	$200
Purchase orders	2
Receiving reports	2
Setups	1
Inspections	1
Machine hours	10

Note that the costs indicated are *for all 10 motors*—they are *not* per motor.

REQUIRED

a. Calculate the cost of the Kromer job using the new ABC system.

b. Calculate the cost of the Kromer job assuming the company used a traditional costing system with labor cost as the only allocation base.

c. Briefly explain why costs are higher or lower using the ABC system in part a compared to the traditional system in part b.

ANSWER

a.

Cost Pool	Overhead Rate
Direct labor related	$ 0.40 per direct labor dollar
Material ordering	$ 20.00 per purchase order
Material inspection	$150.00 per receiving report
Equipment setup	$200.00 per setup
Quality control	$200.00 per inspection
Machine related	$ 20.00 per machine hour
Miscellaneous	$ 0.10 per dollar of product costs other than misc.

ABC Cost of Kromer Job

Material		$ 500
Labor		200
Overhead:		
Labor related ($0.40 × $200)	$ 80	
Material ordering ($20 × 2)	40	
Material inspection ($150 × 2)	300	
Setup ($200 × 1)	200	
Quality control ($200 × 1)	200	
Machine related ($20 × 10)	200	
Miscellaneous (.10 × cost other than misc.)	172	
Total overhead		1,192
Total cost		$1,892

Cost other than misc. = $1,720

b. **Traditional Overhead Rate**

Total overhead	$2,900,000
Total labor cost	$1,000,000
Rate	$2.90 per labor dollar

Traditional Cost of Kromer Job

Material	$ 500
Labor	$ 200
Overhead ($2.90 × $200)	$ 580
Total cost	$1,280

c. Costs are higher with ABC because the Kromer job is relatively small and makes use of a number of activities whose costs are not proportionate to volume.

KEY TERMS

Ability to bear costs (211)
Activity-based costing (ABC) (218)
Activity-based management (ABM) (226)
Batch-level activities (220)
Cause-and-effect relationship (210)
Controllable costs (214)
Cost allocation (204)
Cost driver (219)
Cost objective (209)
Cost pool (209)
Direct method of allocating cost (212)
Equity approach to allocation (211)
Facility-level activities (221)
Lump-sum allocations (216)
Product-level activities (221)
Relative benefits approach to allocation (211)
Responsibility accounting system (214)
Unitized (215)
Unit-level activities (220)

SELF-ASSESSMENT (Answers Below)

1. Costs are allocated:

a. To provide information useful for decision making.

b. To reduce frivolous use of resources.

c. To encourage evaluation of internally provided services.

d. To calculate the "full cost" of products/services for GAAP reporting.

e. All of these answer choices are correct.

2. An important concern in forming a cost pool is to:

a. Avoid placing similar costs in the same pool.

b. Limit the number of costs that make up the pool.

c. Ensure that the costs in the pool are homogeneous, or similar.

d. None of these answer choices is correct.

3. In the cost allocation process, an allocation base:
   a. Must be some characteristic that is common to all of the cost objectives.
   b. Ideally should result in cost being allocated based on a cause-and-effect relationship.
   c. Selection is not an easy matter.
   d. All of these answer choices are correct.
4. The direct method of allocating costs:
   a. Allocates service department costs to other service departments.
   b. Allocates only direct costs.
   c. Allocates service department costs to producing departments only.
   d. None of these answer choices is correct.
5. When fixed costs are stated on a per unit basis:
   a. They are called "lump sum" allocations.
   b. Fixed costs may appear to be variable to managers receiving allocations.
   c. Decision making is greatly improved.
   d. All of these answer choices are correct.
6. One way to avoid the problems associated with unitized fixed costs is to:
   a. Not allocate fixed costs.
   b. Use a lump-sum method of allocating fixed costs.
   c. Combine fixed and variable costs in a single cost pool.
   d. None of these answer choices is correct.
7. Controllable costs for the manager of Production Department A include:
   a. Costs of the finance department.
   b. Costs of material and labor used in Department A.
   c. All costs related to Department A's final product.
   d. All of these answer choices are correct.
8. In allocating costs to products, more accurate costing is generally obtained by:
   a. Allocating costs using labor hours as the allocation base.
   b. Having more than one cost pool.
   c. Always using allocation bases that are based on production volume.
   d. None of these answer choices is correct.
9. Cost drivers in activity-based costing:
   a. Are always related to production volume.
   b. Are workers who influence cost control.
   c. Often assign more costs to low-volume products than traditional allocation methods.
   d. None of these answer choices is correct.
10. Most companies that use an activity-based costing system use:
    a. No cost pools.
    b. One or two cost pools.
    c. Two to five cost pools.
    d. More than five cost pools.

ANSWERS TO SELF-ASSESSMENT

1. e 2. c 3. d 4. c 5. b 6. b 7. b 8. b 9. c 10. d

QUESTIONS

1. Is the following statement true: "Cost allocation refers to the process of assigning direct costs"? Discuss.
2. Explain what a cost objective is and give two examples.
3. Explain one possible advantage to having two cost pools for each service department: one for variable costs and one for fixed costs.
4. If a company is allocating cafeteria costs to all departments within the company, what allocation base might result in a cause-and-effect relationship?
5. Why is it generally a good idea to allocate budgeted, rather than actual, service department costs?
6. What is a responsibility accounting system?
7. Why might noncontrollable costs be allocated to a department?
8. Briefly explain how traditional methods of allocating overhead to products might underallocate costs to low-production-volume products.
9. How does activity-based costing differ from the traditional costing approach?
10. When would activity-based costing give more relevant costs than traditional costing systems?

EXERCISES

GROUP WORK

EXERCISE 6-1. [LO 2] Explain how the allocation process can make a fixed cost appear variable, leading to a poor decision.

WRITING

EXERCISE 6-2. [LO 2] Mansard Hotels has five luxury hotels located in Boston, New York, Chicago, San Francisco, and Los Angeles. For internal reporting purposes, each hotel has an income statement showing its revenue and direct expenses. Additionally, the company allocates to each hotel a share of general administrative and advertising costs (e.g., salary of the company president, salary of the company CFO, hotel chain advertising, etc.) based on relative revenue.

REQUIRED

Write a paragraph explaining why the allocation of general administrative and advertising costs to the specific hotels is potentially useful or potentially harmful.

EXERCISE 6-3. [LO 1] The provost at San Francisco University is considering allocating the cost of campus security to the university's various colleges (Arts and Science, Business, Engineering, Nursing, etc.). In this regard, she is considering three allocation bases:

1. College expenses as a percent of total expenses summed across all colleges.
2. Number of college majors as a percent of the total number of students.
3. Square feet of space occupied by the college as a percent of the total square feet summed across all colleges.

REQUIRED

Suppose that the allocation will be subtracted from each college's annual budget and the amount returned to the provost to fund campus police. Explain why the deans of the various colleges are not likely to be in agreement as to which is the "best" allocation.

EXERCISE 6-4. Reasons for Allocating Indirect Costs [LO 1] The Warner Development Company has a security department that provides security services to other departments within the company. Department managers are responsible for working with the head of security to ensure that their departments are protected.

REQUIRED

Explain why Warner might want to allocate security department costs to other departments.

EXERCISE 6-5. Choice of Allocation Base (Cost Driver) for Service Departments [LO 1] Auburn Banking and Loan Company has six service departments:

1. Human Resources (hires employees and manages benefits)
2. Duplicating (performs copy services)
3. Janitorial (provides routine cleaning services)
4. Accounting (provides accounting services)
5. Graphic Design (designs forms)
6. Food Services (provides free breakfast and lunch to employees)

The services are used by the company's two subsidiaries, Auburn Personal Banking and Auburn Business Banking.

REQUIRED

a. Suggest allocation bases to be used in allocating the service department costs to the two subsidiaries.

b. Food services are used by employees in the human resources department. Would a share of food service costs be allocated to human resources under the direct method of allocation?

EXCEL **EXERCISE 6-6. Cost Allocation Process [LO 1]** The Apex Company's copy department, which does almost all of the photocopying for the sales department and the administrative department, budgets the following costs for the year, based on the expected activity of 5,000,000 copies:

Salaries (fixed)	$100,000
Employee benefits (fixed)	12,500
Depreciation of copy machines (fixed)	10,000
Utilities (fixed)	5,000
Paper (variable, 1 cent per copy)	50,000
Toner (variable, 1 cent per copy)	50,000

The costs are assigned to two cost pools, one for fixed and one for variable costs. The costs are then assigned to the sales department and the administrative department. Fixed costs are assigned on a lump-sum basis, 40 percent to sales and 60 percent to administration. The variable costs are assigned at a rate of 2 cents per copy.

REQUIRED

Assuming 4,800,000 copies were made during the year, 2,500,000 for sales and 2,300,000 for administration, calculate the copy department costs allocated to sales and administration.

EXERCISE 6-7. Allocation of Service Department Costs [LO 1] The building maintenance department for the Taylor Manufacturing Company budgets annual costs of $5,250,000 based on the expected operating level for the coming year. The costs are allocated to two production departments. Taylor is considering two allocation bases for assignment of costs to departments: (1) square footage and (2) direct labor hours. The following data relate to the potential allocation bases:

	Production Dept. 1	Production Dept. 2
Square footage	30,000	40,000
Direct labor hours	40,000	30,000

REQUIRED

Calculate the costs allocated to the production departments using each allocation base. Comment on which allocation base is preferable.

EXCEL **EXERCISE 6-8. Allocation of Service Department Costs [LO 1]** The Marvin Company has three service departments, S1, S2, and S3, and two production departments, P1 and P2. The following data relate to Marvin's allocation of service department costs:

	Budgeted Costs	Number of Employees
S1	$4,500,000	90
S2	3,000,000	60
S3	2,700,000	40
P1		200
P2		300

Service department costs are allocated by the direct method. The number of employees is used as the allocation base for all service department costs.

REQUIRED

a. Allocate service department costs to production departments.

b. Calculate the total service department cost allocated to each production department.

EXERCISE 6-9. Problems Associated with Cost Allocation [LO 2] Custom Metal Works received an offer from a big-box retail company to purchase 3,000 metal outdoor tables for $220 each. Custom Metal Works accountants determine that the following costs apply to the tables:

Direct material	$125
Direct labor	50
Manufacturing overhead	70
Total	$245

Of the $70 of overhead, $14 is variable and $56 relates to fixed costs. The $56 of fixed overhead is allocated as $1.12 per direct labor dollar.

REQUIRED

a. What will be the real effect on profit if the order is accepted?

b. Explain why managers who focus on reported cost per unit may be inclined to turn down the order.

EXERCISE 6-10. Responsibility Accounting, Controllable Costs [LO 1, 2] Vance Mason, the manager of the service department at the Proton Electronics Company, is evaluated based on the profit performance of his department. The profit of the department is down this year because the service department's share of allocated general and administrative costs (allocated based on relative sales dollars) is much higher than last year. In the current year, service revenue has increased slightly while sales of handheld electronic game devices, the company's major product, have decreased substantially.

REQUIRED

a. Explain why the allocation of general and administrative costs to the service department is higher in the current year.

b. Discuss how this situation relates to a responsibility accounting system and controllable costs.

EXERCISE 6-11. Problems with Cost Allocation [LO 1, 2] Auburn Banking and Loan Company has six service departments—human resources, duplicating, janitorial, accounting, graphic design, and food services—whose costs are allocated to the company's two subsidiaries, Auburn Personal Banking and Auburn Business Banking, on the basis of their relative sales.

REQUIRED

a. Suppose you are the president of Auburn Business Banking. Will you perceive the allocated service department costs to be fixed costs, variable costs, or mixed costs?

b. In performing incremental analysis related to expanding or contracting her business, will the president of Auburn Business Banking tend to overestimate or underestimate incremental costs? Explain.

EXERCISE 6-12. Problems Associated with Too Few Cost Pools [LO 2] Morton Manufacturing allocates factory overhead using one cost pool with direct labor hours as the allocation base. Morton has two production departments, P1 and P2. The new accountant at Morton estimates that next year, the total factory overhead costs will be $5,000,000, and approximately 500,000 direct labor hours will be worked. The accountant also estimates that P1 will use 200,000 direct labor hours, and there will be about $3,000,000 in overhead costs in P1. P2 will use 300,000 direct labor hours, and there will be $2,000,000 in overhead costs in P2. Morton has two products, A1 and B1. It takes two direct labor hours in P1 and three direct labor hours in P2 to complete one unit of A1. It takes one direct labor hour in P1 and four direct labor hours in P2 to complete one unit of B1.

REQUIRED

Which product will be undercosted and which will be overcosted with the one-cost-pool system? Support your answer with appropriate calculations. Round all amounts 2 decimal places.

EXERCISE 6-13. Cost Allocation and Opportunity Cost [LO 1] Auburn Banking and Loan Company has a graphic design department that designs loan forms and other documents used by the company's two subsidiaries, Auburn Personal Banking and Auburn Business Banking. For practical purposes, the costs of the graphic design department are primarily fixed and relate to the salaries of the department's two employees.

REQUIRED

Analyze the following four independent cases:

a. Assume there is no allocation of graphic design costs to the subsidiaries. Jobs requested by the subsidiaries are completed promptly (generally by the next business day). How does the allocation (which is zero) compare to the opportunity cost of using design services?

b. Assume there is no allocation of graphic design costs to the subsidiaries. Jobs requested by the subsidiaries generally take weeks to complete; the subsidiaries often go outside the company for design services. How does the allocation (which is zero) compare to the opportunity cost of using design services?

c. Assume subsidiaries receive an allocation of $60 per design hour. Jobs requested by the subsidiaries generally take weeks to complete; the subsidiaries often go outside the company for design services rather than wait for jobs to be completed. They generally pay $80 per hour outside the company. How does the allocation ($60 per design hour) compare to the opportunity cost of using design services?

d. Assume subsidiaries receive an allocation of $60 per design hour. Although the graphic design department is busy, jobs requested by the subsidiaries are completed promptly (generally by the next business day). How does the allocation ($60 per design hour) compare to the opportunity cost of using design services?

EXERCISE 6-14. Activity-Based Costing [LO 2] The following are six cost pools established for a company using activity-based costing. The pools are related to the company's products using cost drivers.

Cost pools:

1. Inspection of raw materials
2. Production equipment repairs and maintenance
3. Raw materials storage
4. Plant heat, light, water, and power
5. Finished product quality control
6. Production line setups

REQUIRED

For each of the preceding cost pools, identify a possible cost driver.

EXERCISE 6-15. Relating Cost Pools to Products Using Cost Drivers [LO 1, 2] Power Electronics manufactures portable power supply units. Power has recently decided to use an activity-based approach to cost its products. Production line setups is a major activity at Power. Next year Power expects to perform 2,000 setups at a total cost of $4,200,000. Power plans to produce 800 units of product EP150, which will require two setups.

REQUIRED

How much setup cost will be allocated to each unit of EP150 produced?

EXERCISE 6-16. Relating Cost Pools to Products Using Cost Drivers [LO 1, 2] Classic Attire is the designer and manufacturer of prom dresses. The president of Classic wants to switch to an activity-based approach in the upcoming year to assign prices to the gowns. Production line setups are a major activity at Classic. Next year Classic expects to perform 1,500 setups at a total cost of $105,000. Classic plans to produce 325 dresses of the A128 design, which will require three setups.

REQUIRED

How much setup cost will be allocated to each dress of the A128 design that is produced?

EXERCISE 6-17. Activity-Based Management [LO 2] The Eldon Company has two production plants. Recently, the company conducted an ABM study to determine the cost of activities involved in processing orders for parts at each of the plants.

REQUIRED

How might an operations manager use this information to manage the cost of processing orders?

EXERCISE 6-18. Activity-Based Management [LO 2] Hearthstone Appliances supplies parts for laundry and kitchen appliances. Customer orders are placed over the Internet and are generally filled in 1 or 2 days using express mail services.

Angela Farnsworth, a consultant with ABM Services, has been asked to conduct an ABM study of inventory management at Hearthstone Appliances. In this regard she has determined that the cost of filling customer orders in the past year consisted primarily of $300,000 of salary expense related to five workers who pick parts from the warehouse and $450,000 of salary expense related to six workers who pack the orders for shipment. In the past year, the company filled 125,000 orders. Based on work performed for a very large chain of auto supply stores, Angela has determined a benchmark cost of $4.50 per order.

REQUIRED

a. Comment on the advisability of comparing the costs at Hearthstone Appliances to those at an auto supply chain store.

b. Angela has observed the following: Workers go to a box that contains individual customer order sheets. They take the bottom order (the oldest) and go into the warehouse with a handcart and a box. They then fill the order and carry the parts to a packing station. Can you suggest ways of improving this process?

PROBLEMS

PROBLEM 6-1. Number of Cost Pools [LO 1] Icon.com sells software and provides consulting services to companies that conduct business over the Internet. The company is organized into two lines of business (software and consulting), and profit statements are prepared as follows:

	Software	Consulting
Sales	$15,000,000	$8,000,000
Less direct costs	6,000,000	4,000,000
Less allocated costs	5,250,000	1,750,000
Income before taxes	$ 3,750,000	$2,250,000

Direct costs include costs that are easily associated with each line of business. For software, this includes the salary of programmers, the cost of computers used by programmers, and the cost of software manuals sold to customers. For consulting, direct costs include consultant salaries, computer costs, and travel costs. Allocated costs include costs that are not directly traced to the business units. These costs include employee benefits, rent, telecommunications costs, and general and administrative costs, such as the salary of the CEO of Icon.com.

At the start of 2017, allocated costs were estimated as follows:

Employee benefits	$2,500,000
Rent	1,000,000
Telecommunications	500,000
General and administrative costs	3,000,000
Total	$7,000,000

In the past, allocations have been based on headcount (the number of employees in each business unit). Software had 375 employees and consulting had 125 employees. The new controller of Icon.com believes that the key driver of employee benefits and telecommunications costs is headcount. However, rent is driven by space occupied, and general and administrative costs are driven by relative sales. Icon.com rents 40,000 square feet; approximately 20,000 is occupied by software employees and 20,000 by consulting personnel.

REQUIRED

a. Prepare profit reports for software and consulting assuming the company allocates costs using headcount, space occupied, and sales as allocation bases. Compare the new levels of profit to the levels that result using a single allocation base (headcount). Round to six decimal places.

b. Which provides the best information on profitability: a single overhead cost pool with headcount as the allocation base, or multiple cost pools using headcount, sales, and space occupied?

PROBLEM 6-2. Number of Cost Pools [LO 1] The Kiddo Company manufactures and ships children's stuffed animals across the nation. The following are profit statements for the company's two lines of business:

	Stock Stuffed Animals	Custom Stuffed Animals
Sales	$7,500,000	$5,000,000
Less direct costs	2,500,000	4,000,000
Less allocated costs	3,375,000	1,125,000
Income (loss) before taxes	$1,625,000	($ 125,000)

Costs that are easily associated with each line of business are included in the direct costs. Allocated costs include costs that are not directly traced to the business units. These costs include employee benefits, rent, telecommunications costs, and general and administrative costs, such as the salary of the CEO of Kiddo.

At the start of 2017, allocated costs were estimated as follows:

Employee benefits	$1,500,000
Rent	1,500,000
Telecommunications	500,000
General and administrative costs	1,000,000
Total	$4,500,000

In the past, allocations have been based on headcount (the number of employees in each business unit). There were 240 employees in Stock and 80 employees in Custom. The new controller of Kiddo believes that the key driver of employee benefits and telecommunications costs is headcount. However, rent is driven by space occupied, and general and administrative costs are driven by relative sales. Kiddo rents 20,000 square feet; approximately 10,000 is occupied by Stock employees and 10,000 by Custom personnel.

REQUIRED

a. Prepare profit reports for Stock and Custom, assuming the company allocates costs using headcount, space occupied, and sales as allocation bases. Compare the new levels of profit to the levels that result using a single allocation base (headcount). Round to two decimal places.

b. Which provides the best information on profitability: a single overhead cost pool with headcount as the allocation base, or multiple cost pools using headcount, sales, and space occupied?

PROBLEM 6-3. Allocated Cost and Opportunity Cost [LO 1] Binder Manufacturing produces small electric motors used by appliance manufacturers. In the past year, the company has experienced severe excess capacity due to competition from a foreign company that has entered

Binder's market. The company is currently bidding on a potential order from Dacon Appliances for 6,000 Model 350 motors. The estimated cost of each motor is $45, as follows:

Direct material	$25
Direct labor	5
Overhead	15
Total	$45

The predetermined overhead rate is $3 per direct labor dollar. This was estimated by dividing estimated annual overhead ($15,000,000) by estimated annual direct labor ($5,000,000). The $15,000,000 of overhead is composed of $6,000,000 of variable costs and $9,000,000 of fixed costs. The largest fixed cost relates to depreciation of plant and equipment.

REQUIRED

a. With respect to overhead, what is the opportunity cost of producing a Model 350 motor?

b. Suppose Binder can win the Dacon business by bidding a price of $39 per motor (but no higher price will result in a winning bid). Should Binder bid $39?

c. Discuss how an allocation of overhead based on opportunity cost would facilitate an appropriate bidding decision.

PROBLEM 6-4. Allocated Cost and Opportunity Cost [LO 1] Brennen produces a mint syrup used by gum and candy companies. Recently, the company has had excess capacity due to a foreign supplier entering its market. Brennen is currently bidding on a potential order from Quality Candy for 5,000 cases of syrup. The estimated cost of each case is $23, as follows:

Direct material	$ 9
Direct labor	5
Overhead	9
Total	$23

The predetermined overhead rate is $1.80 per direct labor dollar. This was estimated by dividing estimated annual overhead ($1,080,000) by estimated annual direct labor ($600,000). The $1,080,000 of overhead is composed of $270,000 of variable costs and $810,000 of fixed costs. The largest fixed cost relates to depreciation of plant and equipment.

REQUIRED

a. With respect to overhead, what is the opportunity cost of producing a case of syrup?

b. Suppose Brennen can win the Quality Candy business by bidding a price of $19 per case (but no higher price will result in a winning bid). Should Brennen bid $19?

c. Discuss how an allocation of overhead based on opportunity cost would facilitate an appropriate bidding decision.

ETHICS

PROBLEM 6-5. Cost-Plus Contracts, Allocations, and Ethics [LO 1] Pelton Instruments manufactures a variety of electronic instruments that are used in military and civilian applications. Sales to the military are generally on a cost-plus-profit basis with profit equal to 10 percent of cost. Instruments used in military applications require more direct labor time because "fail-safe" devices must be installed. (These devices are generally omitted in civilian applications.)

At the start of the year, Pelton estimates that the company will incur $75,000,000 of overhead, $7,500,000 of direct labor, and 750,000 machine hours. Consider the Model KV10 gauge that is produced for both civilian and military uses:

	Civilian	Military
Direct material	$3,000	$3,500
Direct labor	$ 900	$1,200
Machine hours	100	100

REQUIRED

a. Calculate the cost of civilian and military versions of Model KV10 using both direct labor dollars and machine hours as alternative allocation bases.

b. Explain why Pelton Instruments may decide to use direct labor as an overhead allocation base.

c. Is it ethical for Pelton to select an allocation base that tends to allocate more of overhead costs to government contracts? Explain.

PROBLEM 6-6. Allocating Service Department Costs [LO 1] World Airlines has three service departments: (1) ticketing, (2) baggage handling, and (3) engine maintenance. The service department costs are estimated for separate cost pools formed by department and are allocated to two revenue-producing departments: (1) domestic flights and (2) international flights. World does not differentiate between fixed and variable costs in making allocations. The following data relate to the allocations:

	Budgeted Data	
	Costs	Air Miles
Ticketing	$4,000,000	
Baggage handling	$2,000,000	
Engine maintenance	$9,000,000	
Domestic flights		7,500,000
International flights		22,500,000

REQUIRED

a. Allocate the service department costs to the revenue-producing departments using air miles as the allocation base.

b. Evaluate the cause-and-effect relationship resulting from the use of air miles as the allocation base. In which of the cost pools do you think the cause-and-effect relationship is the strongest? Suggest alternative allocation bases for the two remaining cost pools with the weakest cause-and-effect relationship.

PROBLEM 6-7. Allocating Service Department Costs [LO 1] Armstrong Industries produces electronic equipment for the marine industry. Armstrong has two service departments (maintenance and computing) and two production departments (assembly and testing). Maintenance costs are allocated on the basis of square footage occupied, and computing costs are allocated on the basis of the number of computer terminals. The following data relate to allocations of service department costs:

	Maintenance	Computing	Assembly	Testing
Service department costs	$700,000	$900,000		
Square footage			84,000	36,000
Terminals			6	14

REQUIRED

Allocate the service department costs to production departments using the direct method.

PROBLEM 6-8. Allocating Service Department Costs [LO 1] Snowcap Electronics is a manufacturer of data storage devices. Snowcap consists of two service departments (maintenance and computing) and two production departments (assembly and testing). Maintenance costs are allocated on the basis of square footage occupied, and computing costs are allocated on the basis of the number of computer terminals. The following data relate to allocations of service department costs:

	Maintenance	Computing	Assembly	Testing
Service department costs	$600,000	$1,000,000		
Square footage			100,000	50,000
Terminals			30	60

REQUIRED

Allocate the service department costs to production departments using the direct method. Round to two decimal places.

EXCEL **PROBLEM 6-9. Choice of Allocation Base, Problems with Cost Allocation [LO 1]** Tilden Financial Services has two divisions, Financial Planning and Business Consulting. The firm's accountants are in the process of selecting an allocation base to allocate centrally provided personnel costs to the divisions. Two allocation bases have been proposed: salary and headcount (number of employees). Personnel costs are expected to be $1,500,000. The following data relate to the allocation:

	Financial Planning	Business Consulting
Salaries	$15,000,000	$5,000,000
Headcount	200	50

REQUIRED

a. Prepare a schedule showing the allocations to the two divisions using each allocation base.

b. Referring to your answer to part a, explain why allocations are sometimes considered arbitrary.

PROBLEM 6-10. Cost Allocation and Apparent Profitability [LO 1] Simon Products manufactures jewelry settings and sells them to retail stores. In the past, most settings were made by hand, and the overhead allocation rate in the prior year was $12 per labor hour ($2,700,000 overhead ÷ 225,000 labor hours). In the current year, overhead increased by $800,000 due to acquisition of equipment. Labor, however, decreased by 50,000 hours because the equipment allows rapid creation of the settings. One of the company's many customers is a local jewelry store, Jasmine's Fine Jewelry. This store is relatively small, and the time to make an order of jewelry pieces is typically less than 10 labor hours. On such jobs (less than 10 labor hours), the new equipment is not used, and thus the jobs are relatively labor intensive.

REQUIRED

a. Assume that in the current year, the company continues to allocate overhead based on labor hours. What would be the overhead cost of a 10-labor-hour job requested by Jasmine's Fine Jewelry? How does this compare to the overhead cost charged to such a job in the prior year?

b. Assume that the price charged for small jobs does not change in the current year. Are small jobs less profitable than they were in the past?

PROBLEM 6-11. Activity-Based Costing [LO 2] The Summit Manufacturing Company produces two products. One is a recreational whitewater kayak molded from plastic and designed to perform as a durable whitewater play boat. The other product is a high-performance competition kayak molded with high-tech fiberglass materials that are very light. The recreation kayak is uniform in its dimensions and style. However, the competition kayak is custom designed to fit the individual (e.g., rocker and cockpit size are adjusted).

Most of the sales come from the recreation kayaks, but recently sales of the competition kayaks have been increasing. The following information is related to the products for the most recent year:

	Recreation Kayak	Competition Kayak
Sales and production (number of kayaks)	1,000	200
Sales price per kayak	$650	$800
Unit costs:		
Direct materials	175	225
Direct labor	125	125
Overhead*	175	175
Total unit cost	475	525
Gross profit	$ 175	$275
Overhead* costs:		
Building depreciation	$ 35,000	
Equipment depreciation	35,000	
Materials ordering	25,000	
Quality control	20,000	
Maintenance and security	20,000	
Setup and drafting	35,000	
Supervision	40,000	
Total overhead	$210,000	
Overhead rate based on direct labor dollars:		
Total overhead	$210,000	
Total labor ($125 × 1,000) + ($125 × 200)	$150,000	

* Overhead rate = $1.40 per direct labor dollar.

Victoria Mason, the president of Summit Manufacturing, is concerned that the traditional cost system used by Summit may not be providing accurate cost information and that the sales price of the competition kayak might not be enough to cover its true cost.

REQUIRED

a. The traditional system that Summit is using assigns 83 percent of the $210,000 total overhead to the recreational kayak because 83 percent of the direct labor dollars are spent on the recreational kayaks. Discuss why this might not be an accurate way to assign overhead to kayaks.

b. Discuss how Summit might be able to improve cost allocation by using an ABC system.

c. Assume that Summit retains a consultant to create an activity-based costing system, and the consultant develops the following data:

			Driver Activity	
Cost Pool	Amount	Driver	Recreational Kayaks	Competition Kayaks
Building	$ 35,000	Square footage	8,000	2,000
Equipment	35,000	Machine hours	4,250	750
Materials ordering	25,000	Number of orders	200	100
Quality control	20,000	Number of inspections	300	150
Maintenance and security	20,000	Square footage	8,000	2,000
Setup and drafting	35,000	Number of setups	30	60
Supervision	40,000	Direct labor cost	$125,000	$25,000
	$210,000			

Determine the overhead allocation to each line of kayaks using an activity-based costing approach, and compute the total unit costs for each model kayaks. Round to three decimal places.

d. Discuss why activity-based allocations are different from those generated by the traditional allocation method used by Summit.

PROBLEM 6-12. Activity-Based Costing [LO 2] The Cheesecake Shoppe is a national bakery that is known for its strawberry cheesecake. It makes 12 different kinds of cheesecake as well as many other types of bakery items. It has recently adopted an activity-based costing system to assign manufacturing overhead to products. The following data relate to its strawberry cheesecake and the ABC cost pools:

Strawberry Cheesecake:

Annual production	19,500 units
Direct materials per unit	$10
Direct labor per unit	$2

Cost Pool	Cost	Cost Driver
Materials ordering	$ 72,000	Number of purchase orders
Materials inspection	75,000	Number of receiving reports
Equipment setup	105,000	Number of setups
Quality control	69,000	Number of inspections
Other	100,000	Direct labor cost
Total manufacturing overhead	$421,000	

Annual activity information related to cost drivers:

Cost Pool	All Products	Strawberry Cheesecake
Materials ordering	8,000 orders	100
Materials inspection	375 receiving reports	60
Equipment setup	3,000 setups	30
Quality control	3,000 inspections	150
Other	$2,000,000 direct labor	$39,000

REQUIRED

a. Calculate the overhead rate per unit of activity for each of the five cost pools.

b. Calculate the total overhead assigned to the production of the strawberry cheesecake.

c. Calculate the overhead cost per unit for the strawberry cheesecake. Round to three decimal places.

d. Calculate the total unit cost for the strawberry cheesecake. Round to three decimal places.

e. Suppose that the Cheesecake Shoppe allocates overhead by a traditional production volume-based method using direct labor dollars as the allocation base and one cost pool. Determine the overhead rate per direct labor dollar and the per unit overhead assigned to the strawberry cheesecake. Discuss the difference in cost allocations between the traditional method and the activity-based costing approach. Round to three decimal places.

PROBLEM 6-13. Activity-Based Costing at a Service Company [LO 2] Tannhauser Financial is a banking services company that offers many different types of checking accounts. It has recently adopted an activity-based costing system to assign costs to various types of checking accounts. The following data relate to one type of checking account, the money market checking account, and the ABC cost pools:

Total Number of Checking Accounts	221,750
Number of Money Market Checking Accounts	70,000

Checking account cost pools:

Cost Pool	Cost	Cost Driver
Returned check costs	$3,000,000	Number of returned checks
Checking account reconciliation costs	60,000	Number of account reconciliation requests
New account setup	780,000	Number of new accounts
Copies of cancelled checks	300,000	Number of cancelled check copy requests
Web site maintenance (for online banking)	225,000	Per product group (type of checking account)
Total checking account costs	$4,365,000	

Annual activity information related to cost drivers:

Cost Pool	All Products	Money Market Checking
Returned checks	200,000 returned checks	18,000
Check reconciliation costs	3,000 checking account reconciliations	420
New accounts	60,000 new accounts	20,000
Cancelled check copy requests	80,000 cancelled check copy requests	50,000
Web site costs	10 types of checking accounts	1

REQUIRED

a. Calculate the cost rate per cost driver activity for each of the five cost pools. Round to two decimal places.

b. Calculate the total cost assigned to the money market checking account. Round to two decimal places.

c. Suppose that Tannhauser Financial allocates overhead using the number of checking accounts as the allocation base and one cost pool. Determine the cost rate per checking account and the per account cost assigned to the money market checking account. Discuss the difference in cost allocations between this method and the activity-based costing approach.

PROBLEM 6-14. Traditional Allocation versus ABC Allocation of Manufacturing Overhead Costs [LO 1, 2] TriTech Company has been allocating overhead to individual product lines based on each line's relative shares of direct labor hours. For the upcoming year, the company estimated that manufacturing overhead will be $1,800,000 and estimated direct labor hours will be 120,000. The company also has the following estimates:

Cost Pool	Cost Driver	Total Amount	Total Amount of Activity
Maintenance costs	Direct labor hours	$ 700,000	120,000
Setup costs	Number of setups	500,000	200
Engineering costs	Number of design changes	600,000	400
		$1,800,000	

Among many other products, TriTech has two switches, Standard and Elite switches. Standard switches are a high-volume product that the company makes in large batches, while Elite switches are a specialty product that is fairly low in sales volume.

Information about Standard and Elite usage of the different activities follows:

	Standard	Elite
Direct labor hours	3,000	300
Number of setups	1	14
Number of design changes	2	20

REQUIRED

a. Calculate the predetermined overhead rate based on direct labor hours (traditional allocation). Use this predetermined overhead rate to calculate the amount of overhead to apply to Standard and Elite switches, based on their usage of direct labor hours.

b. Calculate the individual ABC pool rates by taking the total amount of overhead for each cost pool and dividing that total by the total amount of activity for that pool. Allocate overhead to each of the two products using these three activity rates.

c. Compare the overhead calculated in part a to that calculated in part b. Why are they different? Which allocation method (traditional or ABC) most likely results in a better estimate of product cost?

PROBLEM 6-15. Activity-Based Costing—Comprehensive Problem [LO 2] The Riverdale Printing Company prints limited edition art books with production runs of 15,000 to 100,000. It has recently adopted an activity-based costing system to assign manufacturing overhead to products. The following data relate to one product, *Art of Design*, and the ABC cost pools:

Art of Design:

Annual production	40,000 units
Direct materials per unit	$37
Direct labor per unit	$8

Manufacturing overhead cost pools:

Cost Pool	Cost	Cost Driver
Materials ordering	$ 840,000	Number of purchase orders
Materials inspection	525,000	Number of receiving reports
Equipment setup	2,500,000	Number of setups
Quality control	1,000,000	Number of inspections
Other	25,000,000	Direct labor cost
Total manufacturing overhead	$29,865,000	

Annual activity information related to cost drivers:

Cost Pool	All Books	*Art of Design*
Materials ordering	120,000 orders	1,200
Materials inspection	2,100 receiving reports	315
Equipment setup	125 setups	1
Quality control	5,000 inspections	500
Other	$12,500,000 direct labor	$320,000

REQUIRED

a. Calculate the overhead rate per unit of activity for each of the five cost pools.

b. Calculate the total overhead assigned to the production of the *Art of Design*. Round to two decimal places.

c. Calculate the overhead cost per unit for the *Art of Design.*

d. Calculate the total unit cost for the *Art of Design.*

e. Suppose that Riverdale Printing allocates overhead by a traditional production volume-based method using direct labor dollars as the allocation base and one cost pool. Determine the overhead rate per direct labor dollar and the per unit overhead assigned to the *Art of Design.* Discuss the difference in cost allocations between the traditional method and the activity-based costing approach.

PROBLEM 6-16. (Appendix) Activity-Based Management [LO 2] Talbot Partners is a consulting firm with clients across the nation. Within the company is a travel group that arranges flights and hotel accommodations for its over 2,000 consultants. The cost of operating the travel group (excluding the costs associated with actual travel such as hotel cost and air fare) amounts to approximately $1,500,000.

Recently, Talbot Partners conducted an ABM study that has determined the following:

1. Each consultant takes approximately 15 business trips per year.
2. On average, 30 percent of trips are rescheduled due to conflicts and poor planning.
3. The travel group employs 15 individuals at $50,000 each to book travel. In addition, there is a travel manager and an assistant travel manager.
4. Benchmarking with a Talbot Partners' client indicates that the client incurs $35 cost per completed trip to book travel.

REQUIRED

a. Evaluate the cost incurred by Talbot Partners compared to the benchmark cost.

b. Talbot Partners is planning a process improvement initiative aimed at reducing scheduling conflicts. What would be the savings if rescheduling could be reduced by 50 percent? Assume that the only variable cost in travel services is the wages paid to employees who book travel.

PROBLEM 6-17. (Appendix) Activity-Based Management [LO 2] Primary Savings and Loan of Denver is conducting an ABM study of its teller operations. In this regard, the company has identified the following major activities performed by bank tellers:

1. Process deposits
2. Process withdrawals
3. Process requests for certificates of deposit
4. Answer customer questions related to balances, overdrafts, interest rates, etc.
5. Print out customer activity statements
6. Provide access to safe deposit boxes
7. Reconcile cash drawer

The company benchmarked its operations against banks in other cities and has found that it has many more tellers in comparison to banks of similar size. Further, the company has a relatively unsophisticated Web site and call center.

REQUIRED

a. How do the company's Web site and call center affect the demand for teller activities and the cost of teller services?

b. Identify two or three ways that technology can be used to reduce the cost of teller services.

PROBLEM 6-18. (Appendix) Activity-Based Management [LO 2] Each month, senior managers at Vermont Wireless Technologies review cost reports for the company's various departments. The report for the human resource (HR) group for April is as follows:

Human Resources
April 2017

Salaries and benefits	$80,000
Supplies	2,400
Depreciation of office equipment	1,700
Total	$84,100

Jason Fox, the new vice president of operations, expressed his dissatisfaction with the report at a meeting with the company president, CFO, and controller. "This report is garbage," he began. "It shows that $80,000 is being spent on salaries in HR, but it doesn't provide any information on what we're paying for. We need to know the activities of HR and what they cost. How are we supposed to manage the activities without that information? At my previous company, we routinely did activity-based management studies, and they really helped us get a handle on operations and our costs."

Maxwell Davies, the controller, responded that he'd get to work on ABM studies right away. Two weeks later, his staff had developed the following information for the HR operation:

Activities in HR	Monthly Cost
General administration of department	
Salary of HR head	$10,000
Salary of assistant to HR head	5,000
Depreciation of equipment	300
Supplies	200
	$15,500
Benefits administration	
Salary of administrator	$ 8,000
Depreciation of equipment	250
Supplies	400
	$ 8,650
HR Web site development/maintenance	
One half-time staff person	$ 4,000
Depreciation of equipment	500
Supplies	200
	$ 4,700
Operations	
Salary of five clerks who process paperwork related to hiring, retirements, terminations	$18,000
Depreciation of equipment	700
Supplies	500
	$19,200
Training	
Salary of six staff members who train new employees on company policies	$35,000
Depreciation of equipment	650
Supplies	400
	$36,050
Total	$84,100

Additional Information: The company has approximately 6,000 employees and annual employee turnover of approximately 15 percent. New employee training is a half day session and 2 hours are required to process paperwork for new hires and terminations.

REQUIRED

Comment on the insights provided by the ABM study to date. Where's the low-hanging fruit? In other words, what activities appear to be good candidates for further study and significant cost savings?

CASE

6-1 EASTSIDE MEDICAL TESTING [LO 2]

Eastside Medical Testing performs five different tests (T1–T5) to detect drug use. Most clients are referred to the company by potential employers who pay for the tests. Revenue and costs related to the tests, for the most recent fiscal year, are detailed in the table below.

Setting up equipment to conduct a test is the responsibility of three highly skilled technicians, one of whom is Emmet Wilson, founder and owner of the company. Tests T2 to T5 are high-volume tests that are conducted in batches of 100 tests per batch. Thus, for example, T5 is run approximately three times a day to annually process 92,000 tests in 920 batches. T1 is a test with relatively low demand. However, it is run almost every day (350 runs per year), so that results can be quickly communicated to employers. This fast turnaround represents a significant competitive advantage for the company.

Nuclear Systems, Inc., is one of the few companies that requires T1. Indeed, it accounted for almost half of the 3,500 T1 tests conducted in the past year. Recently, Ron Worth, vice president of operations at Nuclear Systems, questioned the relatively high price being charged for T1. In a letter to Emmet Wilson he noted:

> We pay $35 for each T1 test, which is about 40% higher than your next most expensive test. Is this charge warranted? Frankly, this isn't just a matter of dollars and cents. We believe that we are being taken advantage of because we are one of the few companies that requires the test, and you are one of the few companies that provide it. If we believed that the high price was justified in terms of significantly higher costs, we would not be writing this letter.

Before responding to Worth's letter, Emmet reviewed the revenue and cost data presented in the table below. As indicated, T1 produced a profit of $5.90 per test, which was much higher than the profit per test of any of the other procedures. However, since taking a day-long continuing education course at City College (titled ABC and Managing by the Right Numbers!), Emmet has wondered whether the profitability of tests is being distorted by the company's simple approach to allocating overhead—overhead allocation is based on direct labor cost. Direct labor consists of wages and benefits paid to relatively unskilled technicians who prepare samples for testing. This cost, $325,650, is only 9.6 percent of total overhead. With help from his bookkeeper, Emmet began to analyze overhead costs in an attempt to calculate the ABC cost of the five tests. In the past year, overhead amounted to $3,386,760, as follows:

Overhead	Costs
Setup labor	$ 925,760
Equipment	1,476,000
Rent	390,000
Billing	235,000
Clerical	160,000
Other	200,000
Total	$3,386,760

Emmet's analysis of these six overhead cost categories was as follows:

Profitability of Tests for the Fiscal Year Ending December 31, 2017

	T1	T2	T3	T4	T5	Total
Number of tests per year	3,500	52,000	72,000	80,000	92,000	299,500
Number of runs	350	520	720	800	920	3,310
Price per test	$ 35.00	$ 26.00	$ 22.00	$ 21.00	$ 20.00	
Less:						
Material cost	12.00	10.50	7.50	7.35	5.85	
Direct labor at $18 per hour	1.50	1.00	1.10	1.10	1.10	
Overhead at $10.40 per labor hour	15.60	10.40	11.44	11.44	11.44	
Total cost	29.10	21.90	20.04	19.89	18.39	
Profit per test	$ 5.90	$ 4.10	$ 1.96	$ 1.11	$ 1.62	
Total profit	$20,650	$ 213,200	$141,120	$ 88,800	$ 148,120	$ 611,890
Total overhead	$54,600	$540,8000	$823,680	$915,200	$1,052,480	$3,386,760
Total labor	$ 5,250	$ 52,000	$ 79,200	$ 88,000	$ 101,200	$ 325,650

Setup labor ($925,760). This amount is essentially the salary and benefits paid to Emmet and the two other skilled technicians who set up equipment for testing batches of T1 to T5. Emmet believes that the number of runs (batches of tests) is a valid driver for this cost pool. In the past year, there were 3,310 runs.

Equipment ($1,476,000). This amount is depreciation on equipment used to process the tests. All of the major pieces of equipment are used in each test. (In other words, no major piece of equipment is used exclusively for any individual test.) Emmet believes that the amount of direct labor cost is a valid driver for this cost pool. This follows because equipment hours vary with direct labor hours and direct labor cost. In the past year, total direct labor was $325,650.

Rent ($390,000). This amount is the annual rent on the facility occupied by Eastside Medical Testing. Emmet believes that the number of tests (299,500 in the prior year) is a valid driver for this cost pool since each test benefits equally from the incurrence of rent expense.

Billing ($235,000). This amount is the annual salary and benefits of two billing clerks as well as a variety of other charges (e.g., billing software costs). Emmet believes that the number of tests (299,500 in the prior year) is a valid driver for this cost pool since each test requires a separate billing charge.

Clerical ($160,000). This amount is the annual salary and benefits of two general clerical employees who process orders for supplies, file records, and so on. Emmet believes that the number of tests (299,500 in the prior year) is a valid driver for this cost pool since each test benefits equally from the incurrence of clerical expense.

Other ($200,000). This amount includes the salary and benefits of the bookkeeper, depreciation on office equipment, utilities, and so on. Emmet believes that the number of tests (299,500 in the prior year) is a valid driver for this cost pool since each test benefits equally from the incurrence of these expenses.

REQUIRED

a. Based on Emmet's assumptions, calculate the ABC cost per unit and profit per unit of each test. Round to 4 decimal places.

b. Should Emmet lower the price of the T1 test, or keep the current price and risk losing the business of Nuclear Systems?

c. Assume that Emmet, based on his ABC analysis, decides not to lower the price of the T1 test. What will be the effect on annual company profit if the company loses the business of Nuclear Systems (i.e., T1 tests decrease by 1,750)?

CASE

6-2 QuantumTM [LO 2]

QuantumTM manufactures electronic testing and measurement instruments. Many products are custom-designed with recent orders for function generators, harmonic analyzers, logic analyzers, temperature measurement instruments, and data-logging instruments. The company prices its instruments at 30 percent over estimated cost (excluding administrative and selling costs).

Recently, senior management has noted that its product mix has changed. Specifically, the company is receiving fewer large orders for instruments that are relatively simple to produce, and customers are saying that the company is not price competitive. The company is, however, receiving more small orders for complex instruments, and customers appear quite happy to pay QuantumTM's price. This situation was discussed at a weekly management meeting. Jason Norton, VP of operations, blamed the company's antiquated cost accounting system. "Look," he said, "if you have bad cost information, you're going to have bad prices, and we're still doing product costing the way companies did it in the 1930s. I've been reading articles about activity-based costing, and they indicate that out-of-date costing systems make simple products look too costly and complex products too cheap. If that's true, it would explain why we're not price competitive for simple products."

The meeting ended with a decision to hire a consultant to conduct a preliminary ABC study to determine how a switch to ABC would affect product cost. The consulting firm selected two recent orders for study: a 900-unit order for a temperature-monitoring device and an order for 1 harmonic analyzer. The costs and prices charged were as follows:

	Temperature Monitor	Harmonic Analyzer
Component cost per unit	$ 250	$2,500
Direct labor per unit	25	500
Overhead per unit	120	2,500
Cost per unit	395	5,500
Markup at 30%	119	1,650
Price per unit	$ 514	$7,150
Number of units	900	1
Value of order	$462,600	$7,150

In the current system, overhead is applied based on an estimate of $50,000,000 of annual overhead and $10,000,000 of direct labor cost. The consultants have broken the $50,000,000 of annual overhead down into six cost pools and identified related cost drivers as indicated in Exhibit 1. The consultants have also found that the monitor and analyzer make use of the cost drivers as indicated in Exhibit 2.

REQUIRED

a. Based on the consultants' work to date, calculate the ABC cost per unit of each product.

b. The consultants have completed their job, and QuantumTM has adopted an ABC system as indicated in Exhibit 1. Recently, the company received an order for a unique data-logging device. The device will require $9,000 of components and $3,000 of direct labor along with the following requirements:

Use related to a data logging device:	
Number of design hours	27
Number of unique parts	17
Number of inspections	12
Number of setups	1
Machine hours	10

The customer has indicated that it currently has a low bid from another company of $22,000. Calculate the ABC cost of the data-logging device.

c. Suppose QuantumTM meets its competitor's price and gets the job. What will be the impact on company profit? In answering this question, make the following assumptions:

1. 40 percent of design costs are fixed, and 60 percent vary with design hours.
2. 30 percent of material ordering and handling costs are fixed, and 70 percent vary with the number of unique parts.
3. 50 percent of inspection costs are fixed, and 50 percent are variable.
4. 80 percent of setup costs are fixed, and 20 percent are variable.
5. 20 percent of labor-related costs are fixed, and 80 percent are variable.
6. Prices charged to this customer or other customers in the future will not be impacted by the current deal. This follows because each order is unique.

EXHIBIT 1
Cost pools and drivers

Cost Pools	Annual Cost	Annual Driver Value
Product design	$ 8,000,000	160,000 design hours
Material ordering and handling	10,000,000	125,000 unique part's
Inspection	3,500,000	560,000 inspections
Setup	2,500,000	80,000 setups
Labor-related overhead	8,000,000	$10,000,000 direct labor
Depreciation of plant and equipment	18,000,000	225,000 machine hours
	$50,000,000	

EXHIBIT 2
Use of cost driver

The following values relate to the entire order of 900 monitors (this is not per monitor):

Number of design hours	47
Number of unique parts	17
Number of inspections	225
Number of setups	1
Machine hours	112

The following values relate to the order for 1 analyzer:

Number of design hours	110
Number of unique parts	25
Number of inspections	20
Number of setups	1
Machine hours	7

7

THE USE OF COST INFORMATION IN MANAGEMENT DECISION MAKING

Jon Jensen is the owner/operator of Jensen's Rapid Copy, a large copy center located near Eastern State University.

Currently, Jensen's Rapid Copy is open from 6 A.M. until 8 P.M. 7 days per week. However, Jon is considering two alternatives: (1) staying open until midnight or (2) staying open 24 hours a day.

To properly make this decision, Jon should perform incremental analysis. We touched on this topic in Chapter 1 and in subsequent chapters. Now we discuss it in more detail.

©Photoraldz/Shutterstock

LEARNING OBJECTIVES

1. Explain the role of incremental analysis (analysis of incremental costs and revenues) in management decisions, and define sunk cost, avoidable cost, and opportunity cost and understand how to use these concepts in analyzing decisions.
2. Analyze decisions involving joint costs, and discuss the importance of qualitative considerations in management decisions.

INCREMENTAL ANALYSIS

Decision Making/ Incremental Analysis

All decisions involve a choice among alternative courses of action. In Chapter 1, we learned that the solution to all business problems involves **incremental analysis**—the analysis of the *incremental* revenue and the *incremental* costs incurred when one decision alternative is chosen over another. **Incremental revenue** is the additional revenue received as a result of selecting one decision alternative over another. **Incremental cost** is the additional cost incurred as a result of selecting one decision alternative over another. If an alternative yields an incremental profit (the difference between incremental revenue and incremental cost), then it should be selected. Incremental costs sometimes are referred to as **relevant costs**, because they are the only costs that are *relevant* to consider when analyzing decision alternatives. They are also referred to as **differential costs**, because they are the costs that differ between decision alternatives.

LEARNING OBJECTIVE 1

Explain the role of incremental analysis (analysis of incremental costs and revenues) in management decisions, and define sunk cost, avoidable cost, and opportunity cost and understand how to use these concepts in analyzing decisions.

Let's go over an example of incremental analysis to ensure that the approach is understood. The example we'll consider is the decision faced by Jon Jensen at Rapid Copy. Later we'll apply incremental analysis to somewhat more complicated decisions.

Currently, Jensen's Rapid Copy is open from 6 A.M. until 8 P.M. Let's compare this to the alternative of extending hours until midnight. In this case, there is a choice between two alternatives: closing at 8 P.M., which is the status quo, or closing at midnight. Incremental analysis of this decision is presented in Illustration 7-1. Note that there are three columns. In the first column, we show the revenue and costs associated with the status quo (decision alternative 1) for a one-year time horizon. In the second column, we show the revenue and costs associated with the decision to stay open until midnight (decision alternative 2). In the third column, we show the difference in the revenue and costs between the two decision alternatives. This is the incremental revenue and incremental costs associated with the decision to stay open later. Since we are using a one-year time horizon, this is obviously the incremental revenue and costs associated with that time period. We could also perform the analysis for multiple years. However, when multiple years are considered, it is generally important to consider the time value

ILLUSTRATION 7-1

Incremental analysis of decision to extend hours of operation until midnight

	Alternative 1 Current Hours	Alternative 2 Extend Hours to Midnight	Incremental Revenue and Costs (Alternative 2 minus Alternative 1)
Revenue	$3,600,000	$3,888,000	$288,000
Less:			
Labor	576,000	604,800	28,800
Paper, toner, and other supplies	2,520,000	2,721,600	201,600
Utilities	26,640	28,771	2,131
Insurance	7,800	8,250	450
Depreciation	60,000	60,000	–0–
Rent	55,000	55,000	–0–
Other fixed costs	3,000	3,000	–0–
Total expense	3,248,440	3,481,421	232,981
Profit	$ 351,560	$ 406,579	$ 55,019

of money. That is, we need to take into account the fact that a dollar today is worth more than a dollar in the future. We'll go into that topic in Chapter 9.

As indicated in Illustration 7-1, if hours are extended, revenue will increase by $288,000. This is the incremental revenue. However, labor, paper, toner and other supplies, utilities, and insurance will increase. The total increase in expense is $232,981. This is the incremental cost of extending hours. Incremental profit, the difference between incremental revenue and incremental cost, is $55,019. Since incremental profit is positive, the second alternative (extending hours) should be selected.

Note that depreciation, rent, and other fixed costs are not incremental in this decision, since none of these costs changed. Thus, they are not relevant to the decision at hand. This is not to say that a fixed cost is never incremental. As we will see in later examples, sometimes decisions have a major impact on operations and cause costs that are normally considered to be fixed to change. For example, suppose expanded operations required Jon Jensen to rent additional space to store supplies. In this case, rent (which is normally considered to be a fixed cost) would, in fact, be an incremental cost.

Incremental analysis can also be extended beyond two decision alternatives. Recall that Jon is also considering the option of keeping the copy center open 24 hours per day. Now there are three choices: close at 8 P.M., close at midnight, or stay open 24 hours. There are several ways we can deal with the third choice. We can compare it to the status quo and see if it yields an incremental profit greater than the incremental profit associated with staying open until midnight, which is $55,019; if so, it is preferred to the midnight alternative. Or we can compare the all-day alternative directly to the midnight option, which, as we know, dominates the status quo. Let's do the latter. The analysis is presented in Illustration 7-2. As indicated, the incremental revenue associated with staying open 24 hours is $36,000. However, the incremental cost is $69,717. Thus, if Jon were to stay open 24 hours, he would lose $33,717 compared to staying open until midnight. Another way of saying this is: "The incremental profit of alternative 2 over alternative 3 is $33,717." Jon's best decision of the three alternatives, therefore, is to stay open until midnight.

A third way to determine the best alternative is to calculate the profit under each of the three alternatives. In that approach, the best alternative is the one with the highest profit, and the difference between its profit and the profit of any other alternative is its

ILLUSTRATION 7-2
Incremental analysis of the decision to stay open 24 hours versus staying open until midnight

	Alternative 2 Stay Open until Midnight	Alternative 3 Stay Open 24 Hours	Incremental Revenue and Costs (Alternative 3 minus Alternative 2)
Revenue	$3,888,000	$3,924,000	$36,000
Less:			
Labor	604,800	648,800	44,000
Paper, toner, and other supplies	2,721,600	2,746,800	25,200
Utilities	28,771	29,038	267
Insurance	8,250	8,500	250
Depreciation	60,000	60,000	–0–
Rent	55,000	55,000	–0–
Other fixed costs	3,000	3,000	–0–
Total expense	3,481,421	3,551,138	69,717
Profit	$ 406,579	$ 372,862	($33,717)

ILLUSTRATION 7-3
Incremental analysis of three alternatives: status quo, open until midnight, and open 24 hours

	Alternative 1 Current Hours	Alternative 2 Stay Open until Midnight	Alternative 3 Stay Open 24 Hours
Revenue	$3,600,000	$3,888,000	$3,924,000
Less:			
Labor	576,000	604,800	648,800
Paper, toner, and other supplies	2,520,000	2,721,600	2,746,800
Utilities	26,640	28,771	29,038
Insurance	7,800	8,250	8,500
Depreciation	60,000	60,000	60,000
Rent	55,000	55,000	55,000
Other fixed costs	3,000	3,000	3,000
Total expense	3,248,440	3,481,421	3,551,138
Profit	$ 351,560	$ 406,579	$ 372,862
Incremental profit of alternative 2 over alternatives 1 and 3	$55,019 (Alternative 1 – Alternative 2)		$33,717 (Alternative 2 – Alternative 3)

incremental profit. This is the approach presented in Illustration 7-3. Note that alternative 2 has the highest profit, and its incremental profit compared to alternative 1 is $55,019, which is what we calculated in Illustration 7-1. Its incremental profit compared to alternative 3 is $33,717, which is what we calculated in Illustration 7-2.

ANY QUESTIONS?

Q: The focus on incremental analysis makes it seem like decisions are pretty cut and dry and based just on "running the numbers." I've talked to business people who say that "gut feel" plays a very important role in the major decisions they make.

A: When making an important business decision, it's always a good idea to perform incremental analysis. But often there are important incremental benefits and incremental costs that are difficult, if not impossible, to quantify. Managers shouldn't ignore them, and that's where "gut feel" plays a role. We'll discuss this in a bit more detail at the end of the chapter, in the section *Qualitative Considerations in Decision Analysis*.

When Your Boss Asks, "What Does This Product (Service) Cost?" You Should Say, "Why Do You Want to Know?"

If you're ever in a situation where your boss asks you how much a product or service costs, you should reply: "Why do you want to know?" While that reply may seem a bit rude, it makes an important point about incremental analysis. There is no single cost number that is relevant for all decisions. Thus, you need to know what decision your boss is planning to make so you can identify the incremental cost information that is applicable to the decision. Suppose your boss is trying to decide whether to accept a special order for a particular product. In this case, your boss wants to know whether the incremental cost of producing the order will exceed the incremental revenue from accepting it. Some costs, such as the salary of a production supervisor, will not change as a result of accepting the order and should not be considered as an incremental cost.

However, your boss may be considering dropping the product. If the product is dropped, the supervisor may be laid off, and the cost savings related to the supervisor's salary are incremental. Thus, whether supervisory salary is an incremental cost and relevant to a decision depends on the decision being made. So, whenever, you're asked what a product or service costs, you need to respond: "Why do you want to know?"

TEST YOUR **KNOWLEDGE**

Which of the following is likely to be an incremental cost associated with increasing a planned production run of 1,000 units to 1,010 units?

a. Setup costs.
b. Depreciation of equipment.
c. Inspection costs.
d. Material costs.

Correct answer is d.

ANALYSIS OF DECISIONS FACED BY MANAGERS

Now that we know how to apply incremental analysis, let's practice the approach in the context of three decisions that managers frequently face:[1]

1. The decision to engage in additional processing of a product
2. The decision to make or buy a product
3. The decision to drop a product line

Additional Processing Decision

Occasionally manufacturers must decide whether to sell a product in a partially completed stage or incur the additional processing costs required to complete the product. As an example, consider Bridge Computer, a manufacturer of personal computers. Bridge Computer has already decided to discontinue its Model 250 computer. Currently, it has 5,000 partially completed units on hand. To date, the company has spent $800 per unit, or $4,000,000, to bring these computers to their current stage of completion. The company estimates that costs of $400 per unit must be incurred to complete the computers. The costs are summarized below:

Bridge Computer
Costs of Model 250 Computer

	Costs per Unit Incurred to Date	Costs per Unit to Complete
Material	$300	$200
Labor	200	100
Variable overhead	100	100
Fixed overhead	200	–
	$800	$400

[1] Another decision that managers frequently face is the pricing of special orders. This decision is presented in Chapter 8.

Because the company has announced that the Model 250 is going to be discontinued, the price of the computer has fallen. If the units are completed, they can be sold for only $1,000 per unit. That is less than the total cost of producing the computers—$1,200 per unit ($800 cost to date plus $400 of additional cost). An alternative to finishing the units is to sell them as they are. A small computer assembly company in another state is willing to buy the units in their current partial state of completion for $500 per unit.

Which action should be taken? Should the computers be sold in their current state of completion, or should the additional processing costs be incurred? Without a thorough understanding of accounting information and incremental analysis, a manager at Bridge Computer might conclude that further processing is not appropriate. After all, with further processing, total costs will amount to $1,200 per unit, which is more than the selling price of $1,000 per unit.

The error of this conclusion is revealed by incremental analysis. The facts for our analysis are presented in Illustration 7-4. Note that the illustration contains three columns. The first column lists the revenue and costs related to selling the computers in their current state of completion (Alternative 1). The second column lists the revenue and costs related to selling completed computers (Alternative 2). The third column lists the incremental revenue and costs that will be incurred by completing the computers.

ILLUSTRATION 7-4

Incremental analysis of additional processing decision

Bridge Computer
Incremental Analysis of Additional Processing

	Sell in Current State of Completion (Alternative 1)	Complete Processing (Alternative 2)	Incremental Revenue and Costs (Alternative 2 minus Alternative 1)	
Revenue	$500	$1,000	$500	← Incremental revenue associated with Alternative 2
Less:				
Prior production costs				
Material	300	300	0	
Labor	200	200	0	
Variable overhead	100	100	0	
Fixed overhead	200	200	0	
	800	800	0	
Additional processing costs				
Material	0	200	200	
Labor	0	100	100	
Variable overhead	0	100	100	
	0	400	400	← Incremental cost associated with Alternative 2
Gain (loss) per unit	($300)	($ 200)	$100	← Incremental profit associated with Alternative 2

We'll begin by examining incremental revenue. Recall that incremental revenue is simply the difference in revenue between two alternatives. Bridge Computer can sell completed units for $1,000 each, whereas it can sell the units in their current state of completion for $500 each. Thus, incremental revenue of $500 per unit is associated with choosing Alternative 2 and completing processing.

Now let's turn to incremental cost. Before going any further, we need to recall another cost term from Chapter 1—*sunk costs*, or costs incurred in the past. Sunk costs are not incremental costs. Since they've already been incurred, they won't increase or decrease with the choice of one alternative over another. In the case of Bridge Computer, the prior production costs are sunk costs, not incremental costs. Thus, they do not enter our analysis.

What, then, are the incremental costs for Bridge Computer? An incremental cost, remember, is the difference in cost between two alternatives. The $400 cost of completing the units ($200 material, $100 labor, and $100 variable overhead) will be incurred if the units are completed; thus, $400 is the incremental cost associated with completing processing.

You can see that by choosing Alternative 2, the company will be better off by $100 per unit ($500 incremental revenue – $400 incremental cost). In total, the incremental profit of completing the units is $500,000 (100 × 5,000 units). As we noted earlier, if an alternative yields an incremental profit, it should be selected.

LINK TO **PRACTICE**

Sell Partially Completed Superyacht?

Here's an interesting "additional processing" decision from the buyer's (rather than the seller's perspective). Available in 2014 in Whangarei, New Zealand is project U77, a "superyacht" with 10 staterooms for 20 guests. It's for sale of $24.9 million, but the problem is it's only 50 percent finished. A potential buyer must calculate the incremental cost of completing the yacht, add that to the purchase price and compare the total to the cost of buying a completed yacht. Let's suppose the yacht could be completed for $30 million and a fully completed similar yacht would cost $60 million. In this case, buying the partially completed yacht is a "good deal!" The total cost would only be $54.9 million versus $60 million for a yacht that's already completed.

Source: Partially-built superyacht project U77 for sale at Fraser Yachts and Burgess. http://www.boatinternational.com/2014/06/04/partially-built-superyacht-project-u77-for-sale-at-fraser-yachts-and-burgess/

Make-or-Buy Decisions: The General Refrigeration Example

Most manufactured goods are made up of numerous components. In some cases, a company may purchase one or more of the components from another company. This may lead to considerable savings if the outside supplier is particularly efficient at manufacturing the component and can offer it at a reasonable price. Two decision alternatives arise in this situation: make or buy the component. No incremental revenues are involved. Therefore, the analysis of this decision concentrates solely on incremental costs.

Consider the situation faced by Wendy Grant, manager of the Tennessee plant of General Refrigeration, a company that manufactures and sells refrigeration units used by food processors and grocery stores. One of the main components of a refrigeration unit is a compressor. Recently, Wendy received an offer from Dillard Compressor Corporation to supply 50,000 compressors at $310 per unit. Last year, when her plant produced 50,000 compressors, the following costs were incurred:

Cost of Manufacturing 50,000 Compressors	
Variable costs:	
Direct material ($100 per unit)	$ 5,000,000
Direct labor ($120 per unit)	6,000,000
Variable overhead ($80 per unit)	4,000,000
Total variable cost	15,000,000
Fixed costs:	
Depreciation of building	600,000
Depreciation of equipment	800,000
Supervisory salaries	500,000
Other	350,000
Total fixed cost	2,250,000
Total cost	$17,250,000
Cost per unit	$ 345

Additional analysis reveals the following: (1) The market value of the machinery used to produce the compressors is approximately zero. (2) Five of the six production supervisors will be fired if production of compressors is discontinued. However, one of the supervisors, who has more than 10 years of service, is protected by a clause in a labor contract and will be reassigned to other duties, although his services are not really needed. His salary is $110,000.

At first, you might assume that General should buy the compressors rather than manufacture the units internally since the company can buy the units for $310 each, whereas the cost of manufacturing them is $345 each ($17,250,000 ÷ 50,000 units). However, careful consideration of the incremental costs reveals that it is cheaper to manufacture the compressors internally.

LINK TO PRACTICE

Boeing's Global Outsourcing Strategy Blamed for 3-Year Delay in 787

In developing the 787 Dreamliner, Boeing set up a large and complex global supply chain with strategic partners in China, Japan, Italy, Sweden, South Korea, and other countries. The plane has 30 percent international content, which is more than any other plane the company has produced.

Outsourcing key technologies and components turned out to be disastrous. Boeing Commercial Airplanes Chief Jim Albaugh conceded, "We spent a lot more money in trying to recover than we ever would have spent if we'd tried to keep the key technologies closer to home." Some analysts estimate that the outsourcing decision ended up costing Boeing $12 to $18 billion on top of what Boeing had planned to spend. As of 2011, Boeing was 3 years late in delivering a plane that is critical to the long-run success of the company.

Source: "A Prescient Warning to Boeing on 787 Trouble," *The Seattle Times,* February 6, 2011, p. D-1.

To demonstrate, we'll work through an incremental analysis, which is presented in Illustration 7-5. Like previous examples, Illustration 7-5 uses a three-column format. The first two columns present the costs of the two alternatives, while the third column presents the incremental costs. Another option is to use a single-column format that concentrates

ILLUSTRATION 7-5
Incremental analysis of make-or-buy decision

Incremental Cost Analysis

	Cost of Manufacturing 50,000 Compressors	Cost of Buying 50,000 Compressors	Incremental Cost (Savings)
Variable costs:			
Direct material	$ 5,000,000	–0–	($ 5,000,000)
Direct labor	6,000,000	–0–	(6,000,000)
Variable overhead	4,000,000	–0–	(4,000,000)
Total variable cost	15,000,000	–0–	(15,000,000)
Fixed costs:			
Depreciation of building	600,000	600,000	–0–
Depreciation of equipment	800,000	800,000	–0–
Supervisory salaries	500,000	110,000	(390,000)
Other	350,000	350,000	–0–
Total fixed costs	2,250,000	1,860,000	(390,000)
Cost of buying compressors	–0–	15,500,000	15,500,000
Total	$17,250,000	$17,360,000	$ 110,000

only on the incremental costs and benefits. A single-column analysis of the make-or-buy decision faced by the General Refrigeration Company is presented in Illustration 7-6.

A key issue in our analysis involves determining which of the costs listed earlier are, in fact, incremental costs. Clearly, none of the $15,000,000 of variable manufacturing costs will be incurred if the compressors are purchased outside the company. Thus, this is an incremental cost *savings* between the two alternatives.

What about the fixed costs? Let's consider them item by item. The fixed costs associated with depreciation on the building and equipment do not represent a cost savings. The costs of purchasing the building and equipment were incurred in prior periods. Remember that the approach to analyzing decisions requires consideration of only the incremental revenues and costs of decision alternatives. The sunk costs related to purchasing the building and the pieces of equipment are not incremental costs because they have already been incurred and will not change no matter which decision alternative is selected.

The example assumes that fixed costs classified as "other" are also irrelevant sunk costs. But note that not all fixed costs are irrelevant sunk costs. Some fixed costs are **avoidable costs**—costs that can be avoided if a particular action is undertaken. In our example, if compressors are purchased outside the company, the salaries of five production supervisors will be saved. The saving totals $390,000 (total supervisory salaries of $500,000 less the $110,000 that must still be paid to the supervisor who will be retained). In other words, supervisory salaries of $390,000 represent an avoidable cost and thus an incremental cost.

ILLUSTRATION 7-6
Single-column format for incremental analysis

Incremental Cost Analysis

Cost of buying compressors outside (50,000 units @ $310)		$15,500,000
Cost savings (avoidable if compressors purchased outside):		
Variable costs	$15,000,000	
Supervisory salaries (salaries of 5 of 6 supervisors)	390,000	(15,390,000)
Excess cost of buying compressors outside		$ 110,000

LINK TO PRACTICE

PACCAR Decides to Make as Well as Buy!

PACCAR is one of the largest truck manufacturers in the United States and Europe. Its Kenworth and Peterbilt trucks, which are sold primarily in North America, were powered by engines made by either Cummins or Caterpillar. Apparently, the company performed incremental analysis and determined that the incremental benefits of making its own engines outweigh the incremental costs. Thus, the company built a $400 million engine factory in Columbus, Mississippi.

One of the benefits of making its own engines is that the company can work more closely with dealers to ensure timely delivery of parts when trucks come in for repair. That's not too often, however. PACCAR trucks typically run for over a million miles, and engine overhauls may not be needed for 800,000 miles.

We can see, then, that $15,000,000 of variable costs and $390,000 of fixed costs can be eliminated if the compressors are purchased from Dillard Compressor Corporation, for a total cost savings of $15,390,000. But the cost of purchasing the compressors from Dillard is $15,500,000 (50,000 units × $310). The difference is $110,000 ($15,500,000 purchase price − $15,390,000 cost saving), and the General Refrigeration Company would be $110,000 worse off if it decided to buy rather than make the compressors. Before a final decision is reached, however, qualitative factors should be considered. We'll discuss these factors later in the chapter.

A cost that must be considered in decision making is an opportunity cost. An **opportunity cost** is the value of benefits forgone by selecting one decision alternative over another. For example, if you chose to purchase a $1,000 stereo system rather than investing in a certificate of deposit (CD), the potential interest that could have been earned on the CD is an opportunity cost associated with buying the stereo. Since opportunity costs differ depending on which decision alternative is selected, they are also incremental costs and are relevant in evaluating decision alternatives.

Suppose that the Tennessee plant is currently spending $500,000 per year to rent space for manufacturing metal shelving, which is used in the refrigeration units. If production of compressors is discontinued, the company will move the shelving operation to space currently occupied by the compressor operation. Thus, in continuing to produce the compressors, the company gives up rent savings of $500,000. The forgone rent savings represents an opportunity cost. An analysis that includes this opportunity cost

LINK TO PRACTICE

Indian Wireless Company Outsources to U.S. and European Firms!

The make-or-buy decision that we just analyzed for General Refrigeration is often referred to as an outsourcing decision. That's because the component under consideration may be *sourced* from *outside* the company. Outsourcing isn't just for components, however. Services may also be outsourced. Consider the actions taken by Bharti Airtel, the largest wireless company in India. In 2003, the company was ramping up from 3 million to more than 25 million subscribers. The company realized that it couldn't build its network fast enough to take on this volume.

To manage the tremendous growth, Bharti Airtel outsourced its entire network to Sweden's Ericsson, Germany's Siemens, and Finland's Nokia. The result is that the company no longer needs to worry about buying and maintaining equipment. Instead, it pays a fee based on traffic and customer service. Bharti Airtel also signed a 10-year, $750 million contract with IBM. Now IBM handles the company's information technology, billing, and management of customer accounts. This was an interesting development since we often think of U.S. firms outsourcing to Indian companies rather than Indian companies outsourcing to U.S. and European firms.

Source: Clay Chandler, "Wireless Wonder," *Fortune*, January 22, 2007, pp. 131–132.

ILLUSTRATION 7-7
Make-or-buy analysis with opportunity costs considered

Incremental Cost Analysis

Cost of buying compressors outside (50,000 units @ $310)		$15,500,000
Cost savings (avoidable if compressors purchased outside)	$15,000,000	
Variable costs		
Supervisory salaries (salaries of 5 or 6 supervisors)	390,000	
Opportunity cost of using the plant to produce compressors (forgone rent savings)	500,000	(15,890,000)
Net savings resulting from buying the compressors outside		($ 390,000)

is presented in Illustration 7-7. According to this analysis, purchasing the compressors outside is the best alternative because it results in a net annual cost saving of $390,000.

Dropping a Product Line

Dropping a product line is a very significant decision and one that receives a great deal of attention. The proper approach to analyzing the problem is to calculate the change in income that will result from dropping the product line. If income will increase, the product line should be dropped. If income will decrease, the product line should be kept. This amounts to comparing the incremental revenues and costs that result from dropping the product line.

Let's consider an example involving a retailer. Mercer Hardware sells three product lines: tools, hardware supplies, and garden supplies. Illustration 7-8 presents a product line income statement for the prior year. To arrive at net income for each product line, both direct fixed costs and allocated fixed costs are deducted from each product line's contribution margin.

Direct fixed costs are fixed costs that are directly traceable to a product line. For example, the salary of a worker who spends 100 percent of his or her time working in the tool section of the hardware store is a direct fixed cost to the tool product line.

Allocated fixed costs are those fixed costs that are not directly traceable to an individual product line. These costs are also referred to as **common costs** because they are incurred for the common benefit of all product lines. An example of an allocated fixed

ILLUSTRATION 7-8
Product line income statement for Mercer Hardware

Mercer Hardware
Product Line Income Statement
For the Year Ended December 31, 2017

	Tools	Hardware Supplies	Garden Supplies	Total
Sales	$120,000	$200,000	$80,000	$400,000
Cost of goods sold	81,000	90,000	60,000	231,000
Gross margin	39,000	110,000	20,000	169,000
Other variable costs	2,000	4,000	1,000	7,000
Contribution margin	37,000	106,000	19,000	162,000
Direct fixed costs	8,000	5,000	3,500	16,500
Allocated fixed costs	24,000	40,000	16,000	80,000
Total fixed costs	32,000	45,000	19,500	96,500
Net income (loss)	$ 5,000	$ 61,000	($ 500)	$ 65,500

ILLUSTRATION 7-9

Effect of dropping garden supplies at Mercer Hardware

	Income with Garden Supplies				Income without Garden Supplies			Difference
	Tools	Hardware Supplies	Garden Supplies	Total	Tools	Hardware Supplies	Total	
Sales	$120,000	$200,000	$80,000	$400,000	$120,000	$200,000	$320,000	($80,000)
Cost of goods sold	81,000	90,000	60,000	231,000	81,000	90,000	171,000	(60,000)
Gross margin	39,000	110,000	20,000	169,000	39,000	110,000	149,000	(20,000)
Other variable costs	2,000	4,000	1,000	7,000	2,000	4,000	6,000	(1,000)
Contribution margin	37,000	106,000	19,000	162,000	37,000	106,000	143,000	(19,000)
Direct fixed costs	8,000	5,000	3,500	16,500	8,000	5,000	13,000	(3,500)
Allocated fixed costs	24,000	40,000	16,000	80,000	30,000	50,000	80,000	–
Total fixed costs	32,000	45,000	19,500	96,500	38,000	55,000	93,000	(3,500)
Net income	$ 5,000	$ 61,000	($ 500)	$ 65,500	($ 1,000)	$ 51,000	$ 50,000	($15,500)

cost is the salary of the owner/manager of the hardware store. Mercer Hardware allocates common fixed costs to product lines based on their relative sales revenues. For example, sales of tools are 30 percent of sales ($120,000 tool sales ÷ $400,000 total sales). Thus, of the $80,000 of common costs, $24,000 (30% of $80,000) is allocated to tools.

In examining the product line income statement, the owner of Mercer Hardware observes that the garden supplies line is currently showing a loss of $500. Would dropping this product line increase the profitability of the hardware store? To answer this question, we turn again to incremental analysis. As indicated in Illustration 7-9, sales revenue will decline by $80,000 if garden supplies are dropped. However, some costs will decrease or be eliminated altogether. Cost of goods sold will decrease by $60,000, and other variable costs will decrease by $1,000. Whether the direct fixed costs will decrease depends on the nature of these costs. For purposes of this example, assume that the direct fixed cost of $3,500 for garden supplies represents the wages paid to a part-time employee. If the garden supplies product line is dropped, this employee will not be retained by the store. In this case, the direct fixed cost of $3,500 is avoidable and represents a cost savings achieved by dropping garden supplies.

LINK TO PRACTICE

Spike TV Drops Impact Wrestling

For TV stations, each show is a product, and in 2015, Spike TV dropped a product called "Total Nonstop Action (TNA) Impact Wrestling." Speculation is that Spike's leadership believes that TNA can't grow its brand against WWE (World Wrestling Entertainment), and Spike doesn't want a product that can't grow.

Source: TNA News: The Real Reason Spike TV Decided To Drop Impact Wrestling Finally Revealed. http://www.inquisitr.com/1529412/the-real-reason-spike-tv-is-dropping-tna-wrestling/

Allocated common fixed costs are generally not avoidable. Thus, no cost savings will be achieved with respect to the $16,000 of fixed costs allocated to garden supplies. For example, one component of the allocated fixed cost is rent of the hardware store. The rent will not decrease simply because one of the product lines is eliminated. Another allocated fixed cost is the cost of electricity. This cost is also unlikely to decrease if garden supplies are eliminated, because the store will still need approximately the same amount of heat and light. If garden supplies are eliminated, the share of fixed costs allocated to tools and hardware supplies will simply increase.

To summarize, the analysis of incremental costs and revenues indicates that income of $15,500 will be lost if garden supplies are dropped:

Incremental Analysis Dropping Garden Supplies	
Lost sales	($80,000)
Cost savings:	
Cost of goods sold	60,000
Other variable costs	1,000
Direct fixed costs	3,500
Total cost savings	64,500
Net loss from dropping	($15,500)

Beware of the Cost Allocation Death Spiral!

Whenever you analyze a decision involving dropping a product or service, remember that common fixed costs are not incremental. This will allow you to avoid what is sometimes referred to as the *cost allocation death spiral.* In many cases, products or services may not appear to be profitable because they receive allocations of common fixed costs. But what will happen to the common costs if the product or service is dropped? They'll be allocated over the remaining products and services. That may result in another product or service appearing to be unprofitable.

Consider Mercer Hardware as an example. If the company had decided to drop garden supplies, the $80,000 of common fixed costs would have been allocated over tools and hardware supplies. The new allocation would be $6,000 higher for tools, and it no longer would appear profitable—it would show a $1,000 loss. But what will happen to the common costs if it's dropped? That's right, they'll be allocated to hardware supplies. Before long, the store (which is currently profitable) would be out of business!

Summary of Incremental, Avoidable, Sunk, and Opportunity Costs

A number of costs terms have been used earlier, and in this section we briefly review them. Recall that the basic approach to decision making is to compare decision alternatives in terms of costs and revenues that are incremental. Costs that can be *avoided* by taking a particular course of action are always incremental costs and, therefore, relevant to the analysis of a decision. Costs that are *sunk* (i.e., already incurred and not reversible) are never incremental costs because they do not differ among the decision alternatives. Therefore, they are not relevant in making a decision.

Students of managerial accounting often assume that fixed costs are equivalent to sunk costs and are thus irrelevant (i.e., are not incremental costs), but this is not always the case. Fixed costs may be sunk and, therefore, irrelevant. Fixed costs may not be sunk but still irrelevant. Finally, fixed costs may not be sunk and may be relevant. Examples of these three possibilities are presented in Illustration 7-10.

Finally, *opportunity costs* represent the benefit forgone by selecting a particular decision alternative over another. By their nature, they are always incremental costs, and they must be considered when making a decision. To illustrate opportunity costs, consider the Mercer Hardware example presented earlier. In this example, the company is considering dropping the garden supplies product line. Suppose that if garden supplies are dropped, more space can be devoted to selling tools, sales of tools will increase, and the contribution margin associated with tools will increase by $20,000. In this case, there is a $20,000 opportunity cost associated with the decision to keep the garden supplies

ILLUSTRATION 7-10
Fixed costs and decision relevance

Fixed Costs	Classification
Depreciation on equipment already purchased	Sunk and irrelevant (not incremental)
President's salary, which will not change for both action A and action B	Not sunk but still irrelevant (not incremental)
Salary of supervisor who will be retained if action A is taken and fired if action B is taken	Not sunk and relevant (incremental)

product line. This opportunity cost would make dropping the product line desirable rather than undesirable. Recall that our previous analysis indicated a \$15,500 decrease in income from dropping the product line. However, considering the \$20,000 opportunity cost due to forgone sales of tools, it appears that the store will be better off by \$4,500 (i.e., \$20,000 – \$15,500) if garden supplies are dropped.

LINK TO PRACTICE

Ronald H. Coase's Contribution to Incremental Analysis

Ronald H. Coase was one of the early academics to state that the approach to solving all business problems involves incremental analysis. In 1938, while he was on the faculty of the London School of Economics, Coase wrote a series of 12 articles published in the *Accountant* titled "Business Organization and the Accountant." In the articles, Coase laid out his thinking on incremental analysis and decision making. (A shortened version of these articles is available at www.econlib.org/library/NPDBooks/Thirlby/bcthLS5.html.)

In the series of articles, Coase wrote, "The first point that needs to be made and strongly emphasized is that attention must be concentrated on the variations which will result if a particular decision is taken, and the variations that are relevant to business decisions are those in costs and/or receipts." In other words, the costs and incremental revenues relevant to business decisions are incremental costs and incremental revenues. Coase also went on to clarify that opportunity costs are relevant to every decision because they are incremental costs.

©AP/Wide World Photos

While Coase thought his ideas where somewhat obvious (especially to academics), he had critics. Indeed, S. W. Rowland, the head of the accounting department at the London School of Economics, gave his colleague a public rebuke in an address where he criticized Coase's emphasis on opportunity costs. As Coase wrote in a 1989 article published in the *Journal of Accounting and Economics* ("Accounting and the Theory of the Firm"), Rowland "opened his reference to my articles with the following sentences: 'If I particularize I do so with pure objectivity. I notice cases where the impact of economic studies on accounting lays greater emphasis on the speculative element than on experiences.' He then proceeded to ridicule the opportunity cost concept after completely misunderstanding what I had said."

Later in his career, Coase received wide recognition for his research, especially his work on transaction costs and property rights, and in 1991 he was awarded the Nobel Prize in Economics.

TEST YOUR KNOWLEDGE

Which of the following is true?

a. Opportunity costs are never incremental costs.
b. Opportunity costs are always incremental costs.

Correct answer is b.

LEARNING OBJECTIVE 2

Analyze decisions involving joint costs, and discuss the importance of qualitative considerations in management decisions.

DECISIONS INVOLVING JOINT COSTS

When two or more products *always* result from common inputs, they are known as **joint products**. The costs of the common inputs are referred to as **joint costs**. Joint costs are common in the food processing, extractive, and chemical industries. For example, in the dairy processing business, the common input of raw milk is converted into cream, skim milk, and whole milk. For lumber companies, the common input of a log is converted into various grades of lumber. For fuel companies, the common input of crude oil is converted into a variety of fuels and lubricants.

A graphical treatment of a joint products and joint costs problem is presented in Illustration 7-11. In the illustration, joint costs are incurred, leading to two joint products. The stage of production at which individual products are identified is referred to as the **split-off point**. Beyond this point, each product may undergo further separate processing and may incur additional costs.

Allocation of Joint Costs

For financial reporting purposes, the cost of the common inputs must be allocated to the joint products. However, care must be taken to ensure that the resulting information does not mislead managers about the profitability of the joint products. For example, suppose a lumber company spends $600 for an oak log and $20 to saw the log into two grades of lumber. The process results in 500 board feet of grade A lumber that sells for $1 per board foot and 500 board feet of grade B lumber that sells for $0.50 per board foot. How should the $620 joint cost be allocated to the joint products? One approach might be to allocate the cost based on the physical quantity of output. Since the production process results in equal quantities of physical output, it might seem reasonable to allocate an equal share of the joint cost to each of the grades of lumber. In this case, both the grade A lumber and the grade B lumber would show a cost of $310. This allocation could lead managers to think that grade B lumber is not profitable and should be scrapped—after all, its cost is $310, while revenue from its sale is only $250. But this logic is faulty. If the grade B lumber were scrapped, the company would lose $250 that helped cover the joint cost of $620.

It is important to realize that the total joint cost will be incurred no matter what the company does with the joint products beyond the split-off point. Because the joint cost

ILLUSTRATION 7-11
Joint costs and joint products

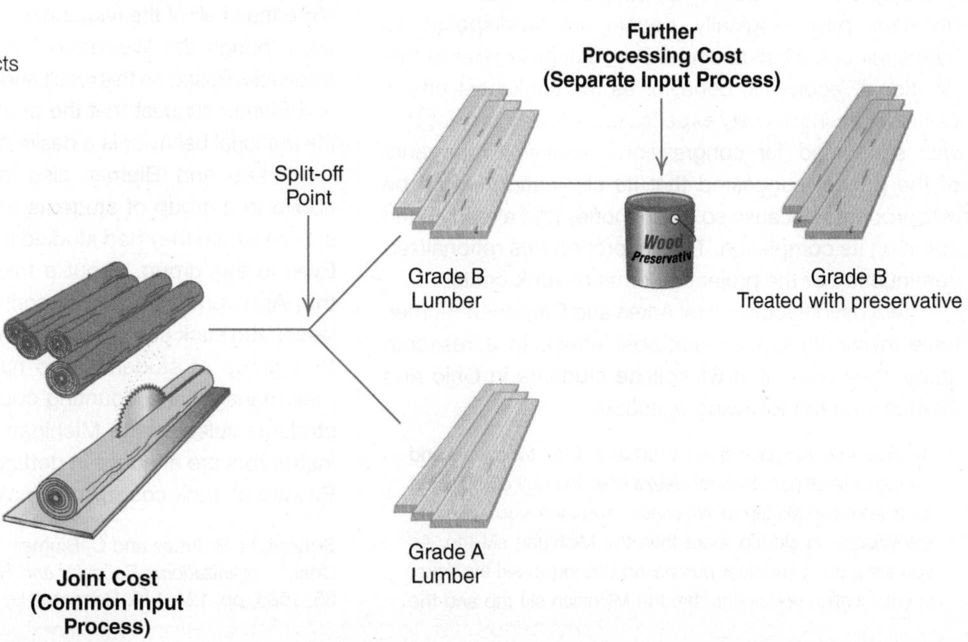

is not incremental to production of an individual joint product, it is irrelevant to any decision regarding an individual joint product. However, the joint cost is relevant to decisions involving the joint products as a group. If the total revenue from the sale of the joint products is less than the joint cost, production of all of the joint products should cease.

A better way of allocating the joint cost is to use the **relative sales value method.** With this method, the amount of joint cost allocated to products depends on the relative sales values of the products at the split-off point:

$$\text{Joint cost allocated to product A} = \frac{\text{Sales value of A}}{\text{Sales value of A} + \text{Sales value of B}} \times \text{Joint cost}$$

$$\text{Joint cost allocated to product B} = \frac{\text{Sales value of B}}{\text{Sales value of A} + \text{Sales value of B}} \times \text{Joint cost}$$

In the previous example, the grade A lumber would receive an allocation of $413.33 [i.e., $620 × ($500 ÷ $750)]. The grade B lumber would receive an allocation of $206.67 [i.e., $620 × ($250 ÷ $750)]. A good feature of this method is that the amount of joint cost allocated to a product cannot exceed its sales value at the split-off point (unless the amount of joint cost is greater than the sales value of the joint products, in which case they should not be produced). Thus, products that make a positive contribution to covering joint cost will not look unprofitable.

The costs allocated to the two grades of lumber using the physical quantity and the relative sales value approaches are compared in Illustration 7-12. In particular, note that for grade B lumber, the physical quantity approach yields a negative gross margin of $60, whereas the relative sales value approach yields a positive gross margin of $43.33.

LINK TO PRACTICE

The Sunk Cost Effect

When managers make decisions, they need to be careful that they are not influenced by sunk costs. That's difficult because, psychologically, people are predisposed to take sunk costs into account. Psychologists refer to this "irrational" economic behavior as the sunk cost effect. Consider an immensely expensive waterway project that was scheduled for congressional review. Proponents of the project suggested that its elimination would be inappropriate because so much money had already been spent on its completion. That is, proponents rationalized continuation of the project in terms of sunk costs!

Two psychologists, Hal Arkes and Catherine Blumer, have investigated the sunk cost effect. In a research study, they presented 61 college students in Ohio and Oregon with the following question:

> Assume that you have spent $100 on a ticket for a weekend ski trip to Michigan. Several weeks later you buy a $50 ticket for a weekend ski trip to Wisconsin. You think you will enjoy the Wisconsin ski trip more than the Michigan ski trip. As you are putting your just-purchased Wisconsin ski trip ticket in your wallet, you notice that the Michigan ski trip and the Wisconsin ski trip are for the same weekend! It's too late to sell either ticket, and you cannot return either one. You must use one ticket and not the other. Which trip will you go on?

More than half of the respondents chose the Michigan trip, even though the Wisconsin trip was identified as more enjoyable. Based on this result and other experiments, Arkes and Blumer suggest that the psychological justification for the irrational behavior is a desire not to appear wasteful.

Arkes and Blumer also presented the question above to a group of students enrolled in an economics course where they had studied the concept of sunk cost. Even in this group, about a third favored the Michigan trip. Apparently, training in economics does not greatly lessen the sunk cost effect. However, I gave the question to a group of students who had studied sunk cost in their managerial accounting course. Almost none of the students selected the Michigan trip. Maybe accounting instructors are effective in getting across the message—Beware of sunk costs when making decisions!

Source: H. R. Arkes and C. Blumer, "The Psychology of Sunk Cost," *Organizational Behavior and Human Decision Processes* 35, 1985, pp. 124–140. Reprinted by permission of Elsevier.

ILLUSTRATION 7-12

Comparison of physical quantity and relative sales value approaches to allocation of joint costs

Joint cost:		
Cost of log	$600.00	
Cost of sawing	20.00	
Total	$620.00	
Joint process yields:		
500 board feet of grade A lumber selling for $1.00 per board foot		
500 board feet of grade B lumber selling for $.50 per board foot		
Results using physical quantities to allocate joint costs:		
	Grade A	**Grade B**
Sales revenue		
500 b.f. × $1.00	$500.00	
500 b.f. × $.50		$250.00
Cost		
$620 × (500 b.f. ÷ 1.000 b.f.)	310.00	
$620 × (500 b.f. ÷ 1.000 b.f.)		310.00
Gross margin	$190.00	($ 60.00)
Results using relative sales values to allocate joint costs:		
	Grade A	**Grade B**
Sales revenue		
500 b.f. × $1.00	$500.00	
500 b.f. × $.50		$250.00
Cost		
$620 × ($500 ÷ $750)	413.33	
$620 × ($250 ÷ $750)		206.67
Gross margin	$ 86.67	$ 43.33

Additional Processing Decisions and Joint Costs

Suppose the manager of a lumber company is considering whether to pressure treat grade B lumber so that it will be resistant to rot. The additional processing costs per board foot will be $0.20. The pressure-treated lumber can be sold for $0.75 per board foot, compared with $0.50 for untreated lumber. Should the additional processing be undertaken? Ask yourself, "What will be the incremental revenue and the incremental costs?" The incremental revenue will be $0.25 per board foot (i.e., $0.75 – $0.50). The incremental cost will be $0.20. Therefore, the incremental profit will be $0.05, indicating that the further processing is warranted.

Where do the joint costs enter into this decision? They don't, because they are not incremental! Whether further processing will take place or not, the company must obtain a log and cut it into grade A and grade B lumber (unless the company wants to get out of the business of producing both grades of lumber).

QUALITATIVE CONSIDERATIONS IN DECISION ANALYSIS

The solutions to the problems just presented have focused on the *quantitative* features of the decision situations. In particular, we have concentrated on quantitative differences in costs and revenues among decision alternatives. However, most important problems have one or more features that are very difficult, if not impossible, to quantify. These *qualitative* aspects of the problem must receive the same careful attention as the quantitative components.

The importance of qualitative considerations can be illustrated in the context of the make-or-buy decision discussed earlier. Recall that the Tennessee plant of the General Refrigeration Company was considering whether to continue producing compressors or purchase them from another firm. The goal of our analysis was to determine whether

LINK TO PRACTICE

Qualitative Considerations in Outsourcing to China

Labor rates in China are about 10 percent of those in the United States, and raw material costs may also be much lower. Therefore, it's not surprising that many U.S. companies have outsourced manufacturing to China even though transportation costs back to the United States may be significant.

However, companies that are considering outsourcing should give careful consideration to qualitative factors (those factors that are very difficult or impossible to quantify). For example, it may be that the items produced in China are of somewhat lower quality, which could damage a U.S. company's reputation. Other problems may arise because, when buying from China, ocean freight is generally the preferred means of delivering goods. This can add 4 to 6 weeks to delivery time compared to shipments by truck and rail inside the United States. Because of this long delivery time, high-volume shipments are the norm.

This, however, leads to higher inventory holding costs. And the U.S. buyer faces a risk that inventory may become obsolete before all of it is sold. Also, consider the risk of a manufacturing defect in the shipment. That's obviously a much greater problem when the volume is 20,000 units as opposed to 500.

Source: Adapted and reprinted with permission from "The China Syndrome" by Mitchell Quint and Dermot Shorten from the Spring 2005 issue of *Strategy & Business* magazine, published by Booz & Comp. Inc, www.strategy-business.com.

it would cost General Refrigeration more to produce the compressors or to buy them from an outside supplier. However, our analysis only considered the easily quantifiable differences in costs between the two decision alternatives. In addition, there are qualitative benefits and costs associated with using an outside supplier.

Perhaps the primary benefit of using an outside supplier is that the adverse effect of a downturn in business is less severe. Suppose there is a temporary downturn in the demand for refrigeration units. In this case, General Refrigeration can simply order fewer compressors from its outside supplier, thus avoiding a major cost. In contrast, if General Refrigeration continues to manufacture the compressors and a temporary downturn in business is experienced, it is much more difficult to eliminate some of the fixed costs associated with manufacturing the compressors. For example, the company probably cannot eliminate the fixed costs of supervisors if the downturn is thought to be only temporary. Experienced supervisors are difficult to find, and they cannot be hired and fired based on temporary fluctuations in business.

A disadvantage of using an outside supplier is the associated loss of control over the production process. Purchased items may not be of sufficiently high quality, and delivery schedules may not be honored. Furthermore, knowing that it would be costly for the company to restart internal production, the outside supplier may believe that it has the company over a barrel and that it can raise prices significantly in the future. Also, employee morale may suffer when a company decides to purchase a component outside and employees are fired or transferred as a result. The cost to the firm of reduced morale is difficult to quantify, but it may have a significant effect on the quantity and quality of the products produced by remaining employees.

Decision Making INSIGHT

Throughout the book, and in particular in this chapter, we've stressed the idea that decision making relies on incremental analysis. A problem with implementing this approach, however, is that some incremental costs and incremental benefits are very difficult to quantify. What if a decision has a negative impact on employee morale? How will we quantify this as an incremental cost? Or what if a decision has a positive impact on customer satisfaction? How do we go from knowledge of this qualitative benefit to an estimate of incremental revenue? Whenever you make a decision, carefully think about items that are difficult to quantify. These so-called qualitative factors may be the most important aspect of the decision.

SUMMARY OF **LEARNING OBJECTIVES**

LEARNING OBJECTIVE 1 Explain the role of incremental analysis (analysis of incremental costs and revenues) in management decisions, and define sunk cost, avoidable cost, and opportunity cost and understand how to use these concepts in analyzing decisions.

Decisions involve a choice between two or more alternatives. The best decision can be determined by comparing alternatives in terms of the costs and revenue items that differ between them. These costs and revenues are referred to as incremental costs and revenues.

Sunk costs are costs that have been incurred in the past and are irrelevant to present and future decisions. Avoidable costs are costs that can be avoided by taking a particular action. The term *opportunity cost* refers to the benefit forgone by selecting a particular decision alternative over another. Avoidable costs and opportunity costs are always incremental and relevant in decision analysis.

LEARNING OBJECTIVE 2 Analyze decisions involving joint costs, and discuss the importance of qualitative considerations in management decisions.

Joint costs are the costs of common inputs that result in two or more joint products. Joint costs are not relevant to analyzing decisions that involve only one of the joint products, because they are only incremental to producing all of the joint products. In analyzing decisions related to further processing beyond the split-off point, consider only the incremental revenue (the extra revenue related to further processing) and incremental costs (the costs incurred beyond the split-off point).

A variety of qualitative factors (e.g., quality of goods, employee morale, and customer service) need to be considered in making a decision. Qualitative factors are often even more important than costs and benefits that are easy to quantify.

APPENDIX

LEARNING OBJECTIVE A1

Understand the five-step approach to the Theory of Constraints (TOC).

THE THEORY OF CONSTRAINTS

In this chapter, we focused on the general approach to decision making: incremental analysis. Here we discuss decisions related to constraints and show how large increases in profit can be achieved by elimination of bottlenecks in production processes. Specifically, we will focus on the Theory of Constraints (TOC), which is an approach to production and constraint management developed by Eli Goldratt.[2]

To facilitate our discussion, let's consider the production process of Dwyer Electronics, a producer of electronic measurement instruments. Production takes place in four departments, as indicated in Illustration A7-1. Subassemblies are produced in Departments 1 and 2. The subassemblies are transferred to Department 3, which makes and tests connections and installs the subassemblies in housing units. Units are then transferred to Department 4, which completes final testing and packages units for shipping.

THE FIVE-STEP PROCESS OF TOC

Goldratt specifies a five-step process for dealing with constraints. In this section, we discuss the steps.

Step 1: Identify the Binding Constraint

The first step in the TOC process is to identify the bottleneck or binding constraint. This is the process that limits throughput. (*Throughput* is the amount of inventory produced in a period.) Every manufacturing company has a binding constraint unless capacity in all departments exceeds

[2] For additional information on TOC, see E. Goldratt and J. Cox, *The Goal* (Croton-on-Hudson, NY: North River Press, 1984). Also see D. Smith, *The Measurement Nightmare, How the Theory of Constraints Can Resolve Conflicting Strategies, Policies, and Measures* (Boca Raton, FL: St. Lucie Press/APICS Series on Constraints Management, 2000).

ILLUSTRATION A7-1
Production flow at Dwyer Electronics

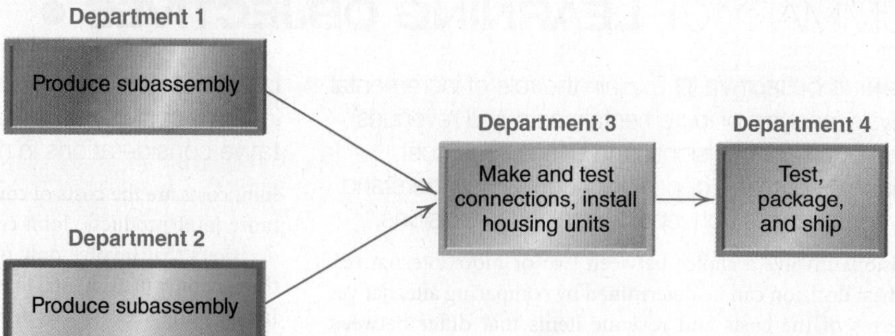

demand for the company's product. And in this case, demand is the binding constraint. For Dwyer Electronics, let's assume that Department 3 is the bottleneck. Management has identified this department as the bottleneck since production from Departments 1 and 2 is stacking up in front of the Department 3 work area.

In the TOC, the department that is the bottleneck is equated to a drum since it "beats a rhythm" that coordinates the production in other departments. At Dwyer Electronics, the production in Departments 1 and 2 should be tied to the needs of Department 3. Even though they can produce more than Department 3, there is no need for them to do so. ***Production beyond the needs of Department 3 just ties up company funds in excess work-in-process inventory.***

Step 2: Optimize Use of the Constraint

The second step is to optimize use of the constraint. This requires that the company use the constraint to produce products with the ***highest contribution margin per unit of the constraint.***[3] Consider the following two testing instruments produced by Dwyer:

	Model A70	Model B90
Selling price per unit	$1,000	$2,000
Variable costs per unit:		
Direct materials	400	900
Direct labor	200	300
Contribution margin per unit	**400**	**800**
Fixed costs per unit	100	300
Profit per unit	$ 300	$ 500
Time to complete 1 unit in Dept. 3	.1 hour	.3 hour
Contribution margin per hour in Dept. 3	$4,000	$2,667
	($400 ÷ .1 hour)	($800 ÷ .3 hour)

Which product optimizes use of the constraint, Model A70 or Model B90? The answer is Model A70. Note that its contribution margin is $400 per unit but it only takes .1 hour to produce a unit in Department 3, which is the constrained department. Thus, each hour this product generates $4,000 of incremental profit. So if managers of Dwyer face a choice between using scarce time in Department 3 to produce Model A70 or Model B90, they should definitely choose Model A70.

[3] Goldratt takes the somewhat extreme position that the only variable cost is material. While this is undoubtedly true in some situations, it is also undoubtedly true that in other situations, additional cost elements are variable. For example, in the production of aluminum, which requires a great deal of electricity, power is clearly a variable cost.

Step 3: Subordinate Everything Else to the Constraint

The third step is to subordinate everything else to the constraint. This means that managers of Dwyer should focus their attention on trying to loosen the constraint and not concentrate on process improvements in other departments. Why, for example, should managers work to improve processes 1, 2, or 4 if they are not limiting production? Only the binding constraint limits production, and attention should be focused completely on this department.

There are a number of things that managers can do to loosen the constraint in Department 3. For example, suppose the workers in Department 3 all take their breaks at the same time. Capacity could be gained by staggering breaks. And note that this would generate substantial sums of money. Product Model A70 generates $4,000 per hour. If breaks are staggered and the company gains an hour a day of additional capacity in Department 3, then it is generating an additional $20,000 of profit per week (5 hours × $4,000 per hour).

Step 4: Break the Constraint

The fourth step in the TOC process is to break the constraint. This can be accomplished in many ways. Here are some examples:

- Cross-train workers in Departments 1 and 2 so they can help out in Department 3.
- Outsource some of Department 3's work.
- Purchase additional equipment for Department 3.
- Hire additional workers for Department 3.
- Train workers in Department 3 so that they can perform their jobs more efficiently.

Step 5: Identify a New Binding Constraint

The final step is to identify a new binding constraint. Once the constraint is broken in Department 3, either Department 1, 2, or 4 will become the bottleneck. Or, if the company has excess capacity in all departments, it should focus its attention on building demand.

IMPLICATIONS OF TOC FOR INSPECTIONS, BATCH SIZES, AND ACROSS-THE-BOARD CUTS

TOC has implications for a number of decisions faced by managers. Here we'll discuss three: implications for inspections, batch sizes, and across-the-board cuts.

Inspections. Time in a constrained department should never be wasted. Thus, whenever possible, inspections should take place *before* work is transferred to a constrained department. That way, the valuable time of the constrained department will not be wasted working on defective items.

Batch Sizes. In recent years, many companies have gone to small batch sizes to gain flexibility in responding to new orders and to avoid producing large quantities of defective items if a process goes out of control. However, when a production process is a binding constraint, it may be better to have large batch sizes. The reason is that then the valuable time of the constrained department is not wasted setting up equipment for numerous small batches of production.

Across-the-Board Cuts. The decision to have across-the-board cuts is completely at odds with TOC. Cuts in nonbottleneck departments may make sense, but across-the-board cuts, even to the department that is the binding constraint, can have a severe, negative impact on profit. Recall that at Dwyer Electronics, each hour gained in Department 3 results in $4,000 of incremental profit if the time is spent producing Model A70. Likewise, each hour lost reduces profit by $4,000. If an across-the-board cut reduced capacity by the equivalent of just an hour a day, more than a $1 million of profit would be lost in a year (1 hour × 5 days per week × 52 weeks × $4,000 per hour = $1,040,000).

YOU GET WHAT YOU MEASURE

YOU GET WHAT YOU MEASURE AND TOC

As you know, a major theme of this book is: "You get what you measure!" In other words, performance measures drive the behavior of managers. TOC points out that performance measures related to production volume (e.g., units produced per hour) can have a negative impact on shareholder value *when they are applied to nonbottleneck departments*. Suppose at Dwyer Electronics, the company measures and rewards Departments 1 and 2 for units produced per hour. In this case, the departments have an incentive to produce more items than Department 3 can deal with since it is a bottleneck. The result will be large levels of work-in-process inventory accumulating in front of Department 3. That excess inventory is an investment of shareholder funds, but shareholders will not receive a reasonable return on the investment since it serves no useful purpose. Remember: Be careful of performance measures that encourage overproduction in nonbottleneck departments!

REVIEW PROBLEM 1

Bainbridge Harbor Service currently operates a walk-on ferry service between Bainbridge Island and downtown Seattle. Five days per week, the schedule is as follows:

Morning

7 A.M.	Ferry departs Bainbridge, arrives in Seattle at 7:30 A.M. Returns empty to Bainbridge.
8:15 A.M.	Ferry departs Bainbridge, arrives in Seattle at 8:45 A.M.

Evening

5:15 P.M.	Ferry departs Seattle, arrives in Bainbridge at 5:45 P.M. Returns empty to Seattle.
6:30 P.M.	Ferry departs Seattle, arrives in Bainbridge at 7:00 P.M.

The cost of a round-trip ticket is $30, and only round-trip tickets are sold. Profit last year was as follows:

Revenue (40 round-trip fares per day × $30 × 52 weeks × 5 days)		$312,000
Depreciation	20,000	
Dock rental	12,000	
Fuel	62,400	
Captain	90,000	
Mate	55,000	
Bookkeeping	15,000	
Miscellaneous	10,400	264,800
Profit		$ 47,200

The distance between Bainbridge and Seattle is 5 miles, the boat's fuel efficiency is 1 mile per gallon, and the cost of a gallon of fuel is estimated at $4. Bookkeeping costs are fixed, as is the annual rental of dock space on both sides. Miscellaneous costs vary with miles.

The company is now considering offering a 10 A.M. trip to Seattle on Saturday morning with a return trip at 3 P.M., on Saturday afternoon. The round-trip fare will remain at $30, and the company estimates 15 fares per day. A captain will be paid $300 per day, and a mate will be paid $150 per day.

REQUIRED

What is the annual incremental profit (loss) associated with the Saturday trips?

ANSWER

Incremental revenue:	
(15 round-trip fares per day × \$30 × 52 weeks)	\$23,400
Incremental costs:	
Fuel (5 miles per crossing × 2 × \$4 per gallon × 52 weeks)	2,080
Captain (\$300 × 52)	15,600
Mate (\$150 × 52)	7,800
Miscellaneous (see below)	693
	26,173
Incremental loss:	(\$ 2,773)

Given that there is an incremental loss, the Saturday trips should not be undertaken.

Current miles per year:
6 crossings per day × 5 miles per crossing × 5 days per week × 52 weeks = 7,800 miles per year.
\$10,400 annual miscellaneous ÷ 7,800 miles = \$1.3333 per mile.
Miles for Saturday trips = 2 crossings per day × 5 miles per crossing × 52 weeks = 520 miles.
520 miles × \$1.3333 = \$693.

REVIEW PROBLEM 2

Mayfield Software has a 2,000-square-foot cafeteria located on the lower level of Building 3, the company's largest building. The vice president of operations for Mayfield insists that meal prices be reasonable so workers will stay on campus and avoid wasting time driving to restaurants with slow service. Employees at Mayfield are generally happy with the quality of food and the level of service in the cafeteria. Still, Mayfield is considering outsourcing to Regal Food Service. Mayfield is expanding and realizes that the future success of the company will require increased focus on its core competencies (and food service is not a core competency!).

A cafeteria profit report for 2017 follows. In the report, the cafeteria is charged \$20 per year per square foot for space and 3 percent of sales for general overhead (to cover the centrally administered costs of Mayfield Software, such as legal, brand advertising, salary of the CFO, etc.). All business units receive the same 3 percent charge.

Cafeteria Profit Report for 2017

Sales		\$1,095,000
Less expenses:		
Cost of food and supplies	\$657,000	
Salaries	342,000	
Space charge	40,000	
Depreciation of equipment	6,000	
General overhead charge	32,850	1,077,850
Cafeteria profit		\$ 17,150

The terms of the agreement with Regal (which has not yet been signed) call for Regal to provide similar-quality meals and service at the same prices that were charged in 2017. Regal will use the current cafeteria space and existing equipment without cost. Regal will keep 96 percent of sales revenue and remit 4 percent of sales revenue back to Mayfield. Regal will pay for all food and supplies and hire and pay the salaries of all staff including the cafeteria manager, cooks, and servers.

REQUIRED

Evaluate the annual financial impact of the outsourcing decision assuming sales in the coming year, under Regal, will be the same as in 2017.

ANSWER

Incremental Revenue and Costs	
Lost sales	($1,095,000)
4% payment from Regal	43,800
Food savings	657,000
Salary savings	342,000
Net effect	($ 52,200)

Food services should not be outsourced since the effect is to reduce profit by $52,200. Note that the general overhead charge is not included in the analysis because these costs will not actually change due to the outsourcing decision. Thus, they are not incremental costs.

KEY TERMS

Avoidable costs (263)
Common costs (265)
Differential costs (256)
Incremental analysis (256)
Incremental cost (256)
Incremental revenue (256)
Joint costs (269)
Joint products (269)
Opportunity cost (264)
Relative sales value method (270)
Relevant costs (256)
Split-off point (269)

SELF-ASSESSMENT (Answers Below)

1. Differential costs are sometimes referred to as __________ costs.

2. Which of the following costs should **not** be taken into consideration when making a decision?
   a. Opportunity costs.
   b. Sunk costs.
   c. Relevant costs.
   d. Differential costs.

3. Which of the following is often **not** a differential cost?
   a. Material.
   b. Labor.
   c. Variable overhead.
   d. Fixed overhead.

4. True or false? Fixed costs are never incremental costs.

5. Which of the following is **not** relevant when considering whether or not to drop a product?
   a. The contribution margin.
   b. Qualitative factors.
   c. The potential impact on demand for other products.
   d. Allocated common costs.

6. Opportunity costs are:
   a. Never incremental costs.
   b. Always incremental costs.
   c. Sometimes sunk costs.
   d. None of these answer choices is correct.

7. The joint costs incurred in a joint product situation:
   a. Are incurred before the split-off point.
   b. Are incurred after the split-off point.
   c. Should be allocated based on physical attributes only.
   d. None of these answer choices is correct.

8. A joint product's cost is $18, which includes $6 of allocated joint cost. Its sales price is $16. In this case:
   a. Profit will improve if the company discontinues production of the product.
   b. The company should sell as few of the items as possible to minimize the loss on sales.
   c. The data are misleading because the $6 allocated joint cost will be incurred even if the product is discontinued.
   d. All of these answer choices are correct.

9. (Appendix) According to the Theory of Constraints, optimizing use of a constraint requires:
   a. Production of the product with the highest profit per unit.
   b. Production of the product with the shortest production time.
   c. Production of the product with the highest contribution margin.
   d. Production of the product with the highest contribution margin per unit of the constrained resource.

10. (Appendix) True or false? Generally, parts should be inspected prior to being sent to a department that is a bottleneck.

ANSWERS TO SELF-ASSESSMENT

1. relevant **2.** b **3.** d **4.** false **5.** d
6. b **7.** a **8.** c **9.** d **10.** true

QUESTIONS

1. What are differential costs and revenues?
2. Why are sunk costs irrelevant in decision making?
3. What are avoidable costs?
4. Why are opportunity costs relevant when making decisions?
5. What is the proper approach to analyzing whether a product line should be dropped?
6. Give an example of a fixed cost that is not sunk but is still irrelevant.
7. What is a qualitative advantage of making rather than buying a component?
8. Why is the relative sales value a more logical basis for allocating joint costs than physical quantity?
9. (Appendix) Why are batch sizes generally larger in bottleneck departments?
10. (Appendix) Why is the bottleneck department referred to as a drum in the Theory of Constraints?

EXERCISES

GROUP WORK

EXERCISE 7-1. [LO 1] Describe a decision and provide an example of a fixed cost that is incremental in the context of the decision. Then provide an example of a fixed cost that is not incremental in the context of the decision.

WRITING

EXERCISE 7-2. [LO 1] Jordan Walken owns and operates an electronics store in Seattle, Washington. Her accountant has prepared a product line income statement that is reproduced below. (Jordan's two lines are music devices and accessories.) In preparing the income statement, the accountant allocated all common costs, including rent, Jordan's salary and the salary of her two assistants, utilities, and other common costs based on relative sales (rounded to thousands). Her reason: "Each product line needs to cover its share of common costs."

In light of this report, Jordan is considering eliminating accessories and concentrating solely on the sale of music devices (although, she does not expect an increase in music device sales).

	Music Devices	Accessories	Total
Sales	$970,000	$150,000	$1,120,000
Cost of merchandise	705,000	120,000	825,000
Gross margin	265,000	30,000	295,000
Rent	43,000	7,000	50,000
Salaries	198,000	32,000	230,000
Utilities	6,000	1,000	7,000
Other	5,000	1,000	6,000
Total	252,000	41,000	293,000
Income before taxes	$ 13,000	($ 11,000)	$ 2,000

REQUIRED

Analyze the effect on profit of dropping accessories. Then write a paragraph explaining the role of common costs in your analysis and how allocation of common costs can lead to the cost allocation death spiral.

EXERCISE 7-3. [LO 1] Go to the financial glossary Investorwords.com at www.investorwords.com and look up the phrases *sunk cost* and *opportunity cost*.

REQUIRED

Why are sunk costs never relevant to a decision whereas opportunity costs are always relevant?

EXCEL **EXERCISE 7-4. Incremental Analysis [LO 1]** Rustic Interiors, an interior design company, has experienced a drop in business due to an increase in interest rates and a corresponding slowdown in remodeling projects. To stimulate business, the company is considering exhibiting at the Middleton Home and Garden Expo. The exhibit will cost the company $15,000 for space. At the show, Rustic Interiors will present a slide show on a laptop, pass out brochures that were printed previously (the company printed more than needed), and show its portfolio of previous jobs.

The company estimates that revenue will increase by $40,000 over the next year as a result of the exhibit. For the previous year, profit was as follows:

Revenue		$212,500
Less:		
Design supplies	$18,000	
Salary of Samantha Spade (owner)	82,000	
Salary of Kim Bridesdale (full-time employee)	56,000	
Rent	19,000	
Utilities	7,000	
Depreciation of office equipment	4,000	
Printing of advertising materials	800	
Advertising in *Middleton Journal*	3,000	
Travel expenses other than depreciation of autos	3,000	
Depreciation of company cars	10,000	202,800
Net income		$ 9,700

REQUIRED

Calculate the impact of the exhibit on company profit. Should the company exhibit at the home show?

EXCEL **EXERCISE 7-5. Incremental Analysis [LO 1]** Each year, Knight Motors surveys 7,600 former and prospective customers regarding satisfaction and brand awareness. For the current year, the company is considering outsourcing the survey to RBG Associates, which has offered to conduct the survey and summarize results for $35,000. Craig Knight, the president of Knight Motors, believes that RBG will do a higher-quality job than his company has been doing but is unwilling to spend more than $10,000 above current costs. The head of bookkeeping for Knight has prepared the following summary of costs related to the survey in the prior year:

Mailing	$17,500
Printing (done by Lester Print Shop)	6,000
Salary of Pat Fisher, part-time employee who stuffed envelopes and summarized data when surveys were returned (130 hours × $16)	2,080
Share of depreciation of computer and software used to track survey responses and summarize results	1,200
Share of electricity/phone/etc. based on square feet of space occupied by Pat Fisher vs. entire company	600
Total	$27,380

REQUIRED

What is the incremental cost of going outside vs. conducting the survey as in the past? Will Craig Knight accept the RBG offer?

EXCEL **EXERCISE 7-6. Incremental Analysis and Opportunity Costs [LO 1, 2]** Finn's Seafood Restaurant has been approached by New England Investments, which wants to hold an employee recognition dinner next month. Lillian Sumner, a manager of the restaurant, agreed to a charge of $72 per person, for food, wine, and dessert, for 175 people. She estimates that the cost of unprepared food will be $36 per person and beverages will be $14 per person.

To be able to accommodate the group, Lillian will have to close the restaurant for dinner that night. Typically, she would have served 190 people with an average bill of $56 per person. On a typical night, the cost of unprepared food is $20 per person and beverages are $17 per person. No additional staff will need to be hired to accommodate the group from New England Investments.

REQUIRED

a. Calculate the incremental profit or loss associated with accepting the New England Investments group.

b. What was the opportunity cost of accepting the New England Investments group?

c. Should Lillian have considered any qualitative factors in her decision? Explain.

EXERCISE 7-7. Make-or-Buy Decision: Relevant Costs [LO 1] The Tufanzi Furniture Company manufactures leather furniture. The manufacturing process uses a variety of metal pieces, such as brackets, braces, and casters. Carla Reid, the resource officer of Tufanzi, has been asked to determine whether it is advisable to purchase these pieces rather than make them internally (the current practice). Identify which of the following items are relevant to her decision.

a. The original cost of equipment currently used to make metal pieces.

b. The market value of equipment currently used to make metal pieces.

c. The cost of buying metal pieces from suppliers.

d. The space freed up if metal pieces are not made internally.

e. The salary of the president of Tufanzi Furniture.

f. The quality of the metal pieces made internally.

g. The quality of the metal pieces purchased from suppliers.

h. Depreciation on equipment used to make metal pieces (ignore taxes).

i. The labor contract with production workers.

j. The selling prices of furniture pieces.

EXERCISE 7-8. Make-or-Buy Decision [LO 1] The Howell Corporation produces an executive jet for which it currently manufactures a fuel valve; the cost of the valve is indicated below:

	Cost per Unit
Variable costs	
Direct material	$ 950
Direct labor	650
Variable overhead	300
Total variable costs	$1,900
Fixed costs	
Depreciation of equipment	500
Depreciation of building	200
Supervisory salaries	300
Total fixed costs	1,000
Total cost	$2,900

The company has an offer from Duvall Valves to produce the part for $2,100 per unit and supply 1,000 valves (the number needed in the coming year). If the company accepts this offer and shuts down production of valves, production workers and supervisors will be reassigned to other areas where, unfortunately, they really are not needed. The equipment cannot be used elsewhere in the company, and it has no market value. However, the space occupied by the production of the valve can be used by another production group that is currently leasing space for $55,000 per year.

REQUIRED

Should the company make or buy the valve?

EXERCISE 7-9. Sunk, Avoidable, and Opportunity Costs [LO 1] Consider the information in Exercise 7-8 and identify the following statements as true or false.

a. Supervisory salary is an avoidable cost if the company decides to buy the valves.

b. Depreciation of building is an avoidable cost if the company decides to buy the valves.

c. The $55,000 cost of leasing space is an opportunity cost associated with continuing production of the valve.

d. The depreciation of equipment is an opportunity cost associated with continuing production of the valve.

e. Depreciation of building is a sunk cost even if the company continues with production of the valve.

f. Supervisory salary is a sunk cost even if the company continues with production of the valve.

EXERCISE 7-10. Dropping a Product: Relevant Costs [LO 1] E-Teller manufactures ATM machines. Recently the company has begun manufacturing and marketing a machine that can recognize customer fingerprints. Demand for this machine is very strong, and the chief executive officer of E-Teller is considering dropping production of the company's original model, which relies on bankcards and passwords. This will give the company increased capacity to devote to the new model. Which of the following items are relevant to the CEO's decision to drop the old model machine?

a. The original cost of equipment used to manufacture the old model.

b. Depreciation of the equipment used to manufacture the old model (ignore taxes).

c. The CEO's salary.

d. The time it takes to manufacture each model.

e. The production manager's salary.

f. The selling price of the new model.

g. The variable cost of producing the new model.

h. The cost of retraining personnel to make the newer model.

i. Depreciation of the factory building allocated to the old model.

EXERCISE 7-11. Additional Processing Decision [LO 1] DataPoint, Inc. has decided to discontinue manufacturing its Quantum model personal organizer. Currently the company has a number of partially completed personal organizers on hand. The company has spent $110 per unit to manufacture these organizers. To complete each unit, costs of $14 for material and $16 for direct labor will be incurred. In addition, $10 of variable overhead and $32 of allocated fixed overhead (relating primarily to depreciation of plant and equipment) will be added per unit.

If the DataPoint Company completes the organizers, it can sell them for $130 per unit. Another manufacturer is interested in purchasing the partially completed organizers for $107 per unit and converting them into inventory tracking devices.

Determine whether DataPoint should complete the personal organizers or sell them in their current state.

EXERCISE 7-12. Make-or-Buy Decision [LO 1, 2] Imperial produces whirlpool tubs. Currently the company uses internally manufactured pumps to power water jets. Imperial has found that 40 percent of the pumps have failed within their 12-month warranty period, causing huge warranty costs. Because of the company's inability to manufacture high-quality pumps, management is considering buying pumps from a reputable manufacturer that also will bear any related warranty costs. Imperial's unit cost of manufacturing pumps is $80 per unit, which includes $18 of allocated fixed overhead (primarily depreciation of plant and equipment). Also, the company has spent an average of $20 (labor and parts) repairing each pump returned. Imperial can purchase pumps for $85 per pump.

REQUIRED

During 2017, Imperial plans to sell 15,000 whirlpools (requiring 15,000 pumps). Determine whether the company should make or buy the pumps and the amount of cost savings related to the better alternative. What qualitative factors should be considered in the outsourcing decision?

EXERCISE 7-13. Dropping a Product Line [LO 1] Computer Village sells computer equipment and home office furniture. Currently the furniture product line takes up approximately 50 percent of the company's retail floor space. The president of Computer Village is trying to decide whether the company should continue offering furniture or concentrate on computer equipment. Below is a product line income statement for the company. If furniture is dropped, salaries and other direct fixed costs can be avoided. In addition, sales of computer equipment can increase by 13 percent without affecting direct fixed costs. Allocated fixed costs are assigned based on relative sales.

	Computer Equipment	Home Office Furniture	Total
Sales	$1,400,000	$1,100,000	$2,500,000
Less cost of goods sold	900,000	800,000	1,700,000
Contribution margin	500,000	300,000	800,000
Less direct fixed costs:			
Salaries	175,000	175,000	350,000
Other	60,000	60,000	120,000
Less allocated fixed costs:			
Rent	13,440	10,560	24,000
Insurance	3,360	2,640	6,000
Cleaning	3,920	3,080	7,000
President's salary	72,800	57,200	130,000
Other	6,720	5,280	12,000
Net income	$ 164,760	($ 13,760)	$ 151,000

REQUIRED

Determine whether Computer Village should discontinue the furniture line and the financial benefit (cost) of dropping it.

EXERCISE 7-14. Qualitative Factors in Decision Making [LO 2] For each of the following situations, indicate a qualitative factor that should be considered prior to making a decision:

a. A company that produces and sells bottled water is considering outsourcing its bottling operation. The company will still source the water and deliver it to bottling companies.

b. A wine producer is considering dropping its premium brand wine and concentrating exclusively on less costly wines.

c. A software company currently has a large facility for producing videos used in games and advertisements. The company is considering shutting down the facility and using resources provided by other companies.

EXERCISE 7-15. Joint Cost Allocation with Physical Quantity of Output [LO 2] Bailey Products produces two joint products (A and B). Prior to the split-off point, the company incurs costs of $6,000. Product A weighs 30 pounds, and Product B weighs 120 pounds. Product A sells for $100 per pound, and Product B sells for $35 per pound.

REQUIRED

a. Based on a physical measure of output, allocate joint costs to Products A and B.

b. Compare the costs to the selling prices. Should the company sell products whose selling price is less than the allocated joint cost?

EXERCISE 7-16. Joint Cost Allocation with Relative Sales Values [LO 2] Bailey Products produces two joint products (A and B). Prior to the split-off point, the company incurs costs of $6,000. Product A weighs 30 pounds, and Product B weighs 120 pounds. Product A sells for $100 per pound, and Product B sells for $35 per pound.

REQUIRED

a. Based on relative sales values at the split-off point, allocate joint costs to Products A and B.

b. Under what condition would the cost allocated using relative sales values be greater than the selling price of a joint product?

EXERCISE 7-17. Allocating Joint Costs [LO 2] The American Produce Company purchased a truckload of cantaloupes (weighing 4,000 pounds) for $900. American Produce separated the cantaloupes into two grades: superior and economy. The superior-grade cantaloupes had a total weight of 3,200 pounds, and the economy-grade cantaloupes totaled 800 pounds. American Produce sells the superior-grade cantaloupes at $0.50 per pound, and the economy-grade ones at $0.20 per pound.

REQUIRED

Allocate the $900 cost of the truckload to the superior-grade and economy-grade cantaloupes using the physical quantity method and the relative sales value method.

EXERCISE 7-18. (Appendix) Calculating the Value of Loosening a Constraint [LO A1] At RM Sharpton, the engraving department is a bottleneck, and the company is considering hiring an extra worker, whose salary will be $55,000 per year, to mitigate the problem.

With the extra worker, the company will be able to produce and sell 7,000 more units per year. The selling price per unit is $14. Cost per unit currently is $8 as follows:

Direct material	$2.75
Direct labor	1.00
Variable overhead	.25
Fixed overhead (primarily depreciation of equipment)	4.00
Total	$8.00

REQUIRED

Calculate the annual financial impact of hiring the extra worker.

PROBLEMS

ETHICS

PROBLEM 7-1. Decision Making and Ethics [LO 1, Ethics] Joan Paxton, VP of marketing for Supertone Recording Equipment, has developed a marketing plan for presentation to the company's president. The plan calls for television ads, something the company has never used. As part of her presentation, she will indicate the impact of the TV ads on company profit as follows:

Incremental sales from increased exposure		$9,600,000
Less:		
Incremental cost of goods sold	$4,200,000	
Cost of TV ads	3,100,000	7,300,000
Incremental profit		$2,300,000

While Joan is quite confident in the cost of the ads and the incremental cost of goods sold if sales are $9,600,000, she is quite uncertain about the sales increase. In fact, she believes that her estimate is on the high side. However, she also believes that if she puts in a more conservative estimate, such as $7,000,000, the president will not go along with the TV ads even though they still will generate substantial profits at $7,000,000 of incremental sales.

REQUIRED

Is it unethical of Joan to bias her estimate of incremental sales on the high side, given that she believes the ultimate outcome is in the best interest of the company?

PROBLEM 7-2. Incremental Analysis of Outsourcing Decision [LO 1, 2] Oakland College is considering outsourcing grounds maintenance. In this regard, Oakland has received a bid from Highline Grounds Maintenance for $300,000 per year. Highline states that its bid will cover all services and planting materials required to "keep Oakland's grounds in a condition comparable to prior years." Oakland's cost for grounds maintenance in the preceding year were $309,000, as follows:

Salary of three full-time gardeners	$195,000
Plant materials	80,000
Fertilizer	10,000
Fuel	12,000
Depreciation of tractor, mowers, and other miscellaneous equipment	12,000
Total	$309,000

If Oakland College outsources maintenance, it will be able to sell equipment for $30,000, and the three gardeners will be laid off.

REQUIRED

a. Analyze the 1-year financial impact of outsourcing grounds maintenance.

b. How will savings in the second year differ from those in year 1?

c. Discuss qualitative factors that should be considered in the decision.

PROBLEM 7-3. Incremental Analysis of Outsourcing Decision [LO 1, 2] Selzer & Hollinger, a legal services firm, is considering outsourcing its payroll function. It has received a bid from ABC Payroll Services for $22,000 per year. ABC Payroll will provide all payroll processing, including employee checks and payroll tax reporting. Selzer & Hollinger's costs for payroll processing in-house over the past year were as follows:

Cost	Amount
Payroll clerk (part time)	$12,000
Annual cost of payroll processing software updates	1,000
Human resources manager's salary	80,000
Depreciation of computers used in payroll processing	2,000
Annual payroll tax update seminar costs for one employee	1,500

Currently the payroll clerk works only on payroll processing, and will be laid off if payroll is outsourced. The human resources manager spends 25 percent of her time currently on payroll-related issues. The computers would remain and be used for other tasks if payroll is outsourced.

REQUIRED

a. What is the annual impact of outsourcing payroll? Will the company save money or spend extra money if payroll is outsourced?

b. What qualitative factors should be considered in this decision?

EXCEL **PROBLEM 7-4. Make-or-Buy Decision [LO 1]** For most construction projects, Bradley Heating and Cooling buys sheet metal and forms the metal into heating/cooling ducts as needed. The company estimates the costs of making and installing ductwork for the Kerry Park shopping mall to be as follows:

Materials	$35,000
Labor to form ductwork	4,000
Labor to install ductwork	10,000
Miscellaneous variable costs	1,500
Fixed costs allocated based on labor hours	3,000
Total cost	$53,500

The fixed costs relate to the company's building, equipment, and office staff. The company plans to bill the Kerry Park developer $68,000 for services. Bradley is currently behind schedule on other projects and is paying a late penalty of $1,200 per day. Walt Bradley, the owner of Bradley Heating and Cooling, is considering ordering prefabricated ductwork for the Kerry Park job. The prefabricated ductwork will cost $42,000 (including the cost of sheet metal). If Walt buys the prefabricated ductwork, he'll be able to reassign workers to another project and avoid five days of late fees.

REQUIRED

Should Bradley make the ductwork or buy it prefabricated?

PROBLEM 7-5. Keep-or-Buy Decision, Sunk Costs [LO 1, 2] Susan Crossing purchased a used Ford Focus for $12,000. Since purchasing the car, she has spent the following amounts on parts and labor:

New stereo system	$1,500
New paint job	2,500
New tires	1,200
New muffler	250
Total	$5,450

Unfortunately, the car needs a few major repairs now; among other things, the brake rotors and pads must be replaced, and the radiator has sprung a leak. (A new radiator is needed.) The repairs are estimated to cost $2,500.

Susan has looked around at other used cars and has found a used Honda Civic for $10,500 that is in very good condition and is approximately the same age as the Ford Focus. Susan can sell the Ford Focus "as is" for $8,500.

REQUIRED

a. In trying to decide whether to repair the Ford Focus or buy the Honda Civic, Susan is upset because she has already spent $17,450 on the Focus. The car seems like it costs too much to sell at such a large loss. How would you react to her dilemma?

b. Assuming that Susan would be equally happy with either the Ford Focus or the Honda Civic, should she buy the Civic or repair the Focus? Explain your answer.

c. Are there any qualitative factors that might enter into this decision? Explain.

PROBLEM 7-6. Make-or-Buy Decision [LO 1] The Curtis Corporation is beginning production of Mighty Mint, a new mouthwash in a small spray container. The product will be sold to wholesalers and large drugstore chains in packages of 30 containers for $20 per package. Management allocates $225,000 of fixed manufacturing overhead costs to Mighty Mint. The manufacturing cost per package of 30 containers for expected production of 100,000 packages is as follows:

Direct material	$ 8.00
Direct labor	3.50
Overhead (fixed and variable)	3.50
Total	$15.00

The company has contacted a number of packaging suppliers to determine whether it is better to buy or manufacture the spray containers. The lowest quote for the containers is $1.90 per 30 units. It is estimated that purchasing the containers from a supplier will save 10 percent of direct materials, 20 percent of direct labor, and 15 percent of variable overhead. Curtis's manufacturing space is highly constrained. By purchasing the spray containers, the company will not have to lease additional manufacturing space, which is estimated to cost $17,000 per year. If the containers are purchased, one supervisory position can be eliminated. Salary plus benefits for this position are $72,000 per year.

REQUIRED

Should Curtis make or buy the containers? What is the incremental cost (benefit) of buying the containers as opposed to making them?

PROBLEM 7-7. Additional Processing Decision and Qualitative Factors [LO 1, 2] Mulan Carpet produced 1,200 yards of its economy-grade carpet. In the coloring process, there was a pigment defect, and the resulting color appeared to be faded. The carpet normally sells for $15 per yard: $7 of variable cost per yard and $6 of fixed cost per yard have been assigned to the carpet.

The company realizes that it cannot sell the carpet for $15 per yard through its normal channels, unless the coloring process is repeated. The incremental cost of the process is $2 per yard. However, Practical Home Solutions is willing to buy the carpet in its current faded condition for $9 per yard.

REQUIRED

a. Should Mulan repeat the coloring process or sell the carpet to Practical Home Solutions?

b. Suppose Practical Home Solutions is willing to buy the carpet for $14 per yard if Mulan's brand is associated with the carpet by means of a tag indicating the carpet was produced by Mulan (a highly regarded producer). Would you accept Practical Home Solutions's offer if you were the president of Mulan?

EXCEL **PROBLEM 7-8. Additional Processing Decision with a Production Constraint [LO 1]** Mega Chemical Company produces ZylexA and a related product called ZylexB. ZylexB, which sells for $17.00 per gallon, is made from a base of ZylexA plus additional ingredients. It takes 25 minutes to manufacture a gallon of ZylexA and an additional 10 minutes to manufacture a gallon of ZylexB. ZylexA sells for $11.00 per gallon. The cost per gallon of manufacturing ZylexA and the additional costs to convert it into ZylexB are:

	ZylexA	Additional Cost to Convert ZylexA into ZylexB
Material	$2.00	$1.75
Labor	2.50	0.50
Variable overhead	2.25	1.10

Both products have been successful, and demand for both products is strong and beyond the company's capacity. Since it takes additional time to manufacture ZylexB, the vice president of production is trying to determine whether ZylexB should be produced.

REQUIRED

Which product makes the largest contribution to company profit, given a capacity constraint measured in terms of production time?

PROBLEM 7-9. Dropping a Product Line [LO 1, 2] Pantheon Gaming, a computer enhancement company, has three product lines: audio enhancers, video enhancers, and connection-speed accelerators. Common costs are allocated based on relative sales. A product line income statement follows:

Pantheon Gaming
Income Statement
For the Year Ended December 31, 2017

	Audio	Video	Accelerators	Total
Sales	$1,200,000	$2,450,000	$2,400,000	$6,050,000
Less cost of goods sold	730,000	1,435,000	2,070,000	4,235,000
Gross margin	470,000	1,015,000	330,000	1,815,000
Less other variable costs	53,000	69,000	20,000	142,000
Contribution margin	417,000	946,000	310,000	1,673,000
Less direct salaries	155,000	175,000	65,000	395,000
Less common fixed costs:				
Rent	11,970	25,830	25,200	63,000
Utilities	4,370	9,430	9,200	23,000
Depreciation	5,890	12,710	12,400	31,000
Other administrative costs	79,230	170,970	166,800	417,000
Net income	$ 160,540	$ 552,060	$ 31,400	$ 744,000

Since the profit for accelerator devices is relatively low, the company is considering dropping this product line.

REQUIRED

a. Determine the annual impact on profit of dropping accelerator products.
b. Discuss the potential qualitative effects of discontinuing the sale of accelerator products.

PROBLEM 7-10. Drop a Product/Opportunity Cost [LO 1] Midwestern Sod produces two products, fescue grass and Bermuda grass:

	Fescue Grass	Bermuda Grass
Selling price per square yard	$3.00	$3.85
Variable cost per square yard (water, fertilizer, maintenance)	.85	1.57

The company has 130,000 square yards of growing space available. In the past year, the company dedicated 65,000 square yards to fescue and 65,000 square yards to Bermuda grass. Annual fixed costs are $130,000, which the company allocates to products based on relative growing space.

Martha Lopez, the chief financial officer of Midwestern Sod, has suggested that in the coming year, all 130,000 square yards should be devoted to Bermuda grass. The president vetoed her suggestion, saying, "I know that right now home construction is booming in our area, and we can sell all the grass we can produce, irrespective of what type. But you know a lot of developers really like that fescue grass, and I'd hate to disappoint them by not offering it."

REQUIRED

What is the opportunity cost of the president's decision to stick with both types of grass?

PROBLEM 7-11. Drop a Product Decision [LO 1] Lennon Fans manufactures three model fans for industrial use. The standard selling price and cost of each fan follow:

	Model 501	Model 541	Model 599
Selling price	$6,300	$12,000	$15,200
Unit cost:			
Material	1,650	5,450	7,050
Direct labor	850	2,700	4,900
Overhead	880	3,518	7,036
Unit profit (loss)	$2,920	$ 332	($ 3,786)

Essentially, all overhead costs are fixed. Some of the fixed overhead costs are direct costs to particular models, and others are common fixed costs.

Estimated Total Overhead

	Model 501	Model 541	Model 599	Total
Direct fixed	$5,000,000	$2,000,000	$1,000,000	$ 8,000,000
Common fixed				5,000,000
Total				$13,000,000

Lennon allocates overhead costs to products using a single overhead rate developed as follows. Estimated total overhead is divided by estimated direct labor cost. This results in an overhead rate per labor dollar. This rate is used to assign standard overhead to products.

Below are estimates of sales and direct labor. These values imply an overhead rate of $1.3146 per labor dollar ($13,000,000 ÷ $9,889,000).

	Model 501	Model 541	Model 599	Total
Estimated unit sales	1,100	2,300	560	3,960
Estimated labor	$935,000	$6,210,000	$2,744,000	$9,889,000

REQUIRED

a. Because Model 599 is showing a loss, the controller of Lennon has asked you to analyze whether it should be dropped. You should assume that direct fixed costs will be avoided if a model is dropped but common fixed costs will not be avoided if the model is dropped.

b. Explain why the method used to allocate costs at Lennon results in unreasonably high charges to the Model 599 fan.

PROBLEM 7-12. Cost Allocation Death Spiral [LO 1] Carpets Unlimited produces and sells three lines of carpet: economy, standard, and deluxe. Jeff Choi, the chief financial officer of the company, has prepared the following report on the profitability in the past year. In the report, fixed costs are allocated based on yards of carpet.

	Economy	Standard	Deluxe	Total
Yards of carpet	30,000	45,000	75,000	150,000
Sales	$325,000	$700,000	$1,525,000	$2,550,000
Less variable costs (dye, yarn, labor, etc.)	175,000	430,000	925,000	1,530,000
Less fixed costs (depreciation, supervisory salaries, etc.)	162,000	243,000	405,000	810,000
Profit (loss)	($ 12,000)	$ 27,000	$ 195,000	$ 210,000

Upon seeing the report, Matt Williams, the president of Carpets Unlimited, suggested that the company should consider dropping the economy grade and concentrate on the two other lines. Jeff replied, however, that would lead to the cost allocation death spiral.

REQUIRED

a. Revise the report assuming the company drops the economy grade.

b. If either the standard or the deluxe grades is reporting a loss in part a, revise the report assuming that it is also dropped.

c. Explain what Jeff means by the "cost allocation death spiral."

PROBLEM 7-13. Joint Costs and Decision Making [LO 2] Sylvan Wood Products purchases alder logs for $100 per log. After the bark is stripped, the log is spun on a veneer cutter, which peels thin layers of wood (referred to as veneer) that are sold to furniture manufacturers for $150 per 3′ × 30′ sheet of veneer. The peeled log (referred to as a peeler) is sold for $50 to companies that use the logs to construct outdoor play equipment. On average, each alder log yields one 3′ × 30′ sheet of veneer and (obviously) one peeled log. The cost of processing each log into a sheet of veneer and a peeled log is $35 in addition to the $100 cost of the alder log. On average, a peeled log weighs 60 pounds, and an average 3′ × 30′ sheet of veneer weighs 10 pounds.

REQUIRED

a. Suppose Sylvan were to allocate all joint costs based on the weight of the joint products. Calculate expected profit per sheet of veneer and per peeler.

b. The profit per peeler in part a is negative. Does this imply that the company should not sell them?

c. Suppose Sylvan were to allocate all joint costs based on the relative sales values of the joint products. Calculate expected profit per sheet of veneer and per peeler.

d. Briefly explain why the relative sales value approach is the preferred method for allocating joint costs.

PROBLEM 7-14. Joint Costs and Additional Processing [LO 2] Good Earth Products produces orange juice and candied orange peels. A 1,000-pound batch of oranges, costing $500, is transformed using labor of $50 into 100 pounds of orange peels and 300 pints of juice. The company has determined that the sales value of 100 pounds of peels at the split-off point is $350, and the value of a pint of juice (not pasteurized or bottled) is $0.40. Beyond the split-off point, the cost of sugar-coating and packaging the 100 pounds of peels is $60. The cost of pasteurizing and packaging the 300 pints of juice is $250. A 100-pound box of candied peels is sold to commercial baking companies for $600. Each pint of juice is sold for $1.75.

REQUIRED

a. Allocate joint costs using the relative sales values at the split-off point, and calculate the profit per 100-pound box of sugar-coated peels and the profit per pint of juice. Round to the nearest dollar.

b. What is the incremental benefit (cost) to the company of sugar-coating the peels rather than selling them in their condition at the split-off point?

c. What is the incremental benefit (cost) to the company of pasteurizing and packaging a pint of juice rather than selling the juice at the split-off point?

PROBLEM 7-15. Joint Costs [LO 2] Gavin West is a commercial fisherman, and he has just returned from a trip off the coast of Maine. He has calculated the cost of his catch as follows:

Wages of deckhands	$35,000
Gavin's wage	18,000
Food, medical supplies, etc.	7,000
Depreciation of netting and other equipment	5,400
Depreciation of boat	12,600
Fuel	18,000
Total	$96,000

Gavin's nets yielded a catch of 15,000 pounds of salmon, 23,000 pounds of halibut, and 37,000 pounds of flounder. Salmon sells for $9 per pound, halibut for $6 per pound, and flounder for $3 per pound.

REQUIRED

a. Allocate joint costs based on weight. With these costs, what is the profit associated with each type of fish?

b. Allocate joint costs based on relative sales values. With these costs, what is the profit associated with each type of fish? (Note: Round percentages to 3 decimal places.)

c. Gavin is considering turning the flounder into fish paste. The incremental cost of this operation is $10,000. Each pound of flounder yields 1/2 pound of paste, and the paste sells for $6 per pound. Will Gavin be better off selling the flounder or turning it into paste? What role does the allocated joint cost play in this decision?

PROBLEM 7-16. Joint Costs [LO 2] Northwest Minerals operates a mine. During July, the company obtained 500 tons of ore, which yielded 250 pounds of gold and 62,500 pounds of copper. The joint cost related to the operation was $500,000. Gold sells for $950 per ounce, and copper sells for $2.50 per pound.

REQUIRED

a. Allocate the joint costs using relative weight (rounded to 4 decimal places). With these costs, what is the profit associated with each mineral? What is the drawback of this approach?

b. Allocate the joint costs using the relative sales values (rounded to 4 decimal places). With these costs, what is the profit associated with each mineral?

c. With the relative sales value approach to allocation, what is the smallest value of joint cost that would result in copper showing a loss? What is the smallest value of joint cost that would result in gold showing a loss?

PROBLEM 7-17. (Appendix) Batch Size Decision and Constraints [LO A1] At Dalton Playground Equipment, the powder-coating process is a bottleneck. Typically, it takes approximately 2 hours to switch between jobs. The time is spent cleaning nozzles and paint tanks and recalibrating equipment. Currently the company runs relatively small batch sizes through the process but is considering increasing them to reduce setup time.

With small batch sizes, powder coating can process approximately 2,000 units per 8-hour shift, and products have an average contribution margin of $60. With large batch sizes, powder coating can process approximately 2,300 units per 8-hour shift.

REQUIRED

a. Calculate the additional profit associated with running larger batch sizes through the powder-coating process.

b. What potential problems are created by the larger batch sizes?

PROBLEM 7-18. (Appendix) Managing Constraints [LO 1, A1] Reece Herbal Supplements purchases, in bulk, a variety of dietary supplements that the company bottles, packages, and ships to health-food stores and drugstores around the country. The company has a good reputation, and its products are in high demand. Last year the company purchased mechanical packaging equipment for $300,000 and reduced its shipping department by two people, eliminating an annual salary expense of $120,000. When it works, the equipment packages product 20 percent faster than the previous manual system. Unfortunately, the equipment has broken down on many occasions for up to four hours. Normally (when the packaging equipment is working), the company packages 2,500 bottles per hour, and the average contribution margin per bottle is $0.60. The general manager of operations has suggested that the company rehire the two packaging workers as backup for the new packaging system. The company president doesn't think this is a good idea, since the workers will be "sitting around doing nothing for 30 hours per week!"

REQUIRED

Comment on the general manager's suggestion and the president's reaction. Support your answer with an estimate of the financial impact of rehiring the two workers.

CASE

7-1 PRIMUS CONSULTING GROUP [LO 1, 2]

Primus is a firm of consultants that focuses on process reengineering and quality improvement initiatives. Northwood Industries has asked Primus to conduct a study aimed at improving on-time delivery. Normal practice for Primus is to bill for consultant time at standard rates plus actual travel costs and estimated overhead. However, Northwood has offered a flat $75,000 for the job. Currently, Primus has excess capacity so it can take on the Northwood job without turning down other business and without hiring additional staff. If normal practices were followed, the bill would be:

Classification	Hours	Rate	Amount
Partner	90	$260	$23,400
Senior consultant	125	$160	20,000
Staff consultant	160	$ 90	14,400
Travel costs			21,000
Overhead at $30 per nonpartner hour			8,550
Total			$87,350

Overhead (computer costs, rent, utilities, paper, copying, etc.) is determined at the start of the year by dividing estimated annual overhead costs ($2,400,000) by total estimated nonpartner hours (80,000 hours). Approximately 20 percent of the total amount is variable costs. All Primus employees receive a fixed wage (i.e., there is no compensation for overtime). Annual compensation in the previous year amounted to the following:

	Per Hour
Partner	$250
Senior consultant	$150
Staff consultant	$ 80

REQUIRED

What will be the effect on company profit related to accepting the Northwood Industries job? What qualitative factors should be considered in the decision whether to accept the job or not?

CASE

7-2 FIVE STAR TOOLS [LO A1]

(Note: This case relates to the appendix on the Theory of Constraints.)

Five Star Tools is a small family-owned firm that manufactures diamond-coated cutting tools (chisels and saws) used by jewelers. Production involves three major processes. First, steel "blanks" (tools without the diamond coating) are cut to size. Second, the blanks are sent to a chemical bath that prepares the tools for the coating process. In the third major process, the blanks are coated with diamond chips in a proprietary process that simultaneously coats and sharpens the blade of each tool. Following the coating process, each tool is inspected and defects are repaired or scrapped.

In the past 2 years, the company has experienced significant growth and growing pains. The company is at capacity in the coating and sharpening process, which requires highly skilled workers and expensive equipment. Because of the bottleneck created by this operation, the company has missed deadlines on orders from several important customers.

Maxfield Turner, the son of Frederick Turner, founder of Five Star Tools, is the president of the company. Over lunch he and Betty Spence, vice president of marketing, discussed the situation. "We've got to do something," Betty began. "If we don't think we can meet a customer's order deadline, we should turn down the business. We can't simply keep customers waiting for product or we'll develop a reputation as an unreliable supplier. You know as well as I do that this would be devastating to our business."

"I think there may be another approach, Betty," replied Max. "Some of our products are exceptionally profitable. Maybe we should concentrate on them and drop some of the less profitable ones. That would free up our production resources. Or maybe we can figure out a way to run more product through the coating process. If we could just loosen that constraint, I know we could improve our response time and profitability. I'll tell you what I'll do. I'll get the accounting department to prepare an analysis of product profitability. That should help us figure out which products to concentrate on. And I'll get the production people thinking about how to free up some time in coating. We'll meet early next month and try to get a handle on how to deal with our production constraints."

REQUIRED

a. What steps can be taken to loosen the constraint in coating and sharpening?

b. Consider Model C210 and Model D400 chisels. Which product should be emphasized if the constraint in coating and sharpening cannot be loosened?

c. Focusing only on the Model C210 chisel and the model D400 chisel, what would be the benefit to the firm of gaining one more hour of production time in coating and sharpening?

d. In coating and sharpening, the operator begins by inspecting items that have arrived from the chemical bath. If rough edges or blemishes are detected, the operator smooths and/or buffs the items before actual coating or sharpening takes place. (Note that this process is in addition to the inspection that takes place at a separate inspection station following coating and sharpening.)

In order to save valuable time in coating and sharpening, management is considering forming a separate inspection station before the coating and sharpening process. The inspection station can utilize existing smoothing and buffing equipment, and it can be staffed on an as-needed basis by an employee who normally works in the chemical bath area, which has excess capacity (so the employee will not be missed for brief periods). Management estimates that this action will free up 240 hours in coating and sharpening ([an average of 5 minutes per hour × 8 hours per day × 360 operating days per year]/60). Management has calculated that the average contribution margin per unit for its products is $300. The average contribution margin per hour spent in coating and sharpening is $850.

Based on this information, estimate the incremental profit per year associated with adding the new inspection station.

	Model C210 Chisel		Model D400 Chisel	
Selling price		$500		$850
Less variable costs:				
Direct labor	$ 85		$180	
Direct material	150		180	
Variable overhead	15	250	60	420
Contribution margin		250		430
Less allocated fixed costs		185		230
Profit per unit		$ 65		$200
Time in coating and sharpening to produce 1 unit		.2 hours		.8 hours

8

PRICING DECISIONS, CUSTOMER PROFITABILITY ANALYSIS, AND ACTIVITY-BASED PRICING

Nancy Sanchez, vice president of marketing for Priced Right Office Supplies, recently attended a management training seminar where the instructor made the following point:

All customers are not the same—some are highly profitable and some are marginally profitable at best. To be successful, companies need to analyze the profitability of customers. Marginally profitable customers should be charged increased prices or their business should be dropped. The highly profitable customers—those are the ones you want to focus on. Direct your marketing campaigns toward them and you'll be on your way to achieving major increases in shareholder value!

Driving home from the seminar, Nancy thought about what she had learned and changes that needed to be made at Priced Right. In particular, she thought about her company's approach to pricing. Currently, the company charges all customers a 10 percent markup over the cost of products ordered. But some customers are much more difficult to deal with than others. In particular, some customers want frequent deliveries of relatively small orders. This means that relatively more time is spent picking and packing their orders, and delivery costs are higher. "What we need to do," Nancy decided, "is determine the profitability of our various customers and then come up with a more rational approach to pricing. First thing tomorrow, I'll set up a team with members from distribution, marketing, and accounting to work on customer profitability, measurement, and pricing."

Pricing decisions are often the most difficult decisions that managers face, and in this chapter we will examine them in some detail. We begin by discussing the profit-maximizing price from the standpoint of economic theory. Then we discuss pricing special orders and prices set by marking up costs as well as determining the target cost for a new product. We conclude the chapter with a discussion of measuring customer profitability and activity-based pricing—two topics that relate directly to the problem Nancy Sanchez is facing at Priced Right Office Supplies.

Antonprado/iStockphoto

LEARNING OBJECTIVES

1. Compute the profit-maximizing price for a product or service, and perform incremental analysis related to pricing a special order.
2. Explain the cost-plus approach to pricing and why it is inherently circular for manufacturing firms. Also, explain the target costing process for a new product.
3. Analyze customer profitability, and explain the activity-based pricing approach.

LEARNING OBJECTIVE 1

Compute the profit-maximizing price for a product or service, and perform incremental analysis related to pricing a special order.

THE PROFIT-MAXIMIZING PRICE

Economic theory suggests that the quantity demanded of a product or service is a function of the price that is charged and that generally, the higher the price, the lower the quantity demanded. If managers can estimate the quantity demanded at various prices (admittedly a difficult but not an impossible task), determining the optimal price is relatively straightforward. Simply subtract variable costs from price to obtain the contribution margin, multiply the contribution margin by the quantity demanded, subtract fixed costs, and estimate profit. The price with the highest profit should be selected. This is much simpler than it sounds. Consider the following example.

Next month, Test Technologies will begin to market a new electronic testing device called the Model TM20. The variable costs of producing and marketing the device are $1,500 per unit, and fixed costs are $7,000,000 per year. The market research team at Test Technologies estimate demand at various prices as indicated in Illustration 8-1. Note that with a price of $6,000 per unit, the quantity demanded is only 1,000 units whereas demand increases to 19,000 units if the price is dropped to $2,500 per unit. By subtracting the variable cost of $1,500 per unit from each price we obtain the contribution margin per unit, which we multiply by the quantity demanded to estimate the total contribution margin. From the total contribution margin, we subtract fixed costs of $7,000,000 to obtain a measure of profit. In this case, the optimal price would be $3,500 per unit, because this price yields the highest total profit ($17,000,000 per year).[1]

The most difficult part of determining the profit-maximizing price is determining the demand function, which is the relation between price and the quantity demanded. While this is as much art as science, a number of approaches can be used. For example, Test Technologies could ask sales managers in various regions to estimate the quantities they can sell at various prices and then sum their responses to estimate the total quantity demanded at various prices. Or the company could test-market the product with a number of potential customers and experiment with various prices. From this experience, the company would extrapolate to the entire market for the product. Still, it must be admitted that estimating the demand function is quite challenging, and that's why

ILLUSTRATION 8-1

Estimating the profit-maximizing price

A	B	C	D = A − C	E = B × D	F	G = E − F
Price per Unit	**Quantity Demanded**	**Variable Cost per Unit**	**Contribution Margin per Unit**	**Total Contribution Margin**	**Fixed Costs**	**Profit**
$6,000	1,000	$1,500	$4,500	$ 4,500,000	$7,000,000	($ 2,500,000)
5,500	2,000	1,500	4,000	8,000,000	7,000,000	1,000,000
5,000	4,000	1,500	3,500	14,000,000	7,000,000	7,000,000
4,500	6,000	1,500	3,000	18,000,000	7,000,000	11,000,000
4,000	9,000	1,500	2,500	22,500,000	7,000,000	15,500,000
3,500	12,000	1,500	2,000	24,000,000	7,000,000	17,000,000
3,000	15,000	1,500	1,500	22,500,000	7,000,000	15,500,000
2,500	19,000	1,500	1,000	19,000,000	7,000,000	12,000,000

[1] The approach to pricing in Illustration 8-1 is equivalent to an approach you may have learned in economics; namely, select a price such that marginal revenue equals marginal cost.

LINK TO PRACTICE

Pricing Strategy: Apple's Approach to Pricing

While economic theory plays an important role in pricing decisions, so too does strategy. Two strategic approaches to pricing are *skimming* and *market penetration*. With a skimming strategy, the initial price of a product is set higher than competing products. With skimming, a company can take advantage of consumers willing to pay a high price to be first to have an exciting new product. This segment is often referred to as *early adopters*. After introduction, the price is lowered to capture additional customers at a lower price point. With a market penetration strategy, price is set lower than competing products. The idea is to rapidly achieve high volume and economies of scale.

According to an article in Techpinions, Apple has added a twist to the skimming strategy. It introduces products at a high price point, but then defends the price (rather than lowering it to gain penetration) by updating them in future iterations. As an example, the average price of the iPhone remained quite stable for 6 years.

The strategy seems to be working. In 2012, for example, Apple had 69 percent of all the total profit in the mobile phone market. And it obtained this level of performance with only 8 percent market share!

Source: John Kirk, "Android's Penetration vs. Apple's Skimming Marketing Strategies," *Techpinions* (March 21, 2013).

© EdStock/iStockphoto

some companies turn to a simple approach: cost-plus pricing, which we discuss later in the chapter. Now let's turn to the pricing of special orders and return to a concept we've stressed throughout the book: incremental analysis.

PRICING SPECIAL ORDERS

Companies occasionally receive what are called *special orders*. These are orders for goods or services that are not considered part of a company's normal business. The price charged for a special order is not expected to affect prices charged in the normal course of business, and, thus, the price may deviate substantially from what is common. Indeed, as we'll see, a company may be better off charging a price that is actually below full cost.

LINK TO PRACTICE

Pricing Power More Important Than Management

Warren Buffett, the widely respected and frequently quoted CEO of Berkshire Hathaway, has bought or invested in hundreds of companies. Along the way, he's become one of the wealthiest individuals in the world. So what does Buffett look for when he considers an investment opportunity? He looks at the company's pricing power. According to Buffett, "If you've got the power to raise prices without losing business to a competitor, you've got a very good business. And if you have to have a prayer session before raising the price by 10 percent, then you've got a terrible business." Buffett also believes that truly great businesses don't require good management, and he sometimes doesn't even consider who's in charge when he makes an investment!

Source: Andrew Frye and Dakin Campbell, "Buffett: Not Much Stock in Who Runs Company," *The Seattle Times*, February 19, 2011, p. A 15.

Decision Making/ Incremental Analysis

Consider a situation faced by Premier Lens Company, which manufactures camera lenses. Its lenses are sold through camera shops with a variety of mounting adapters to fit most popular 35-millimeter digital cameras. Recently, Blix Camera has asked Premier to produce 20,000 lenses for its compact 35-millimeter digital camera. The lens is identical to the Model A lens that Premier currently sells for $85. However, the model to be produced will substitute the Blix name for the Premier name stamped on the lens.

In the past year, Premier sold 280,000 units of the Model A. However, the company has been operating at only 75 percent of practical capacity and can easily accommodate production of the 20,000 additional units. The standard cost of producing the Model A is $75.

Model A Lens Standard Unit Cost

Direct material	$30.00
Direct labor	15.00
Variable overhead	10.00
Fixed overhead	20.00
Total	$75.00

Blix Camera has offered to buy the 20,000 lenses for $73 each. Since the total standard cost is $75, it appears that the special order should be turned down. However, the incremental analysis presented in Illustration 8-2 indicates that the special order will make a substantial contribution to company income.

The special-order decision presents two alternatives: accept or reject the special order. Since the income from the main business is the same under both alternatives, it is *not incremental* and need not be considered in the decision. The most obvious incremental item is the revenue associated with the special order. If Premier accepts the order, its revenue will increase by $1,460,000. In addition, direct material, direct labor, and variable overhead will increase by $1,100,000 if the special order is accepted. These costs are incremental, because they will be incurred if the special order is accepted and they will not be incurred if the special order is not accepted. Since incremental revenue exceeds incremental cost by $360,000, it appears to be quite beneficial to accept the special order.

ILLUSTRATION 8-2
Incremental analysis of special lens order

Incremental revenue (20,000 × $73)		$1,460,000
Less incremental costs:		
Direct material (20,000 × $30)	$600,000	
Direct labor (20,000 × $15)	300,000	
Variable overhead (20,000 × $10)	200,000	1,100,000
Net benefit of special order		$ 360,000

Note that in the calculation of the net benefit of accepting the special order, none of the fixed costs of production is considered to be incremental costs. This is because these costs will be incurred whether the special order is accepted or not. This assumption seems reasonable given that the Premier Lens Company has excess capacity. However, suppose the management of Premier anticipates some increase in fixed costs if the special order is accepted. By how much could fixed costs increase before acceptance of the special order would be inadvisable? As long as fixed costs increase by less than $360,000, the excess of incremental revenue over incremental cost, acceptance of the special order will increase company income.

TEST YOUR KNOWLEDGE

Which of the following is true?

a. In pricing special orders, fixed costs typically are not relevant.

b. In pricing special orders, fixed costs typically are relevant.

Correct answer is a.

LEARNING OBJECTIVE 2

Explain the cost-plus approach to pricing and why it is inherently circular for manufacturing firms. Also, explain the target costing process for a new product.

COST-PLUS PRICING

Perhaps in part because of the difficulty of estimating demand functions, many companies use so-called **cost-plus pricing**. With a cost-plus approach, the company starts with an estimate of product cost (typically excluding any selling or adminstrative costs) and adds a markup to arrive at a price that allows for a reasonable level of profit. To illustrate cost-plus pricing, suppose the Chicago Pump Company produces a variety of pumps used in the mining industry. The company has recently introduced the Model L50 pump. To produce the pump, the company must incur $1,000,000 of annual fixed costs and variable costs of $200 per unit. The company estimates that it can sell 10,000 pumps annually and marks up cost by 30 percent. In this case, as indicated in the top section of Illustration 8-3, the price will be $390 per unit, which includes total cost of $300 and markup of $90.

The obvious advantage of a cost-plus pricing approach is that it is simple to apply. Also, if a sufficient quantity can be sold at the specified price, the company will earn a reasonable profit. However, the approach also has limitations.

ILLUSTRATION 8-3
Cost-plus pricing for Model L50 pump

Estimated quantity demanded in units	10,000
Total fixed costs	$1,000,000
Fixed costs per unit ($1,000,000 ÷ 10,000)	$100
Variable costs per unit	200
Total cost per unit	300
Markup at 30%	90
Price	$390
Suppose the actual quantity demanded is less (say 9,000 units)	9,000
Total fixed costs	$1,000,000
Fixed costs per unit ($1,000,000 ÷ 9,000)	$111
Variable costs per unit	200
Total cost per unit	311
Markup at 30%	93
Price	$404

An obvious difficulty is choosing what markup percent to use. Is 30 percent an appropriate markup, or should 10 percent, 20 percent, or 40 percent be used? Determination of an appropriate markup requires considerable judgment, and experimentation with different markups may be necessary before a final decision is reached.

Another problem is that cost-plus pricing is inherently circular for manufacturing firms.[2] You must estimate demand to determine fixed manufacturing cost per unit so that you can mark up cost to obtain a price. However, the price affects the quantity demanded; the higher the price, the lower the quantity demanded for most products. What would happen if demand for the Model L50 pump produced by Chicago Pump actually turned out to be 9,000 units? In this case, the cost per pump, as indicated in the bottom half of Illustration 8-3, would increase (because fixed costs would be spread over fewer units) and the price would be increased to $404. But what will happen to the quantity demanded when the price is increased? That's right, fewer units will be purchased, the cost per unit will go up, and the cost-plus price will be increased, resulting in lower demand! This circular process (increased price, decreased demand, increased cost per unit, increased price) is obviously not a strategy used by successful companies.

ANY **QUESTIONS?**

Q: When I was shopping at an office supply store the other day, I noticed that many product prices end in 99. For example, printer paper sold for $39.99 a case, ballpoint pens were $7.99 per dozen, and message books were $4.99 each. Why the focus on 99?

A: Most managers believe that human nature has a significant impact on purchase decisions. And human nature, some believe, makes consumers treat certain digits as extraneous information. Take the case of the paper selling for $39.99 a case. Conventional wisdom is that although the price is very close to $40 per case, consumers will ignore the 99 and simply classify the price as being in the $30 range. Alternatively, some managers think that a price ending in 99 makes a product look like it's on sale and, therefore, more attractive to consumers.

LINK TO **PRACTICE**

Pricing Treasure Hunt Items at Costco

Costco has around 4,000 items at each warehouse store. Generally, 3,000 are there every day and 1,000 are referred to as "treasure hunt" items. These items are constantly changing and lead consumers to think they'd better buy them while they're shopping or they'll miss out on a great deal. According to Jim Sinegal, past CEO of Costco, consumers recognize that a Coach handbag (a treasure hunt type item) selling for $159 is a great deal since it would be $300 at a department store. Treasure hunt items keep customers coming back and create a positive buzz among consumers.

Source: Brendan Byrnes, "Jim Sinegal on Costco's Pricing Magic," *The Motley Fool* (August 8, 2013).

[2]Cost-plus pricing is not inherently circular for retail firms. Such firms typically mark up the cost of merchandise from suppliers, which is a variable cost. They do not mark up fixed cost per unit, which would require an estimate of the quantity demanded *before* setting price.

TARGET COSTING

Manufacturing companies are always searching for ways to cut costs. Unfortunately, once a new product is designed (the product's features are specified, detailed engineering plans are made, and manufacturing of the product is ready to commence), it is very difficult to make changes that will reduce costs. In fact, it is commonly accepted that 80 percent of a product's costs cannot be reduced once it is designed. The primary reason for this state of affairs is that product features drive costs. Consider the case of KC Home Appliances. The company is bringing a new coffeemaker to market designed with an automatic burr grinder, a water filter, and a stainless steel carafe that keeps coffee warm for 6 hours. These features will largely determine the cost of manufacturing the coffeepot, and it will be very difficult to reduce them once the coffeepot is being produced. Indeed, costs related to purchases of equipment to produce the grinders, filters, and carafes are sunk costs and cannot be changed.

To confront this difficulty, a number of companies have turned to **target costing**, which is an integrated approach to determining product features, product price, product cost, and product design that helps ensure a company will earn a reasonable profit on new products. The target costing process is presented in Illustration 8-4. The process

ILLUSTRATION 8-4
The target costing process

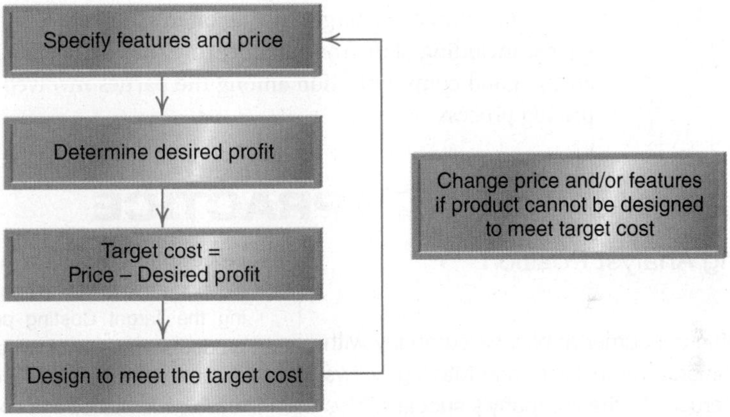

LINK TO PRACTICE

Insull's Most Radical Innovation Wasn't Technology—It Was Pricing!

Samuel Insull was Thomas Edison's right-hand business partner, taking care of financing, operations, hirings, firings, and mergers. In 1892, he left his position with Edison and became the president of a small electricity producer. The problem for the company back then, as it is for many companies today, was the mismatch between capacity and spikes in demand during peak usage hours. Insull solved that problem by charging different rates to consumers to boost demand when usage tended to be slow, primarily in the evenings when companies were shut down for the night. It was obvious that Insull was charging consumers less than the average cost per kilowatt-hour. But Insull knew that he was building demand and that the fixed cost per hour would drop, making huge power stations feasible and profitable.

Sir Harold Evans, the author of *They Made America* (Little, Brown, 2004), refers to this action as "the single most significant innovation in the single most important technological advance of the 20th century." By 1898 Insull had bought out all the power generators in downtown Chicago. Fifteen years later his company, then known as Commonwealth Edison, had become the dominant energy company in the Midwest.

Source: Nicholas G. Carr, "Suits to the Rescue," *Strategy + Business*, Spring 2005, pp. 26–29.

ILLUSTRATION 8-5
Target cost of KC Home Appliances's new coffeemaker

Quantity demanded given features	50,000 units
Price given features	$200
Required profit margin per unit (30% × $200)	60
Target cost	$140

begins with a careful analysis of competing products and customer needs and wants. This leads to a specification of product features and a price that the company believes will be attractive to customers, given the product features. Suppose KC Home Appliances determines that, given the features of its new coffeemaker, it can sell 50,000 units per year at $200 each. The second step in the target costing process is to specify a desired level of profit. Suppose that KC wants a profit margin of 30 percent or, alternatively, a profit of $60. The price and the desired profit determine the target cost, which is $140 (see Illustration 8-5). Finally, the product engineering department, working with substantial input from the cost accounting department, develops a detailed design for a product that can be produced for $140 or less. If the product cannot be produced for $140 per unit, then the company will reconsider features and price. For example, the company may decide to slightly lower its price and go with a plastic carafe as opposed to a more expensive stainless steel carafe.

Companies using target costing often set up cross-functional product development teams, including staff from engineering, marketing, and cost accounting. This helps ensure good communication among the parties involved in the product development/pricing process.

LINK TO **PRACTICE**

Target Costing Analyst Position at Whirlpool

Whirlpool, a leading consumer appliance company with brands such as Amana, KitchenAid, and Maytag, views target costing as crucial to the company's success. This is clear from reading an ad placed online for a product target costing analyst:

> The Product Target Costing Analyst will be a highly visible position, reporting to the Product Target Costing Manager. This role will focus on assisting project teams in the logical and systematic conversion of customer or product requirements into total affordable system solutions through the administration of the Target Costing process and necessary analytical support. The Target Costing analyst will have a working knowledge of applying the Target Costing process for new and existing products and will provide support to project analysis tasks to facilitate the process enabling project teams to reach performance and cost targets.
>
> Excellent communication and teaming skills will be required for the necessary interfacing with Project Management and counterparts/management in Marketing, GCD, Finance, Engineering, Manufacturing and Procurement. The desired outcome is the initiation of a world-class Target Costing process enabling sustainable competitive advantage in product cost.

Source: Posted on Jobing.com, January 22, 2012.

LEARNING OBJECTIVE 3
Analyze customer profitability, and explain the activity-based pricing approach.

ANALYZING CUSTOMER PROFITABILITY: REVISITING THE PRICED RIGHT OFFICE SUPPLIES CASE

Recall that in the chapter opener, Nancy Sanchez, vice president of Priced Right Office Supplies, wanted to know the profitability of various customers as a basis for setting prices and targeting marketing campaigns. To accomplish her objective, she needs a **customer profitability measurement (CPM) system**. With a CPM system, the indirect

ILLUSTRATION 8-6

Graphical presentation of customer profitability measurement

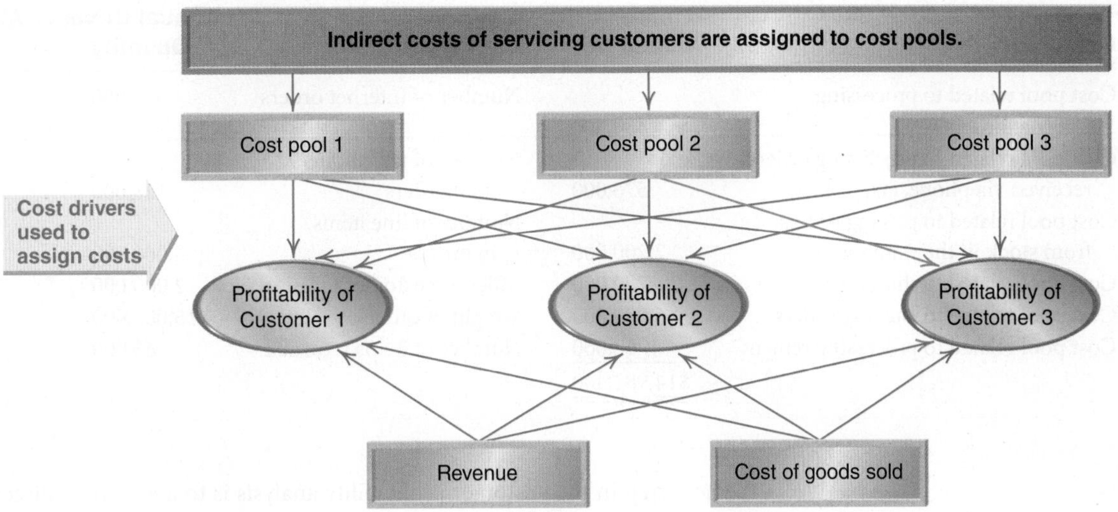

costs of servicing customers (including the cost of processing orders, the cost of handling returns, the cost of shipments, etc.) are assigned to cost pools. Using cost drivers, these costs are then allocated to specific customers. Subtracting these costs and product costs from customer revenue yields a measure of customer profitability. A graphical presentation of CPM is presented in Illustration 8-6.

You probably notice a connection between activity-based costing (ABC) presented in Chapter 6 and CPM. In Chapter 6, we used ABC to allocate costs to products and services. In this section, we're going to use ABC to allocate costs to customers so that we can determine the full cost of serving them. To facilitate our discussion of customer profitability measurement, we will consider the situation facing Nancy Sanchez at Priced Right Office Supplies. Assuming her company has a reasonably sophisticated computerized information system, it can easily trace sales revenue and cost of goods sold to individual customers. The challenging task will be to trace the indirect costs of serving customers to individual customers.[3]

Suppose the team that investigated CPM at Priced Right Office Supplies determined the cost pools and cost drivers indicated in Illustration 8-7. In total, indirect costs amount to $14,982,400 per year. The first two cost pools relate to the costs of processing Internet orders versus orders placed by phone, fax, or mail. Note that the cost per Internet order is substantially less ($1.20 per order versus $4.50 per order). The next cost pool relates to the costs incurred in picking orders from stock in the warehouse. More time is spent as the number of different items in the order increases since different items are stored in different locations in the warehouse, and each line on an order form relates to a specific item. Thus, the cost driver is the number of line items in an order. The final three cost pools relate to shipping and packing orders and processing returned merchandise.

[3]See L. Brem and V. G. Narayanan. "Owens and Minor (A) and (B)," *Harvard Business School Cases* (2000) for a description of customer profitability measurement at the company Owens and Minor. These cases also discuss an activity-based pricing system that we will cover at the end of this chapter.

ILLUSTRATION 8-7

Cost pools and drivers for indirect costs to service customers at Priced Right Office Supplies

Cost Pools	Annual Cost	Cost Driver	Annual Driver Quantity	Allocation Rate
Cost pool related to processing Internet orders	$ 434,400	Number of Internet orders	362,000	$1.20
Cost pool related to processing orders received via phone, fax, or mail	576,000	Number of fax/phone/ mail orders	128,000	$4.50
Cost pool related to picking orders from stock in the warehouse	7,200,000	Number of line items in orders	8,000,000	$0.90
Cost pool related to shipping	720,000	Miles to customer location	2,000,000	$0.36
Cost pool related to packing orders	6,000,000	Weight of order	15,000,000	$0.40
Cost pool related to processing returns	52,000	Number of items returned	65,000	$0.80
	$14,982,400			

The next step in the customer profitability analysis is to apply the indirect costs to specific customers. Consider the two customers analyzed in Illustration 8-8. Although Customers 1 and 2 have about the same level of sales, Customer 2 imposes more than twice as much indirect costs on Priced Right Office Supplies ($8,294 for Customer 2 versus $3,498 for Customer 1). This results because Customer 2 places more orders and uses

ILLUSTRATION 8-8

Customer profitability analysis for two customers

Customer 1		
Revenue		$732,600
Less cost of goods sold		666,000
Gross margin		66,600
Less indirect costs:		
165 Internet orders × $1.20	$ 198	
20 fax orders × $4.50	90	
2,500 line items × $0.90	2,250	
1,200 miles × $0.36	432	
900 pounds × $0.40	360	
210 items returned × $0.80	168	3,498
Customer profit		$ 63,102
Profit as a percent of sales		8.61%
Customer 2		
Revenue		$727,650
Less cost of goods sold		661,500
Gross margin		66,150
Less indirect costs:		
0 Internet orders × $1.20	$ -0-	
320 fax orders × $4.50	1,440	
5,100 line items × $0.90	4,590	
3,300 miles × $0.36	1,188	
870 pounds × $0.40	348	
910 items returned × $0.80	728	8,294
Customer profit		$ 57,850
Profit as a percent of sales		7.95%

LINK TO PRACTICE

How to Fix Unprofitable Customers

Before giving up on unprofitable customers, a company should consider ways to "fix" them. Here are three suggestions from Jiwoong Shin and K. Sudhir, professors at the Yale School of Management:

1. *Reduce services.* For example, for low profitability customers, the Royal Bank of Canada will conduct a check trace taking 3 to 5 days. The same service for a more profitable customer is 1 day.
2. *Charge fees for costly services.* For example, some banks now charge for paper statements while online statements are free.
3. *Educate customers to use less-costly services.* Discuss with customers how ordering in small batches, requesting expedited deliveries, and cancelling orders all increase supplier costs. Such discussion may lead to avoidance of these behaviors.

Source: Jiwoong Shin and K. Sudhir, "Should You Punish or Reward Current Customers?" *MIT Sloan Management Review* (Fall, 2013).

the more costly fax method rather than the Internet. Customer 2 also orders a greater variety of items (indicated by its 5,100 line items), which leads to higher order-picking costs. Finally, more miles are traveled to deliver orders for Customer 2, and Customer 2 returns more merchandise.

Priced Right Office Supplies could perform the same analysis for all of its customers and then sort them into groups based on their relative profitability. The most profitable customers may receive special treatment (e.g., occasional calls/visits from the president of Priced Right Office Supplies, special discounts or promotions, etc.) to ensure their continued business. The company may also study the characteristics of the most profitable customers in an effort to gain a better understanding of how to expand business to similar customers. With respect to the least profitable customers, the company may increase prices, try to move them to less costly service (e.g., require that they place orders over the Internet ordering system), or even drop them.

TEST YOUR KNOWLEDGE

A customer profitability measurement (CPM) system:

a. Allocates indirect costs to individual customers.
b. Traces revenue to individual customers.
c. Traces cost of goods sold to individual customers.
d. All of these answer choices are correct.

Correct answer is d.

LINK TO PRACTICE

Sprint Drops Customers for Excessive Use of Customer Service

In some cases, customer profitability is negatively impacted by customers making an excessive number of calls to customer service. Sprint Nextel, the nation's third largest wireless service provider, identified 1,000 customers who were making an average of 25 calls to customer service per month. That rate is 40 times higher than average. After identifying the customers, Sprint "fired" them! In a letter to the customers, Sprint stated, "The number of inquiries you have made to us . . . has led us to determine that we are unable to meet your current wireless needs."

Source: Samar Srivastava, "Sprint Drops Clients over Excessive Inquires," *Wall Street Journal*, July 7, 2007, p. A3.

TEST YOUR KNOWLEDGE

Which type of customer is likely to be more profitable?

a. Customer A makes frequent small purchases each month of many different items via faxed orders.

b. Customer B makes major purchases of a few items each month via the Internet.

Correct answer is b.

CUSTOMER PROFITABILITY AND PERFORMANCE MEASURES

YOU GET WHAT YOU MEASURE

To focus the attention of managers on improving customer profitability, companies need to use performance measures. Remember, as we've said many times, "You get what you measure!"

Here are some examples of performance measures that will grab the attention of managers and drive them to improve customer profitability:

- Percent of customers who are not profitable
- Dollar loss for customers who are not profitable
- Average profit per customer
- Number of customer service requests per 100 customers
- Percent of customers who return items
- Dollar value of returned merchandise

Consider the measure *percent of customers who return items*. If this measure is highly visible and recognized as important, managers will try to reduce it, which in turn, will improve the profitability of customers. But how do you reduce returns? One approach may be to train sales people so that they sell the right products to meet customers' needs. Or processes may need to be improved in the fulfillment system to ensure that orders are filled correctly.

ACTIVITY-BASED PRICING

The same type of information used to analyze customer profitability can form the basis for an activity-based pricing system. Essentially, **activity-based pricing** is an approach to pricing in which customers are presented with separate prices for services they request in addition to the cost of goods they purchase. This causes customers to carefully consider the services they request and may lead them to impose less cost on their suppliers. Some companies refer to activity-based pricing as menu-based pricing since customers are presented with a menu of prices related to the various services they request in addition to the products they purchase.

Let's see how an activity-based pricing system might work at Priced Right Office Supplies. Suppose that, based on the study of indirect costs presented in Illustration 8-7, the company set the prices for services indicated in Illustration 8-9. As you can see, the company proposes to charge customers $1.25 for every order placed via the Internet whereas phone, fax, or mail orders are priced at $4.75 per order. Each line item in an order is associated with picking an item from the warehouse, and the company charges $1 for this activity. Delivery charges are $0.40 per mile ($0.04 higher than cost), packing

ILLUSTRATION 8-9
Activity-based pricing for indirect cost at Priced Right Office Supplies

Charge for Internet orders	$1.25
Charge for phone, fax, or mail orders	$4.75
Charge per line item in an order	$1.00
Delivery charge per mile	$0.40
Packing charge per pound	$0.50
Per item restocking charge for returned merchandise	$1.00

is $0.50 per pound ($0.10 higher than cost), and the company charges $1 to restock a returned item ($0.20 higher than cost).

Some customers might object to this pricing scheme, arguing that the price they pay for the goods they purchase should cover these costs. There are a number of ways to deal with this resistance. The company could lower its prices for goods (at least slightly) and then encourage customers to make fewer but larger purchases to reduce their overall costs. Customers could also be encouraged to limit the variety of goods they purchase, since variety leads to separate line items on order forms and higher cost (e.g., does the customer really need 10 different pens in four different colors?). Alternatively, the company might decide just to use the activity-based pricing approach for its less profitable customers. Then the most profitable customers, who are still paying just for the goods they purchase, will perceive that they are getting a "break" because they are valued customers. And the least profitable customers will be paying for the extra costs they impose on the company.

Decision Making INSIGHT

When making a pricing decision about a product you manufacture, don't get overly focused on the current cost per unit. The quantity demanded is affected by the price, and this quantity changes the cost per unit because fixed costs are spread out over more or fewer units.

Ideally, you want to determine the price that maximizes profit. The profit-maximizing approach we learned in this chapter can be difficult to implement because of difficulty in estimating the relation between the quantity demanded and price. However, at a minimum, it provides a useful framework for thinking about pricing decisions since it takes into account price, demand, variable costs, and fixed costs.

SUMMARY OF LEARNING OBJECTIVES

LEARNING OBJECTIVE 1 Compute the profit-maximizing price for a product or service, and perform incremental analysis related to pricing a special order.

The first step in computing the profit-maximizing price is to estimate the quantity demanded at various prices. Then subtract variable costs from price to determine the contribution margin per unit. From the total contribution margin, subtract fixed costs to determine profit. The price that yields the highest profit is the profit-maximizing price.

Special orders will yield an incremental profit as long as the selling price exceeds the incremental cost of filling the order. Fixed costs that are not affected by the special order are irrelevant to the decision as to whether the order should be taken.

LEARNING OBJECTIVE 2 Explain the cost-plus approach to pricing and why it is inherently circular for manufacturing firms. Also, explain the target costing process for a new product.

In cost-plus pricing, the full cost per unit is determined and price is set by adding a prespecified markup to the cost. This process is circular for manufacturing firms in that the quantity demanded, which is needed to estimate full cost per unit, is determined prior to setting the price, which has a major impact on the quantity demanded.

Using target costing, companies analyze the marketplace and decide on a set of features and a price point for their product. They subtract a desired profit level from the price to solve for the target cost. The product is then designed to meet the target cost when it is produced. If the target cost cannot be achieved, the company may reconsider the set of features and the price or decide not to go ahead with the product.

LEARNING OBJECTIVE 3 Analyze customer profitability, and explain the activity-based pricing approach.

The profitability of a customer depends not just on what is purchased but also on the set of services provided to the customer (e.g., order processing, shipping, handling returns, etc.). To analyze the profitability of a customer, the cost of such services must be subtracted from the customer's gross margin. This requires that service costs must be grouped into cost pools and related cost drivers must be identified so that the cost per unit of service can be allocated to specific customers.

In activity-based pricing, customers are presented with a menu of prices and are charged for *services* provided to them (in addition to being charged for the goods they purchase). The charge for such services usually is determined based on an analysis of their costs. Since they are charged for specific services, customers will carefully consider the services they request and may end up imposing less cost on suppliers.

REVIEW PROBLEM 1

Heartland Tools is a large Midwest company that designs and manufactures dies, jigs, fixtures, roll-form tooling, and special machines. Equipment used by the company includes milling machines, HeliArc welders, drill presses, hydraulic presses, and heat treatment ovens. Due to intense competition from foreign companies, the firm currently has substantial excess capacity, and in the prior year, the company laid off 545 employees.

To price its product, the company estimates design and product costs and marks the total up by 40 percent to cover administrative and marketing costs and to earn a profit. Product costs include material, labor, depreciation of equipment, and other overhead. The costs in the "other overhead" cost pool are primarily fixed costs.

Costs are estimated as follows:

1. Design costs	Based on estimated engineering hours times a rate of $40 per hour.
2. Material	Estimate of the actual cost of materials.
3. Labor	Estimate of actual direct labor costs (estimate of actual hours multiplied by the wage rate of employees likely to be assigned to the job).
4. Depreciation of manufacturing equipment	Based on predetermined overhead rates for each type of equipment. For each type of equipment, the company divides estimated annual depreciation by estimated annual hours of use.

Equipment Type	Annual Depreciation	Annual Hours of Use
Milling	$6,000,000	4,000
Welding	$2,000,000	8,000
Drill press	$1,000,000	5,000
Hydraulic press	$4,000,000	4,000
Heat treatment	$5,000,000	4,000

5. Other manufacturing overhead (i.e., other than depreciation)	Estimated as $50 per direct labor hour.

The company is currently pricing a job for Preston Manufacturing. A preliminary bid form indicates the following:

Preliminary/Incomplete Cost Estimate and Bid for Preston Manufacturing

Material		$25,000
Direct labor	28 hours × $25	$ 700
	15 hours × $18	$ 270
	25 hours × $30	$ 750
Design time	18 hours	
Milling time	9.0 hours	
Welding time	5.0 hours	
Drill press time	7.0 hours	
Hydraulic press time	6.5 hours	
Heat treat time	2.0 hours	
Other overhead		______
Estimated total cost		______
Markup at 40%		______
Bid		______

REQUIRED

a. Estimate total cost and the bid price with the 40 percent markup.

b. Preston has told Heartland that it will use another supplier if Heartland's bid is over $50,000. Heartland's CFO strongly objects to a $50,000 price since it will not even cover full costs. Evaluate the CFO's position. Should the company price the job at $50,000?

ANSWER

a. Cost-Plus Price for Preston Manufacturing

Material			$25,000
Direct labor	28 hours × $25	$ 700	
	15 hours × $18	270	
	25 hours × $30	750	1,720
Design time	18 hours × $40		720
Milling time	9.0 hours × $1,500	13,500	
Welding time	5.0 hours × $250	1,250	
Drill press time	7.0 hours × $200	1,400	
Hydraulic press time	6.5 hours × $1,000	6,500	
Heat treatment time	2.0 hours × $1,250	2,500	25,150
Other overhead	68 direct labor hours × $50		$ 3,400
Estimated total cost			$55,990
Markup at 40%			22,396
Bid			$78,386

Equipment Type	Annual Depreciation	Annual House of Use	Overhead Rate
Milling	$6,000,000	4,000	$1,500
Welding	$2,000,000	8,000	$ 250
Drill press	$1,000,000	5,000	$ 200
Hydraulic press	$4,000,000	4,000	$1,000
Heat treatment	$5,000,000	4,000	$1,250

b. It appears that the only costs that are likely to be incremental are those related to design, material, and labor. Assuming this is the case, the company will generate an incremental profit of $22,560 at a price of $50,000. Given that the company is operating below capacity (and assuming this "low" price does not negatively impact future prices to Preston or other customers), charging $50,000 for the job is a good decision.

Incremental revenue		$50,000
Incremental costs		
Design costs	$ 720	
Material	25,000	
Direct labor	1,720	27,440
Incremental profit		$22,560

REVIEW PROBLEM 2

Automated Packaging Solutions is a distributor of high-speed packaging systems that include conveyor belts, automated wrapping equipment, box loading systems, and other high-speed equipment. The following steps are required for a "typical" order:

1. Meet with customer to determine requirements.
2. Design a preliminary system.
3. Meet with customer to discuss the preliminary system.
4. Revise design and fax to customer for final approval.
5. Pick components from stock or source from suppliers.
6. Ship to customer.
7. Supply installation service as required. Note that some customers perform the installation with no help from Automated Packaging Solutions.

While this is a "typical" sequence, some customers simply place orders to replace broken components or for specific components needed to upgrade their systems. In these cases, no design work is needed.

Currently, the company prices most orders to achieve a 30 percent gross margin [(Sales − Component costs) ÷ Sales = 30%]. Put another way, the company marks up component cost by 1.42857. However, the company vice president of marketing, Paxton Taylor, recently attended a seminar on customer profitability measurement. She is concerned that the approach may be severely limiting the company's financial performance. According to the seminar presenter, the cost-plus approach has a major flaw:

> Cost-plus assumes that each customer imposes costs on your company in proportion to product costs. That's simply not true. Some customers are great—they buy a product, use it, and come back for more. Others, well, you know the problem customers. They buy a product, return it, ask for a redesign, want their order to be expedited and then they want a ton of customer service. You need to identify these customers and then "fire them" or charge them for the value-added services they demand.

The seminar convinced Paxton that the time was right to implement an activity-based costing approach to measure customer profitability. She got agreement from the company president and the CFO and signed an agreement with Activity Analysis Consulting (AAC) to have Brian Hart, a senior consultant, design a customer profitability measurement (CPM) system.

Paxton was amazed that Brian and his AAC staff were able to develop the CPM system in only 3 days. On the first day, Brian explained the idea of CPM and interviewed employees to determine key activities and how much time they spend on them. On the second day, Brian finalized a set of cost pools and drivers and allocated costs to the pools (see Exhibit 1). On the third day, the AAC staff designed an Excel-based template that Automated Packaging Systems can use to calculate the profitability of any customer. Later the next week, Brian presented an analysis of three customers using the new tool (see Exhibit 2).

EXHIBIT 1

Cost pools and drivers

Activities	Annual Cost	Driver	Driver Quantity	Cost per Driver Unit
Order processing	$ 637,859	No. of orders	16,258	$39.234
Pulling parts from stock	1,485,648	No. of parts picked	113,806	13.054
Shipping	1,405,793	No. of orders	16,258	86.468
Expediting	304,430	No. of expedited orders	4,177	72.882
Problem order activities	104,500	No. of problem orders	2,363	44.223
Engineering	482,351	No. of engineering hours	10,380	46.469
Installation activities	90,879	Hours of installation	1,985	45.783
Business sustaining activities	1,015,650	No. of orders	16,258	62.471
Total overhead	**$5,527,110**			

Order processing. Includes labor, depreciation of office equipment, depreciation of building, etc.

Pulling parts from stock. Includes labor, depreciation of equipment, depreciation of warehouse, etc.

Shipping. Includes labor related to packing orders and loading trucks, depreciation of forklift trucks, and payment to shipper.

Expediting. Includes premium for air and next day shipping.

Problem order activities. Estimate calculated as Total wages paid to customer service representatives × Percent of time they spend on "problem orders".

Engineering. Includes labor, drafting supplies, depreciation of computers, software, etc.

Installation activities. Includes labor used for installations and expenses related to small tools.

Business sustaining activities. Includes all costs other than cost of components and the seven other cost pools. Items include executive salaries, accounting and legal expenses, depreciation of the office building and furniture and fixtures, etc.

EXHIBIT 2

Analysis of three customers

Customer Profitability Analysis

	Customer A	Customer B	Customer C
Actual customer sales	$25,000.00	$15,000.00	$2,000.00
Cost of goods sold	17,500.00	10,500.00	1,400.00
Gross margin	7,500.00	4,500.00	600.00
Gross margin percent	30%	30%	30%
Other Cost Drivers			
Order processing	1	2	4
Pulling parts from stock	30	10	4
Shipping	1	2	4
Expediting	—	—	4
Problem order activities	1	—	—
Engineering	102	6	—
Installation activities	20	10	—
Business sustaining activities	1	2	4
Other costs	6,279.51	1,243.53	1,096.44
ABC customer profitability	$ 1,220.49	$ 3,256.47	($ 496.44)
Profit percent of sales	4.88%	21.71%	–24.82%

Note:

Customer A purchased a single, relatively complex system.

Customer B purchased two relatively simple systems.

Customer C purchased single components on four occasions to replace broken parts. The customer requested expediting to get their system up and running as quickly as possible.

REQUIRED

a. Show the details of the calculation of the "other costs" (amounting to $6,279.51) for Customer A.

b. Paxton Taylor recently stated that she "now knows the true costs of serving each customer." Is this the case? What does the term *true cost* mean to Paxton? What *should* the term mean?

c. Paxton has now reviewed the profitability of each customer, and she finds that they generally fit into one of three categories:

- Customers purchasing large, complex systems (like Customer A) whose profit as a percent of sales ranges from 3 to 7 percent
- Customers purchasing relatively simple systems (like Customer B) whose profit as a percent of sales ranges from 15 to 25 percent and
- Customers purchasing one or two components (like Customer C) who generate a negative profit

Next week, Paxton will have a meeting with Bill Ruben, CFO, to discuss the analysis. She believes that Bill will recommend dropping sales to customers who purchase only one or two components, and she believes that this action will increase company profit.

Do you agree that profit will increase if the company drops Customer C types? Explain.

d. Suppose that at the meeting, Bill Ruben recommends not only dropping Customer C types but also phasing out sales to Customer A types so that more attention can be paid to the "sweet spot" (i.e., Customer B types).

1. Why might Bill's recommendation hurt the profitability of Automated Packaging Solutions?

2. What type of analysis would you suggest be performed prior to adopting Bill's recommendation? Be specific as to what exactly the analysis will involve.

ANSWER

a.

Order processing	$ 39.23 (1 × $39.234)
Pulling	391.62 (30 × $13.054)
Shipping	86.47 (1 × $86.468)
Expediting	—
Problem order	44.22 (1 × $44.223)
Engineering	4,739.84 (102 × $46.469)
Installation	915.66 (20 × $45.783)
Business sustaining	62.47 (1 × $62.471)
Total	$6,279.51

b. True cost is a very nebulous term. There is no "true cost" applicable to all decisions. There is, however, a true incremental cost applicable to each specific decision. Paxton most likely means she has a better full cost number where "better" is still a bit vague.

c. The cost associated with Customer C is:

Order processing	$ 156.94
Pulling	52.22
Shipping	345.87
Expediting	291.53
Problem order	—
Engineering	—
Installation	—
Business sustaining	249.88
Total	$1,096.44

Some of these costs (especially business-sustaining and some order processing costs) will not go away if the business is dropped. More importantly, if the company doesn't supply parts (that's what C ordered), then they may lose type A and B sales. This suggests keeping C customers—perhaps with increased prices for shipping and expediting.

d. 1. The company may enter a cost allocation death spiral. Much of the costs allocated to A and C don't go away and are allocated to B. In other words, the company may lose more revenue than it gains in cost savings.

2. Not surprisingly, an incremental analysis should be performed. The company needs to calculate:

- Lost revenue from A and C
- Cost savings from dropping A and C
- Incremental effect on B sales
- Incremental effect on B costs

KEY TERMS

Activity-based pricing (306)
Cost-plus pricing (299)
Customer profitability measurement (CPM) system (302)
Target costing (301)

SELF-ASSESSMENT (Answers Below)

1. To determine the profit-maximizing price, a manager must:

a. Estimate the quantity demanded for various prices.
b. Estimate variable costs.
c. Estimate both the quantity demanded for various prices and variable costs.
d. None of these answer choices is correct.

2. Cost-plus pricing:

a. Leads to profit maximization.
b. Is inherently circular for manufacturing firms.
c. Is difficult to perform.
d. None of these answer choices is correct.

3. Target costing:

a. Requires specification of desired level of profit.
b. Targets specific costs for reduction.
c. Is used primarily with products that are already in production.
d. Leads to profit maximization.

4. Customer profitability is measured as:

a. Revenue – Cost of goods sold.
b. Revenue – Indirect manufacturing costs.
c. Revenue – Cost of goods sold – Indirect service costs.
d. Revenue – Cost of goods sold – Indirect manufacturing costs.

5. With activity-based pricing:

a. Customers face a menu of prices for various services.
b. Customers are encouraged to consider the costs they impose on a supplier.
c. Customers may be charged less if they request less product variety in their orders.
d. All of these answer choices are correct.

6. The formula for target cost is:

a. Price – Desired profit.
b. Desired profit ÷ Price.
c. Absorption cost × Profit percentage.
d. Desired profit – Absorption cost.

7. Typically, which departments are involved in setting target costs?

a. Engineering.
b. Marketing.
c. Cost accounting.
d. All of these answer choices are correct.

8. Which of the following is an advantage of cost-plus pricing?

a. The selection of a markup percent is easily done.
b. The method is simple to apply.
c. The cost-plus pricing method is inherently circular.
d. All of these are advantages to the cost-plus pricing method.

9. When is it beneficial for companies to accept an order that is priced at less than the product's full cost?

a. When the company is operating at capacity.
b. When incremental revenue exceeds incremental cost.
c. It is always advantageous to have higher sales.
d. It is never beneficial to accept an order that is priced below full cost.

10. Cost-plus pricing includes which of the following costs?

a. Manufacturing costs.
b. Selling costs.
c. Administrative costs.
d. All of these costs are included in cost-plus pricing.

ANSWERS TO SELF-ASSESSMENT

1. c **2.** b **3.** a **4.** c **5.** d **6.** a **7.** d **8.** b **9.** b **10.** a

QUESTIONS

1. According to economic theory, how would a manager determine the profit-maximizing price for a product or service?
2. Why is cost-plus pricing inherently circular for a manufacturing firm?
3. To implement target costing for a new product, companies often set up a cross-functional team with members from engineering, marketing, and cost accounting. Why is a cross-functional team desirable when implementing the target costing approach?
4. How is cost allocation used in customer profitability analysis?
5. Explain why less profitable customers may become more profitable if a supplier switches to activity-based pricing.
6. Explain the target costing process. How is it calculated?
7. Explain how the profit-maximizing price is calculated. Why is the profit-maximizing price extremely difficult to calculate for an actual product?
8. What is a "special order"? How does whether a company is operating at capacity or not matter in deciding whether to accept the special order?
9. What are the disadvantages of the cost-plus approach to pricing?
10. What is the lowest per unit price on a special order that a company could accept and still not show a loss from the special order?

EXERCISES

GROUP WORK

EXERCISE 8-1. [LO 1, 2] Consider a company that manufactures and sells personal computers (let's call the company Bell Computers). Recently the company lowered its prices dramatically. The company is very efficient and needs only 5 days of inventory, collects its receivables within 30 days, and has suppliers who are willing to wait 59 days for payment. A competitor commenting on the aggressive pricing stated, "We're in a commodity business, and a price war in a commodity business is really dumb."

REQUIRED

Discuss the competitor's comment that lowering prices is a dumb move by Bell Computers.

WRITING

EXERCISE 8-2. [LO 3] The Brindle Corporation is considering an initiative to assess customer profitability. The company's CFO, John Bradley, stated his position as follows: "I strongly suspect that some of our customers are losers—in other words, they're not covering product costs and service costs. Think about our Weston account. Weston places a ton of small orders, and they're always asking us to expedite them. Then our accounting department has to follow up because Weston misplaces billing records, which really slows down their payments. We're going to make a $1,000,000 investment in CRM [customer relationship management] software to help us assess customer profitability, but I'm confident that the investment will really pay off when it helps us identify this type of loser customer."

The position of the company's marketing vice president, Jerry Brown, is quite different. "This $1,000,000 investment is a waste of money. We'll go through the exercise and find out that some customers are more profitable than others, but we're not going to change a thing. Even the less profitable customers make a contribution to covering overhead, and we're not going to drop a single one."

REQUIRED

Write one or two paragraphs elaborating on the arguments of the CFO and the marketing vice president. In your discussion, consider the fact that the bonus compensation of the marketing VP is based on sales volume. Could this be influencing Jerry's position?

EXERCISE 8-3. [LO 1] The Portland Brewing Company is a small craft brewer that produces five standard varieties of beer. The beers sell for $6 per six-pack, and the company currently sells 10,000 six-packs per month.

The company is considering producing a seasonal beer that will be sold in October, November, and December. The company estimates that at $6 per six-pack, the company will sell 2,000 six-packs. At $7 per six-pack, sales will be 1,000 six-packs. The company also estimates that sales of the seasonal beer will eat into sales of its standard items. Specifically, for every 1,000 six-packs of the seasonal beer that are sold, 300 six-packs of the standard varieties will not be sold. The variable production costs of all beers is $1.20 per six-pack.

REQUIRED

Calculate the incremental profit associated with the two selling prices under consideration for the seasonal beer (i.e., $6 and $7 per six-pack). Should Portland Brewing produce the beer and, if so, what price should the company charge?

EXERCISE 8-4. Profit-Maximizing Price [LO 1] The editor of *Spunk* magazine is considering three alternative prices for her new monthly periodical. Her estimate of price and quantity demanded are:

Price	Quantity Demanded
$7.95	25,000
$6.95	31,000
$5.95	37,000

Monthly costs of producing and delivering the magazine include $95,000 of fixed costs and variable costs of $2.20 per issue.

REQUIRED

Which price will yield the largest monthly profit?

EXERCISE 8-5. Profit-Maximizing Price [LO 1] Erin Hamill is the owner/operator of a tanning salon. She is considering four prices for a weekly tanning pass. Her estimate of price and quantity demanded are:

Price	Quantity Demanded
$12.50	330
$11.50	380
$10.50	390
$ 9.50	430

Monthly costs of providing the tanning service include $1,750 of fixed costs and variable costs of $2.50 per service.

REQUIRED

Which price will yield the largest monthly profit?

EXERCISE 8-6. Analyzing a Special Order [LO 1] PowerDrive produces a hard disk drive that sells for $175 per unit. The cost of producing 25,000 drives in the prior year was:

Direct material	$ 725,000
Direct labor	475,000
Variable overhead	225,000
Fixed overhead	1,500,000
Total cost	$2,925,000

At the start of the current year, the company received an order for 3,000 drives from a computer company in China. Management of PowerDrive has mixed feelings about the order. On one hand, they welcome the order because they currently have excess capacity. Also, this is the company's first international order. On the other hand, the company in China is willing to pay only $125 per unit.

REQUIRED

What will be the effect on profit of accepting the order?

EXERCISE 8-7. Analyzing a Special Order [LO 1] Budget Tax Service prepares tax returns for small businesses. The cost of preparing 800 tax returns in the prior year was:

Direct labor	$360,000
Variable overhead	320,000
Fixed overhead	250,000
Total cost	$930,000

At the start of the current year, the company received an offer from Advantage Business, a firm that provides bundled services to businesses. Advantage wants Budget Tax Service to prepare tax returns for its 150 small-business clients. Budget Tax Service has the capacity to prepare up to 1,000 returns in a given year, so this special order would not take away revenue from any of Budget Tax Service's current clients. Advantage is willing to pay $900 per tax return.

REQUIRED

What will be the effect on Budget Tax Service's profit if it agrees to prepare returns for the 150 clients of Advantage Business?

EXERCISE 8-8. Analyzing a Special Order Service Company [LO 1] Flamingos to Go is a service company owned by Irvin Vonnet that will "plant" plastic flamingos on a special day in people's yards to help celebrate and advertise birthdays, births, anniversaries, and other important milestones. The average delivery is priced at $75. The costs of providing 775 deliveries in the past year were:

Direct labor	$13,950
Variable overhead	9,300
Fixed overhead (advertising costs, phone service, insurance)	17,000
Total cost	$40,250

At the start of the current year, Irv received a phone call from the local Rotary club. The club would like to contract with Flamingos to Go to have flamingos delivered to the yards of each of its members in the upcoming year; this contract would provide an additional 130 deliveries for Flamingos to Go. However, the club wants a special price since it is ordering a large number of deliveries; it has said it would like a price of $57 per delivery. Flamingos to Go can make up to 1,000 deliveries per year without incurring additional fixed costs.

REQUIRED

What will be the affect on profit if Irv accepts the special order?

EXERCISE 8-9. Cost-Plus Pricing [LO 2] World View is considering production of a lighted world globe that the company would price at a markup of 25 percent above full cost. Management estimates that the variable cost of the globe will be $80 per unit and fixed costs per year will be $240,000.

REQUIRED

a. Assuming sales of 1,200 units, what is the full cost of a globe, and what is the price with a 25 percent markup?

b. Assume that the quantity demanded at the price calculated in part a is only 600 units. What is the full cost of the globe, and what is the price with a 25 percent markup?

c. Is the company likely to sell 600 units at the price calculated in part b?

EXERCISE 8-10. Cost-Plus Pricing [LO 2] The chief engineer at Future Tech has proposed production of a portable electronic storage device to be sold at a 30 percent markup above its full cost. Management estimates that the fixed costs per year will be $210,000, and the variable cost of the storage device will be $15 per unit.

REQUIRED

a. Assuming production and sales of 60,000 units, what is the full cost of a storage device, and what is the price with a 30 percent markup?

b. Assume that the quantity demanded at the price calculated in part a is only 40,000 units and only 40,000 units are produced. What is the full cost of the storage device, and what is the price with a 30 percent markup?

c. Compare the selling prices computed in parts a and b; does the selling price increase, decrease, or stay the same when the number of units produced and sold decreases? Why does this change occur?

EXERCISE 8-11. Target Costing [LO 2] Use the Web and search for information on how companies are implementing target costing. Find an example of how target costing has actually been used at a company and summarize that company's experience in a few paragraphs.

EXERCISE 8-12. Target Costing [LO 2] A cross-functional team at Mazzor Systems is developing a new product using the target costing methodology. Product features in comparison to competing products suggest a price of $2,800 per unit. The company requires a profit of 25 percent of selling price.

REQUIRED

a. What is the target cost per unit?

b. Suppose the engineering and cost accounting members of the team determine that the product cannot be produced for the cost calculated in part a. What is the next step in the target costing process?

EXERCISE 8-13. Target Costing [LO 2] A new product is being designed by an engineering team at Odin Security. Several managers and employees from the cost accounting department and the marketing department are also on the team to evaluate the product and determine the cost using a target costing methodology. An analysis of similar products on the market suggests a price of $150 per unit. The company requires a profit of 35 percent of selling price.

REQUIRED

a. What is the target cost per unit?

b. The members of the team subsequently determine that the product cannot be produced for the cost calculated in part a. What is the next step in the target costing process? Does the new product get eliminated from consideration now?

EXERCISE 8-14. Target Costing [LO 2] The product design team at New Time Products is in the process of designing a clock using target costing. Product features in comparison to competing products suggest a price of $35 per unit. The company requires a profit of 30 percent of selling price.

REQUIRED

a. What is the target cost per clock?

b. Suppose it appears that the clocks cannot be manufactured for the target cost. What are some of the options that the company should consider?

EXERCISE 8-15. Customer Profitability Analysis [LO 3] Delta Products has determined the following costs:

Order processing (per order)	$ 6
Additional handling costs if order marked rush (per order)	$11
Customer service calls (per call)	$12
Relationship management costs (per customer per year)	$3,500

In addition to these costs, product costs amount to 85 percent of sales. In the prior year, Delta had the following experience with one of its customers, Johnson Brands:

Sales	$55,000
Number of orders	250
Percent of orders marked rush	70%
Calls to customer service	160

REQUIRED

Calculate the profitability of the Johnson Brands account.

EXERCISE 8-16. Activity-Based Pricing [LO 3] Refer to the information in Exercise 8-15. For the coming year, Delta Products has told Johnson Brands that it will be switched to an activity-based pricing system or it will be dropped as a customer. In addition to regular prices, Johnson will be required to pay:

Order processing (per order)	$ 7
Additional handling costs if order marked rush (per order)	$13
Customer service calls (per call)	$17

REQUIRED

a. Calculate the profitability of the Johnson Brands account if activity is the same as in the prior year.

b. Assume that Johnson Brands decides to accept the activity-based pricing system offered by Delta Products. What changes will likely be made by Johnson?

EXCEL **EXERCISE 8-17. Customer Profitability Analysis [LO 3]** The Triumph Corporation has analyzed its customer and order handling data for the past year and has determined the following costs:

Order processing cost per order	$ 9
Additional costs if order must be expedited (rushed)	$ 11
Customer technical support calls (per call)	$ 13
Relationship management costs (per customer per year)	$1,800

In addition to these costs, product costs amount to 80 percent of sales. In the prior year, Triumph had the following experience with one of its customers, the Julius Company:

Sales	$22,000
Number of orders	170
Percent of orders marked rush	80%
Calls to technical support	90

REQUIRED

Calculate the profitability of the Julius Company account.

EXERCISE 8-18. Activity-Based Pricing [LO 3] Refer to the information in Exercise 8-17. For the coming year, the Triumph Corporation has told the Julius Company that it will be switched to an activity-based pricing system or it will be dropped as a customer. In addition to regular prices, Julius will be required to pay:

Order processing (per order)	$11
Additional handling costs if order marked rush (per order)	$20
Technical support calls (per call)	$21

REQUIRED

a. Calculate the profitability of the Julius Company account if activity is the same as in the prior year.

b. Is it realistic to expect Julius's activity to be the same this year as the previous year if activity-based pricing is instituted? How might the Julius Company react to the new pricing scheme? How might its order behavior change as a result of the new fees?

PROBLEMS

EXCEL

PROBLEM 8-1. Determining the Profit-Maximizing Price [LO 1] Spencer Electronics has just developed a low-end electronic calendar that it plans to sell via a cable channel marketing program. The cable program's fee for selling the item is 20 percent of revenue. For this fee, the program will sell the calendar over six 10-minute segments in September.

Spencer's fixed costs of producing the calendar are $160,000 per production run. The company plans to wait for all orders to come in, then it will produce exactly the number of units ordered. Production time will be less than 3 weeks. Variable production costs are $28 per unit. In addition, it will cost approximately $5 per unit to ship the calendars to customers.

Marsha Andersen, a product manager at Spencer, is charged with recommending a price for the item. Based on her experience with similar items, focus group responses, and survey information, she has estimated the number of units that can be sold at various prices:

Price	Quantity
$85	15,000
$75	20,000
$65	30,000
$55	45,000
$45	65,000

REQUIRED

a. Calculate expected profit for each price.

b. Which price maximizes company profit?

PROBLEM 8-2. Determining the Profit-Maximizing Price [LO 1] Elite Kitchenware has come out with a new line of dishes that it plans to test market through a series of demonstrations at the local mall throughout the month of August. If the demonstrations result in enough sales, the program will be expanded to other malls in the region. The cost of the demonstrations is a flat fee of $1,500 to the mall owner/operator and a commission of 25 percent of revenue to the person giving the demonstrations. (The demonstrator will not receive any salary beyond this commission.)

Elite Kitchenware's fixed costs of producing the dishes are $7,000 per production run. The company plans to wait for all orders to come in, then it will produce exactly the number of units ordered. (There will be no beginning or ending inventory.) Variable production costs are $15 per set of dishes. In addition, it will cost approximately $10 per set to ship the dishes to customers.

Beverly Slater, a product manager at Elite Kitchenware, is charged with recommending a price for the item. Based on her experience with similar items, focus group responses, and survey information, she has estimated the number of units that can be sold at various prices:

Price	Quantity
$65.99	450
$55.99	725
$45.99	800
$35.99	1,000
$25.99	1,300

REQUIRED

a. Calculate expected profit for each price.

b. Which price maximizes company profit?

ETHICS **PROBLEM 8-3. Ethics and Pricing Decisions [LO 1]** LowCostDrugs.com is an online drugstore. Recently the company used a computer program to analyze the purchase behavior of customers sorted by zip code and found that customers in some zip codes are, on average, less price sensitive than customers in other zip codes. Accordingly, the company has raised prices by 3 percent for the customers in the less-price-sensitive zip codes. Note that zip code is automatically identified when a customer comes to the company Web site.

REQUIRED

Is it ethical for LowCostDrugs.com to charge some customers a higher price based on its analysis of prior purchasing behavior?

PROBLEM 8-4. Determining the Profit-Maximizing Price [LO 1] RoverPlus, a pet product superstore, is considering pricing a new RoverPlus-labeled dog food. The company will buy the premium dog food from a company in Indiana that packs the product with a RoverPlus label. Rover pays $9 for a 50-pound bag delivered to its store.

The company also sells Royal Dog Food (under the Royal Dog Food label), which it purchases for $12 per 50-pound bag and sells for $20.99. The company currently sells 26,000 bags of Royal Dog Food per month, but that is expected to change when the RoverPlus brand is introduced.

The company will continue to price the Royal Dog Food brand at $20.99. The quantity of RoverPlus and the quantity of Royal Dog Food that will be sold at various prices for Royal are estimated as:

Price RoverPlus	Quantity RoverPlus	Quantity Royal
$ 9.99	36,000	12,000
$10.99	35,500	12,300
$11.99	35,000	12,500
$12.99	34,000	13,000
$13.99	31,000	14,000
$14.99	26,000	15,000
$15.99	16,000	16,000
$16.99	11,000	20,000
$17.99	6,000	22,000

For example, if RoverPlus is priced at $9.99, the company will sell 36,000 bags of RoverPlus and 12,000 bags of Royal at $20.99. If the company prices RoverPlus at $17.99, it will sell 6,000 bags of RoverPlus and 22,000 bags of Royal at $20.99. This is 4,000 fewer bags of Royal than is currently being sold.

REQUIRED

a. Calculate the profit-maximizing price for the RoverPlus brand, taking into account the effect of the sales of RoverPlus on sales of the Royal Dog Food brand.

b. At the price calculated in part a, what is the incremental profit over the profit earned before the introduction of the RoverPlus-branded dog food?

PROBLEM 8-5. Determining the Profit-Maximizing Price [LO 1] Adagio Music Publishing is a boutique company that publishes and prints sheet music for composers and also records and sells CDs of their compositions. Adagio is considering purchasing a line of CDs from a well-regarded composer, Jacques Elles, from another company, to be sold under the Adagio Music label. Adagio pays $6 for a CD to be delivered to its store.

The company also sells CDs of the composer Julian West, which it purchases for $7 per CD and sells for $16. The company currently sells 800 Julian West CDs per month, but that is expected to change when the Elles CD is introduced.

The company will continue to price the Julian West CD at $16. The quantity of Elles CDs and the quantity of West CDs that will be sold at various prices for Elles is estimated as:

Price Elles CD	Quantity Elles CD	Quantity West CD
$10	950	200
$11	900	275
$12	825	350
$13	725	395
$14	550	475
$15	460	525
$16	300	575
$17	200	625
$18	125	675

For example, if the Elles CD is priced at $10, the company will sell 950 CDs by Elles and 200 CDs by West at $16. If the company prices the Elles CD at $18, it will sell 125 CDs by Elles and 675 CDs by West at $16. This is 125 fewer West CDs than is currently being sold.

REQUIRED

a. Calculate the profit-maximizing price for the Jacques Elles CD, taking into account the effect of the sales of the Elles CD on sales of the Julian West CD.

b. At the price calculated in part a, what is the incremental profit over the profit earned before the introduction of the Jacques Elles CD?

PROBLEM 8-6. Cost-Plus Pricing [LO 2] The Wendel Stove Company is developing a "professional"-model stove aimed at the home market. The company estimates that variable costs will be $2,700 per unit and fixed costs will be $12,600,000 per year.

REQUIRED

a. Suppose the company wants to set its price equal to full cost plus 30 percent. To determine cost, the company must estimate the number of units it will produce and sell in a year. Suppose the company estimates that it can sell 6,000 units. What price will the company set?

b. What is odd about setting the price based on an estimate of how many units will be sold?

c. Suppose the company sets a price as in part a, but the number of units demanded at that price turns out to be 5,000. Revise the price in light of demand for 5,000 units.

d. What will happen to the number of units that will be sold if the price is raised to the one you calculated in part c?

e. Explain why setting price by marking up cost is inherently circular for a manufacturing firm.

PROBLEM 8-7. Cost-Plus Pricing [LO 2] The product design team of Cervantes Golf is in the process of designing a new model of golf bag cart. The company estimates that variable costs will be $33 per unit and fixed costs will be $850,000 per year.

REQUIRED

a. Suppose the company wants to set its price equal to full cost plus 35 percent. To determine cost, the company must estimate the number of units it will produce and sell in a year. Suppose the company estimates that it can sell 8,500 units. What price will the company set?

b. Suppose the company sets a price as in part a, but the number of units demanded at that price turns out to be 6,250. Revise the price in light of demand for 6,250 units.

c. Compare the two prices you just calculated; why are the prices different? What is likely to happen to the quantity demanded if the company is forced to raise its price to the price calculated in part b?

PROBLEM 8-8. Cost-Plus Pricing [LO 2] Emerson Ventures is considering producing a new line of hang gliders. The company estimates that variable costs will be $400 per unit and fixed costs will be $400,000 per year.

REQUIRED

a. Emerson has a pricing policy that dictates that a product's price must be equal to full cost plus 50 percent. To calculate full cost, Emerson must estimate the number of units it will produce and sell in a year. At the beginning of the year, Emerson estimates that it will sell 1,600 gliders and sets its price according to that sales and production volume. What is the price?

b. Right after the beginning of the year, the economy takes a dive and Emerson finds that demand for their gliders has fallen drastically. Emerson revises its sales and production estimate to just 1,000 gliders for the year. According to company policy, what price must now be set?

c. What is likely to happen to the number of gliders sold if Emerson follows company policy and raises the glider price to that calculated in part b?

d. Why is setting price by marking up cost inherently circular for a manufacturing firm?

PROBLEM 8-9. Target Costing [LO 2] Baker Plumbing Fixtures is developing a preplumbed acrylic shower unit. The team developing the product includes representatives from marketing, engineering, and cost accounting. To date, the team has developed a set of features that it plans to incorporate in the unit, including a seat, two shower heads, four body sprays, and a steam unit. With this set of features, the team believes that a price of $5,000 will be attractive in the marketplace. Baker seeks to earn a per unit profit of 30 percent of selling price.

REQUIRED

a. Calculate the target cost per unit.

b. The team has estimated that the fixed production costs associated with the product will be $2,500,000, and variable costs to produce and sell the item will be $2,500 per unit. In light of this, how many units must be produced and sold to meet the target cost per unit?

c. Suppose the company decides that only 1,400 units can be sold at a price of $5,000 and, therefore, the target cost cannot be reached. The company is considering dropping the steam feature, which adds $800 of variable cost per unit. With this feature dropped, the company believes it can sell 2,500 units at $4,000 per unit. Will Baker be able to produce the item at the new target cost or less?

PROBLEM 8-10. Target Costing [LO 2] Symphony Sound is designing a portable recording studio to be sold to consumers. The team developing the product includes representatives from marketing, engineering, and cost accounting. The recording studio will include sound-canceling monitor headphones, audio recording and enhancement software, several instrumental and vocal microphones, and portable folding acoustic panels. With this set of features, the team believes that a price of $4,700 will be attractive in the marketplace. Symphony Sound seeks to earn a per unit profit of 25 percent of selling price.

REQUIRED

a. Calculate the target cost per unit.

b. The team has estimated that the fixed production costs associated with the product will be $1,800,000, and variable costs to produce and sell the item will be $2,900 per unit. In light of this, how many units must be produced and sold to meet the target cost per unit?

c. Suppose the company decides that only 2,000 units can be sold at a price of $4,700 and, therefore, the target cost cannot be reached. The company is considering dropping the folding acoustic panels, which add $650 of variable cost per unit. With this feature dropped, the company believes it can sell 2,600 units at $4,000 per unit. Will Symphony Sound be able to produce the item at the new target cost or less?

PROBLEM 8-11. Analyzing Customer Profitability [LO 3] Lauden Conference Solutions specializes in the design and installation of meeting and conference centers for large corporations. When bidding on jobs, the company estimates product cost and direct labor for installers and marks up the total cost by 35 percent. On a recent job for Orvieto Industries, the company set its price as follows:

Product costs including podiums, seating, lighting, etc.	$175,000
Installer salaries	25,000
Total	200,000
Markup at 35 percent	70,000
Bid price	$270,000

The job turned out to be a big hassle. Orvieto requested 25 change orders, although the dollar value of the products it requested changed very little. The company also returned 33 items that had extremely minor flaws (scratches that were barely visible and would be expected in normal shipping). Orvieto also requested seven meetings with designers taking 40 hours before its plan was finalized. Normally, only two or three meetings are necessary.

Alison Jackson, controller for Lauden, decided to conduct a customer profitability analysis to determine the profitability of Orvieto. She grouped support costs into three categories with the following drivers:

Driver	Annual Value of Driver	Annual Cost
Change orders	850 change orders	$212,500
Number of returns	1,000 product returns	70,000
Design meeting hours	1,300 meeting hours	78,000

REQUIRED

a. Calculate the indirect service costs related to the job performed for Orvieto Industries.

b. Assuming that Orvieto Industries causes a disproportionate amount of indirect service costs, how should Lauden deal with this situation?

PROBLEM 8-12. Activity-Based Pricing [LO 3] Consider the information in Problem 8-11. Lauden Conference Solutions has decided to adopt an activity-based pricing scheme. On future jobs, the company will charge a 35 percent markup on the sum of product costs plus installer salaries. In addition, the company will charge $300 per change order, $90 per product return for products that are in excellent condition, and $85 per meeting hour with a Lauden conference room designer.

REQUIRED

a. What would the profit be on the order from Orvieto in Problem 8-11?

b. Identify pros and cons of adopting the activity-based pricing scheme.

CASE

8-1 PRESTON CONCRETE [LO 1, 2]

Preston Concrete is a major supplier of concrete to residential and commercial builders in the Pacific Northwest. The company's policy is to price deliveries at 25 percent over full cost per cubic yard (including an allowance for administrative costs). At the start of 2017, the company estimated costs as follows:

Material costs = $75 per cubic yard

Delivery costs = $500,000 per year + $10 (mile) + $50 (truck hour)

Yard operation costs = $300,000 per year + $17 per cubic yard

Administrative costs = $2,000,000 per year

Delivery costs include a rate per mile, recognizing that more miles result in more gas and maintenance costs, and a rate per truck hour since, even if a delivery truck is kept waiting at a job site, the truck must be kept running (so the concrete mix will not solidify) and the driver must be paid. At the start of 2017, the company estimated that it would deliver 500,000 cubic yards.

REQUIRED

a. On October 28, Fairview Construction asked Preston to deliver 6,000 cubic yards of concrete. The job will require driving 8,400 miles and 300 truck hours. What will the price be if Preston follows its normal pricing policy?

b. A sharp increase in interest rates has reduced housing starts and the demand for concrete. Fairview has indicated that it will sign a firm order agreement only if the price is $115 per cubic yard. Should Preston accept the order? Briefly indicate factors that, while hard to quantify, should be taken into account in this decision.

CASE

8-2 GALLOWAY UNIVERSITY MEDICAL CENTER PHARMACY [LO 1]

Galloway University Medical Center (GUMC) has a top-rated medical facility that draws patients from a three-state area. On the day of discharge from the GUMC hospital, most patients fill their prescriptions from the GUMC pharmacy. However, when it comes time to renew them, they turn to a local pharmacy because that is more convenient than driving back to the GUMC pharmacy. To encourage prescription renewals, GUMC is considering offering either free overnight delivery or reduced prices on renewal orders.

Currently, the GUMC pharmacy has revenue of $54,990,000 per year on 846,000 orders. The gross margin (price minus cost of drugs) is approximately 25 percent. Free overnight delivery is expected to cost $9 per order and result in 125,000 renewal orders per year. To deal with the increased volume, the pharmacy will need to hire two pharmacists at $90,000 each per year and an additional staff person (to handle shipping) at $50,000 per year.

Alternatively, the pharmacy can generate 125,000 renewal orders per year by offering 20 percent off the prices of renewal orders. With this option, two pharmacists must be hired, but no additional staff person will be needed.

REQUIRED

Estimate the impact on annual pharmacy profit of free overnight delivery and 20 percent off on renewals. Which option should be selected?

9

CAPITAL BUDGETING AND OTHER LONG-RUN DECISIONS

For several years, Steve Wilson, president of Wilson Air, has operated a successful business flying passengers between Seattle and resorts in Idaho and around Washington State.

Now Steve thinks it's time to consider adding to his fleet of three seven-passenger aircraft. "Look," he explains to his chief accountant, Ellen Ortega, "with another plane, we can service 3,500 additional round-trip passengers a year. At an average fare of $200, that's $700,000!" "But don't forget," Ellen points out, "a new plane will cost around $1,000,000, operating cost will be nearly $400,000 per year, and, after 5 years, that $1,000,000 plane will only be worth $500,000. It's not clear that buying another plane is a good business decision."

This chapter extends the discussion of decision making in Chapter 7 to include problems like the one facing Steve Wilson. Steve is considering investing cash *today* in order to receive cash in the *future*. Obviously, Steve will require a total cash inflow that is larger than his initial outflow, since he wants to earn a return on his investment in the plane. Here we discuss how to determine whether future cash inflows are sufficient to earn a *satisfactory* return.

We begin our discussion by focusing on capital budgeting decisions. Essentially, these are decisions related to investments in property, plant, and equipment. As you will see, the approach to the proper analysis of these decisions requires that we take into account the fact that a dollar today is worth more than a dollar tomorrow. In other words, we must consider the time value of money. After we learn about capital budgeting decisions and time value of money approaches to decision making, we will use the same techniques to evaluate other long-run decisions. Since these decisions also affect cash flows across multiple years, we will need to take the time value of money into account in analyzing them.

Medioimages/Photodisc/Getty Images

LEARNING OBJECTIVES

1. Define capital expenditure decisions and capital budgets and evaluate investment opportunities using the net present value approach and the internal rate of return approach.
2. Calculate the depreciation tax shield and evaluate long-run decisions, other than investment decisions, using time value of money techniques.
3. Use the payback period and the accounting rate of return methods to evaluate investment opportunities, and explain why managers may concentrate erroneously on the short-run profitability of investments rather than their net present values.

LEARNING OBJECTIVE 1

Define capital expenditure decisions and capital budgets and evaluate investment opportunities using the net present value approach and the internal rate of return approach.

CAPITAL BUDGETING DECISIONS

Individuals make investments in their homes, automobiles, major appliances, furniture, and other long-lived assets. Companies also make investments in long-lived assets. Examples of investment decisions are presented in Illustration 9-1. In each example, a firm is considering investing in one or more assets that will affect its operations for several years.

Investment decisions are extremely important because they have a major, long-term effect on a firm's operations. When BMW decided to expand its South Carolina plant, it made an investment in additional productive capacity that will affect its labor and transportation costs for many years to come. Labor to build the cars is supplied by American rather than German workers, so labor costs are largely determined by business conditions in the United States rather than in Germany. Transportation costs are greatly reduced for cars sold in the United States because cars can be shipped from South Carolina rather than continental Europe.

The investment decisions of small companies are also extremely important. Consider a small print shop that decides to make an investment in a computerized printing machine. The cost of the machine may represent 50 percent or more of the company's total assets. But the cost savings from the investment in new technology may make the difference between being a solid competitor in its market or being on the verge of financial failure.

Investment decisions involving the acquisition of long-lived assets are often referred to as **capital expenditure decisions** because they require that capital (company funds) be expended to acquire additional resources. Investment decisions are also called **capital budgeting decisions**. Most firms carefully analyze the potential projects in which they may invest. The process of evaluating the investment opportunities is referred to as capital budgeting, and the final list of approved projects is referred to as the **capital budget**.

EVALUATING INVESTMENT OPPORTUNITIES: TIME VALUE OF MONEY APPROACHES

Crucial to an understanding of capital budgeting decisions is an understanding of the *time value of money*. In evaluating an investment opportunity, a company must know not only *how much* cash it receives from or pays for an investment but also *when* the cash is received or paid. The time value of money concept recognizes that it is better to receive a dollar today than it is to receive a dollar next year or any other time in the future. This is because the dollar received today can be invested so that at the end of the year, it amounts to more than a dollar.

In an investment decision, a company invests money today in the hopes of receiving more money in the future. Obviously, the company would not invest money in a project unless it expected the total amount of funds received in the future to exceed the amount of the original investment. But by *how much* must the future cash flows exceed the original investment? Because money in the future is not equivalent to money today, we need to develop a way of converting future dollars into their equivalent current, or present, value. The techniques developed to equate future dollars to current dollars are referred to as present value techniques or time value of money methods.

ILLUSTRATION 9-1

Examples of investment decisions

1. Duke Energy invests in 400 roof-top solar panel installations.
2. Pfizer invests in a $294 million biotechnology factory in Ireland.
3. Lotte Hotel Chain invests in a new hotel in Moscow.
4. Nordstrom invests in a new store in New Jersey.
5. Starbucks invests in a new product: instant coffee.

LINK TO PRACTICE

Royal Caribbean International Invests $1.4 Billion in Cruise Ship

Royal Caribbean International invested $1.4 billion in the construction of the world's largest ship, the *Allure of the Seas*. The ship, launched in December 2010, is 1,187 feet long and 16 decks high, and it holds more than 6,000 passengers and 2,000 crew members.

In making this investment, Royal Caribbean decided that the net future cash inflows generated by the ship would earn a satisfactory return on the cost of building it.

Stock Connection/SuperStock

It may seem odd to have launched a luxury cruise ship in 2010 since this was just after the great recession. But keep in mind that the decision to build the ship started in 2006, when the order was placed with a shipyard in Finland. And to gain economies of scale, Royal Caribbean ordered two nearly identical ships, the *Allure* and its sister ship, the *Oasis* (which is 2 inches shorter!).

Source: Toni Schlesinger, "A City on the Sea," *New York Times*, February 13, 2011.

Some readers of this book will have been introduced to present value techniques in their study of financial accounting and the valuation of long-term debt. We review the basics in the next section, "Basic Time Value of Money Calculations." After that, we discuss two approaches for evaluating investments that take into account the time value of money: the net present value method and the internal rate of return method.

Basic Time Value of Money Calculations

Suppose you invest $100 at an interest rate of 10 percent. At the end of one year, you will have $110.

$$\$100 \times (1 + .10) = \$110$$

Now let's turn this problem around. Suppose you require a return of 10 percent on your investments. How much is a payment of $110, one year from now, worth today? A little algebra (dividing both sides by 1 + .10) indicates that it is worth $100. In other words, if your required return is 10 percent, the present value of $110 received 1 year from now is $100. Put another way, $100 is the amount you would have to invest today, at an interest rate of 10 percent, to have $110 at the end of 1 year:

$$\$100 = \frac{\$110}{(1 + .10)}$$

Now suppose you invest $100 at 10 percent for 2 years. At the end of the first year, you will have $100 times (1 + .10). At the end of the second year, you will have this new amount times (1 + .10), which equals $121:

$$\$100 \times (1 + .10) \times (1 + .10) = \$100(1 + .10)^2 = \$121$$

Turning this problem around, if you require a return of 10 percent on your investments, then how much is a payment of $121, 2 years from now, worth today? The answer is $100:

$$\$100 = \frac{\$121}{(1 + .10)^2}$$

You may note that a pattern is emerging. In general, if your required rate of return is r, the present value (P) of any amount (F) received n years in the future is:

$$P = \frac{F}{(1+r)^n}$$

That is, to calculate the present value (P) of an amount (F) received n years in the future, we divide F by 1 plus the required rate of return (r) raised to the nth power.

Let's try out the formula. What is the present value of $1,000 received 5 years from now if your required rate of return is 12 percent? To answer the question, we divide $1,000 (the amount received in the future) by 1 plus the required return raised to the fifth power, since the cash is received at the end of year 5. The answer is $567.43:

$$\begin{aligned} P &= \frac{F}{(1+r)^n} \\ &= \frac{\$1{,}000}{(1+.12)^5} \\ &= \frac{\$1{,}000}{1.7623417} \\ &= \$567.43 \end{aligned}$$

To simplify calculations, managers can use present value tables to look up present value factors (also called discount factors).[1] Present value factors are simply calculations of $\frac{1}{(1+r)^n}$. Thus, to calculate the present value of a future amount, you can multiply the future amount by the present value factor.

For example, let's consider again the present value of $1,000 received 5 years from now if the required rate of return is 12 percent. The present value factor, or discount factor, is $\frac{1}{(1+r)^n}$. Substituting values into this equation and rounding the result to four places, we find that the factor is:

$$\begin{aligned} \text{Present value factor} &= \frac{1}{(1+r)^n} \\ &= \frac{1}{1.7623417} \\ &= .5674 \end{aligned}$$

Rather than working through the calculation of present value factors, we can turn to the present value of $1 table, Table B9-1 in Appendix B of this chapter. Going across the top of the table to a discount rate of 12 percent and down five rows (since the amount is to be received 5 years in the future), we come to a present value factor of .5674, the same as the value we calculated. Now we can find the present value itself by multiplying the factor times $1,000 (the amount to be received at the end of 5 years):

$$\begin{aligned} \text{Present value} &= \$1{,}000 \times \text{Present value factor} \\ &= \$1{,}000 \times .5674 \\ &= \$567.40 \end{aligned}$$

[1] Managers can also use financial calculators and spreadsheet programs rather than tables of present value factors. In fact, this is what most managers do. We discuss use of Excel® to perform present value calculations in Appendix A of this chapter.

TEST YOUR **KNOWLEDGE**

Using the previous formula, what is the present value of $500 received 2 years in the future if you desire a return of 10 percent?

a. $413.20. b. $468.58. c. $471.60. d. $480.30.

Correct answer is a ($\$500 \times [1 \div (1 + .10)^2]$).

The Net Present Value Method

The time value of money forms the basis of the net present value method for evaluating capital investments.

Decision Making/ Incremental Analysis

Steps in the NPV Method. The first step in using the net present value method is to identify the amount and time period of each cash flow associated with a potential investment. Investment projects have both cash inflows (which are positive) and cash outflows (which are negative). Consistent with our discussion in Chapter 8, the only relevant cash flows are those that are *incremental*—the cash flows that will be incurred if the project is undertaken. Cash flows that have already been incurred are sunk and have no bearing on a current investment decision.

The second step is to equate or discount the cash flows to their present values using a required rate of return. The required rate of return is discussed later. For now, simply assume that the **required rate of return** (also called the hurdle rate) is the minimum return that top management wants to earn on investments.

The third and final step is to evaluate the net present value. The sum of the present values of all cash flows (inflows and outflows) is the **net present value (NPV)** of the investment. If the NPV is zero, the investment is generating a rate of return exactly equal to the required rate of return. Thus, the investment should be undertaken. If the NPV is positive, it should also be undertaken because it is generating a rate of return that is even greater than the required rate of return. Investment opportunities that have a negative NPV are not accepted because their rate of return is less than the required rate of return. A graphical presentation of the NPV approach to evaluating investments is presented in Illustration 9-2.

An Example of the NPV Approach. An example will show how the NPV approach is used. Suppose an auto repair shop is considering purchasing automated paint-spraying equipment. The company estimates that the equipment will last 5 years. Each year it will save the company $2,000 in paint wasted in the current manual spraying operation. It will also reduce labor costs by $20,000. It is estimated that the machine will require

ILLUSTRATION 9-2
NPV approach to evaluating investments

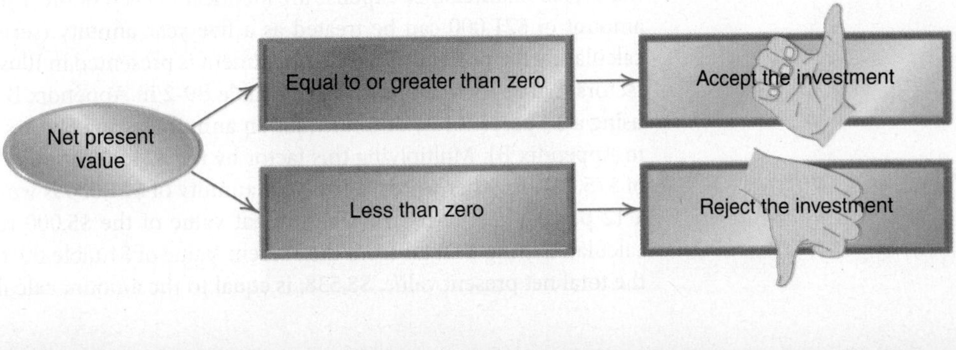

ILLUSTRATION 9-3

Evaluation of automated paint-spraying equipment

Time Period	Present 0	Year 1	Year 2	Year 3	Year 4	Year 5	
Cash flow							
Purchase price	($70,000)						
Labor saving		$20,000	$20,000	$20,000	$20,000	$20,000	
Paint saving		$ 2,000	$ 2,000	$ 2,000	$ 2,000	$ 2,000	
Maintenance		($ 1,000)	($ 1,000)	($ 1,000)	($ 1,000)	($ 1,000)	
Residual value						$ 5,000	
Total cash flow	($70,000)	21,000	$21,000	$21,000	$21,000	$26,000	
PV factor (Table in Appendix B)	×1.000	×.8929	×.7972	×.7118	×.6355	×.5674	
Total	($70,000)	$18,751	$16,741	$14,948	$13,346	$14,752	= $8,538 (NPV)

maintenance costs of $1,000 per year. The machine costs $70,000, and it is expected to have a residual value (also called salvage value) of $5,000 at the end of 5 years. Top management has determined that the required rate of return is 12 percent. Should the company invest in the new equipment?

The cash flows related to the investment opportunity are presented on the timeline at the top of Illustration 9-3. In analyzing the cash flows, we make the assumption that all cash inflows and outflows (other than the cash outflow of $70,000 for purchasing the equipment) occur at the end of a year. To simplify analysis, managers commonly make this assumption, and it is unlikely to introduce significant error, even though cash flows actually take place throughout the year (not just at year-end).

Illustration 9-3 also includes present value (PV) factors for each year's cash-flow total. Consider first the $70,000 cash outflow created by the purchase of the spraying equipment. Note that the present value factor associated with the $70,000 purchase price is 1.0000. Because this amount is going to be spent immediately, it is already expressed in terms of its present value. Now consider the cash flows in year 1. In this year, the net cash inflow is $21,000. The present value factor for an amount received at the end of year 1 using a 12 percent rate of return is .8929 (see Table B9-1 in Appendix B). Multiplying the present value factor by the cash inflow of $21,000 indicates that the present value of the net cash inflow in year 1 is $18,751. The net present value of the investment in spraying equipment is found by summing the present values of the cash flows in each year. This amounts to $8,538. Because the net present value is positive, the company should go ahead with plans to purchase the equipment.

In the preceding problem, the $20,000 labor savings, the $2,000 paint savings, and the $1,000 maintenance expense are identical in each of the 5 years. Thus, the net annual amount of $21,000 can be treated as a five-year annuity (series of equal payments) in calculating the present value. This treatment is presented in Illustration 9-4. Present value factors that apply to annuities are in Table B9-2 in Appendix B. The present value factor, using a 12 percent rate of return, for an annuity lasting 5 years is 3.6048 (see Table B9-2 in Appendix B). Multiplying this factor by the $21,000 annuity indicates a present value of $75,701. In other words, a five-year annuity of $21,000 is worth $75,701 if you require a 12 percent rate of return. The present value of the $5,000 residual value in year 5 is calculated using a factor from the Present Value of $1 table B9-1 (Appendix B). Note that the total net present value, $8,538, is equal to the amount calculated in Illustration 9-3.

ILLUSTRATION 9-4

Evaluation of automated paint-spraying equipment using present value of an annuity approach

Item	Cash Flow	Present Value Factor	Present Value
Purchase price	($70,000)	1.0000	($70,000)
Labor, paint, and maintenance	$21,000 per year for 5 years	3.6048	75,701
Residual value	$5,000 at end of year 5	.5674	2,837
		Net present value	$ 8,538

Present value of an annuity of $1 table. Table B9-2 in Appendix B.

Present value of $1 table. Table B9-1 in Appendix B.

LINK TO PRACTICE

NPV of Livengood Gold Mine Depends on Estimates

In 2011, International Tower Hill, the owner of the Livengood gold mine near Fairbanks, Alaska, released a preliminary economic analysis of the mine showing a net present value of $1.2 billion. This analysis used a 5 percent required rate of return, a 23-year life, a gold price of $1,100 per ounce and estimated capital expenditures of $1.6 billion.

A new feasibility study was conducted in 2013, and estimated capital expenditures related to construction grew to $2.7 billion. In addition, ongoing capital expenditures were estimated at $667 million and reclamation and closure costs were estimated at $353 million. At this point, NPV would only be positive if gold prices were $1,600 per ounce or higher. In June, 2015, International Tower Hill was still working to determine if "optimization" of the project would yield a positive NPV. In June, 2015 gold prices were "only" $1,200 per ounce.

This demonstrates the inherent uncertainty in estimates of cash inflows and outflows related to major projects.

Sources: Press Release, International Tower, Alaska, August 23, 2011; Anthony Vaccaro, "ITH's Livengood Struggles at Today's Gold Price, The Northern Miner, August 8, 2013.

Comparing Alternatives with NPV. It is relatively easy to evaluate decision alternatives with the NPV approach. Essentially, we calculate the NPV of each alternative and select the one with the highest NPV. The difference between the NPVs of any two alternatives is the incremental value of the highest NPV investment.

Consider an alternative to the investment we have just considered. Let's call the previous investment A and the alternative B. The alternative piece of equipment will also last 5 years. Each year it will save the company $3,000 in paint wasted in the current manual spraying operation, and it will reduce labor costs by $27,000 per year. It will require $4,000 of annual maintenance. Thus, the net savings each year is $26,000:

Paint savings	$ 3,000
Labor savings	27,000
Maintenance	(4,000)
Net annual savings	$26,000

The cost of the machine is $80,000, and it will have a residual value of $7,000. The alternative investments are evaluated in Illustration 9-5. As indicated, alternative B has the highest NPV, $17,697, and, thus, it is the preferred alternative. Its incremental value over alternative A is the difference in their NPVs, which is $9,159.

Another way to evaluate alternatives is to compute the present values of their incremental cash flows. This is presented in the bottom panel of Illustration 9-5. As indicated, alternative B has an incremental outflow related to the purchase price of $10,000. However, it has positive incremental cash flows related to labor, paint, and maintenance

ILLUSTRATION 9-5
Evaluation of alternatives using NPV

Comparison of Each Alternative's NPV

Alternative A	Cash Flow	12% Factor	Present Value
Purchase price	($70,000)	1.0000	($70,000)
Labor, paint, and maintenance	$21,000 per year for 5 years	3.6048	75,701
Residual value	$5,000 at end of year 5	0.5674	2,837
		NPV	$ 8,538

Alternative B	Cash Flow	12% Factor	Present Value
Purchase price	($80,000)	1.0000	($80,000)
Labor, paint, and maintenance	$26,000 per year for 5 years	3.6048	93,725
Residual value	$7,000 at end of year 5	0.5674	3,972
		NPV	$17,697

$9,159 Incremental Value of Alternative B

Analysis of Incremental Cash Flows of Alternative B versus Alternative A

Incremental Cash Flows of B versus A	Cash Flow	12% Factor	Present Value
Purchase price	($10,000)	1.0000	($10,000)
Labor, paint, and maintenance	$5,000 per year for 5 years	3.6048	18,024
Residual value	$2,000 at end of year 5	0.5674	1,135
		NPV	$ 9,159

Note: Present value factors are in Tables B9-1 and B9-2 of Appendix B.

each year of $5,000 ($26,000 of savings for B versus $21,000 for A). Also, it has an incremental salvage value of $2,000. Applying present value factors to these incremental cash flows again shows us that the incremental value of alternative B is $9,159 greater compared to alternative A. While the approach you take will yield the same answer, students seem to make fewer errors when they calculate each alternative's NPV and compare these values to determine which alternative is best.

The Internal Rate of Return Method

The internal rate of return method is an alternative to net present value for evaluating investment possibilities. Like net present value, it takes into account the time value of money. Specifically, the **internal rate of return (IRR)** is the rate of return that equates the present value of future cash flows to the investment outlay. In other words, it is the return that makes the NPV equal to zero. If the IRR of a potential investment is equal to or greater than the required rate of return, the investment should be undertaken. In Illustration 9-6, the IRR approach to evaluating investments is outlined.

Consider a simple case where $100 is invested to yield $60 at the end of year 1 and $60 at the end of year 2. What rate of return equates the two-year, $60 annuity to $100?

ILLUSTRATION 9-6

IRR approach to evaluating investments

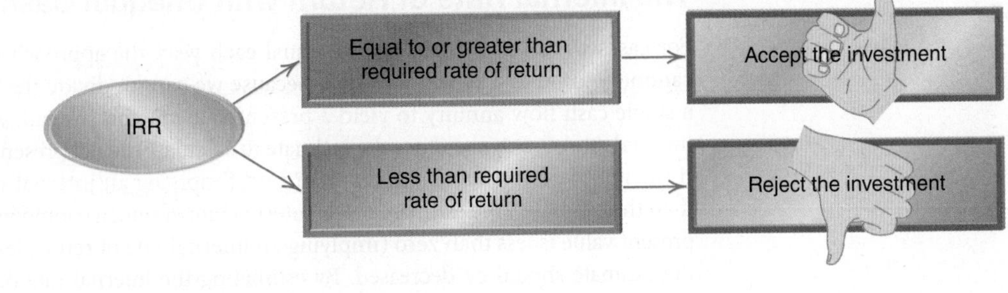

Recall that when we performed present value analysis for previous annuities, we multiplied a present value factor by the annuity to solve for a present value. That is:

$$\text{Present value} = \text{Present value factor} \times \text{Annuity}$$

In the current case, we set the present value equal to the initial outlay for the investment. Then, we can solve for the present value factor and use it to look up the rate of return implicit in the investment:

$$\text{Present value factor} = \frac{\text{Initial outlay}}{\text{Annuity amount}}$$

With a \$100 cost of the investment and a \$60 annuity, the present value factor is 1.667:

$$1.6667 = \frac{\$100}{\$60}$$

Because the \$60 is to be received in each of 2 years, we use the annuity table (Table B9-2 in Appendix B) to look up the internal rate of return. In the row in Table B9-2 for two periods, we find a present value factor of 1.6681 (very close to 1.6667) in the column for a 13 percent rate of return. Thus, the IRR on this investment is approximately 13 percent. If the required rate of return is 13 percent or less, the investment should be undertaken.

Insight into the IRR can be gained by using it to calculate the net present value of the project. If we evaluated the previous project using a 13 percent required rate of return, what would be the net present value? The answer is zero, because the internal rate of return equates the present value of future cash flows to the investment outlay:

Item	Cash Flow	Present Value Factor	Present Value
Cash flow	\$ 60	1.6681 Table B9-2, Appendix B	\$100.09
Initial investment	(\$100)	1.0000	(100.00)
		Difference (due to rounding)	\$ .09

TEST YOUR **KNOWLEDGE**

A potential investment should be undertaken if:

a. The NPV is zero or positive.

b. The IRR is equal to or greater than the required rate of return.

c. Both a and b are true.

Correct answer is c.

The Internal Rate of Return with Unequal Cash Flows

For cases where cash flows are not equal each year, the approach previously presented cannot be used to calculate the IRR, because we cannot divide the initial investment by a single cash flow annuity to yield a present value factor. Instead, we must estimate the internal rate of return and use the estimate to calculate the net present value of the project. If the net present value is greater than zero (implying an internal rate of return greater than the estimate), the estimate of the internal rate of return should be increased. If the net present value is less than zero (implying an internal rate of return less than the estimate), the estimate should be decreased. By estimating the internal rate of return in this **trial-and-error** fashion, it is possible to eventually arrive at the actual internal rate of return.

LINK TO **PRACTICE**

College Education Yields 15% Return

In this chapter, we focus on business investments and how to calculate their internal rates of return. The same procedures can be applied to calculate the IRR on an investment in a college education. Indeed, the calculation was performed by the Brookings Institution, a nonprofit public policy organization based in Washington, DC. According to a paper it published in 2011, a four-year college degree had a return of 15.2 percent. Interestingly, this is more than double the average return to investments in stocks since 1950 and more than five times the return to corporate bonds. While the study didn't specifically address the return on investments in an undergraduate *business* degree or an MBA, it wouldn't be surprising if they were quite a bit higher than 15 percent!

Source: Michael Greenstone and Adam Looney, "Where is the Best Place to Invest $102,000—In Stocks, Bonds, or a College Degree?" *Brookings*, June 25, 2011.

Let's consider an example to illustrate the method. Suppose a company is considering changes in its production process that will involve purchasing several pieces of equipment costing a total of $120,000. The changes are expected to yield cost savings of $49,500 in year 1; $45,000 in year 2; $35,000 in year 3; $22,000 in year 4; and $19,600 in year 5:

Time Period	0	1	2	3	4	5
Cash Flow	($120,000)	$49,500	$45,000	$35,000	$22,000	$19,600

The company wants to evaluate the potential project in terms of its internal rate of return. The first step is to estimate what the internal rate of return is likely to be. Since the cash flow is fairly large in relation to the initial investment, a reasonable guess as to the internal rate of return might be 14 percent. However, when we calculate the net present value of the investment as in Illustration 9-7 using 14 percent, we see that the present value is a positive $4,880. Thus, the true internal rate of return is greater than 14 percent. As a next approximation, we can try 20 percent. However, with this rate of return, the present value is a negative $8,761. This indicates that our second estimate of the internal rate of return was too high.

At this point, we know that the internal rate of return is somewhere between 14 percent and 20 percent. Thus, as a further attempt, we might try 16 percent. The present value using a rate of 16 percent is $26. This is sufficiently close to zero to allow us to conclude that the internal rate of return is approximately 16 percent. If management of the company believes that a return of 16 percent is sufficient, then the company should go ahead with the project.

It may appear that the need to estimate the internal rate of return using a trial-and-error approach presents a significant obstacle to its use. Actually, this is not the case. A spreadsheet program such as Excel® and even some pocket calculators

ILLUSTRATION 9-7

Calculating the IRR when there are unequal cash flows

		14%		20%		16%	
Time Period	**Cash Flows**	**Factor for 14%**	**Present Value**	**Factor for 20%**	**Present Value**	**Factor for 16%**	**Present Value**
0	($120,000)	1	($120,000)	1	($120,000)	1	($120,000)
1	$ 49,500	0.8772	$ 43,421	0.8333	$ 41,248	0.8621	$ 42,674
2	$ 45,000	0.7695	$ 34,628	0.6944	$ 31,248	0.7432	$ 33,444
3	$ 35,000	0.6750	$ 23,625	0.5787	$ 20,255	0.6407	$ 22,425
4	$ 22,000	0.5921	$ 13,026	0.4823	$ 10,611	0.5523	$ 12,151
5	$ 19,600	0.5194	$ 10,180	0.4019	$ 7,877	0.4761	$ 9,332
		Total	$ 4,880		($ 8,761)		$ 26

contain functions that easily estimate the internal rate of return of a project. The user simply inputs the cash flow information, and the IRR is computed automatically.

Summary of Net Present Value and Internal Rate of Return Methods

Although both the net present value method and the internal rate of return method take into account the time value of money, they differ in their approach to evaluating investment alternatives. With net present value, any investment with a zero or positive net present value should be undertaken. With the internal rate of return method, any investment with an internal rate of return equal to or greater than the required rate of return should be undertaken.[2]

CONSIDERING "SOFT" BENEFITS IN INVESTMENT DECISIONS

When managers make investment decisions, it is important that they consider so-called soft benefits in addition to a project's NPV or IRR. Soft benefits are benefits that are difficult to quantify.[3] Consider a situation faced by Dynamic Medical Equipment. The company is considering production of a high-tech wheelchair. The wheelchair would take advantage of advances in lightweight graphite construction techniques pioneered in the manufacturing of tennis racquets and design improvements suggested by athletes competing in wheelchair events. Suppose that in evaluating the project, the finance department fails to consider the fact that production of the high-tech wheelchair will improve the firm's reputation as an industry leader committed to innovation. Such a reputation is clearly valuable, since it has a positive effect on sales of the firm's entire product line. However, the value is also very difficult to quantify. Or consider the fact that producing the wheelchair will introduce new construction techniques that will help the firm produce future products made from graphite. This may be a major benefit to the firm, but it is very difficult to quantify.

[2] Under some circumstances, the net present value and the internal rate of return methods may be inconsistent with one another in evaluating the desirability of an investment opportunity. This potential problem is discussed in introductory corporate finance texts.

[3] Firms may also have difficulty quantifying certain costs. For example, an investment in a new manufacturing process may result in additional pollution, the cost of which is hard to quantify. If "soft costs" are ignored in investment analysis, companies will tend to overinvest.

LINK TO PRACTICE

Use of NPV and IRR by CFOs

John Graham and Campbell Harvey of Duke University conducted a survey of chief financial officers (CFOs) to assess their use of capital budgeting techniques. According to their results, 74.9 percent of CFOs always or almost always use NPV and 75.7 percent always or almost always use IRR. Moreover, large companies are significantly more likely to use NPV than small companies. After NPV and IRR, the payback method (discussed later in this chapter) is the most frequently used capital budgeting technique with 56.7 percent of the CFOs stating that they always or almost always use it.

Source: J. Graham and C. Harvey, "How Do CFOs Make Capital Budgeting and Capital Structure Decisions," *Journal of Applied Corporate Finance,* Spring 2002, pp. 8–22. Reprinted by permission of Blackwell Publishing Ltd.

Ignoring soft benefits may lead firms to pass up investments that are of strategic importance, especially investments in advanced manufacturing technology. For example, investment in robotics may be needed to reduce product defects. And defect-free production may be a source of competitive advantage. However, the NPV analysis of the investment may focus on the cash savings resulting from a reduction in labor, which is relatively easy to quantify, and ignore the cash savings resulting from increased product demand, which is relatively hard to quantify.

As a further example, consider an investment in a flexible manufacturing system. Such systems are generally highly automated and often involve computer-controlled equipment. They are configured so that machines can be easily adjusted to produce a number of different products or variations of standard products. With a flexible manufacturing system, companies can easily respond to custom orders that meet the exact specifications of their individual customers. Flexible manufacturing systems also improve delivery times on orders and allow companies to introduce new products quickly. But while being able to improve delivery times and introduce new products quickly may greatly improve a company's competitive position, these benefits are quite difficult to quantify in dollar terms.

Calculating the Value of Soft Benefits Required to Make an Investment Acceptable

Managers should make a reasonable effort to calculate the cash value of soft benefits when analyzing investment opportunities. However, in some cases, they may decide that quantifying the benefits is too costly. In these cases, if the NPV of a potential investment is negative, managers should calculate the amount of additional cash inflows needed to have a positive NPV. Then, if managers believe that the value of soft benefits, while uncertain, will clearly exceed the additional cash inflows, they can decide to fund the investment.

For example, suppose the high-tech wheelchair project at Dynamic Medical Equipment has a NPV of negative $80,000. In calculating the NPV, the finance department used a required rate of return of 15 percent and assumed that the project would have a 10-year life. After 10 years, the chair will be out of date and replaced in the product line. As we know, the finance department did not consider soft benefits in calculating the NPV. But what must be the value of the soft benefits each year before the wheelchair is an acceptable investment? The calculation needed to answer this question is presented in Illustration 9-8.

The present value of the soft benefits must be at least $80,000 before the project is acceptable. Using the present value of an annuity table, we find that the discount factor for 10 periods at 15 percent is 5.019. This implies that as long as the soft benefits are worth at least $15,939 per year, the project should be funded. Managers at Dynamic Medical Equipment will likely find this analysis very useful. For example, while they may be unable to specify the exact value of the soft benefits, there may be general agreement that the value will certainly exceed $16,000 each year. If this is the case, then the

ILLUSTRATION 9-8

Calculation of soft benefits needed to make the investment acceptable

$$\text{Needed present value} = \text{Discount factor} \times \text{Value of benefits}$$

$$\text{Value of benefits} = \frac{\text{Needed present value}}{\text{Discount factor}}$$

$$\text{Value of benefits} = \frac{\$80{,}000}{5.019}$$

$$\text{Value of benefits} = \$15{,}939$$

LINK TO PRACTICE

Soft Benefits Related to Investing in ERP System

As discussed in Chapter 1, enterprise resource planning (ERP) systems are complex and comprehensive systems used to computerize inventory control, manage company supply chains, and automate customer support and other key business functions. Such systems can cost more than $1 million and receive careful consideration before purchase decisions are made. In running the numbers, managers find it difficult to take into account a number of soft benefits. According to an article by Kenneth Murphy and Steven Simon, these benefits may include reduced number of customer complaints, improved customer satisfaction, improved customer retention, early identification of market trends, and support of organizational change.

Neustockimages/iStockphoto

The authors also did a case study of an ERP decision and found that after quantifying one soft benefit, customer satisfaction, the IRR increased from 39.2 percent to 124 percent!

Source: Kenneth E. Murphy and Steven John Simon, "Intangible Benefits Valuation in ERP Projects," *Information Systems Journal,* 2002, pp. 301–320.

wheelchair appears to be a good investment. However, there may be general agreement that while there certainly will be some soft benefit, the value is unlikely to exceed even $10,000 per year. If this is the case, then the wheelchair is not a good investment.

ESTIMATING THE REQUIRED RATE OF RETURN

In the problems presented earlier, we simply stated a required rate of return that could be used to calculate an investment's net present value or that could be compared with an investment's internal rate of return. In practice, the required rate of return must be estimated by management. Under certain conditions, the required rate of return should be equal to the cost of capital for the firm. The **cost of capital** is the weighted average of the costs of debt and equity financing used to generate capital for investments. The cost of debt arises because interest must be paid to individuals, banks, and other companies that lend money to the firm. Essentially, the cost of equity is the return demanded by shareholders for the risk they bear in supplying capital to the firm. Estimating the cost of capital, especially the cost due to equity capital, is a challenge even to sophisticated financial managers.[4] Because of this difficulty, many managers use their judgment to determine the required rate of return, following the general principle that the more risky the investment, the higher the required rate of return.

[4] Complications arise, for example, because some debt issues allow for conversion to common stock. Also, some companies have multiple classes of stock with different voting rules and other features that make calculation of the cost of equity capital difficult.

LINK TO **PRACTICE**

Cost of Capital for Various Business Sectors

The Stern School of New York University has a website that lists the cost of capital by business sector. The values provide you with a good feel for differences in the cost of capital across companies.

http://people.stern.nyu.edu/~adamodar/New_Home_Page/datafile/wacc.htm

Some examples as of January 2015 are:

Aerospace/defense	7.93%
Apparel	7.09%
Auto parts	8.44%
Brug. (Biotechnology)	8.25%
Entertainment	7.09%
Food processing	6.78%
Semiconductor	8.58%
Telecoms Equipment	8.69%

ADDITIONAL CASH FLOW CONSIDERATIONS

To be useful in investment analysis, both the net present value and the internal rate of return methods require a proper specification of cash flows. It is particularly important to remember that *only cash inflows and outflows, not revenues and expenses*, are discounted back to present value. Thus, if a sale is expected to occur in period 1 but the collection of the sale is not anticipated until period 2, the cash flow that is discounted back to present value is a period 2 cash flow, even though the related revenue will be recorded in period 1. Similarly, if a cash payment is anticipated at the start of period 1 to purchase an asset, and related depreciation is to be recorded in periods 1 through 5, only the start of period 1 cash outflow is used in the net present value analysis. Depreciation is a legitimate business cost, but it does not require a cash outflow in the period in which it is recorded. Present value analysis is concerned only with cash flows.

In this section, we consider two special topics related to cash flows. The first deals with depreciation. Although depreciation does not have a direct effect on cash flows, it does have an indirect effect because of taxes. The second topic deals with the effect of inflation on cash flows.

LEARNING OBJECTIVE 2

Calculate the depreciation tax shield and evaluate long-run decisions, other than investment decisions, using time value of money techniques.

Cash Flows, Taxes, and the Depreciation Tax Shield

In all of the previous examples, we ignored the effect of income taxes on cash flows. However, tax considerations play a major role in capital budgeting decisions, and we discuss them here. If an investment project generates taxable revenue, cash inflows from the project will be reduced by the taxes that must be paid on the revenue. Similarly, if an investment project generates tax-deductible expenses, cash inflows from the project will be increased by the tax savings resulting from the decrease in income taxes payable.

Earlier we stated that depreciation is not relevant in a present value analysis of an investment opportunity because it is not a cash flow. But although depreciation does not *directly* affect cash flow, it *indirectly* affects cash flow because it reduces the amount of tax a company must pay. That is, it acts to shield income from taxes. The term **depreciation tax shield** is used to refer to the tax savings resulting from depreciation.

As an example, suppose the Mando Party Supply Company is considering a new product, custom-imprinted T-shirts. Imprinting will require an investment in equipment costing $100,000. Each year, the company expects sales to amount to $70,000 and expenses (other than depreciation on the equipment) to amount to $40,000. Depreciation calculated on a straight-line basis for the expected 10-year life of the equipment is $10,000 per year. The company has a 40 percent tax rate.[5] Assume that revenue is collected in

[5] Our discussion and examples assume a 40 percent tax rate. This assumption ignores complexities in tax rates and rules in practice that may change from year to year. However, the assumption allows us to more clearly convey the essential role of taxes in investment decisions.

the period earned and expenses other than depreciation are paid in the period incurred. Thus, net income and cash flows related to the investment are as follows:

Net Income

Revenue		$70,000
Less:		
Operating expense other than depreciation	$40,000	
Depreciation	10,000	50,000
Income before taxes		20,000
Income taxes (40% tax rate)		8,000
Net income		$12,000

Cash Flows

Revenue	$70,000
Less taxes on revenue	(28,000)
Less expenses other than depreciation	(40,000)
Plus tax savings related to expenses other than depreciation	16,000
Plus tax savings related to depreciation ($10,000 × .40)	4,000
Cash flow	$22,000

Note that revenue increases cash inflows by $70,000 but taxes on the revenue decrease cash flows by $28,000. Expenses other than depreciation reduce cash flows by $40,000 but, since they reduce taxable income by $40,000, they also *save* taxes of $16,000. Now note that depreciation expense does not reduce cash flows—that's because depreciation is a noncash expense. However, it does reduce taxable income and thus results in a cash inflow equal to the amount of depreciation times the tax rate ($10,000 × .40 = $4,000). Thus, there is a depreciation tax shield of $4,000.

In the example, we calculated cash flows in a rather circuitous way because we wanted to show the depreciation tax shield. A much more direct way would be to simply add depreciation back to net income as follows:

Net income	$12,000
Plus depreciation	10,000
Cash flow	$22,000

We add depreciation back because it is the only item in the calculation of Mando Party Supply's net income that is not a cash flow.

Because the project is fairly risky, top management of Mando Party Supply has set a required rate of return of 16 percent. The net present value calculation for the investment under consideration is presented in Illustration 9-9. Note that because the amounts of revenue, expense, and tax are the same each year, we can work with the net amount and treat it as a 10-year annuity with a required rate of return of 16 percent. Because the net present value is a positive $6,330, the investment in the equipment should be undertaken.

The fact that depreciation reduced taxes had a significant effect on the value of the investment project. With depreciation of $10,000 and a 40 percent tax rate, we saw that there is a $4,000 tax savings each year due to depreciation. The present value of this "tax shield" over 10 years at 16 percent is $19,333 ($4,000 × present value factor of 4.8332). Thus, it is apparent that without the tax shield afforded by depreciation, the investment would not have a positive net present value and would not be worth undertaking.

ILLUSTRATION 9-9
NPV analysis taking taxes into account

Item		Cash Flow	Present Value Factor	Present Value
Initial investment		($100,000)	1,000	($100,000)
Revenue	$70,000			
Expense (other than depreciation)	(40,000)			
Taxes	(8,000)	22,000	4.8332	106,330
Net present value				$ 6,330

Table B9-2, Appendix B

LINK TO PRACTICE

Depreciation Tax Shield at Delta Air Lines

Federal tax laws (with certain restrictions that we won't go into) allow companies to carry losses backward to reduce previous taxes paid and receive a refund. If the losses cannot be carried back, they can be carried forward to offset future income in the determination of federal income taxes.

The use of tax loss carry forwards appears to be particularly useful to Delta Air Lines. In 2013, the company had income of $2.7 billion excluding special items. However, it was not required to pay federal income taxes. The reason—it had more than $15 billion in tax loss carry forwards related to previous years when the company had significant losses.

How would this affect the value of the depreciation tax shield for an investment in equipment in January 2014 that results in depreciation expense in 2014 and 2015? Since the company isn't going to pay taxes in 2014 or 2015, it is clear that the incremental depreciation related to the investment will not save taxes in these years, and there is no depreciation tax shield in 2014 or 2015.

Adjusting Cash Flows for Inflation

An additional topic that must be addressed in estimating the cash flows of investments is how to handle inflation. During the 1970s and early 1980s, the United States experienced double-digit inflation. Because high rates of inflation are still common in many foreign countries, it may be quite important to consider inflation when estimating the cash flows associated with investment opportunities.

Inflation can be taken into account by multiplying the current level of cash flow by the expected rate of inflation. For example, if an investment is expected to yield a cash flow in period 1 of $100 and the rate of inflation is expected to be 5 percent per year in the foreseeable future, then a reasonable estimate of the cash flow would be $105 ($100 × 1.05) in period 2, $110.25 ($105 × 1.05) in period 3, $115.76 in period 4, and so forth. Estimates of inflation can be obtained from financial journals or can be purchased for a fee from firms that specialize in economic forecasts.

If inflation is ignored in net present value analysis, many worthwhile investment opportunities may be rejected. Why? Because current rates of return for debt and equity financing already include estimates of future inflation. For example, banks charge higher rates of interest on loans to companies when they estimate that inflation will be high. Suppose a company uses its current costs of debt and equity financing (which are high because a high rate of inflation is expected) to determine its required rate of return. Now, if the company does not take inflation into account in estimating future cash inflows, the cash inflows will be relatively low, whereas the required rate of return will be relatively high. The result may be that suitable projects will appear to have a negative net present value.

ILLUSTRATION 9-10

Other long-run decisions

1. Decision to outsource grounds maintenance
2. Decision to drop a product line
3. Decision to buy rather than make a subcomponent of a product
4. Decision to conduct a multiyear advertising campaign
5. Decision involving customers paying for goods with alternative payment plans (e.g., large upfront payment and smaller annual payments versus small upfront payment and larger annual payments)

OTHER LONG-RUN DECISIONS

So far we have discussed capital budgeting decisions that involve investments in long-lived assets, and we have shown how to analyze them using time value of money techniques: specifically, the net present value method and the internal rate of return method. In addition to being used to analyze capital budgeting decisions, time value of money techniques are also applicable to the analysis of other long-run decisions. Long-run decisions are those that affect the cash flows of a number of future periods. Since cash flows occur in the future and a dollar today is worth more than a dollar tomorrow, the NPV and IRR methods are applicable to these types of decisions. Examples of long-run decisions that are not investment decisions but should be analyzed using NPV or IRR are listed in Illustration 9-10.

Let's consider an example that shows how time value of money techniques can be used to analyze a decision other than a capital budgeting decision. Suppose that Accelerator Consulting is considering signing a contract to sponsor a golf tournament in Phoenix. The contract specifies that Accelerator will pay $600,000 at the start of each of 5 years. In return, the tournament will be called the Accelerator Open when it is broadcast on television and there will be highly visible signage around the clubhouse and course. Additionally, Accelerator will receive free catering and seats on the 18th hole so the company can entertain customers and other VIPs.

Accelerator estimates that over the 5 years, exposure from the tournament will increase revenue by $2,000,000, $3,000,000, $4,000,000, $5,000,000, and $6,000,000. The company's normal pretax profit margin (pretax profit divided by revenue) is 20 percent, and the company's tax rate is 40 percent. The company would like to earn a 10 percent return related to the event. Should the company agree to sponsor the tournament? Analysis of the decision using NPV and IRR is presented in Illustration 9-11. Note that the NPV is a positive $141,048. Thus, Accelerator should sponsor the tournament. The illustration also shows that the IRR on the project is 14.59 percent. This was calculated using the IRR function in Excel® as demonstrated in Appendix A.

ANY **QUESTIONS?**

Q: In Chapter 7, we analyzed decisions much like those described in Illustration 9-10 and in the example related to Accelerator Consulting, but we focused on incremental revenues and incremental costs rather than cash inflows and outflows, and we didn't use NPV. Why could we ignore the time value of money in Chapter 7 but we have to use it in this chapter?

A: In Chapter 7, we analyzed incremental revenues and incremental costs. An underlying assumption, which was not spelled out because it would have been confusing then, is that the incremental revenues were also incremental cash inflows, and the incremental costs were also incremental cash outflows. Also, we assumed that the time value of money wasn't important to analyzing the decision. This could be because the decision affected only one or two periods, so ignoring the time value of money wouldn't result in a significant error. Or, it may have been that the decision alternatives did not require significant investments and one alternative clearly dominated the others because its incremental profit was the highest in all years.

ILLUSTRATION 9-11

Evaluation of decision to sponsor a golf tournament

Cash Flows	Present	Year 1	Year 2	Year 3	Year 4	Year 5	
Payments	($600,000)	($600,000)	($600,000)	($600,000)	($600,000)	—	
Tax savings from payments	—	240.000[a]	240,000	240,000	240,000	240,000	
Additional pretax profit exluding payments	—	400,000[b]	600,000	800,000	1,000,000	1,200,000	
Additional taxes related to additional pretax profit	—	(160,000)[c]	(240,000)	(320,000)	(400,000)	(480,000)	
Cash flows	($600,000)	($120,000)	$ —	$120,000	$240,000	$ 960,000	
PV factor (Table B9-1, Appendix B)	×1.0000	×0.9091	×0.8264	×0.7513	×0.6830	×0.6209	
Total	($600,000)	($109,092)	$ -0-	$ 90,156	$163,920	$ 596,064	= $141,048 (NPV)
							14.59% (IRR)[d]

[a]Equals $(600,000) × .4.
[b]Equals $2,000,000 × .2.
[c]Equals $400,000 × .4.
[d]Calculated using Excel®, as described in Appendix A.

LEARNING OBJECTIVE 3
Use the payback period and the accounting rate of return methods to evaluate investment opportunities, and explain why managers may concentrate erroneously on the short-run profitability of investments rather than their net present values.

SIMPLIFIED APPROACHES TO CAPITAL BUDGETING

The net present value and the internal rate of return methods are widely used in industry to evaluate capital projects. However, many companies continue to use other, simpler, approaches to evaluating capital projects. Two of these approaches, the payback period method and the accounting rate of return method, are discussed in this section. As you will see, both of these methods have significant limitations in comparison to net present value and internal rate of return.

Payback Period Method

The **payback period** is the length of time it takes to recover the initial cost of an investment. Thus, if an investment opportunity costs $1,000 and yields cash flows of $500 per year, it has a payback period of 2 years. If an investment costs $1,000 and yields cash flows of $300 per year, it has a payback period of 3⅓ years. All else being equal, a company would like to have projects with short payback periods.

One approach to using the payback method is to accept investment projects that have a payback period less than some specified requirement. However, this can lead to extremely poor decisions. For example, suppose a company has two investment opportunities, both costing $1,000. The first investment yields cash flows of $500 per year for 3 years and has a payback period of 2 years. The second investment yields no cash flows in the first 2 years but has cash flows of $1,000 in the third year and $4,000 in the fourth year. Thus, it has a payback period of 3 years. Obviously, the second investment is preferable. However, if the company has a 2-year payback requirement, it will select the first investment and reject the second. The problem is that the payback

LINK TO PRACTICE

Payback on Home Solar Power

What's the payback on an investment in a home solar panel project? That depends on the number of panels, local cost of electricity, and other factors. But, here's an example from a homeowner in southeastern Pennsylvania. Kevin Tofel added solar panels to his four-bedroom house at a cost of $51,865. After a federal tax credit and a state rebate, the net cost was only $29,205. His typical electric bill had been around $2,500 per year. Thus, he estimated that his payback period would be around 11.7 years ($29,205 ÷ $2,500). After he made the investment, Tofel sold his gas powered car and bought an electric vehicle. He saved on gas and had no incremental electricity costs as his system had plenty of capacity. This made his actual payback period even lower.

Source: Kevin C. Tofel, "Adding an Electric Car Cut the Payback Point of Our Solar Panel Investment in Half," GIGAOM, May 12, 2013.

method *does not take into account the total stream of cash flows* related to an investment. It only considers the stream of cash flows up to the time the investment is paid back. Thus, in this example, the payback period method ignores the $4,000 cash inflow in the fourth year of the second investment.

A further limitation of the payback method is that it *does not consider the time value of money*. Consider two investments, each with a cost of $1,000. The first yields cash flows of $700 in the first year, $300 in the second year, and $300 in the third year. Thus, it has a payback of 2 years. The second investment yields cash flows of $300 in the first year, $700 in the second year, and $300 in the third year. Thus, it also has a payback period of 2 years. But although both investments have the same payback period (implying they are equally valuable), the first investment is actually more favorable, because the $700 cash inflow is received in the first year rather than the second year. In fact, the first investment has an internal rate of return of 17 percent, whereas the second investment has an internal rate of return of only 14 percent.

Although the payback method has significant limitations, some companies may find it useful, particularly if they have cash flow problems. Companies with cash flow problems may need to focus on investments that quickly return cash in order to avoid bankruptcy.

Accounting Rate of Return

The **accounting rate of return** is equal to the average after-tax income from a project divided by the average investment in the project:

$$\text{Accounting rate of return (ARR)} = \frac{\text{Average net income}}{\text{Average investment}}$$

Here the average investment is simply the initial investment divided by 2.[6] The accounting rate of return can be used to evaluate investment opportunities by comparing their accounting rates of return with a required accounting rate of return. The primary limitation of this approach is that, like the payback period method, it ignores the time value of money.

Consider two investment alternatives facing a firm with a cost of capital of 15 percent and a 40 percent tax rate. Both require investments in equipment costing $100,000, and

[6] Note that if an investment in a project has scrap value, the average investment is equal to (initial investment plus scrap value) ÷ 2. Also, some textbooks define the denominator to be the *initial investment* rather than the *average investment*. For our purposes, however, we will use the average investment in the denominator.

ILLUSTRATION 9-12

Net income and cash flow data for alternative projects

	Project 1	Project 2
Year 1		
Revenue	$90,000	$ 70,000
Less: Operating expenses other than depreciation	20,000	20,000
Depreciation	50,000	50,000
Income before taxes	20,000	0
Taxes	8,000	0
Net income	12,000	0
Plus: depreciation	50,000	50,000
Cash flow	$62,000	$ 50,000
Year 2		
Revenue	$90,000	$110,000
Less: Operating expenses other than depreciation	20,000	20,000
Depreciation	50,000	50,000
Income before taxes	20,000	40,000
Taxes	8,000	16,000
Net income	12,000	24,000
Plus: depreciation	50,000	50,000
Cash flow	$62,000	$ 74,000

both generate cash flows for 2 years. The investments are identical except that, while both have total revenue over 2 years of $180,000, project 1 has $90,000 of revenue in the first year, while project 2 has $70,000. In the second year, project 1 again has $90,000 of revenue, while project 2 has $110,000. Illustration 9-12 presents the net incomes and cash flows of the two alternatives for the 2 years. We assume that all revenue items are collected in the period earned and all expense items (other than depreciation) are paid in the period incurred. Thus, the difference between net income and cash flow is simply the amount of depreciation.

Based on the information, it is easy to calculate the accounting rate of return for each project, as indicated in Illustration 9-13. Both have identical accounting rates of return of 24 percent, indicating that the two projects are equally desirable. When we take into account the time value of money, however, it is clear that project 1 is more desirable than project 2. As indicated in Illustration 9-14, using a cost of capital of 15 percent, the net present value of project 1 is $793.40, whereas project 2 has a negative net present value of $568.60. Thus, taking into account the time value of money, project 1 is an acceptable investment while project 2 is not acceptable.

ILLUSTRATION 9-13

Comparison of ARRs for alternative projects

$$\text{Accounting rate of return (ARR)} = \frac{\text{Average net income}}{\text{Average investment}}$$

$$\text{ARR for project 1} = \frac{(\$12{,}000 + \$12{,}000) \div 2}{(\$100{,}000 \div 2)} = .24$$

$$\text{ARR for project 2} = \frac{(\$0 + \$24{,}000) \div 2}{(\$100{,}000 \div 2)} = .24$$

ILLUSTRATION 9-14
NPV comparison of alternative projects

Project 1

Time Period	Cash Flow	Present Value Factor	Present Value
-0-	($100,000)	1.0000	($100,000.00)
1	$ 62,000	.8696	53,915.20
2	$ 62,000	.7561	46,878.20
		Net present value	$ 793.40

Project 2

Time Period	Cash Flow	Present Value Factor	Present Value
-0-	($100,000)	1.0000	($100,000.00)
1	$ 50,000	.8696	43,480.00
2	$ 74,000	.7561	55,951.40
		Net present value	($ 568.60)

TEST YOUR KNOWLEDGE

Compared to NPV, both the accounting rate of return and the payback method suffer from a failure to consider:

a. Soft benefits. b. Unexpected consequences. c. The time value of money.

Correct answer is c.

The Accounting Rate of Return Is Not a Reliable Estimate of the Internal Rate of Return. Some people think that while the accounting rate of return ignores the time value of money, it still provides a *reasonably* accurate estimate of a project's internal rate of return. This is **not** the case. Using Excel™ (see Apprendix A), we can easily calculate the IRR of project 1 in Illustration 9-14 to be 15.62 percent. Recall that this is the rate that makes the NPV of the project equal to zero. The accounting rate of return provided a return of 24 percent, which is more than 50 percent greater than the internal rate of return. This clearly demonstrates that the accounting rate of return need not be a reasonable estimate of a project's real economic return, which is measured by IRR.

CONFLICT BETWEEN PERFORMANCE EVALUATION AND CAPITAL BUDGETING

YOU GET WHAT YOU MEASURE

An NPV greater than zero or an IRR greater than the required rate of return informs managers that an investment opportunity will increase their firm's value. Thus, managers who wish to maximize shareholder wealth should use these present value techniques to evaluate investments. However, in some companies, managers may be discouraged from using present value techniques for evaluating investments because of the way in which their own performance is evaluated.

For example, an investment may result in high amounts of depreciation in the early years of its life. At the same time, in these early start-up years, revenues may be quite low, resulting in low profits or even losses. However, revenues in later years may be large enough to ensure that the project has a positive net present value. If a manager knows that job performance is evaluated in terms of reported accounting income, he or she may fear being fired because of the low initial profits of this investment. If this is the case, the manager will likely ignore the fact that a project has a positive net present value and concentrate instead on reported income.

To illustrate this, suppose a manager is considering producing a new product that requires an investment of $1,000,000 in equipment. Depreciation on the equipment will be recorded using the straight-line method. Based on a 10-year life, depreciation will be $100,000 per year. The product is not expected to sell well in the early years. Expected first-year revenue is only $40,000. However, by the end of the seventh year, expected revenue is up to $400,000 per year. In addition to depreciation, there are $40,000 of other expenses each year. The company has a 10 percent required rate of return.

Illustration 9-15 is a net present value analysis of the investment. The net present value is $26,998, indicating that the project should be undertaken. However, will the

ILLUSTRATION 9-15

Net present value analysis of new product[a]

	Year 1	Year 2	Year 3	Year 4	Year 5
Revenue	$ 40,000	$ 60,000	$100,000	$150,000	$200,000
Less: Operating expenses other than depreciation	40,000	40,000	40,000	40,000	40,000
Depreciation	100,000	100,000	100,000	100,000	100,000
Net income	(100,000)	(80,000)	(40,000)	10,000	60,000
Plus: depreciation	100,000	100,000	100,000	100,000	100,000
Cash flow	$ 0	$ 20,000	$ 60,000	$110,000	$160,000

	Year 6	Year 7	Year 8	Year 9	Year 10
Revenue	$300,000	$400,000	$400,000	$400,000	$400,000
Less: Operating expenses other than depreciation	40,000	40,000	40,000	40,000	40,000
Depreciation	100,000	100,000	100,000	100,000	100,000
Net income	160,000	260,000	260,000	260,000	260,000
Plus: depreciation	100,000	100,000	100,000	100,000	100,000
Cash flow	$260,000	$360,000	$360,000	$360,000	$360,000

Time Period	Cash Flows	Factor for 10%	Present Value
0	($1,000,000)	1.0000	($1,000,000)
1	0	0.9091	0
2	20,000	0.8264	16,528
3	60,000	0.7513	45,078
4	110,000	0.6830	75,130
5	160,000	0.6209	99,344
6	260,000	0.5645	146,770
7	360,000	0.5132	184,752
8	360,000	0.4665	167,940
9	360,000	0.4241	152,676
10	360,000	0.3855	138,780
	Net present value		$ 26,998

[a]Note that the example is simplified and ignores taxes. Therefore, there is no depreciation tax shield. Also, the example assumes that revenue is collected in the period earned and other expenses are paid in the period incurred.

manager be motivated to undertake this project, which is in the best interest of the company? Note that the project shows a substantial loss in each of the first 3 years. The manager may fear that this will reflect badly on his or her performance, perhaps leading to dismissal from the firm. If this is the case, the manager may opt to pass up this valuable investment opportunity.

At least a partial solution to this problem is to make sure managers realize that, if they approve projects with positive net present values that lower reported income in the short run, evaluations of their performance and their compensation will take the expected *future* benefits into account. Managers must be confident that their performance will be evaluated with respect to the long-run profitability of the firm, or they will not take a long-run perspective in evaluating capital projects.

At some firms, top managers are required to hold stock in the company they work for. The idea behind the requirement is that it aligns the interests of managers with the interests of shareholders. These managers will tend to take actions that maximize the value of the firm, because increasing firm value increases their own wealth. It is hoped that these managers will tend to focus on present value techniques in evaluating investments because these techniques identify investments that increase the firm's value.

WILSON AIR EXAMPLE REVISITED

At the beginning of the chapter, Steve Wilson, president of Wilson Air, was trying to decide whether he should purchase another plane. At this point, we have developed the tools needed to analyze problems like the one facing Steve.

Recall that a new plane costs $1,000,000. The residual value of the plane after 5 years will be $500,000, and annual depreciation using the straight-line method is $100,000. Revenue will increase by $700,000 per year, and operating costs (ignoring depreciation and taxes) will be $400,000. Revenue will be collected in the period earned, and operating costs other than depreciation will be paid in the period incurred. Assume the income tax rate is 40 percent. What is the net present value of the investment in the plane if the required rate of return is 10 percent? The answer is $144,426, as shown in Illustration 9-16. Because the NPV is positive, the investment should be undertaken.

ILLUSTRATION 9-16
Present value of investment in plane

Item		**Cash Flow**	**Present Value Factor**	**Present Value**
Purchase price		($1,000,000)	1.0000	($1,000,000)
Revenue	$700,000			
Less:				
Operating expenses other than depreciation	400,000			
Depreciation	100,000			
Income before income taxes	200,000			
Income taxes	80,000			
Net income	120,000			
Plus: depreciation	100,000			
Annual cash flow		220,000	3.7908	833,976
Residual value		500,000	.6209	310,450
		Net present value		$ 144,426

Appendix B, Table B9-2, 10%, 5 years

Appendix B, Table B9-1, 10%, 5 years

Decision Making INSIGHT

Capital budgeting decisions involve estimation of incremental cash inflows and outflows. Since the cash flows don't occur in the same periods and because a dollar today is worth more than a dollar tomorrow, we need to take into account the time value of money by using the net present value (NPV) approach or the internal rate of return (IRR) approach.

However, managers may not make investments in projects with substantial NPVs (or projects with IRRs greater than the required rate of return) because they are evaluated in terms of short-run accounting profit, which may decrease when the projects are undertaken.

SUMMARY OF LEARNING OBJECTIVES

LEARNING OBJECTIVE 1 Define capital expenditure decisions and capital budgets and evaluate investment opportunities using the net present value approach and the internal rate of return approach.

Capital expenditure decisions are investment decisions involving the acquisition of long-lived assets. A capital budget is the final list of approved acquisitions.

Two of the primary methods for evaluating investment opportunities, which take into account the time value of money, are the net present value method (NPV) and the internal rate of return method (IRR). The net present value method equates all cash flows to their present values. If the sum of the present values of cash inflows and outflows (i.e., the NPV) is zero or positive, the return on the investment equals or exceeds the required return and the investment should be made.

The internal rate of return method calculates the rate of return that equates the present value of the future cash flows to the initial investment. If this rate of return is equal to or greater than the required rate of return, the investment is warranted.

LEARNING OBJECTIVE 2 Calculate the depreciation tax shield and evaluate long-run decisions, other than investment decisions, using time value of money techniques.

In analyzing cash flows for a net present value analysis or an internal rate of return analysis, remember that depreciation is not a cash flow but the tax savings generated by depreciation are relevant to the analysis. The tax savings owing to depreciation are referred to as the depreciation tax shield.

NPV and IRR are also used to evaluate long-run decisions that are not capital budgeting decisions. Examples include outsourcing decisions and decisions related to multiyear advertising campaigns.

LEARNING OBJECTIVE 3 Use the payback period and the accounting rate of return methods to evaluate investment opportunities, and explain why managers may concentrate erroneously on the short-run profitability of investments rather than their net present values.

The payback method evaluates capital projects in terms of how quickly the initial investment is recovered by future cash inflows. The accounting rate of return method evaluates capital projects in terms of the ratio of average after-tax accounting income to the average investment. Both of these methods have the major limitation that they ignore the time value of money.

Managers who want to maximize shareholder wealth should evaluate investment opportunities using the net present value method or the internal rate of return method. In some cases, however, projects with a positive net present value or with an internal rate of return greater than required may have a negative effect on short-run income. Although these projects may be quite valuable to the long-run success of the firm, managers may not approve them because they fear that their own job performance will receive negative evaluations if short-run income is reduced.

APPENDIX A

USING EXCEL® TO CALCULATE NPV AND IRR

In this appendix, you will see how to use functions in Excel® to calculate the net present value (NPV) and internal rate of return (IRR) of investment opportunities. Let's focus on the data related to the paint-spraying equipment example presented in Illustration 9-3.

ILLUSTRATION A9-1

Input data into Excel®

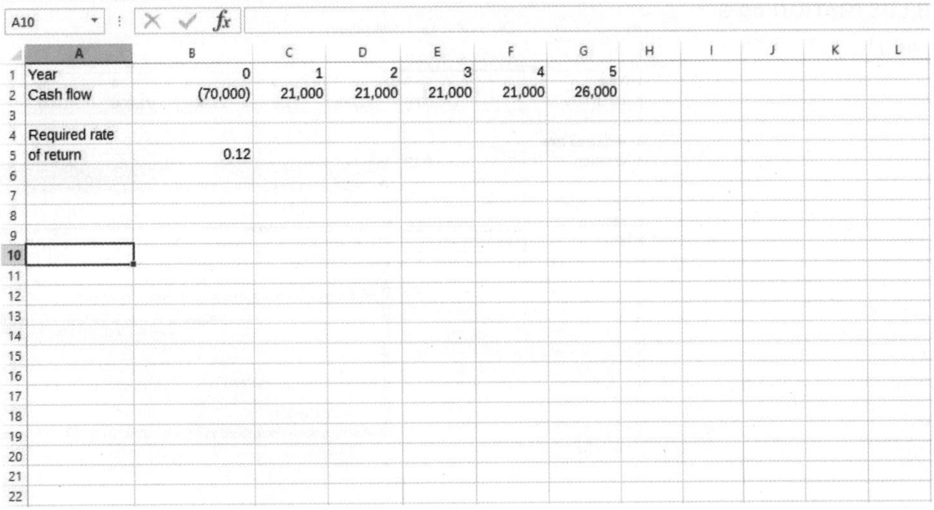

The first step in performing present value calculations in Excel® is to input the relevant cash flows into a spreadsheet: cells B2–G2 in Illustration A9-1. As indicated, purchase of the paint-spraying equipment requires a $70,000 payment at time 0. The company buying the equipment will save $21,000 each year for 5 years and sell the equipment for $5,000 at the end of the fifth year. Thus, the cash inflow at the end of year 5 is $26,000 ($21,000 + $5,000). The required rate of return on the investment is 0.12, which we input in cell B5.

To calculate net present value, we need to input the NPV function into a cell; click on cell B8. Now click on Formulas, then click on Financial, and then click on NPV, which is one of the programs in the Financial section. The first item we input into the NPV function is the required rate of return, which is in cell B5. The NPV function calculates the present value of cash flows assuming the first cash flow occurs at the *end* of year 1. So, be careful: Don't include the cash flow at time 0 at this point. Simply input the cash flows from C2 through G2. At this point, your screen should be similar to the one in Illustration A9-2.

ILLUSTRATION A9-2

Using the NPV function

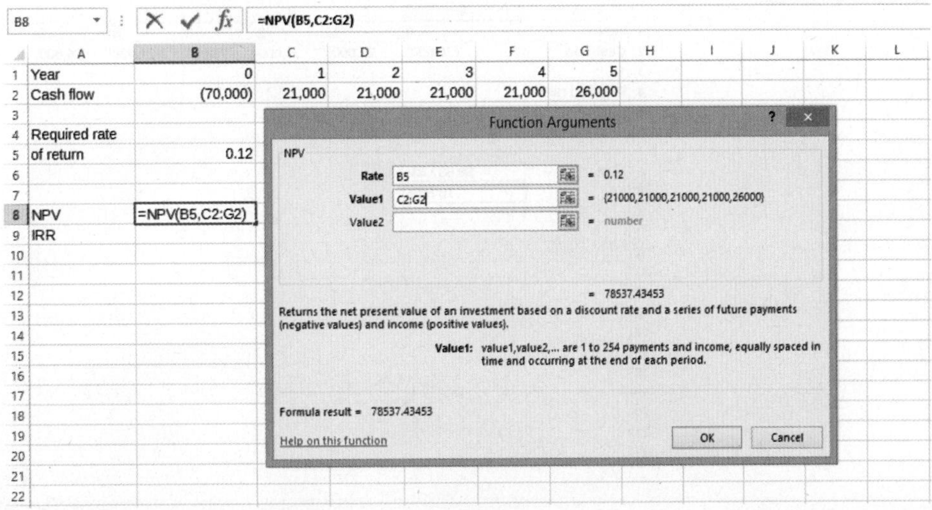

ILLUSTRATION A9-3
Using the IRR function

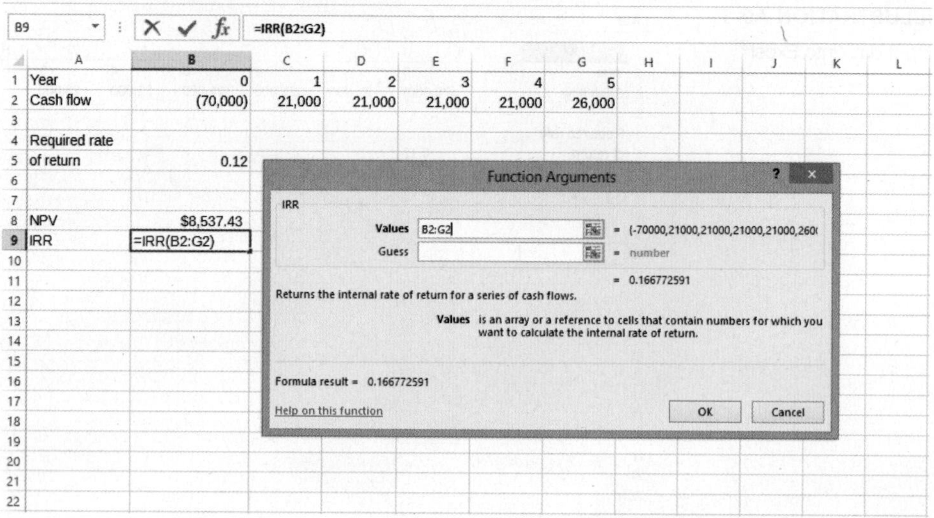

Now click OK, go back to cell B8, and add the cash flow occurring at time 0, which is in cell B2. As you can see, this gives us the project's NPV of $8,537.43.

Let's turn our attention now to the IRR function and put it in cell B9. Go to the Function button, click the Financial Category, and click the IRR function name. Now input B2:G2, which highlights the project's cash flows. Then, if you want, input an estimated internal rate of return. This estimate just helps the program have an efficient starting point for calculating the IRR. You can generally ignore this step, and we will do that here (see Illustration A9-3).

Once you click OK, Excel® will calculate the internal rate of return, which is 16.68 percent in this example (see Illustration A9-4).

Since the NPV is positive and the IRR is greater than the required rate of 12 percent, the project should be undertaken.

ILLUSTRATION A9-4
NPV and IRR results

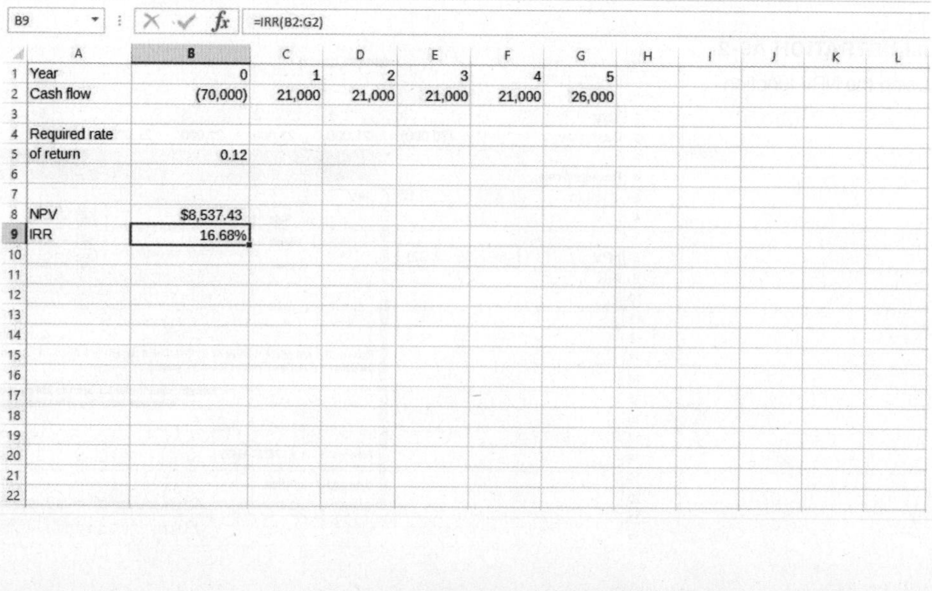

APPENDIX B

TABLE B9-1

Present value of $1 due in *n* periods

	6%	7%	8%	9%	10%	11%	12%	13%	14%	15%	16%	20%	30%
1	0.9434	0.9346	0.9259	0.9174	0.9091	0.9009	0.8929	0.8850	0.8772	0.8696	0.8621	0.8333	0.7692
2	0.8900	0.8734	0.8573	0.8417	0.8264	0.8116	0.7972	0.7831	0.7695	0.7561	0.7432	0.6944	0.5917
3	0.8396	0.8163	0.7938	0.7722	0.7513	0.7312	0.7118	0.6931	0.6750	0.6575	0.6407	0.5787	0.4552
4	0.7921	0.7629	0.7350	0.7084	0.6830	0.6587	0.6355	0.6133	0.5921	0.5718	0.5523	0.4823	0.3501
5	0.7473	0.7130	0.6806	0.6499	0.6209	0.5935	0.5674	0.5428	0.5194	0.4972	0.4761	0.4019	0.2693
6	0.7050	0.6663	0.6302	0.5963	0.5645	0.5346	0.5066	0.4803	0.4556	0.4323	0.4104	0.3349	0.2072
7	0.6651	0.6227	0.5835	0.5470	0.5132	0.4817	0.4523	0.4251	0.3996	0.3759	0.3538	0.2791	0.1594
8	0.6274	0.5820	0.5403	0.5019	0.4665	0.4339	0.4039	0.3762	0.3506	0.3269	0.3050	0.2326	0.1226
9	0.5919	0.5439	0.5002	0.4604	0.4241	0.3909	0.3606	0.3329	0.3075	0.2843	0.2630	0.1938	0.0943
10	0.5584	0.5083	0.4632	0.4224	0.3855	0.3522	0.3220	0.2946	0.2697	0.2472	0.2267	0.1615	0.0725
11	0.5268	0.4751	0.4289	0.3875	0.3505	0.3173	0.2875	0.2607	0.2366	0.2149	0.1954	0.1346	0.0558
12	0.4970	0.4440	0.3971	0.3555	0.3186	0.2858	0.2567	0.2307	0.2076	0.1869	0.1685	0.1122	0.0429
13	0.4688	0.4150	0.3677	0.3262	0.2897	0.2575	0.2292	0.2042	0.1821	0.1625	0.1452	0.0935	0.0330
14	0.4423	0.3878	0.3405	0.2992	0.2633	0.2320	0.2046	0.1807	0.1597	0.1413	0.1252	0.0779	0.0254
15	0.4173	0.3624	0.3152	0.2745	0.2394	0.2090	0.1827	0.1599	0.1401	0.1229	0.1079	0.0649	0.0195
16	0.3936	0.3387	0.2919	0.2519	0.2176	0.1883	0.1631	0.1415	0.1229	0.1069	0.0930	0.0541	0.0150
17	0.3714	0.3166	0.2703	0.2311	0.1978	0.1696	0.1456	0.1252	0.1078	0.0929	0.0802	0.0451	0.0116
18	0.3503	0.2959	0.2502	0.2120	0.1799	0.1528	0.1300	0.1108	0.0946	0.0808	0.0691	0.0376	0.0089
19	0.3305	0.2765	0.2317	0.1945	0.1635	0.1377	0.1161	0.0981	0.0829	0.0703	0.0596	0.0313	0.0068
20	0.3118	0.2584	0.2145	0.1784	0.1486	0.1240	0.1037	0.0868	0.0728	0.0611	0.0514	0.0261	0.0053

TABLE B9-2

Present value of an annuity of $1 per period

	6%	7%	8%	9%	10%	11%	12%	13%	14%	15%	16%	20%	30%
1	0.9434	0.9346	0.9259	0.9174	0.9091	0.9009	0.8929	0.8850	0.8772	0.8696	0.8621	0.8333	0.7692
2	1.8334	1.8080	1.7833	1.7591	1.7355	1.7125	1.6901	1.6681	1.6467	1.6257	1.6052	1.5278	1.3609
3	2.6730	2.6243	2.5771	2.5313	2.4869	2.4437	2.4018	2.3612	2.3216	2.2832	2.2459	2.1065	1.8161
4	3.4651	3.3872	3.3121	3.2397	3.1699	3.1024	3.0373	2.9745	2.9137	2.8550	2.7982	2.5887	2.1662
5	4.2124	4.1002	3.9927	3.8897	3.7908	3.6959	3.6048	3.5172	3.4331	3.3522	3.2743	2.9906	2.4356
6	4.9173	4.7665	4.6229	4.4859	4.3553	4.2305	4.1114	3.9975	3.8887	3.7845	3.6847	3.3255	2.6427
7	5.5824	5.3893	5.2064	5.0330	4.8684	4.7122	4.5638	4.4226	4.2883	4.1604	4.0386	3.6046	2.8021
8	6.2098	5.9713	5.7466	5.5348	5.3349	5.1461	4.9676	4.7988	4.6389	4.4873	4.3436	3.8372	2.9247
9	6.8017	6.5152	6.2469	5.9952	5.7590	5.5370	5.3282	5.1317	4.9464	4.7716	4.6065	4.0310	3.0190
10	7.3601	7.0236	6.7101	6.4177	6.1446	5.8892	5.6502	5.4262	5.2161	5.0188	4.8332	4.1925	3.0915
11	7.8869	7.4987	7.1390	6.8052	6.4951	6.2065	5.9377	5.6869	5.4527	5.2337	5.0286	4.3271	3.1473
12	8.3838	7.9427	7.5361	7.1607	6.8137	6.4924	6.1944	5.9176	5.6603	5.4206	5.1971	4.4392	3.1903
13	8.8527	8.3577	7.9038	7.4869	7.1034	6.7499	6.4235	6.1218	5.8424	5.5831	5.3423	4.5327	3.2233
14	9.2950	8.7455	8.2442	7.7862	7.3667	6.9819	6.6282	6.3025	6.0021	5.7245	5.4675	4.6106	3.2487
15	9.7122	9.1079	8.5595	8.0607	7.6061	7.1909	6.8109	6.4624	6.1422	5.8474	5.5755	4.6755	3.2682
16	10.1059	9.4466	8.8514	8.3126	7.8237	7.3792	6.9740	6.6039	6.2651	5.9542	5.6685	4.7296	3.2832
17	10.4773	9.7632	9.1216	8.5436	8.0216	7.5488	7.1196	6.7291	6.3729	6.0472	5.7487	4.7746	3.2948
18	10.8276	10.0591	9.3719	8.7556	8.2014	7.7016	7.2497	6.8399	6.4674	6.1280	5.8178	4.8122	3.3037
19	11.1581	10.3356	9.6036	8.9501	8.3649	7.8393	7.3658	6.9380	6.5504	6.1982	5.8775	4.8435	3.3105
20	11.4699	10.5940	9.8181	9.1285	8.5136	7.9633	7.4694	7.0248	6.6231	6.2593	5.9288	4.8696	3.3158

REVIEW PROBLEM 1

Summit Maintenance Technology sells a software package that companies can use to manage their facility and equipment maintenance functions. Features include work order tracking, maintenance history reporting, repair history reporting, and parts inventory management. The software is used mainly by large organizations such as airports, manufacturing plants, office complexes, hospitals, and commercial bakeries. A unique aspect of Summit's product is that it has a very intuitive interface and can be accessed via the Web with Summit providing application servers, database servers, and security. Thus, firms that implement the system do not need to add information technology staff or equipment.

Currently Summit is negotiating with Ogden National Airport, which has considerable maintenance challenges. For example, the airport has six employees whose sole job is relamping (i.e., replacing light bulbs). In total, the maintenance department at Ogden has 45 employees who maintain escalators, elevators, trams, lighting, and perform painting and other miscellaneous maintenance duties.

Craig Bradley, a senior manager at Ogden National Airport, has held a series of meetings with Summit and has identified the following cost savings:

1. The company can avoid purchasing a server costing $10,000 next year.
2. Due to better tracking, parts inventory can be reduced. The effect on purchases is $30,000, $20,000, and $10,000 over the next 3 years.
3. The company will need one less maintenance employee with an annual salary and benefits of $60,000.
4. The company is currently paying $5,000 per year to upgrade its maintenance software.

Craig anticipates that the charges to Ogden for software and consulting services will be as follows:

Initial costs—$90,000 "program fee" plus $55,000 consultant charges for systems integration and customization of reports

Ongoing costs—$14,000 annual program fee after the initial year plus $6,000 per year consulting charges for ongoing customization beyond the initial year

REQUIRED

Calculate the net present value (NPV), assuming a required rate of return of 15 percent. Also calculate the internal rate of return (IRR). In performing your calculations, use a three-year time horizon and ignore taxes.

Should Ogden invest in the new software?

ANSWER

Time	0	1	2	3
Initial program fee	(90,000.00)			
Initial consulting charges	(55,000.00)			
Ongoing charges		(20,000.00)	(20,000.00)	(20,000.00)
IT equipment		10,000.00		
Parts inventory		30,000.00	20,000.00	10,000.00
Maintenance employee		60,000.00	60,000.00	60,000.00
Old software upgrade		5,000.00	5,000.00	5,000.00
Total	(145,000.00)	85,000.00	65,000.00	55,000.00
Present value factors at 15%	1.0000	0.8696	0.7561	0.6575
	(145,000.00)	73,916.00	49,146.50	36,162.50
NPV	14,225.00			
IRR, in %	21.33			

Note: IRR calculated using Excel®, as explained in Appendix A.

Since the NPV is greater than zero and the IRR is greater than the required rate of return, Ogden should invest in the software.

REVIEW PROBLEM 2

United Insurance of Hawaii is building a new facility to house its staff of 500 in downtown Honolulu. The company prides itself on a commitment to sustainability, and, in this regard, it is considering two alternatives that will reduce its demand for electricity generated using fossil fuel.

The first alternative is to install solar panels on the roof of the building. The company estimates that this alternative will cost $1,000,000 and save the company $280,000 per year in electricity costs. The panels are expected to have a five-year life.

The second alternative is to utilize nanotechnology to produce a photovoltaic material that can be installed over windows. This alternative is more expensive, $1,500,000, but is expected to save $400,000 per year over its five-year life.

REQUIRED

Use the NPV approach to determine the better alternative. Assume the company desires a return of 12 percent.

ANSWER

Solar Panels	Cash Flow	12% Factor	Present Value
Purchase price	($1,000,000)	1.0000	($1,000,000)
Energy savings	$280,000 per year		
	for 5 years	3.6048	1,009,344
		NPV	$ 9,344

$67,424

Nanotechnology	Cash Flow	12% Factor	Present Value
Purchase price	($1,500,000)	1.0000	($1,500,000)
Energy savings	$400,000 per year		
	for 5 years	3.6048	1,441,920
		NPV	($ 58,080)

As indicated, the investment in solar panels is the better alternative. It has an incremental NPV of $67,424 over the investment in nanotechnology.

KEY TERMS

Accounting rate of return (345)
Capital budget (328)
Capital budgeting decisions (328)
Capital expenditure decisions (328)
Cost of capital (339)
Depreciation tax shield (340)
Internal rate of return (IRR) (334)
present value (NPV) (331)
Payback period (344)
Required rate of return (331)
Trial-and-error (336)

SELF-ASSESSMENT (Answers Below)

1. Which of the following is **not** a capital expenditure decision?

a. Building a new factory.
b. Purchasing a new piece of equipment.
c. Purchasing a computer system.
d. All of the above are capital expenditure decisions.

2. Which of the following methods equates future dollars to current dollars?

a. Net present value method.
b. Accounting rate of return.
c. Payback period method.
d. All of these answer choices are correct.

3. If you require a return of 8 percent, the present value of \$100 received 2 years from now would be calculated as:

   a. $\frac{\$100}{(.08)^2}$.   b. $\frac{(1+.08)^2}{\$100}$.

   c. $\$\frac{100}{(1+.08)^2}$.

   d. None of these answer choices is correct.

4. If the net present value of a project is zero, the project is earning a return equal to:

   a. Zero.

   b. The rate of inflation.

   c. The accounting rate of return.

   d. The required rate of return.

5. An investment should be made if:

   a. The IRR is equal to or greater than the required rate of return.

   b. The IRR is equal to or greater than zero.

   c. The IRR is greater than the accounting rate of return.

   d. The IRR is greater than the present value factor.

6. The cost of capital is:

   a. The cost of debt financing.

   b. The cost of equity financing.

   c. The weighted average of the costs of debt and equity financing.

   d. The internal rate of return.

7. A piece of equipment costs \$100,000 and has a five-year life. Assuming straight-line depreciation and a 40 percent tax rate, this investment:

   a. Will generate a positive cash inflow at time 0.

   b. Will have a negative depreciation tax shield.

   c. Will generate a \$40,000 expense each year but will not affect cash flows beyond year 0.

   d. Will generate a depreciation tax shield equivalent to an annual cash inflow of \$8,000 for 5 years.

8. A project with a useful life of 5 years requires an investment of \$100,000 and yields after-tax income of \$40,000 per year for 5 years. Assuming the investment has no value at the end of 5 years, the accounting rate of return is:

   a. 40 percent.

   b. 20 percent.

   c. 10 percent.

   d. None of these answer choices are correct.

9. A project requires a \$2,000,000 investment and has an internal rate of return of 20 percent. The cost of capital is only 15 percent. A manager with a short-run orientation may still reject this investment if:

   a. The net present value is positive.

   b. The rate of inflation is high.

   c. The accounting rate of return is high.

   d. Accelerated depreciation leads to reported losses in the early years of the investment's useful life.

10. A project has unequal cash flows, and a manager guesses that the internal rate of return will be 10 percent. If the net present value is positive at 10 percent, then:

    a. The internal rate of return is greater than 10 percent.

    b. The internal rate of return is less than 10 percent.

    c. The internal rate of return is exactly 10 percent.

    d. None of these answer choices is correct.

ANSWERS TO SELF-ASSESSMENT

1. d **2.** a **3.** c **4.** d **5.** a **6.** c **7.** d **8.** d **9.** d **10.** a

QUESTIONS

1. What is a capital expenditure decision?
2. Why is it important to take into account the time value of money when making capital budgeting decisions?
3. What are the two approaches for evaluating investments that take into account the time value of money?
4. How do the net present value and the internal rate of return methods differ in their approach to evaluating investment alternatives?

5. What is the cost of equity financing?
6. How are cash flows affected as a result of the tax consequences of depreciation?
7. What are the advantages of evaluating projects using the net present value and internal rate of return methods instead of the payback and accounting rate of return methods?
8. Why may managers concentrate on the short-run profitability of investments rather than their net present values?
9. How is the internal rate of return (IRR) determined if there are uneven cash flows?
10. Why does the failure to consider soft benefits discourage investment?

EXERCISES

EXERCISE 9-1. [LO 1] Explain why interest expense is not treated as a cash outflow in capital budgeting decisions made using net present value (NPV) analysis.

GROUP WORK

WRITING

EXERCISE 9-2. [LO 1, 3] Sally Omar is the manager of the office products division of Wallace Enterprises. In this position, her annual bonus is based on an appraisal of return on investment (ROI) measured as Division income ÷ End-of-year division assets (net of accumulated depreciation).

Currently, Sally is considering investing $40,000,000 in modernization of the division plant in Tennessee. She estimates that the project will generate cash savings of $6,550,000 per year for 8 years. The plant improvements will be depreciated over 8 years ($40,000,000 ÷ 8 years = $5,000,000). Thus, the annual effect on income will be $1,550,000 ($6,550,000 – $5,000,000).

REQUIRED

Using a discount rate of 10 percent, calculate the NPV of the modernization project. Then calculate the ROI of the project each year over its eight-year life. (Calculate ROI as effect on income divided by end-of-year book value. Note that the value of ROI is not defined at the end of year 8 when book value is zero.) Finally, write a paragraph explaining why Sally may not make the investment even though it has a positive NPV.

EXERCISE 9-3. [LO 1] Generally speaking, the cost of capital for a food-processing company is lower than the cost of capital for a company that runs casinos. Briefly expain why this is the case.

EXCEL

EXERCISE 9-4. Using Present Value Tables [LO 1] What is the present value of $850 per year for 6 years if the required return is 11 percent (answer using Table B9-2 in Appendix B).

EXERCISE 9-5. Using Present Value Tables [LO 1] Examine Table B9-1 in Appendix B. Explain why the numbers decrease as you move from left to right in a given row. Explain why the numbers decrease as you move from top to bottom in a given column.

EXERCISE 9-6. Calculate Present Value [LO 1] Suppose you face the prospect of receiving $1,200 per year for the next 7 years plus an extra $950 payment at the end of 7 years. Determine how much this prospect is worth today if the required rate of return is 15 percent.

EXERCISE 9-7. Calculate Present Value [LO 1] Mary Martinez is ready to retire and has a choice of three pension plans. Plan A provides for an immediate cash payment of $350,000. Plan B provides for the payment of $40,000 per year for 8 years and the payment of $200,000 at the end of year 8. Plan C will pay $35,000 per year for 8 years. Mary Martinez desires a return of 8 percent. Determine the present value of each plan and select the best one.

EXERCISE 9-8. Calculate Net Present Value [LO 1] An investment that costs $85,000 will return $35,000 per year for 5 years. Determine the net present value of the investment if the required rate of return is 12 percent. (Ignore taxes.) Should the investment be undertaken?

EXERCISE 9-9. Calculate the Internal Rate of Return [LO 1] An investment that costs $200,000 will reduce operating costs by $35,000 per year for 12 years. Determine the internal rate of return of the investment (ignore taxes). Should the investment be undertaken if the required rate of return is 18 percent?

EXERCISE 9-10. Calculate the Internal Rate of Return [LO 1] Tanya Sinclair, owner of Sinclair Fine Wine, is considering investing $195,000 in a temperature-controlled wine storage room. She plans to rent space to customers and expects to generate $55,000 annually (rental charges less miscellaneous expenses other than depreciation).

REQUIRED

a. Assuming Tanya wishes to evaluate the project with a five-year time horizon, what is the internal rate of return of the investment? (Ignore taxes.)

b. Should Tanya make the investment if her required rate of return is 10 percent?

EXERCISE 9-11. Depreciation Tax Shield [LO 2] Strauss Corporation is making a $90,000 investment in equipment with a five-year life. The company uses the straight-line method of depreciation and has a tax rate of 40 percent. The company's required rate of return is 15 percent.

REQUIRED

What is the present value of the tax savings related to depreciation of the equipment?

EXERCISE 9-12. Cash Flow Implications of Tax Losses [LO 2] WesternGear.com is expected to have operating losses of $350,000 in its first year of business and $270,000 in its second year. However, the company expects to have income before taxes of $400,000 in its third year and $650,000 in its fourth year. The company's required rate of return is 14 percent.

REQUIRED

Assume a tax rate of 35 percent and that current losses can be used to offset taxable income in future years. What is the present value of tax savings related to the operating losses in years 1 and 2?

EXERCISE 9-13. Net Present Value with Taxes [LO 1, 2] Great Northern Fishing Company is contemplating the purchase of a new smoker. The smoker will cost $60,000 but will generate additional revenue of $34,000 per year for 6 years. Additional costs, other than depreciation, will equal $12,000 per year. The smoker has an expected life of 6 years, at which time it will have no residual value. Great Northern uses the straight-line method of depreciation for tax purposes. Determine the net present value of the investment if the required rate of return is 14 percent and the tax rate is 40 percent. Should Great Northern make the investment in the smoker?

EXERCISE 9-14. Calculate the Payback Period [LO 3] The Sunny Valley Wheat Cooperative is considering the construction of a new silo. It will cost $126,000 to construct the silo. Determine the payback period if the expected cash inflows are $21,000 per year.

EXERCISE 9-15. Calculate the Accounting Rate of Return [LO 3] The Herbolt Company is considering a new line of business. Starting the business will require an initial investment in equipment of $355,000. It is expected that the new business will increase net income by $32,000 per year for 5 years. The equipment will be depreciated over a 5-year period using straight-line depreciation with no residual value. Determine the accounting rate of return of the new business.

EXERCISE 9-16. IRR and Unequal Cash Flows [LO 1] Newport Department Store is considering development of an e-commerce business. The company estimates that development will require an initial outlay of $1,300,000. Other cash flows will be as follows:

Year 1	($750,000)
Year 2	$221,000
Year 3	$850,000
Year 4	$950,000
Year 5	$940,000

REQUIRED

Assuming the company limits its analysis to 5 years, estimate the internal rate of return of the e-commerce business. Should the company develop the e-commerce business if the required rate of return is 14 percent?

EXERCISE 9-17. IRR and Unequal Cash Flows [LO 1] A company is making an investment of $2,500,000 that will yield the following cash flows:

Year 1	$ 250,000
Year 2	$ 440,000
Year 3	$ 650,000
Year 4	$ 850,000
Year 5	$1,102,765

REQUIRED

What is the internal rate of return of the investment?

EXERCISE 9-18. Soft Benefits [LO 1] Reece Jewelry has 45 stores in major malls around the country. The company is considering starting an online business, ReeceJewelry.com, which will require a substantial investment in technology.

REQUIRED

Identify a potential benefit of the online business that would be difficult to quantify in a net present value analysis.

PROBLEMS

EXCEL

PROBLEM 9-1. Present Value Analysis [LO 1, 2] James Hardy recently rejected a $20,000,000, five-year contract with the Vancouver Seals hockey team. The contract offer called for an immediate signing bonus of $7,500,000 and annual payments of $2,500,000. To sweeten the deal, the president of player personnel for the Seals has now offered a $22,000,000, five-year contract. This contract calls for annual increases and a balloon payment at the end of 5 years.

Year 1	$ 2,500,000
Year 2	2,600,000
Year 3	2,700,000
Year 4	2,800,000
Year 5	2,900,000
Year 5 balloon payment	8,500,000
Total	$22,000,000

REQUIRED

Suppose you are Hardy's agent and you wish to evaluate the two contracts using a required rate of return of 15 percent. In present value terms, how much better is the second contract?

PROBLEM 9-2. Calculate Net Present Value [LO 1] Memory Florist is considering replacing an old refrigeration unit with a larger unit to store flowers. Because the new refrigeration unit has a larger capacity, Memory estimates that it can sell an additional $9,000 of flowers a year. (The cost of the flowers is $5,000). In addition, the new unit is energy efficient and should save $2,500 in electricity each year. It will cost an extra $4,000 per year for maintenance. The new refrigeration unit costs $25,000 and has an expected life of 10 years. The old unit is fully depreciated and can be sold for an amount equal to disposal cost. At the end of 10 years, the new unit has an expected residual value of $6,000. Determine the net present value of the investment if the required rate of return is 14 percent. (Ignore taxes.) Should the investment be undertaken?

PROBLEM 9-3. Choosing among Alternative Investments [LO 1] Albert Shoe Company is considering investing in one of two machines that attach heels to shoes. Machine A costs $70,000 and is expected to save the company $20,000 per year for 6 years. Machine B costs $95,000 and is expected to save the company $25,000 per year for 6 years. Determine the net present value for each machine and decide which machine should be purchased if the required rate of return is 13 percent. Ignore taxes.

EXCEL

PROBLEM 9-4. Present Value and "What If" Analysis [LO 1] National Cruise Line is considering the acquisition of a new ship that will cost $200,000,000. In this regard, the president of the company asked the CFO to analyze cash flows associated with operating the ship under two alternative itineraries: Itinerary 1, Caribbean Winter/Alaska Summer and Itinerary 2, Caribbean Winter/Eastern Canada Summer. The CFO estimated the following cash flows, which are expected to apply to each of the next 15 years:

	Caribbean/Alaska	Caribbean/Eastern Canada
Net revenue	$120,000,000	$105,000,000
Less:		
Direct program expenses	(25,000,000)	(24,000,000)
Indirect program expenses	(20,000,000)	(20,000,000)
Nonoperating expenses	(21,000,000)	(21,000,000)
Add back depreciation	115,000,000	115,000,000
Cash flow per year	$169,000,000	$155,000,000

REQUIRED

a. For each of the itineraries, calculate the present values of the cash flows using required rates of return of both 12 and 16 percent. Assume a 15-year time horizon. Should the company purchase the ship with either or both required rates of return?

b. The president is uncertain whether a 12 percent or a 16 percent required return is appropriate. Explain why, in the present circumstance, spending a great deal of time determining the correct required return may not be necessary.

c. Focusing on a 12 percent required rate of return, what would be the opportunity cost to the company of using the ship in a Caribbean/Eastern Canada itinerary rather than a Caribbean/Alaska itinerary?

PROBLEM 9-5. Net Present Value and Taxes [LO 1, 2] Penguin Productions is evaluating a film project. The president of Penguin estimates that the film will cost $20,000,000 to produce. In its first year, the film is expected to generate $16,500,000 in net revenue, after which the film will be released to video. Video is expected to generate $10,000,000 in net revenue in its first year, $2,500,000 in its second year, and $1,000,000 in its third year. For tax purposes, amortization of the cost of the film will be $12,000,000 in year 1 and $8,000,000 in year 2. The company's tax rate is 35 percent, and the company requires a 12 percent rate of return on its films.

REQUIRED

What is the net present value of the film project? To simplify, assume that all outlays to produce the film occur at time 0. Should the company produce the film?

EXCEL **PROBLEM 9-6. Internal Rate of Return and Taxes [LO 1]** The Boston Culinary Institute is evaluating a classroom remodeling project. The cost of the remodel will be $350,000 and will be depreciated over 6 years using the straight-line method. The remodeled room will accommodate five extra students per year. Each student pays annual tuition of $22,000. The before-tax incremental cost of a student (e.g., the cost of food prepared and consumed by a student) is $2,000 per year. The company's tax rate is 40 percent, and the company requires a 12 percent rate of return on the remodeling project.

REQUIRED

Assuming a six-year time horizon, what is the internal rate of return of the remodeling project? Should the company invest in the remodel?

PROBLEM 9-7. Net Present Value, Internal Rate of Return, Payback, Accounting Rate of Return, and Taxes [LO 1, 2, 3] Adrian Sonnetson, the owner of Adrian Motors, is considering the addition of a paint and body shop to his automobile dealership. Construction of a building and the purchase of necessary equipment is estimated to cost $800,000, and both the building and equipment will be depreciated over 10 years using the straight-line method. The building and equipment have zero estimated residual value at the end of 10 years. Sonnetson's required rate of return for this project is 12 percent. Net income related to each year of the investment is as follows:

Revenue	$650,000
Less:	
Material cost	70,000
Labor	150,000
Depreciation	80,000
Other	10,000
Income before taxes	340,000
Taxes at 40%	136,000
Net income	$204,000

REQUIRED

a. Determine the net present value of the investment in the paint and body shop. Should Sonnetson invest in the paint and body shop?

b. Calculate the internal rate of return of the investment (approximate).

c. Calculate the payback period of the investment.

d. Calculate the accounting rate of return.

PROBLEM 9-8. Choosing among Alternative Investments [LO 1] Pronto Cleaners, a chain of dry cleaning stores, has the opportunity to invest in one of two dry cleaning machines. Machine A has a four-year expected life and a cost of $30,000. It will cost an additional $6,500 to have the machine delivered and installed, and the expected residual value at the end of 4 years is $4,000. Machine B has a 4-year expected life and a cost of $55,000. It will cost an additional $7,000 to have the machine delivered and installed, and the expected residual value at the end of four years is $6,000. Pronto has a required rate of return of 14 percent. Additional cash flows related to the machines are as follows:

Machine A

Item	Year 1	Year 2	Year 3	Year 4
Labor saving	$25,000	$25,000	$25,000	$25,000
Power saving	1,500	1,500	1,500	1,500
Chemical saving	3,000	3,000	3,000	3,000
Additional maintenance	(1,200)	(1,200)	(1,200)	(1,200)
Additional miscellaneous	(2,500)	(2,500)	(2,500)	(2,500)

Machine B

Item	Year 1	Year 2	Year 3	Year 4
Labor saving	$32,000	$32,000	$32,000	$32,000
Power saving	2,000	2,000	2,000	2,000
Chemical saving	3,500	3,500	3,500	3,500
Additional maintenance	(1,500)	(1,500)	(1,500)	(1,500)
Additional miscellaneous	(2,700)	(2,700)	(2,700)	(2,700)

REQUIRED

a. Ignoring taxes, determine the net present value of investing in Machine A.

b. Ignoring taxes, determine the net present value of investing in Machine B.

c. Which, if any, machine should be purchased?

PROBLEM 9-9. Net Present Value and Taxes [LO 1, 2] Drake Limousine Service is considering acquisition of an additional vehicle. The model under consideration will cost $160,000 and have a five-year life and a $45,000 residual value. The company anticipates that the effect on annual net income will be as follows:

Revenue		$120,000
Less expenses:		
Driver	40,000	
Fuel	9,000	
Maintenance	2,000	
Insurance	1,800	
Depreciation	23,000	
Miscellaneous	2,000	
Total expense		77,800
Income before taxes		42,200
Taxes at 40%		16,880
Net income		$ 25,320

REQUIRED

Calculate the net present value of the investment assuming the company has a required rate of return of 14 percent. Should the company invest in the new limousine?

PROBLEM 9-10. Net Present Value and Taxes [LO 1, 2] Island Ferry plans to expand operations by acquiring another boat. It has a bid of $950,000 from a boat manufacturer to provide a boat that can carry 40 passengers. The boat has an expected life of 7 years with an expected residual value for financial reporting and tax purposes of $50,000. Island Ferry has a tax rate of 40 percent and uses straight-line depreciation for tax purposes. Its required rate of return is 10 percent. The following annual cash flows relate to the investment in the new boat:

Item	Cash Flow
Passenger revenues	$325,000
Labor cost	(90,000)
Fuel cost	(16,000)
Maintenance cost	(15,000)
Miscellaneous cost	(4,000)
Taxes	?

REQUIRED

Calculate the net present value of the investment in the boat. Should the company make the investment?

PROBLEM 9-11. Quantifying Soft Benefits [LO 1] Pritchard Manufactured Products is considering investing in a flexible manufacturing system that will enable the company to respond rapidly to customer requests. Ben Jarvis, the controller of Pritchard, has estimated that the system will have a nine-year life and a net present value of negative $600,000. However, he admits that he did not take into account the potential sales increases that will result from improvement in on-time delivery. According to Ben, "This is just too hard to estimate."

REQUIRED

Using a nine-year life and a required return of 10 percent, what must be the annual value of the soft benefits associated with the project to yield a zero net present value? Assume that there is general agreement that the annual "soft" benefits will yield at least $120,000 in additional net cash flows. In this case, should the investment be undertaken?

PROBLEM 9-12. Comprehensive Capital Budgeting Problem [LO 1, 3] Van Doren Corporation is considering producing a new temperature regulator called Digidial. Marketing data indicate that the company will be able to sell 45,000 units per year at $30. The product will be produced in a section of an existing factory that is currently not in use.

To produce Digidial, Van Doren must buy a machine that costs $500,000. The machine has an expected life of 6 years and will have an ending residual value of $15,000. Van Doren will depreciate the machine over 6 years using the straight-line method for both tax and financial reporting purposes.

In addition to the cost of the machine, the company will incur incremental manufacturing costs of $370,000 for component parts, $425,000 for direct labor, and $200,000 of miscellaneous costs. Also, the company plans to spend $150,000 annually to advertise Digidial. Van Doren has a tax rate of 40 percent, and the company's required rate of return is 15 percent.

REQUIRED

a. Compute the net present value.
b. Compute the payback period.
c. Compute the accounting rate of return.
d. Should Van Doren make the investment required to produce Digidial?

PROBLEM 9-13. Comprehensive Capital Budgeting Problem [LO 1] True Fresh Grocery operates a chain of 40 grocery stores. Currently the company is considering starting a new division, TrueFresh.com, to provide home delivery services. Customers will be able to order groceries by phone or using the Internet, and TrueFresh.com will deliver them within 24 hours at a price guaranteed to be identical to the prices charged in the company's stores.

The company has projected revenue and cost related to this business for the next 7 years, as follows:

	Year 1	Year 2	Year 3	Year 4	Year 5	Year 6	Year 7
Revenue	$1,700,000	$1,870,000	$2,057,000	$2,262,700	$2,488,970	$2,737,867	$3,011,654
Less expenses:							
Cost of merchandise	1,120,000	1,175,000	1,200,000	1,200,000	1,260,000	1,300,000	1,375,000
Salaries	350,000	365,000	380,750	397,000	414,652	432,884	462,030
Depreciation	60,000	60,000	60,000	60,000	60,000	60,000	60,000
Miscellaneous	23,333	21,667	20,917	28,000	27,015	28,783	27,970
Total expense	1,553,333	1,621,667	1,661,667	1,685,000	1,761,667	1,821,667	1,925,000
Income before taxes	146,667	248,333	395,333	577,700	727,303	916,200	1,086,654
Taxes at 40%	58,667	99,333	158,133	231,080	290,921	366,480	434,662
Net income	$ 88,000	$ 149,000	$ 237,200	$ 346,620	$ 436,382	$ 549,720	$ 651,992

The business will require an initial investment in delivery trucks and other equipment of $500,000. The trucks and equipment will be depreciated over a seven-year life using straight-line depreciation with a residual value of $80,000.

REQUIRED

Assume that True Fresh has decided to limit its analysis to 7 years. Calculate the net present value of the new business using a 14 percent required rate of return. Should True Fresh make the investment in the new business?

PROBLEM 9-14. Net Present Value and Inflation [LO 1, 2] Edward Laren, an accountant with Tenergy Industries, prepared the following analysis of an investment in manufacturing equipment:

Cost savings:	
Labor savings	$ 525,000
Reduction in rework materials	125,000
Other	60,000
Total	710,000
Additional taxes related to cost savings	(239,750)
Tax savings related to depreciation of new equipment	161,000
Annual cash flow	$ 631,250
Present value at 10 percent for 5 years	$ 2,392,934
Cost of equipment	(2,300,000)
Net present value	$ 92,934

Edward's boss, Megan Mangione, reviewed the calculation and made the following observation: "Ed, you've assumed that there won't be inflation, but inflation is built into our 10 percent cost of capital. I think it's reasonable to assume that labor and costs other than depreciation will increase by 4 percent per year. Why don't you redo the analysis with that assumption?"

REQUIRED

a. What does Megan Mangione mean by "inflation is built into our 10 percent cost of capital"?

b. Redo Edward Laren's analysis assuming an inflation rate of 4 percent. Should the company make the investment in the equipment?

PROBLEM 9-15. Internal Rate of Return with Uneven Cash Flows [LO 1] Based on the information in Problem 9-14, what is the internal rate of return of the investment, assuming an inflation rate of 4 percent applicable to labor and costs other than depreciation? Should the company make the investment if its cost of capital is 10 percent?

PROBLEM 9-16. Risk and Cost of Capital [LO 1] Talich Industries is considering investing in an automated welding system. The system employs a 300-watt laser with fiber optic beam delivery to weld dissimilar metals. The specifications of the system indicate that it can make hundreds of welds per minute—significantly faster than the company's current welding equipment—and improve the quality of welds.

In the recent past, Talich has evaluated investments using a 12 percent cost of capital. However, the automated welding system is not in general use. While the company expects that it will result in significant labor savings and improve quality leading to increased sales, the cash flows are not at all certain.

REQUIRED

Assume that the cash inflows associated with the automated welding system are more risky than those associated with the company's typical investment. Should the company evaluate the investment using the cost of capital of 12 percent, or should a higher or lower rate be used? Briefly explain the basis for your answer.

PROBLEM 9-17. Conflict between Performance Evaluation and Use of NPV [LO 3] Division managers at Creighton Aerospace are evaluated and rewarded based on ROI (return on investment) targets. In the current year, Delmar Richards, the president of the commercial products division, has an ROI target of 12 percent. If the division has an ROI of 12 percent or greater, Delmar will receive 250,000 options on Creighton stock in addition to a base salary of $400,000.

The commercial products division is considering a major investment in product development, which has a net present value of $25,000,000. However, the investment will have a negative effect on reported profit over the next 2 years, after which the investment will begin to have a significant positive effect on firm profitability for the next 8 years.

REQUIRED

a. Discuss the potential conflict between the company's evaluation/compensation system and Delmar's focus on the NPV of the investment in product development.

b. Suppose Delmar currently holds stock in Creighton Aerospace with a market value of $1,250,000 and has options on 500,000 shares (awarded in previous years). Is this likely to acerbate or mitigate the conflict you discussed in part a?

PROBLEM 9-18. Internal Rate of Return with Uneven Cash Flows [LO 1] Palermo Pizzeria is considering expanding operations by establishing a delivery business. This will require the purchase of an oven that will cost $50,000, including installation. The oven is expected to last 5 years, have a $5,000 residual value, and will be depreciated using the straight-line method. Cash flows associated with the delivery business are as follows:

Item	Year 1	Year 2	Year 3	Year 4	Year 5
Revenue	$65,000	$66,300	$78,230	$88,000	$95,238
Ingredients	(25,100)	(27,600)	(30,392)	(33,441)	(36,695)
Salary	(24,900)	(26,900)	(28,900)	(30,900)	(32,800)
Additional misc.	(2,100)	(2,300)	(2,500)	(2,700)	(2,800)
Residual value					5,000

In addition to the above, there are tax consequences related to the new business, and the company's tax rate is 40 percent.

REQUIRED

Calculate the internal rate of return for the delivery business. (*Hint:* Try a range of rates between 8 percent and 15 percent.) Should Palermo Pizzeria invest in the delivery business if the required rate of return is 10 percent?

CASE

9-1 ETHICS CASE: JUNIPER PACKAGING SOLUTIONS. [LO 1]

Juniper Packaging Solutions provides custom packaging products to companies all over the United States. With five production facilities, the company produces cardboard boxes, plastic and steel drums, aluminum bottles, and absorbent pouches and bags. Companies using their products ship everything from chemicals in 55-gallon containers to biological specimens in tamper-evident pouches.

Spencer Williams is the vice president in charge of the Maryland production facility, and in the last year he's become concerned about plant performance. The plant needs a long lead time for orders, and defect rates have increased—both of which hurt customer satisfaction. In Spencer's opinion, the problems are the result of outmoded production equipment. Recently Spencer's team of production managers identified three pieces of state-of-the-art equipment that they believe will turn the plant around and make it the most efficient of the company's five plants. Unfortunately, the price tag of the equipment is $2,000,000 and the company has a freeze on capital expenditures greater than $500,000. The freeze was mandated by the company chief executive officer (CEO) after third-quarter earnings dropped by 10 percent due to a weakening of the Asian economy and reduced shipments to Japan and Korea by several of Juniper's major customers.

Spencer and the controller of the Maryland plant both believe that the new equipment is absolutely necessary for the company to maintain customer satisfaction and market share. Together they've devised a plan to circumvent the capital expenditure freeze. Each piece of equipment is actually a "system" with multiple components (e.g., conveyor belt, box molding unit, box taping unit, etc.). Spencer will ask the equipment manufacturers to break each system into components and submit multiple bills (e.g., a separate bill for the conveyor, a separate bill for the box molding unit, etc.) each less than $500,000. The plant controller will then approve the expenditures as being consistent with the guidelines that only prohibit expenditures on equipment costing more than $500,000.

REQUIRED

Is the plan devised by Spencer and the CFO ethical? In answering this question, assume that Spencer and the controller are both firmly convinced that the new equipment will increase shareholder value.

CASE

9-2 SERGO GAMES [LO 1, 2]

Sergo Games produces a variety of action games including a flight simulation game, Airport 10, which sold more than 800,000 copies in the past year. The programs are run on computers, and the company operates an in-house production facility that manufactures and packages CDs for shipment to customers.

In 2017, the production plant prepared 2,600,000 CDs and incurred the following costs:

Units processed	2,600,000
Labor	$ 900,000
Material	4,800,000
Supervisory salaries	350,000
Depreciation of equipment	420,000
Heat, light, phone, etc.	200,000
Total	$6,670,000

Leslie Eastman, an accounting manager, has been given the responsibility to analyze outsourcing the production of CDs. Her report is provided below.

REQUIRED

Should production of CDs be outsourced? Unlike Leslie, support your answer with appropriate calculations.

Sergo Games

April 19, 2018

TO: Shane Santiago, CFO

FROM: Leslie Eastman

SUBJECT: Outsourcing CD production

In 2017, total production and packaging costs were $6,670,000, or $2.57 per CD. The low-cost outside bidder for this business was XLS. They are a highly respected firm, and their offer is $2.52 per CD. Although the savings related to outsourcing is only $0.05 per CD, with annual production of 2,600,000 units, this amounts to $130,000 per year. The present value with a five-year horizon and a 11 percent cost of capital is $480,467. Thus, I recommend that we outsource CD production.

You asked me to determine the selling price of the production equipment. I had a representative of XLS walk through the facility. In his opinion, the equipment is dated, and he believes that the market value is essentially zero. At any rate, his company is not interested in purchasing the equipment even if we select them as a supplier. If we outsource, I do not believe that we can use the production facility for another purpose. As you know, the building is run down, and it's not a suitable space even for programmers!

Finally, I want to mention another aspect of the problem that enhances the appeal of outsourcing. We currently have equipment with a book value of $2,000,000 and an average remaining life of 5 years. This generates approximately $400,000 per year of depreciation. If we outsource, we'll have a $2,000,000 tax loss, which will save us approximately $700,000 (assuming a 35 percent tax rate). Thus, the total value of outsourcing is $1,180,467 (i.e., $480,467 + $700,000).

Please call me if you have any questions regarding my analysis.

10

BUDGETARY PLANNING AND CONTROL

Preston Joystick produces a joystick that is the top choice for many serious gamers.

At a meeting of key managers, Alan Renton, president of Preston Joystick, reviewed the past successes and failures of his firm. "As you know," he concluded, "we've begun a new marketing campaign, and I am confident that next year sales will increase by at least 20 percent." Jack North, the production manager, seemed caught off guard by this good news. "Look, Alan," he said, "if you really think sales are going to take off, we've got to plan for the increase. I'll have to hire additional workers, and the people in purchasing will need to buy more parts so we don't run out." Pam Smith, vice president of finance, chimed in. "Also, more sales means more inventory, and more inventory means we'll have to borrow additional funds to finance the expansion. I'll need some lead time to arrange the loan."

The meeting ended with everyone agreeing that more attention should be devoted to planning company activities. Alan went back to his office convinced that without a plan to guide and coordinate company activities, the coming year would be a series of near disasters. "The marketing, production, and finance people need to know what is anticipated so we can operate effectively and efficiently," he concluded.

In business, **budgets** are the formal documents that quantify a company's plans for achieving its goals. The entire planning and control process of many companies is built around budgets. This chapter illustrates the preparation of several budgets that are in common use. The chapter also describes the role of budgets in the performance evaluation process and discusses a number of issues associated with budgets.

Squaredpixels/Istock/Getty Images Plus

LEARNING OBJECTIVES

1. Discuss the use of budgets in planning and control.
2. Prepare the budget schedules that make up a master budget.
3. Explain why flexible budgets are needed for performance evaluation, and discuss the conflict between the planning and control uses of budgets.

LEARNING OBJECTIVE 1

Discuss the use of budgets in planning and control.

USE OF BUDGETS IN PLANNING AND CONTROL

At companies from Microsoft to Marriott, from Walmart to Wendy's, budgets are a high priority. As mentioned, the entire planning and control process of many companies is built around budgets. This section describes how budgets are used in planning and control.

Planning

Budgets are useful in the planning process because they enhance *communication* and *coordination*. The process of developing a formal plan—that is, a budget—forces managers to consider carefully their goals and objectives and to specify means of achieving them. Budgets become the vehicle for communicating information about where the company is heading, and they aid coordination of managers' activities. For example, the marketing department may prepare a budget that includes estimates of sales for each month of a future year. The production department may use the information contained in this budget to schedule workers and material deliveries. Thus, the necessary coordination of product sales and product production is achieved.

Control

Budgets are useful in the control process because they provide a basis for *evaluating performance*. To control a company—to make sure it is heading in the proper direction and operating efficiently—it is essential to assess the performance of managers and the operations for which they are responsible. Often performance evaluation is carried out by comparing actual performance with planned or budgeted performance.

Significant deviations from planned performance are associated with three potential causes:

1. **It is possible that the plan or budget was poorly conceived.** If a budget is not carefully developed, it should not be surprising that actual results are different from planned results.
2. **It is possible that although the budget was carefully developed, conditions have changed.** For example, if the economy were to take a sudden downturn, actual sales might be less than budgeted sales.
3. **It is possible that managers have done a particularly good or poor job managing operations.** If this is the case, the managers will be rewarded for good performance (e.g., given a bonus or a promotion) or punished for poor performance (e.g., given reduced responsibility or even fired).

YOU GET WHAT YOU MEASURE

A graphic presentation of the role of budgets in the planning and control process appears in Illustration 10-1. As you study this illustration, remember that **you get what you measure!** This idea is central to an understanding of the control process. If managers know that their performance will be evaluated with respect to the budget, they are likely to work especially hard to achieve budgeted goals. Thus, it is critical that the budgeted goals be well thought out and clearly communicated to managers

DEVELOPING THE BUDGET

Budgets are prepared for departments, for divisions of a company, and for the company as a whole. Often the group within a company that is responsible for approval of the various budgets is the **budget committee**. This committee consists of senior managers, including the president, the chief financial officer, the vice president for operations, and the controller. Typically, the budget committee works with departments to develop realistic

ILLUSTRATION 10-1

Role of budgets in the planning and control process

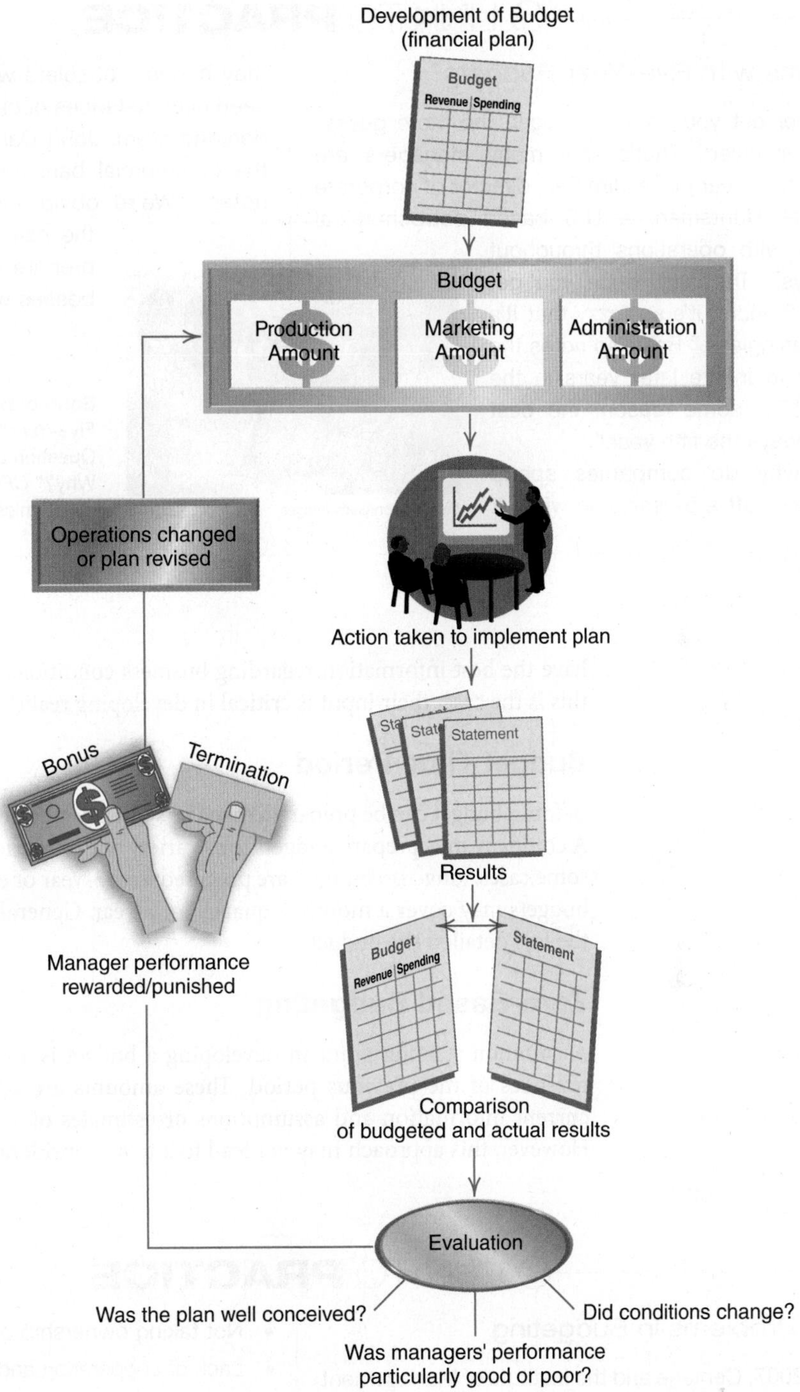

plans that are consistent with overall company goals. In some cases, however, the budget committee may impose a budget without soliciting input from department managers.

The extent to which departments are consulted relates to the distinction between top-down and bottom-up approaches to the development of a budget. In a top-down approach, budgets are developed at higher organizational levels without substantial input from lower-level managers. In a bottom-up approach, lower-level managers are the primary source of information used in setting the budget. Most managers believe a successful budgeting process requires a bottom-up approach. After all, lower-level managers often

LINK TO PRACTICE

Problems with Five-Year Budgets

The farther out you go in a budget, the more guesswork is involved. That's why many managers are opposed to 5-year plans. Jim Bell, director of corporate finance at Huntsman, a U.S.-based petrochemical company with operations throughout Asia, says, "Truthfully, once you get out past 2 years, it's so fuzzy that it's fairly meaningless." Bell also notes the tendency to inflate later years in the budget. "For some reason, the best year is always the fifth year."

So why do companies spend months to craft a 5-year plan when it may become obsolete within 6 months when unforeseen circumstances occur? One reason is that lenders demand them. John Daniels, senior vice president in the commercial banking group at Bank of America, notes: "We're obviously asking so we understand the risk of a deal." And some CFOs prepare them simply because their bosses want one!

Digital Vision/Getty Images

Source: Based on Kris Frieswick, "The Five-Year Itch: For CFOs, the Biggest Question about Doing Five-Year Plans Is, Why?" *CFO Asia*, March 2003. Reprinted by permission.

have the best information regarding business conditions affecting their departments. If this is the case, their input is critical in developing realistic financial plans.

Budget Time Period

Before a budget can be prepared, managers must decide on an appropriate budget period. A company may prepare budgets for a variety of time periods, depending on its needs. In some cases, long-run budgets are prepared for a 3-year or even a 5-year period. Short-run budgets may cover a month, a quarter, or a year. Generally, the longer the time period, the less detailed the budget.

Zero-Based Budgeting

A common starting point in developing a budget is a consideration of the costs and revenues of the previous period. These amounts are adjusted up or down based on current information and assumptions or estimates of what will happen in the future. However, this approach may *not* lead to a fresh consideration of activities.

LINK TO PRACTICE

People Problems in Budgeting

In spring 2007, Centage and the Institute of Management and Administration conducted a survey of chief financial officers (CFOs) from more than 20 industries regarding their budgeting practices. According to the respondents, the number one budgeting pain point was dealing with managers. In particular, the CFOs faulted managers for:

- Not taking ownership or being accountable.
- Lack of cooperation and/or participation.
- Lack of understanding of the process or what's required.
- Not meeting deadlines.
- Padding their budgets/providing unrealistic numbers.

OJO Images/SUPERSTOCK

Source: Centage/IOMA, *Budgeting Survey: Benchmarks & Issues*, 2008.

So-called **zero-based budgeting** is a method of budget preparation that requires budgeted amounts to be justified by each department at the start of each budget period, even if the amounts were supported in prior budget periods. That is, managers must start from zero in developing their budgets. This results in a fresh consideration of the validity of budget amounts, but the technique is time-consuming and expensive. Although zero-based budgeting has gained some support in governmental budgeting, it is not widely practiced by business enterprises.

LEARNING OBJECTIVE 2

Prepare the budget schedules that make up a master budget.

THE MASTER BUDGET

The **master budget** is a comprehensive planning document that incorporates a number of individual budgets. Typically, it includes budgets for sales, production, direct materials, direct labor, manufacturing overhead, selling and administrative expenses, capital acquisitions, and cash receipts and disbursements, as well as a budgeted income statement and a budgeted balance sheet.

In this section, we present examples of each of these components of a master budget. For purposes of the example, budgetary information is prepared by quarter for Preston Joystick. As you will see, the various budgets are interrelated. In particular, the sales budget influences the production budget. The production budget, in turn, influences the material purchases budget, the direct labor budget, and the manufacturing overhead budget. The relationships among the various budgets are presented in Illustration 10-2.

Sales Budget

The first step in the budget process involves preparation of sales forecasts and development of a sales budget. This budget comes first because other budgets cannot be prepared without an estimate of sales. For example, managers preparing the production budget must have an estimate of future sales before they can determine what level of production will be necessary to meet demand.

ILLUSTRATION 10-2

Relationships among various budgets that comprise the master budget

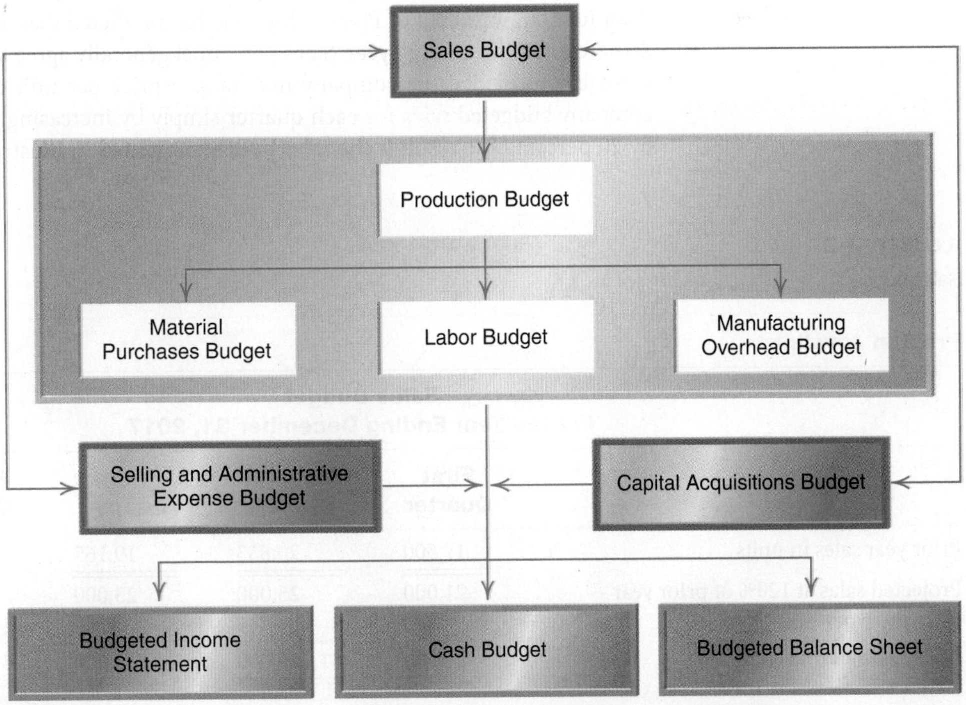

LINK TO PRACTICE

Budget Process in Great Britain

In 2002, *Financial Director* (a business magazine) and Hyperion (a software company) conducted a survey of financial managers in Great Britain. Here are some of the major findings:

- Budget holders involved in preparing their budgets are more likely to take ownership of the results.
- Bottom-up budgeting is more common than "imposed" top-down budgets.
- The budget process is being completed much more quickly than 4 years ago.
- Large organizations believe that there is too little accountability when plans are not achieved.
- Half of the large companies surveyed believe there is some "game playing" in negotiating budgets.
- Large companies believe their budgets are too detailed.

Source: "Budgeting; More of the Same," *Financial Director*, November 2002, p. 41. Reprinted by permission of VNU.

Companies use numerous methods to estimate sales. Very large companies may hire economists to prepare sales forecasts using sophisticated mathematical models that take into consideration the rate of inflation, national capital expenditures, and other economic data. Smaller companies may develop forecasts based on an analysis of the trend in their own sales data. Trade journals or magazines exist for almost every industry, and they may provide useful information for developing sales forecasts. Typically, these journals contain information on past industry sales. They may also make predictions about the growth of the industry. Sales personnel may be another good source of information for forecasting sales. Some companies periodically ask all of their salespersons to estimate sales in their territories for the coming year. These estimates may be highly accurate if the salespersons make their estimates based on thorough knowledge of their customers' needs. In general, forecasts of sales are part science and part art. The forecasts of even the most sophisticated mathematical models are often adjusted based on the professional judgment of experienced managers.

Based on the trend of sales and taking into account a planned marketing campaign, Alan Renton, president of Preston Joystick, has predicted that unit sales will increase by 20 percent in the coming year. Sales personnel generally agree that this level of increase is realistic provided the company maintains a price per unit of $45. Accordingly, the company budgeted sales for each quarter simply by increasing prior year sales in units by 20 percent. The result is the sales budget presented in Illustration 10-3.

ILLUSTRATION 10-3
Sales budget

Preston Joystick

Sales Budget
For the Year Ending December 31, 2017

	First Quarter	Second Quarter	Third Quarter	Fourth Quarter	Year
Prior year sales in units	17,500	20,833	19,167	18,333	75,833
Projected sales at 120% of prior year	21,000	25,000	23,000	22,000	91,000
Sales price per unit	$ ×45	$ ×45	$ ×45	$ ×45	$ ×45
Budgeted sales revenue	$945,000	$1,125,000	$1,035,000	$990,000	$4,095,000

Production Budget

Once the sales budget has been prepared, the production budget can be developed. In deciding how much to produce, managers must take into account how much they expect to sell, how much is in beginning inventory, and how much they want in ending inventory.[1]

The quantity that must be produced can be calculated from the following formula:

Finished units to be produced	=	Expected sales in units	+	Desired ending inventory of finished units	−	Beginning inventory of finished units

Preston Joystick would like the ending inventory of finished goods to be equal to 10 percent of next quarter's sales. In the first quarter, Preston estimates that 21,000 units will be sold; 2,500 units are needed in ending inventory (i.e., 10 percent of 25,000 units expected to be sold in the second quarter). Thus, a total of 23,500 units are required. However, the company has 2,100 units in beginning inventory, so only 21,400 units must be produced. The production budget for Preston Joystick is presented in Illustration 10-4.

TEST YOUR **KNOWLEDGE**

Mason Manufacturing expects to sell 10,000 units in the first quarter and 14,000 in the second quarter. The company desires ending inventory equal to 20 percent of the next quarter's sales, and finished goods on hand at the start of the first quarter equals 2,000 units. How many units should be produced in the first quarter?

a. 14,000. b. 16,000. c. 10,800. d. 12,000.

Correct answer is c (10,000 + 2,800 − 2,000) = $10,800.

ILLUSTRATION 10-4

Production budget

Preston Joystick

Production Budget
For the Year Ending December 31, 2017

	First Quarter	Second Quarter	Third Quarter	Fourth Quarter	Year
Unit sales[a]	21,000	25,000	23,000	22,000	91,000
Plus desired ending inventory of finished units[b]	2,500	2,300	2,200	2,400[c]	2,400
Total needed	23,500	27,300	25,200	24,400	93,400
Less beginning inventory of finished units	2,100	2,500	2,300	2,200	2,100
Units to be produced	21,400	24,800	22,900	22,200	91,300

[a]Information from sales budget in Illustration 10-3.
[b]Equals 10 percent of next quarter's sales.
[c]Based on estimate of sales in the first quarter of the following year.

[1] Preston Joystick does not have a significant amount of Work in Process inventory. Thus, we do not need to take work in process into account in our calculations of anticipated production.

Direct Material Purchases Budget

The amount of direct materials that must be purchased depends on the amount needed for production and the amount needed for ending inventory. Obviously, a company needs some direct materials on hand at the end of the period for use in production at the start of the subsequent period (although, as explained in Chapter 2, the amount would be small in a just-in-time environment). The amount that must be purchased can be calculated using the following formula:

Required purchases of direct materials	=	Amount required for production	+	Desired ending inventory of direct materials	−	Beginning inventory of direct materials

Preston Joystick has established a policy of maintaining direct materials inventory equal to 10 percent of the amount required for production in the subsequent quarter. In the first quarter, the company plans on producing 21,400 units. Each unit requires parts costing $6. In addition, $14,880 of parts must be on hand at the end of the quarter (i.e., 10 percent of the amount required for next quarter's production), but $12,840 of parts are on hand at the start of the quarter. Thus, $130,440 of parts must be purchased in the first quarter. This information is presented in the purchases budget, Illustration 10-5.

Direct Labor Budget

The direct labor budget for Preston Joystick presents direct labor cost by quarter. Direct labor cost is calculated by multiplying the number of units produced each quarter by the labor hours per unit and the rate per hour. In the first quarter, the company expects to produce 21,400 units, and 1 labor hour per unit is required. At a rate of $15 per labor hour, this amounts to $321,000. Preston estimates that, on average, each employee works 480 hours per quarter. This information can be used to estimate the approximate number of employees needed each quarter. In the first quarter, 21,400 labor hours are required. Since an average employee works 480 hours per quarter, approximately 45 employees

ILLUSTRATION 10-5

Direct material purchases budget

Preston Joystick

Direct Material Purchases Budget
For the Year Ending December 31, 2017

	First Quarter	Second Quarter	Third Quarter	Fourth Quarter	Year
Units to be produced[a]	21,400	24,800	22,900	22,200	91,300
Cost of parts per unit	$ ×6	$ ×6	$ ×6	$ ×6	$ ×6
Cost of parts needed for production	$128,400	$148,800	$137,400	$133,200	$547,800
Plus desired ending inventory of parts[b]	14,880	13,740	13,320	14,700[c]	14,700
Total needed	143,280	162,540	150,720	147,900	562,500
Less beginning inventory of parts	12,840	14,880	13,740	13,320	12,840
Cost of purchases	$130,440	$147,660	$136,980	$134,580	$549,660

[a]Information from production budget in Illustration 10-4.
[b]Equals 10 percent of parts required for next quarter's production.
[c]Based on estimate of parts required for production in the first quarter of next year.

ILLUSTRATION 10-6
Direct labor budget

Preston Joystick

Direct Labor Budget
For the Year Ending December 31, 2017

	First Quarter	Second Quarter	Third Quarter	Fourth Quarter	Year
Direct labor hours per unit	1.0	1.0	1.0	1.0	1.0
Labor rate per hour	$ ×15	$ ×15	$ ×15	$ ×15	$ ×15
Direct labor cost per unit	15	15	15	15	15
Units to be produced[a]	×21,400	×24,800	×22,900	×22,200	×91,300
Direct labor cost	$321,000	$372,000	$343,500	$333,000	$1,369,500
Total hours	21,400	24,800	22,900	22,200	
Average hours per quarter per employee	÷480	÷480	÷480	÷480	
Approximate number of employees needed	45	52	48	46	

[a]Information from production budget in Illustration 10-4.

will be needed for production. The direct labor budget for Preston Joystick is presented in Illustration 10-6.

Note that the direct labor budget indicates that 52 employees are needed in the second quarter, whereas only 45 are needed in the first quarter. With this information, the company may decide to adjust its production plans to keep employment stable. If new employees are hired in the second quarter, operations may not be efficient. And if several of these employees are fired in the third quarter, when only 48 employees are needed, morale may suffer. A better idea may be to hire part-time workers or have full-time employees work overtime.

Manufacturing Overhead Budget

Preston Joystick separates variable and fixed costs in the budget for manufacturing overhead. The cost per unit of production of each variable cost item is multiplied by the quantity produced each quarter. The fixed costs are identical each quarter except for the amount of depreciation. This cost increases in the third and fourth quarters because of planned acquisitions of equipment that increase the level of depreciation.

The manufacturing overhead budget is presented in Illustration 10-7. Note that in the budget, we subtract depreciation from total overhead to determine the amount of cash paid out for overhead each quarter. This information will be used when we prepare the budget for cash receipts and disbursements.

Selling and Administrative Expense Budget

To this point, we have presented only the sales budget and production-related budgets. However, budget information is also needed for selling and administrative expenses. Preston Joystick estimates that these expenses are all fixed. The 2017 selling and administrative expense budget is presented in Illustration 10-8.

Budgeted Income Statement

Much of the information contained in the budgets already described is utilized in the preparation of a *budgeted income statement*. This budget is presented in Illustration 10-9. As you

ILLUSTRATION 10-7
Manufacturing overhead budget

Preston Joystick

Manufacturing Overhead Budget
For the Year Ending December 31, 2017

	First Quarter	Second Quarter	Third Quarter	Fourth Quarter	Year
Units to be produced[a]	21,400	24,800	22,900	22,200	91,300
Variable costs:					
Indirect material ($2 per unit)	$ 42,800	$ 49,600	$ 45,800	$ 44,400	$182,600
Indirect labor ($1.50 per unit)	32,100	37,200	34,350	33,300	136,950
Other variable costs ($1.00 per unit)	21,400	24,800	22,900	22,200	91,300
Total variable overhead	96,300	111,600	103,050	99,900	410,850
Fixed costs:					
Supervisory salaries	90,000	90,000	90,000	90,000	360,000
Depreciation of plant and equipment[b]	20,000	20,000	26,000	28,000	94,000
Other	5,000	5,000	5,000	5,000	20,000
Total fixed overhead	115,000	115,000	121,000	123,000	474,000
Total overhead	211,300	226,600	224,050	222,900	884,850
Less depreciation	20,000	20,000	26,000	28,000	94,000
Cash payments for overhead	$191,300	$206,600	$198,050	$194,900	$790,850

Estimated overhead rate = annual overhead ÷ annual production = $884,850 ÷ 91,300 = $9.69 per unit

[a]Information from production budget, Illustration 10-4.
[b]Increase in third and fourth quarter due to acquisition of additional equipment. See capital acquisitions budget in Illustration 10-10.

can see, the sales figures come directly from the sales budget (Illustration 10-3). Cost of goods sold requires a calculation of the unit cost of production. The direct material budget indicates that material cost is $6 per unit (Illustration 10-5). The direct labor budget indicates that direct labor is $15 per unit. And the manufacturing overhead

ILLUSTRATION 10-8
Selling and administrative expense budget

Preston Joystick

Selling and Administrative Expense Budget
For the Year Ending December 31, 2017

	First Quarter	Second Quarter	Third Quarter	Fourth Quarter	Year
Salaries	$160,000	$160,000	$160,000	$160,000	$ 640,000
Advertising	70,000	70,000	70,000	70,000	280,000
Depreciation of office equipment	5,000	5,000	5,000	5,000	20,000
Other	15,000	15,000	15,000	15,000	60,000
Total	250,000	250,000	250,000	250,000	1,000,000
Less depreciation	5,000	5,000	5,000	5,000	20,000
Cash disbursements for selling and administrative expense	$245,000	$245,000	$245,000	$245,000	$ 980,000

ILLUSTRATION 10-9
Budgeted income statement

Preston Joystick

Budgeted Income Statement
For the Year Ending December 31, 2017

	First Quarter	Second Quarter	Third Quarter	Fourth Quarter	Year
Sales[a]	$945,000	$1,125,000	$1,035,000	$990,000	$4,095,000
Less cost of goods sold[b]	644,490	767,250	705,870	675,180	2,792,790
Gross margin	300,510	357,750	329,130	314,820	1,302,210
Less selling and administrative expenses[c]	250,000	250,000	250,000	250,000	1,000,000
Net income	$ 50,510	$ 107,750	$ 79,130	$ 64,820	$ 302,210

[a]Information per sales budget, Illustration 10-3.
[b]First quarter calculation is: 21,000 units × $30.69 = $644,490.
[c]Information per selling and administrative expense budget in Illustration 10-8.

budget indicates that manufacturing overhead is $9.69 per unit. Thus, the unit cost of production is $30.69:

Direct materials	$ 6.00 (Illustration 10-5)
Direct labor	15.00 (Illustration 10-6)
Manufacturing overhead	9.69 (Illustration 10-7)
Total	$30.69 per unit

Management should carefully consider the budgeted income statement to make sure that anticipated profit is consistent with company goals. If budgeted profit is less than the amount management considers satisfactory, steps may be taken to increase sales and reduce costs. Perhaps the advertising campaign can be expanded to further increase sales. Or perhaps material costs can be reduced through negotiations with suppliers. If management decides to take steps to increase profit, then the previous budgets will need to be adjusted to reflect the anticipated changes.

Capital Acquisitions Budget

Decision Making/ Incremental Analysis

Recall that in Chapter 9 we discussed how to make decisions with respect to long-lived assets such as plant and equipment. The recommended approach was to identify incremental cash flows and evaluate them in terms of their net present value (NPV) and/or the internal rate of return (IRR). Decisions involving long-lived assets often are called capital expenditure decisions, and the final list of approved projects is documented in the *capital acquisitions budget.*

Acquisitions of capital assets must be carefully planned, in part because they may substantially reduce cash reserves. Preston Joystick anticipates purchases of office equipment and machinery during the coming year, and this is reflected in the capital acquisitions budget presented in Illustration 10-10.

Cash Budget

In the cash budget, managers plan the amount and timing of cash flows. The information in this budget is a necessary supplement to the information presented in the budgeted

ILLUSTRATION 10-10
Capital acquisitions budget

Preston Joystick

Capital Acquisitions Budget
For the Year Ending December 31, 2017

	First Quarter	Second Quarter	Third Quarter	Fourth Quarter	Year
Office equipment (5-year life)	$10,000	—	—	—	$ 10,000
Machinery (5-year life)	—	—	$120,000[a]	$40,000[b]	160,000
Total	$10,000	—	$120,000	$40,000	$170,000

[a]Increases depreciation by $6,000 in third quarter [i.e., ($120,000 ÷ 5-year life) × 1/4 for third quarter]. See manufacturing overhead budget in Illustration 10-7.

[b]Increases depreciation by $2,000 in fourth quarter [i.e., ($40,000 ÷ 5-year life) × 1/4 for fourth quarter]. See manufacturing overhead budget in Illustration 10-7.

income statement. It is quite possible for a company to project a substantial amount of net income and still face financial distress because its entire set of plans imply more cash outflows than cash inflows. For example, a considerable amount of income may be recognized when a major sale is made. However, the cash received in payment for the sale may not arrive for many months. Or consider a company that makes a major equipment purchase. Although cash reserves may be reduced immediately by the *total* cost of the equipment, current period income will be reduced by only a *fraction* of the cost of the equipment (i.e., by the amount of depreciation). By carefully planning cash receipts and disbursements, companies can anticipate cash shortages and arrange to borrow funds to enhance their cash positions. Or if cash surpluses are anticipated, companies can seek additional investment opportunities or consider paying higher dividends to shareholders.

To prepare an estimate of cash collections, management must determine the percent of credit sales revenue that is collected in the period of sale and the percent collected in the subsequent period. The percentages usually can be estimated based on past collection experience. Preston Joystick has only credit sales. Fifty percent of the sales revenue is collected in the quarter of sale, and 50 percent is collected in the next quarter.

To prepare an estimate of cash disbursements, management must determine the percent of material purchases that is paid in the period of purchase and the percent that is paid in the subsequent period. Preston Joystick determines that 70 percent is paid in the quarter of purchase and 30 percent is paid in the subsequent quarter. The company has determined that, for practical purposes, all other disbursements are made in the quarter in which the related cost is incurred.

In preparing a cash budget, it is important to remember that some expenses do not require cash outlays. For example, depreciation is part of manufacturing overhead, but it does not require a current outlay of cash. Cash is disbursed when an asset is purchased, not when depreciation is recorded. Another example of a noncash expense is the amortization of prepaid insurance. Cash is disbursed when the insurance is purchased, not when the expense is recognized through the amortization of prepaid insurance.

In the cash budget for Preston Joystick, Illustration 10-11, note that cash disbursed for manufacturing overhead in the first quarter is only $191,300. This is $20,000 less than the $211,300 of overhead cost planned for the first quarter in the manufacturing overhead budget, Illustration 10-7. The $20,000 is the amount of depreciation in the first quarter.

ILLUSTRATION 10-11
Cash budget

Preston Joystick

Cash Budget
For the Year Ending December 31, 2017

	First Quarter	Second Quarter	Third Quarter	Fourth Quarter	Year
Cash receipts					
Collection of credit sales[a]					
4th quarter prior year	$430,435				$ 430,435
1st quarter ($945,000)	472,500	$ 472,500			945,000
2nd quarter ($1,125,000)		562,500	$ 562,500		1,125,000
3rd quarter ($1,035,000)			517,500	$ 517,500	1,035,000
4th quarter ($990,000)				495,000	495,000
Total cash receipts	902,935	1,035,000	1,080,000	1,012,500	4,030,435
Cash disbursements					
Purchases of materials[b]					
4th quarter prior year	36,180				36,180
1st quarter ($130,440)	91,308	39,132			130,440
2nd quarter ($147,660)		103,362	44,298		147,660
3rd quarter ($136,980)			95,886	41,094	136,980
4th quarter ($134,580)				94,206	94,206
Total disbursement for purchases	127,488	142,494	140,184	135,300	545,466
Payment for direct labor[c]	321,000	372,000	343,500	333,000	1,369,500
Payment for manufacturing overhead[d]	191,300	206,600	198,050	194,900	790,850
Payment for sell. & adm. expense[e]	245,000	245,000	245,000	245,000	980,000
Capital acquisitions[f]	10,000		120,000	40,000	170,000
Total cash disbursements	894,788	966,094	1,046,734	948,200	3,855,816
Excess of receipts over disbursements	8,147	68,906	33,266	64,300	174,619
Plus beginning cash balance	20,000	28,147	97,053	130,319	20,000
Ending cash balance	$ 28,147	$ 97,053	$ 130,319	$ 194,619	$ 194,619

[a]See Illustration 10-3 for sales information; 50% collected in quarter of sale and 50% collected in subsequent quarter.
[b]See Illustration 10-5 for purchase information; 70% paid in quarter of purchase and 30% paid in subsequent quarter.
[c]See Illustration 10-6 for labor cost information.
[d]Does not include depreciation indicated in manufacturing overhead budget (Illustration 10-7), since depreciation does not require a cash outlay.
[e]Does not include depreciation indicated in selling and administrative expense budget (Illustration 10-8), since depreciation does not require a cash outlay.
[f]See capital acquisitions budget (Illustration 10-10).

TEST YOUR KNOWLEDGE

Mason Manufacturing expects sales of $100,000 in the first quarter and $140,000 in the second quarter. The company collects 70 percent of sales in the quarter sold and 30 percent in the subsequent quarter.

What are expected cash collections in the second quarter?

a. $128,000. b. $30,000. c. $98,000. d. $142,000.

Correct answer is a [(.3 × $100,000) + (.7 × $140,000) = $128,000].

As indicated in the illustration, the anticipated cash flows fluctuate significantly from quarter to quarter. The result is that at the end of the first quarter, the cash balance is expected to be only $28,147, whereas the cash balance at the end of the fourth quarter is expected to be $194,619. Obviously, a low cash balance is dangerous because the company may not have enough funds to pay employees and suppliers. Thus, Preston Joystick may wish to consider borrowing money to improve its cash position in the first quarter. The cash budget alerts management to such potential problems well in advance. This gives management sufficient time to arrange a loan on favorable terms. As the budget indicates, the loan can be repaid easily in the fourth quarter, when cash reserves are high.

Excessively large cash balances generally should be avoided because they earn little if any interest. If a company is building up financial reserves for expansion (purchasing a major piece of equipment or even another company), excess cash generally will be invested in low-risk, highly marketable securities. If the company is not building up reserves to expand, the excess cash may be distributed to shareholders as dividends.

Budgeted Balance Sheet

The last component of the master budget that we consider is the *budgeted balance sheet.* This budget is simply a planned balance sheet (sometimes called a pro forma balance sheet). Managers can use this budget to assess the effect of their planned decisions on the future financial position of the firm. The budgeted balance sheet for Preston Joystick is presented in Illustration 10-12.

ILLUSTRATION 10-12
Budgeted balance sheet

Preston Joystick

Budgeted Balance Sheet
December 31, 2017

Current Assets	
Cash[a]	$ 194,619
Accounts receivable[b]	495,000
Raw material inventory[c]	14,700
Finished goods inventory[d]	73,656
Property, plant, and equipment (net)	620,000
Total assets	$1,397,975
Current Liabilities	
Accounts payable[e]	$ 40,374
Stockholders' Equity	
Common stock	906,456
Retained earnings	451,145
Total liabilities and stockholders' equity	$1,397,975

[a]Ending balance per cash receipts and disbursements budget (Illustration 10-11).
[b]50% of 4th quarter sales not yet collected per cash receipts and disbursements budget (Illustration 10-11).
[c]See direct material purchases budget in Illustration 10-5.
[d]Per the production budget (Illustration 10-4), 2,400 units of finished goods are required. The cost per unit is $30.69 ($6 of direct material per Illustration 10-5; $15 of direct labor per Illustration 10-6; and $9.69 of manufacturing overhead per Illustration 10-7).
[e]30% of 4th quarter purchases of materials not yet paid per cash receipts and disbursements budget (Illustration 10-11).

LINK TO **PRACTICE**

Address Cash Flow Uncertainty with a Revolving Loan

Many companies know they are going to need to borrow money when they must stock up on inventory in anticipation of peak demand. This follows because the cash collected from related sales may be weeks or months after the necessary payment for purchases of inventory.

A problem is that companies are often uncertain as to the exact amount they will need to borrow and when the loan will be needed. In such cases, companies often set up a revolving loan (also known as a *revolver*) with a bank. With a revolving loan, the bank sets up a credit limit and a company can borrow up to that limit at a specified rate of interest. If the credit limit isn't reached, a company can borrow additional funds without reapplying for a new loan.

USE OF COMPUTERS IN THE BUDGET PLANNING PROCESS

The budget committee may review a budget and decide that it is inconsistent with company goals. This conclusion may lead managers to explore a variety of actions that affect future costs and revenues. If the managers decide to make changes, then they must also revise the budget. Since budgets are highly interdependent, a change in one can affect several others.

Computers are very useful in this situation. Most companies that use budgets define the budget relationships in a computer model using a spreadsheet program such as Excel® or a custom program specifically designed for them. With computerized budget information, an item in a budget can be changed, and the computer can recalculate that budget and any other budget affected by the change. Obviously, this results in a substantial savings in time and managerial effort.

"What if" analysis, discussed in Chapter 4, is also facilitated when budgets are prepared using a spreadsheet program. Suppose the management of Preston Joystick wants to know *what* the cash balance will be in the fourth quarter *if* sales in the first quarter are 22,000 instead of the 21,000 units budgeted. If all of the budgetary relationships have been properly specified in a spreadsheet, the answer can be found simply by changing the sales figure in the first-quarter sales budget from 21,000 to 22,000 and letting the computer recalculate the cash balance in the fourth quarter cash receipts and disbursements budget.

LINK TO **PRACTICE**

Spreadsheets for Budgeting

Most large companies use sophisticated software packages for budgeting, such as those by SAP or Oracle. Most small companies, however, turn to relatively simple spreadsheets when preparing budgets. According to a survey by *CFO Magazine*, the percentage of companies relying solely on spreadsheets for budgeting is only 30 percent when annual revenue is more than $1 billion. When annual revenue is less than $100 million, the percent jumps to 78 percent.

The problem with spreadsheets is that they don't have the controls of the more sophisticated software packages. Still, companies can protect their spreadsheet budgets by password protection, hosting spreadsheets on protected servers, and locking cells in spreadsheets.

Source: Based on Tim Reason, "Budgeting in the Real World," *CFO*, July 2005.

LEARNING OBJECTIVE 3

Explain why flexible budgets are needed for performance evaluation, and discuss the conflict between the planning and control uses of budgets.

BUDGETARY CONTROL

Our discussion of the master budget and its components gave you some indication of how budgets are used in the planning process to communicate company goals and coordinate diverse activities. Budgets, as noted earlier, also facilitate *control* of operations. Next, we discuss that function in more detail.

Budgets as a Standard for Evaluation

Budgets facilitate control by providing a standard for evaluation. The standard is the budgeted amount, against which actual results are compared. Differences between budgeted and actual amounts are referred to as **budget variances**, and reports that indicate budget variances are referred to as *performance reports*. If budgeted and actual costs are approximately equal, no action needs to be taken because results are consistent with management's expectations. However, if actual costs differ from budgeted costs by a material amount, management should launch an investigation to determine the cause of the difference.

How would performance be evaluated if budgets were not prepared? Most likely, actual performance in the current period would be compared with actual performance in the prior period. This is obviously an inferior approach because conditions may change significantly from one period to the next, making a comparison of the two periods meaningless. For example, suppose Preston Joystick evaluates the performance of the marketing department by comparing sales in the current year with sales in the past year. Further, suppose sales in the prior year are 75,833 units and actual sales in the current year are 85,000 units. An evaluation of performance based on a comparison with the prior year would lead to a favorable evaluation of the marketing department, because sales are up by approximately 12 percent. However, senior managers at Preston anticipated that, given an expanded advertising campaign, the company should have sales of 91,000 units, a 20 percent increase that is reflected in the budget. A comparison of actual sales to budgeted sales indicates that rather than receiving a favorable evaluation, the marketing department should be asked to explain why actual sales are only 85,000 units instead of the 91,000 units forecasted.

Static and Flexible Budgets

In evaluating performance by using budgets, care must be taken to make sure that the level of activity used in the budget is equal to the *actual* level of activity. Let's consider an example to see why this is the case. Suppose the manager responsible for manufacturing overhead at Preston Joystick is evaluated at the end of the first quarter by comparing the actual level of overhead cost to the overhead costs budgeted at the start of the year. This comparison is presented in Illustration 10-13.

The analysis implies that the manager responsible for overhead costs has not done a good job of cost control. After all, total variable overhead costs are $15,300 higher than planned, and total fixed overhead costs are $500 higher than planned. However, note that actual production was 25,000 units, whereas planned production was only 21,400 units. The extra production may be due to an unexpected increase in sales necessitating increased production. With the increase in production, an increase in variable costs is expected. Fixed costs, however, would be expected to remain the same. Since changes in cost are expected when actual production is different from planned production, the analysis presented is not very useful for evaluating performance.

The budget presented in Illustration 10-13 is referred to as a **static budget** because it is not adjusted for the actual level of production. A more appropriate analysis of performance would make use of a **flexible budget**, which is a set of budget relationships

ILLUSTRATION 10-13
Performance evaluation with a static budget

Preston Joystick

Performance Report, Manufacturing Overhead
Static Budget Comparison
First Quarter, 2017

	Static Budget	Actual	Variance
Units produced	21,400	25,000	3,600
Variable costs:			
Indirect materials (budgeted at $2 per unit)	$ 42,800	$ 49,000	($ 6,200)
Indirect labor (budgeted at $1.50 per unit)	32,100	38,000	(5,900)
Power and light (budgeted at $1 per unit)	21,400	24,600	(3,200)
Total variable costs	96,300	111,600	(15,300)
Fixed costs:			
Supervisory salaries	90,000	90,200	(200)
Depreciation on plant and equipment	20,000	20,300	(300)
Other	5,000	5,000	-0-
Total fixed cost	115,000	115,500	(500)
Total overhead	$211,300	$227,100	($15,800)

( ) denotes unfavorable variance.

that can be adjusted to various activity levels. Thus, flexible budgets take into account the fact that when production increases or decreases, variable costs change. Fixed costs, however, stay the same. Consider a company that anticipates variable production costs of $10 per unit and fixed production costs of $500,000. With this cost structure, flexible budgets for production levels of 20,000 units, 30,000 units, and 40,000 units can be prepared as in Illustration 10-14.

In Illustration 10-15, a flexible budget is used to evaluate the performance of the manager responsible for manufacturing overhead at Preston Joystick. Note that the variable costs are adjusted to the actual level of units produced. The fixed costs are at the same level as in the static budget, because they are not expected to change when production increases or decreases. Comparison of actual overhead costs with the overhead costs in a flexible budget is potentially more revealing about the manager's ability to control costs. Actual variable costs are $900 less than the *flexible* budget amount. This contrasts sharply with the $15,300 amount by which actual costs were greater than the *static* budget amount for variable costs. The variance with respect to fixed costs is still $500 more than budgeted—the same as in the static budget comparison.

ILLUSTRATION 10-14
Flexible budgets for various production levels

Preston Joystick

Flexible Budgets for Production
Levels of 20,000, 30,000, and 40,000 Units

Units produced	20,000	30,000	40,000
Variable costs ($10 per unit)	$200,000	$300,000	$400,000
Fixed costs	500,000	500,000	500,000
Total	$700,000	$800,000	$900,000

ILLUSTRATION 10-15

Performance evaluation with a flexible budget

Preston Joystick

Performance Report, Manufacturing Overhead
Flexible Budget Comparison
First Quarter, 2017

	Flexible Budget	Actual	Variance
Units produced	25,000	25,000	-0-
Variable costs:			
Indirect materials (budgeted at $2 per unit)	$ 50,000	$ 49,000	$1,000
Indirect labor (budgeted at $1.50 per unit)	37,500	38,000	(500)
Power and light (budgeted at $1 per unit)	25,000	24,600	400
Total variable costs	112,500	111,600	900
Fixed costs:			
Supervisory salaries	90,000	90,200	(200)
Depreciation on plant and equipment	20,000	20,300	(300)
Other	5,000	5,000	-0-
Total fixed cost	115,000	115,500	(500)
Total overhead	$227,500	$227,100	$ 400

( ) denotes unfavorable variances.

INVESTIGATING BUDGET VARIANCES

As noted at the beginning of the chapter, significant deviations from the budget (i.e., significant variances) may have three causes:

1. The budget may not have been well conceived.
2. Conditions may have changed.
3. Managers may have performed their jobs particularly well or poorly.

If the budget is not carefully developed with reasonable estimates of cost, it should not be surprising if actual costs are not equal to the budgeted amounts. In this case, budget variances should not be blamed on the manager responsible for meeting the budget.

Even if the budget is carefully developed, the company may nonetheless experience unforeseen and unavoidable price increases. As a result, the actual costs will be different from budgeted costs.

Finally, budget variances are sometimes due to inefficiencies resulting from poor management techniques or decisions. In this case, top management may adjust the compensation of the manager responsible for meeting the budget (e.g., reduce or eliminate his or her bonus compensation) and suggest ways the manager can improve the performance of his or her operation. In some cases, it may be necessary to fire a manager who is incapable of improving.

The cause of a variance cannot be determined without an investigation. However, because of the cost of investigation, it is not practical to investigate all budget variances. A **management by exception** approach is more economical. Under this approach, only exceptional variances are investigated. Generally, variances that are large in absolute dollars or relative to budgeted amounts are considered exceptional. It is important to point out that both exceptional "unfavorable" *and* exceptional "favorable" variances should be investigated. For example, in the performance report in Illustration 10-15, there is a $1,000 "favorable" variance for indirect materials, indicating that actual costs are less

LINK TO **PRACTICE**

Using Rolling Budgets to Deal with Changes in Economic Conditions

Many companies find that shortly after they prepare their annual budget, it's out of date. The problem is unanticipated changes in economic conditions. To deal with this situation, companies such as Electrolux and General Electric have turned to so-called rolling budgets. At the start of their fiscal year, the companies prepare an annual budget covering four quarters, based on best estimates of what they expect to occur. At the end of the first quarter, a new annual budget is prepared that covers the remaining three quarters and the first quarter of the following year. This new budget takes into account information on changes in economic conditions that come to light in the first quarter which may affect spending for capital acquisitions as well as product mix and prices. The process is then repeated each quarter. Rolling budgets also can be updated monthly if desired.

To implement rolling budgets, companies must have a good handle on fixed and variable expenses so they can predict how unanticipated changes in sales will affect costs in the revised budget.

For more information, see Marc P. Lynn and Roland L. Madison, "A Closer Look at Rolling Budgets," *Management Accounting Quarterly,* Fall 2004, and Randy Myers, "Budgets on a Roll," *Journal of Accountancy,* December 2001.

than budgeted costs. This seems to indicate a favorable state of affairs. However, it is possible that cheap, low-quality materials are being used. This could result in substandard products that damage the reputation of the company.

ANY **QUESTIONS?**

Q: The chapter provides an example of a "favorable" variance from the budget that is actually unfavorable from the standpoint of increasing shareholder value. Can there also be "unfavorable" variances that are associated with increasing shareholder value?

A: It is quite possible that an "unfavorable" budget variance could be due to an action that increased shareholder value. For example, suppose a manager decides to spend much more on customer service than budgeted. But the outcome of the additional expenditures is that the company makes great strides in customer satisfaction and sales increase dramatically. In this case, there's an unfavorable variance, but the action that generated the variance increased shareholder value.

CONFLICT IN PLANNING AND CONTROL USES OF BUDGETS

As previously discussed, budgets are used for both planning and control. With respect to planning, they communicate company goals and help coordinate various activities. With respect to control, they focus the attention of managers on meeting or beating budget targets. This is because a manager's total compensation, including his or her bonus, may depend on meeting or beating budget targets.

Unfortunately, there is an inherent conflict when budgets are used for both planning and control. The result of the conflict is that managers may: (1) pad their budgets and (2) shift income between periods to increase their compensation.[2] Both problems are discussed in the next section.

[2] The well-known economist Michael Jensen has an excellent discussion of the two problems (and their solution) in his article "Corporate Budgeting Is Broken—Let's Fix It," *Harvard Business Review,* November 2001. Illustration 10-16 is taken from this article.

Why Budget-Based Compensation Can Lead to Budget Padding and Income Shifting

Illustration 10-16 helps understanding of the two related problems. The illustration shows a common budget-based compensation scheme in which a manager receives a "hurdle" bonus once he or she hits a target, which is commonly 80 percent of budgeted performance. (Here the budget could be in sales dollars, units of output, profit, or some other performance measure. For our purposes, we will assume the performance measure is profit.) Performance better than 80 percent of budgeted profit results in additional "variable" bonus compensation until a cap is reached. This is commonly 120 percent of the budget. At this point, no additional compensation is earned for the budget period under consideration.

Now let's examine the two potential problems. Recall that managers who are evaluated with respect to a budget are likely to provide information used in setting it. This follows because they are likely to have better information about costs and revenues than their superiors. This leads to the first problem, which is that managers have an incentive to pad a budget and create budget **slack**—that is, a budget with targets that are easy to achieve. That's because the lower the budget target, the more likely it is that the managers will receive the hurdle bonus and the maximum variable bonus. Managers can create slack by lowering their forecasts of sales and increasing their forecasts of costs.

The second problem relates to the fact that managers who are evaluated with respect to the budget may have an incentive to shift income from one period to another. Consider a manager who estimates that it is unlikely he or she will meet the hurdle target. This manager has an incentive to shift income from a future period into the current period so that the hurdle target (80 percent of the budget) is reached and the hurdle bonus is received. This might be done by cutting back research and development expenditures in the current year and delaying them until a future year. Or a manager could recognize revenue in the current year on goods that are not going to be shipped until the start of the next year. This latter option violates generally accepted accounting principles (GAAP)

ILLUSTRATION 10-16
Common budget-based compensation scheme

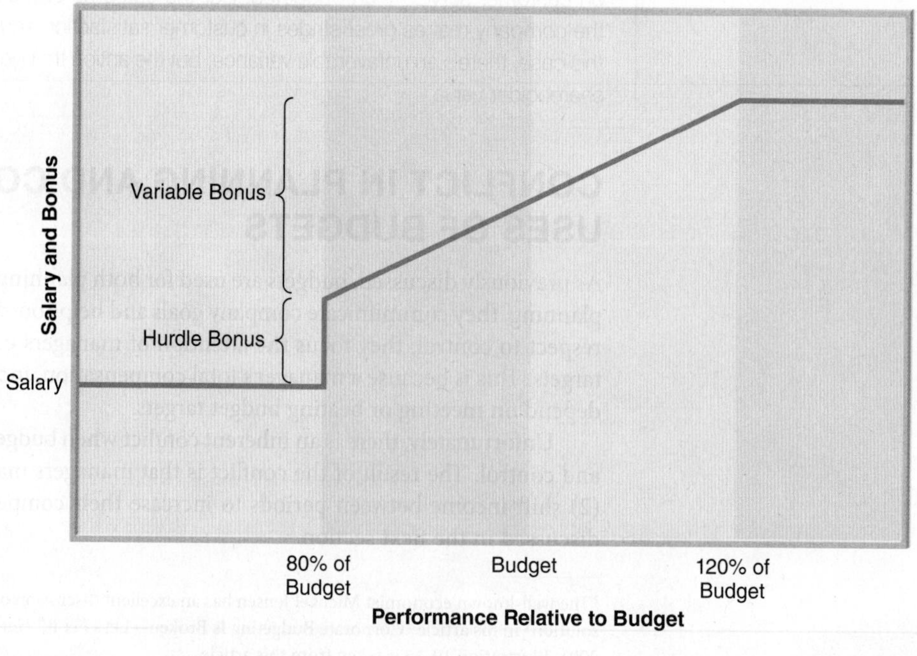

and is, most likely, illegal. But the action has been used over the years by a number of ethically challenged managers.

Now consider a manager who estimates that the performance of his or her business unit is likely to exceed 120 percent of the budget target. This manager has an incentive to shift income from the current period to a future period. The excess performance (performance in excess of 120 percent of the budget) won't help the manager's compensation since the bonus is capped once 120 percent of the budget is reached. The manager might delay shipments scheduled at year-end so that revenue won't be recognized in the current period but will be recognized at the start of the next year, when goods are finally shipped. The extra revenue in the next year will make achievement of the budget target in that year relatively easy.

A factor that deters both budget padding and income shifting is the chance of getting caught. There is always a chance that senior managers will detect that a lower-level manager has padded a budget and punish this behavior by, for example, firing him or her. That certainly reduces the incentive to build in excessive budget slack. With respect to income shifting, there is also a chance that it will be detected and punished by higher-level managers. And if the income shifting is illegal, penalties may be stiff indeed.

Perhaps the best that can be done to mitigate the conflict between the planning and control uses of budgets is to assure managers that their performance in comparison to the budget will be fairly evaluated and compensated. Managers should be confident that they will be allowed to comment on the real causes of budget variances and tell their side of the story.

EVALUATION, MEASUREMENT, AND MANAGEMENT BEHAVIOR

YOU GET WHAT YOU MEASURE

Managers pay close attention to those aspects of their jobs that are measured and evaluated. Thus, it is important to quantify in budgets key "success factors" for the company. Historically, budgets primarily have included dollar amounts. However, including some nonmonetary measures of performance in the budget is likely to be advantageous. For example, if a key aspect of a company's success is high-quality, defect-free products, it may be useful to budget the number of defects and the number of customer complaints at levels consistent with high quality. The actual number of defects and complaints can be compared with the budgeted quantities to evaluate performance. Or if a company is

LINK TO **PRACTICE**

Ratcheting and the Ability to Achieve Budget Targets

Some managers worry that beating their budgeted earnings targets may lead superiors to make their budgets harder to achieve in the next budget period. That practice, know as *ratcheting*, is thought to create an incentive problem in that it motivates managers to avoid striving to beat budgeted earnings by a significant margin.

Recent research by Mahlendorf, Matejaka, and Schäffer documents that favorable performance relative to the target is, indeed, associated with increases in the target. However, it appears that this isn't a major obstacle in that well-performing managers are able to repeatedly meet these higher targets. Thus, while ratcheting exists, it doesn't appear to create negative incentives for the best managers.

Source: Matthias Mahlendorf, Michal Matejka, and Utz Schäffer, "Target Ratcheting, Incentives, and Achievability of Earnings Targets." Working Paper (August 2014).

experiencing problems with employee absenteeism, it may be useful to budget an acceptable number of days missed and compare actual days missed with the target. Remember, **you get what you measure!**

THE PRESTON JOYSTICK CASE REVISITED

At the start of the chapter, Alan Renton, president of Preston Joystick, noted: "The marketing, production, and financing people need to know what is anticipated so we can operate effectively and efficiently." How can Alan plan and coordinate the activities of his company?

As you know from reading the preceding material, the answer lies in developing budgets. Once a sales budget is produced, the production group can develop budgets for labor, material, and overhead that are consistent with the production level needed to meet expected sales. Once these budgets are produced, the finance group can prepare budgets that take into account the cash inflows and outflows anticipated in the sales and production budgets as well as the cash flows related to selling and administrative activities and capital acquisitions.

Decision Making INSIGHT

Budget-based compensation schemes can encourage budget padding (e.g., overestimation of expense and underestimation of revenue). But can this hurt decision making? Absolutely. Suppose a manager underestimates next year's sales so that his or her budgeted income target will be relatively easy to beat. Since the sales figures in the budget are used to prepare the production budget, production managers may fail to make optimal hiring and material acquisition decisions. The result could be needless overtime and more costly rush orders for materials when sales turn out to be higher than anticipated by the people in production.

SUMMARY OF LEARNING OBJECTIVES

LEARNING OBJECTIVE 1 Discuss the use of budgets in planning and control.

Budgets are useful in the planning process because they enhance communication and coordination. Budgets are also useful in the control process because they provide a standard for evaluating performance.

LEARNING OBJECTIVE 2 Prepare the budget schedules that make up a master budget.

The master budget is a comprehensive planning document and usually includes budgets for sales, production, direct materials, direct labor, manufacturing overhead, selling and administrative expenses, capital acquisitions, cash receipts and disbursements, a budgeted income statement, and a budgeted balance sheet. These budgets are highly interrelated in that the amounts presented in one budget may be dependent on the amounts in one or more other budgets.

LEARNING OBJECTIVE 3 Explain why flexible budgets are needed for performance evaluation, and discuss the conflict between the planning and control uses of budgets.

In evaluating performance, flexible budgets should be used because they present amounts adjusted to the actual level of production. Comparing actual performance with a static budget is not very useful because variable costs are expected to differ from the budget if actual production is different from the production level indicated in the static budget.

The fact that budgets are used for both planning and performance evaluation presents a difficulty in that managers who participate in the development of their own budgets may tend to understate budgeted revenues and overstate budgeted expenses. The result is a budget that is easy to achieve and contains budget slack. Managers may also shift income from one budget period to the next to improve their chances of receiving the hurdle bonus and the maximum variable bonus.

REVIEW PROBLEM 1

Boston Accounting Services provides accounting services to small businesses. The following data relate to the preparation of a master budget for January 2017.

1. At the end of 2016, the company's general ledger indicated the following balances:

Cash	$ 62,000	Accounts payable	$ 40,000
Accounts receivable	48,000	Note payable	10,000
Equipment (net)	80,000	Common stock	50,000
		Retained earnings	90,000
Total	$190,000		$190,000

2. Revenue in December 2016 was $80,000, and revenue budgeted for January 2017 is $70,000.
3. Forty percent of revenue is collected in the month earned, and 60 percent is collected in the subsequent month. The receivable balance at the end of 2016 reflects revenue earned in December 2016.
4. Monthly expenses (excluding interest expense) are budgeted as follows: salaries, $50,000; rent, $3,000; depreciation of equipment, $3,000; utilities, $1,000; other, $2,000.
5. Expenses are paid in the month incurred. Purchases of equipment are paid in the month after purchase. The $40,000 payable at the end of 2016 represents money owed for the purchase of equipment in December 2016. No purchases of equipment are anticipated for January.
6. The note is at 10 percent per annum and requires monthly interest payments of $83. The entire principal must be paid in October 2017.
7. The tax rate is 35 percent. Taxes are paid as incurred.

REQUIRED

Complete the following budgets:

a. **Cash Budget**
For January 2017

Cash Receipts	
Collection of December 2016 revenue	$
Collection of January 2017 revenue	
Total cash receipts	
Cash Disbursements	
Payment of salaries	
Payment of rent	
Payment of utilities	
Payment of other expenses	
Payment for purchases of computer equipment	
Payment of interest on note	
Payment of taxes	
Total cash disbursements	
Plus beginning cash balance	
Ending cash balance	$

b. **Budgeted Income Statement**
For January 2017

Revenue		$
Less:		
Salaries	$	
Rent		
Utilities		
Other expenses		
Depreciation		
Interest expense		
Total expense		
Income before taxes		
Taxes on income at 35%		
Net income		$

c. **Budgeted Balance Sheet**
As of January 31, 2017

Assets	
Cash	$
Accounts receivable	
Equipment (net)	
Total assets	$
Liabilities	
Accounts payable	$
Note payable	
Total liabilities	
Stockholders' Equity	
Common stock	
Retained earnings	
Total stockholders' equity	
Total liabilities and stockholders' equity	$

ANSWER

a. **Cash Budget**
For January 2017

Cash Receipts	
Collection of December 2016 revenue (.6 × $80,000)	$48,000
Collection of January 2017 revenue (.4 × $70,000)	28,000
Total cash receipts	76,000
Cash Disbursements	
Payment of salaries	50,000
Payment of rent	3,000
Payment of utilities	1,000
Payment of other expenses	2,000
Payment for purchases of computer equipment	40,000
Payment of interest on note	83
Payment of taxes	3,821
Total cash disbursements	(99,904)
Plus beginning cash balance	62,000
Ending cash balance	$38,096

b. **Budgeted Income Statement**
For January 2017

Revenue		$70,000
Less:		
Salaries	$50,000	
Rent	3,000	
Utilities	1,000	
Other expenses	2,000	
Depreciation	3,000	
Interest expense	83	
Total expense		59,083
Income before taxes		10,917
Taxes on income at 35%		3,821
Net income		$ 7,096

c. **Budgeted Balance Sheet**
As of January 31, 2017

Assets	
Cash	$ 38,096
Accounts receivable (.6 × $70,000)	42,000
Equipment (net) ($80,000 – $3,000)	77,000
Total assets	$157,096
Liabilities	
Accounts payable	$ —
Note payable	10,000
Total liabilities	10,000
Stockholders' Equity	
Common stock	$ 50,000
Retained earnings ($90,000 + 7,096)	97,096
Total stockholders' equity	147,096
Total liabilities and stockholders' equity	$157,096

REVIEW PROBLEM 2

The results of operations for the Jackson Manufacturing Company for the fourth quarter of 2016 were as follows:

Sales		$600,000
Less variable cost of sales		240,000
Contribution margin		360,000
Less fixed production costs	$ 65,000	
Less fixed selling and administrative expenses	105,000	170,000
Income before taxes		190,000
Less taxes on income		76,000
Net income		$114,000

Note: Jackson Manufacturing uses the variable costing method. Thus, only variable production costs are included in inventory and cost of goods sold. Fixed production costs are charged to expense in the period incurred.

The company's balance sheet as of the end of the fourth quarter of 2016 was as follows:

Cash	$200,000
Accounts receivable	120,000
Inventory	400,000
Total current assets	720,000
Property, plant, and equipment	200,000
Less accumulated depreciation	100,000
Total assets	$820,000
Accounts payable	$ 12,000
Common stock	600,000
Retained earnings	208,000
Total liabilities and stockholders' equity	$820,000

Additional information:

1. Sales and variable costs of sales are expected to increase by 10 percent in the next quarter.
2. All sales are on credit with 80 percent collected in the quarter of sale and 20 percent collected in the following quarter.
3. Variable cost of sales consists of 50 percent materials, 30 percent direct labor, and 20 percent variable overhead. Materials are purchased on credit: 90 percent are paid for in the quarter of purchase, and the remaining amount is paid for in the quarter after purchase. The inventory balance is not expected to change. Also, direct labor and variable overhead are paid in the quarter the expenses are incurred.
4. Fixed production costs (other than $10,000 of depreciation) are expected to increase by 5 percent. Fixed production costs requiring payment are paid in the quarter they are incurred.
5. Fixed selling and administrative costs (other than $5,000 of depreciation expense) are expected to increase by 5 percent. Fixed selling and administrative costs requiring payment are paid in the quarter they are incurred.
6. The tax rate is expected to be 40 percent. All taxes are paid in the quarter they are incurred.
7. No purchases of property, plant, or equipment are expected in the first quarter of 2017.

REQUIRED

a. Prepare a budgeted income statement for the first quarter of 2017.

b. Prepare a budgeted statement of cash receipts and disbursements for the first quarter of 2017.

c. Prepare a budgeted balance sheet as of the end of the first quarter of 2017.

ANSWER

a.

Jackson Manufacturing Company
Budgeted Income Statement
For the Quarter Ended March 31, 2017

Sales		$660,000	10% increase over prior quarter
Less variable cost of sales		264,000	10% increase over prior quarter
Contribution margin		$396,000	
Less fixed production costs	$ 67,750		$10,000 + 1.05 ($65,000 – $10,000)
Less fixed selling and adm.	110,000	177,750	$5,000 + 1.05 ($105,000 – $5,000)
Income before taxes		$218,250	
Less taxes on income		87,300	40% of income before taxes
Net income		$130,950	

b. **Jackson Manufacturing Company**
Cash Budget For the Quarter Ended March 31, 2017

Cash collected from sales:	
$120,000 + .8 ($660,000)[a]	$648,000
Cash payments:	
Payment of material ($12,000 + 0.9 × $132,000)[b]	130,800
Payment for labor[c]	79,200
Payment for variable overhead[d]	52,800
Payment for fixed production costs ($67,750 – $10,000 depreciation)	57,750
Payment for fixed selling and administrative expenses ($110,000 – $5,000 depreciation)	105,000
Payment of income taxes	87,300
Total cash payments	512,850
Excess of receipts over disbursements	135,150
Plus beginning cash balance	200,000
Ending cash balance	$335,150

[a] 20% of prior quarter sales collected in next quarter (0.2 × $600,000) = $120,000
[b] Material used in prior quarter (0.5 × $240,000) = $120,000
10% paid in next quarter $12,000
Material used in current quarter (0.5 × $264,000) = $132,000
[c] Direct labor used (0.3 × $264,000) = $79,200
[d] Variable overhead incurred (0.2 × $264,000) = $52,800

c. **Jackson Manufacturing Company**
Budgeted Balance Sheet As of March 31, 2017

Assets:		
Cash	$335,150	
Accounts receivable	132,000	(0.2 × $660,000)
Inventory	400,000	
Total current assets	867,150	
Property, plant, and equipment	200,000	
Less accumulated depreciation	(115,000)	($100,000 + $10,000 + $5,000)
Total assets	$952,150	
Liabilities and stockholders' equity:		
Accounts payable	$ 13,200	(0.1 × $132,000)
Common stock	600,000	
Retained earnings	338,950	($208,000 + $130,950)
Total liabilities and stockholders' equity	$952,150	

KEY TERMS

Budgets (368)
Budget committee (370)
Budget variances (384)
Flexible budget (384)
Management by exception (386)
Master budget (373)
Slack (388)
Static budget (384)
Zero-based budgeting (373)

SELF-ASSESSMENT (Answers Below)

1. Which of the following statements about budgets is **false**?

a. They are formal documents that quantify a company's plans.

b. They enhance communication and coordination.

c. They are useful in planning but not in control.

d. They provide a basis for evaluating performance.

2. Budgets are useful in the planning process because they enhance ______________ and ______________.

3. Which of the following statements regarding a sales budget is **false**?

   a. Input from the sales force may be useful in predicting sales.

   b. Very large companies may hire economists to help forecast sales.

   c. The sales budget is prepared before the cash receipts and disbursements budget.

   d. The sales budget is developed after the production budget.

4. Which of the following is the correct formula to determine required purchases of direct materials?

   a. Quantity required for production + Desired ending quantity − Beginning quantity

   b. Quantity required for production − Desired ending quantity + Beginning quantity

   c. Quantity required for production + Desired ending quantity + Beginning quantity

   d. Beginning quantity + Purchases − Desired ending quantity

5. Which of the following items do **not** require cash outflow?

   a. Salaries

   b. Purchase of raw materials

   c. Advertising

   d. Depreciation

6. Differences between budgeted and actual amounts are referred to as ______________.

7. A ______________ budget is **not** adjusted for the actual level of production whereas a ______________ budget is adjusted for the actual level of production.

8. Which of the following is true about management by exception?

   a. Only large favorable variances are investigated.

   b. Management by exception is an economical approach to cost control.

   c. Management by exception can be used only with computers.

   d. Large favorable variances should not be investigated.

9. True or false? There is never a conflict between the planning and control use of budgets.

10. Which of the following is **false**?

    a. Including some nonmonetary measures of performance in a budget is not likely to be advantageous.

    b. If a key aspect of a company's success is high-quality, defect-free products, it may be useful to budget the number of defects and the number of customer complaints at levels consistent with high quality.

    c. The actual number of defects and complaints can be compared with the budgeted quantities to evaluate performance.

    d. If a company is experiencing problems with employee absenteeism, it may be useful to budget an acceptable number of days missed and compare actual days missed with the target.

ANSWERS TO SELF-ASSESSMENT

1. c **2.** communication, coordination **3.** d **4.** a **5.** d **6.** budget variances **7.** static, flexible **8.** b **9.** false **10.** a

QUESTIONS

1. Why are budgets useful in the planning process?
2. Why are budgets useful in the control process?
3. What is the difference between the top-down and the bottom-up approach to developing a budget?
4. What is meant by a zero-based budget?
5. How does use of a spreadsheet program facilitate "what if" analysis in budgeting?
6. What are the main purposes of preparing a cash budget?
7. Explain the difference between a static and a flexible budget.
8. The number of defects in a manufacturing process is an example of a nonmonetary measure of employee performance. Describe a financial measure that captures the effect of defects.
9. How would performance be evaluated if there were no budgets?
10. Why is there an inherent conflict between planning and control uses of budgets?

EXERCISES

GROUP WORK

EXERCISE 10-1. [LO 3] Explain why a budget-based compensation scheme may encourage a manager to shift income from the current period to a future period if expected performance is quite high (e.g., greater than 120 percent of budgeted performance). How could the income shifting be accomplished?

WRITING

EXERCISE 10-2. [LO 3] Write a paragraph that explains why a budget-based compensation scheme may lead managers to create budget slack.

EXERCISE 10-3. Order of Budgets [LO 1] Determine the order in which the following budgets are generally prepared.

a. Material purchases budget

b. Sales budget

c. Budgeted income statement

d. Production budget

EXCEL

EXERCISE 10-4. Sales Budget [LO 2] Locksafe Company manufactures burglar-resistant commercial door locks. Recently the company began selling locks on the Web, and the company expects sales to increase dramatically compared with the prior year. For the past year, 2017, unit sales were:

First quarter	23,000 units
Second quarter	28,000 units
Third quarter	27,000 units
Fourth quarter	32,000 units

REQUIRED

Assume that total unit sales for each quarter in 2018 will be 20 percent higher than in 2017 and that the selling price per lock is $25. Prepare a sales budget by quarter for 2018.

EXERCISE 10-5. Sales Budget for Service Company [LO 2] Oregon Adventures provides tours of scenic locations in Oregon. The company expects tours taken to increase dramatically compared with the prior year.

For the past year, 2017, the number of tours given were as follows:

First quarter	6,000
Second quarter	7,000
Third quarter	10,000
Fourth quarter	9,000

REQUIRED

Assume that sales for each quarter in 2018 will be 35 percent higher than in 2017 and that the price per tour is $75. Prepare a sales budget by quarter for 2018.

EXERCISE 10-6. Production Budget [LO 2] VitaPup produces a vitamin-enhanced dog food that is sold in Kansas. The company expects sales to be 13,000 bags in January, 14,900 bags in February, 19,400 bags in March, and 22,000 bags in April. There are 1,300 bags on hand at the start of January. VitaPup desires to maintain monthly ending inventory equal to 15 percent of next month's expected sales.

REQUIRED

Prepare the production budget for VitaPup for the months of January, February, and March.

EXCEL **EXERCISE 10-7. Direct Materials Purchases Budget [LO 2]** Roehler Industrial has estimated that production for the next five quarters will be:

Production Information

1st quarter, 2017	45,000 units
2nd quarter, 2017	41,000 units
3rd quarter, 2017	49,000 units
4th quarter, 2017	38,000 units
1st quarter, 2018	47,000 units

Finished units of production require 6 pounds of raw material per unit. The raw material cost is $7 per pound. There is $283,500 of raw material on hand at the beginning of the first quarter, 2017. Roehler desires to have 15 percent of next quarter's material requirements on hand at the end of each quarter.

REQUIRED

Prepare quarterly direct materials purchases budgets for Roehler Industrial for 2017.

EXERCISE 10-8. Direct Labor Budget [LO 1] Prepare quarterly direct labor budgets for Roehler Industrial for 2017, using the production information in Exercise 10-7. It takes 3.0 hours of direct labor to produce each finished unit of product. Direct labor costs are $20 per hour. Each employee can work 470 hours per quarter.

EXERCISE 10-9. Manufacturing Overhead Budget [LO 2] Prepare quarterly manufacturing overhead budgets for Roehler Industrial for 2017, using the production information from Exercise 10-7. Roehler has overhead costs as follows:

Variable Costs		Fixed Costs per Quarter	
Indirect material	$3.25 per unit	Supervisory salaries	$70,000
Indirect labor	2.20 per unit	Factory depreciation	37,000
Utilities	0.50 per unit	Other	6,000

EXERCISE 10-10. Budgeted Sales and Cash Receipts [LO 2] The Warrenburg Antique Mall budgeted credit sales in the first quarter of 2018 to be as follows:

January	$160,000
February	170,000
March	182,000

Credit sales in December 2017 are expected to be $200,000. The company expects to collect 70 percent of a month's sales in the month of sale and 30 percent in the following month.

REQUIRED

Estimate cash receipts for each month of the first quarter of 2018.

EXERCISE 10-11. Cash Disbursements for Purchases [LO 2] The Warrenburg Antique Mall expects to make purchases in the first quarter of 2018 as follows:

January	$95,000
February	120,000
March	85,000

Purchases in December 2017 are expected to be $92,000. The company expects that 50 percent of a month's purchases will be paid in the month of purchase and 50 percent will be paid in the following month.

REQUIRED

Estimate cash disbursements related to purchases for each month of the first quarter of 2018.

EXERCISE 10-12. Budgeted Sales and Cash Receipts [LO 2] Mississippi Retailers expects credit sales in the next quarter as follows:

April	$ 80,000
May	90,000
June	113,000

Prior experience has shown that 70 percent of a month's sales are collected in the month of sale, 20 percent are collected in the month following sale, and the remaining 10 percent are collected in the second month following sale. February and March sales were $90,000 and $100,000, respectively.

REQUIRED

Estimate budgeted cash receipts for April, May, and June.

EXERCISE 10-13. Cash Disbursements for Purchases [LO 2] Mississippi Retailers expects to make inventory purchases in the next quarter as follows:

April	$60,000
May	70,000
June	95,000

Prior experience has shown that 70 percent of a month's purchases are paid in the month of purchase and 30 percent are paid in the month following purchase. March purchases were $55,000.

REQUIRED

Estimate cash disbursements related to purchases for April, May, and June.

EXERCISE 10-14. Flexible Budget [LO 3] Expected manufacturing costs for Imperial Data Devices are as follows:

Variable Costs		Fixed Costs per Month	
Direct material	$8.00/unit	Supervisory salaries	$17,000
Direct labor	3.50/unit	Factory depreciation	10,500
Variable overhead	1.80/unit	Other factory costs	3,100

REQUIRED

Estimate manufacturing costs for production levels of 12,000 units, 15,000 units, and 17,000 units per month.

EXERCISE 10-15. Performance Report [LO 3] Prepare a performance report for Imperial Data Devices using the budget information from Exercise 10-14 and the next performance information. During the period, Imperial produced 13,000 units and incurred the following costs:

Variable Costs		Fixed Costs per Month	
Direct material	$102,500	Supervisory salaries	$17,750
Direct labor	50,000	Factory depreciation	9,500
Variable overhead	23,000	Other factory costs	3,400

EXERCISE 10-16. Performance Report [LO 2, 3] At the start of 2018, the New Orleans Fine Food Company budgeted before-tax income as follows:

Sales		$550,000
Less:		
Material cost	$100,000	
Labor cost	220,000	
Owner's salary	65,000	
Rent	55,000	
Depreciation	45,000	
Utilities	22,000	507,000
Income before taxes		$ 43,000

Actual before tax income for 2018 was:

Sales		$660,000
Less:		
Material cost	$130,000	
Labor cost	285,000	
Owner's salary	65,750	
Rent	55,000	
Depreciation	45,200	
Utilities	21,000	601,950
Income before taxes		$ 58,050

REQUIRED

Florence Roden, the owner of the company, is pleased that sales were much higher than planned, but she also is concerned that expenses were $94,950 higher than the amounts she budgeted. Should she be concerned with the level of actual expenses? Prepare a performance report that will help her focus on areas needing attention.

EXERCISE 10-17. Conflict in Planning and Control [LO 3] Riemers Jewelry operates 45 stores in major shopping malls around the country, and Walter Chan is the manager of a store in Dallas. The company is in the third quarter of 2017 and is beginning preparation of its fiscal 2018 budget. Typically, the company begins its profit-planning process by asking store managers to forecast sales and expenses. Individual profit plans are developed for each store and aggregated to develop a profit plan for the company as a whole.

In the control process, company executives compare actual profit performance to the plan on a store-by-store basis. Managers of stores that beat their budgeted profit levels are rewarded with significant bonuses.

REQUIRED

Will Walter Chan be motivated to provide unbiased forecasts of revenue and expense for the Dallas store? If not, what will be the direction of the bias for revenue and for expense?

PROBLEMS

PROBLEM 10-1. Master Budget [LO 2] (*Note:* This problem is similar to Review Problem 2, only the numbers have been changed. Students who get stuck should consult the solution to Review Problem 2.)

The results of operations for the Preston Manufacturing Company for the fourth quarter of 2017 were as follows:

Sales		$550,000
Less variable cost of sales		330,000
Contribution margin		220,000
Less fixed production costs	$120,000	
Less fixed selling and administrative expenses	55,000	175,000
Income before taxes		45,000
Less taxes on income		18,000
Net income		$ 27,000

Note: Preston Manufacturing uses the variable costing method. Thus, only variable production costs are included in inventory and cost of goods sold. Fixed production costs are charged to expense in the period incurred.

The company's balance sheet as of the end of the fourth quarter of 2017 was as follows:

Assets:	
Cash	$ 160,000
Accounts receivable	220,000
Inventory	385,000
Total current assets	765,000
Property, plant, and equipment	440,000
Less accumulated depreciation	110,000
Total assets	$1,095,000
Liabilities and owners' equity:	
Accounts payable	$ 66,000
Common stock	540,000
Retained earnings	489,000
Total liabilities and owners' equity	$1,095,000

Additional information:

1. Sales and variable costs of sales are expected to increase by 12 percent in the next quarter.
2. All sales are on credit with 60 percent collected in the quarter of sale and 40 percent collected in the following quarter.
3. Variable cost of sales consists of 40 percent materials, 40 percent direct labor, and 20 percent variable overhead. Materials are purchased on credit. Fifty percent are paid for in the quarter of purchase, and the remaining amount is paid for in the quarter after purchase. The inventory balance is not expected to change. Also, direct labor and variable overhead costs are paid in the quarter the expenses are incurred.
4. Fixed production costs (other than $9,000 of depreciation expense) are expected to increase by 3 percent. Fixed production costs requiring payment are paid in the quarter they are incurred.
5. Fixed selling and administrative costs (other than $7,000 of depreciation expense) are expected to increase by 2 percent. Fixed selling and administrative costs requiring payment are paid in the quarter they are incurred.
6. The tax rate is expected to be 40 percent. All taxes are paid in the quarter they are incurred.
7. No purchases of property, plant, or equipment are expected in the first quarter of 2018.

REQUIRED

a. Prepare a budgeted income statement for the first quarter of 2018.

b. Prepare a cash budget for the first quarter of 2018.

c. Prepare a budgeted balance sheet as of the end of the first quarter of 2018.

PROBLEM 10-2. Master Budget [LO 2] The results of operations for the Garret Bug Spray Manufacturing Company for the fourth quarter of 2017 were as follows (in thousands):

Sales of bug spray		$500,000
Less variable cost of goods sold		280,000
Contribution margin		220,000
Less fixed production costs	$90,000	
Less fixed selling and administrative expenses	50,000	140,000
Income before taxes		80,000
Less taxes on income		32,000
Net income		$ 48,000

Note: Garret uses the variable costing method. Thus, only variable costs are included in the cost of goods sold. Fixed costs are charged to expense in the period incurred.

The company's balance sheet as of the end of the fourth quarter of 2017 was as follows (in thousands):

Assets:		
Cash		$ 30,000
Accounts receivable		250,000
Total current assets		280,000
Fixtures and equipment	$130,000	
Less accumulated depreciation	80,000	50,000
Total assets		$330,000
Liabilities and owners' equity:		
Accounts payable		$ 44,800
Retained earnings		175,000
Common stock		110,200
Total liabilities and owners' equity		$330,000

Additional information:

1. Sales and variable costs of sales are expected to increase by 7 percent in the next quarter.
2. All sales are on credit with 50 percent collected in the quarter of sale and 50 percent collected in the following quarter.
3. Variable cost of sales consists of 40 percent materials, 40 percent direct labor, and 20 percent variable overhead. Materials are purchased on credit. Sixty percent are paid for in the quarter of purchase, and the remaining amount is paid for in the quarter after purchase. There is no inventory. Also, direct labor and variable overhead costs are paid in the quarter the expenses are incurred.
4. Fixed production costs (other than $5,000 of depreciation expense) are expected to increase by 1.5 percent. Fixed production costs requiring payment are paid in the quarter they are incurred.
5. Fixed selling and administrative costs (other than $3,000 of depreciation expense) are expected to increase by 3 percent. Fixed selling and administrative costs requiring payment are paid in the quarter they are incurred.
6. The tax rate is expected to be 40 percent. All taxes are paid in the quarter they are incurred.
7. No purchases of fixtures or equipment are expected in the first quarter of 2018.

REQUIRED

a. Prepare a budgeted income statement for the first quarter of 2018.

b. Prepare a budgeted statement of cash budget for the first quarter of 2018.

c. Prepare a budgeted balance sheet as of the end of the first quarter of 2018.

PROBLEM 10-3. Master Budget [LO 2] Techlabs operates a computer training center. The following data relate to the preparation of a master budget for January 2018.

1. At the end of 2017, the company's general ledger indicated the following balances:

Debits		Credits	
Cash	$ 60,000	Accounts Payable	$ 40,000
Accounts receivable	40,000	Note payable	60,000
Equipment (net)	120,000	Common stock	30,000
		Retained earnings	90,000
Total	$220,000		$220,000

2. Tuition revenue in December 2017 was $80,000, and tuition revenue budgeted for January 2018 is $110,000.

3. Fifty percent of tuition revenue is collected in the month earned, and 50 percent is collected in the subsequent month. The receivable balance at the end of 2017 reflects tuition earned in December 2017.
4. Monthly expenses (excluding interest expense) are budgeted as follows: salaries, $60,000; rent, $4,000; depreciation on equipment, $8,000; utilities, $2,000; other, $800.
5. Expenses are paid in the month incurred. Purchases of equipment are paid in the month after purchase. The $40,000 payable at the end of 2017 represents money owed for the purchase of computer equipment in December 2017.
6. The company intends to purchase $50,000 of computer equipment in January 2018. The anticipated $8,000 per month of depreciation (see number 4) reflects the addition of $2,000 of monthly depreciation related to this purchase.
7. The note is at 15 percent per annum and requires monthly interest payments of $750. The payments are made on the 20th of each month. The principal must be paid in February 2019.
8. The tax rate is 35 percent.

REQUIRED

Complete the following budgets:

a.

Techlabs
Cash Budget
For January 2018

Cash receipts	
Collection of December 2017 tuition	$
Collection of January 2018 tuition	
Total cash receipts	
Cash disbursements	
Payment of salaries	
Payment of rent	
Payment of utilities	
Payment of other expenses	
Payment for purchases of computer equipment	
Payment of interest on note	
Payment of taxes	
Total disbursements	
Excess disbursements over receipts	
Plus beginning cash balance	
Ending cash balance	$

b.

Techlabs
Budget Income Statement
For January 2018

Tuition revenue	$
Less:	
Salaries	
Rent	
Utilities	
Depreciation	
Other	
Interest expense	
Total expense	
Income before taxes	
Taxes on income	
Net income	$

c.

Techlabs
Budgeted Balance Sheet
As of January 31, 2018

Assets	
Cash	$
Accounts receivable	
Equipment (net)	
Total assets	$
Liabilities	
Accounts payable	$
Note payable	
Total liabilities	$
Stockholders' equity	
Common stock	
Retained earnings	
Total stockholders' equity	
Total liabilities and stockholders' equity	$

PROBLEM 10-4. Master Budget [LO 2] The Schrödinger Science Store operates a retail store in a local shopping mall. The results of operations for the fourth quarter of 2017 are as follows:

Sales	$350,000
Less cost of sales	205,000
Gross margin	145,000
Less selling, general, and administrative expenses	50,000
Income before taxes	95,000
Less income taxes	38,000
Net income	$ 57,000

Additional information:

1. Sales and cost of sales are expected to increase by 10 percent, are expected to increase by 12 percent, in each of the next two quarters.
2. 75 percent of sales are collected in the quarter of sale, and 25 percent are collected in the quarter following sale.
3. The balance in accounts receivable at the end of 2017 relates to sales in the fourth quarter of 2017.
4. Inventory purchases in the fourth quarter of 2017 are $200,000.
5. The balance in accounts payable at the end of 2017 relates to purchases in the fourth quarter of 2017.
6. Inventory at the end of 2017 is $150,000. For 2018, the company plans to hold ending inventory equal to 65 percent of subsequent quarter cost of sales.
7. Selling and administrative expenses are expected to increase by $8,000 due to increases in advertising and salaries. All other expenses in this category are expected to remain constant.
8. Fifty percent of inventory purchases are paid in the quarter of purchase, and 50 percent are paid in the following quarter. All other expenses, including taxes, are paid in the quarter incurred.
9. Selling, general, and administrative expense includes $2,500 of depreciation related to furniture and fixtures with a book value (net of accumulated depreciation) of $50,000 at the end of 2017.
10. The tax rate is expected to remain at 40 percent.
11. The cash balance at the end of 2017 is $40,000.
12. Common stock at the end of 2017 is $80,000 and retained earnings is $147,500.
13. Asset accounts are cash, accounts receivable, inventory, and furniture and fixtures. The only liability account is accounts payable. Owner's equity accounts are common stock and retained earnings.

REQUIRED

a. Prepare a budgeted income statement for the first quarter of 2018.

b. Prepare a cash budget for the first quarter of 2018.

c. Prepare a budgeted balance sheet as of the end of the first quarter of 2018.

d. The company is discussing the possibility of opening a new store late in the first quarter of 2018. A store opening would require cash payments of $50,000. Assuming the company wants a minimum cash balance of $30,000 at the end of the first quarter, can a new store be opened without obtaining additional funds?

PROBLEM 10-5. Master Budget [LO 2] The World Restaurant is situated in a local shopping center and serves food of many different cultures. It also caters private functions for companies. The results of operations for the fourth quarter of 2017 are as follows:

Sales	$500,000
Less cost of sales	345,000
Gross margin	155,000
Less selling, general, and administrative expenses	60,000
Income before taxes	95,000
Less income taxes	38,000
Net income	$ 57,000

Additional information:

1. Sales and cost of sales are expected to increase by 13 percent in each of the next two quarters.
2. Eighty percent of sales are collected in the quarter of sale and 20 percent are collected in the quarter following sale.
3. The balance in accounts receivable at the end of 2017 relates to sales in the fourth quarter of 2017.
4. Food purchases in the fourth quarter of 2017 are $346,975.
5. The balance in accounts payable at the end of 2017 relates to purchases in the fourth quarter of 2017.
6. Food inventory at the end of 2017 is $17,000. For 2018, the company plans to hold ending inventory equal to 30 percent of the subsequent quarter's cost of sales.
7. Selling, general, and administrative expenses are expected to increase by $12,000 due to increases in advertising and salaries. All other expenses in this category are expected to remain constant.
8. Seventy-five percent of inventory purchases are paid in the quarter of purchase and 25 percent are paid in the following quarter. All other expenses, including taxes, are paid in the quarter incurred.
9. Selling and administrative expense includes $5,000 of depreciation related to fixtures and equipment with a book value (net of accumulated depreciation) of $60,000 at the end of 2017.
10. The tax rate is expected to remain at 40 percent.
11. The cash balance at the end of 2017 is $40,000.
12. Common stock at the end of 2017 is $25,000 and retained earnings is $105,256.
13. Asset accounts are cash, accounts receivable, inventory, and furniture and fixtures. The only liability account is accounts payable. Owner's equity accounts are common stock and retained earnings.

REQUIRED

a. Prepare a budgeted income statement for the first quarter of 2018.

b. Prepare a cash budget for the first quarter of 2018.

c. Prepare a budgeted balance sheet as of the end of the first quarter of 2018.

d. The company is discussing the possibility of expanding its restaurant to include a Thai section late in the first quarter of 2018. The section's construction would require cash payments of $50,000. Assuming the company wants a minimum cash balance of $15,000 at the end of the first quarter, can a new section be added without obtaining additional funds?

PROBLEM 10-6. Budgeted Income Statement [LO 2] Modern Healthcare, a group practice clinic with 10 physicians, had the following income in 2017:

Revenue		$3,250,000
Less operating expenses:		
Salaries		
Physicians	$1,300,000	
Nurses	152,000	
Nursing aide	68,500	
Receptionist	50,000	
Accounting services	45,000	
Training	120,000	
Supplies	250,000	
Phone and fax	3,750	
Insurance	275,000	
Depreciation	242,000	
Utilities	19,800	
Miscellaneous	66,000	
Total operating expenses		2,592,050
Income before taxes		657,950
Less taxes on income		230,283
Net income		$ 427,668

The following changes are expected in 2018:

1. The clinic is expecting a 2 percent decline in revenues because of increasing pressure from insurance companies.
2. Physicians are planning to hire a physician assistant at a salary of $50,000 per year.
3. Training costs are expected to increase by $15,000.
4. Supplies are expected to increase to be 10 percent of revenue.
5. Phone, fax, and insurance amounts will stay the same.
6. Depreciation expense will increase by $20,000 per year, since the clinic is planning to purchase equipment for $125,000.
7. Utilities and miscellaneous expenses are expected to increase by 5 percent next year.
8. Taxes on income will be 35 percent.

REQUIRED

Prepare a budgeted income statement for Modern Healthcare for the year 2018.

PROBLEM 10-7. Budgeted Income Statement [LO 2] Pinnacle Engineering, an acclaimed chemical engineering team of engineers, chemists, and other scientists, had the following income in 2017:

Revenue		$3,550,000
Less operating expenses:		
Salaries	$2,400,000	
Accounting services	63,000	
Training	182,000	
Supplies	175,000	
Phone and fax	3,850	
Insurance	303,000	
Depreciation	220,000	
Utilities	35,000	
Miscellaneous	7,100	
Total operating expenses		3,388,950
Income before taxes		161,050
Less taxes on income		64,420
Net income		$ 96,630

The following changes are expected in 2018:

1. The company is expecting a 12 percent increase in revenues because of increasing demand in the marketplace for its services.
2. Training costs are expected to increase by $50,000.
3. Supplies are expected to increase to 8 percent of revenue.
4. Phone, fax, accounting services, and insurance amounts will stay the same.
5. Depreciation expense will increase by $9,000 per year, since the company is planning to purchase equipment for $75,000.
6. Pinnacle is planning to hire a laboratory technician at a salary of $36,000 per year.
7. Utilities and miscellaneous expenses are expected to increase next year by 10 percent.
8. Taxes on income will be 40 percent.

REQUIRED

Prepare a budgeted income statement for Pinnacle Engineering for fiscal year 2018.

PROBLEM 10-8. Combined Production and Purchases Budgets [LO 2] Super Clean produces and sells stain remover. Information about the budget for the year 2018 is as follows:

1. The company expects to sell 57,000 bottles of stain remover in the first quarter, 65,000 in the second quarter, 105,000 in the third quarter, and 42,000 in the fourth quarter.
2. A bottle of stain remover requires 6 ounces of Chemical A and 11 ounces of Chemical B.
3. For 2018, the desired ending inventory of finished goods is equal to 12 percent of next quarter's sales, whereas the desired ending inventory for material is 15 percent of next quarter's production requirements.
4. There are 7,000 bottles of stain remover, 25,000 ounces of Chemical A, and 60,000 ounces of Chemical B on hand at the beginning of the first quarter.
5. At the end of the fourth quarter, the company must have 10,000 bottles of stain remover, 35,000 ounces of Chemical A, and 85,000 ounces of Chemical B to meet its needs in the first quarter of 2018.
6. The cost of Chemical A is $0.13 per ounce, the cost of Chemical B is $0.08 per ounce, and the selling price of the stain remover is $10.50 per bottle.
7. The cost of direct labor is $0.80 per bottle, and the cost of variable overhead is $1.20 per bottle. Fixed manufacturing overhead is $65,000 per quarter.
8. Variable selling and administrative expense is 5 percent of sales, and fixed selling and administrative expenses is $42,000 per quarter.

REQUIRED

a. Prepare a production budget for each quarter of 2018.

b. Prepare a material purchases budget for each quarter of 2018.

c. Prepare a budgeted income statement for each quarter of 2018 (ignore taxes).

PROBLEM 10-9. Combined Production and Purchases Budgets [LO 2] Fenzel Slide Oil produces a lubricant, SlickTone, which is used on trombone slides. Information about the budget for the year 2018 is as follows:

1. The company expects to sell 7,000 bottles of SlickTone in the first quarter, 6,000 in the second quarter, 10,000 in the third quarter, and 8,000 in the fourth quarter.
2. A bottle of SlickTone requires 6 ounces of Chemical A and 3.5 ounces of Chemical B.
3. For the first, second, and third quarters of 2018, the desired ending inventory of finished goods is equal to 8 percent of next quarter's sales, whereas the desired ending inventory for material is 12 percent of next quarter's production requirements.
4. There are 1,600 bottles of SlickTone, 4,800 ounces of Chemical A, and 2,400 ounces of Chemical B on hand at the beginning of the first quarter.

5. At the end of the fourth quarter, the company must have 1,000 bottles of SlickTone, 8,000 ounces of Chemical A, and 4,000 ounces of Chemical B to meet its needs in the first quarter of 2019.
6. The cost of Chemical A is $1.05 per ounce, the cost of Chemical B is $0.15 per ounce, and the selling price of SlickTone is $12.00 per bottle.
7. The cost of direct labor is $0.55 per bottle, and the cost of variable overhead is $0.75 per bottle. Fixed manufacturing overhead is $3,000 per quarter.
8. Variable selling and administrative expense is 4 percent of sales and fixed selling and administrative expense is $3,000 per quarter.

REQUIRED

a. Prepare a production budget for each quarter of 2018.

b. Prepare a material purchases budget for each quarter of 2018.

c. Prepare a budgeted income statement for each quarter of 2018 (ignore taxes).

PROBLEM 10-10. Cash Budget [LO 2] In the fourth quarter of 2017, Casey Wholesalers had the following net income:

Sales	$650,000
Less cost of sales	300,000
Gross margin	350,000
Selling and administration	250,000
Income before taxes	100,000
Income taxes	35,000
Net income	$ 65,000

Purchases in the fourth quarter amounted to $375,000.

Estimated data for Casey Wholesalers, Inc. for 2018 are as follows:

	Quarter 1	Quarter 2	Quarter 3	Quarter 4
Sales	$725,000	$805,000	$875,000	$968,000
Cost of sales	350,000	420,000	500,000	580,000
Purchases	410,000	450,000	525,000	600,000
Selling and administration	250,000	250,000	250,000	250,000

Taxes are 35 percent of pretax income and are paid in the quarter incurred. Sixty percent of sales are collected in the quarter of sale and 40 percent are collected in the next quarter. Eighty percent of purchases are paid in the quarter of purchase and 20 percent are paid in the next quarter. Selling and administrative expenses are paid in the quarter incurred except for $10,000 of depreciation included in selling and administrative expense. A capital expenditure for $75,000 is planned for the fourth quarter of 2018.

REQUIRED

Prepare a cash budget for each quarter of 2018.

PROBLEM 10-11. Cash Budget [LO 2] In the fourth quarter of 2017, Eurofit Cycling, a bike shop, had the following net income:

Sales	$550,000
Less cost of sales	250,000
Gross margin	300,000
Selling and administration	70,000
Income before taxes	230,000
Income taxes	80,500
Net income	$149,500

Purchases in the fourth quarter amounted to $195,000.

Estimated data for Eurofit Cycling for 2018 are as follows:

	Quarter 1	Quarter 2	Quarter 3	Quarter 4
Sales	$400,000	$475,000	$550,000	$600,000
Cost of sales	170,000	185,000	220,000	230,000
Purchases	160,000	200,000	225,000	267,000
Selling and administration	67,000	69,000	71,000	73,000

Taxes are 35 percent of pretax income and are paid in the quarter incurred. Fifty percent of sales are collected in the quarter of sale and 50 percent are collected in the next quarter. Seventy percent of purchases are paid in the quarter of purchase and 30 percent are paid in the next quarter. Selling and administrative expenses are paid in the quarter incurred except for $7,000 of depreciation included in selling and administrative expense. A capital expenditure for $20,000 is planned for the fourth quarter of 2018.

REQUIRED

Prepare a cash budget for each quarter of 2018.

PROBLEM 10-12. Budget Relationships [LO 2] The accountant at Supreme Audio resigned while he was in the midst of preparing the budget for 2018. His work papers indicated the following:

Budgeted Sales and Inventory Purchases for 2018

	Quarter 1	Quarter 2	Quarter 3	Quarter 4	Total
Sales in 2017	$256,000	$300,000	$290,000	$368,000	$1,214,000
Expected sales in 2018	$320,000	$	$	$	$
Cost of sales	$192,000	$	$	$	$
Beginning inventory	$ 69,500	$	$	$	$
Ending inventory	$	$	$	$	$
Purchases	$	$	$	$	$

Assumptions:

Sales will increase by 25 percent over 2017.
Cost of sales equals 75 percent of sales.
For 2018, ending inventory should equal 35 percent of the cost of sales for the next quarter.
Sales in the first quarter of 2019 will be $300,000.

REQUIRED

Fill in the missing information to determine the sales and purchases budgets for 2018.

PROBLEM 10-13. "What If" Analysis Using a Spreadsheet [LO 2] Javier Andreas is in the process of developing a spreadsheet to budget annual sales and purchases of inventory for his company, The Backyard Place, a retail store that sells lighting, furniture, and other amenities for the backyard. In 2017, sales were as follows:

Quarter 1	Quarter 2	Quarter 3	Quarter 4
$254,000	$275,000	$320,000	$205,000

Inventory at the end of 2017 is $27,800.

REQUIRED

Help Javier build a spreadsheet that will allow him to examine the impact on purchases of inventory of the following three items:

1. *Sales growth from 2017 to 2018.* Javier believes that quarterly sales will grow by 8 percent in 2018 compared to the corresponding quarter in 2017, and sales in the first quarter of 2019

will be 8 percent higher than in the corresponding quarter in 2018. However, he would also like to explore the effect on purchases of alternative growth rates. Thus, your spreadsheet must allow you to change this value and observe the effect on all other values.

2. *Inventory on hand at the end of each quarter for 2018.* Javier is tentatively planning to have ending inventory equal to 15 percent of the cost of sales needed for the next quarter. He would also like to explore the effect on purchases of alternative rates. Thus, your spreadsheet must allow you to change this value and observe the effect on purchases.
3. *Cost of goods sold.* Javier estimates that cost of goods sold as a percent of sales will be 35 percent. He would also like to explore the effect on purchases of different rates. Thus, your spreadsheet must allow you to change this value. After you have developed your spreadsheet, calculate purchases in the first quarter through the fourth quarter of 2018 for the following combinations:

Combination 1—Sales growth of 10 percent, ending inventory of 22 percent of next quarter's cost of goods sold, cost of goods sold of 33 percent of current quarter's projected sales

Combination 2—Sales growth of 15 percent, ending inventory of 24 percent of next quarter's cost of goods sold, cost of goods sold of 28 percent of current quarter's projected sales

Combination 3—Sales growth of 9 percent, ending inventory of 34 percent of next quarter's cost of goods sold, cost of goods sold of 40 percent of current quarter's projected sales

PROBLEM 10-14. Budgeting Process [LO 3] Debra Green is the division manager of the Consumer Banking Division of Pennywise Bank. Each year Debra submits an annual budget to Barney Stringer, the bank's chief financial officer. Debra's bonus, salary increases, and promotion opportunities are based on how her performance compares with budgeted divisional income. Debra has to negotiate the budget with the CFO each year.

In the past, Barney has insisted that Debra underestimated revenue and overestimated expenses, whereas Debra tells Barney that he is expecting too much from her division.

During 2017, the Consumer Banking Division had a record year, and Debra received a huge bonus. For 2018, Barney insisted that Debra's budget be at least equal to the prior year's performance level. Debra stated that the prior year was exceptional and performance could not be repeated. After getting into a rather heated argument, they scheduled a meeting with the president and CEO of the bank to resolve their conflict.

REQUIRED

a. Explain why Barney and Debra have conflicting opinions.

b. If you were the president of Pennywise Bank, how would you resolve the argument between Barney and Debra?

PROBLEM 10-15. Performance Report [LO 1, 2, 3] The Customer Support Department at Silvan.com budgeted for the following costs in June, assuming 35 customer consultants responding to 11,200 customer calls:

Salaries of customer consultants	$160,000
Salaries of supervisors	30,000
Office space charge	5,000
Depreciation on equipment	7,000
Total	$202,000

The department is located in a wing of the company's new office building and has space to accommodate extra customer consultants. Each customer consultant works at a computer/telecommunications center. Depreciation on equipment relates to the equipment used by each customer consultant.

During the month of June, the department handled 14,000 customer calls and incurred the following costs:

Salaries of customer consultants	$182,000
Salaries of supervisors	30,250
Office space charge	5,000
Depreciation on equipment	8,000
Total	$225,250

REQUIRED

a. Making assumptions about fixed and variable costs, prepare a performance report comparing actual costs with flexible budget costs applicable to handling 14,000 customer calls.

b. List possible causes for significant variances in the performance report.

c. In addition to the variances calculated above, what nonfinancial measures could be used to evaluate the Customer Support Department?

PROBLEM 10-16. Performance Report [LO 3] The Watch and Timepiece Division of Geraldo Jewelers had significant problems in 2018. Sales and production were down by almost 35 percent as compared with the budget. Manufacturing was plagued by quality problems and had frequent customer complaints. Timothy Atlee, the division's manager, recently received a report comparing his division's actual costs with the costs in the master budget prepared at the start of 2018. Surprisingly, actual costs were less than budgeted, indicating favorable variances.

Timothy was upbeat when told that the president had scheduled a meeting with him to discuss the Watch and Timepiece Division's performance. Although sales were down, at least he could point to a large number of favorable cost variances.

REQUIRED

Briefly explain why the variances are positive, and discuss what John should know about flexible budgets. Assuming that the president understands flexible budgets, will the president be impressed by the favorable cost variances?

PROBLEM 10-17. Conflict in Planning and Control [LO 3] Franz Manteca is the president of Max Storage Devices, a wholly owned subsidiary of Vanguard Industries. His annual salary is $600,000. In addition, he receives a $200,000 bonus if Max Storage's profit exceeds 75 percent of budget. He also receives 1 percent of any profit over 75 percent of budget. His total bonus is capped when Max Storage's profit exceeds 120 percent of budget.

REQUIRED

a. Each year, Franz spends hours negotiating the profit budget for Max Storage Devices with the senior management team of Vanguard Industries. Invariably he claims that their sales estimates are too high and their cost estimates are too low. They in turn claim that Franz is padding his budget. In this context, what is meant by *budget padding*? Explain why Franz may indeed have an incentive to pad his budget. Provide an example of how budget padding may hurt company performance.

b. For the current year, the profit budget was set at $45,000,000. Late in the fourth quarter of the current year, Franz received a report from Max Storage's CFO indicating that actual profit would be close to $62,000,000. Franz then ordered that planned shipments for the last 2 weeks of the quarter be delayed until the start of the next year. Why did Franz take this step? What is the effect of this action on shareholder value?

PROBLEM 10-18. Budgeting and Nonmonetary Measures [LO 1] The Xtreme Board Company manufactures skateboards. The president of the company, Greg Conklin, believes: "You get what you measure!" Accordingly, he would like to include a number of nonmonetary measures related to factors that affect the success of the company in the annual budget. In

Greg's opinion, this will get his management team focused on important success factors, and the budgeted amounts can be compared to actual values at year-end to determine whether goals have been achieved.

REQUIRED

Suggest four nonmonetary measures that Greg Conklin can include in the annual budget for Xtreme Board Company.

CASE

10-1 ETHICS CASE: COLUMBUS PARK—WASTE TREATMENT FACILITY [LO 3]

As manager of the waste treatment facility for the city of Columbus Park, Illinois, Ann Paxton is in the process of preparing an annual expense budget. While eating lunch at her desk, she thought about the coming year. "Next year, my department will probably be asked to process some 9,000,000 gallons of waste. Our variable costs are about $.20 per gallon, and our fixed costs are about $2,400,000. So, the total cost should be somewhere around $4,200,000. I better submit a budget of around $4,900,000. The city's tax revenues are down and the city controller will probably reduce whatever budget I submit by 10 percent. And what if I end up incurring higher expenses than anticipated? A new labor contract, for instance, could increase costs by more than $300,000. Or waste could be 500,000 gallons higher than estimated. The last thing I want is to incur more costs than budgeted. I've got to stay within budget to have any chance for a promotion out of this stinking department!"

REQUIRED

Discuss whether it is ethical for Ann to submit a budget for an amount higher than the cost expected to be incurred.

CASE

10-2 ABRUZZI OLIVE OIL COMPANY [LO 1]

The Abruzzi Olive Oil Company is a small producer of premium olive oil. Cheryl Sounders, the owner of Abruzzi, is currently developing a budget spreadsheet to explore the impact of various sales goals on production.

In 2017, the company had monthly sales as follows:

Month	Sales (gallons)
January	9,200
February	9,000
March	9,400
April	8,600
May	8,000
June	8,500
July	8,200
August	7,500
September	8,900
October	9,300
November	9,200
December	9,600

At a planning meeting in November 2017, Jay Peters, the marketing manager for Abruzzi, told Cheryl that he expected monthly sales to increase by 5 to 15 percent in the coming year. But in late December 2017, Jay rushed into Cheryl's office with some good news. "Cheryl, I just had a meeting with Consolidated Restaurants, and they're considering an order for 1,250 gallons each month for all of 2018."

"Gosh," Cheryl replied, "that's an exciting bit of news, but I'm concerned about whether we have the capacity to accept such a large order. I'll prepare budgets assuming we don't get the Consolidated business but we increase monthly sales by 5, 10, or 15 percent. Then I'll assume the Consolidated order comes through, and on top of that we have monthly sales increases of 5, 10, and 15 percent. This should give us a good idea of whether we'll bump up against capacity." Jay thought that this sounded fine, but he wondered whether Cheryl had the time to do this much work. Cheryl indicated that the analysis was relatively easy since she was preparing the budget on a spreadsheet and each analysis would require only a simple change.

REQUIRED

a. Using a spreadsheet, prepare the six monthly budget schedules that Cheryl suggested (i.e., monthly budgets with and without the Consolidated business assuming other sales increases of 5, 10, and 15 percent). As a general rule, Cheryl likes to have ending inventory equal to 12 percent of next month's sales. Assume that the company ended 2017 with an inventory of 1,500 gallons of olive oil. In order to calculate ending inventory at the end of December 2018, assume that sales in January 2019 will be the same as December 2018 sales.

b. Suppose that capacity is 12,000 gallons. Is the company likely to encounter a capacity problem?

c. Abruzzi sells its oil for $25 per gallon. The variable cost per gallon is $10. What will be the annual impact on profit of obtaining the Consolidated business (assuming that there is no capacity problem)?

11

STANDARD COSTS AND VARIANCE ANALYSIS

At the start of the year, Darrington Ice Cream budgeted material costs at $2 per gallon.

During the year, the company produced 1,000,000 gallons, and the material cost was approximately $2,200,000. Linda Evert, director of operations, immediately called a meeting of the plant manager and the production supervisor. Linda's opening statement grabbed their attention. "What's going on? Our actual costs are 10 percent higher than budgeted." Both managers assured her that the increased costs were not due to waste in the use of materials. The plant manager was confident that the increased costs resulted from a sudden jump in sugar and milk prices. And, he observed, "Price changes are beyond our control. Talk to the guys in purchasing—they'll back me up on the price increase."

Linda went back to her office and continued to think about the situation. "What would really be useful," she concluded, "would be a report that broke the material cost increase out into two parts: the part due to using more material than planned and the part due to paying a higher price than planned. I wonder if Jane in the accounting department can help out with the calculations."

Fortunately, Linda was on the right track. An accountant could help her with the needed calculations and, ultimately, help the company develop a standard costing system. In such systems, manufactured goods are not recorded at their actual product cost but rather at the cost that *should have been incurred* to produce the items. This cost is referred to as the standard cost.

A primary benefit of a standard costing system is that it allows managers to compare differences between standard and actual costs. Such differences are referred to as standard cost variances. For material costs, the standard cost variances distinguish between the variance due to a difference between the actual price and the standard price and the variance due to a difference between the actual quantity of raw material and the standard quantity. Standard costing systems also generate variances for direct labor and manufacturing overhead. Large or unusual variances are investigated by management to determine whether production is inefficient. If problems exist, corrective action can be taken. Thus, standard costs play an important role in *controlling operations* as well as in determining *product costs*. This chapter illustrates both of these uses of standard costs.

©ASA studio/Shutterstock

LEARNING OBJECTIVES

1. Explain how standard costs are developed, and calculate and interpret variances for direct material and direct labor.
2. Calculate and interpret variances for manufacturing overhead, and calculate the financial impact of operating at more or less than planned capacity.
3. Discuss how the management-by-exception approach is applied to the investigation of standard cost variances. Also, explain why a favorable variance may be unfavorable, how process improvements may lead to unfavorable variances, and why evaluation in terms of variances may lead to overproduction.

LEARNING OBJECTIVE 1

Explain how standard costs are developed, and calculate and interpret variances for direct material and direct labor.

STANDARD COSTS

The term **standard cost** refers to the cost that management believes *should be incurred* to produce a good or service under anticipated conditions. A tool manufacturing company may set a standard cost for the production of a hammer, whereas a bank may set a standard cost for processing a check. In the following examples, we concentrate on standard costing in a manufacturing setting. But much of the discussion also applies to service companies, such as banks, that also use standard costs.

Standard Costs and Budgets

Some accountants use the terms **budgeted cost** and standard cost interchangeably. However, the term *standard cost* often refers to the cost of a single unit, whereas the term *budgeted cost* often refers to the cost, at standard, of the total number of budgeted units. The cost information contained in budgets must be consistent with standard costs. For example, suppose the standard cost of a unit of production is:

STANDARD COST PER UNIT	
Direct material (2 lb. at $5 per lb.)	$10.00
Direct labor (3 hours at $10 per hour)	30.00
Manufacturing overhead ($5 per labor hour)	15.00
Standard cost per unit	$55.00

If the budget for direct material purchases calls for purchasing 5,000 pounds of raw material, the budget would show an expected cost of $25,000 (i.e., 5,000 pounds at the standard price of $5 per pound). Similarly, if the direct labor budget is prepared for an expected production level of 1,000 units, it would indicate 3,000 hours of labor costing $30,000.

LINK TO **PRACTICE**

Starbucks Uses Standard Costs

When we think of companies that use standard costing, manufacturing companies, such as Boeing and General Motors, and chemical producers, such as Dow Chemical, come to mind. But even companies in the food services industry use standard costing. For example, Starbucks uses standard costing to control the cost of beans in its roasting operation. Beans lose weight in the roasting process because water is evaporated from them. The company sets a standard weight loss and compares that to the actual loss in weight for a batch of roasted beans.

© andrearoad/iStockphoto

Development of Standard Costs

Standard costs for material, labor, and overhead are developed in a variety of ways. The standard quantity of material may be specified in engineering plans that provide detailed lists of raw materials needed in production. For some companies, the standard quantity of raw material actually is specified in recipes or formulas. This is the case in large commercial bakeries and other companies that manufacture food products. The standard price of the materials often is determined from price lists provided by suppliers.

The standard quantity of direct labor can be determined by time-and-motion studies conducted by industrial engineers. In time-and-motion studies, standard labor hours are determined based on observation of workers under simulated or actual working conditions. Standard labor hours can also be estimated from an analysis of past data. For example, suppose a company developed the following information on production and labor hours:

	PRODUCTION IN UNITS	LABOR HOURS
1st quarter, 2018	2,025	6,500
2nd quarter, 2018	2,500	7,400
3rd quarter, 2018	2,100	6,800
4th quarter, 2018	2,600	7,900
Total	9,225	28,600

Based on these data, the average time to produce one unit is approximately 3.10 hours (28,600 hours ÷ 9,225 units). If the company does not anticipate any major changes in the production process, this average could be used as the standard quantity of labor. However, if the company has operated inefficiently in the past, basing current standards on past performance will result in standards that do not reflect efficient production practices. The standard labor wage rates usually are set at the rates management expects to pay the various categories of workers. In many cases, the wage rates are set equal to the rates specified in labor contracts.

Developing standard costs for overhead involves procedures similar to the ones used to develop the predetermined overhead rates discussed earlier in the book. Dividing the amount of anticipated overhead by the standard quantity of the allocation base results in a standard cost of overhead. For example, suppose a company anticipates that $60,000 of overhead will be incurred if the company works 5,000 standard labor hours. In this case, the standard overhead rate would be $12 per standard labor hour. At companies that use activity-based costing, standard costs are developed for a number of overhead cost drivers, such as the number of setups, the number of purchase orders, and the number of shipments received.

LINK TO **PRACTICE**

How Often Do Companies Update Standards?

According to a survey of 12 companies conducted by KPMG in the United Kingdom, increased economic volatility is leading companies to update their standard costs more frequently. Most update standard costs on an annual basis. But changes in commodity raw material prices, foreign exchange movements, and partial or full factory closures may require updates throughout the year.

Source: Based on KPMG, "Standard Costing: Insights from Leading Companies," *Financial Management,* February 2010.

Ideal versus Attainable Standards

In developing standard costs, some managers emphasize **ideal standards**, whereas other managers emphasize **attainable standards**. Ideal standards are developed under the assumption that no obstacles to the production process will be encountered. Thus, they do not allow for a breakdown of equipment that would increase the quantity of labor hours or defects in raw material that would increase the quantity of material required for production. Ideal standards are sometimes referred to as perfection standards because they

LINK TO PRACTICE

Standard Costing—In the Beginning

An early presentation of standard costing came in 1908 when John Whitmore, an American accountant, published a paper in the *Journal of Accountancy* on a standard costing system for a shoe factory. He suggested that the leather used to make shoes should be recorded at a "proper cost," his term for standard cost. He also noted that the variance between proper cost and actual cost could be due to differences between the standard price and actual price of leather or to differences between the standard quantity of leather and the actual quantity of leather used in production.

Comstock/Getty Images

emphasize production in a "perfect" environment. However, if a company expects occasional equipment failure, occasional substitution of inexperienced for experienced workers, and some raw material defects, then standards should be set at a level that allows for the cost of these events. Currently attainable standards are standard costs that take into account the possibility that a variety of circumstances may lead to costs that are greater than ideal.

Managers who support ideal standards believe they motivate employees to strive for the best possible control over production costs. Such managers argue that if the cost of defects and breakdowns is built into the standards, the result will be an acceptance of defects and breakdowns rather than an effort to eliminate them. However, because they do not allow for *expected* deviations from ideal conditions, ideal standards may not be useful for planning. If equipment breakdowns and defects are a fact of life, then it makes sense to plan for their associated costs. Most managers support the use of attainable standards.

A GENERAL APPROACH TO VARIANCE ANALYSIS

Companies that have standard costing systems can analyze the difference between a standard and an actual cost, referred to as a **standard cost variance**, to determine whether operations are being performed efficiently. The analysis—referred to as **variance analysis**—generally involves decomposing (breaking down) the difference between standard and actual cost into two components. For direct material, the two components are the material price and the material quantity variances. For direct labor, the two components are the labor rate variance and the labor efficiency variance. And for manufacturing overhead, the two components are the overhead volume variance and the controllable overhead variance.

Variance analysis helps companies control operations by highlighting potential problems in operations. In the following sections, we examine the variance calculations for the Vulcan Polymer Company, a producer of a synthetic rubber compound used in molding operations. The standard cost for a 50-gallon drum of the compound (the standard production unit) is as follows:

Material	
400 pounds @ $10 per pound	$4,000
Labor	
4 hours @ $15 per hour	60
Overhead	
$50 per unit	50
Total per 50-gallon drum	$4,110

MATERIAL VARIANCES

The difference between standard and actual material cost can be divided into two material variances: a material price variance and a material quantity variance. The formulas used to calculate the variances are presented in Illustration 11-1 and are discussed next.

ILLUSTRATION 11-1

Direct material variance formulas

Actual Material Cost	Actual Quantity at Standard Price	Standard Material Cost
$AQ^P \times AP$	$AQ^P \times SP$	$SQ \times SP$
200,000 lb. × \$9.90	200,000 lb. × \$10	180,000 lb. × \$10
\$1,980,000	\$2,000,000	\$1,800,000

$(AP - SP)\,AQ^P$
(\$20,000) favorable
Material Price Variance

$AQ^U \times SP$
181,000 × \$10
\$1,810,000

$(AQ^U - SQ)\,SP$
\$10,000 unfavorable
Material Quantity Variance

AQ^P = Actual quantity of material *purchased*
AP = Actual price paid for materials
AQ^U = Actual quantity *used* in production
SP = Standard price for materials
SQ = Standard quantity of material for the actual level of production

Note: In computing the material price variance, use the actual quantity of material purchased (AQ^P). In computing the material quantity variance, use the actual quantity of material used (AQ^U).

Material Price Variance

The **material price variance** is equal to the difference between the actual price per unit of material (AP) and the standard price per unit of material (SP) times the actual quantity of material purchased (AQ^P):

$$\text{Material price variance} = (AP - SP)AQ^P$$

Let's see how to calculate this variance for the Vulcan Polymer Company. Suppose the company purchased 200,000 pounds of material and actually paid \$9.90 per pound rather than the standard price of \$10. In this case, there would be a favorable \$20,000 material price variance:

$$\begin{aligned}\text{Material price variance} &= (AP - SP)AQ^P \\ &= (\$9.90 - \$10.00)200{,}000 \\ &= (\$20{,}000)\text{favorable}\end{aligned}$$

In thinking about this variance, note that material costs \$0.10 less per pound than planned, and this saving is realized on 200,000 pounds purchased. That is why the material price variance is labeled *favorable*. The actual price per pound is less than the standard price.

In the variance formulas presented in this chapter, negative variances will be favorable and positive variances will be unfavorable. Rather than concentrating on the sign of the variance, however, you can simply remember that:

- Actual prices or quantities greater than standard are labeled *unfavorable.*
- Actual prices or quantities less than standard are labeled *favorable.*

Material Quantity Variance

The **material quantity variance** is equal to the difference between the actual quantity of material used (AQ^U) and the standard quantity of material allowed for the number of units produced (SQ) times the standard price of material (SP):

$$\text{Material quantity variance} = (AQ^U - SQ)SP$$

Suppose Vulcan Polymer produces 450 of the 50-gallon drums of molding compound. The standard quantity of material is 400 pounds per drum. Thus, the standard quantity of material allowed for the 450 units produced is 180,000 pounds (i.e., 450 drums × 400 lb. per drum). Recall that the standard price of material is \$10 per pound. Thus, if 181,000 pounds of material are actually used, the material quantity variance is \$10,000 and unfavorable:

$$\begin{aligned}\text{Material quantity variance} &= (AQ^U - SQ)SP \\ &= (181{,}000 - 180{,}000)\$10 \\ &= \$10{,}000 \text{ unfavorable}\end{aligned}$$

In other words, 1,000 extra pounds are used at a standard cost of \$10 per pound. Note that the material quantity variance is labeled *unfavorable.* This is because more material is actually used than called for by the standards. This is considered an unfavorable outcome because it has a negative effect on company profit.

LINK TO **PRACTICE**

You Get What You Measure!

YOU GET WHAT YOU MEASURE

A purchasing manager at a large Midwestern manufacturing firm recounted how he had identified a new material that would result in higher quality and cost savings for the company. However, the material would cost a bit more than the standard price of the current inferior material. Buying the new material would make the purchasing department look bad because it would be charged with a material price variance. Any savings in manufacturing would be credited to the manufacturing department.

Guess what happened. The company stuck with the inferior material. This example illustrates that placing too much emphasis on price variances when evaluating performance ultimately can hurt company profitability.

Rather than concentrating only on purchase price variances, purchasing managers should also focus on developing strong relationships with suppliers that lead to on-time deliveries and minimal quality problems and performance measures that encourage that focus should be considered.

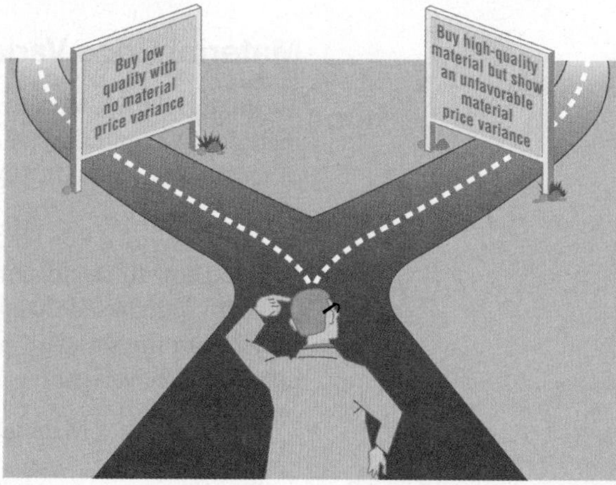

DIRECT LABOR VARIANCES

As we just saw, there are two material variances: a material price variance and a material quantity variance. Similarly, there are two direct labor variances: a labor rate variance and a labor efficiency variance. The formulas used to calculate these variances are presented in Illustration 11-2 and are discussed next.

ILLUSTRATION 11-2
Direct labor variance formulas

Actual Labor Cost	Actual Quantity at Standard Rate	Standard Labor Cost
AH × AR	AH × SR	SH × SR
1,700 hours × $15.50	1,700 hours × $15	1,800 hours × $15
$26,350	$25,500	$27,000

Labor Rate Variance	Labor Efficiency Variance
$850 unfavorable	($1,500) favorable
(AR − SR) AH	(AH − SH) SR

AH = Actual hours worked
AR = Actual wage per hour
SR = Standard wage rate per hour
SH = Standard hours for the actual level of production

Labor Rate Variance

The **labor rate variance** is equal to the difference between the actual wage rate (AR) and the standard wage rate (SR) times the actual number of labor hours worked (AH). This variance is very similar to the material price variance:

$$\text{Labor rate variance} = (\text{AR} - \text{SR})\text{AH}$$

The standards for Vulcan Polymer call for a standard wage rate of $15 per hour. Suppose that the actual wage rate is $15.50, and 1,700 hours are worked. In this case, the labor rate variance is an unfavorable $850:

$$\begin{aligned}\text{Labor rate variance} &= (\text{AR} - \text{SR})\text{AH} \\ &= (\$15.50 - \$15.00)\,1{,}700 \\ &= \$850 \text{ unfavorable}\end{aligned}$$

In other words, the company paid $0.50 more per hour than planned for each of the 1,700 hours worked.

Labor Efficiency Variance

The **labor efficiency variance** is equal to the difference between the actual number of hours worked (AH) and the standard labor hours allowed for the number of units produced (SH) times the standard labor wage rate (SR). This variance is similar to the material quantity variance.

$$\text{Labor efficiency variance} = (\text{AH} - \text{SH})\text{SR}$$

The Vulcan Polymer Company used 1,700 hours to produce 450 units. Standards call for 4 hours per unit at a standard wage rate of $15 per hour. Thus, the standard number of hours for 450 units is 1,800 (450 units × 4 hours per unit). In this case, the labor efficiency variance is $1,500 favorable:

$$\begin{aligned}\text{Labor efficiency variance} &= (\text{AH} - \text{SH})\text{SR} \\ &= (1{,}700 - 1{,}800)\$15 \\ &= (\$1{,}500)\text{favorable}\end{aligned}$$

In other words, the company worked 100 hours less than planned, saving $15 per hour at the planned rate.

LEARNING OBJECTIVE 2

Calculate and interpret variances for manufacturing overhead, and calculate the financial impact of operating at more or less than planned capacity.

OVERHEAD VARIANCES

The total variance for manufacturing overhead is the difference between the overhead applied to inventory at standard and actual overhead costs. The total overhead variance can be separated into an overhead volume variance and a controllable overhead variance.[1] The formulas for the overhead variances are presented in Illustration 11-3 and are discussed next.

ILLUSTRATION 11-3

Manufacturing overhead variance formulas

Actual Overhead Cost	Flexible Budget Overhead	Overhead Applied Using the Standard Rate
	$15,000 + ($20 × 450)	$50 × 450
$23,000	$24,000	$22,500
($1,000) favorable **Controllable Overhead Variance**	$1,500 unfavorable **Overhead Volume Variance**	

Controllable Overhead Variance

The **controllable overhead variance** is the difference between the actual amount of overhead and the amount of overhead that would be included in a flexible budget for the actual level of production. The variance is referred to as *controllable* because managers are expected to be able to control costs so that they are not substantially different from the amount that would be included in the flexible budget:

$$\text{Controllable overhead variance} = \text{Actual overhead} - \text{Flexible budget level of overhead for actual level of production}$$

Suppose the Vulcan Polymer Company expects $15,000 of fixed overhead and $20 of variable overhead per unit. In this case, the flexible budget for the actual level of production (450 units) is $24,000 [$15,000 + ($20 × 450)]. During the period, Vulcan Polymer incurs $23,000 of overhead. Thus, there is a $1,000 favorable controllable overhead variance:

$$\begin{aligned}\text{Controllable overhead variance} &= \text{Actual overhead} - \text{Flexible budget level of overhead for actual level of production}\\ &= \$23{,}000 - [\$15{,}000 + (\$20 \times 450)]\\ &= (\$1{,}000)\text{ favorable}\end{aligned}$$

Again, the variance is labeled *favorable* because the actual amount of cost is less than the amount indicated in the flexible budget.

Detailed Analysis of the Controllable Overhead Variance

To gain insight into the causes of a controllable overhead variance, we can compare details of actual overhead cost to details of overhead costs in a flexible budget. Assume that the details of the $23,000 of actual overhead are as follows:

[1] It is possible to decompose the difference between variable overhead applied at standard and actual variable overhead into a *variable* overhead spending and a *variable* overhead efficiency variance. And the difference between applied and actual *fixed* overhead can be decomposed into a *fixed* overhead budget variance and a *fixed* overhead volume variance. This "four-way analysis" of overhead variances is covered in cost accounting textbooks.

	Actual Overhead Costs
Fixed Overhead Costs	
Rent	$ 3,125
Supervisor salary	7,135
Depreciation	3,725
Other fixed	750
Total	$14,735
Variable Overhead Costs	
Power	$ 4,725
Indirect materials	2,940
Machine maintenance	600
Total	$ 8,265
Total actual overhead	$23,000

Recall the flexible budget = $15,000 of fixed overhead cost + $20 of variable overhead cost per unit.

Now suppose budgeted fixed overhead costs are as follows:

Rent	$ 3,000
Supervisor salary	7,000
Depreciation	4,000
Other fixed	1,000
Total budget fixed costs	$15,000

And suppose budgeted variable overhead costs per unit are:

Power	$10
Indirect materials	6
Machine maintenance	4
Total budget fixed costs	$20

Now let's prepare a flexible budget for overhead at the actual level of production (450 units):

	Flexible Budget Overhead Costs
Fixed Overhead Costs	
Rent	$ 3,000
Supervisor salary	7,000
Depreciation	4,000
Other fixed	1,000
Total	$15,000
Variable Overhead Costs	
Power ($10 × 450)	$ 4,500
Indirect materials ($6 × 450)	2,700
Machine maintenance ($4 × 450)	1,800
Total	$ 9,000
Total flexible budget overhead	$24,000

Now let's compare actual costs to the flexible budget. This analysis is in Illustration 11-4.

Again, we see that the controllable overhead variance is $1,000 favorable. However, we also have gained considerable insight into the cause of the variance. Note that the largest single variance is the favorable $1,200 variance for machine maintenance. Although this variance is favorable, it would be important to investigate why it occurred. It may

ILLUSTRATION 11-4

Details of actual overhead versus overhead in the flexible budget

	Actual Overhead Costs	Flexible Budget Overhead Costs	Variance	
Fixed Overhead Costs				
Rent	$ 3,125	$ 3,000	$ 125	unfavorable
Supervisor salary	7,135	7,000	135	unfavorable
Depreciation	3,725	4,000	(275)	favorable
Other fixed	750	1,000	(250)	favorable
Total	$14,735	$15,000	($ 265)	favorable
Variable Overhead Costs				
Power	$ 4,725	$ 4,500	$ 225	unfavorable
Indirect materials	2,940	2,700	240	unfavorable
Machine maintenance	600	1,800	(1,200)	favorable
Total	$ 8,265	$ 9,000	(735)	favorable
Totals	$23,000	$24,000	($1,000)	favorable

be that the company is cutting back on needed maintenance to show good performance. Actually, this may be damaging in the long run.

Overhead Volume Variance

The **overhead volume variance** is equal to the difference between the amount of overhead included in the flexible budget and the amount of overhead applied to production using the standard overhead rate:

$$\text{Overhead volume variance} = \begin{array}{c}\text{Flexible budget level}\\ \text{of overhead for actual}\\ \text{level of production}\end{array} - \begin{array}{c}\text{Overhead applied to}\\ \text{production using}\\ \text{standard overhead rate}\end{array}$$

Before calculating the volume variance, let's review the calculation of the standard overhead rate. Suppose that at the start of its accounting period, Vulcan Polymer anticipates producing 500 of the 50-gallon drums of compound. Further, the company anticipates having $15,000 of fixed manufacturing overhead and variable overhead equal to $20 per unit. In this case, total expected overhead is $25,000 [$15,000 + ($20 × 500 units)], and the overhead rate is $50 per unit (i.e., $25,000 ÷ 500 units):

$15,000 + ($20 × 500 units)	$25,000
÷ Expected production	500 units
= Standard overhead rate	$ 50 per unit

Note that the standard overhead rate in this example is expressed on a per unit basis. This is because Vulcan Polymer only produces a single product. When multiple products are produced, the overhead rate should be based on labor hours, machine hours, or some other measure of activity that is common to the various products. Or an activity-based costing system can be used with standard rates for each driver of overhead cost.

Computing the Overhead Volume Variance. If Vulcan Polymer actually produces 450 units, $22,500 of standard overhead would be applied to production (450 × $50). However, the flexible budget amount for 450 units of production is $24,000. Thus, the overhead volume variance is $1,500 unfavorable:

$$\text{Overhead volume variance} = \text{Flexible budget level of overhead for actual level of production} - \text{Overhead applied to production using standard overhead rate}$$

$$= 15{,}000 + (\$20 \times 450) \quad - (\$50 \times 450 \text{ units})$$

$$\$1{,}500 \text{ unfavorable} = \$24{,}000 \quad - \$22{,}500$$

Why is this variance labeled *unfavorable?* We turn to that question next.

Interpreting the Overhead Volume Variance. Volume variances do not signal that overhead costs are in or out of control. That signal is provided by the controllable overhead variance, discussed earlier. An overhead volume variance simply signals that the quantity of production was greater or less than anticipated when the standard overhead rate was developed. When more units are produced than anticipated, the amount of overhead applied to inventory exceeds the flexible budget because the amount of fixed cost per unit is being applied to more units than anticipated.

Consider the standard overhead rate of the Vulcan Polymer Company. The rate of $50 per unit is composed of $20 per unit of variable cost and $30 of fixed cost. The $30 of fixed cost per unit results from dividing the expected amount of fixed cost ($15,000) by the anticipated production of 500 units:

STANDARD OVERHEAD RATE	
Variable cost per unit	$20
Fixed cost per unit ($15,000 ÷ 500 expected units)	30
Total	$50

When this rate is applied to 450 units, a fixed cost of $13,500 is applied to inventory rather than the expected amount of fixed cost, which is $15,000. Thus, the amount of fixed cost applied to inventory is $1,500 less than the amount of fixed cost in the flexible budget (which is not affected by the level of activity):

	STANDARD COST APPLIED TO 450 UNITS	FLEXIBLE BUDGET FOR 450 UNITS	DIFFERENCE
Variable cost	$ 9,000 ($20 × 450)	$ 9,000 ($20 × 450)	–0–
Fixed cost	13,500 ($30 × 450)	15,000	$1,500
Total	$22,500	$24,000	$1,500

If the company had anticipated that 450 units would be produced, the fixed cost per unit would have been $33.3333, and the standard overhead rate would have been set at $53.3333:

STANDARD OVERHEAD RATE	
Variable cost per unit	$20.0000
Fixed cost per unit ($15,000 ÷ 450 expected units)	33.3333
Total	$53.3333

With a rate of $53.3333 per unit, $24,000 of overhead would have been applied to the 450 units produced, and the volume variance would be zero.

The usefulness of the volume variance is limited. It signals only that more or fewer units have been produced than planned when the standard overhead rate was set. If more units are produced than were originally planned, the variance is labeled *favorable* because additional production often (but not always) reflects unexpectedly high customer demand (a favorable outcome). If fewer units are produced, the variance is referred to as *unfavorable*.

Calculating the Financial Impact of Operating at More or Less than Planned Capacity

Decision Making/ Incremental Analysis

As just explained, the volume variance really doesn't measure the financial impact of operating at more or less than planned capacity. So you are probably wondering how one would go about calculating the financial impact of producing more or fewer units than planned. To perform the calculation, we return to a familiar concept: incremental analysis.

Recall that at the start of the accounting period, Vulcan Polymer anticipated producing 500 units. As it turned out, the company operated at less than planned capacity and produced only 450 units. Let's assume that a unit (a 50-gallon drum of compound) sells for $5,000. How much profit does the company lose when a unit is not produced and sold? The company obviously loses the selling price per unit, but it saves the variable cost per unit of production. Fixed costs are not saved since they are not affected by production volume. In other words, the company loses the contribution margin per unit. The contribution margin of a 50-gallon drum is $920:

Selling price per unit		$5,000
Less variable costs:		
Material	$4,000	
Labor	60	
Variable overhead	20	4,080
Contribution margin		$ 920

Since 50 units were not produced and sold, Vulcan Polymer lost $46,000 of profit:

Number of units not produced and sold	50
Contribution margin per unit	× $ 920
Financial effect of not producing and selling 50 units	$46,000

Similarly, if 50 units more than planned were produced and sold, the company would have gained $46,000 of incremental profit.

TEST YOUR KNOWLEDGE: COMPREHENSIVE EXAMPLE

Let's apply the information just discussed to the Darrington Ice Cream Company. Recall from the scenario at the start of the chapter that Linda Evert, director of operations for Darrington, was concerned about a 10 percent increase in material cost. The plant manager assured her that the increase was not due to waste in the use of raw materials. The material variances we calculate next will provide insight into the validity of the plant manager's statement.

At the start of the year, Darrington Ice Cream planned on producing 900,000 gallons of ice cream. Production of ice cream requires various raw materials (e.g., milk, cream, sugar, and flavorings). Most likely Darrington develops separate standards for each. To simplify the setting, however, we assume that Darrington uses only one raw material. Each gallon of ice cream requires .8 gallons of raw material costing $2.50 per gallon—

a gallon of ice cream does not require a gallon of raw material, because air is incorporated in the production process. Each gallon of ice cream also requires .125 hours of direct labor costing $12 per hour.

The company estimates that fixed overhead costs will equal $450,000 per year and variable overhead costs will equal $0.25 per gallon. Thus, the standard overhead rate is set at $0.75 per gallon [$0.50 of fixed overhead per gallon ($450,000 ÷ 900,000 gallons) + $0.25 of variable overhead per gallon].

In summary, the standard cost per unit is:

STANDARD COST PER UNIT	
Direct material (.8 gallons × $2.50)	$2.00
Direct labor (.125 hours × $12)	1.50
Manufacturing overhead	.75
Total	$4.25

Actual demand during the year is somewhat greater than anticipated, necessitating production of 1,000,000 gallons. Darrington purchases 810,000 gallons and uses 809,000 gallons of material, at a cost of $2.72 per gallon, to produce the 1,000,000 gallons of ice cream. Actual direct labor costs of $1,573,000 are incurred for 130,000 actual hours. Thus, the actual wage rate is $12.10 per hour ($1,573,000 ÷ 130,000). Finally, actual overhead costs of $680,000 are incurred.

At this point, you should attempt to calculate the standard cost variances for the Darrington Ice Cream data. For your convenience in working through the example and in solving problems at the end of the chapter, a summary of the variance formulas is presented in Illustration 11-5. Some key figures needed in the calculation of the variances for Darrington Ice Cream are summarized in Illustration 11-6.

ILLUSTRATION 11-5

Standard cost variance formulas

Material Price Variance = (AP – SP) AQ^P
AP = actual price per unit of material
SP = standard price per unit of material
AQ^P = actual quantity of material purchased

Material Quantity Variance = (AQ^U – SQ) SP
AQ^U = actual quantity of material used
SQ = standard quantity of material for the actual level of production
SP = standard price per unit of material

Labor Rate Variance = (AR – SR) AH
AR = actual labor rate per hour
SR = standard labor rate per hour
AH = actual hours worked

Labor Efficiency Variance = (AH – SH) SR
AH = actual hours worked
SH = standard hours of labor for the actual level of production
SR = standard labor rate per hour

Controllable overhead Variance = Actual overhead – Flexible budget level of overhead for actual level of production

Overhead Volume Variance = Flexible budget level of overhead for actual level of production – Overhead applied to production using standard overhead rate

ILLUSTRATION 11-6
Summary of data for production of 1,000,000 gallons of ice cream

	Standard Cost Information	Actual Cost Information
Direct material	800,000 gallons at $2.50 per gallon	810,000 gallons purchased at $2.72 per gallon 809,000 gallons used in production
Direct labor	125,000 hours at $12 per hour	130,000 hours at $12.10 per hour
Overhead applied at standard	$0.75 × 1,000,000 gallons = $750,000	
Flexible budget overhead	$450,000 + ($0.25 × 1,000,000 gallons) = $700,000	Actual overhead $680,000

Material Variances

The actual price of material is $2.72 per gallon, whereas the standard price is $2.50 per gallon. The actual quantity of material purchased is 810,000 gallons. Thus, the material price variance is:

$$\begin{aligned}\text{Material price variance} &= (\$2.72 - \$2.50)810{,}000\\ &= \$178{,}200 \text{ unfavorable}\end{aligned}$$

Note that the material price variance is based on the quantity of material *purchased*, not the quantity used.

The actual quantity of material used is 809,000 gallons. Since 1,000,000 gallons of ice cream were produced, and the standard quantity of material per gallon is .8 gallons, the standard quantity of material for the total units produced is 800,000 gallons. The standard price is $2.50 per gallon. Thus, the material quantity variance is:

$$\begin{aligned}\text{Material quantity variance} &= (809{,}000 - 800{,}000)\$2.50\\ &= \$22{,}500 \text{ unfavorable}\end{aligned}$$

Note that these results support the plant manager's contention that the large material variance was not due to wasting materials. Of the total $200,700 unfavorable variance, only $22,500 is due to using more material than planned. Most of the variance is due to paying more per gallon for raw material than planned.

Labor Variances

The actual wage rate is $12.10 per hour, whereas the standard wage rate is $12 per hour. Because 130,000 actual hours are worked, the labor rate variance is:

$$\begin{aligned}\text{Labor rate variance} &= (\$12.10 - \$12)130{,}000\\ &= \$13{,}000 \text{ unfavorable}\end{aligned}$$

The actual quantity of labor is 130,000 hours, whereas the standard quantity of labor for the 1,000,000 gallons produced is 125,000 hours (1,000,000 gallons × .125 hours per gallon). The standard wage rate is $12 per hour. Thus, the labor efficiency variance is:

$$\begin{aligned}\text{Labor efficiency variance} &= (130{,}000 - 125{,}000)\$12 \\ &= \$60{,}000 \text{ unfavorable}\end{aligned}$$

Overhead Variances

The actual amount of overhead is $680,000, whereas the flexible budget amount of overhead for 1,000,000 gallons produced is $700,000 [$450,000 + ($0.25 × 1,000,000 gallons)]. Thus, the controllable overhead variance is:

$$\begin{aligned}\text{Controllable overhead variance} &= \$680{,}000 - \$700{,}000 \\ &= (\$20{,}000) \text{ favorable}\end{aligned}$$

The amount of overhead applied to production is equal to the standard overhead rate of $0.75 per gallon times the 1,000,000 gallons produced. This amounts to $750,000. The flexible budget amount of overhead is $700,000. The difference between the flexible budget amount of overhead and the amount of overhead applied is the overhead volume variance, which is $50,000:

$$\begin{aligned}\text{Overhead volume variance} &= \$700{,}000 - \$750{,}000 \\ &= (\$50{,}000) \text{ favorable}\end{aligned}$$

LEARNING OBJECTIVE 3

Discuss how the management-by-exception approach is applied to the investigation of standard cost variances. Also, explain why a favorable variance may be unfavorable, how process improvements may lead to unfavorable variances, and why evaluation in terms of variances may lead to overproduction.

INVESTIGATION OF STANDARD COST VARIANCES

Once standard cost variances have been computed, how should they be used? It is important to note that standard cost variances do not provide definitive evidence that costs are out of control and that managers are not performing effectively. Rather, they should be viewed as indicators of *potential* problem areas. The only way to determine whether costs are being effectively controlled or not is to investigate the facts behind the variances.

To illustrate, consider again the standard cost variances just computed for Darrington Ice Cream. The variances are summarized in Illustration 11-7. As indicated in the illustration, there is a $178,200 unfavorable material price variance. Does this imply that the purchasing department is not doing a good job of searching for the lowest-cost material consistent with desired quality levels? Not necessarily. Investigation may reveal that price increases were unavoidable. Obviously, the purchasing department can do very little if all of the company's suppliers increase their prices.

ILLUSTRATION 11-7
Variance summary

Darrington Ice Cream

Variance Summary
For the Period Ending December 31, 2016

Material price variance	$178,200	unfavorable
Material quantity variance	22,500	unfavorable
Labor rate variance	13,000	unfavorable
Labor efficiency variance	60,000	unfavorable
Controllable overhead variance	(20,000)	favorable
Overhead volume variance	(50,000)	favorable
Total	$203,700	unfavorable

As another example, consider the $60,000 unfavorable labor efficiency variance indicated in Illustration 11-7. What factors might account for this unfavorable variance? The first explanation that comes to mind may be that the manager responsible for supervising the production workforce has not done a competent job. However, this is just one possibility. Perhaps workers went on strike, and inexperienced substitutes were hired. These substitutes would have a difficult time meeting standard allowable production times even if they were properly supervised. Another possibility is that a new piece of equipment was placed into production during the period. Workers may simply require additional time to become familiar with the new equipment. Which of these, among other possible explanations, is correct can be determined only by an investigation to discover the real cause of the variance.

ANY **QUESTIONS?**

Q: In Chapter 10, we learned that there are three reasons why actual results may be different from the budget. Does the same logic apply to standard cost variances?

A: Yes. Actual costs may differ from standard because:

1. The standards were not properly developed;
2. The standards were properly developed but conditions changed; or
3. Management performance was particularly good (or bad).

An investigation is usually needed to determine which of these factors caused a particular variance.

Management by Exception

Because investigation of standard cost variances is itself a costly activity, management must decide which variances to investigate. Most managers take a management-by-exception approach and investigate only those variances that they deem to be exceptional. Of course, this implies that some criterion for determining what is meant by "exceptional" must be established. The absolute dollar value of the variance or the variance as a percent of actual or standard cost is often used as the criterion.

Suppose, for example, that Darrington Ice Cream decides to investigate any variance in excess of $40,000. This implies that the material price variance, the labor efficiency variance, and the overhead volume variance should be investigated. However, the cause of the overhead volume variance is quite obvious: More units were produced than anticipated when the standard overhead rate was developed. Thus, management need only investigate the material price variance and the labor efficiency variance.

Favorable Variances May Be Unfavorable

The fact that a variance is *favorable* does not mean that it should not be investigated. Indeed, a favorable variance may be indicative of poor management decisions. For example, suppose the price of raw materials increases. In order to avoid an unfavorable material price variance, a manager could order the purchase of cheap, inferior materials. This could generate a favorable material price variance if the price of the inferior goods is less than the standard price of materials. However, the inferior materials may result in undetected product defects and cause the company to lose its reputation as a high-quality producer. If the defects are detected, items would be scrapped or reworked. This would lead to an unfavorable material quantity variance, because additional materials would be used to replace or rework defective items.

Can Process Improvements Lead to *Unfavorable* Variances?

A surprising reason why a firm may have an unfavorable variance is because it engaged in process improvements! Recall that at the Vulcan Polymer Company the standard labor hours for a unit of production is four hours and the company anticipated producing 500 units. Thus, the company anticipates needing 2,000 labor hours and staffs its production department to this level. Now suppose production workers at Vulcan Polymer suggest a change in a manufacturing process such that they can produce a unit with only three hours of labor instead of four, and standards are changed accordingly. If the company produces 500 units, standard labor will be 1,500 hours. But what will actual labor be? Unless the company fires workers, actual labor will still be 2,000 hours and there will be an unfavorable variance. And it will be very difficult to fire workers who just improved the production process!

Company anticipates production of 500 units at 4 labor hours per unit	2,000 labor hours
Less process improvement results in standard labor for 500 units of only 3 hours per unit	1,500 labor hours
Unfavorable labor hour variance	500 labor hours

What the company really needs to do is stimulate demand for its product so it can produce and sell more than 500 units and take advantage of the extra free capacity generated by the process improvement.

Beware: Evaluation in Terms of Variances Can Lead to Excess Production

YOU GET WHAT YOU MEASURE

If you read the appendix on the Theory of Constraints in Chapter 7, you know that a production department in front of a bottleneck department should not produce more units than the bottleneck can handle. If it does, the company will be making an investment in excess work-in-process inventory with a negative impact on shareholder value. However, evaluation in terms of standard cost variances might just encourage such counterproductive behavior.

Let's see why this is the case. Suppose a company has two production departments: assembly and finishing. The company anticipates that both departments will process 1,000 units per month, and standard labor is 1.92 hours per unit in the assembly department. Since assembly anticipates the need for 1,920 labor hours per month, it hires 12 full-time workers (1,920 hours per month ÷ 160 hours per employee per month). Now suppose the finishing department becomes a bottleneck due to sporadic failure of a paint curing device. In this case, the assembly department should cut back its production until the finishing department has solved the problem of the paint curing device. Let's assume that the assembly department cuts back production to 900 units. With 900 units, standard labor hours are only 1,728. But unless the assembly department fires workers, it will have an unfavorable labor hour variance of 192 hours if only 900 units are produced:

Staffing for 1,000 units (1,000 × 1.92 hours per unit)	1,920 hours
Less standard for 900 units needed (900 × 1.92 hours per unit)	1,728 hours
Unfavorable variance unless the assembly department fires workers	192 hours

Since the assembly department does not want to fire workers for a short-term problem, it may go ahead and produce 1,000 units (100 more than needed) to avoid an unfavorable labor efficiency variance. Remember: "You get what you measure!" And if you measure efficiency in terms of the labor efficiency variance, you just might get overproduction in a nonbottleneck department.

RESPONSIBILITY ACCOUNTING AND VARIANCES

As noted previously, the central idea of responsibility accounting is that managers should be held responsible only for costs they can control. The implication for variances is that managers and workers should be held responsible only for *variances* they can control. Thus, a supervisor who can control material usage but has no control over the price paid for materials should be held responsible for the material quantity variance but not for the material price variance. The purchasing agent responsible for buying material at the lowest price consistent with quality considerations should be held responsible for the price variance.

Decision Making INSIGHT

Managers need to assure their subordinates that they recognize that an unfavorable variance does not necessarily imply poor performance. Otherwise, subordinates may make decisions that hurt shareholder value. Let's see why this is the case. Suppose a manager unfairly criticizes a subordinate for having an unfavorable material price variance when, beyond the control of the subordinate, suppliers increase prices. What will happen the next time prices increase? The subordinate may turn to a lower-quality (and lower-price) supplier in an effort to avoid an unfavorable material price variance. That decision, however, could have a major negative impact on shareholder value.

SUMMARY OF LEARNING OBJECTIVES

LEARNING OBJECTIVE 1 Explain how standard costs are developed, and calculate and interpret variances for direct material and direct labor.

Standard costs are developed in a variety of ways. Standard material quantities may be determined by engineering studies. Supplier price lists may be used to determine standard prices of materials. Time-and-motion studies are sometimes used to determine standard labor hours.

The total material variance can be divided into a material price variance and a material quantity variance.

The total labor variance can be divided into labor rate and labor efficiency variances.

LEARNING OBJECTIVE 2 Calculate and interpret variances for manufacturing overhead, and calculate the financial impact of operating at more or less than planned capacity.

The total overhead variance can be divided into an overhead volume variance and a controllable overhead variance.

When a company produces and sells more (fewer) units than planned, the company gains (loses) an amount equal to the contribution margin per unit times the number of units.

LEARNING OBJECTIVE 3 Discuss how the management-by-exception approach is applied to the investigation of standard cost variances. Also, explain why a favorable variance may be unfavorable, how process improvements may lead to unfavorable variances, and why evaluation in terms of variances may lead to overproduction.

Because the investigation of variances is costly, managers only investigate exceptional variances. Variances that are large in absolute dollar value or as a percent of actual or standard cost are generally considered exceptional.

A favorable material price variance may result from buying inferior materials at a price lower than standard.

A process improvement might result in the need for less labor and lower standard labor hours per unit. Then, unless a firm fires workers or increases output, an unfavorable labor efficiency variance will result.

A production department generally should not produce more units than required by downstream production departments. However, if a downstream department is a bottleneck and requires fewer units than planned, the nonbottleneck department will have an unfavorable labor efficiency variance if it decreases production to the level required by the bottleneck (unless it fires or lays off workers).

APPENDIX

LEARNING OBJECTIVE A1

Record standard costs in the accounts of a manufacturing firm.

RECORDING STANDARD COSTS IN ACCOUNTS

Standard costing systems are used to control the operations of manufacturing companies and to determine product costs. In this chapter, we have illustrated the calculation of standard cost variances and discussed how they can be used to evaluate operations. Now we'll see how product costs are recorded at the standard rate in the accounts of a manufacturing company. In a standard costing system, the costs added to the Raw Material Inventory, Work in Process Inventory, Finished Goods Inventory, and Cost of Goods Sold accounts are all recorded at standard rather than actual cost. In the process of recording inventory at standard cost, variances are also calculated and recorded for management's use in performance evaluation. As a concrete example, we will present the entries for recording material, labor, and manufacturing overhead using the information presented for Darrington Ice Cream (see Illustration 11-6).

Recording Material Costs

Darrington Ice Cream purchased 810,000 gallons of raw materials. The company actually paid \$2.72 per gallon, or \$2,203,200. This amount is recorded as a credit to accounts payable. The Raw Material Inventory account, however, is debited for the standard cost of the material purchased. Because the standard price is \$2.50 per gallon, this amounts to \$2,025,000 in total. The difference between actual and the standard cost is the material price variance of \$178,200:

(date)	Raw Material Inventory	2,025,000	
	Material Price Variance	178,200	
	Accounts Payable		2,203,200
	To record material purchases.		

Darrington Ice Cream used 809,000 gallons of material in production. The standard cost of this material (809,000 × \$2.50 = \$2,022,500) is removed from Raw Material Inventory by crediting that account. The standard quantity of material to produce 1,000,000 gallons of ice cream is 800,000 gallons. At the standard price of \$2.50 per gallon, the standard material cost is \$2,000,000. The standard amount is recorded as a debit in Work in Process Inventory. The difference between the debit and the credit is due to the material quantity variance (\$22,500).

Variance accounts are temporary accounts and are always closed before financial statements are prepared. We demonstrate the closing process later. Note that in this example, both the material price variance and the material quantity variance are unfavorable and recorded as debits. Unfavorable variances are associated with increases in the expenses of a company and have a debit balance like expense accounts. Favorable variances are associated with reductions in the expenses of a company and have a credit balance:

(date)	Work in Process Inventory	2,000,000	
	Material Quantity Variance	22,500	
	Raw Material Inventory		2,022,500
	To record material used in production.		

Recording Labor Cost

During the year, 130,000 actual labor hours are worked at a rate of \$12.10 per hour for a total cost of \$1,573,000. The standard number of hours is 125,000, and the standard wage rate is \$12 per hour. Thus, the total standard cost of labor to be added to Work in Process Inventory is \$1,500,000. The difference between the total actual labor cost payable and the total standard labor cost assigned to Work in Process Inventory is the sum of the labor rate and labor efficiency variances:

(date)	Work in Process Inventory	1,500,000	
	Labor Rate Variance	13,000	
	Labor Efficiency Variance	60,000	
	Wages and Salaries Payable		1,573,000
	To record labor cost.		

Recording Manufacturing Overhead

Recording manufacturing overhead in a standard costing system is a three-step process:

1. Actual overhead is recorded in the Manufacturing Overhead account.
2. Overhead is applied to Work in Process Inventory at the standard cost.
3. The difference between actual overhead and overhead applied at standard is closed and overhead variances are identified.

These three steps are illustrated next.

Actual overhead incurred during the year is $680,000. Various accounts (e.g., indirect wages payable, utilities payable, and accumulated depreciation) are credited to record this amount, and the actual cost of overhead is debited in the Manufacturing Overhead account:

(date)	Manufacturing Overhead	680,000	
	Various Accounts		680,000
	To record actual overhead cost.		

Work in Process Inventory is assigned the standard cost of overhead, which is equal to the standard overhead rate times the number of units produced. In the example, this amounts to $750,000 (i.e., 1,000,000 gallons × $0.75 per gallon). When this amount is applied to Work in Process Inventory, Manufacturing Overhead is reduced by the same amount:

(date)	Work in Process Inventory	750,000	
	Manufacturing Overhead		750,000
	To apply overhead cost to inventory at standard.		

At this point, Manufacturing Overhead has been debited for the actual amount of overhead and credited for the amount of overhead applied to Work in Process Inventory at the standard overhead rate. The difference between the actual overhead cost and the standard overhead applied to inventory ($70,000) is equal to the sum of the overhead volume variance and the controllable overhead variance. These two variances are identified when the journal entry to close out Manufacturing Overhead is recorded:

(date)	Manufacturing Overhead	70,000	
	Overhead Volume Variance		50,000
	Controllable Overhead Variance		20,000
	To close out Manufacturing Overhead and record Overhead Variances.		

Recording Finished Goods

At this point, Work in Process Inventory contains the following costs:

Raw material	$2,000,000
Direct labor	1,500,000
Overhead	750,000
Total	$4,250,000

The total of $4,250,000 is equal to the 1,000,000 gallons produced at a standard cost per gallon of $4.25. When the units are completed, the cost is transferred from Work in Process Inventory to Finished Goods Inventory:

(date)	Finished Goods Inventory	4,250,000	
	Work in Process Inventory		4,250,000
	To record completed units in Finished Goods Inventory.		

Recording Cost of Goods Sold

When units are sold, the cost of Finished Goods Inventory is reduced and Cost of Goods Sold is increased by the standard cost of the units sold. Assume that all 1,000,000 gallons of ice cream produced are sold. The standard cost is $4.25 per gallon. Therefore, the entry to record the Cost of Goods Sold is:

(date)	Cost of Goods Sold	4,250,000	
	Finished Goods Inventory		4,250,000
	To record Cost of Goods Sold.		

Closing Variance Accounts

At the end of the accounting period, the temporary variance accounts must be closed. As a practical matter, this is usually accomplished by debiting or crediting the variances to Cost of Goods Sold. Before closing the variance accounts, Cost of Goods Sold is recorded at standard cost. Thus, closing the variances results in the account being adjusted to approximate actual cost. It would be more accurate to adjust Work in Process Inventory and Finished Goods Inventory (as well as Cost of Goods Sold) to actual cost by allocating part of the total variance to these accounts. However, unless the variances are significant and the balances in Work in Process Inventory and Finished Goods Inventory are large relative to Cost of Goods Sold, closing the total variance to Cost of Goods Sold is convenient and not misleading. In the case of Darrington Ice Cream, there is no Work in Process or Finished Goods Inventory at the end of the year. (All of the ice cream produced was sold.) Therefore, the variances are closed to Cost of Goods Sold.

The journal entry to close the variance accounts is as follows. Note that a favorable variance reduces the amount of Cost of Goods Sold, whereas an unfavorable variance increases the account:

(date)	Cost of Goods Sold	203,700	
	Overhead Volume Variance	50,000	
	Controllable Overhead Variance	20,000	
	Material Price Variance		178,200
	Material Quantity Variance		22,500
	Labor Rate Variance		13,000
	Labor Efficiency Variance		60,000
	To close variance accounts to Cost of Goods Sold.		

REVIEW PROBLEM 1

Sterling Steel Company produces steel billets that are sold to specialty steel fabricators. Fixed overhead costs are budgeted at $20,000,000 per year, and variable overhead costs are budgeted at $350 per ton. At the start of the year, the company planned to produce 70,000 tons.

During the year, the company actually produced 60,000 tons and incurred $42,000,000 of overhead costs.

REQUIRED

Calculate the controllable overhead variance and the overhead volume variance.

ANSWER

$$\text{Controllable overhead variance} = \text{Actual overhead} - \text{Flexible budget level of overhead for actual level of production}$$

$$= \$42{,}000{,}000 - (\$20{,}000{,}000 + (\$350 \times 60{,}000 \text{ tons}))$$

$$= \$42{,}000{,}000 - \$41{,}000{,}000$$

$$= \$1{,}000{,}000 \text{ unfavorable}$$

Overhead volume variance = Flexible budget level of overhead for actual level of production − Overhead applied to production using standard overhead rate

= $41,000,000 − ($635.7143 × 60,000 tons)

= $41,000,000 − $38,142,858

= $2,857,142 unfavorable

Note: The standard overhead rate

= [$20,000,000 + ($350 × 70,000 tons)] ÷ 70,000 tons = $635.7143.

REVIEW PROBLEM 2

RampUp Storage Containers produces a 1,000-cubic-foot metal storage unit that is used by storage companies and other businesses needing low-cost, mobile storage units. The units sell for $3,000 per unit.

The company uses a standard costing system. At the start of 2016, standard costs were set as follows:

Standard cost per unit:

Material cost (6 prefabricated metal sheets × $200)	$1,200
Direct labor (10 hours × $20)	200
Overhead ($500 per unit)	500
Total	$1,900

The overhead rate was calculated as follows: At the start of 2016, the company estimated that it would produce and sell 5,000 units and incur $500,000 of variable overhead costs and $2,000,000 of fixed overhead costs:

Variable overhead	$ 500,000
Fixed overhead	2,000,000
Total	2,500,000
Divided by estimated production	5,000
Overhead cost per unit	$ 500

Based on estimated sales, standard costs, and other information, the following budget was prepared:

2016 Budget (Expected Production and Sales of 5,000 Units)

Sales	$15,000,000
Cost of sales	9,500,000
Gross profit	5,500,000
Selling, general, and administrative expense	3,900,000
Income from operations	$ 1,600,000

During 2016, the company received an unexpected large order (1,000 units) from a national storage company. The result was a substantial increase in the number of units produced and sold (6,000 units in total). Of the 6,000 units, 5,000 were sold at the standard price of $3,000 per unit. The 1,000 units sold to the national storage company were sold at $2,800 per unit.

To produce the 6,000 units, the company incurred the following production costs:

Material purchased and used	
(36,200 metal sheets × $200)	$ 7,240,000
Direct labor	
(62,000 hours × $21)	1,302,000
Variable overhead	594,000
Fixed overhead	2,480,000
Total actual production costs	$11,616,000

REQUIRED

a. Calculate the production cost variances and indicate whether they are favorable or unfavorable.

b. Provide a brief interpretation of the overhead volume variance. In other words, answer the question: What is the meaning of an overhead volume variance?

c. Calculate the financial impact of the 1,000 unit special order from the national storage company.

ANSWER

a. Material price variance
(AP – SP) AQ
($200 – $200) 36,200 = -0-

Material quantity variance
(AQ – SQ) SP
(36,200 – 36,000) $200 = $40,000 unfavorable

Labor rate variance
(AR – SR) AH
($21 – $20) 62,000 = $62,000 unfavorable

Labor efficiency variance
(AH – SH) SR
(62,000 – 60,000) $20 = $40,000 unfavorable

Controllable overhead variance
Actual overhead – Flexible budget for actual production
$3,074,000 – [$2,000,000 + $100 (6,000)] = $474,000 unfavorable

Overhead volume variance
Flexible budget for actual production – Overhead applied
[$2,000,000 + $100 (6,000)] – ($500 × 6,000) = ($400,000) favorable

b. The overhead volume variance results from applying a predetermined fixed overhead rate to more or fewer units than originally planned when the rate was determined. If more units are produced than planned, more fixed overhead than anticipated will be applied at the standard rate. If fewer units are produced than planned, less fixed overhead than anticipated will be applied at the standard rate.

c. The selling price per unit for the 1,000 unit order is $2,800

Variable costs at standard are:

Material	$1,200	
Labor	200	
Variable overhead	100	1,500
Contribution margin		$ 1,300

1,000 extra units results in $1,300,000 of incremental profit.

Contribution margin per unit	$ 1,300
Number of units	× 1,000
Incremental profit	$1,300,000

KEY TERMS

Attainable standards (417)
Budgeted cost (416)
Controllable overhead variance (422)
Ideal standards (417)
Labor efficiency variance (421)
Labor rate variance (421)
Material price variance (419)
Material quantity variance (420)
Overhead volume variance (424)
Standard cost (416)
Standard cost variance (418)
Variance analysis (418)

SELF-ASSESSMENT (Answers Below)

1. What is the primary benefit of a standard costing system?

a. It records costs at what should have been incurred.

b. It allows a comparison of differences between actual and standard costs.

c. It is easy to implement.

d. It is inexpensive and easy to use.

2. Which of the following is **not** a way to develop a standard cost?

a. By using a fixed rate that is higher every period.

b. By performing time and motion studies.

c. By analyzing past data.

d. By using what is specified in engineering plans.

3. The total material variance can be divided into a material ________ variance and a material ________ variance.

4. Which of the following statements correctly describes an unfavorable material price variance?

a. Too much material was purchased.

b. A higher price was paid for material purchased compared with the standard price.

c. More material was used than called for by the standard.

d. Less material was used than called for by the standard.

5. True or false? The labor rate variance is equal to the difference between the actual wage rate and the standard wage rate times the standard number of labor hours worked.

6. What does a favorable labor efficiency variance indicate?

a. Labor rates were higher than called for by standards.

b. Inexperienced labor was used, causing the rate to be lower than standard.

c. More labor was used than called for by standards.

d. Less labor was used than called for by standards.

7. What does an unfavorable overhead volume variance mean?

a. Overhead costs are out of control.

b. Overhead costs are in control.

c. Production was greater than anticipated.

d. Production was less than anticipated.

8. True or false? Standard cost variances provide definitive evidence that costs are out of control and managers are not performing effectively.

9. True or false? A favorable variance may be due to a poor management decision.

10. (Appendix) At the end of the accounting period, a journal entry is made to close variance accounts to ________ or ________, ________, and ________.

ANSWERS TO SELF-ASSESSMENT

1. b **2.** a **3.** price, quantity **4.** b **5.** false **6.** d **7.** d **8.** false **9.** true **10.** Cost of Goods Sold, Work in Process, Finished Goods, Cost of Goods Sold

QUESTIONS

1. What role do standard costs play in controlling the operations of a business?

2. How are standard costs developed for direct materials, direct labor, and manufacturing overhead?

3. What is the difference between an ideal standard and an attainable standard?

4. "You get what you measure!" If so, what problem might be created by managers attempting to achieve favorable material price variances?

5. How might a favorable material price variance or a favorable labor rate variance be related to an unfavorable material quantity variance?

6. Should managers investigate only unfavorable variances?

7. Overhead volume variances do not signal that overhead costs are in or out of control. Do you agree? Explain.

8. What factors should be considered when investigating variances?

9. What is management by exception?

10. What does responsibility accounting imply with respect to holding managers responsible for standard cost variances?

EXERCISES

GROUP WORK

EXERCISE 11-1.[2] **[LO 3]** Five Star Tools is a small family-owned firm that manufactures diamond-coated cutting tools (chisels and saws) used by jewelers. Production involves three major processes. First, steel "blanks" (tools without the diamond coating) are cut to size. Second, the blanks are sent to a chemical bath that prepares the tools for the coating process. In coating, the third major process, the blanks are coated with diamond chips in a proprietary process that simultaneously coats and sharpens the blade of each tool. Following the coating process, each tool is inspected and defects are repaired or scrapped:

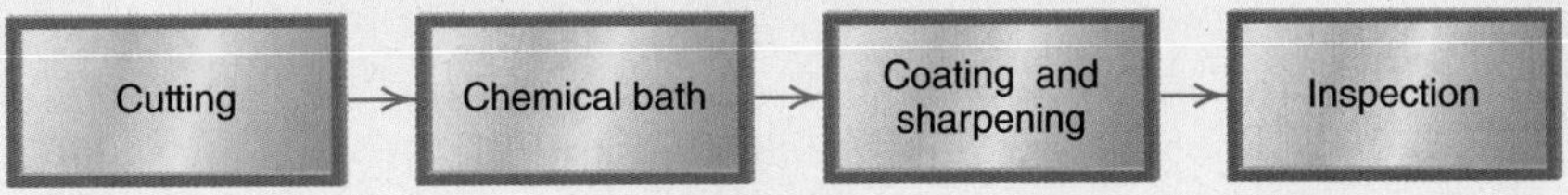

Currently, the chemical bath department is a bottleneck due to intermittent failures related to an antiquated dipping tank. The result is that the department can process only 600 items per hour from the cutting department rather than the 700 items per hour that are normally processed.

REQUIRED

Explain why the cutting department should cut back production from 700 items per hour to 600. Further, explain why if the cutting department does cut back, as it should, it is likely to have an unfavorable labor efficiency variance.

WRITING

EXERCISE 11-2. [LO 3] Write a paragraph explaining how, if workers improve a production process, they actually may generate an unfavorable labor efficiency variance.

EXERCISE 11-3. Calculating Material Variances [LO 1] At Frigicor, the standard price for the M640 electrical relay (a component used in the production of a commercial refrigeration unit) is \$57. Standards call for 2.5 relays per unit of finished product. In July, the company purchased 150 relays for \$8,900. The company used 104 relays in the production of 50 refrigeration units (4 relays were damaged in the installation process).

REQUIRED

Calculate the material price variance and the material quantity variance related to the M640 electrical relay. Indicate whether the variances are favorable or unfavorable.

EXERCISE 11-4. Calculating Labor Variances [LO 1] At Frigicor, the standard quantity of labor is 22 hours per refrigeration unit. The standard wage rate is \$35. In July, the company produced 75 refrigeration units and incurred 2,100 labor hours at a cost of \$69,000.

[2] This exercise is related to a case in Chapter 7 that dealt with decision making and constraints.

REQUIRED

Calculate the labor rate variance and the labor efficiency variance. Indicate whether the variances are favorable or unfavorable.

EXERCISE 11-5. Calculating Overhead Variances [LO 2, 3] The Stanton Supply Company produces cleaning equipment for professional cleaners. At the start of the year, Stanton estimated variable overhead costs to be $13 per unit and total fixed overhead costs at $301,000, based on a volume of 66,000 units. The detail for the overhead estimates follows:

Variable Overhead	
Indirect material ($8)	$ 528,000
Utilities ($2)	132,000
Maintenance ($3)	198,000
Total variable overhead	$ 858,000
Fixed Overhead	
Supervisor salaries	$ 126,000
Depreciation	150,000
Other fixed overhead	25,000
Total fixed overhead	$ 301,000
Total overhead costs	$1,159,000

Actual costs for the year are as follows:

Actual Production	56,000 units
Variable Overhead	
Indirect material	$ 468,500
Utilities	95,000
Maintenance	170,000
Total variable overhead	$ 733,500
Fixed Overhead	
Supervisor salaries	$ 127,000
Depreciation	145,000
Other fixed overhead	26,700
Total fixed overhead	$ 298,700
Total overhead costs	$1,032,200

REQUIRED

Calculate the controllable overhead variances for variable and fixed overhead. As a manager with limited time, which variances would you focus on?

EXCEL **EXERCISE 11-6. Calculating Material Variances [LO 1]** Crown Jewelry produced 1,500 rings during March. The standard cost of each ounce of gold used in a ring is $1,000 per ounce. The standard quantity of material for each ring is a half ounce of gold per ring. The cost of gold purchased and used in March was $788,480 at $1,024 per ounce. Determine the material price variance and the material quantity variance for March. Indicate whether each variance is favorable or unfavorable.

EXERCISE 11-7. Calculating Material Variances [LO 1] WRX uses a standard costing system. For production of a fuel cell, standards call for 4 model RN-3 valves per cell costing $2,300 each. During 2018, the company purchased 250 valves for $587,500. The company used 248 valves in the production of 60 fuel cells (8 valves were ruined through installation error).

REQUIRED

Calculate material price and quantity variances for the model RN-3 valves.

EXERCISE 11-8. Calculating Labor Variances [LO 1] The standard labor cost in the production of a pair of Tukor Brand athletic shoes is .40 hours at $13.00 per hour. During the month of June,

25,000 pairs were produced. Actual labor costs were $111,700 for 8,200 hours. Compute the labor rate and labor efficiency variances for the month of June.

EXERCISE 11-9. Calculating Material and Labor Variances [LO 1] Star Band Uniforms uses a standard costing system. The standard material and labor costs for producing a marching band hat are as follows:

Materials (.90 yards × $12.00)	$10.80
Direct labor (1.2 hours × $14.00)	$16.80

During May, the company produced 3,550 band hats; 4,000 yards of material were purchased for $42,000, and 3,100 yards of material were used in production. Also during May, 4,450 direct labor hours were worked at a cost of $62,000. Calculate material price and quantity variances and labor rate and efficiency variances. Indicate whether the variances are favorable or unfavorable.

EXERCISE 11-10. Calculating Overhead Variances—Service Example [LO 2] Barret Hospital is interested in analyzing overhead related to laundry services. The hospital administrator estimated that monthly fixed costs would be $90,000, and variable costs would be $3.00 per patient day. During the month of September, the hospital had 19,000 patient days. Total laundry costs were $176,000.

REQUIRED

Analyze laundry costs for the month of September, using the procedures for calculating a controllable overhead variance. Is the variance favorable or unfavorable?

EXERCISE 11-11. Calculating Labor and Overhead Variances [LO 1, 2] At the start of 2018, Textile Express Company determined its standard labor cost to be 2.25 hours per unit at $12.00 per hour. The budget for variable overhead was $9 per unit, and budgeted fixed overhead was $15,000 for the year. Expected annual production was 6,000 units. During 2018, the actual cost of labor was $14.25 per hour. Textile Express produced 4,600 units requiring 11,700 direct labor hours. Actual overhead for the year was $50,000.

REQUIRED

Calculate labor rate and efficiency variances and the controllable overhead variance and the overhead volume variance.

EXERCISE 11-12. Investigating Variances [LO 1, 2, 3] At the start of the year, Frigicor estimated that the company would produce 960 refrigeration units during the year (80 per month). Annual fixed overhead costs were estimated to be $1,200,000 ($100,000 per month), and estimated variable overhead costs were estimated to be $1,000 per unit. Standard cost per unit was set at $5,200:

Standard material cost	$ 700
Standard labor cost	1,000
Standard overhead rate per unit	3,500
Total	$5,200

During the year, the company experienced stiff competition and ended up producing and selling only 800 units. Actual annual production costs were $4,511,900, and standard cost variances were as follows:

Summary of Production Variances

Material price variance	$ 8,900	unfavorable
Material quantity variance	34,000	unfavorable
Labor rate variance	(4,600)	favorable
Labor efficiency variance	9,600	unfavorable
Controllable overhead variance	4,000	unfavorable
Overhead volume variance	300,000	unfavorable
Total	$351,900	unfavorable

REQUIRED

Suppose you are the CFO of Frigicor, and you want to determine the cause of significant variances. Given the demands on your time, you don't want to investigate variances that have an obvious explanation or that are less than 1/2 percent of actual production cost. Which variance(s) would you investigate? Explain the basis for your answer.

EXERCISE 11-13. (Appendix) Calculating Material Variances and Recording Material Costs [LO 1] The Quality Cabinet Company uses a standard costing system and produced 2,000 cabinets during May. The standard cost of wood is $22 per linear foot, and the standard quantity for each cabinet is 27 linear feet. During May, the company purchased 57,000 linear feet of wood for $1,140,000, and 55,000 feet were used in production. Determine the material price variance and the material quantity variance, and record the related journal entries for May.

EXERCISE 11-14. (Appendix) Recording Labor Variances [LO 1] The Vanderwaal Company uses a standard costing system. In August, 5,450 actual labor hours were worked at a rate of $12.25 per hour. The standard number of hours is 5,270 and the standard wage rate is $13 per hour. Prepare a journal entry to record labor cost and related variances during the month.

EXERCISE 11-15. (Appendix) Recording Manufacturing Overhead Variances [LO 2] The Linneas Company uses a standard costing system. During 2018, the company incurred actual overhead of $575,000. The standard rate for applying overhead is $4.25 per unit, and 130,000 units were produced in 2018. One-third of the total overhead variance is attributed to the volume variance, and the remainder is attributed to the controllable overhead variance. Prepare the journal entries to record overhead incurred (you should credit "various accounts") and the overhead variances.

EXERCISE 11-16. (Appendix) Closing Variance Accounts [LO 1, 2] The variance summary for Bell Computers is as follows:

Bell Computers

Variance Summary
For the Year Ended December 31, 2018

Material price variance	($ 3,600)	favorable
Material quantity variance	3,900	unfavorable
Labor rate variance	(1,650)	favorable
Labor efficiency variance	5,650	unfavorable
Controllable overhead variance	2,550	unfavorable
Overhead volume variance	4,270	unfavorable
Total	$ 11,120	unfavorable

REQUIRED

Prepare a journal entry to close the variance accounts at Bell Computers. Assume that the total variance is not material and is closed to cost of goods sold.

EXERCISE 11-17. (Appendix) Closing Variance Accounts [LO 1, 2] Refer to the summary of variances in Exercise 11-16. At Bell Computers, the ending balance in Finished Goods Inventory is $117,000; the ending balance in Work in Process Inventory is $54,000, and the balance in Cost of Goods Sold is $437,500.

REQUIRED

Prepare a journal entry to close the variance accounts at Bell Computers. Assume that the total variance is material and is apportioned among Finished Goods Inventory, Work in Process Inventory, and Cost of Goods Sold.

PROBLEMS

PROBLEM 11-1. Material Variances [LO 1, 3] Hank's is a chain of 55 coffee shops. The standard amount of ground coffee per cup is .75 ounces. During the month of September, the company sold 325,000 cups of coffee (reported via electronic cash registers), and the 55 shops reported using 16,800 pounds of coffee. Also during September, the company purchased 19,000 pounds of coffee at a cost of $290,700. The standard price per pound is $15.

REQUIRED

a. Compute material price and quantity variances.

b. Do either or both of the variances warrant investigation?

PROBLEM 11-2. Material Variances [LO 1] T&C Tees is a manufacturer of T-shirts. The standard amount of 100% cotton jersey fabric used to make each T-shirt is 2.3 yards. The standard price per yard of the fabric is $2.75. During last month, T&C purchased 6,200 yards of the jersey fabric for $13,000. The production department used 5,000 yards to produce 1,800 T-shirts during the month.

REQUIRED

a. Compute the material price and quantity variances.

b. Is the material price variance favorable or unfavorable? What might have caused this variance? Is the material quantity variance favorable or unfavorable? How might it be related to the material price variance?

PROBLEM 11-3. Labor Variances: Service Firm [LO 1] Sarah Aiken is the owner of Pretty Paws, a dog-grooming service. At standard, it takes 1 hour to groom each dog. During the month of October, it took Pretty Paws employees 350 hours to groom 300 dogs, at a total labor cost of $4,890. In November, employees spent 355 hours grooming 310 dogs, at a total labor cost of $6,500; in December, 360 hours were used to groom 330 dogs, at a total labor cost of $6,980. The wage rate standard for groomers is $15 per hour.

REQUIRED

a. Calculate the labor rate and efficiency variances for each of the past 3 months.

b. What trends can you spot regarding the variances over the past 3 months? What might be a cause for the labor rate variance? What might be a cause for the labor efficiency variance?

PROBLEM 11-4. Labor Variances: Service Firm [LO 1] K&J Web Designs creates websites for businesses. K&J has a basic website creation package that it offers for a flat fee of $750. This package includes everything that a business would need to have a simple but functional website built. K&J estimates that each of these websites should take, on average, 7.5 hours of Web designer time. K&J pays its Web design employees an average of $42 per hour.

Last month, K&J sold and built 150 websites for $750 each. Web design employees worked a total of 850 hours at a total payroll cost of $42,000.

REQUIRED

a. Calculate the labor rate and efficiency variances for the past month.

b. Calculate the standard amount of contribution margin (sales price less variable labor cost) that K&J would expect to make on an average website.

c. Calculate the actual amount of contribution margin (sales price less variable labor cost) that K&J made, on average, on each website in the past month.

EXCEL **PROBLEM 11-5. Comprehensive Variance Problem [LO 1, 2]** The Hayes Chemical Company produces a chemical used in dry cleaning. Its accounting system uses standard costs. The standards per .5-gallon can of chemical call for 1.20 gallons of material and 1.50 hours of labor. (1.20 gallons of material are needed to produce a .5-gallon can of product due to evaporation.) The standard cost per gallon of material is $6.00. The standard cost per hour for labor is $9.00. Overhead is applied at the rate of $7.75 per can. Expected production is 20,000 cans with fixed overhead per year of $55,000 and variable overhead of $5.00 per unit (a .5-gallon can).

During 2018, 23,000 cans were produced; 35,000 gallons of material were purchased at a cost of $250,000; 30,000 gallons of material were used in production. The cost of direct labor incurred in 2018 was $290,000 based on an average actual wage rate of $8.25 per hour. Actual overhead for 2018 was $220,000.

REQUIRED

a. Determine the standard cost per unit.

b. Calculate material, labor, and overhead variances.

c. List a possible cause for each variance.

PROBLEM 11-6. Comprehensive Variance Problem [LO 1, 2] XO-20 is an oil-based product used to remove rust on bolts and nuts that are stuck. Its accounting system uses standard costs. The standards per .5-liter can of solution call for 0.75 liters of material and 4 hours of labor. (0.75 liters of material are needed due to evaporation in the production process.) The standard cost per liter of material is $2.50. The standard cost per hour for labor is $13.00. Overhead is applied at the rate of $15.375 per can. Expected production is 8,000 cans with fixed overhead per year of $35,000 and variable overhead of $11 per unit (a .5-liter can).

During 2018, 7,800 cans were produced; 13,000 liters of material were purchased at a cost of $60,000; 10,100 liters of material were used in production. The cost of direct labor incurred in 2018 was $376,250, based on an average actual wage rate of $11 per hour. Actual overhead for 2018 was $125,000.

REQUIRED

a. Determine the standard cost per unit. Round to the nearest cent.

b. Calculate material, labor, and overhead variances.

c. List a possible cause for each variance.

PROBLEM 11-7. Comprehensive Variance Problem [LO 1, 2] Dante's Protein Powder produces a dietary supplement. The standard cost of producing one unit is:

Material (1.25 pounds × $2.50)	$ 3.13
Labor (1.2 hours × $10)	12.00
Overhead	11.60
Total	$26.73

Standard variable overhead is $8.00 per unit, and fixed annual overhead is $90,000. At the start of 2018, expected production was 25,000 units. During 2018, 30,000 units were produced. The following information, related to actual costs incurred in 2018, is available:

1. Purchased 40,000 pounds of material for $85,000.
2. Used 38,750 pounds of material.
3. Worked 35,300 labor hours costing $375,000.
4. Actual overhead incurred was $327,000.

REQUIRED

a. Show the calculation of the standard overhead rate per unit.

b. Calculate all material, labor, and overhead variances.

c. Prepare a variance summary, and briefly comment on variances that should be investigated.

PROBLEM 11-8. Comprehensive Variance Problem: Service Firm [LO 1] Selzer & Hollinger, a low-cost legal firm, has set time standards for each of the two basic legal services it offers, which include the following:

	Attorney Time	Paralegal Time
Business incorporation	2.5 hours @ $125 per hour	4 hours @ $38 per hour
Will preparation	1.5 hour @ $175 per hour	3 hours @ $25 per hour

Over the past month, Selzer & Hollinger has handled 40 business incorporations and 30 wills. Actual hours and costs follow:

	Costs of Attorneys	Costs of Paralegals
Business incorporation	92 hours @ $140 average attorney cost per hour	135 hours @ $40 average paralegal cost per hour
Will preparation	38 hours @ $180 average attorney cost per hour	95 hours @ $30 average paralegal cost per hour

REQUIRED

a. Calculate the labor rate and labor efficiency variances for attorneys doing business incorporations.

b. Calculate the labor rate and labor efficiency variances for attorneys preparing wills.

c. Calculate the labor rate and labor efficiency variances for paralegals assisting with business incorporations.

d. Calculate the labor rate and labor efficiency variances for paralegals assisting with wills.

PROBLEM 11-9. Comprehensive Variance Problem [LO 1, 2] Bowser Products operates a small plant in New Mexico that produces dog food in batches of 1,500 pounds. The product sells for $6 per pound. Standard costs for 2018 are:

Standard direct labor cost = $15 per hour
Standard direct labor hours per batch = 10 hours
Standard price of material A = $0.35 per pound
Standard pounds of material A per batch = 800 pounds
Standard price of material B = $0.55 per pound
Standard pounds of material B per batch = 250 pounds
Fixed overhead cost per batch = $500

At the start of 2018, the company estimated monthly production and sales of 50 batches. The company estimated that all overhead costs were fixed and amounted to $25,000 per month. During the month of June 2018 (typically a somewhat slow month), 42 batches were produced (not an unusual level of production for June). The following costs were incurred:

Direct labor costs were $7,800 for 460 hours.
37,500 pounds of material A costing $8,500 were purchased and used.
12,000 pounds of material B costing $5,600 were purchased and used.
Fixed overhead of $23,000 was incurred.

REQUIRED

a. Calculate variances for material, labor, and overhead.

b. Prepare a summary of the variances. Does the unfavorable overhead volume variance suggest that overhead costs are out of control?

PROBLEM 11-10. Comprehensive Variance Problem [LO 2, 3, 4, 6] The Antikron Company produces rubber seals used in the aerospace industry. Standards call for 3 pounds of material at $2.50 per pound for each seal. The standard cost for labor is 1.5 hours at $15 per hour. Standard overhead is $10 per unit. For the year 2018, expected production is 130,000 seals with fixed overhead of $130,000 and variable overhead of $9 per seal. During 2018, a total of 125,000 seals were produced. The company purchased 455,000 pounds of material for $1,150,000. Production required 425,000 pounds of material. The cost of direct labor incurred was $2,900,000 with an actual average wage rate of $15.25 per hour. Actual overhead for the year was $900,000.

REQUIRED

a. Determine the standard cost per seal.

b. Calculate the material, labor, and overhead variances.

c. Prepare a summary of the variances, and indicate which variances should be investigated.

PROBLEM 11-11. Labor Variances [LO 1] Northwest Medical Testing draws blood samples from approximately 1,500 clients each month. The standard time for a technician to draw and prepare a blood sample for testing is 20 minutes. The standard wage rate for technicians is $40 per hour. During August, Northwest hired a temporary employee at $60 per hour to fill in for a technician who quit unexpectedly. During the month, technicians processed 1,250 samples and were paid $22,100 for 425 hours of work related to drawing and preparing blood samples.

REQUIRED

Calculate labor rate and efficiency variances for August, and comment on whether labor costs for technicians appear to be in control or out of control.

PROBLEM 11-12. Setting Standards and Assigning Responsibility for Variances [LO 1] Recycled Plastics manufactures a plastic dimensional lumber product from recycled plastic milk jugs. The company purchases consumer-recycled milk jugs in 700-pound bales and then shreds them into small pieces in its grinding department. Once ground, the plastic pieces are mixed in a hopper and extruded into shaped boards in the extrusion department. When the boards are cooled, they are used much as wood lumber would be used to build picnic tables and park benches in the fabrication department.

Recycled Plastics has grown from a small five-person operation to a company employing more than 100 people. The company also contains a sales department, an accounting department, an administration department, and a purchasing department. The president and owner of the company, Alan Roberts, would like to institute a standard cost system; at this point, he has been setting prices based on his rough pen-and-paper estimates of costs.

REQUIRED

a. What standards could be set within each of the three production departments of the company? How should standards be set? Who should be involved in setting the standards?

b. What benefits might Recycled Plastics receive from adopting a standard costing system? What disadvantages or problems might arise from adopting a standard costing system?

PROBLEM 11-13. Variance Analysis [LO 3] Will Norton, the general manager of Cummings Manufactured Siding, is reviewing a monthly variance summary. The summary reveals a large favorable material price variance and large unfavorable material quantity and labor efficiency variances. All other variances are small. Will's initial instinct is to reward the purchasing manager with a substantial bonus and withhold the plant manager's monthly bonus until material quantity and labor efficiency variances improve.

REQUIRED

a. Should Will act according to his initial instinct?

b. What scenario(s) other than good performance in purchasing and poor performance in manufacturing could lead to the same variances as those noted?

c. What should Will do to determine whether the purchasing manager's performance is especially good and the plant manager's performance is poor?

PROBLEM 11-14. Labor and Overhead Variance Analysis [LO 1, 2] The Dudley Travel Agency has found that, on average, its travel agents take 2 hours to serve each client and that those travel agents are paid a standard rate of $30 per hour.

The following table contains the labor data for the Dudley Travel Agency for 2018:

	Estimated (expected)	Actual
Number of clients served	5,200	5,000
Travel agent hours	10,400	10,200
Travel agent wages	$312,000	$298,000
Fixed overhead	$75,000	$80,000
Variable overhead	$22 per travel agent hour	$23 per travel agent hour

REQUIRED

a. Calculate the labor rate and efficiency variances.

b. Calculate the controllable overhead variance and the overhead volume variance.

c. What might have caused each variance?

PROBLEM 11-15. Variance Analysis—Nonmonetary Measures [LO 3] XcomSoftware operates a 24-hour help line to answer customer questions. To control the cost of operations, the company compares the actual time required to answer customer questions with a standard time of 6 minutes per customer call. Monthly bonuses are awarded if the standard is achieved.

In the past 5 months, the number of calls has decreased from approximately 6,000 to approximately 5,000. The average time per call has decreased from 6.5 minutes to 4.80 minutes. However, a software magazine recently gave the company a poor evaluation in an article that reviewed the support that software companies provide customers.

REQUIRED

a. Does the favorable variance for response time indicate good performance?

b. What might account for the "improvement" in performance related to time per call and the poor rating of customer support?

PROBLEM 11-16. Relationships among Variances [LO 3] In her review of annual production variances, Amy Abel, CFO of Chanceworth Manufacturing, noted that there was a $80,000 favorable material price variance, a $70,000 unfavorable material quantity variance, an $90,000 favorable labor rate variance, and a $180,000 unfavorable labor efficiency variance. From her previous discussions with factory supervisors and other managers, she knows that the purchasing department was able to buy materials at a bargain price. However, the material often failed stress tests, and a large number of items needed to be reworked. Also, the company had a brief strike. During the strike, the company hired a number of inexperienced, temporary replacement workers at wage rates significantly below those paid to the striking workers.

REQUIRED

a. Explain how the favorable material price variance and the favorable labor rate variance may be related to the unfavorable material quantity variance and the unfavorable labor efficiency variance.

b. Would you characterize the favorable material price variance as indicative of a good decision by the purchasing department?

PROBLEM 11-17. Interpreting the Overhead Volume Variance; Calculating the Financial Impact of Operating below Capacity [LO 2] The National Battery Company produces a wide variety of batteries for home, automobile, and marine use. One example of its many products is the Road Guardian automobile battery. The standard cost for this battery is as follows:

Standard Cost, Road Guardian	
Material	$ 5.00
Labor	4.00
Overhead	11.00
Total	$20.00

At the start of the current year, 2018, the company estimated that it would incur $48,000,000 of overhead costs and $6,000,000 of direct labor costs. Thus, $8 of overhead is applied at standard for each dollar of direct labor. Overhead is essentially completely fixed, which reflects the high level of investment in automated manufacturing.

During 2018, the company experienced a labor strike that severely limited production, and standard labor cost was only $5,200,000. At a recent meeting in early January 2019, C. W. Rogers, the president of National, asked the company controller, Walter Cox, to estimate the effect of the strike on company profit. The following morning, Walter sent the president a memo:

Date: January 7, 2019
To: C.W.
From: Walter
Subject: Effect of strike on company profit

As you know, profit in 2018 was greatly affected by a strike, which reduced productive capacity. The way to measure the impact of the reduced capacity is to examine the overhead volume variance. At the start of the year, we budgeted overhead to be $48,000,000. Actual overhead was $46,000,000 so we had a favorable overhead budget variance of $2,000,000. However, we applied only $41,600,000 of overhead to inventory ($8 overhead rate × $5,200,000 standard labor). Thus, we had an unfavorable overhead volume variance of $6,400,000.

Actual Overhead	Budgeted Overhead*	Applied Overhead
$46,000,000	$48,000,000	$41,600,000 ($8 × $5,200,000)

$2,000,000 Favorable $6,400,000 Unfavorable

*Note that budgeted overhead does not need to be adjusted for actual production since overhead costs are, for practical purposes, fixed. Thus, overhead in a static budget and in a flexible budget are equal.

In my opinion, the $6,400,000 unfavorable volume variance tells the story of our poor profit performance. If we had not had the strike, production would have been at a higher level (a level requiring $6,000,000 of standard labor cost), and this variance would have been avoided.

C.W., I realize that you are not an accountant, so please call me if you have any questions about my analysis.

REQUIRED

Suppose the strike limited production of the Road Guardian battery—a battery for which there is excess demand. Without the strike, 700,000 more of these batteries could have been produced and sold ($800,000 of direct labor not available × $4 of labor per battery). The selling price of the battery is $44. Taking this into account, calculate the effect of the strike on company profit, and comment on the controller's analysis.

PROBLEM 11-18. (Appendix) Recording Standard Costs [LO 1, 2] Bechtel Technical Clothing produces parkas used by arctic explorers, mountain climbers, and people living in Minnesota. The company uses a standard costing system, and standards call for 2.5 yards of material at $55 per yard for each parka. The standard cost for labor is 3.5 hours at $35 per hour. Standard overhead is $14 per unit. For the year 2018, expected production is 8,000 parkas with fixed overhead of $60,000 and variable overhead of $6.50 per parka.

During 2018, 8,500 parkas were manufactured. The company purchased 24,000 yards of material at a cost of $1,375,000. Production required 22,300 yards of material. The cost of direct labor was $1,000,000 for 27,500 hours. Actual overhead for the year was $90,000.

REQUIRED

a. Prepare a journal entry to record the purchase of material.

b. Prepare a journal entry to record material used in production.

c. Prepare a journal entry to record direct labor.

d. Prepare a journal entry to record actual overhead and overhead applied.

e. Prepare a journal entry to close the variances in requirements a through d to Cost of Goods Sold.

CASE

11-1 JACKSON SOUND [LO 3]

Jackson Sound produces amplifiers and mixing boards in a modern production facility. The company is well known for its quality products. Each item is thoroughly tested before it leaves the plant. Workers are highly skilled. The company considers direct labor to be a fixed cost because it does not reduce the workforce when there is a small downturn in business, and it can accommodate production increases of up to 10 percent due to excess capacity.

In the production process, workers in the circuit department prepare circuit boards that are sent to the case department for installation in custom cases. In the past 6 months, the workers in the circuit department have pursued a number of process improvement initiatives that have resulted in much shorter production times. For example, the Model LE7 amplifier used to require 12.5 standard labor hours in the circuit department, but the standard was revised last month to only 10.4 standard hours.

Although the circuit department has made production improvements, the chief financial officer of the company, Christopher Carlson, is concerned about a major buildup of in-process inventory that is occurring between the circuit department and the case department. "What's going on?" he asked his assistant, Megan Welles. "I was walking through the plant yesterday and I saw a tremendous amount of in-process inventory. I thought we had implemented a JIT system and we were working to balance our production processes. That investment in work in process is just going to drag down company performance."

Megan replied that the source of the problem might be related to the process improvements and the fact that bonuses for production workers are tied to standard cost performance. Christopher, however, didn't see how a process improvement could actually make things worse.

REQUIRED

Assume that the company is reluctant to fire workers in the circuit department even if they are not really needed. (After all, they have just worked hard to improve productivity.) Given the production improvements and the institution of new standards, explain why the circuit department has an incentive to overproduce (i.e., produce more output than can be handled by the case department). (*Hint:* If the circuit department does not overproduce, what will be the effect of the process improvements on the labor efficiency variance?)

CASE

11-2 CHAMPION INDUSTRIES [LO 1, 2, 3]

Stan Holbert, the purchasing manager for Champion Industries, recently attended a meeting with a potential supplier, Wallace Materials. At the meeting, a Wallace manager demonstrated a material that was easier to handle and shape than the material currently used by Champion Industries.

Current standards call for 10 pounds of material per unit, costing $23 per pound. Direct labor per unit is 2.5 hours at $30 per hour. The new material will cost $25 per pound. However, only 8 pounds of material will be needed per unit due to reduced waste. Also, direct labor per unit will be reduced to 0.75 hour because the new material is less toxic and easier to handle.

REQUIRED

a. Assume that annual production is 150,000 units. Calculate the cost savings associated with using the new material.

b. Stan knows that because of an overworked accounting department, standard costs will not be updated in a timely manner. Suppose that the company switches to the new material. What are the expected material and labor variances if standards are not updated?

c. Suppose purchase price variances play a prominent role in the evaluation of Stan's job performance. Will he be inclined to suggest use of the new material?

12

DECENTRALIZATION AND PERFORMANCE EVALUATION

Action Industries is a diversified corporation whose divisions manufacture office products, home products, janitorial supplies, storage containers, and a variety of plastic products.

At a recent meeting of the board of directors of Action Industries, Bill Stern, president and CEO, rose to address board members. "As I'm sure you know," he began, "Marie Greco is doing a really superb job as manager of our Home Products division. Five years ago, we gave her a mandate to turn this sleepy division around, and we granted her the authority to make the key decisions that would improve the division's performance. The result is that her division has increased profit by 10 to 15 percent each year, and her division has gone from being our fifth to our second largest! Marie's operation is really making a contribution to our bottom line. Maybe it's time to think of moving her into corporate. The position of VP of Operations is opening up, and I want a results-oriented person in the job."

At this point, Alister Hurd, the founder and chairman of the board of Action Industries, spoke up. "Bill, I'm not so sure that Home Products is a top performer. After all, we expect profit to increase with the size of a division. Is the profit of Home Products that great if we take our investment into account? I think it's time we moved away from our focus on division profit and growth in profit. When I talk to my friends at other companies, I find they focus on ROI, and some of them are starting to use EVA and the balanced scorecard approach to evaluating performance. I wonder if our approach is out of step with current thinking. We need to be sure that our performance measures are giving us a clear picture of performance and driving the right manager behaviors." The meeting ended with Bill committed to a thorough review of alternative performance measures, which he would present at the next board meeting.

Sebastian Duda/Shutterstock

LEARNING OBJECTIVES

1. Explain the advantages and disadvantages of decentralization, explain why companies evaluate the performance of subunits and subunit managers, and identify cost centers, profit centers, and investment centers.
2. Calculate and interpret return on investment (ROI), residual income (RI), and economic value added (EVA).
3. Explain the potential benefits of using a balanced scorecard to assess performance, and discuss how a strategy map can be used to communicate the linkages among the measures in a balanced scorecard.

As firms increase in size and complexity, business segments or subunits (such as the Home Products division at Action Industries) are organized and the managers of the segments are granted decision-making authority so that the firm will function efficiently and effectively. Firms that grant substantial decision-making authority to the managers of subunits are referred to as **decentralized organizations**. Likewise, firms that do not grant substantial decision-making authority to the managers of subunits are referred to as centralized organizations.

Most firms are neither totally centralized nor totally decentralized. Decentralization is a matter of degree. To the extent that more decision-making authority is delegated to subunit managers, a firm is more decentralized. Action Industries is a decentralized organization in that substantial decision-making authority has been given to Marie Greco, the manager of the Home Products division.

In this chapter, we examine various types of subunits, and we illustrate how performance evaluation can be used to control the behavior of subunit managers. The goal is to ensure that subunit managers make decisions that are in the best interest of the entire firm.

LEARNING OBJECTIVE 1

Explain the advantages and disadvantages of decentralization, explain why companies evaluate the performance of subunits and subunit managers, and identify cost centers, profit centers, and investment centers.

WHY FIRMS DECENTRALIZE

Firms decentralize for a number of reasons. Here we look first at what firms hope to gain by decentralizing. Then we examine some disadvantages of decentralization.

Advantages of Decentralization

A primary reason for decentralization is that subunit managers have *better information* than top management and they can *respond more quickly* to changing circumstances. Consider an electronics firm that has two primary divisions: a copier division and a camera division. Division managers report to top management responsible for both divisions. As shown in Illustration 12-1, each division operates in a unique environment. Competition, customer needs, and the supply of workers and raw materials are different for each of these product lines.

Suppose a new personal copier is to be introduced in the coming year, and a pricing decision must be made. Who has superior information as to an appropriate price to charge—the manager of the copier division or top management? Because of his or her daily involvement with the market for copiers, the manager of the division probably has a better understanding of how the market will react to a particular price. If this is

ILLUSTRATION 12-1

Firm and subunit environments

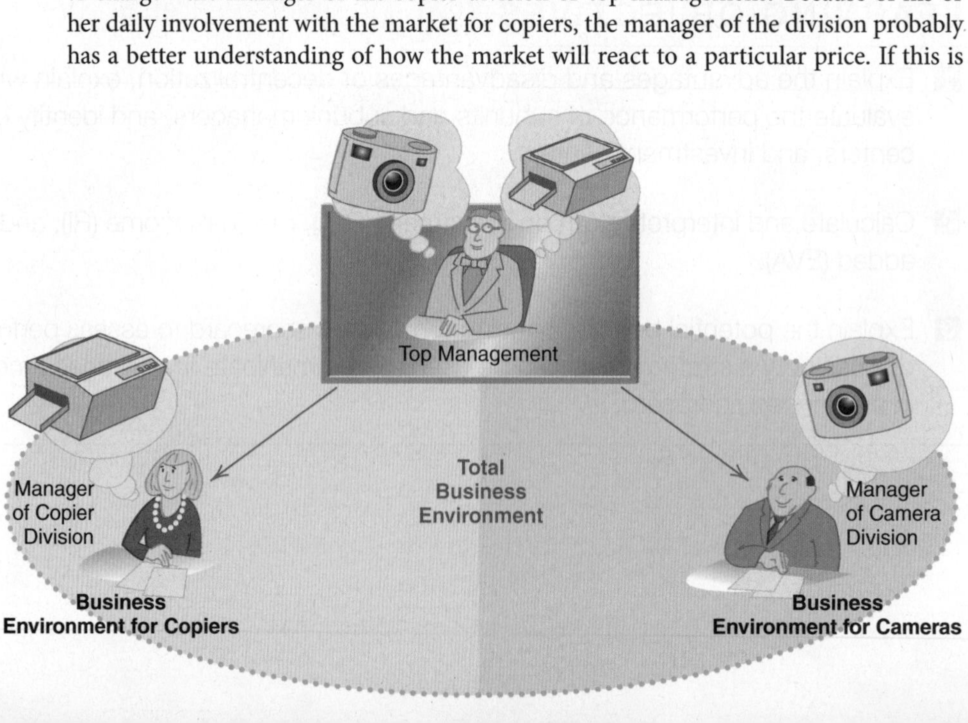

the case, then the pricing decision should be delegated to the division manager, further enhancing the decentralization of the firm.

Suppose the manager of the camera division learns that a supplier of camera lenses is facing excess capacity and is willing to supply the division with lenses at a bargain price. In a decentralized organization, the manager can react quickly to this opportunity and increase the profitability of the division and the firm. However, if the firm is more centralized, the manager of the division may have to present the facts to top management, which will make the decision as to whether the lenses should be purchased. This can be a time-consuming process, and by the time a decision is made, the supplier may no longer have excess capacity. Worse, other camera companies may take advantage of the situation and gain a competitive edge.

Some firms decentralize because they believe that managers who are given significant decision-making authority are *more motivated* and work harder than managers in centralized organizations. If managers are given broad decision-making responsibility, they may identify so strongly with their subunits that they work as hard as they would if they actually owned the business.

Finally, decentralized organizations provide excellent *training* for future top-level executives. Subunit managers in decentralized organizations are used to making important decisions and taking responsibility for their actions. Thus, when high-level positions in the firm need to be filled, the firm has a ready supply of managers with the required decision-making experience.

Disadvantages of Decentralization

Although decentralization has several beneficial features, it may create problems. One potential problem is that decentralization may result in a costly *duplication of activities*. For example, two subunit managers may decide to develop their own purchasing departments when one purchasing department would be more economical. Or each major subunit may have its own sales force, when a single coordinated sales force would be more effective.

A second problem with a decentralized organization is that managers of subunits may pursue personal goals that are incompatible with the goals of the company as a whole. This problem is referred to as a **lack of goal congruence**. An example of a goal congruence problem is empire building. Some managers derive substantial satisfaction from running large subunits (their *empires*). Perhaps this satisfaction comes from impressing friends and business associates with the number of employees and the size of the facilities under their control. However, maximizing the size of the subunit, which satisfies the manager's personal goal, may be incompatible with the overall company goal of profit maximization. Bigger operations are not necessarily more profitable operations.

To control goal congruence problems in decentralized organizations, companies evaluate the performance of subunit managers. As we will see later in this chapter, the evaluation process should encourage managers of subunits to take actions that are in the interest of the company as a whole. That is, performance evaluation should encourage managers to behave as if their own personal goals are congruent with the goals of the company as a whole.

A summary of these advantages and disadvantages of decentralization is presented in Illustration 12-2.

ILLUSTRATION 12-2

Some advantages and disadvantages of decentralization

Advantages of Decentralization

1. Better information, leading to superior decisions
2. Faster response to changing circumstances
3. Increased motivation of managers
4. Excellent training for future top-level executives

Disadvantages of Decentralization

1. Costly duplication of activities
2. Lack of goal congruence

WHY COMPANIES EVALUATE THE PERFORMANCE OF SUBUNITS AND SUBUNIT MANAGERS

Decentralization leads naturally to the need to evaluate subunits and their managers. These evaluations serve different purposes, as explained next.

Decision Making/ Incremental Analysis

Evaluating Subunits

Evaluation of subunits is undertaken to identify successful operations and areas needing improvement. If an operation is deemed successful, top management may perform incremental analysis to determine whether the operation should be expanded. If an operation is viewed as underperforming, top management may perform incremental analysis to determine whether the operation should be eliminated or whether funds should be invested to improve it.

YOU GET WHAT YOU MEASURE

Evaluating Subunit Managers

The reason we evaluate subunit managers is that the evaluation influences their behavior. As first discussed in Chapter 1, "You get what you measure!" In other words, performance measures can be used to drive the behavior of managers.

For example, suppose Marie Greco, the manager of the Home Products division of Action Industries, has historically been evaluated in terms of *total sales*. In the current year, she is also being evaluated in terms of *sales to new customers*. Do you think her behavior will change? Quite likely, she will spend more time focusing the attention of her sales team on developing *new* customers because she will want to perform at a high level with respect to the new performance measure. If developing new customers is critical to the company's success, then it is a good idea to encourage this behavior by focusing on the new performance measure—sales to new customers.

Keep in mind that it is possible to have a good manager and a bad subunit. A manager may do all that is reasonably possible to improve a subunit, but the subunit may not be a line of business that the company believes has good long-run profit potential. In this case, the company may reward the performance of the manager but still exit the subunit's line of business.

Responsibility Accounting and Performance Evaluation

The discussion of cost allocation in Chapter 6 introduced the topic of *responsibility accounting*, a technique that holds managers responsible only for costs and revenues that they can control. This idea should play a prominent role in the design of accounting systems used to evaluate the performance of managers in a decentralized organization. To implement responsibility accounting in a decentralized organization, costs and revenues are traced to the organizational level where they can be controlled.

For example, consider the information presented for the Jones Tool Company in Illustration 12-3. Jones Tool produces a variety of small tools in two plants: the Eastern Plant and the Western Plant. Each plant has a plant manager who is responsible for operations. Currently, two production shifts are run each day, with work supervised by individuals with the title *production supervisor*. A vice president of manufacturing is responsible for production in both the Eastern Plant and the Western Plant.

The illustration indicates, in a simplified setting, how implementation of responsibility accounting would suggest that costs be accumulated for assessing performance. Only labor costs and material costs are traced to the individual shift supervisors. This follows because at the Jones Tool Company, the production supervisors make numerous decisions that affect

ILLUSTRATION 12-3

Tracing costs to the organizational level where they can be controlled

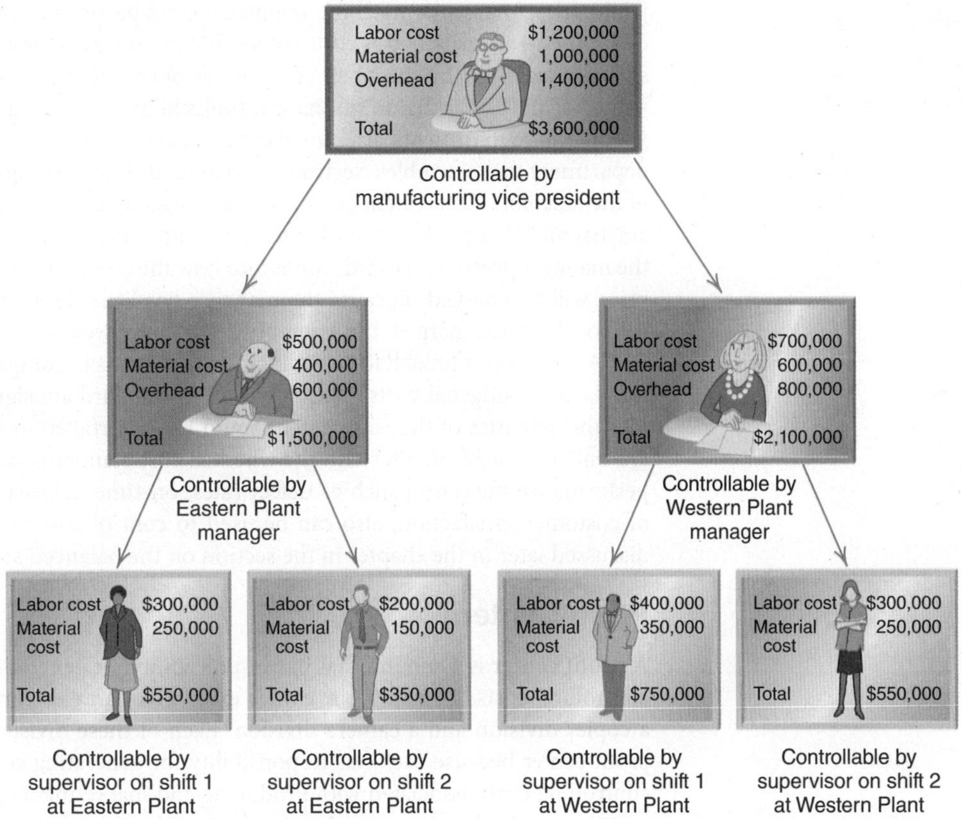

the amount of labor and material costs incurred. However, plant overhead costs are not traced to the supervisors, because these supervisors are not involved in decisions that affect the amount of overhead incurred. Instead, overhead costs are traced to the individual plant managers, who can control overhead costs. The manager of the Eastern Plant, for example, is responsible for $500,000 of labor costs ($300,000 from the first shift and $200,000 from the second shift), $400,000 of material costs ($250,000 from the first shift and $150,000 from the second shift), and $600,000 of overhead costs incurred in the Eastern Plant.

The vice president of manufacturing is responsible for all of the costs incurred at both the Eastern Plant and the Western Plant. Therefore, all production costs are traced to the vice president. For example, the overhead costs traced to the vice president are $1,400,000, which includes $600,000 from the Eastern Plant and $800,000 from the Western Plant.

COST CENTERS, PROFIT CENTERS, AND INVESTMENT CENTERS

Subunits are organizational units with identifiable collections of related resources and activities. A subunit may be a department, a subsidiary, or a division. Subunits are sometimes referred to as **responsibility centers**, defined as organizational units responsible for the generation of revenue and/or the incurrence of costs. Responsibility centers typically are classified as being cost centers, profit centers, or investment centers. Let's look at the types of performance measures that are appropriate for each of these subunits.

Cost Centers

A **cost center** is a subunit that has responsibility for controlling costs but does not have responsibility for generating revenue. Most service departments (e.g., photocopying, janitorial services, the machine maintenance department, and the computer services department) are classified as cost centers. The managers of these departments are responsible for making sure that their services are provided at a reasonable cost to the company, but they typically do not have responsibility for generating revenue for the firm. Production departments also are classified as cost centers. As an example, consider a department that assembles electronic components into desktop computers. The manager of the assembly department certainly is responsible for making sure that the computers are assembled at the lowest cost consistent with acceptable quality standards. However, the manager probably has little input into how the computers will be marketed and what price will be charged. Because the manager has little direct control over the quantity sold or the price charged, the assembly department would be considered a cost center.

A common approach to controlling cost centers is to compare their actual costs with standard or budgeted costs. If variances from standard are significant, an investigation into the activities of the cost center should be undertaken to determine whether costs are out of control or, alternatively, whether cost standards need to be revised. Other performance measures, such as defect rates, on-time delivery statistics, and measures of customer satisfaction, also can be used to control cost centers. Such measures are discussed later in the chapter in the section on the balanced scorecard.

Profit Centers

A **profit center** is a subunit that has responsibility for generating revenue as well as for controlling costs. Consider our earlier example of an electronics firm that consists of a copier division and a camera division. Each of these divisions can be classified as a profit center because each has responsibility for generating revenue through sales and controlling costs associated with producing and marketing its products.

Because both revenues and costs (the two elements that determine profit) are under the control of the profit center manager, the performance of the profit center can be evaluated in terms of profitability. Evaluation in terms of profitability is useful because it motivates managers to focus their attention on ways of maximizing profit-center profitability.

Companies use a variety of methods to evaluate the profitability of profit centers. Income earned in the current year may be compared with an income target or budget. Or income earned may be compared with income earned in the prior year. Some firms evaluate profit centers using **relative performance evaluation**. Relative performance evaluation of profit centers involves evaluating the profitability of each profit center relative to the profitability of other, similar profit centers.

For example, the Chicken King Company operates 10 fast-food restaurants in a major midwestern city. Each outlet (restaurant) is treated as a profit center because it is responsible for generating revenue (sales of chicken sandwiches, sodas, ice cream, etc.) and controlling costs (food costs, labor, heat and light, etc.). If each outlet is *reasonably* similar in terms of size, appearance, and menu, comparing the income earned by each outlet with the income earned by other outlets may be a useful means of assessing the effectiveness of outlet managers.

Investment Centers

An **investment center** is a subunit that is responsible for generating revenue, controlling costs, and investing in assets. Because it is responsible for revenue, costs, and investment, an investment center is charged with earning income consistent with the amount of assets invested in the segment. Most divisions of a company can be treated as either profit centers or investment centers. If the division manager can significantly influence decisions affecting investment in divisional assets, the division should be considered an investment center. If the division manager cannot influence investment decisions, the division should be considered a profit center. Since Marie Greco, the manager of the

LINK TO PRACTICE

Subunits at Nordstrom

Think about the subunits at Nordstrom. The company has 117 full-line stores selling apparel, shoes, and accessories for women, men, and children. In addition, the company operates 142 discount stores under the name Nordstrom Rack. There also are two Jeffrey boutiques and one Last Chance clearance store. Each of these subunit groups is a profit center or an investment center, depending on how much autonomy the managers have over investments. The individual stores (e.g., the Nordstrom store in San Francisco) are also profit centers or investment centers. The advertising, maintenance, and accounting departments at Nordstrom are cost centers. Managers in these subunits are responsible for controlling their costs, but they do not have responsibility for generating revenue.

Home Products division of Action Industries, is granted authority to make investment decisions, her operation is an investment center.

Investment center managers generally play a major role in determining the level of inventory, the level of accounts receivable, and the investment in equipment and other assets held by the investment center. Thus, it seems reasonable to hold them responsible for earning a return on these assets. However, although investment center managers play a major role, they generally are not given complete autonomy in investing in assets. Typically, central management has final approval of all major investments. Guidelines may specify that investment center managers must have central management approval for all investments greater than some specified dollar amount (e.g., investments greater than $200,000).

TEST YOUR KNOWLEDGE

Classify each of the following subunits as being (most likely) a cost center, a profit center, or an investment center.

a. Kmart corporation, a subsidiary of Sears Holdings Corporation.

b. The unit responsible for physical security on the Microsoft campus in Redmond, Washington.

c. The manager of men's shoes at the Nordstrom store in Dallas.

Correct answers are: a. investment center; b. cost center; c. profit center.

LEARNING OBJECTIVE 2

Calculate and interpret return on investment (ROI), residual income (RI), and economic value added (EVA).

EVALUATING INVESTMENT CENTERS WITH ROI

One of the primary tools for evaluating the performance of investment centers is **return on investment (ROI)**. ROI is calculated as the ratio of investment center income to invested capital. The idea of evaluating performance using ROI was developed in the early part of the twentieth century by Du Pont (known then as the DuPont Powder Company) and has now gained widespread acceptance.[1]

ROI has a distinct advantage over income as a measure of performance. It focuses the attention of managers not only on income (the numerator of ROI) but also on investment (the denominator of ROI). Suppose two business units earn the same income—$100,000. A performance measure based solely on income would rate the two units as equally successful. However, suppose the first business unit required an investment in assets of $1,000,000, while the second business unit required only $500,000. The second unit has performed much better than the first because it required only half

[1]See H. Thomas Johnson and Robert S. Kaplan, *Relevance Lost: The Rise and Fall of Management Accounting* (Boston: Harvard Business School Press, 1987), Chapter 4.

LINK TO **PRACTICE**

The Focus on ROI and Shareholder Value Is Not the Same in France, Germany, and Japan as It Is in the United States and Great Britain

Managers in the United States and Great Britain focus intensely on financial measures of performance such as ROI. They do so because they believe that actions increasing ROI lead to increases in shareholder value, and increasing *shareholder* value is their primary responsibility. This is not the case, however, in France, Germany, and Japan. In these countries, managers believe that they should focus their attention on the welfare of all company *stakeholders*, including employees, customers, suppliers, and citizens of the cities where they operate in addition to investors/shareholders. This can lead to differing decisions in these countries. For example, in the United States and Great Britain, managers may cut wages to increase profit and ROI and pump up stock prices, increasing the wealth of investors. In France, Germany, and Japan, however, such cuts may be viewed less favorably because they hurt a major stakeholder group: employees. Thus, the focus on ROI is much less in these countries compared to the United States and Great Britain.

Source: "Companies Not for Shareholders Alone," editorial from *Yomiuri Shimbun*, October 24, 2005. Reprinted by permission of *Yomiuri Shimbun*.

the investment to earn the same level of income. This allows the company to invest the funds not required by the second unit in another project and earn additional income:

	Business Unit 1	Business Unit 2
$\text{ROI} = \dfrac{\text{Income}}{\text{Invested capital}}$	$\dfrac{\$100{,}000}{\$1{,}000{,}000} = .10, \text{ or } 10\%$	$\dfrac{\$100{,}000}{\$500{,}000} = .20, \text{ or } 20\%$

Note that unlike income, ROI does not rate these two units as equally successful. The first unit has an ROI of only 10 percent while the second unit has a much higher ROI of 20 percent.

Some companies break ROI down into two components: profit margin and investment turnover:

$$\text{ROI} = \frac{\text{Income}}{\text{Invested capital}} = \underset{\textbf{Profit Margin}}{\frac{\text{Income}}{\text{Sales}}} \times \underset{\textbf{Investment Turnover}}{\frac{\text{Sales}}{\text{Invested capital}}}$$

Profit margin is the ratio of income to sales, while **investment turnover** is the ratio of sales to invested capital. Breaking down ROI into these components clearly indicates to managers that there are two ways in which ROI can be improved. Managers can take actions to improve the income earned on each dollar of sales (i.e., increase the margin), or managers can take actions to generate more sales for each dollar invested (i.e., increase turnover).

Measuring Income and Invested Capital When Calculating ROI

In calculating ROI, companies measure "income" in a variety of ways (net income, income before interest and taxes, controllable profit, etc.). For purposes of this book, and consistent with the practice of many companies, we'll measure investment center income as **net operating profit after taxes**, known by the abbreviation **NOPAT**.

Because NOPAT is focused on *operating* profit after taxes, it excludes interest expense, which is a nonoperating expense. Therefore, to calculate NOPAT, we must add interest expense back to net income and adjust tax expense accordingly. Consider the data in Illustration 12-4, which relates to the Home Products division of Action Industries. As indicated, net income is $3,900,000. We add back interest expense of $1,000,000, and we subtract the tax savings on interest equal to the 35 percent tax rate times $1,000,000. The

ILLUSTRATION 12-4
Calculation of investment center income and invested capital for the Home Products division of Action Industries

Net Income	
Sales	$40,000,000
Less cost of goods sold	25,000,000
Gross margin	15,000,000
Less selling and administrative expenses	8,000,000
Income from operations	7,000,000
Less interest expense	1,000,000
Income before taxes	6,000,000
Less taxes	2,100,000
Net income	$ 3,900,000
NOPAT	
Net income	$ 3,900,000
Plus interest expense	1,000,000
Less tax savings related to interest (equals .35 × $1,000,000)	350,000
NOPAT	$ 4,550,000
Invested Capital	
Book value of total assets	$96,000,000
Less noninterest-bearing current liabilities	5,000,000
Invested capital	$91,000,000
ROI = NOPAT ÷ Invested capital	0.05 or 5%

result is a NOPAT value of $4,550,000. A benefit of using NOPAT is that it does not hold the investment center manager responsible for interest expense. This is appropriate because investment center managers frequently do not have responsibility for decisions related to financing their operations. Also, using NOPAT facilitates comparisons of multiple investment centers because it is not influenced by differences in how the investment centers are financed.

As with "income," companies measure "invested capital" in a variety of ways (total assets, total assets after adding back accumulated depreciation, total assets less current liabilities, etc.). We'll measure invested capital as total assets less **noninterest-bearing current liabilities (NIBCL)**. NIBCL are current liabilities that do not require interest payments. Thus, they include accounts payable, income taxes payable, accrued liabilities, and a number of other items. Noninterest-bearing current liabilities are deducted from the total assets because they are a "free" source of funds and reduce the cost of the investment in assets. As indicated in Illustration 12-4, invested capital calculated as total assets less noninterest-bearing current liabilities is $91,000,000. Thus, ROI (the ratio of NOPAT to invested capital) is only 5 percent, which is likely to be less than the company's cost of capital.

ANY **QUESTIONS?**

Q: In Illustration 12-4, NOPAT is calculated by adding interest back to net income and then subtracting the tax savings on interest. Why not just take income from operations and then subtract related taxes? You get the same answer:

Income from operations (see Illustration 12-4)	**$7,000,000**
Less taxes at 35%	**2,450,000**
NOPAT	**$4,550,000**

A: It is perfectly fine to start with income from operations and then subtract related taxes. As you can see, you get the same answer. However, some income statements do not break out an "income from operations" number. In such cases, *you* have to first calculate income from operations and then subtract related taxes. Either approach works—just remember that NOPAT does not include interest expense.

Given the low ROI earned by the Home Products division, it is appropriate for Alister Hurd, the chairman of the board, to question the performance of the operation. While Home Products is generating a substantial profit, the profit is low relative to the level of investment in the operation. That is the essential insight provided by ROI.

Problems with Using ROI

In spite of its advantages, using ROI can present problems. One problem with ROI is that investment in assets typically is measured using historical costs. Recall that the historical cost of total assets is affected by depreciation of plant and equipment. As assets become fully depreciated, the measure of investment becomes very low, and ROI becomes quite large. This makes comparison of investment centers using ROI difficult.

Consider two investment centers that are alike in all respects except one: Investment Center 1 was started 5 years ago, and its investment in fixed assets is substantially depreciated, whereas Investment Center 2 was started in the current year. Both earn exactly the same level of net operating profit after taxes, $100,000. As indicated in Illustration 12-5, the ROI of Investment Center 1 is 29.41 percent, while the ROI of Investment Center 2 is 23.81 percent. The difference of 5.6 percent is due to the fact that the fixed assets of Investment Center 1 are substantially depreciated. Thus, its investment base is much lower than the investment base of Investment Center 2.

Now suppose additional funds become available to invest in either of the two business segments. Will Investment Center 1 earn a higher return than Investment Center 2 on the incremental investment? Although Investment Center 1 has the higher ROI, the two business segments are identical in all respects except for the age of their equipment. Thus, we would expect both segments to generate the same income with the funds. The point is that using ROI to rank the attractiveness of investment centers can be difficult if the remaining useful lives of their depreciable assets are very different.

Some critics of ROI have suggested that undue emphasis on ROI may lead managers to delay the purchase of modern equipment needed to stay competitive. Old equipment has a low carrying value because it is substantially depreciated. Thus, the denominator of ROI (total assets less noninterest-bearing current liabilities) is low, and ROI is high. If new equipment is purchased, it may significantly raise the level of investment and reduce ROI. If managers are evaluated in terms of ROI, they may fear that the decline in ROI will lead to low ratings of their job performance. In situations like this, managers may fail to purchase equipment necessary for the long-run success of the company.

ILLUSTRATION 12-5

Comparison of investment centers with differences in accumulated depreciation

		Investment Center 1		Investment Center 2
NOPAT		$100,000		$100,000
Investment:				
Cash		$ 20,000		$ 20,000
Accounts receivable		80,000		80,000
Inventory		150,000		150,000
Plant and equipment				
Cost	$200,000		$200,000	
Less accumulated depreciation	100,000	100,000	20,000	180,000
Total assets		350,000		430,000
Less noninterest-bearing current liabilities		10,000		10,000
Invested capital		$340,000		$420,000
ROI		$ 29.41%		$ 23.81%

Recall that in an earlier chapter, we recommended that investment alternatives should be evaluated in terms of their net present values. Investment opportunities with positive net present values should be undertaken while investment opportunities with negative net present values should be rejected. However, if the performance of managers is evaluated using ROI, they may not be motivated to invest in projects with positive net present values. The reason is that, in the short run, projects with positive net present values may have low levels of income and correspondingly low ROIs. If managers are evaluated in terms of ROI, they will be quite concerned about how ROI will be affected by additional investments. The result is that managers with currently high ROI may consider the effect on ROI, instead of net present value, in evaluating investment alternatives.

LINK TO **PRACTICE**

Did Boeing's Focus on ROI Lead to Excessive Outsourcing?

In developing the 787 Dreamliner, Boeing implemeted a global outsourcing strategy of unprecedented scale. The plan was to drive down costs by having companies around the world design and build key components of the aircraft, which would then be assembled by Boeing in the United States. Unfortunately, the strategy backfired. Analysts estimate that the strategy cost Boeing $12 to $18 billion more than the company planned to invest in the project.

At a meeting with students at Seattle University, Jim Albaugh, CEO of Boeing Commercial Airplanes, candidly told them that the decision to outsource at such a scale (a decision made before he took over) may have been driven in part by focusing excessively on RONA (return on net assets). This measure is very similar to the measure we've been discussing, ROI.

Suppose you were a manager at Boeing in the late 1990s, when the Dreamliner was being conceived. Why might you have wanted to engage in outsourcing if your performance was going to be evaluated by using ROI? One way to increase ROI is to reduce assets (the denominator in ROI). By outsourcing, Boeing thought it could shift the cost of building facilities and other assets to suppliers and thus increase ROI.

Source: "A 'Prescient' Warning to Boeing on 787 Trouble," *The Seattle Times*, February 6, 2011, pp. D1, D6.

Problems of Overinvestment and Underinvestment: You Get What You Measure!

A related problem with ROI is that managers of investment centers with high ROIs may be unwilling to invest in assets that will earn a return that is satisfactory to central management if that return is less than their current, high, ROI. That is, managers with currently high ROIs may underinvest. As illustrated later, this problem can be minimized by evaluating managers using residual income or economic value added (EVA). For now, let's compare the tendency for underinvestment, which is related to the use of ROI as a performance measure, to the tendency for overinvestment, which is related to the use of profit as a performance measure.

YOU GET WHAT YOU MEASURE

Evaluation in Terms of Profit Can Lead to Overinvestment. As discussed in Chapter 9, we would like managers to invest in assets that earn a return in excess of the cost of capital. But remember, "You get what you measure!" If we evaluate managers in terms of growth in profit, they may be motivated to make investments that earn a return that is less than the cost of capital—that is, they may overinvest in assets.

I may not be a very good manager, but I can increase the profit of any company as long as shareholders will provide me with the assets to make investments. And while I'm increasing profit, I'll be decreasing shareholder value! How will I achieve these apparently conflicting outcomes? I'll do it by growing the company and investing in projects that earn returns that are less than the cost of capital (i.e., I'll do it by overinvesting). For example, suppose the cost of capital relevant to my subunit is 9 percent, and the subunit

ILLUSTRATION 12-6
Subunits with high ROIs may pass up investments with ROIs greater than the cost of capital if the return is less than their current high ROI

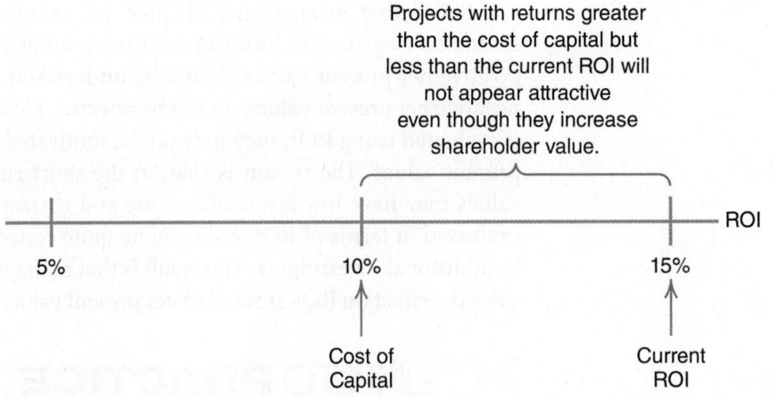

currently earns a profit of $100,000 on an investment of $1,000,000. This means the subunit is earning a 10 percent return. Now I'll grow the subunit using funds provided by shareholders (so there is no interest charge to reduce my profit!). Suppose I double the size of the investment in my subunit to $2,000,000 and earn a profit of $150,000. Note that I've had a 50 percent increase in profit, so my performance will look good if I'm evaluated in terms of growth in profit. But what return have I earned on the incremental investment of $1,000,000? The increase in profit is only $50,000, so I only earned a return of 5 percent, which is less than the cost of capital.

Evaluation in Terms of ROI Can Lead to Underinvestment. Perhaps an obvious solution to the overinvestment problem is to evaluate managers in terms of ROI. Managers won't want to take on projects that have a low return just to increase profit if they are evaluated in terms of the return they earn. As we have just seen, however, ROI has its own set of problems, and one of them is that it may lead managers to underinvest—that is, they may pass up projects that earn a return that is greater than the cost of capital.

Suppose you were the manager of a subunit with an ROI of 15 percent and a cost of capital of 10 percent. If you were evaluated in terms of ROI, would you take on a new project that had a return of 12 percent? Probably not. Although the project has a return greater than the cost of capital and will increase shareholder wealth, it will lower your reported ROI and possibly reflect negatively on your performance. In fact, you may try to get rid of some of your current projects that are earning a return greater than 10 percent but less than 15 percent in an effort to increase your reported ROI. Note that ROI is most likely to lead to underinvestment for high-performing subunits; those are the ones that are earning returns much greater than the cost of capital. And these are exactly the subunits that are good candidates for expansion! Shareholders want these managers to invest in all projects that have returns greater than the cost of capital. But the managers will not want to invest in projects that have returns higher than the cost of capital but less than their current high returns. The reason: The investments will lower their current high ROI, which suggests that their performance is declining (see Illustration 12-6).

EVALUATION USING ECONOMIC VALUE ADDED (EVA)

An approach to solving overinvestment and underinvestment problems involves the use of a performance measure known as economic value added (EVA). Firms that use EVA typically tie bonus compensation to the measure. Thus, managers become very focused on achieving high levels of EVA. EVA was developed based on a concept known as residual income, which was developed in the 1930s and is generally attributed to General Electric. In the next section, we will review residual income and then consider the extension to EVA.

Residual Income (RI)

Residual income (RI) is the net operating profit after taxes of an investment center in excess of its required profit. And required profit is equal to the investment center's required rate of return times the level of investment in the center (i.e., RI = NOPAT– Required profit). Generally, the required rate of return is the cost of capital for the investment center. Although a number of alternative measures of investment exist, we'll use total assets minus noninterest-bearing current liabilities as a measure of investment. Under these conditions, the formula for calculating residual income is:

$$\text{Residual income} = \text{NOPAT} - \text{Required Profit}$$

$$= \text{NOPAT} - \text{Cost of capital} \times \text{Investment}$$

$$= \text{NOPAT} - \text{Cost of capital} \times (\text{Total assets} - \text{NIBCL})$$

Here NIBCL stands for noninterest-bearing current liabilities. Why is NIBCL deducted from total assets to determine the level of investment? The answer is that these liabilities are a free source of funds. Suppose you open an audio/video store and purchase $1,000,000 of inventory. Further, suppose your suppliers agree that you do not have to pay for the inventory until it is sold. Thus, you have total assets of $1,000,000 related to inventory and $1,000,000 of accounts payable (a noninterest-bearing current liability). But what is your investment in the inventory? The answer, of course, is zero, and this is precisely what you will calculate if you measure investment as total assets less NIBCL.

Revisiting the Situation at Action Industries. Consider the situation of the Home Products division of Action Industries presented at the start of the chapter. As we saw in Illustration 12-4, it has NOPAT of $4,550,000 and invested capital (total assets minus NIBCL) of $91,000,000. Assume that cost of capital for Home Products is 12 percent. In this case, residual income is a loss of $6,370,000.

$$\begin{aligned}\text{Residual income} &= \text{NOPAT} - \text{Required profit}\\ &= \text{NOPAT} - \text{Cost of capital} \times \text{Investment}\\ &= \text{NOPAT} - \text{Cost of capital} \times (\text{Total assets} - \text{NIBCL})\\ &= \$4{,}550{,}000 - (12\% \times \$91{,}000{,}000)\\ &= \$4{,}550{,}000 - \$10{,}920{,}000\\ &= (\$6{,}370{,}000)\end{aligned}$$

The Home Products division had a net operating profit after taxes of $4,500,000, but given that the company had an investment of $91,000,000, it should have had net operating profit after taxes of at least $10,920,000. Thus, the company has a negative residual income of $6,370,000. So instead of helping improve the company's economic well-being, the division has destroyed more than $6,000,000 of shareholder value! This is clear only after we calculate an appropriate level of income given the investment in the Home Products division.

Solving the Overinvestment and Underinvestment Problems

RI has the potential to solve the overinvestment problem and the underinvestment problem. Let's see how. Suppose a project comes along that will earn a return on its incremental investment of 9 percent. Would the manager make the investment? Not if the manager is evaluated using RI and the cost of capital is 10 percent. Since the manager receives a capital charge on investments of 10 percent, the manager knows that residual income will be reduced if the investment is made. Thus, there is no incentive for overinvestment. Now suppose a project comes along that will earn a return of 11 percent. Will

LINK TO PRACTICE

Companies That Have Used EVA

Here are a number of well-known companies that have used EVA:

Bausch & Lomb	Eli Lilly	Rubbermaid
Best Buy	Georgia-Pacific	Sprint
Boise Cascade	Herman Miller	Steelcase
Briggs & Stratton	JCPenney	Toys "Я" Us
Coca-Cola	Monsanto	U.S. Postal Service
Dresser Industries	Olin	Whirlpool
		Whole Foods

An excellent website for information on EVA is by EVANOMICS, at http://evanomics.com.

the manager make the investment? The answer is yes, since residual income will increase (because the capital charge is less than the amount earned by the project). Thus, there is no incentive to underinvest.

Economic Value Added (EVA)

Economic value added, better known as simply **EVA**, is a performance measure developed by the consulting firm Stern Stewart. In essence, EVA is simply residual income adjusted for what Stern Stewart refers to as "accounting distortions" that arise from following generally accepted accounting principles (GAAP). A primary distortion is

LINK TO PRACTICE

Deere & Company Uses SVA Rather Than EVA

Several companies use measures that are similar to EVA. For example, Deere & Company uses a measure it calls shareholder value added or SVA. Its calculation is:

Operating profit − (Cost of assets × Average assets)

Here operating profit is similar if not identical to NOPAT, and cost of assets is essentially the company's weighted average cost of capital. What's different is that the cost of assets is multiplied by average assets rather than assets less noninterest-bearing current liabilities. Thus, the company does not take into account the benefit of free sources of funds (NIBCL). According to the company's chief financial officer, this was done because the company believes the focus on assets alone is more intuitive to people who work in factories. For 2014, the company calculated SVA for its equipment operation to be $2.437 billion:

SVA billions: $4.297 − .12 × $15.493 = $2.438

Here operating profit is $4.297 billion, the cost of assets is 12 percent, and average assets is $15.493 billion.

Neither EVA nor SVA is required under generally accepted accounting principles. Thus, Deere is somewhat unique in that it publishes SVA in the company's annual report, which can be obtained at the company's website under Investor Relations.

related to research and development (R&D). GAAP requires that R&D be expensed in the period incurred. However, in many if not most cases, R&D creates benefits for future periods. Thus, with EVA, R&D is capitalized as an asset and amortized over the future periods that benefit from the incurrence of the R&D. An advantage of this approach is that managers are less tempted to cut R&D, an act that increases short-term income but destroys shareholder value. Marketing programs that benefit future periods are also capitalized under EVA although the cost of such programs is expensed under GAAP. In total, there are more than 100 adjustments that Stern Stewart might make on a particular EVA consulting engagement. However, in practice, the number of adjustments is likely to be 5 or less.

The adjustments made using EVA affect both the computation of NOPAT and the computation of investment. Thus, the formula for EVA is:

$$\text{EVA} = \text{NOPAT}^{\text{adjusted}} - (\text{Cost of capital} \times \text{Investment}^{\text{adjusted}})$$

EVA Example. Let's review the calculation of EVA using the example of Spider Connectivity Products, a company that manufactures and sells a variety of connectivity products used in the audio/video, telecom, and computer industries (e.g., fiber-optic cables, FireWire products, USB devices, high-definition video and audio cables, modular plugs). The company's financial information is presented in Illustration 12-7.

Note that between 2016 and 2017, net income increased from $3,266,000 to $3,334,000. Is that increase consistent with good performance? Let's calculate EVA for both years to help us answer that question. In doing so, we'll assume that research and development (R&D) has a 3-year life with one-third amortized in the year it's incurred.

The calculation of EVA is presented in Illustration 12-8. Basically, the calculation of EVA is a three-step process. First we calculate adjusted NOPAT, then we calculate adjusted investment, and third we calculate EVA as Adjusted NOPAT – (Cost of capital × Adjusted investment). Note that in calculating adjusted NOPAT for 2017, we start with income before taxes and add back interest and the current-period R&D. Unless we add back interest, we will be double-counting a financing charge. (Interest would be deducted from income, and it would be deducted again when we multiply the cost of capital times the level of investment to calculate the return.) R&D is added back because we treat R&D as an intangible asset in EVA. We then deduct R&D expense related to amortizing the current and prior years' R&D amounts over 3 years (i.e., we deduct one-third of R&D from 2017, 2016, and 2015). Note that this results in adjusted NOPAT of $3,359,000 for 2017.

Now let's go on to the second step: calculation of adjusted investment. We start with total assets and then add unamortized R&D. Only one-third of R&D in 2017 became an expense so two-thirds is still an intangible asset. Of the R&D in 2016, one-third was expensed in 2016, and one-third was expensed in 2017, which means that one-third remains an intangible asset at the end of 2017. In total, adjusted investment is $19,122,000 for 2017.

The last step is to calculate EVA. Assuming a cost of capital of 18 percent (the cost of capital for technology companies is often quite high), EVA is equal to a loss of $83,000. A similar process is followed to calculate EVA for 2016. Here we find that EVA is a positive $376,000.

Now, why is it that accounting profit is up in 2017 but EVA is down? Look at what happened to the level of investment. It went from $16,940,000 to $19,122,000. Although income is up in 2017, *it's not up enough* given the increased investment, especially in accounts receivable and inventory. This is an important insight provided by EVA: Firms need to have earnings consistent with their cost of capital and their investment in assets. Most likely, if the senior managers of Spider Connectivity Products were evaluated and compensated based on EVA, they would have paid more attention to the investment the company was making in additional assets and analyzing whether the investment was likely to result in a payoff greater than the cost of capital.

ILLUSTRATION 12-7
Financial information for Spider Connectivity Products

Comparative Income Statements (in thousands)	2017	2016
Sales	$29,059	$27,287
Less:		
Cost of sales	19,361	17,981
Research and development	1,400	1,600
Selling, general and administrative expense	3,031	2,537
Interest expense	138	144
Income before income taxes	5,129	5,025
Less income taxes	1,795	1,759
Net income	$ 3,334	$ 3,266

Comparative Balance Sheets (in thousands)	2017	2016
Assets		
Cash and cash equivalents	$ 147	$ 1,286
Accounts receivable	4,588	2,568
Inventory	3,420	1,902
Prepaid expenses	47	45
Total current assets	8,202	5,801
Land	1,342	1,342
Building, furniture, fixtures (net)	8,438	8,523
Total noncurrent assets	9,780	9,865
Total assets	$17,982	$15,666
Liabilities		
Accounts payable	$ 209	$ 199
Accrued liabilities	57	45
Taxes payable	60	49
Current portion of long-term debt	175	188
Total current liabilities	501	481
Long-term debt	795	863
Total liabilities	1,296	1,344
Stockholders' Equity		
Common stock	5,080	5,080
Retained earnings	11,606	9,242
Total stockholders' equity	16,686	14,322
Total liabilities and stockholders' equity	$17,982	$15,666

Note: Research and development was $1,500,000 in 2015 and $1,400,000 in 2014.

LINK TO PRACTICE

Focus on EVA Affects Key Decisions across an Organization

David Hoover is the CEO of Ball Corporation, a company that produces metal and plastic packaging for beverages, foods, and household products. When the company experienced strong stock price appreciation, Hoover attributed the result in part to a focus on EVA. According to Hoover, the focus on EVA led the company to divest from a glass business that was not earning a return in excess of the cost of capital. And even workers in the company's beverage-can plants and people on the line can explain EVA and actions they can take to increase NOPAT or reduce investments (the key drivers of increases in EVA). According to Christopher Manuel, an analyst with KeyBanc Capital Markets, too many companies don't consider the cost of capital when they make decisions. He believes that Hoover, however, has done all the right things to make the focus on EVA work.

For 2014, Bell reported EVA of $190.7 million in its annual report. This was an increase of 28 percent. For purposes of its EVA calculation, Bell uses a capital charge of 9 percent. This was an increase of 28 percent over the previous year.

Source: Based on Don Durfee, "The Top Spot," *CFO Magazine*, October 2005.

ILLUSTRATION 12-8

EVA calculations for Spider Connectivity Products

Step 1		Step 2		Step 3	
2017					
Income before taxes	$5,129	Total assets	$17,982	Adjusted NOPAT	$3,359
Add interest expense	138	Plus unamortized R&D		Less cost of capital ×	
Add current period R&D	1,400	2017: 2/3 × $1,400	933	adjusted investment	
Less amortization of prior R&D		2016: 1/3 × $1,600	533	(.18 × $19,122)	(3,442)
2017: 1/3 × $1,400	(467)		19,448	EVA	($ 83)
2016: 1/3 × $1,600	(533)	Less NIBCL			
2015: 1/3 × $1,500	(500)	Accounts payable	(209)		
	5,167	Accrued liabilities	(57)		
Less taxes at 35%	(1,808)	Taxes payable	(60)		
Adjusted NOPAT	$3,359		(326)		
		Adjusted Investment	$19,122		
2016					
Income before taxes	$5,025	Total assets	$15,666	Adjusted NOPAT	$3,425
Add interest expense	144	Plus unamortized R&D		Less cost of capital ×	
Add current period R&D	1,600	2016: 2/3 × $1,600	1,067	adjusted investment	
Less amortization of prior R&D		2015: 1/3 × $1,500	500	(.18 × $16,940)	(3,049)
2016: 1/3 × $1,600	(533)		17,233	EVA	$ 376
2015: 1/3 × $1,500	(500)	Less NIBCL			
2014: 1/3 × $1,400	(467)	Accounts payable	(199)		
	5,269	Accrued liabilities	(45)		
Less taxes at 35%	(1,844)	Taxes payable	(49)		
Adjusted NOPAT	$3,425		(293)		
		Adjusted Investment	$16,940		

ANY **QUESTIONS?**

Q: In our operations management class, we learned about inventory holding costs and how some companies are using just-in-time methods to reduce them. Obviously, evaluation in terms of EVA creates an incentive to reduce inventory and related holding costs since reducing inventory reduces investment and increases EVA. Is this also the case if managers are evaluated in terms of GAAP profit?

A: Students often wonder where inventory holding costs are on a traditional GAAP income statement. The answer is that they show up on a traditional income statement only to the extent that the investment in inventory is financed with debt. Then the company has interest expense that reflects the cost of investment in inventory financed by the debt. But if the investment in inventory is financed with equity, the income statement and the GAAP measure of profit will not reflect the cost of holding inventory. That's because a GAAP measure of income does not show a capital charge for equity capital.

This is not the case with EVA. With EVA, the cost of capital (which includes the cost of both debt and equity capital) is multiplied by the investment in inventory, so the cost of holding inventory is reflected in EVA whether the inventory is financed with debt, equity, or, as is most likely, a combination of the two. And managers have an incentive to control this inventory-holding cost by reducing the investment in inventory.

LINK TO PRACTICE

Use of EVA at Whole Foods

In its 2014 annual filing with the Securities and Exchange Commission (Form 10-K), Whole Foods notes that new store projects must meet an economic value added (EVA) hurdle. Essentially, the company estimates what a potential store's EVA will be using 8 percent as the weighted average cost of capital. New store projects are considered only if the estimated cumulative EVA of the proposed store is positive in 5 years.

LEARNING OBJECTIVE 3

Explain the potential benefits of using a balanced scorecard to assess performance, and discuss how a strategy map can be used to communicate the linkages among the measures in a balanced scorecard.

USING A BALANCED SCORECARD TO EVALUATE PERFORMANCE

A problem with assessing performance with financial measures like profit, ROI, and EVA is that these financial measures are backward looking. In other words, today's financial measures tell you about the accomplishments and failures of the past. And the lag may be quite long. Suppose you work for a biotech company and have a tremendous day at the office: You develop a drug that cures the common cold. When will this tremendous accomplishment play out in accounting earnings? Given the regulatory process, it's likely that the drug will not be marketed and profit recognized for more than 10 years! Now suppose a new CEO is hired 10 years from now. Even if the executive performs poorly, it's likely that profit, ROI, and EVA will be high. It won't be because of the CEO's performance. It will be because of accomplishments that took place in the distant past. Illustration 12-9 graphically presents the backward-looking nature of financial performance measures.

An approach to performance measurement that also focuses on what managers are doing today to create future shareholder value is the balanced scorecard, a technique developed by Robert Kaplan, a Harvard professor, and David Norton, a consultant.[2] Essentially, a **balanced scorecard** is a set of performance measures constructed for four dimensions of performance. As indicated in Illustration 12-10, the dimensions are financial, customer, internal processes, and learning and growth. Having financial measures is critical even if they are backward looking. After all, they have a great effect on the evaluation of the company by shareholders and creditors. Customer measures examine the company's success in meeting customer expectations. Internal process measures examine the company's success in improving critical business processes. And learning and growth measures examine the company's success in improving its ability to adapt, innovate, and grow. The customer, internal processes, and learning and growth measures generally are thought to be predictive of *future* success (i.e., they are not backward looking).

ILLUSTRATION 12-9

Financial performance measures are "backward looking"

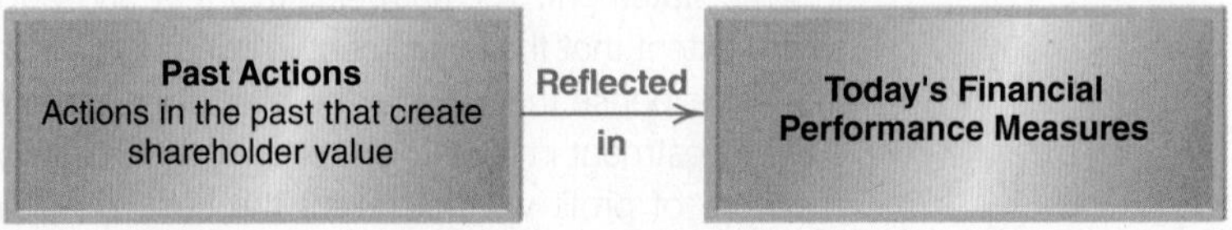

[2] Seminal articles on the balanced scorecard include Robert S. Kaplan and David Norton, "The Balanced Scorecard—Measures That Drive Performance," *Harvard Business Review,* January–February 1992, and Robert S. Kaplan and David Norton, "Putting the Balanced Scorecard to Work," *Harvard Business Review,* September–October 1993.

ILLUSTRATION 12-10
The balanced scorecard

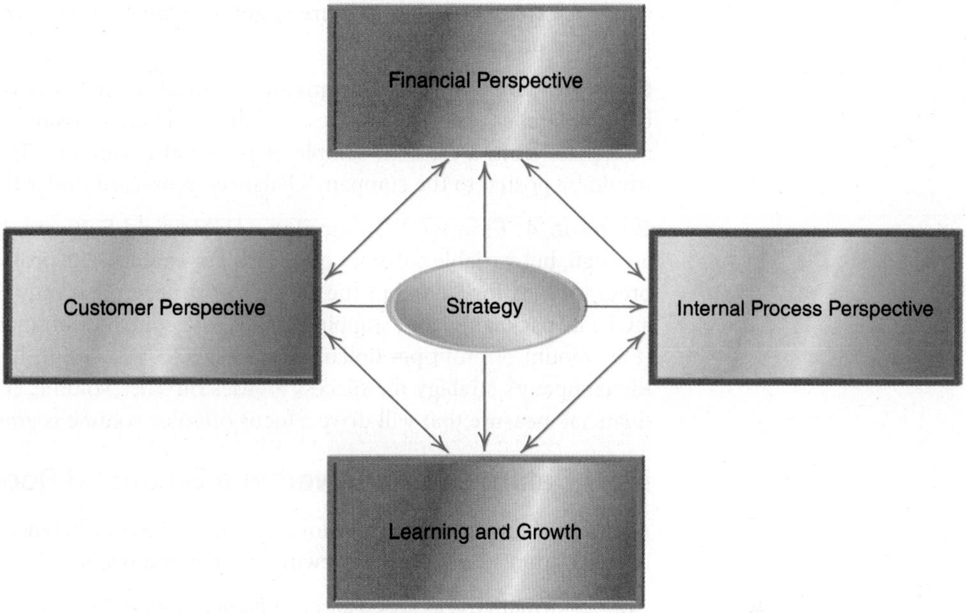

Tying the Balanced Scorecard Measures to the Strategy for Success. Typically, a company using a balanced scorecard will develop three to five performance measures for each dimension. To the extent possible, the measures on a balanced scorecard should be tied to a company's strategy for success. For example, consider the customer dimension. If it is critical to success that the company's product be easy to use, the company may survey customers to measure this aspect of performance. If on-time delivery is critical to customers, then it will be used as a performance measure. With respect to internal processes, a company may decide that it needs to reduce the number of defective units produced. In this case, number of defects might be an appropriate measure for the internal process dimension. With respect to the learning and growth dimension, a company may decide that to remain innovative, it is crucial to retain its highly skilled workforce. In this case, a measure of employee job satisfaction might be an appropriate measure for the learning and growth dimension. Another potential learning and growth measure is the number of new products developed.

As you well know, "You get what you measure!" and companies need measures that drive behaviors consistent with their strategy for success. Let's consider four scenarios for a software company, to further illustrate how performance measures are tied to strategy for each dimension of a balanced scorecard.

Scenario 1. Learning and Growth Dimension. At Mayfield Software, many of the product managers are former programmers who have little or no training in business management. The company believes that to continue to grow sales and adapt to changes in the industry, these managers need to become more knowledgeable about business concepts and practices. In this case, the company might develop a learning and growth measure that assesses the average number of hours of business training received by a product manager. Also, the company might survey product managers and have them rate the quality of business training provided by the company.

Scenario 2. Internal Process Dimension. Mayfield Software has been severely hampered by viruses that shut down all computer systems for 15 days in the prior year. This led to delays and provided an advantage to a competitor that was first to market with a product that was also under development by Mayfield. In this case, the company might develop an internal process measure that assesses the company's ability to detect and block viruses. Such a measure might be *number of hours computers are locked down to prevent the spread of a virus.*

Scenario 3. Customer Dimension. Critical to the success of Mayfield Software is brand awareness. In this case, the company might commission a survey to measure brand awareness from a random sample of potential customers. The results of the measure would be posted to the company's balanced scorecard under the customer dimension.

Scenario 4. Financial Dimension. At Mayfield Software, fixed costs such as R&D are high, but variable costs are quite low. For example, its project management software program sells for $200, but the variable cost per unit is only $5 (including the cost of a CD, its packaging, and shipping). Thus, the contribution margin ratio of the product (the amount of profit per dollar of sales) is 97.5 percent. In light of this cost structure, the company's strategy for success focuses on sales volume. In this case, an important financial measure that will drive a focus on sales volume is *growth in sales.*

How Balance Is Achieved in a Balanced Scorecard

A variety of potential measures for each dimension of a balanced scorecard are indicated in Illustration 12-11. After reviewing these measures, note how "balance" is achieved:

1. Performance is assessed across a *balanced set of dimensions* (financial, customer, internal processes, and learning and growth).
2. *Quantitative* measures (e.g., number of defects) are balanced with *qualitative* measures (e.g., ratings of customer satisfaction).
3. There is a balance of *backward-looking* measures (e.g., financial measures like growth in sales) and *forward-looking* measures (e.g., number of new patents as a learning and growth measure).

ILLUSTRATION 12-11
Examples of measures for the four perspectives of a balanced scorecard

		Measures
Financial	Is the company achieving its financial goals?	Operating income Return on assets Sales growth Cash flow from operations Reduction of administrative expense
Customer	Is the company meeting customer expectations?	Customer satisfaction Customer retention New customer acquisition Market share
Internal Processes	Is the company improving critical internal processes?	On-time delivery Defect rate Time to fill orders Lead time Number of suppliers Material turnover Percent of practical capacity
Learning and Growth	Is the company improving its ability to innovate?	Amount spent on employee training Employee satisfaction Employee retention Number of new products New product sales as percent of total sales Number of patents

YOU GET WHAT YOU MEASURE

Underlying the balanced scorecard is an idea that we have emphasized throughout this book: "You get what you measure!" If you believe that customer satisfaction is critical for success, then you had better measure it so that managers will focus their attention on it. If you believe that reducing cycle time (the time it takes to make a product) is critical for success, then drive your managers to reduce cycle time by evaluating their performance in relation to this aspect of performance.

DEVELOPING A STRATEGY MAP FOR A BALANCED SCORECARD

A **strategy map** is a diagram of the relationships across the four dimensions of a balanced scorecard (learning and growth, customer, internal process, and financial) of the strategic objectives the company has developed to create shareholder value. It is useful to test the soundness of the strategy and how it is linked to measures on the scorecard (do the relationships make sense?), and it is useful to communicate strategic objectives to employees.

As an example, suppose that Mayfield Software has determined that a key driver of shareholder value is increased sales and has determined that increased sales will be achieved only if customers are satisfied. In the past, customer satisfaction has been low because they could not get accurate and fast responses to their questions at the company's customer call center. The problem is that employees at the call center are not well trained. Let's look at Illustration 12-12 to see how a strategy map works.

Starting with the learning and growth perspective, note that the goal is to improve employee skills at the call center. The measure the company has chosen is the percentage of employees receiving training. Next look at the internal processes perspective. Here the goal is to have fast and accurate responses to customer questions. The related measure is the time to answer customer calls with no additional follow-up. Note that an arrow connects the strategic objective of the learning and growth perspective to the strategic objective of the internal process perspective. That's because the company anticipates a cause-and-effect relationship. More training will improve accuracy and speed in the call center. Now look at the customer perspective. Here the goal is to improve customer satisfaction, and the measure is obtained via a survey of

ILLUSTRATION 12-12

Partial strategy map for Mayfield Software

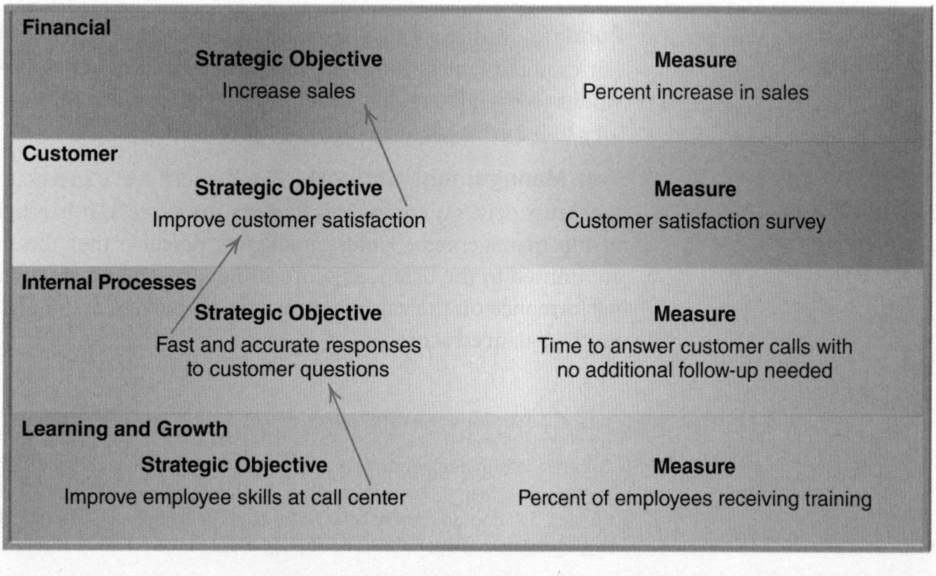

customers. The arrow linking the objective of the internal processes perspective to the customer perspective shows that the company expects satisfaction to increase because of improvements at the call center. Finally, look at the financial perspective. Here the objective is an increase in sales, and the measure is the percentage increase in sales over the previous year. The arrow connecting the customer objective to the financial objective indicates that the company expects that an increase in customer satisfaction will lead to sales increases.

The partial strategy map in Illustration 12-12 is developed showing only one objective for each perspective. There are likely to be multiple objectives for each perspective of the balanced scorecard, and a complete strategy map would show all of the linkages among them.[3]

KEYS TO A SUCCESSFUL BALANCED SCORECARD: TARGETS, INITIATIVES, RESPONSIBILITY, FUNDING, TOP MANAGEMENT SUPPORT

It's probably pretty obvious that just having a number of performance measures is not going to drive a company's strategy for success. Here are some of the key items that are necessary for a successful balanced scorecard.

Targets. For each measure, there should be a target so managers know what they are expected to achieve. For example, for the financial measure "percent growth in sales," the target might be 15 percent.

Initiatives. For each measure, the company must identify actions that will be taken to achieve the target. Refer to Illustration 12-12 and note the learning and growth measure "Percent of employees receiving training." Here the target might be 100 percent. But what is the nature of the training? The company must develop a training program initiative to make sure that the employees receive the right kind of training.

Responsibility. A particular employee must be given responsibility and be held accountable for successfully implementing each initiative. Without this accountability, successful implementation of key initiatives is unlikely.

Funding. Initiatives also must be funded appropriately or they will not be successful. For example, unless funds are provided to develop an appropriate training program, it would seem unlikely that the employees at Mayfield Software will gain the skills necessary to improve performance at the call center.

Top Management Support. Finally, to have a successful balanced scorecard, one that truly drives a company's strategy for success, it is crucial to have the full support of top management. Unless managers perceive that the president and the CEO are committed to the balanced scorecard approach and are giving careful consideration to performance on the various measures, employees are not likely to focus their attention on the balanced scorecard.

---

[3] For more information on strategy maps, see Robert Kaplan and David Norton, "Having Trouble with Your Strategy? Then Map It," *Harvard Business Review,* September 2000, and Christopher Ittner and David Larcker, "Coming Up Short on Nonfinancial Performance Measurement," *Harvard Business Review,* November 2003. Also, a great deal of information on strategy maps can be found on the web.

LINK TO PRACTICE

Brigham and Women's Hospital Receives Award for Its Balanced Scorecard

Balanced scorecards are not just for profit-oriented businesses. In 2005, Brigham and Women's Hospital (a major teaching hospital affiliated with Harvard Medical School in Boston) received an award for its scorecard at a business intelligence and data warehousing conference. According to Sue Schade, chief information officer for the hospital, the scorecard allows staff at every level to see how their efforts, "affect patient care and satisfaction as well as the overall financial health of the organization. Staff at every level—from administrators and division chiefs to individual physicians, nurses, and other front-line clinicians—can see how their day-to-day efforts affect patient care and satisfaction as well as the overall financial health of our organization."

The hospital's nearly 900 employees have access to 35 metrics on the hospital's overall scorecard. Also, many of the hospital's clinical specialties have their own scorecards.

According to the hospital's website, measures in their balanced score card in 2015 included: quality of care, safety and infection control, patient satisfaction, and financial performance.

Source: Business Wire, Inc., *Brigham and Women's Hospital Honored in 2005 World Class Solutions Awards,* Las Vegas, October 26, 2005.

Decision Making INSIGHT

In the chapter, we saw that various financial performance measures can cause managers to make poor investment decisions. Evaluation in terms of growth in profit can lead to overinvestment (making investments that should not be made because the return is too low). Evaluation in terms of return on investment (ROI) can lead to underinvestment (not making investments that earn an adequate return) for business units with high current ROIs. Arguably, evaluation in terms of economic value added (EVA) influences managers to make good investment decisions since EVA increases when managers take on projects that earn a return in excess of the cost of capital.

SUMMARY OF LEARNING OBJECTIVES

LEARNING OBJECTIVE 1 Explain the advantages and disadvantages of decentralization, explain why companies evaluate the performance of subunits and subunit managers, and identify cost centers, profit centers, and investment centers.

Decentralization may lead to better information, faster responses to changing circumstances, and increased motivation of managers. Decentralized organizations also may provide excellent training for future top-level executives. However, decentralization may lead to costly duplication of activities and problems of goal congruence.

Companies evaluate the performance of subunits to identify successful operations and areas needing improvement. Companies evaluate subunit managers to influence the behavior of the managers (because you get what you measure).

Finally, managers of cost centers are responsible only for controlling costs. Managers of profit centers are responsible for generating revenue as well as for controlling costs. Investment center managers are responsible for income and the level of assets used to generate income.

LEARNING OBJECTIVE 2 Calculate and interpret return on investment (ROI), residual income (RI), and economic value added (EVA).

Return on investment is calculated as the ratio of investment center income to invested capital. We measure income as net operating profit after taxes (NOPAT), and we measure invested capital as total assets less noninterest-bearing current liabilities.

Managers who are evaluated in terms of profit know that it is easy to increase profit by growing their company and taking on projects that earn a low return (i.e., overinvesting). In this case, profit increases, but the return is not adequate. If managers are evaluated in terms of ROI and their operation is already earning a high ROI, they may be reluctant to take on projects that earn a return greater than the cost of capital but lower than the current ROI. In this case, the managers are underinvesting.

Residual income is equal to the net operating profit after taxes of an investment center in excess of the profit required for the level of investment. EVA is conceptually similar, although adjustments are made for accounting distortions such as expensing R&D costs.

LEARNING OBJECTIVE 3 Explain the potential benefits of using a balanced scorecard to assess performance, and discuss how a strategy map can be used to communicate the linkages among the measures in a balanced scorecard.

A balanced scorecard assesses performance with respect to four dimensions: financial, customer, internal processes, and learning and growth. The specific measures should be linked to a company's strategy for success. Whereas financial measures focus on past performance, the other dimensions assess what the company is doing to create future shareholder value.

A strategy map is a diagram of the relationships, across the four dimensions of a balanced scorecard, of the strategic objectives the company has developed to create shareholder value. By identifying these linkages, top management can ensure that its strategy makes sense. The map also is a useful tool to communicate the company's strategy to employees.

APPENDIX

LEARNING OBJECTIVE A1

Discuss the use of market price, variable cost, full cost plus profit, and negotiation in setting transfer prices.

TRANSFER PRICING

In many cases, subunits of a company "sell" goods or services to other subunits within the same company. For example, a university print plant may sell printing services to other university departments. Similarly, a car manufacturing company may have one division that produces cars and another division that produces a variety of auto batteries. Most likely the car-producing division will use auto batteries produced by the battery division.

The price that is used to value internal transfers of goods or services is referred to as a **transfer price**. If the battery division transfers 10,000 batteries to the car division at a transfer price of $15 per unit, the battery division will have revenue of $150,000. However, this revenue is only recognized for internal reporting purposes. For external financial reporting purposes, a company cannot recognize revenue on the sale of goods between responsibility centers within the firm, because the revenue has not been realized.

Revenue, for financial reporting purposes, is realized when goods or services are sold to customers outside the firm. Sales within a company are not "arm's length" transactions (transactions entered into by unrelated parties). Without this restriction, companies could inflate sales and income by engaging in numerous unnecessary internal sales transactions.

In practice, a number of different approaches are taken to setting transfer prices. The primary alternatives in practice are transfer prices based on: (1) market prices, (2) variable costs, (3) full cost plus profit, and (4) negotiated prices. These alternatives are discussed next. Which of the transfer prices is most appropriate depends on the circumstances. What is desired is a transfer price that will lead the subunit managers to make decisions that maximize firm value. The transfer price that motivates the best decisions is the *opportunity cost of producing an item and transferring it inside the company*. Recall that an opportunity cost is the forgone benefit (increased cost) of selecting one alternative over another.

MARKET PRICE AS THE TRANSFER PRICE

For purposes of discussion, let's assume that the subunits buying and selling internally are divisions of a company. In some cases, the producing division transfers a product internally to a buying division and also sells the same product outside the firm. For example, the battery division of the auto company may sell batteries to various auto supply companies and also "sell" batteries internally to the car-producing division.

When the product is sold outside the firm, a market price exists, and it can be used as the transfer price. The external market price is an excellent internal transfer price because it allows both the buying division and the selling division to be treated as "stand-alone," independent companies. Generally, market prices are perceived as fair and reasonable by both the buying and the selling divisions. The buying division cannot complain that the transfer price is too high, because it represents the same price the buying division would have to pay in the open market. For the same reason, the selling division cannot complain that the transfer price is too low.

In some cases, the selling division experiences cost savings from selling internally rather than in an external market. For example, shipping costs may be reduced if the buying division is close to the selling division. Advertising costs may also be lower, and reduced production costs may be achieved if the selling division finds it easier to schedule production for internal sales than for external sales. If cost savings exist, the market price should be reduced by the cost savings to arrive at the transfer price.

Consider an example. Suppose the Processor division of Tectron Manufacturing produces a microprocessor that it sells to a large number of companies at a market price of $300 each. The Computer division of Tectron produces personal computers that utilize the microprocessor produced by the Processor division. By selling the microprocessor internally, the Processor division saves approximately $2 per unit in shipping costs and $1 per unit in manufacturing costs. In this case, a reasonable transfer price would be $297 (i.e., $300 market price less the $3 cost savings):

Market price	$300
Savings due to reduced shipping costs	(2)
Savings due to reduced manufacturing costs	(1)
Adjusted transfer price	$297

MARKET PRICE AND OPPORTUNITY COST

Earlier, we suggested that the best transfer price should be the *opportunity cost of producing an item and transferring it to the buying division*. When a market price exits, it is a good transfer price because it is equal to the opportunity cost.

Suppose the Sweet Company is composed of two divisions. The Syrup division produces corn syrup, and the Candy division produces a variety of candies using corn syrup as a sweetener. The Syrup division can sell corn syrup to outside buyers for $8 per gallon. If the market price is used as a transfer price for sales of corn syrup from the Syrup division to the Candy division, the transfer price, too, will be $8. But is $8 the opportunity cost of transferring the corn syrup from the Syrup division to the Candy division?

An opportunity cost is the forgone benefit or increased cost of selecting one alternative over another. What benefit is forgone by transferring corn syrup internally? The answer is that the $8 that could be earned selling the corn syrup externally is forgone when the corn syrup is transferred to the Candy division. Thus, the opportunity cost is equal to the market price of the transferred product.

To illustrate, suppose that 1 gallon of syrup is used to produce every 10 pounds of rock candy manufactured by the Candy division. The rock candy sells for $50 for a 10-pound container. Variable costs are as follows:

10-Pound Container	
Variable production cost excluding corn syrup	$43
Transfer price of corn syrup	8
Total variable cost per container	$51

In this situation, because the candy sells for $50 for a 10-pound container, the Candy division has a negative contribution margin of $1 per container and will not be willing to produce rock candy.

Now suppose the Candy division argues that if the transfer price of corn syrup is reduced to $5 (the variable cost of producing corn syrup), its variable costs will only be $48, and rock candy will have a positive contribution margin. Should the transfer price be lowered? The answer is no. The income of the Syrup division and the total income of the Sweet Company will be reduced if the Candy division is subsidized by a transfer price lower than the market price. If the Candy division cannot earn a profit paying a transfer price equal to what it would pay for syrup in the open market, then consideration should be given to eliminating the product.

The effect on the company's contribution margin of lowering the transfer price and transferring the syrup inside to the Candy division is presented in Illustration A12-1. If the transfer price

ILLUSTRATION A12-1
Analysis of lowering the transfer price below the market price

Sell Syrup at Market Price

Contribution Margin of Syrup Division per Gallon of Syrup		Contribution Margin of Candy Division per 10-Pound Container	Contribution Margin of Company
Selling price	$ 8		
Variable cost	(5)		
Cont. margin	$ 3	-0-[a]	$ 3

Transfer Syrup to Candy Division at $5

Contribution Margin of Syrup Division per Gallon of Syrup		Contribution Margin of Candy Division per 10-Pound Container		Contribution Margin of Company
Transfer price	$ 5	Selling price	$50	
Variable cost	(5)	Own variable costs	(43)	
Cont. margin	$-0-	Transfer price	(5)	
		Cont. margin	$ 2	$ 2

[a] Contribution margin is zero because Candy division will not demand any corn syrup at a transfer price of $8

is the market price of $8, the Candy division will not find production of rock candy profitable. No syrup will be demanded by the Candy division, and all syrup will be sold in the marketplace. In this case, the Syrup division will earn $3 of contribution margin on every gallon of syrup, the Candy division will earn no contribution margin, and the contribution margin of the company as a whole will be $3. Alternatively, if the syrup is transferred to the Candy division at a transfer price of $5, the Syrup division will earn no contribution margin because the transfer price will be equal to the variable cost of producing the syrup. For each gallon of syrup, however, the Candy division can produce a 10-pound container of rock candy that sells for $50. The Candy division will have $43 of variable costs in addition to the $5 transfer price it must pay for each gallon of syrup. Thus, the Candy division will earn a contribution margin of $2. The contribution margin to the company will also be $2 because the Syrup division will have a contribution margin of zero. Note that although the Candy division is certainly better off with a transfer price of $5, the Syrup division is worse off, and the company as a whole is worse off by $1 for each gallon of syrup transferred at the $5 transfer price.

VARIABLE COST AS THE TRANSFER PRICE

In some cases, the transferred product is unique and is not sold by the producing division in the open market. Obviously, no market price exists, and some other transfer price must be chosen. The variable cost of producing the transferred good may be the best transfer price in this situation. The reason for selecting the variable cost of production as the transfer price is that it conveys accurate opportunity cost information. When no external market exists, the opportunity cost of producing and selling an item internally is simply the variable costs of producing the item.[4] Each time an additional unit is produced, the company must incur additional costs equal to the variable cost of production.

Again, knowing the opportunity cost of the transferred product can lead the Buying division to make well-informed decisions. For example, suppose the Buying division is considering a request for a special order from a customer. To produce the product, the Buying division must use a component that will be supplied by another division of the firm (the Selling division). In

[4] This assumes that the Selling division has excess capacity. If I does not, the opportunity cost must include the income lost on items that cannot be produced when capacity is used to produce goods for internal transfer.

addition to the transfer price, the Buying division will incur variable production costs of $50 per unit. Further, the Selling division will incur variable costs of $25 in producing the component. What is the minimum price that could be accepted for the special order? The answer is $75, which is equal to the $50 of variable cost incurred by the Buying division plus the $25 of variable cost incurred by the Selling division. Any price above $75 will increase the overall contribution margin of the company and its income.

But suppose the transfer price is set at an amount greater than the variable cost of the Selling division. For example, suppose the transfer price is set at $40. In this case, the manager of the Buying division will perceive that the minimum acceptable selling price for the special order is $90, not $75. The $90 amount is equal to the $40 transfer price paid for each unit by the Buying division plus the other variable costs incurred by the Buying division, which are equal to $50. The special order would be turned down by the manager of the Buying division at prices between $75 and $90, at a definite loss of income for the company as a whole. A failure to know the real opportunity cost of production may thus lead to poor decisions by the Buying division manager.

FULL COST PLUS PROFIT AS THE TRANSFER PRICE

A very significant problem with using variable cost as the transfer price is that the Selling division cannot earn a profit on production of the transferred product. Thus, use of variable cost as a transfer price may not be acceptable to division managers. For this reason, many companies add a profit margin to the full cost of an item and use the resulting amount as the transfer price.

For example, suppose the variable cost of producing an item for internal sale to a Buying division is $100 per unit. Further, 1,000 units are expected to be transferred in the coming year, and fixed costs per year will amount to $200,000. The fixed costs relate to depreciation on equipment that is not currently being used to capacity. In this case, the full cost per unit is $300 ($100 variable cost and $200 fixed cost). At a transfer price of $300, the Selling division will just break even on the internal transfer. However, suppose the company utilizes a transfer pricing policy whereby the transfer price is equal to full cost plus 10 percent of full cost. In this case, the transfer price will be $330, and the Selling division will earn income of $30 on each item produced.

Although full cost plus profit may be more acceptable as a transfer price to division managers, the transfer price may not measure the opportunity cost of producing the transferred product. As we saw earlier, this can result in decisions that do not maximize the profitability of the whole company. Suppose the Buying division of the company just described must incur $400 of variable costs in addition to the transfer price. The market price for the item produced by the Buying division is $690. The Buying division will not continue producing the product unless it makes a positive contribution toward covering its fixed costs. With a transfer price of $330, the contribution margin faced by the Buying division is a negative $40 ($690 selling price less variable cost of $400 and transfer price of $330). Thus, the Buying division will be inclined to drop the product. However, the product does, in fact, make a positive contribution to firm income. The selling price of $690 is greater than the variable cost of the Buying division ($400) plus the variable cost of the Selling division ($100) by $190. Thus, the company as a whole is actually better off by $190 for each unit sold:

	Transfer Price Equals Full Cost Plus Profit	Transfer Price Equals Variable Cost
Selling price of final product	$690	$690
Less: variable cost of the Buying division except for the transfer price	400	400
Less: transfer price	330	100
Contribution margin of Buying division	($ 40)	$190

NEGOTIATED TRANSFER PRICES

As discussed at the start of this chapter, one of the benefits of decentralization is that managers who are delegated significant decision-making responsibility tend to be highly motivated. To encourage the sense of autonomy, some companies allow division managers to negotiate a transfer price. This presents the subunit managers with the same situation faced by an independent business that must negotiate a price for specialized items. However, the resulting transfer price may reflect the relative negotiating skills of the subunit managers and fail to reflect the underlying opportunity cost associated with producing goods and transferring them internally.

LINK TO PRACTICE

Transfer Pricing at Starbucks

At Starbucks, the world's largest coffee chain, all the coffee it uses worldwide is bought by a Starbucks' subsidiary in Switzerland. Although the coffee is never transported through Switzerland, the subsidiary then sells the coffee to Starbucks' units operating in other countries at a transfer price including a 20 percent markup. That way, the profit related to the 20 percent markup gets taxed in Switzerland, which has a low corporate tax rate, rather than a country with a higher rate. European regulators opened an investigation of Starbucks' management of international taxes in 2014.

Source: Tom Fairless, "Huge Profit Stokes Concerns Over Starbucks's Tax Practices in Europe," *The Wall Street Journal*, April 6, 2015. Available at: http://www.wsj.com/articles/starbuckss-tax-practices-draw-european-scrutiny-1428363189.

TRANSFER PRICING AND INCOME TAXES IN AN INTERNATIONAL CONTEXT

When goods are transferred between profit centers in different countries, the income tax situations in the countries may create incentives for relatively high or relatively low transfer prices. For example, suppose the tax rate in Country A is 10 percent, whereas the tax rate in Country B is 40 percent. Holding everything else constant, this creates an incentive to have high transfer prices when goods are transferred from a profit center in Country A to a profit center in Country B. With this approach, the profit center in Country A will have relatively high income (which is taxed at a low rate), and the profit center in Country B will have relatively low income (which is taxed at a high rate). Thus, overall taxes of company income for the two profit centers will be reduced. If goods were to be transferred from a profit center in Country B to a profit center in Country A, there would be an incentive for a relatively low transfer price. The Internal Revenue Service in the United States and the taxing authorities in other countries are aware of these incentives and try to make sure that transfer prices are not unreasonably high or low in response to the incentives created by differences in income tax rates between countries.

REVIEW PROBLEM 1

Merlin Appliances, founded by Morgan D. Edwards in 1976, is a closely held company that operates five stores in Michigan selling refrigerators, stoves, washers and dryers, and other household appliances. The company's stock is owned by various members of the Morgan D. Edwards family, and five family members serve on the board of directors. The president and CEO of Merlin is David Bell. David, who is not a family member, was hired in 2016 and is responsible for all day-to-day company decisions. He reports to Brandon Edwards, who is chairman of the board.

At the end of fiscal 2017, David was asked to prepare a brief memo to the board reviewing the company's performance. A copy of the memo is presented below along with comparative financial statements. A board meeting is scheduled for early February at which time the board will review company performance and David's compensation including his performance bonus for 2017.

Merlin Appliances

Selection, Service, and Magically Low Prices
Serving Michigan Residents Since 1976

January 26, 2018

TO:	Board of Directors of Merlin Appliances
FROM:	David Bell, President and CEO
SUBJECT:	Financial performance in fiscal 2017

At the start of 2017 we discussed the fact that the market for appliances was likely to be soft due to economic conditions in the state of Michigan. Specifically, at the start of 2017, unemployment was high and several major companies had made plans for substantial job cuts. In light of this, I am very happy to report that we have had an outstanding year. Sales have increased by 7.68 percent, and profit is up by 14.11 percent.

How was this accomplished? Here's a brief outline of the three strategies we employed—I'll review them in detail at the February 7 board meeting.

1. Market research indicated that sales could be increased if we held the line on prices, displayed a wider selection of items at each store, and had more items available in our warehouse so that we could offer 1- or 2-day delivery. This strategy was implemented, with obvious good results, in early 2017.
2. We adjusted our quarterly sales events. In addition to offering our normal discounts at these events, we also offered terms with no payments (and no interest charges) for 6 months. This strategy was successful in attracting customers who might have delayed purchases in the current year.
3. We retired all short-term and all long-term debt. As you know, we had cash reserves of approximately $1.6 million at the end of 2016. (The money had been accumulated in anticipation of expansion, but expansion plans have been put on hold.) Paying down debt reduces company risk and appears to be a good use of the funds.

I also want to note that our exceptional performance in fiscal 2017 could not have been achieved without the support of the 138 Merlin team members whose hard work and dedication to the company's success is evident in every sale and every delivery!

Finally, as you know, we paid out approximately $1,000,000 in dividends in fiscal 2017—no dividends were paid in 2015, and dividends in 2016 were only $500,000.

See you on February 7.

Comparative Income Statements	2017	2016	% Change
Sales	$27,659,548	$25,687,240	7.68%
Less:			
Cost of sales	19,361,684	17,981,068	
Selling, general and administrative expense	5,531,910	5,137,448	
Interest expense	—	144,711	
Income before income taxes	$ 2,765,954	$ 2,424,013	
Less income taxes	968,084	848,405	
Net income	$ 1,797,870	$ 1,575,608	14.11%

Comparative Balance Sheets	2017	2016
Assets		
Cash and cash equivalents	$ 147,636	$ 1,586,250
Accounts receivable	2,990,221	2,568,724
Inventory	2,420,211	1,997,896
Prepaid expenses	47,399	45,265
Total current assets	5,605,467	6,198,135
Land	1,342,350	1,342,350
Building, furniture, fixtures (net)	8,438,088	8,523,321
Total noncurrent assets	9,780,438	9,865,671
Total assets	$15,385,905	$16,063,806
Liabilities		
Accounts payable	$ 210,240	$ 199,790
Accrued liabilities	57,010	45,685
Taxes payable	60,690	49,321
Current portion of long-term debt	—	188,754
Total current liabilities	327,940	483,550
Long-term debt		1,258,360
Total liabilities	327,940	1,741,910
Stockholders' Equity		
Common stock	5,079,315	5,079,315
Retained earnings	9,978,650	9,242,581
Total stockholders' equity	15,057,965	14,321,896
Total liabilities and stockholders' equity	$15,385,905	$16,063,806

REQUIRED

a. Evaluate performance in fiscal 2017 and 2016 in terms of economic value added (EVA). Assume a weighted average cost of capital of 15 percent in 2017 and 14 percent in 2016. Briefly comment on whether this evaluation supports a significant bonus for David Bell.

b. Suppose that the entire increase in net operating profit after taxes in 2017 is due to having more inventory and "no payments or interest" for 6 months, which led to an increase in accounts receivable. Evaluate the impact of these strategies in terms of their impact on EVA using a 15 percent cost of capital.

ANSWER

a.

	2017	2016
Net income	$ 1,797,870	$ 1,575,608
Add interest		144,711
Less taxes related to interest		(50,649)
NOPAT	$ 1,797,870	$ 1,669,670

	2017	2016
Investment		
Total assets	$15,385,905	$16,063,806
Less NIBCL:		
Accounts payable	(210,240)	(199,790)
Accrued liabilities	(57,010)	(45,685)
Taxes payable	(60,690)	(49,321)
Investment	15,057,965	15,769,010
Cost of capital	0.15	0.14
Required NOPAT	2,258,695	2,207,661
EVA (NOPAT – Required NOPAT)	($ 460,825)	($ 537,991)

Note that, alternatively, NOPAT could have been calculated as:

	2017	2016
Income before taxes	$ 2,765,954	$ 2,424,013
Add interest	-0-	144,711
	2,765,954	2,568,724
Less taxes	968,084	899,053
NOPAT	$ 1,797,870	$ 1,669,671

The slight difference between the calculation here and above for 2016 is due to rounding.

It does not appear that a substantial bonus is warranted since EVA is negative in 2017 indicating that shareholder value has actually declined. This follows because net operating profit is less than the level required given the investment in the company. Note that EVA was also negative in 2016. Also note that EVA and residual income are identical in this problem since there are no adjustments for "accounting distortions."

b. The company increased inventory. And the policy of no payments or interest for 6 months increased accounts receivable. Together, these two items increased investment by $843,812. With a 15 percent cost of capital, NOPAT would need to increase by $126,572 to break even. In actuality, NOPAT increased by $128,200 for a net benefit of $1,628. While positive, this rather small amount is hardly in line with the financial gains claimed in David Bell's memo:

Increase in inventory ($2,420,211 – $1,997,896)	$422,315
Increase in receivables ($2,990,221 – $2,568,724)	421,497
Increase in investment	843,812
Cost of capital	× .15
Required additional NOPAT	126,572
Less actual additional NOPAT ($1,797,870.00 – $1,669,670.15)	128,200
Net benefit	$ 1,628

REVIEW PROBLEM 2

Ransom Apparel is a men's casual clothing company. The company has set aggressive targets in both sales growth and return on investment for the coming year. The company's strategy for achieving these goals includes a campaign aimed at building brand recognition. It is also seeking improvements in product quality and on-time delivery from manufacturers in China and Vietnam as well as expansion of the product line to include three styles of jeans, which will complement the company's line of silk shorts and slacks. A number of limited edition items is also part of the company's strategy.

To bolster its brand, the company plans to provide limited edition items to celebrities in Los Angeles, San Diego, Chicago, and New York. The company hopes that the celebrities will be seen around town and in fashion magazines such as *GQ*.

REQUIRED

Based on this limited information, provide two objectives and two measures for each perspective of the balanced scorecard. Using a strategy map, show how the objectives are related across the four dimensions of a balanced scorecard. Note that a number of alternative measures could be appropriate—the ones provided in the answer are simply examples of such alternatives.

ANSWER

Measures for the various objectives are shown below in the strategy map. The logic behind the strategy map is:

1. Development of limited edition items should improve the odds of celebrities wearing the company's products and being highlighted in trend-setting magazines such as *GQ*.
2. Development of a new line of jeans should lead to an increase in sales as the product line is expanded.
3. Improved on-time delivery from suppliers should increase sales since the company is more likely to meet its own delivery schedules to customers.
4. Improved product quality should improve ROI since the company will have lower costs associated with returns.
5. If trend-setters wear the brand, brand recognition is expected to improve.

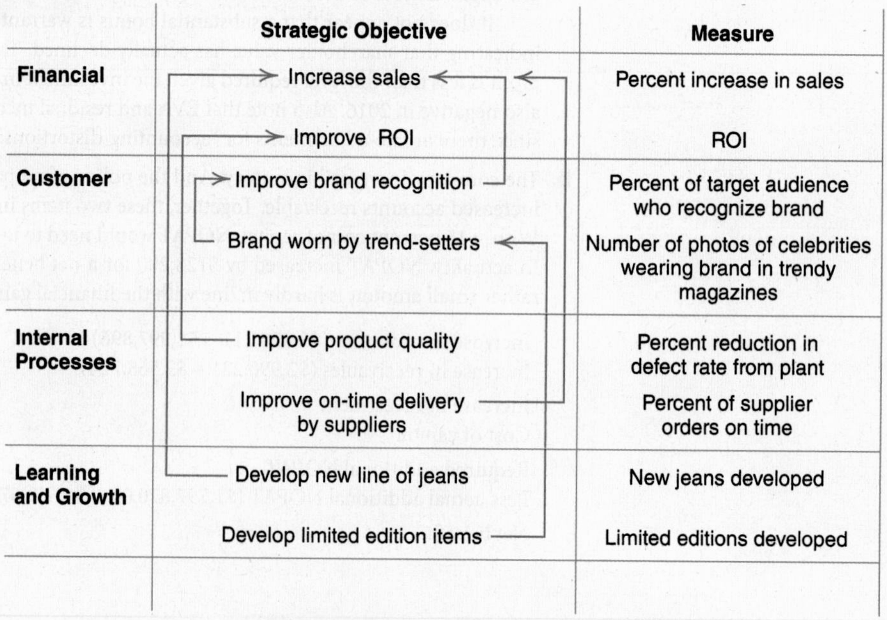

KEY TERMS

Balanced scorecard (468)
Cost center (455)
Decentralized organization (452)
Economic value added (EVA) (464)
Investment center (456)
Investment turnover (458)
Lack of goal congruence (453)
Noninterest-bearing current liabilities (NIBCL) (459)
Net operating profit after taxes (NOPAT) (458)
Profit center (456)
Profit margin (458)
Relative performance evaluation (456)
Residual income (RI) (463)
Responsibility centers (455)
Return on investment (ROI) (457)
Strategy map (471)
Transfer price (Appendix, 474)

SELF-ASSESSMENT (Answers Below)

1. Which of the following is **not** a reason for having decentralized organizations?

a. Better information at the local level leads to superior decisions.

b. Goal congruence is enhanced.

c. Quicker response to changing circumstances.

d. Increased motivation of managers.

2. An investment center is responsible for:

a. Investing in long-term assets.

b. Controlling costs.

c. Generating revenues.

d. All of these answer choices are correct.

3. A cost center is responsible for:

a. Investing in long-term assets.

b. Controlling costs.

c. Generating revenues.

d. All of these answer choices are correct.

4. Use of profit as a performance measure:

a. May lead to overinvestment in assets.

b. Is appropriate for an investment center.

c. Is appropriate as long as profit is calculated using GAAP.

d. Encourages managers to finance operations with debt rather than equity.

5. Cost centers are often evaluated using:

a. Variance analysis.

b. Operating margin.

c. Return on investment.

d. Residual income.

6. Profit centers often are evaluated using:

a. Investment turnover.

b. Income targets or profit budgets.

c. Return on investment.

d. Residual income.

7. Investment centers often are evaluated using:

a. Time and motion studies.

b. Return on investment.

c. Residual income/EVA.

d. Both (b) and (c) are used.

8. Which of the following is a problem in using return on investment to evaluate managers?

a. Managers of investment centers with high ROIs may not invest in some projects with returns greater than the required rate of return.

b. Managers may overinvest in high-ROI projects.

c. Managers' morale may suffer from being evaluated.

d. None of these answer choices is correct.

9. Which of the following is a true statement regarding the evaluation of an investment center?

a. Return on investment may be high because of old equipment that is fully depreciated.

b. Residual income does not take into account the level of investment in fixed assets.

c. Return on investment does not take into account the level of investment in fixed assets.

d. None of these answer choices is correct.

10. (Appendix) The transfer price that motivates the best decisions is one that measures:

a. The full cost of goods produced.

b. The opportunity cost of producing and transferring an item.

c. The selling division's variable cost.

d. None of these answer choices is correct.

ANSWERS TO SELF-ASSESSMENT

1. b **2.** d **3.** b **4.** a **5.** a **6.** b
7. d **8.** a **9.** a **10.** b

QUESTIONS

1. List four advantages related to decentralization of a firm's operations.
2. List two disadvantages associated with decentralization of a firm's operations.
3. What is empire building in a managerial context?
4. How could costly duplication of activities occur in a decentralized operating environment?
5. Discuss goal congruence and how it impacts the decision to decentralize.
6. Distinguish among cost centers, profit centers, and investment centers.
7. What is the difference between residual income and EVA?
8. What is the problem with using only financial measures of performance?
9. Provide two measures for each perspective of a balanced scorecard.
10. (Appendix) Explain the advantages of using market price as a transfer price.

EXERCISES

GROUP WORK

EXERCISE 12-1. [LO 2] Explain why, in the calculation of EVA, the profit measure used (NOPAT) excludes interest expense.

WRITING

EXERCISE 12-2. [LO 2] Write a paragraph explaining why, in the calculation of a company's EVA, noninterest-bearing current liabilities are subtracted from total assets to determine investment.

EXERCISE 12-3. Why Firms Decentralize [LO 1] The Lyndstrom Glass Company is a manufacturer of automotive glass and glass products used in the home. Discuss the advantages of forming two divisions (an Automotive division and a Home Products division) and allowing the division managers substantial decision-making autonomy.

EXERCISE 12-4. Responsibility Centers and Performance Measures [LO 1] Department managers at Nadaire Department Stores are allowed considerable discretion in sourcing and pricing products based on local tastes and competition. They are also responsible for staffing their departments.

REQUIRED

Suggest two financial performance measures that would be useful in evaluating the performance of department managers at Nadaire Department Stores.

EXERCISE 12-5. Responsibility Centers [LO 1] A major software company has established customer service centers in India, Ireland, and Israel to provide support to its U.S. customers with foreign operations. The prices that the company charges for software reflect estimated costs in operating the centers (i.e., there is no separate charge for service).

REQUIRED

How should these centers be organized: as cost centers, profit centers, or investment centers? Support your answer.

EXERCISE 12-6. Responsibility Centers [LO 1] Samson Software operates a training facility that offers classes in the use of its software products. Historically, the classes have been offered at a modest charge that covers the cost of the instructor's salary but not overhead related to the training facility (e.g., janitorial cost, utilities, rent, and administration).

Latoya Johnsen had recently been named director of customer training, and she will be given considerable freedom in operating the training facility and in marketing classes. Top management at Samson, however, has told Latoya that they want her operation to earn a before-tax profit of at least $500,000.

REQUIRED

Discuss the wisdom of requiring the training operation to earn a profit.

EXERCISE 12-7. Calculating ROI [LO 2] Davenport Mills is a division of Iowa Woolen Products. For the most recent year, Davenport had net income of $20,000,000. Included in income was interest expense of $1,400,000. The operation's tax rate is 40 percent. Total assets of Davenport Mills are $235,000,000, current liabilities are $52,000,000, and $36,000,000 of the current liabilities are noninterest bearing.

REQUIRED

Calculate NOPAT, invested capital, and ROI for Davenport Mills.

EXCEL **EXERCISE 12-8. Calculating ROI [LO 2]** For fiscal year 2017, LaundryMate Products had income as follows:

Sales	$55,000,000
Less:	
Cost of goods sold	38,400,000
Selling and administrative expense	5,700,000
Interest expense	1,000,000
Income before taxes	9,900,000
Less income taxes	3,465,000
Net income	$ 6,435,000

Total assets were $97,000,000, and noninterest-bearing current liabilities were $3,200,000. The company has a required rate of return on invested capital equal to 10 percent.

REQUIRED

Calculate NOPAT, invested capital, and ROI for LaundryMate Products, and comment on the company's profitability.

EXERCISE 12-9. Calculating Residual Income [LO 2] For fiscal year 2018, Katherine's Department Store had net income of $6,000,000. Interest expense was $2,250,000, and the company's tax rate on income was 40 percent. Total assets were $80,000,000, and noninterest-bearing current liabilities were $6,700,000. The company's cost of capital (required rate of return) is 10 percent.

REQUIRED

Calculate NOPAT, invested capital, and residual income for Katherine's Department Store and comment on the company's profitability.

EXERCISE 12-10. Evaluating Investment Centers with Residual Income [LO 2] Lakeside Hospital is a division of Superior Healthcare that is organized as an investment center. In the past year, the hospital reported an after-tax income of $3,500,000. Total interest expense was $1,650,000, and the hospital's tax rate was 35 percent. Hospital assets totaled $35,000,000, and noninterest-bearing current liabilities were $11,400,000. Superior has established a required rate of return equal to 18 percent of invested capital.

REQUIRED

Calculate the residual income/EVA of Lakeside Hospital.

EXERCISE 12-11. Evaluating Investment Centers; ROI versus RI [LO 2] Consider the following data, which relate to the two divisions of McIntyre Products:

	Division 1	Division 2
Total assets	$69,000,000	$23,000,000
Noninterest-bearing current liabilities	4,500,000	2,300,000
NOPAT	12,000,000	5,900,000
Required rate of return	11%	10%

REQUIRED

Compare the two divisions in terms of return on investment and residual income. In the past year, which division has created the most wealth for McIntyre shareholders?

EXERCISE 12-12. Overinvestment and Underinvestment [LO 2] Consider two companies: Quantum Products and Aquafin Products. Senior managers at Quantum Products are evaluated in terms of increases in profit. In fiscal 2017, Quantum Products had a net operating profit after taxes of $4,600,000 and invested capital of $26,000,000. In fiscal 2018, the company had net operating profit after taxes of $6,000,000 and invested capital of $47,500,000. Senior managers at Aquafin Products are evaluated in terms of ROI. In fiscal 2018, ROI was 15 percent while the cost of capital was only 10 percent. Near the end of fiscal 2018, managers had an opportunity to make an investment that would have yielded a return of 14 percent. However, the senior managers did not support making the investment.

REQUIRED

a. Explain why the senior managers at Quantum Products have an incentive to overinvest.

b. Explain why the senior managers at Aquafin Products have an incentive to underinvest.

EXERCISE 12-13. Adjusting NOPAT and Adjusting Investment in the Calculation of EVA [LO 2] The following income statements and other information are available for the Schneider Company:

	2017	2016	2015
Sales	$380,000,000	$250,000,000	$190,000,000
Less cost of goods sold	210,000,000	120,000,000	91,000,000
Gross margin	170,000,000	130,000,000	99,000,000
Less:			
Selling and administrative costs	27,500,000	24,750,000	19,580,000
Research and development	15,600,000	12,400,000	9,450,000
Income from operations	126,900,000	92,850,000	69,970,000
Less taxes on income	38,070,000	27,855,000	20,991,000
Net income	$ 88,830,000	$ 64,995,000	$ 48,979,000
Total assets	$715,000,000	$665,000,000	$441,000,000
Noninterest-bearing current liabilities	14,000,000	11,300,000	9,880,000
Cost of capital	12%	12%	12%

REQUIRED

Calculate EVA for 2017. Assume that for purposes of calculating EVA, the company capitalizes research and development expenditures and amortizes them over 3 years, including the year they are incurred. For external reporting purposes, research and development is expensed in the year incurred, as indicated in the income statements above.

EXERCISE 12-14. Balanced Scorecard [LO 3] Some advocates of the balanced scorecard have argued that managing a company with just financial performance measures is like driving a car and just looking in the rearview mirror. That's why they recommend customer, internal processes, and learning and growth measures that, they believe, focus attention on what a company is doing today to create future value.

REQUIRED

Explain the analogy between financial measures and driving using just the rearview mirror.

EXERCISE 12-15. Customer-Focused Measures for a Balanced Scorecard [LO 3] Major's Fitness Club operates a 20,000-square-foot facility in Dallas. For the coming year, the company is considering development of a balanced scorecard.

REQUIRED

Help the company by identifying three customer-focused measures that can be used on the balanced scorecard. Discuss the key items related to a successful balanced scorecard.

EXERCISE 12-16. (Appendix) Transfer Pricing in Healthcare, Market Price [LO A1] Paramount Medical Services has two outpatient clinics and a pathology laboratory, which are organized as separate profit centers. When the pathology laboratory conducts tests ordered by the clinics, the clinics are charged the basic market price of the tests. The managers of the clinics object to this practice and argue that because they are all part of the same company, they should be charged for the cost of the procedures rather than market price.

REQUIRED

Support the use of market prices or cost-based prices for charging clinics for tests performed by the pathology laboratory.

EXERCISE 12-17. (Appendix) Transfer Pricing, Full Cost Plus Profit [LO A1] The Champion Chemical Company has a number of divisions that produce and market paints, varnishes, and other chemical products. The company also has a small plant that manufactures metal containers for the divisions' various products. The plant, which has substantial excess capacity, is organized as a cost center and transfers containers to the divisions at cost.

Eduardo Sanchez, the container plant manager, has approached the corporate executive committee with the suggestion that the plant he administers be organized as a profit center. This would be accomplished by changing the transfer price to be equal to full cost plus a markup of 10 percent.

REQUIRED

Comment on Eduardo's suggestion. Could his proposal lead to suboptimal decisions from the standpoint of the company as a whole?

PROBLEMS

PROBLEM 12-1. Cost Centers and Performance Measures [LO 1, 3] Magellan Materials manufactures metal and plastic gutters for use in commercial and residential construction. Production occurs in two separate plants. Distribution is from a central warehouse, and there is a centrally managed sales office. Both production plants are currently treated as cost centers, and their budgets are prepared in close consultation with the central office. Analysis of standard cost variances is used as a control mechanism in the two plants.

REQUIRED

a. Explain how budgets and variance analysis provide a means of controlling cost in the production plants.

b. List four nonfinancial performance measures that plant managers can use to assess the operations they control.

PROBLEM 12-2. Investment Centers and Performance Measures [LO 1, 2] LEO Corporation has five divisions, each of which is managed by a divisional president who reports to the chief executive officer of LEO. LEO is decentralized, and divisional presidents are granted authority to make investments under $3,000,000 without prior approval by the CEO.

REQUIRED

Suggest three financial performance measures that could be used to evaluate the divisions and the divisional presidents.

PROBLEM 12-3. Return on Investment [LO 2] Consider the following information for McKinley and Son:

	12/31/2017	12/31/2018
Total assets	$55,000,000	$62,000,000
Noninterest-bearing current liabilities	1,100,000	1,320,000
Net income	3,300,000	3,426,000
Interest expense	726,000	770,000
Tax rate	35%	35%

REQUIRED

a. Evaluate the company in terms of ROI.

b. While income has increased in fiscal 2018, is it clear that the company's performance has improved?

PROBLEM 12-4. Residual Income/Economic Value Added [LO 2] Consider the following information for Executive Electronics:

	12/31/2017	12/31/2018
Total assets	$12,650,000	$12,100,000
Noninterest-bearing current liabilities	550,000	572,000
Net income	770,000	880,000
Interest expense	2,310,000	330,000
Tax rate	40%	40%
Required rate of return	10%	12%

REQUIRED

a. Evaluate the company in terms of residual income (RI), which is equivalent to EVA since there are no adjustments for accounting distortions.

b. While income has increased in fiscal 2018, is it clear that the company's performance has improved?

c. (Optional) Explain why the required rate of return increased in fiscal 2018. (*Hint:* Note that while total assets are approximately the same in both years, interest expense has declined sharply in 2018.)

PROBLEM 12-5. Return on Investment, Effect of Depreciation [LO 2] The chief operating officer of the Wisconsin Corporation is considering the effect of depreciation on the company's ROI. In the most recent year, net operating profit after taxes was $35,000,000 and investment (total assets of $460,000,000 less noninterest-bearing current liabilities of $20,000,000) was $440,000,000.

REQUIRED

a. Assuming that total assets will decline each year by 6 percent due to depreciation of plant and equipment but NOPAT will remain constant, calculate ROI for each of the next 5 years.

b. Explain why evaluation in terms of ROI may lead managers to delay purchases of equipment that, in the long run, will be needed to remain competitive.

EXCEL **PROBLEM 12-6. Return on Investment, Profit Margin, and Investment Turnover [LO 2]** Consider the following information for HandyCraft Stores for 2017 and 2018:

	2017	2018
Total assets	$59,500,000	$56,430,000
Noninterest-bearing current liabilities	4,400,000	4,950,000
Net income	3,650,000	4,950,000
Interest expense	2,420,000	2,975,000
Sales	66,000,000	96,250,000
Tax rate	40%	40%

REQUIRED

a. Compute ROI for both years.

b. Break ROI down into profit margin and investment turnover.

c. Comment on the change in financial performance between 2017 and 2018.

EXCEL **PROBLEM 12-7. ROI and EVA [LO 2, 3]** ELN Waste Management has a subsidiary that disposes of hazardous waste and a subsidiary that collects and disposes of residential garbage. Information related to the two subsidiaries follows:

	Hazardous Waste	Residential Waste
Total assets	$15,300,000	$87,000,000
Noninterest-bearing current liabilities	3,300,000	13,200,000
Net income	1,870,000	6,600,000
Interest expense	1,375,000	8,030,000
Required rate of return	10%	13%
Tax rate	40%	40%

REQUIRED

a. Calculate ROI for both subsidiaries.

b. Calculate EVA for both subsidiaries. Note that since no adjustments for accounting distortions are being made, EVA is equivalent to residual income.

c. Which subsidiary has added the most to shareholder value in the last year?

d. Based on the limited information, which subsidiary is the best candidate for expansion? Explain.

PROBLEM 12-8. EVA [LO 2] Atomic Electronics is considering instituting a plan whereby managers will be evaluated and rewarded based on a measure of economic value added (EVA). Before adopting the plan, management wants you to calculate what EVA will be in 2018, based on financial forecasts for 2018 and prior financial data.

	Fiscal Forecast 2018
Total assets	$ 60,500,000
Noninterest-bearing current liabilities	23,100,000
Sales	110,000,000
Net income	6,050,000
Interest expense	1,320,000
Research and development	2,640,000
Tax rate	35%
Cost of capital	15%

Research and development expenditures in 2016 and 2017 were $1,200,000 and $2,100,000, respectively. In calculating EVA, prior research and development will be capitalized and amortized assuming a 3-year life (i.e., one-third will be expensed in the year incurred, and two-thirds will be capitalized and expensed in the following 2 years).

REQUIRED

a. Explain why it is important to capitalize research and development if managers are to be rewarded based on EVA.

b. Calculate forecasted EVA for 2018.

c. Will management be likely to support use of EVA as a financial performance measure?

PROBLEM 12-9. EVA and Control of the Investment in Company Assets [LO 2] Poseidon Electronics operates 10 stores in Washington, Oregon, and California, selling consumer electronics including stereo equipment and home theater systems. The following financial information is available for 2018 and 2017:

	2018	2017
Income from operations	$ 990,000	$ 935,000
Net income	590,040	557,700
Interest expense	6,600	5,500
Total assets	4,400,000	3,850,000
Noninterest-bearing current liabilities	319,000	308,000
Tax rate	40%	40%
Cost of capital	12%	12%

REQUIRED

a. Although net income has increased by 6 percent, a shareholder evaluating the company's financial performance asserts that, in spite of the increase, financial performance has deteriorated in 2018. Support this assertion with appropriate calculations of EVA. Note that no adjustments are needed for accounting distortions.

b. Management asserts that the increased investment in the company's assets was clearly warranted since income increased. Briefly evaluate this assertion.

c. Briefly explain why evaluation in terms of EVA will drive managers to focus on carefully evaluating the investment in assets while this will not be the case if managers are evaluated in terms of growth in profit.

PROBLEM 12-10. Economic Value Added and the Balanced Scorecard [LO 2, 3] The Spectrum Book Company has two divisions: The Brick and Mortar division sells books through more than 100 bookstores throughout the United States; the Internet division was formed 18 months ago and sells books via the Internet. Data for the past year are:

	Brick and Mortar Division	Internet Division
Total assets	$162,000,000	$15,480,000
Noninterest-bearing current liabilities	7,020,000	2,520,000
Interest expense	1,260,000	418,500
Net income (loss)	27,810,000	(1,125,000)
Tax rate	40%	–0–
Cost of capital	10%	12%

REQUIRED

a. Evaluate the two divisions in terms of economic value added (EVA).

b. Explain why it might be better to evaluate the Internet division in terms of a balanced scorecard rather than just using EVA.

c. Consider the customer and internal processes dimensions of the balanced scorecard. Suggest two measures for each dimension that would be appropriate for the Brick and Mortar division and two measures for each dimension that would be appropriate for the Internet division.

d. A strategy map diagrams the relationship across the dimensions of the balanced scorecard. Identify the potential links between the customer and internal processes dimensions you identified in part c.

PROBLEM 12-11. Growth in Profit and Overinvestment [LO 2] Consider the following data related to the financial performance of Royal Company:

000s	2015	2016	2017	2018
Net income	$ 3,750	$ 4,313	$ 5,088	$ 6,105
% change in income	–0–	15%	18%	20%
Total assets	$37,500	$47,925	$63,750	$87,500

Between 2015 and 2018, income increased by 63 percent, showing a significant increase in income each year. In light of this performance, the board of directors has awarded large bonuses to senior executives. However, the stock price has fallen from $73 per share in 2015 to $56 per share at the end of 2018.

REQUIRED

a. Calculate ROI for each year. To simplify the calculation, assume that there is no interest expense and there are no noninterest-bearing current liabilities (thus, net income equals NOPAT and total assets are a reasonable measure of investment).

b. Explain why the stock price has dropped and why rewarding managers based on increases in profit can lead to overinvestment.

c. Calculate economic value added for 2015 to 2018, using a cost of capital (required return) of 9.5 percent. Does performance measured in terms of EVA help explain the decline in stock price?

PROBLEM 12-12. The Balanced Scorecard [LO 3] The strategy for success at Sassy Jeans calls for rapid growth, a limited number of units for each design to enhance exclusivity, perfect fit, on-time delivery to customers, retaining employees who contribute to innovation, and control of inventory.

REQUIRED

a. Keeping in mind the Sassy Jeans' strategy for success, suggest one performance measure for each dimension of a balanced scorecard.

b. Identify the links between the measures (strategy map) you identified in part a.

PROBLEM 12-13. You Get What You Measure and a Balanced Scorecard [LO 3] Kasper Industries produces custom molds that are used by producers of molded products (e.g., ski boots and snowboards). Many of its customers use just-in-time (JIT) manufacturing, and on-time delivery of the molds is critical because production is halted if the molds are not available when needed. In the past, managers (including Maria Patterson, the vice president of operations) at Kasper have been rewarded based on financial performance. This has led to actions that are not consistent with maximizing shareholder value. Near the end of each quarter, Maria evaluates expected profit in relation to the company's profit goal. If expected profit is below the goal, she rushes into production customer orders that have a high profit margin, even if the orders are not due for two or three weeks. Thus, deliveries of high-profit-margin jobs are often early and deliveries of low-profit-margin jobs (displaced in Kasper's production schedule) are often late. The company has not performed well on a dimension of performance that is critical for long-run success.

REQUIRED

a. A consultant to Kasper Industries has suggested that the company use a balanced scorecard. Suggest a customer measure and an internal process measure that will help the company track its performance with respect to on-time delivery and other improvements that meet the needs of customers.

b. Suppose that Maria Patterson continues to manage production to meet short-run profit goals. Explain how her actions will be detected by the customer and internal process measures you suggested in part a.

PROBLEM 12-14. (Appendix) Transfer Pricing [LO A1] The Leviathan Steel Company has a coal-mining subsidiary in West Virginia. A substantial amount of the coal produced by the subsidiary is used by Leviathan's steel foundries located in Pennsylvania.

REQUIRED

a. Recommend and defend a transfer price (market price, variable cost, or full cost plus profit) for the coal shipped by the mining subsidiary to the foundries.

b. Indicate how the price you recommended in part a compares with the opportunity cost related to using the coal internally.

PROBLEM 12-15. (Appendix) Decentralization and Transfer Pricing [LO A1] The City of Medina Park operates a plumbing and electrical maintenance department, responsible for maintaining all water and electric service functions in buildings owned by the city. The city administration is concerned about the rising costs of the maintenance department, which is currently organized as a cost center. Charlotte Daugherty, the manager of the maintenance department, says that many of the department's service calls are strictly nuisance calls. She cites examples of numerous calls for defective electrical outlets, which turn out to be unplugged equipment, burned-out lightbulbs (which can easily be changed by the users), and drains clogged by coffee grounds. In Charlotte's opinion, these nuisance calls would be avoided if the departments using her department's services were "billed." Essentially, Charlotte suggests that there be a transfer price related to using her department's services and that the price should approximate the cost of these services in the market ($50–$65 per hour of service time). This would turn her operation into a profit center, and, she believes, her department would operate more efficiently because demand for services would decline and she would need fewer employees.

REQUIRED

Evaluate Charlotte's proposal. Do you support use of a transfer price for maintenance services? If so, should the price approximate the market price of service or should it be based on cost?

PROBLEM 12-16. (Appendix) Transfer Pricing [LO A1] Montana Woolen Products has two divisions: a Fabric division that manufactures woolen fabrics and a Clothing division that manufactures woolen dresses, coats, shirts, and accessories. All fabric used by the Clothing division is supplied by the Fabric division, which also supplies fabric to outside companies.

REQUIRED

a. Suggest a transfer price for the fabric assuming that the Fabric division is operating at only 60 percent of capacity due to a surge in popularity of "easy-care" fabrics made of polyester and rayon.

b. Suggest a transfer price for fabric assuming that the Fabric division is operating at capacity due to a revival of consumer interest in natural products and development of lightweight, wrinkle-resistant woolen fabrics.

c. Explain how your choices in parts a and b are related to the opportunity cost concept.

PROBLEM 12-17. ROI and Investment Decisions [LO 2] Sarah Jones, the manager of the Teen division of the Eve Clothing Company, was evaluating the acquisition of a new embroidery machine.

The budgeted operating income of the Teen division was $5,000,000 with total assets of $33,000,000 and noninterest-bearing current liabilities of $1,500,000. The proposed investment would add $1,027,500 to operating income and would require an additional investment of $5,250,000. The targeted rate of return for the Teen division is 14 percent. (Ignore taxes in this problem.)

REQUIRED

a. Compute the ROI of:

1. The Teen division if the embroidery machine is not purchased.

2. The Teen division if the embroidery machine is purchased.

b. Compute the residual income of:

1. The Teen division if the embroidery machine is not purchased.

2. The Teen division if the embroidery machine is purchased.

c. Will Sarah decide to invest in the embroidery machine if her performance is evaluated in terms of ROI? Why or why not?

PROBLEM 12-18. Comparing Performance Evaluation Methods [LO 2] Top management of the Gates Corporation is trying to construct a performance evaluation system to use to evaluate each of its three divisions. This past year's financial data are as follows:

	Division A	Division B	Division C
Total assets	$927,500	$18,725,000	$11,156,250
Noninterest-bearing current liabilities	52,500	2,187,500	1,050,000
Net income	178,500	1,820,000	1,365,000
Interest expense	52,500	1,925,000	1,225,000
Tax rate	40%	40%	40%
Required rate of return	10%	12%	14%

REQUIRED

a. How would the divisions be ranked (from best to worst performance) if the evaluation were based on net income?

b. How would the divisions be ranked (from best to worst performance) if the evaluation were based on ROI?

c. How would the divisions be ranked (from best to worst performance) if the evaluation were based on residual income?

CASE

12-1 HOME VALUE STORES [LO2]

Home Value Stores operates 264 membership warehouse stores in the United States, Europe, and Asia. The company offers low prices on a limited selection of household and grocery products. In the past year, sales increased by approximately 10.8 percent and net earnings increased by 6.4 percent. The company opened only two stores in 2017 and 2018 and closed one of its stores due to poor performance. Jack Davidson and Michael Prine are on the board of directors of Home Value and serve on the company's compensation committee. At a recent lunch meeting, they discussed the company's performance. (See the table on the next page for a balance sheet and an income statement.) Both were pleased with the increase in profit and decided to recommend a contract extension and a substantial six-figure bonus for the company's CEO. They anticipated, however, that the third member of the compensation committee, Tanya Barrett, would object to the bonus. Tanya believes that accounting profit is a poor measure of future firm performance. In her opinion, the company should be focused on what it is doing today to create future value for shareholders. She has also pointed out that, although the company showed quarterly profit increases, its stock price remained flat.

REQUIRED

a. To prepare for an upcoming board meeting, Tanya has asked you to evaluate financial performance for 2017 and 2018, taking into account both the level of investment and the cost of capital. Specifically, she would like you to calculate the level of profit (loss) that was earned in excess of the amount required given the investment in the company. Assume that the cost of capital is 15 percent. Is it clear that the company has had superior financial performance?

b. In fiscal 2019, the CEO of Home Value Stores retired. His successor is concerned that warehouse managers do not understand how their actions are linked to the company's strategy and how they can affect future firm value. In his opinion, while monthly earnings are important, managers are focused almost exclusively on how their actions affect these numbers. Suggest a performance measurement technique that can be used to address the new CEO's concerns.

Comparative Financial Statements: Home Value Stores (in thousands)

	2018	2017
Sales	$26,360,000	$23,800,000
Merchandise costs	20,680,000	17,900,000
Operating, general and administrative	3,220,000	3,600,000
Rent	235,000	220,000
Depreciation and amortization	211,000	200,500
Interest expense	110,000	90,000
Total	24,456,000	22,010,500
Earnings before taxes	1,904,000	1,789,500
Taxes	666,400	626,325
Net earnings	$ 1,237,600	$ 1,163,175
Assets		
Cash and temporary investments	$ 90,000	$ 60,000
Receivables	358,000	202,000
Inventories	1,944,000	1,405,000
Prepaid and other current assets	193,000	118,000
Total current assets	2,585,000	1,785,000
Land	260,000	140,000
Buildings and equipment (net)	640,000	450,000
	900,000	590,000
Total assets	$ 3,485,000	$ 2,375,000
Liabilities and Shareholders' Equity		
Accounts payable	$ 540,000	$ 500,000
Current portion of long-term debt	91,000	80,000
Accrued income taxes	98,000	89,000
Total current liabilities	729,000	669,000
Long-term debt	810,000	600,000
Total liabilities	1,539,000	1,269,000
Shareholders' Equity		
Common stock	775,000	674,000
Retained earnings	1,171,000	432,000
Total shareholders' equity	1,946,000	1,106,000
Total liabilities and shareholders' equity	$ 3,485,000	$ 2,375,000

CASE

12-2 WIN TECH MOTORS [LO 2]

In 2016, five retired software developers opened an auto dealership in Redmond, Washington, which they named WinTechMotors. The company specializes in high-end sports and luxury autos and has one of the largest inventories of used Porsches on the West Coast. (Typically, 75 Porsches are in stock). The inventory is listed on the company's website and the company has shipped cars to online customers as far away as Florida, although most customers are located in Washington, Oregon, and California. In 2017, an industry publication (*Motor Watch*) listed WinTech as the fastest-growing luxury auto dealership on the West Coast. Comparative income statements and balance sheets are presented in the table on the right. As indicated, the company had sales of $15,120,000 in 2017 (a 25 percent increase over 2016) and net income of $326,950 (a 91 percent increase over 2016). The owners were delighted with the company's financial performance and quite proud that they had developed a successful business. However, at a recent meeting, their company's external accountants introduced them to the concept of EVA and noted that, with an assumed weighted average cost of capital of 12 percent, their EVA had been negative in both years. Accordingly, the owners have contracted with an EVA consultant to help them with financial planning.

REQUIRED

a. Calculate EVA for 2017 and 2016, using a cost of capital of 12 percent. No adjustments for accounting distortions are needed. Explain why sales and income have increased substantially in 2017 and yet EVA is negative. What is not captured in income that is captured in EVA?

b. The owners realize they must cut back on inventory to earn a zero or positive EVA in the coming year. To get a handle on this, they would like you to calculate the maximum amount of inventory that could have been on hand at the end of 2017 for the company to achieve a zero level of EVA.

c. Assume the average car has a cost of $75,000. Also assume that sales, expenses, assets (except inventory), and liabilities are roughly the same in 2018 as in 2017. How many cars must be cut from inventory to achieve zero EVA in 2018?

Comparative Financial Statements: Win Tech Motors

	2017	2016
Sales	$15,120,000	$12,105,000
Less cost of autos sold	13,618,000	10,894,000
Gross margin	1,502,000	1,211,000
Less selling and administrative expense	936,000	889,200
Interest	63,000	58,500
Income before taxes	503,000	263,300
Income taxes	176,050	92,155
Net income	$ 326,950	$ 171,145
Increase in sales	24.91%	
Increase in net income	91%	
Assets		
Cash and short-term investments	$ 58,500	$ 63,000
Receivables	355,500	288,000
Inventory	5,625,000	5,040,000
Current assets	6,039,000	5,391,000
Building and equipment (net)	860,400	855,000
Other assets	48,600	54,000
Total assets	$ 6,948,000	$ 6,300,000
Liabilities and Shareholders' Equity		
Accounts payable	$ 276,300	$ 117,000
Short-term debt payable	81,000	67,500
Taxes payable	103,500	36,000
Current liabilities	460,800	220,500
Long-term debt payable	625,500	544,500
Total liabilities	1,086,300	765,000
Retained earnings	821,700	495,000
Common stock	5,040,000	5,040,000
Total liabilities and shareholders' equity	$ 6,948,000	$ 6,300,000

GLOSSARY

A

Ability to bear costs (6) The notion in cost allocation that the allocation base should result in more costs being allocated to products, services, or departments that are more profitable.

Absorption costing (5) An approach to product costing that includes direct material, direct labor, and both fixed and variable manufacturing overhead in product cost. Also referred to as *full costing*. The alternative to absorption costing is variable costing, which includes direct material, direct labor, and variable (but not fixed) manufacturing overhead.

Account analysis (4) A method of estimating cost behavior that requires professional judgment to classify costs as either fixed or variable. The total of the costs classified as variable are divided by a measure of activity to calculate the variable cost per unit of activity. The total of the costs classified as fixed provides the estimate of fixed cost.

Accounting rate of return (9) The average after-tax income from a project divided by the average investment.

Activity-based costing (ABC) (2, 6) A method of assigning overhead costs that identifies key activities and accumulates the costs associated with them. Cost drivers (volume- or nonvolume-related measure of activity) are used to assign the various cost categories to products or services.

Activity-based management (ABM) (6) A management approach that involves analyzing and costing activities with the goal of improving efficiency and effectiveness. See also activity-based costing.

Activity-based pricing (8) An approach to pricing in which customers are presented with separate prices for services they request in addition to the cost of goods they purchase. Activity-based pricing is also referred to as menu-based pricing since customers are presented with a menu of prices related to the various services they request in addition to the products they purchase.

Administrative expenses (2) Expenses associated with the firm's general management. These include the salaries of the company president and accounting personnel, depreciation of the general office building, depreciation of office equipment, and the cost of supplies.

Allocation base (2) The measure of activity used to calculate an overhead rate. Also referred to as a cost driver.

Attainable standards (11) A standard that takes into account the possibility that a variety of circumstances may lead to costs that are greater than ideal.

Avoidable costs (7) Costs that can be avoided if a company takes a particular action.

B

Balanced scorecard (12) A set of performance measures (linked to a company's strategy) for four categories: financial, customer, internal processes, and learning and growth.

Batch-level activities (6) Activities required to produce another batch of a product.

Break-even point (4) The number of units a company must sell to earn a zero profit.

Budget (1, 10) A formal document that quantifies a company's plan for achieving its goals.

Budget committee (10) The group responsible for preparing budgets.

Budget variance (10) The difference between budgeted and actual cost.

Budgeted cost (11) The cost, at standard, for a number of budgeted units.

C

Capital budget (9) The final list of approved investments.

Capital budgeting decision (9) Investment decision involving the acquisition of long-lived assets. See also capital expenditure decision.

Capital expenditure decision (9) Investment decision involving the acquisition of long-lived assets. See also capital budgeting decision.

Cause-and-effect relationship (6) An allocation of cost to the cost objective that caused it to be incurred.

Chief financial officer (CFO) (1) The senior executive responsible for both accounting and financial operations.

Chief information officer (CIO) (1) The manager responsible for a company's information technology and computer systems.

Committed fixed costs (4) Fixed costs that cannot be easily changed in the short run.

Common costs (7) Costs incurred for the benefit of multiple departments or products.

Computer-controlled manufacturing system (2) Highly automated manufacturing system that uses computers to control equipment and generally increases the flexibility and accuracy of the production process.

Contribution margin (4) The difference between sales and variable costs.

Contribution margin ratio (4) The contribution margin divided by sales or the contribution margin per unit divided by the selling price.

Controllable cost (1, 6) A cost that a manager can influence by the decisions he or she makes.

Controllable overhead variance (11) The difference between the amount of overhead that would be included in a flexible budget for the actual level of production and the actual amount of overhead.

Controller (1) The top accounting executive responsible for financial and managerial accounting information and tax filings.

Conversion costs (3) Conversion costs include both labor and overhead. Frequently, they are assumed to be added evenly throughout the production process.

Cost allocation (6) Cost allocation is the process of identifying indirect costs and assigning them to cost objectives such as departments or products.

Cost center (12) A business segment responsible for controlling costs, not for generating revenues.

Cost driver (2, 6) A measure of the activity, related to a cost pool, that is used to allocate cost.

Cost objective (6) The object of cost allocation.

Cost of capital (9) The weighted average of the costs of debt and equity financing used to generate capital for investments.

Cost of goods available for sale (2) The sum of the beginning balance in Finished Goods plus the cost of goods manufactured.

Cost of goods manufactured (2) The cost of items that have been completed in the current accounting period.

Cost per equivalent unit (3) The sum of the cost in beginning Work in Process and the cost incurred in the current period divided by the sum of the units completed and the equivalent units in ending Work in Process.

Cost pool (2, 6) A grouping of overhead costs based on the major activity that created them. Also, a grouping of individual costs whose total is allocated using one allocation base.

Cost-plus pricing (8) An approach to pricing in which a prespecified markup is added to cost in order to determine price.

Cost-volume-profit (C-V-P) analysis (4) The analysis of how costs and profit change when volume changes.

Customer profitability measurement (CPM) system (8) A system in which the indirect costs of serving customers including the cost of processing orders, the cost of handling returns, the cost of shipments, etc., are assigned to cost pools. Using cost drivers, these costs are then allocated to specific customers. Subtracting these costs as well as product costs from customer revenue yields a measure of customer profitability.

Customer relationship management (CRM) systems (1) Systems that automate call centers and customer services. The systems also provide customer data analysis and support of e-commerce storefronts.

D

Decentralized organization (12) A firm that grants substantial decision-making authority to the managers of subunits.

Depreciation tax shield (9) The tax savings resulting from depreciation.

Differential costs (7) Costs that differ between decision alternatives.

Direct cost (1) A cost that is directly traceable to a product, activity, or department.

Direct labor cost (2) The cost of labor that is directly traced to items produced.

Direct material cost (2) The cost of all materials and parts that are directly traced to items produced.

Direct method (13) Method of preparing the statement of cash flows in which the operating activities section is in a format similar to that of an income statement.

Direct method of allocating cost (6) A method of allocating service department costs to production departments that does not allow for allocation of costs among service departments.

Discretionary fixed costs (4) Fixed costs that management can easily change in the short run.

E

Economic value added (EVA) (12) A performance measure equal to net operating profit after taxes (adjusted for accounting distortions) less a charge based on the level of investment.

Enterprise resource planning (ERP) systems (1) Systems that computerize inventory and production planning, support accounting, human resources, and various e-commerce applications.

Equity approach to allocation (6) An attempt to allocate costs in a way that is fair to interested parties.

Equivalent units (3) Partially completed units expressed as a comparable number of whole units.

F

Facility-level activities (6) Activities that support all other activities including unit-level, batch-level, and product-level activities.
Financial leverage (14) Portion of a firm's assets financed with debt as opposed to equity—the more debt, the higher the financial leverage.
Financing activities (13) Classification in the statement of cash flows related to issuing and repurchasing stock, issuing long-term debt, paying off loans to debt holders, and making dividend payments.
Finished Goods Inventory (2) The cost of goods that are completed and ready to sell.
Fixed cost (1, 4) Costs that do not change when there is a change in business activity.
Flexible budget (10) A budget that is adjusted for the actual level of activity.
Full cost (2, 5) An approach to product costing that includes direct material, direct labor, and both fixed and variable manufacturing overhead in product cost. Also referred to as *absorption costing*. The alternative to full costing is variable costing which includes direct material, direct labor, and variable (but not fixed) manufacturing overhead.

H

High-low method (4) A method of estimating fixed and variable cost components in which a straight line is fitted to the data points representing the highest and lowest levels of activity.
Horizontal analysis (14) An analysis that focuses on the dollar value and percentage changes in financial statement amounts across time.

I

Ideal standards (11) Standards developed under the assumption that no obstacles to the production process will be encountered.
Incremental analysis (1, 7) An analysis of the revenues and costs that will change if a decision alternative is selected.
Incremental cost (1, 7) Costs that increase or decrease if a decision alternative is selected.
Incremental revenue (1, 7) Revenue that increases or decreases if a decision alternative is selected.
Indirect costs (1) A cost that either is not directly traceable to a product, activity, or department or is not worth tracing.
Indirect labor cost (2) All labor costs that are not directly traced to items produced.
Indirect materials (2) Materials and parts that are not directly traced to items produced.
Indirect method (13) Method of preparing the statement of cash flows in which the operating activities section is a reconciliation of net income and net cash provided by operating activities.
Internal rate of return (IRR) (9) The rate of return that equates the present value of future cash flows to the investment outlay.
Investing activities (13) Classification in the statement of cash flows related to the buying and selling of long-term assets.
Investment center (12) A business segment responsible for generating revenue, controlling costs, and investing in assets.
Investment turnover (12) A performance measure equal to sales divided by invested capital.

J

Job cost sheet (2) A form used to accumulate the cost of producing an item for order or for inventory.
Job-order costing system (2) A system of accounting for product cost used by companies that produce individual products or batches of products that are unique.
Joint costs (7) The costs of the common inputs that result in two or more products.
Joint products (7) Two or more products that arise from common inputs.
Just-in-time (JIT) manufacturing (2) A manufacturing system designed to minimize inventories of raw materials and works in process. In a JIT system, goods are manufactured just before they are sold and purchases are made just before goods are needed in production.

L

Labor efficiency variance (11) The difference between the standard labor hours allowed for the number of units produced and the actual number of labor hours worked times the standard labor wage rate.
Labor rate variance (11) The difference between the standard and actual wage rates times the actual number of labor hours worked.
Lack of goal congruence (12) A situation where managers pursue personal goals that are incompatible with the goals of the company as a whole.
Lump-sum allocations (6) Allocations of fixed costs in which predetermined amounts are allocated regardless of changes in the level of activity.

M

Management by exception (1, 10) Policy by which managers investigate departures (or variances) from planned results that appear to be exceptional; they do not investigate minor departures (or variances) from the plan.

Management Discussion and Analysis (MD&A) (14) The section of the annual report where firm management discusses the reason for changes in the results of operations, asset accounts, and other matters.

Managerial accounting (1) Accounting that stresses concepts and procedures relevant to preparing reports for internal users of accounting information. It focuses on information that is useful in planning, control, and decision making.

Manufacturing costs (2) All costs associated with the production of goods (i.e., direct material, direct labor, and manufacturing overhead).

Manufacturing overhead (2) The costs of manufacturing activities other than direct material and direct labor.

Margin of safety (4) The difference between the expected level of sales and break-even sales.

Master budget (10) A comprehensive planning document that incorporates a number of individual budgets.

Material price variance (11) The difference between the standard and actual prices per unit of material times the actual quantity of material used.

Material quantity variance (11) The difference between the standard quantity of material allowed for the number of units produced and the actual quantity of material used times the standard price of the material.

Material requisition form (2) A form used to authorize the release of materials for production.

Mixed cost (4) Cost that contain both variable and fixed cost elements.

N

Net present value (NPV) (9) The sum of the present values of all cash flows (alternatively, the present value of future cash inflows less the cost of an investment).

Noncontrollable costs (1) Costs that a manager cannot influence.

Noninterest-Bearing Current Liabilities (NIBCL) (12) Current liabilities that do not require interest payments (i.e., accounts payable, income taxes payable, and accrued liabilities, among other items).

Nonmanufacturing costs (2) Costs that are not associated with the production of goods (e.g., selling and administrative costs).

NOPAT (12) Net operating profit after taxes.

O

Operating activities (13) Classification in the statement of cash flows related to the production and delivery of goods and services.

Operating leverage (4) Level of fixed versus variable costs in a firm's cost structure. Firms that have relatively high levels of fixed cost are said to have high operating leverage.

Opportunity cost (1, 7) The values of benefits foregone by selecting one decision alternative over another.

Overapplied overhead (2) The excess of overhead applied to inventory using a predetermined rate over actual overhead incurred.

Overhead allocation (2) The process of assigning overhead to specific cost objectives (e.g., products or departments).

Overhead allocation rate (2) A measure of overhead cost divided by a measure of the overhead allocation base.

Overhead applied (2) The amount of overhead assigned to jobs.

Overhead volume variance (11) The difference between the amount of overhead applied to production at standard and the amount of overhead included in a flexible budget for the actual level of production.

P

Payback period (9) The length of time it takes to recover the initial cost of an investment.

Performance report (1) A report used to evaluate managers and the operations they control. Frequently, performance reports involve a comparison of planned and actual results.

Period cost (2) Cost identified with accounting periods rather than with goods produced (i.e., nonmanufacturing costs).

Predetermined overhead rate (2) The estimated level of overhead cost divided by the estimated level of the allocation base.

Present value analysis (9) A method of investment analysis that expresses future cash flows in terms of their value today.

Process costing system (2) A product costing system used by companies that produce large numbers of identical items in a continuous production process.

Product costing systems (2) An integrated set of documents, ledgers, accounts, and accounting procedures used to measure and record the cost of manufactured products.

Product costs (2) Costs assigned to goods produced (i.e., manufacturing costs).

Product-level activities (6) Activities required to initiate production of a product regardless of the number of units or batches of the product.
Production cost report (3) A report in a process costing system that provides a reconciliation of units and a reconciliation of costs as well as the details of the cost per equivalent unit calculations.
Profit center (12) A business segment responsible for generating revenue and controlling costs. It is not responsible for investing in assets.
Profit equation (4) Equation that states that profit is equal to revenue (selling price times quantity) minus variable cost (variable cost per unit times quantity) minus total fixed cost.
Profit margin (12) Net income divided by revenue.

R

Raw Materials Inventory (2) An account that includes the cost of materials on hand that are used to produce a company's products.
Regression analysis (4) A statistical technique that can be used to estimate the intercept (an estimate of fixed cost) and the slope (an estimate of variable cost) of a cost equation.
Relative benefits approach to allocation (6) The notion in cost allocation that the allocation base should result in more cost being allocated to the cost objectives that benefit most from incurring the cost.
Relative performance evaluation (12) The evaluation of a subunit in comparison to similar subunits within a company.
Relative sales value method (7) A method of allocating joint costs in which the allocation is based on the relative sales value of the products at the split-off point.
Relevant costs (7) The only cost items that managers need to consider when analyzing decision alternatives because they differ between decision alternatives.
Relevant range (4) The range of activity for which estimates and predictions are likely to be accurate.
Required rate of return (9) The minimum acceptable return on an investment; also referred to as a hurdle rate.
Residual income (RI) (12) A performance measure equal to NOPAT less a charge for the level of investment.
Responsibility accounting system (6) A system of accounting that traces revenues and costs to organizational units and individuals with related responsibility for generating revenue and controlling costs.
Responsibility centers (12) Organizational units responsible for the generation of revenue or for the incurrence of costs.
Return on investment (ROI) (12) A performance measure equal to investment center income divided by invested capital.

S

Scattergraph (4) A graph of costs at various activity levels.
Selling costs (2) Costs associated with securing and filling customer orders.
Slack (10) Amounts (padding) managers include in budgets to assure that budgeted goals can be easily achieved.
Split-off point (7) Stage of production when joint products are individually identifiable.
Standard cost (11) The cost that management believes should be incurred to produce a good or service under anticipated conditions.
Standard cost variance (11) The difference between standard cost and actual cost.
Static budget (10) A budget that is not adjusted for the actual level of activity.
Step costs (4) Costs that are fixed for a range of volume but increase to a higher level when the upper bound of the range is exceeded.
Step fixed costs (4) A step cost for which the range of activity is relatively large before there is an increase in cost.
Step variable costs (4) A step cost for which the range of activity is relatively small before there is an increase in cost.
Strategy map (12) A diagram of the relationships, across the four dimensions of a balanced scorecard, among strategic objectives that create shareholder value.
Sunk costs (1) Costs incurred in the past—they are irrelevant to current decisions.
Supply chain management (SCM) systems (1) Software systems that support the planning of the best way to fill orders and help tracking of products and components among companies in the supply chain.

T

Target costing (8) An integrated approach to determining product features, product price, product cost, and product design that helps ensure a company will earn a reasonable profit on new products. Target cost is equal to price less desired profit and the product is designed to achieve the target cost.
Time tickets (2) Forms completed by workers to keep track of the amount of time spent on each job.

Total quality management (TQM) (2) Programs designed to ensure high-quality products that involve listening to customers' needs, making products right the first time, reducing defective products, and encouraging workers to improve their production processes continuously.
Transfer price (Appendix) (12) The price used to value internal transfers of goods or services.
Transferred-in costs (3) The cost a preceding processing department incurs and transfers to the next processing department.
Treasurer (1) Company official who has custody of cash and funds invested in various marketable securities. In addition to money management duties, the treasurer is generally responsible for maintaining relationships with investors, banks, and other creditors.

U

Underapplied overhead (2) The amount by which actual overhead exceeds the amount applied to inventory using a predetermined overhead rate.
Unit-level activities (6) Activities required to produce an incremental unit of output.
Unitized fixed costs (6) Fixed costs stated on a per unit basis.

V

Value chain (1) The internal operations of a company and its relationships and interactions with suppliers and customers aimed at creating maximum value for the least possible cost.
Variable cost (1) A cost that increases or decreases in response to increases or decreases in business activity.
Variable costing (5) An alternative to full costing in which only variable production costs are included in inventory: Fixed production costs are treated as period costs.
Variable costs (4) Those costs that increase or decrease in proportion to increases or decreases in business activity.
Variance analysis (11) An analysis of the difference between actual and standard cost.
Vertical analysis (14) An analysis that focuses on various financial statement account balances as a percent of some base. The base is sales when analyzing income statement accounts and total assets when analyzing balance sheet accounts. Vertical analysis is also referred to as common size analysis.

W

"What-if" analysis (4) An examination of the results of various courses of action.
Work in Process Inventory (2) An account that includes the cost of goods that are only partially complete.

Z

Zero base budgeting (10) A method of budget preparation that requires each department to justify budgeted amounts at the start of each budget period, even if the amounts were supported in prior periods.

INDEX

For entries on pages 496–570, please go to *WileyPLUS* to access Chapters 13 and 14.

D